The Canadian Anthology of Social Studies

Issues and Strategies for Teachers

Roland Case
Penney Clark

Editors

Pacific Educational Press
Vancouver Canada

Pacific Educational Press
Faculty of Education
University of British Columbia
Vancouver, B.C. V6T 1Z4
Telephone (604) 822-5385
Facsimile (604) 822-6603
E-mail <cedwards@interchange.ubc.ca>

First published in 1997 by:
Field Relations and Teacher In-service Education
Faculty of Education
Simon Fraser University
Burnaby, British Columbia V5A 1S6
Telephone (604) 291-3808
Facsimile (604) 291-5882
Web: http://www.sfu.ca/frtise/
E-mail: patricia_holborn@sfu.ca

Pacific Educational Press would like to acknowledge the ongoing support of the Department of Canadian Heritage towards its publishing program and the expertise brought to the development and publication of this book by the Field Relations Office of the Simon Fraser University Faculty of Education.

Canadian Cataloguing in Publication Data
The Canadian anthology of social studies

   Previous ed. published by: Simon Fraser University, Faculty of
Education, Field Relations and Teacher In-Service Education.
   Includes bibliographical references.
   ISBN 1-895766-39-7

   1. Social sciences--Study and teaching. I. Case, Roland, 1951- II.
Clark, Penney, 1950-
H62.5.C3C32 1999   300'.71'071   C99-910333-4

Project coordination: Patricia Holborn
Design and production: Lenore Ogilvy & Kathie Wraight
Cover design: Instructional Media Centre, Simon Fraser University
Printed and bound in Canada

99 00 01 02   6 5 4 3 2 1

TABLE OF CONTENTS

SECTION TWO : ENDS AND MEANS

SECTION THREE : IMPLEMENTATION

INSTRUCTIONAL PLANNING

LEARNING RESOURCES

STUDENT ASSESSMENT

To Emily and Ian and Susan

FOREWORD

Originally, the word "anthology" meant a collection of flowers. It has subsequently come to refer to a collection of the "flowers" of verse. We further extend the metaphor to the "flowers" of professional and scholarly thinking. Like a bouquet, this anthology of 41 articles by 27 teachers and teacher educators from the Maritimes to British Columbia has the diversity and richness that comes only from a multiplicity of viewpoints and experiences. So too, like a carefully arranged bouquet, rather than compete with one another the different perspectives complement and accentuate the features of the others in the collection. In this respect we are especially proud of both the harmony and the diversity of ideas in this volume. Collectively they speak of a powerful and exciting vision of social studies. As well they blend in a particularly satisfying manner countless very specific, practical suggestions with important discussions of the foundational issues at the heart of social studies teaching.

The anthology is compiled from existing articles, revised versions of previously published works and specially commissioned work. Much of the collection has been used in modified form for several years in social studies methodology classes for elementary and secondary teachers. With a few exceptions the articles speak to issues of concern across the grade spectrum. Because of its considerable scope, we believe the collection will also be of value as a professional reference for practicing teachers and curriculum developers working in social studies.

In an undertaking such as this many individuals deserve thanks for the crucial contributions they have made. We appreciate especially the authors of the works found in this anthology. We believe they are some of the finest educators and teacher educators in Canadian social studies and their writings reflect this expertise. Vivian Rossner of the Centre for Distance Education at Simon Fraser University put the bug in our ears about publishing this collection and Patricia Holborn of the Field Relations office paved the way for the project. Neil Smith and Peter Seixas provided us with helpful feedback which we endeavoured to follow. Craig Harding did much early work looking for "flowers" to include in this collection and Kathie Wraight did much late night work making the collection look right. Hani Ping was as conscientious as ever in her library work and technical support for this project. Several of the articles in this collection were developed initially for a project funded by the Public Participation Program of the Canadian International Development Agency. Our artwork emerges from a group of talented students from Caulfeild Elementary School, West Vancouver which includes Keri Brothers, Jacquie Brown, Laura Brown, Meghan Cook, Katie Gregory, Mairin Kerr, Robyn Stephens, Emily White, Stephanie Wise and, especially, Fenella Brandvold and Audra Mitchell whose works are the centrepiece for our cover design. Lastly we are grateful for the encouraging comments and helpful suggestions from many of our students whose support kept us going when it seemed the project would never end.

Roland Case
Penney Clark

SECTION ONE :

FOUNDATIONS

▶ A COHERENT VISION

▶ DISCIPLINE-BASED STRANDS

▶ CONCERN-BASED STRANDS

▶ DIMENSION-BASED STRANDS

Challenges and Choices Facing Social Studies Teachers

Neil Smith

The challenges and choices facing social studies teachers are neither new nor simple. What goals will we emphasize? What methods shall we employ to achieve these goals? How will we engage students in their learning? This article invites social studies teachers to think in broad terms about what is needed to make social studies a valuable and interesting educational experience for students.

Whether we love social studies or are a reluctant teacher of the subject, all of us can benefit from looking afresh at what this subject means to us and our students. We may need to reconcile our personal orientation and predisposition to social studies with new possibilities that may appear foreign or daunting. In some respects this is because of our past socialization to the subject; each of us comes to the role of a social studies teacher having already experienced thousands of hours of "teacher training" while participating as a student in elementary and secondary school. During this time, images of what social studies means and how it is supposed to be taught have been etched on our minds. These experiences will likely have profoundly shaped our approach to teaching the subject. As the old adage goes, "We teach as we were taught." Reassured by our own social studies experiences, many of us may ask: "Surely these established patterns of social studies are still adequate?" I believe not. Even if we personally enjoyed social studies in elementary and secondary school, the subject as a whole has not been largely successful. According to John Goodlad's seminal study of over 1000 North American classrooms, social studies is one of the least popular of all commonly taught subjects. Upper elementary students liked it less than any other subject (1984, pp. 210-212). At the secondary level Goodlad observed that:

> The topics commonly included in the social sciences appear as though they would be of great human interest. But something strange seems to have happened to them on the way to the classroom. The topics of study become removed from their intrinsically human character, reduced to the dates and places readers will recall memorizing for tests. (Goodlad, 1984)

It is also disturbing that students generally perceive social studies to be one of the most difficult subjects despite the fact that critical thinking is found to be frequently absent from classroom instruction and student evaluation. Studies of British Columbia social studies teachers, for example, found that the importance they attach to critical thinking is not adequately reflected in the teaching strategies they use in their classrooms (Bognar, Cassidy, Lewis & Manley-Casimir, 1991; Case, 1993).

Our challenge—and it is a difficult one—is for each of us to recognize and understand both the strengths and the limitations of our inherited visions of social studies and then to build upon and beyond these experiences to enliven social studies for more of our students. I offer three typical vignettes of social studies teaching as a way of beginning a critical conversation about the what and how of social studies. These "snapshots" of teaching practice invite us to recognize ourselves in them and then to look both for the positive elements and, as importantly, for the areas where improvement is possible.

VIGNETTE #1: FINDING THE FACTS

"Okay, let's turn to page 83 in the text, please." James quietly groans and slouches a little lower in his seat. Glancing to the front he recognizes the predictable signals. Ms. Knowles is about to launch into today's discussion. James' slight anxiety about having not read the assigned chapter on early Canadian immigration for homework is balanced by his confidence that most of his friends are probably in the same boat.

He opens the textbook and begins to flip through the pages. With a quick glance up at Knowles, James is reminded that she is an okay teacher. In fact, most kids quite like her. She is sincere and always keen about the subject. But all her enthusiasm aside, she isn't able to excite most students about this stuff. For most of them, the definition of social studies is "a school way to talk about the dead."

Knowles' first question dislodges James from his musings. "What main factors caused the Canadian government to open the gates to huge numbers of immigrants at the turn of this century?" Her eyes scan the room. James hasn't a clue. He mentally replays his survival strategy: if Knowles looks in his direction for an answer, he will first avert his eyes; if she asks him, he will look up politely with a shy, vacant look on his face, fumble through the pages and mutter that he doesn't remember that part of the chapter. Be polite and uninformed. That usually suffices. He will stay in Knowles' good books, and she probably won't bother him again for the rest of the lesson.

The teacher-directed questioning now begins in earnest. Page by page the information emerges from the memories of the "regulars"—those five students who always seem to appreciate the discussion and who recall the information well enough to offer intelligent comments. Slowly, relentlessly, Knowles extracts the desired facts and painfully reconstructs them like the pieces of a jigsaw puzzle. Finally, it is proclaimed that the chapter had been "covered," James muses that this chapter like the others before it had been "buried," and will be resurrected very briefly at test time. The writing assignment is then scribed on the board: "Describe in two paragraphs

how early twentieth century immigrants contributed to the development of Canada." James spends the next fifteen minutes summarizing a few key ideas remembered from the discussion: that early Canadian immigrants became hard-working farmers who had opened up the prairies for growing food, and also who worked tirelessly on the construction of the national railroad. He receives some help from Alex, an 'A' student sitting beside him. He then scans the text, finds one or two other ideas and copies them verbatim into his assignment. Enough to hold up the 'A-' average, he thinks to himself. After staring dreamily into the pages of the text for a few minutes, and after a drink at the water fountain, James sighs deeply and heads off to the library where he is expected to continue his research project on building the Canadian Pacific Railway.

In reviewing this vignette, it is important first to acknowledge the attributes. The teacher was perceived by James as both knowledgeable and genuine in her approach to the teaching of social studies. She systematically exposed students to important background facts that might serve as a platform from which students could build greater understanding of Canadian history. And for a handful of students the class discussion was a successful way of doing this—of making personal sense of the information contained in their reading assignment.

The lesson, however, raises several basic questions. What organizing themes or concepts frame students' investigations? There is no evidence that the information amounts to anything more than a series of facts. It may be what Walter Parker (1989, p. 40) calls "teaching by mentioning" or the "parade of facts" approach—"the teacher tells students a few facts about a person or event and then moves on to telling a few facts about another person or event." What new perspectives—economic, social, historical—are students being asked to apply to the information studied? Again, the larger picture—the general significance of the events—is seemingly neither apparent to nor appreciated by most students. What level of responsibility or accountability does each student have in their learning? The lesson relies heavily on the textbook, with the teacher engaging students in a "search and rescue" attempt to discover the facts from within its chapters. This methodology tacitly seems to encourage compliance from most students, doing little to increase the number of students actively participating in the discussion or thinking critically about underlying issues. Although the lesson is presented clearly and represents a solid effort to introduce new knowledge, students have little opportunity or motivation to connect this knowledge to previously learned facts and concepts. Nor does it appear to serve as a segue to subsequent investigations that may invoke fuller and more critical analysis.

With this lesson we are left to conjecture how it might

be extended beyond the mere acquisition of facts to learning that would be both compelling and challenging for students. This challenge brings us to a second vignette, one that moves outside the textbook to the world beyond the classroom.

VIGNETTE #2: TREKKING THROUGH TOWN

Mr. Stevens is upbeat. He is continually drumming up enthusiasm among his young students for their community study, tirelessly opening up new avenues for exploring local organizations. Mr. Stevens quickly steps out of the line of children and parent helpers in front of the school and checks off each student's name. After a quick review of the field trip rules, the class walks single-file for three blocks, soon reaching the local firehall where the chief and four firefighters are awaiting their visit.

For the next hour the class tours the facility. The hosts explain their jobs, telling students some of the funny and sad things that they encounter in their work. They describe the different pieces of firefighting equipment. Children slide down the firepole from half-ceiling height, try on rubber boots and coats, and clamber onto the firetruck. When asked by the firechief if students have any special questions, silence ensues, broken only when one student asks if all firefighters were permitted to drive the truck. Another then asks if the chief has ever seen anyone die, and then a third asks what the firefighters do all day and night when there are no emergency calls. At this point, the allotted time is up, and the class heads back to school and arrives just in time for P.E. class in the gym.

For the next social studies class, the class visits the local grocery store and spends time talking with the available staff. They tour the back of the store, look at the butchers' work area, examine the throw-away vegetable section and visit the offices. After a brief conversation with the manager, students return to class and resume other activities. The study proceeds in a similar fashion for three weeks, with field trips to two local businesses, the town hall and a farm. Also, three parents volunteer as guest speakers to explain their occupations. The students listen, and the teacher encourages them to ask the guests questions about their work. At the end of the unit, Mr. Stevens presents a summative assignment: "Pick your favourite job or organization and write five things about it."

A number of positive features are apparent in this scenario. Students are actively engaged in the experience, at least insofar as they all participate with genuine interest in how each of the organizations function. The teacher is committed to providing students with positive experiences that carry them beyond the textbooks and into the real workings of their community. He is well organized and uses a great variety of community resources. Students clearly expand their general knowledge of occupations in their community.

While the levels of student enthusiasm in this scenario are higher than those reported in the first vignette, many of the same questions must be asked. To what extent are students motivated *to learn* from these experiences? Kieran Egan (1986, pp. 5-19) contends that children are typically underwhelmed with the study of everyday commonplace experience, and that greater learning potential exists within the more distant worlds of fantasy and imagination. When social studies concepts are taught in the context of legends and mythology, for example, students are propelled by the power of story to consider important lessons about honour and shame, trust and betrayal and other fundamental human notions. Egan believes these to be far more relevant and motivating than a trip to the firehall could ever be. (For more on this point, see Egan's two articles in this anthology: "Resisting the Erosion of Education" and "Story Forms and Romantic Perspectives.") Involving students in direct experiences, as portrayed in the field study vignette, should not be assumed to be educationally sound merely by virtue of students' level of activity.

A related concern is student accountability. In the field trip activities, what responsibility do students have for their learning? Similar to James' experience in the first scenario, these students are participating in a free ride, albeit with legs moving, but with little perceived obligation or motivation to engage in an investigation. The field study may have been enriched by having students select specific investigations to complete during the experience. After collecting their data during the trip, students might then each be responsible for reporting the results to the class. The field "trip" could thereby be transformed into a field "study" and be the source of fresh concepts and ideas emerging from well constructed investigations. This comes as a result of the teacher working with students to decide upon the most interesting and challenging questions to guide their inquiry.

In the field study lesson, what insights of importance have students gained? What new knowledge or concepts have students acquired through these activities? Although they may pick up tidbits of information incidentally, it is unclear from the vignette that students either entered or exited the field experiences with a rich context for framing and extending their study. The experiences appear as serial pop-up activities with only a modest expectation that students will interconnect or apply this information to some larger question or problem. It is too large a stretch to expect that students will make these connections on their own. Engaging children in direct experiences for the sake of active learning without helping them make the important connections may be interpreted as largely providing entertainment. John Dewey (1938), the twentieth century advocate of experiential education, exhorted teachers to legitimate active learning by systematically linking it with reflective practice and helping students make meaning of their experience by drawing conclusions for the experiences. The main message: direct experiences such as field trips must be linked closely to concepts and theories through reflective thought. But this brings us back to our primary question.

What will make the teaching of social studies a motivating and educationally significant experience for students? It is frequently suggested that schooling should do more to help students learn how to learn and to assess knowledge critically, solve problems and make sound decisions. The third vignette seems to more directly address this vision of social studies teaching. But, as we review the attributes and problems, we will see that it too is cause for some concern.

VIGNETTE #3: TACKLING THE BIG ISSUES

It seemed a bit funny. Grade fours reading fairy stories in social studies, especially the old version of "The Three Little Pigs." Then Mrs. Arnell—"Ms. A" as students call her—reads to them the version of the tale told from the wolf's point of view. In this story, "The True Story of the Three Little Pigs," the Wolf defends his badly tarnished reputation. Students begin to understand how selected events may be interpreted and reported in very different ways, depending on the point of view taken. Students compare the events of the classic version of the tale with the wolf's version and prepare to take on the different roles of the story characters in a simplified mock trial. The trial is to determine if the wolf is innocent or guilty of first degree murder in the death of two pigs.

The Wolf (the defendant), who pleads not guilty, works with his legal defense team to recreate the events of the story and to select information which supports his innocence. Crown Counsel and her team of students are given one hour to study the case and develop arguments why Wolf is guilty of premeditated murder. The judge and jury study the general background of the case and learn their responsibilities in the trial proceedings.

The next day, Wolf's trial is held. The teacher videotapes the proceedings, and using jointly-generated criteria helps students assess their own and peers' presentations. "Interesting," the students think, "a lot of work and even a bit of fun. But, so what does doing this have to do with what they are supposed to be studying about early Canadian history?"

Ms. A starts the third day's class with a story and drawings of Captain Cook's first encounters with the "Nootka" peoples of the west coast of Canada in the late eighteenth century. She summarizes the European views of the key events and, for homework, asks students to read Cook's accounts in the textbook. The next day she provides students with an entirely different perspective—this time from some of the recently published accounts of Maquinna and the Nuu Cha Nulth peoples who were the inhabitants of Friendly Cove on Vancouver Island. These accounts present an entirely different side of the story—passed on through oral tradition—with detailed descriptions of humiliation and assaults endured by the coastal peoples at the hands of European explorers.

Ms. A. then asks the class to compare the two versions of "The Three Little Pigs" with the two versions of the encounters between Cook and the Nuu Cha Nulth people. She helps them learn to use the proper language to compare the fictional with the historical events, and to refine their rough ideas so they are able to write in their journals about the similarities and differences between them.

At this point, students prepare for a second mock trial, this time with Captain Cook charged with destroying the way of life of an indigenous people. Students employ the same model used for the Wolf's trial. Each student, first independently, then in a group, researches events related to the first contact in Friendly Cove. They write a summary of these events and with the help of a small group of peers construct arguments either defending or prosecuting Cook. As a culminating activity, they present their arguments in a mock trial.

Clearly, students are actively engaged in a series of diverse activities. Each student has individual personal responsibility in the learning tasks. Students such as James in the first vignette would have difficulty evading this kind of assignment. To succeed in the mock trials, for example, each student is required to produce written arguments based on research and analysis, and then present these in a persuasive manner. It was intended that students would develop these skills first in relation to the fairy tale, and later by applying them to historical events related to European and aboriginal contact on the west coast of Canada. The objectives for the lesson extended well beyond the text of a classic piece of children's literature. Building on Egan's use of story and literature as a vehicle to teach important concepts, students learned about "points of view" by comparing the traditional version of the fairy tale with its modern counterpart. The teacher invited students to think critically—asking them to analyze information, decide what information would support their arguments, create and present arguments and, ultimately, make ethical judgments about an important historical figure. All is well thus far. So what are the problems in this teaching scenario?

The concerns with this vignette are found in the manner in which students are cast into an extremely complex historical context with insufficient background knowledge, concepts and skills to analyze the issues competently.

If students are to get beyond a superficial indictment or vindication of Captain Cook, they need a more thorough knowledge of both peoples involved: the Nuu Cha Nulth peoples—their history, their systems of economic and social survival, their previous and subsequent experiences with waves of European and American traders and their changing attitudes toward the white visitors—and, on the other side, the European explorers—their methods of pursuing trade, the competition that drove their sponsors to expand their boundaries and increase the volume of trade. Without this understanding, students may be unable to responsibily judge whether or not Cook was guilty of destroying a nation of indigenous people.

A related concern stems from the skills and concepts presupposed by the very sophisticated challenges students were given. Expecting each student to successfully develop a cohesive argument may be an immense stretch if students are not coached and supported in the requisite sub-skills. For example, will students recognize when a reason supports a conclusion and when it is largely irrelevant? Can they distinguish unfounded or exaggerated statements from grounded ones? Are students disposed to look at potential counter-arguments to their position or will they quickly reach a conclusion and be closed to all other options? Fundamental, too, is students' appreciation of the ethnocentrism that may colour each group's perceptions of events. Even the question posed—guilty or innocent—may fuel an unproductive "all or nothing" view of an issue that may better be cast in shades of gray. As exciting and challenging as they might appear, the trials and associated debating exercises are highly sophisticated and complex practices that may render superficial outcomes unless preceded by deliberate and comprehensive preparation. The required abilities in critical thinking do not come naturally to most students, and many will need the support of a systematic progression of instruction and guided practice to prepare them for such complex challenges. Thus, although there is much that is educationally exciting about this third vignette, there are significant gaps that may undermine student learning.

As our discussion of these three vignettes suggests, effective social studies teaching is a complex and demanding enterprise. There are many choices to make concerning what to teach and much is involved in making these studies educationally rewarding for our students. In reviewing the three vignettes, we see how each offers a piece of the puzzle, yet each left on its own presents an incomplete picture. Students must acquire knowledge, yet our teaching must reach beyond transmitting factual information to developing thoughtful understanding. There is a need to involve students in mindful exploration of the world around them. This amounts to much more than providing active, hands-on experiences; it requires helping students frame, think about and apply these experiences in meaningful and fruitful ways. As well, there is more to promoting thoughtfulness then posing provocative issues or dilemmas for discussion; we must identify and carefully develop the requisite skills and knowledge that will empower students to competently and responsibly tackle these challenges. Finally, the diverse curricular and pedagogical decisions regarding what and how to teach social studies must be influenced by one additional consideration—students have to be engaged in and by their social studies before they can be expected to learn what this subject has to offer.

REFERENCES

Bognar, C., Cassidy, C., Lewis, W. & Manley-Casimir, M. (1991). *Social studies in British Columbia: Technical report of the 1989 social studies assessment.* Victoria, BC: Assessment, Examinations and Reporting Branch, Ministry of Education.

Case, R. (1993). *Summary of the 1992 social studies needs assessment.* Victoria, BC: Queen's Printer.

Dewey, J. (1938). *Experience and education.* New York: Free Press.

Egan, K. (1986). *Teaching as story telling.* London, ON: Althouse Press.

Goodlad, J. (1984). *A place called school.* New York: McGraw-Hill.

Parker, W. (1989). How to help students learn history and geography. *Educational Leadership, 47*(3), 39-43.

2

ELEMENTS OF A COHERENT SOCIAL STUDIES PROGRAM

ROLAND CASE

Social Studies Is . . . A Poem

> What is social studies?
> What a question to ask.
> How will I answer?
> What a difficult task.
> Should the focus be religious?
> Early settlers felt it was the key
> The Revolutionary War
> Brought a new philosophy.
> Is social studies history
> With a focus on the past?
> Or sociology
> Where the subject seems so vast!
> Is social studies geography?
> Where we look at population.
> Or is it anthropology?
> Where we look at culture's creation.
> Is social studies political science?
> And a view of government.
> Or is it economics?
> And a view of money spent.
> When I am learning social studies
> Should I start with me?
> This is called the spiral curricula
> And it could hold the key.
> Should my lessons be directed
> By the teacher or me?
> Or can I learn about the subjects
> By my own discovery?
> While writing this poem
> It seems I do digress.
> Overall, I think the definition of social studies
> Should include human development and progress.

Donna Robinson

(cited in Chido, 1990, pp. 466–468; © National Council for the Social Studies. Reprinted by permission.)

As the above poem suggests, there are likely as many answers to the question: "What is social studies?" as there are social studies educators. This lack of consensus is not in itself undesirable—standardization, per se, is not a precondition for a sound social studies program. However, the current diversity of conceptions is not an indication of healthy intellectual disagreement; it is symptomatic of what is widely recognized as a confused mess. As Marion Brady suggests, social studies is in "a chaotic state," little more than "an incredible heap of miscellany" comprised of:

> some odd pieces of the past held together by habit, a few bits of several social sciences (themselves in need of major rethinking), the remnants of a dozen

© National Council for the Social Studies. Reprinted by permission.

ill-digested fads, an assortment of responses to demands of state legislators and special interest groups, and other odds and ends assigned to social studies because they do not seem to fit anywhere else. (1989, p. 80)

This lack of coherence is illustrated in the cartoon above, which shows bewildered educators peering over many jig-saw puzzle pieces. Each piece represents a different dimension of social studies (e.g., citizenship education, global education, sociology, values education, history). The onlookers are at a loss to discover how all the pieces fit together. The caption reads: "It might help if we had a picture of what this is supposed to look like."

This article seeks to help teachers begin to develop a fuller and clearer sense of what social studies can and should be in their own classrooms. It is not imperative that everyone identifies exactly the same picture, although it is important that individual social studies teachers eventually come to a coherent and defensible vision of social studies that drives their teaching. Developing this "picture" is, perhaps, best viewed as a long-term aim that is likely to take years to realize fully. Although building a thoughtful program in social studies is a demanding task, the alternative—what Marion Brady referred to as "a chaotic state" and "an incredible heap of miscellany"—is much less satisfying.

I believe we cannot begin to develop a coherent vision for social studies without understanding three basic features of the subject: the underlying *rationales* for social studies, the *goals* that social studies will promote in order to further the rationale, and the *strands* around

which subject matter is organized to promote the desired goals. In this piece, I consider each of these elements and their relationship to one another in the context of social studies.

RATIONALES FOR SOCIAL STUDIES

The rationale for a program identifies the underlying reason(s) for the program goals. In other words, a rationale for social studies provides the reasons for pursuing the goals discussed above. In this respect the rationale is the "bottom line" of social studies—in the face of uncertainty or conflicting directions, the rationale provides a basis for deciding which direction to pursue. It is commonly suggested that social studies is concerned with preparing citizens, but there is little consensus as to what this means. Four ideals are traditionally offered as "competing" rationales for social studies. Two of the rationales identify specific *social* purposes—that is, their focus is the type of society we hope to promote through social studies—and the other two rationales serve *individual* purposes—these focus on the type of individual that we want social studies to foster.

- **social initiation.** This rationale posits that the primary purpose of social studies is to initiate students into society by transmitting the understandings, abilities and values that students will require if they are to fit into and be productive members of society.

- **social reformation.** This rationale holds that the primary purpose of social studies is to empower students with the understandings, abilities and values necessary to improve or transform their society.

10   *The Canadian Anthology of Social Studies*

- **personal development.** According to this rationale the primary purpose of social studies is to help students develop fully as individuals and as social beings. Its direct purpose is neither to reform society nor to maintain the status quo, but to foster the personal talents and character of each student.
- **academic understanding.** This rationale suggests that the primary purpose of social studies is to introduce students to the bodies of knowledge and forms of inquiry represented in the social science disciplines. Although, many would suggest that understanding the disciplines will enhance personal development and support social initiation and reform, the prime justification for this rationale is the value of understanding the structure and content of the social sciences.

There is a tendency among some teachers to regard discussion of the rationale for a subject as a rather abstract and irrelevant exercise. This attitude is unfortunate and may, in part, contribute to the chaos that Brady talks about in social studies. Getting clear about our rationale—the *raison d'être* or the very reason for doing something—gives us a sense of purpose. Without knowing why we are doing what we do, there is a danger that we will teach a topic for the sake of covering it. The expression "covering the curriculum" sometimes means that teaching is little more than a superficial marching through curricular topics in order to say that one has taught the curriculum. The word curriculum is derived from the word *curricle* which means "the path to follow"—hence, the notion of a *course* of study. Teachers must know where they are going if they are to lead students through the curriculum in a meaningful and educational productive way.

The rationale for a subject serves this very practical function: it gives us a sense of direction—which path to follow—when interpreting and implementing the curriculum. This direction is especially important since most curricula leave teachers considerable latitude in deciding the specifics of what will be taught. Consider the example below of four significantly different units on the same theme, the building of the Canadian Pa-

---

FOUR "VISIONS" OF A CURRICULAR TOPIC: BUILDING THE CANADIAN PACIFIC RAILWAY

Social initiation	Social reformation	Personal development	Academic understanding
To initiate or socialize students so they fit into and are productive members of society.	*To empower and motivate students to work to make the world a better place.*	*To nurture student talents and interests so they can develop satisfying interpersonal relationships and can make sense of their world.*	*To train students' minds by introducing them to the methods and content knowledge of the social science disciplines.*
Topics to be Considered			
• Taming of the Rockies —engineering feats; • The saga of its construction; • Canada's defence against American Manifest Destiny; • The Last Spike at Craigellachie, BC: the linchpin of East and West; • The iron ribbon that binds Canada: fulfilling the Confederation Dream; • Famous people—John A. Macdonald, Donald Smith, William Van Horne, Sanford Fleming, etc.	• Environmental costs the railway—demise of buffalo; • Exploitation of immigrant workers; • Dislocation and abuse of First Nations; • The myths of the nation—the last spike was stolen the first night; • Corruption and greed: the Pacific Scandal • Who really built the CPR: Van Horne or the Chinese?	• Students select any topic of personal interest related to CPR and decide on a way of representing their learning; • Explore potential career choices— engineers, developers, politicians, etc.—by considering the contribution of each to the railway; • Use cooperative activities and role play to develop ability to work with others as students create a mural depicting some aspect of the railway.	• Learn about historical inquiry by developing an account of an event using primary sources; • Learn about geographical inquiry by plotting demographic effects of railway on local terrain or by planning a route using contour maps; • Learn about archaeological inquiry by developing an account of work camp life based on artifacts recovered from a simulated "dig."

cific Railway. As these differing units illustrate, depending upon which rationale is driving the unit, the nature and outcomes of the study would be significantly different.

These units are not simply "doing the CPR" but using the unit on the CPR to promote four significantly different purposes:

- promoting knowledge and pride in the history of Canada (a social initiation rationale);
- encouraging skepticism about the official versions of history and concern for past injustices in Canada (a social reformation rationale);
- nurturing students' ability to work with each other and to plan and carrying out self-directed studies (a personal development rationale);
- introducing students to the methods and criteria used by social scientists in their disciplines (an academic understanding rationale).

Much of the division within social studies stems from a perception that these rationales are inevitably in competition with one another. This is a mistaken perception. These rationales can be construed in ways that are mutually supportive and, indeed, it may be desirable to adopt, to some extent, all four rationales. For example, initiating students into society should not preclude promoting students' capacity to reform society. Surely one of the richest contributions that members of society can make is to improve "the system" as needed, and thoughtful reform is unlikely without a rich appreciation of how and why people and institutions operate as they do. Similarly, greater understanding of the social science disciplines can and should contribute to the other purposes of social studies. For example, understanding the history of our nation and being able to inquire and think carefully about our historical roots are attributes of both productive and reformist citizens. The fact that the four rationales persist as defining purposes for social studies attests to the value that each promises. The challenge for teachers is to determine which aspects from which of the rationales will drive their teaching. Selecting from several rationales and using this composite profile to give purpose to our teaching is not the same as doing whatever comes to mind and finding some after-the-fact justification to rationalize the action—in the latter case, one's social studies teaching may be all over the map, so to speak.

GOALS OF SOCIAL STUDIES

Goals are a second constituent of developing a coherent program. The goals of a program are the direct educational outcomes that are to be promoted. Although the precise wording and ways of categorizing them may differ, generally speaking, social studies is concerned with five general goals.

- **content knowledge.** This goal specifies the breadth and depth of knowledge students should possess about their world. It includes knowledge of *specific facts* (e.g., key figures in local community history,

the capital of Canada, major current events) *generalizations/theories* (e.g., Marxism, environmental determinism, manifest destiny) and *concepts* (e.g., democracy, discrimination, paternalism).

- **critical thinking.** This goal refers to students' abilities and inclinations to competently assess what to believe and to reach defensible decisions about what and how to act. This involves understanding the criteria and procedures for assessing different types of claims (e.g., historical claims, value judgments about human rights, theories about social phenomena) and applying them on a ongoing basis.

- **information gathering and reporting.** This goal specifies the abilities involved in identifying information needs, in competently extracting information from a variety of primary and secondary sources (e.g., textbooks, magazines, other library references, catalogues, artifacts, field trip data, community resources) and in competently representing this information in various forms (e.g., essay, graph, chart, map, timeline, mural, model, debate, oral presentation, audio-visual media).

- **personal and social values.** This goal refers to both personal values (e.g., self-esteem, integrity, personal identity) and social values (e.g., equality, respect for persons, justice, national pride, international solidarity) that are constitutive of healthy individuals, communities and society/world.

- **individual and collective action.** This goal refers to competence in actually solving interpersonal and societal problems (e.g., dealing with siblings and fellow students, combating school- and community-based problems, or acting on national and international concerns). It involves developing students' abilities to analyze problems in their personal lives and in society, plan appropriate courses of action individually and in collaboration with others, put into action their plans, and evaluate the efficacy of their efforts.

Although there would likely be acceptance, in principle, of these general goals, the details of these goals are neither widely understood nor agreed upon. Greater specification of the particular objectives found under each goal is required. For example, does collective action refer to carrying out charitable activities such as fund raising for medical research? Or does it refer to lobbying the school administration or, perhaps, the government to change a policy that is perceived to be unfair? The more detailed elaboration of the contents of each of these goals depends in larger part on the underlying rationale for social studies

As indicated above, a rationale provides direction and substance to the program goals. For example, educators adopting the social initiation rationale *might* be expected to emphasize the fundamental values of harmony, cooperation and national pride; proponents of the social reformation rationale *might* be expected to emphasize values such as social justice and equality. The value of getting clear about the reason(s) for social studies is the help provided in deciding what needs to be taught in each goal area. Consider the goal of individual and collective action. Proponents of social studies as social initiation will be concerned with learning to solve problems that threaten current societal arrangements (e.g., combating the growing violence in society), while advocates of social studies as social reformation will likely focus on problems with the system itself (e.g., changing sexist attitudes towards female politicians). Similarly, proponents of social studies as personal development will be more concerned with issues that students confront in their daily lives (e.g., dealing with a difficult situation involving classmates), whereas advocates of social studies as academic understanding will likely focus on problems arising within disciplinary inquiry (e.g., finding ways to measure and map the elevation of a mountain). The box below provides a sampling of different objectives for each main goal within each of the four traditional rationales for social studies.

ORGANIZING STRANDS FOR SOCIAL STUDIES

I offer the notion of a strand to explain the third element of social studies. The word "strands" refers to the parts that are bound or woven together to form the whole. Strands form the bases for organizing social studies and for determining the emphasis and content of each of the major goals for social studies. The strands in a given social studies program provide the backbone or give shape to the program. Three types of organizing strands are commonly offered: *social science disciplines, social dimensions* and *social concerns.*

Discipline-based strands

Social studies has often been defined in terms of the social science disciplines. In fact, an early definition of social studies was: "Social studies is the social sciences simplified for pedagogical purposes." Discipline-based strands use the structure and contributions of the individual social sciences as the building blocks for social studies. In other words, social studies would promote the understandings, abilities and values associated with

---

ILLUSTRATIVE GOALS FOR EACH RATIONALE

Goals	Social initiation	Social reformation	Personal development	Academic understanding
Content knowledge	• accepted view of world • cultural literacy • rights and responsibilities	• alternative perspectives • exploitation • class/gender bias	• self knowledge • general knowledge	• social science knowledge base • historiography
Information gathering & reporting	• mainstream sources of information • established conventions for presenting information	• accessing alternative sources • persuasive presentation	• mainstream sources of information • exploring personal forms of expression and representation	• use of original sources • field surveys • research papers and other forms academic presentation
Critical thinking	• framed social issues—thinking within "givens" (e.g., how to better contribute to society)	• issues at the foundations of society • deconstructing media	• personal issue analysis • personal viewpoints	• canons of historical reasoning • discipline-based issues
Personal & social values	• patriotism • cooperation • loyalty • respect for others	• equality • social justice • "critical" spirit	• self-esteem • personal pride • personal integrity • taking responsibility	• pursuit of knowledge • intellectual work ethic
Individual & collective action	• community service • school enhancement projects	• political action (lobbying)	• self-help projects community service	• work study • team research projects

---

the social sciences. This include for each of the social sciences: (1) the defining questions or purposes of the discipline, (2) the central concepts and bodies of knowledge, (3) the attitudes and methods of inquiry and (4) the criteria for judging evidence. The justification for discipline-based strands is that they provide the most systematic and rigorous (or disciplined) way of organizing our study of the social world. Typically, history and geography are the major strands in the social studies curriculum, but other social science disciplines are also present to a considerable degree. The most commonly mentioned discipline-based strands are listed below:

- anthropology
- archaeology
- architecture
- economics
- geography
- history
- law
- political science
- psychology
- sociology.

Dimension-based strands

Dimension-based strands divide the social world into different multidisciplinary parts or components. There are many ways in which this pie can be divided, but the justification is that the world does not organize itself according to the social sciences—these disciplines are seen as somewhat narrow or confining ways of studying the world. Instead, it is believed that social studies will be more understandable and relevant to students if the focus is commonplace dimensions of society. In other words, social studies would promote the understandings, abilities and values associated with each of the main components of the world or facets of life that the individual must deal with. The most popular dimension-based strand is the "expanding horizons" approach which divides the curriculum into an increasingly distant set of spheres of experience, starting with the self, then the family, the local community, the region and eventually going to more remote regions in time and space. A sampling of other dimension-based strands are listed below:

- social roles (e.g., citizen, worker, consumer, family member)
- social phenomena (e.g., crime, conflict, play, holidays)
- social institutions (e.g., family, government, religion, sports)
- regional or area studies (e.g., the Middle East, Canadian studies).

Concern-based strands

Concern-based strands focus on the pressing issues or challenges facing students. In other words, social studies would promote the understandings, abilities and values that students need if they are to deal with the priority concerns of their world. The justification for concern-based strands is that the most important issues facing students in local, national and international arenas must be explicitly and fully addressed in multidisciplinary contexts. Over time, as the world encounters new problems, critics of the social studies lament the inattention given this concern in the existing curriculum. As concern for the issue increases, a movement develops which supports infusing this initiative into the curriculum. Rather than dividing the study of society by discipline or by social sector, a concern-based approach focusses on most of the pressing concerns of the age. The most prominent concern-based strands include:

- environmental education
- global education
- human rights education
- multicultural education
- peace education.

The three types of strands are interrelated and overlapping: they provide alternative ways of identifying and organizing the specific objectives for each of the five social studies goals. For example, the topic of war might be addressed historically (e.g., a chronological account starting with World War I and continuing until the end of World War II) or through a peace education approach (e.g., looking generally at the social, economic, psychological and political causes of war, and at ways of avoiding or limiting war). Choosing, a dimension- or concern-based strand does not preclude promoting the kinds of objectives that might be associated with a disciplined-based strand. For example, as part of a community study where students research stories about their personal past and the past of their community, students may also learn about historical interpretation and assessing the reliability of historical sources. Similarly, a study of a global issues may be an educationally effective approach to integrating objectives from history, geography, political science and other social sciences.

It is not always obvious, merely from the topic of a unit of study, what type of strand forms the basis of that unit. For example, a study of Inuit people could be based on various strands. It would be anthropology-based if the prime focus is on the cultural and social interactions of these people (e.g., marriage customs, child rearing practices, treatment of elderly); whereas it would be geography-based if the prime focus was the natural environment of the North and its effects on the Inuit. Alternatively, the topic qualifies as concern-based if the prime focus is on confronting racism (e.g., human rights education) or on promoting cross-cultural understanding (e.g., multicultural education). As should be apparent, any topic may contain elements from several strands of different types.

The prime consideration in selecting strands to use as the backbone of one's social studies program is the extent to which they promote the desired rationale(s) and represent the desired emphases within the goals of social studies. Typically, but not necessarily, the selection of a particular rationale for social studies will influence the decision about the strand. Advocates of the academic understanding rationale are more likely to focus on the discipline-based strands and those promoting the social reformation rationale will likely focus on concern-based strands. Supporters of personal development may be inclined towards dimension-based strands and supporters of social initiation are most likely to focus on either discipline- or dimension-based strands. However, other combinations are possible. For example, some social reformists may decide that a focus on the disciplines is the most effective way of empowering students to improve their society. Alternatively, more than one type of strand may be adopted, especially if more than one rationale is seen as important.

THE TASK AHEAD

It is incumbent on social studies educators to explore and assess the nature and implications of each of these elements—rationale, goals and strands—when developing their social studies programs. To some extent choices will have been dictated by the provincially prescribed curriculum, but most curricula require considerable teacher discretion in deciding what specifically to include and emphasize, and how to organize these for instructional purposes. As a British Columbia Ministry of Education document (1990) noted:

> Curriculum is no longer "ground to be covered." Instead, curriculum evolves from the teacher's mediation between the goals of the program and the curriculum and the individual learning styles, interests and abilities of students. (p. 25)

An earlier British Columbia curriculum guide for secondary social studies explained that "A curriculum is an organized statement of intended learning outcomes that serves as a *framework* for decisions about the instructional process [emphasis added]" (Ministry of Education, 1988, p. 4). In other words, curricula are guidelines to assist teachers in developing a program of study for their own students. This does not mean that we are free to do whatever we wish—we must work within the parameters set out by the curriculum. Notice, if the curriculum identifies, as an outcome, promoting understanding of the building of the CPR, we have an obligation to do so—but, as the earlier example suggests, the form and emphasis of that understanding may vary considerably. Of course, we cannot spend most of our time in social studies on maps simply because we happen to enjoy working on them and they are mentioned in the curriculum. As professionals we have a responsibility to develop a program that is educationally sound and ethically defensible, given our students. In reaching decisions about the substance and shape of our social studies teaching—in deciding upon the rationale, goals and organizing strands—several factors are particularly relevant:

- the needs and expressed wishes of our students
- the expectations embedded in the provincial curriculum;
- the nature of social studies as a subject and the range of purposes that social studies is expected to serve;
- the expressed wishes of the local community;
- the priorities and needs of society generally;
- our own priorities and strengths as an educator.

Developing a coherent and defensible social studies program is not an easy task—it will no doubt evolve over years of teaching and reflection. However, we can begin by thinking about our vision for social studies. If we have only the vaguest idea of what social studies is supposed to look like, how will our students learn from us?

REFERENCES

Brady, M. (1989). *What's worth teaching? Selecting, organizing and integrating knowledge.* Albany: State University of New York Press.

British Columbia Ministry of Education. (1988). *Social studies curriculum guide: Grades 8-11.* Victoria, BC: Author.

British Columbia Ministry of Education. (1990). *The Intermediate Program: Learning in British Columbia.* Victoria, BC: Author.

Chido, J. (1990). Social studies poems. *Social Education, 54*(7), 466-468.

3

Four Purposes of Citizenship Education

Penney Clark
Roland Case

Citizenship has been recognized as the rationale or defining aim of social studies since its inception as a school subject. In 1916, the final report of the Committee on Social Studies of the Commission on the Reorganization of Secondary Education, which marked the formal introduction of social studies in the United States, agreed that the "conscious and constant purpose" of social studies was "the cultivation of good citizenship" (cited in Dougan, 1988, pp. 14-15). Since then citizenship has been called "the primary, overriding purpose" (Barr, Barth & Shermis, 1977) and the "distinctive justification" (Jenness, 1990) of social studies. As Fitzgerald (1979) aptly describes it, again and again social studies reformers have come "reeling back to the old lamppost of citizenship training" (p. 187). In Canada, George Tomkins (1985) claims that "the goal of 'citizenship' probably comes closer than any other to identifying the process that Canadians have usually believed that the social studies should serve" (p. 15). Other Canadian reports affirm that it is the "primary focus" of social studies (Sears, 1994, p. 6).

Unfortunately, general acceptance of citizenship as the *raison d'être* for social studies does not provide much guidance or direction for the subject since there is little agreement as to the ideal citizen. Wilma Longstreet (1985) believes that 'citizenship' is such an amorphous concept that it may be used to legitimize virtually anything in social studies. Others argue that the apparent consensus around citizenship education is almost meaningless because of the widely disparate conceptions of citizenship (Marker & Mehlinger, 1992). Conceptions of citizenship range from "nationalistic loyalty" to "reconstructionism," views which are diametrically opposed (Nelson, 1980).

In this article we outline what we see to be four interrelated rationales of citizenship education which have served at varying times in the history of social studies as the defining purpose of the subject. Before looking at each of these, it is useful to explain why as social studies teachers we should care about which purpose (or mix of purposes), if any, undergirds our teaching.

A Direction for Social Studies

Many of us may be only vaguely aware of an implied vision that molds how we see our subject. Whether aware of it or not, our decisions are shaped by what in 1934 Charles Beard called a frame of reference:

> Every human brought up in society inevitably has in mind a frame of social knowledge, ideas, and ideals—a more or less definite pattern of things deemed necessary, things deemed possible, and things

deemed desirable; and to this frame or pattern, his thought and action will be more or less consciously referred. This frame may be large or small; it may embrace an immense storehouse of knowledge or little knowledge; it may be well organized with respect to categories of thought or confused and blurred in organization; and the ideal element in it may represent the highest or lowest aspirations of mankind. But frame there is in every human mind . . . Since all things known cannot be placed before children in the school room, there must and will be, inevitably, a selection, and the selection will be made with reference to some frame of knowledge and values, more or less consciously established in the mind of the selector. (cited in Thornton, 1991, p. 237)

For teachers, an important element of this frame of reference is our beliefs about the point or ultimate purpose of our subject. In the case of social studies, this is centrally connected with our vision of "good" citizenship. As a result, our decisions about what to teach will likely be informed, consciously or not, by our image of the type of person and world we hope to promote. If our model citizen is essentially someone who is well-informed about social matters, we will devote much of our time to helping students acquire a breadth of information about key topics. If our focus is the ability to make thoughtful ethical decisions about complex issues then we will likely want to engage students in investigating and discussing social issues. Perhaps our ideal citizen is someone who is committed to acting on his or her beliefs. In which case, students might undertake community enhancement projects or implement programs to reduce stereotypical attitudes. Each of these choices should, and likely will, be influenced by an implicit view of what our subject is all about.

For some of us our frame of reference may be so completely established that further discussion will make no difference. For others, however, exploring options may help us become more focussed and resolute in our orientation or, perhaps, cause us to modify our outlook in light of a clearer grasp of the alternative purposes that might be served. If we take seriously our role as educators—not as mere technicians implementing tightly prescribed directives, but as professionals charged with making complex judgments about the intellectual and emotional growth of our students—then we must articulate with some clarity our ultimate educational aims. As Ken Osborne (1991) writes in *Teaching for Democratic Citizenship*:

Good teachers possess a clear vision of education and of what it will do for their students. They are not simply technicians who take prescribed curriculum, or the textbook, and work their students through it. They incorporate the curriculum into their philosophy of education and use what it has to offer in ways that make educational sense. This involves thinking carefully about goals and about how to achieve them, and such thinking inevitably takes a teacher beyond the confines of the classroom. Edu-

cational goals do not exist in a vacuum. They emerge from thinking about what one wants for students and for the society in which they live. (p. 119)

At varying times in the eighty-year history of social studies in North America various rationales of citizenship education have been offered as the guiding purpose for the subject. We believe they are profitably categorized into four camps:[1]

- **citizenship education as social initiation:** passing on the understandings, abilities and values that students require if they are to fit into and be productive members of society;

- **citizenship education as social reformation:** empowering students with the understandings, abilities and values necessary to critique and ultimately improve their society;

- **citizenship education as personal development:** fostering students' personal competencies and interests so that they develop fully as individuals and as social beings;

- **citizenship education as academic understanding:** promoting mastery of the bodies of knowledge and forms of inquiry represented in the social science disciplines so that students have at their disposal the most sophisticated means to make sense of the complex world they face.

Each of these camps themselves comprise variations. For example, the particulars of a social initiation rationale will vary depending on whether we are more liberal or conservative; similarly, social reformers may be radical or moderate in their outlook on the need for social improvement. There is, as well, inevitable blurring of the lines between these camps. At some point an individual's view of a core set of insights and values will differ sufficiently from the majority view such that the individual's vision will cease to fall within the social initiation camp and, instead, amount to a modest form of social reformation. Even pedagogical approaches overlap considerably. Although, for example, social initiation is typically associated with textbook-based programs, and academic understanding with engaging students in conducting original historical or social science research, the reverse is not inconceivable. The point of categorizing different rationales is not to pigeonhole each of us in one camp or another, but to invite reflection about the range of options facing us when deciding upon our ultimate purpose in social studies—*our* reason for teaching the subject.

It is likely—even desirable—that many of us will endorse aspects of all four camps. We might, for example, think that promoting a sense of responsibility for others and recognition of the need to pull one's own weight are part of a core set of values that all citizens ought to abide by. To this extent we have some affinity for the social initiation camp. Perhaps we are concerned that many students are so accepting of mainstream *laissez faire* attitudes which contribute to environmental destruction, exploitation of workers, creation of a desperate underclass and other social ills. In this case, we are espousing elements of a social reformation perspective. We must also decide what is the best preparation for meeting these civic responsibilities. If our inclination is to build from students' feelings, needs, values, issues and problems, we are in effect adopting a personal development view of citizenship. This is certainly a widely-held rationale for social studies, but we may nevertheless be concerned that helping students become "personally fulfilled" may not do enough to prepare them to thoughtfully address the issues that they will encounter. The expression "Those who do not study history are doomed to repeat it" suggests that students who haven't studied much history will have little insight into and context for making sense of contempo-

rary questions. Perhaps, then preparation for civic life should focus on the bodies of knowledge and the rules of sound reasoning and research that drive history and the other social science disciplines. If this is the case, we have moved towards an academic understanding focus for citizenship education.

In formulating our own more specific set of purposes for social studies education, it is useful to view the four traditional camps as positions on two intersecting continuums (as shown in the box below):

- **social acceptance/social change spectrum.** Social initiation and social reformation represent a range of positions on a social acceptance/social change spectrum. At one extreme, the point of citizenship edu-

CITIZENSHIP EDUCATION MATRIX

Social studies rationales have tended to be defined exclusively in terms of one of the continuums either social acceptance/change or child/subject centred. Labeling a view as "social initiation" simply means that the dominant, but by no means exclusive, purpose is social acceptance. The closer a rationale is to the far left "social acceptance" end of the continuum, the greater the emphasis placed on promoting the status quo. As a rationale moves towards the "social change" pole, the emphasis on the status quo diminishes, until at some point the social reformation purpose begins to dominate.

Plotting rationales within a matrix allows us to locate particular camps in light of both sets of poles. For example, the "free school" movement in the 1960s was a radical child-centred approach to education with a strong social change mandate. Consequently, it belongs in the upper right-hand corner of this matrix. Since the public school version of a liberal arts education is strongly subject-centred with a clear social acceptance mandate, it belongs in the lower left-hand quadrant. A view of social studies which is in the very centre of the matrix would give equal weight and attention to all four purposes: getting students to accept certain aspects of society but to challenge others, and nurturing students' individual development in certain domains while seeking mastery of the disciplines.

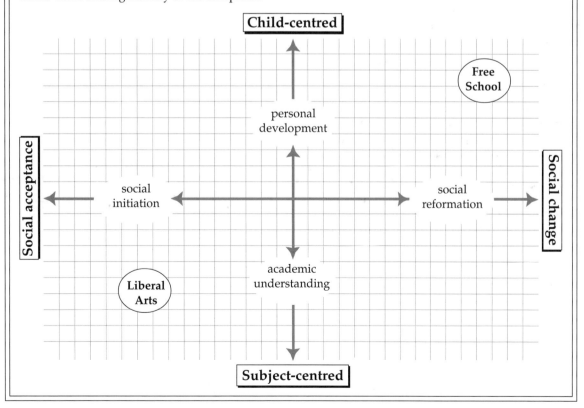

cation is to promote complete conformity with mainstream social norms and practices; at the other extreme, it is to promote total transformation of the social fabric. Seen in this light, the differences between the social initiation and social reformation camps are matters of degree about the extent and depth that citizenship education should encourage social conformity/social transformation.

- **subject-centered/student-centred spectrum**. Personal development and academic understanding represent a range of positions on a subject-centered/student-centred spectrum. At one extreme is a view that the best form of citizenship preparation is achieved by nurturing the whole child by focussing exclusively on students' interests, concerns, problems, values and so on; at the other extreme, the best form of citizenship preparation is thought to be achieved by disciplining the mind exclusively through exposure to the bodies of knowledge and forms of reasoning found in the social sciences.

Let us look at each of the traditional camps of citizenship education and consider how the difference within and between the camps can be explained in terms of where they fall within the matrix created by these two continuums.

THE SOCIAL ACCEPTANCE/ SOCIAL CHANGE SPECTRUM

As indicated above, two of the traditional visions of citizenship education—social intiation and social reformation—can be distinguished by the extent to which conformity with mainstream values, social practices and world view are encouraged.

Citizenship education as social initiation

The most common and long-standing view of the purpose of social studies, for that matter of public schooling generally, has been to promote a core body of beliefs and to instill a set of essential values and skills that are thought necessary to function in and contribute to society (Barr, Barth & Shermis, 1977, p. 59). The socializing role of schooling was prevalent in the 1800s in the teaching of patriotism and character training, which were the primary components of social education at the time. Aspects of it were evident in Canadian social studies curricula in the 1930s and 1940s, in which teachers were urged to use fables and stories about heroes (and occasionally heroines) as a means of inculcating values such as patriotism, loyalty and courage. The "back to basics" movement in the 1970's reinvigorated, in a very conservative voice, the call to provide all students with core knowledge and values. This tradition continues with the recent emphasis on learning the essential facts of our culture and history. E.D. Hirsch (1988) and his cultural literacy movement is an important contemporary American example of this vision. Recent headlines in Canadian newspapers—"Why Canada's Young Adults Need a History Lesson" and "Lack of Common Culture Observed" (MacQueen, 1997, A1, A2)—attest to continuing public interest in promoting knowledge of basic facts of Canadian political and social history.

The social initiation rationale appears to be widely shared by social studies teachers. Jim Leming (1992) believes that in the United States social studies teachers, generally speaking, espouse a conservative version of social initiation involving "the transmission of mainstream interpretations of history and American values" (p. 294). Linda McNeil (1986) found in an ethnographic study of teachers in six schools that a major goal was helping students maintain positive attitudes toward American institutions. In order to achieve this goal teachers avoided content which would expose students to the injustices and inadequacies of economic and political institutions. In a survey of almost 1,800 elementary and secondary social studies teachers in British Columbia, approximately 70 percent supported social initiation as a dominant purpose for social studies (Case, 1993, p. 3). This compared with approximately 57 percent supporting a social reformist role, and 38 percent supporting academic understanding. (Respondents were not asked to comment on a personal development rationale.)

Social initiation does not necessarily require indoctrinating students into a narrow set of beliefs and values. Although nineteenth and early twentieth century versions of social initiation in Canada had a decidedly pro-British assimilationist bent, more recent versions embody a more multicultural, pluralistic aim (Sears, 1994). An individual's perception of the prevailing, mainstream image of a good citizen may be broadminded, including values such as an abiding respect for the rights of others and, in particular, tolerance of individual and cultural differences and freedoms. Nor is social initiation inconsistent with critical thinking; but there are parameters within which this questioning is to occur—students would not be taught or encouraged to question the foundations and received interpretations of our history and dominant world view.

The crucial questions from a social initiation perspective are to what extent and in which ways should the defining purpose of social studies focus on getting students to buy into the generally accepted world view and norms of behaviour. Consider, for example, the following list which several American writers refer to as "a middle of the road interpretation of mainstream val-

> The most common and long-standing view of the purpose of social studies . . . has been to promote a core body of beliefs and to instill a set of essential values and skills that are thought necessary to function in and contribute to society.

ues" in the United States. They cite acceptance of the following values: belief in self-government, the importance of considerable individual freedom, the necessity for hard work, the value of achievement, tolerance and acceptance of differences and the right to make a profit from one's efforts and investments (Barr, Barth & Shermis, 1977, p. 61). Should we encourage students to accept these sorts of social givens? Or should students be taught to question the often unexamined beliefs, values, social practices and structures that undergird our society? For example, would it be beneficial for students to question seriously whether or not Confederation is something to celebrate, whether or not Canada is a token democracy and whether or not students should engage in civil disobedience? These issues are not consistent with the defining premise of social initiation, namely to get students to *internalize* a perspective—to learn about and believe the "received" conception or image of our society, our history and the model citizen.

> Social studies as social reformation has, as its name implies, a focus on encouraging a better society. It posits that there is much to be improved about society and that the role of social studies is to help students acquire the understandings, abilities and values that will launch them on this path.

Citizenship education as social reformation

Social studies as social reformation has, as its name implies, a focus on encouraging a better society. It posits that there is much to be improved about society and that the role of social studies is to help students acquire the understandings, abilities and values that will launch them on this path. Although both social initiation and social reformation would teach students about the history and workings of our nation and the world, their dominant purposes pull in opposing directions. In the case of social initiation, the overriding point is to get students to endorse the implied world view, whereas social reformers believe the emphasis should be to prepare students to critique the existing society. And unlike a social initiation view where the emphasis is on getting students to participate in and contribute to the established ways of operating, a social reformist emphasis is on empowering students to work towards a 'better' society. The reformative position need not imply a radical anarchistic view of social change, but by definition social reform is more controversial than the social initiation position. Leming (1992) and others believe it is for this reason that social reform is espoused more often by university professors than by classroom teachers.

Social studies closest turn towards a social reformation orientation occurred in the 1970's. Jerome Bruner, earlier a proponent of an academic understanding rationale of citizenship education, announced in a 1971 article entitled "*The Process of Education* Revisited," a "moratorium" or at least a "de-emphasis" on teaching the structure of history and instead argued for teaching history in the context of the problems facing Ameri-

can society (p. 21). He identified social problems such as poverty, racism, the unpopular war in Vietnam and the extent to which schools had become "instruments of the evil forces in our society" (p. 20) as desired foci for social studies instruction. Osborne points out that Canada, too, had a "crisis of values" at the time, with the October crisis of 1970, new societal concerns such as sexism, the stirring of discontent among native peoples and a breakdown in federal/provincial relations (1984, p. 95). Others point to Black Studies, Women's Studies and Third World or Development Studies, which have been regularly offered in Ontario as examples of a social reform vision of social studies (van Manen & Parsons, 1985, p. 6). More recently, some environmental education programs have raised critical consideration of local problems such as land use and conservation, as well as larger issues such as overpopulation, pollution and resource depletion.

An important thread of the social reformation camp is teaching students to be what Walter Werner and Ken Nixon call "critically-minded"—to be inclined as a general orientation to ask hard questions about much of what we encounter (1990, p. 2). Students need, for example, to be taught that public media do not simply convey information but, as Neil Postman suggests, they "conceptualize" reality: "They will classify the world for us, sequence it, frame it, enlarge it, reduce it, and argue a case for what it is like" (1979, p. 39). The very fact that public media pay attention to or ignore an event determines what we come to see as important or worth knowing. So too with what gets taught in schools. We shape students' perceptions of what is important in school and in life by celebrating, for example, the individual efforts of famous figures (e.g., Van Horne built the CPR, Cheops built the Great Pyramid) and not the collective toil of ordinary, often exploited people, or by focussing on the military outcomes of battles and not on their environmental outcomes. A social reformer would want students to be critical (in an intellectually healthy way) of the very sources and selection of information—including of their teacher and their textbooks. Whereas a social initiator, even one close to the reformative camp, would want students to be more generally accepting of these sources.

Within the last twenty years a more radical version of social reform—espoused by critical theorists—has appeared in the social studies literature. This version presumes that knowledge is never impartial but *always* represents a value position because it is constructed by people with particular values and interests (Stanley, 1981, 1986). Representing any knowledge as a given or as objectively true obscures its social, economic, political and historical contexts. Social science knowledge shapes our society in conformity with some values and in opposition to others since the dominant culture within our society has a major influence on the development and maintenance of our social institutions. This radical form of social reform calls for "root criticism" of all knowledge in the social sciences, including critical study of gender, race, nationalistic or social class domination of social structures and knowledge (Nelson, 1985, p. 370). Canadian proponents of this conception include van Manen (1980), who invites teachers to broach with their students the "emancipatory" suggestion that "a socially conscious person" ought to engage in "social criticism of all forms of hegemony including the authority of the knowledge and value orientations taught in school" (p. 114).

A second key element in many versions of social reform is the importance of social action. Since the overarching goal is to improve society, students should be assisted in acquiring the abilities and the inclinations to act on their beliefs. There has been a somewhat spotty and ambiguous inclusion of "social action" in Canadian social studies curricula. Fred Newmann's (1975) book, *Education for Citizen Action*, has been influential in urging that students develop "environmental competence" (p. 157) and engage in social action as the natural outcome of considering public issues. The 1981 Alberta curriculum incorporated this notion, with the final step of its inquiry model, "applying the decision," which encouraged students to create plans to implement their decisions (e.g., work to improve school or classroom conditions, provide services to community groups or participate actively in the political process) (Alberta Education, 1981, p. 9). This action component has been retained, although de-emphasized, in the present Alberta curriculum. Recent draft social studies curriculum documents in British Columbia (1996a, 1996b) mandate action projects for students from kindergarten to grade ten. However, it is ambiguous as to the rationale which undergirds this call to involve students in projects outside the classroom. It is consistent with a social initiation rationale to engage students in non-controversial forms of social participation such as cleaning up the litter around the school grounds and raising money for a local charity. A reformative purpose for social action would likely involve students in projects that seek to change, as opposed to merely perpetuate, the way things are done. For example, elementary students have been involved in social reform by writing letters to the newspaper about the way baboons were caged at a Calgary zoo (Dueck, Horvath & Zelinski, 1977) and McDonald's use of styrofoam packaging (Roth, 1991).

THE CHILD-CENTRED/SUBJECT-CENTERED SPECTRUM

Unlike the prior two purposes of citizenship education which have an implied stance towards the status quo—either that the existing state of affairs is basically sound or that it is not and should be changed—the next

two camps that we discuss posit no such assumption. Perpetuating or altering the social order are not their preoccupation. Rather their concern is where to focus in identifying and developing the desired knowledge, abilities and values. Are they found with the child by looking to and working with the range of personal needs and everyday predicaments of students, or do they reside in the subject area, in this case in the storehouse of intellectual insight offered though the social science disciplines?

Citizenship education as personal development

The focus of personal development is on nurturing students so that they are fulfilled, personally and socially. It is believed that the "good" society will follow from creating well-adjusted individuals. Important elements of this tradition are traced to John Dewey's progressivist philosophy. Although as Osborne suggests, "Canadian progressivism spoke in terms of the growth and development of students, of meeting students' needs, of teaching the whole child, and much less of social reform or reconstruction" (1996, p. 42). There is much less a sense of an imposed body of knowledge or predetermined direction for social studies education; the understandings, abilities and attitudes to be developed are very much those that are required to cope with and make sense of students' own lives and experiences. As Shermis explains in this tradition "a problem is not a problem unless an individual senses it as such" (1982, p. 49).

The personal development rationale has had a long history. It can be seen in the 1916 report of the National Education Association Committee on Social Studies in which it was suggested that instruction be organized "not on the basis of the formal social sciences, but on the basis of concrete problems of vital importance to society and of *immediate interest to the pupil* [emphasis added]" (cited in Jenness, 1990, p. 77). This progressive-inspired tradition came into prominence in Canada in the 1930s, a decade during which every province initiated major curricular reform. Revised provincial curricula exemplified new 'child-centred' approaches, which implied correlation of subject matter around the needs and interests of the child. The emphasis was on the 'whole' child who would "grow physically, emotionally and spiritually, as well as mentally" (Newland, 1941, p. 12). Curricula were "activity" oriented, with a focus on group investigation of problems or issues of interest to students, which were intended to promote cooperation, communication and decision-making. Social studies formed the basis of these group investigations, which were called "enterprises" at the elementary level in many provinces (Department of Education, Alberta, 1936, p. 288).

In the 1941 Alberta curriculum, enterprises in grades one to three were to be developed as part of a social studies related theme entitled "How We Adjust Ourselves to Our Immediate Environment to Satisfy Our Basic Human Needs." In grades four to six the theme was "How Man Adjusts Himself in More Remote Environments To Satisfy His Basic Human Needs." Social attitudes and abilities were more important than subject matter content (Department of Education, Alberta, 1941). "The social studies classroom instead of being a place where children 'learn' history, geography and civics, is to be a real laboratory, where co-operation, initiative, originality and responsibility are developed" (Department of Education, Alberta, 1935, p. 36). At the secondary level this approach found expression in programs referred to in different provinces as core curriculum, life adjustment curriculum, or an integration of social studies with language arts and the humanities.

In the 1960s, the values clarification movement was an important addition to the personal development orientation. Values clarification is a model for teaching values developed by Louis Raths, Merrill Harmin and Sidney Simon (1966) which encourages students to choose their own system of values. The values clarification model has been described as "extraordinarily influential" in the development of the 1971 Alberta social studies curricula (Milburn, 1976, p. 222).

The personal development rationale remains in evidence in contemporary social studies, especially in the elementary school. Key features of this vision include: (1) a belief that the content of what is learned is not as significant as students finding what they study personally relevant to their lives, (2) an emphasis on supporting students in pursuing their own directions and developing their own interests, (3) an emphasis on exposing students to a wide range of situations and experiences where they can work out their beliefs and develop their own positions on issues and (4) a priority given to supporting students in feeling confident about themselves and their beliefs over challenging students to think differently or to question their values.

Citizenship education as academic understanding

The definition of social studies which exemplifies the academic understanding rationale is Edgar Wesley's "the social studies are the social sciences simplified for pedagogical purposes" (1937, p. 4). The defining feature of this tradition is not simply or even essentially a matter of acquiring a body of knowledge as it is mastery of the norms and methods used by scholars to gain new knowledge. It is believed that the various social science disciplines have generated the richest insights and investigative techniques for understanding our social world. Hence, acquisition of the understandings, skills and attitudes of social scientists and historians is thought to provide the best preparation for citizenship in a complex world. Unlike the personal development

camp, academic understanding rationales of citizenship education see the disciplines, more than the students, providing the problems worth considering, initiation into the academic traditions are more important than exposure to problems of immediate and personal concern, and coming to one's own conclusions is not as important as coming up with intellectually defensible conclusions.

This tradition came into its own with the publication of Jerome Bruner's slim book, *The Process of Education,* in 1960. Bruner referred to the "structure of the disciplines," by which he meant teaching the component parts or basic structures—the concepts, canons of reasoning and techniques of inquiry—particular to each discipline. He believed that the basic ideas lying at the heart of the disciplines are simple enough for students at any level to grasp. Bruner argued that "intellectual activity anywhere is the same, whether at the frontier of knowledge or in a third-grade classroom" (p. 14). Consequently, rather than simply presenting students with the findings of a discipline, students should take on the role of social scientists and use inquiry techniques of the disciplines to make discoveries themselves. This tradition has been evident in Canada in the texts and other curriculum materials used in the late 1960s and

It is believed that the various social science disciplines have generated the richest insights and investigative techniques for understanding our social world. Hence, acquisition of the understandings, skills and attitudes of social scientists and historians is thought to provide the best preparation for citizenship in a complex world. Unlike the personal development camps, academic understanding visions of citizenship see the disciplines, more than the students, providing the problems worth considering, . . . and coming to one's own conclusions is not as important as coming up with intellectually defensible conclusions.

1970s. It also appeared in texts used for university social studies curriculum and instruction courses, such as *Teaching the Subjects in the Social Studies,* written by Evelyn Moore and Edward Owen (1966). This book points out to the reader that "the authors accept, as a major purpose of the social studies, that elementary school children should begin to learn the thinking patterns, or structure, of the social sciences" (p. v). The authors then go on to say that "a better democratic citizen [is one] who can think historically or geographically, who can think as an economist or as a political scientist, whenever these approaches are relevant to the assessment of contemporary situations" (p. v).

A similar philosophy underlies a 1960's approach to teaching geography in the elementary school:

the child learns, at his own level, the *structure* of geography and the *methods* used by the professional geographer. He will learn of, through use at his own level, the various subjects which contribute to the subject of geography. He will also learn through practice in the field, and later with pictures, to observe details carefully, to record these details in many ways, to analyze the data, and then to synthesize selected data to answer a problem. (Social Studies Advisory Committee, Faculty of Education, University of British Columbia, 1962, p. 139)

While the structure of the disciplines approach has been somewhat discredited,[2] the calls to promote disciplined historical and geography understandings are as strong as they ever were. In fact, there is considerable pressure, including calls from Canadian academics (Seixas, 1994, 1997; see also Egan's articles in this collection), to replace social studies with the teaching of history and geography. As Peter Seixas (1997) argues, students should approach historical accounts critically. Yet this is unlikely to happen as long as students are taught only generic critical thinking or information processing approaches. The distinct challenges of thinking within the disciplines—notions in history, such as what counts as an historically significant event, the difficulties of historical empathy and the bases for accepting historical claims—require discipline-specific instruction. Without a developed capacity for historical thinking, teaching about the past is little more than the "simple accretion of increasing amounts of information" (Seixas, 1994, p. 105). According to proponents of an academic understanding rationale, since the social science disciplines are the most rigorous and insightful forms of inquiry about our social world, they represent the best tools that social studies educators can offer students in preparation for citizenship.

Having a Sense of Purpose

It is evident from the foregoing discussion that the factors which influence the adoption of a particular conception include deep-rooted assumptions about the role of schooling, the perceived nature of challenges facing society and students, personal values of the teacher and theories of knowledge and learning. Because of these ideological divisions, many have dispaired of arriving at a common vision for citizenship education (Marker & Mehlinger, 1992, p. 832). Attempts to reach consensus typically result in statements of purpose that are so vague they provide no helpful direction and are of dubious educational value. For example a 1982 survey of provincial curricula by the Canadian Council of Ministers of Education concluded that the common focus is on inquiry approaches toward a goal of providing "students with the knowledge, skills, values and thought processes which will enable them to participate effectively and responsibly in the ever-changing environment of their community, their country and their world" (p. 4). This statement could

include anything imaginable and can be interpreted to apply to any of the four camps. It is no wonder that it is frequently observed that: "The content of social studies is a smorgasbord of this and that from everywhere; it is as confusing and vague as is the goal of citizenship" (Barr, Barth & Shermis, 1977, p. 2).

Not only is consensus on an identifiable set of desired attributes of citizenship not currently present, the prospects of it are remote. In order to fill this serious gap each of us must of necessity develop our own guiding purpose for social studies.

After reading the above discussion, we may be inclined to actively promote aspects of all four rationales for citizenship education. Perhaps the most appropriate way of framing the challenge is by asking "In what respects should each of these purposes be promoted?" However, we must be careful that this does not amount to unfocussed borrowing from all four camps. Vague and indiscriminate choices have produced the smorgasbord referred to above. Barr, Barth and Shermis, later in the same book, characterize social studies in even less flattering terms, referring to complaints that the subject is "social sludge" and "social stew" and amounts to "a confusing hodge podge" (p. 57). One reason for developing a focussed and discriminating

> One reason for developing a focussed and discriminating vision is that few of the attributes of citizenship that are truly worthwhile can be nurtured quickly. Those that we are most serious about will require considerable thought and effort to bring about. Students will not, for example, develop mastery of the social science disciplines without considerable exposure to the body of knowledge and standards of reasoning in these areas.

sense of purpose is that few of the attributes of citizenship that are truly worthwhile can be nurtured quickly. Those that we are most serious about will require considerable thought and effort to bring about. Students will not, for example, develop mastery of the social science disciplines without considerable exposure to the body of knowledge and standards of reasoning in these areas. Promoting all of the purposes in a half-hearted way may mean that nothing is done very well. Besides, there is never enough time. We must inevitably establish priorities, even if these priorities change over time and depend upon the particular class we are teaching.

The choices we are forced to make each day of our teaching lives should reflect these priorities. Although many of the differences are more matters of emphasis than of mutual exclusivity, in important respects the different purposes require choices among competing objectives. Take, for example, the teaching about Sir John A. Macdonald. Do we explore his personal and political failings in order to debunk the myths of heroes (social reformation) or do we actively enhance his stature in an effort to promote appreciation for national heroes (social initiation)? Alternatively, we might either put the evidence for both sides forward and encourage students to decide for themselves (academic understanding), or leave it entirely up to students to decide whether or not they will study the issue of Macdonald as national hero (personal development).

What is more, unless we actively work to control for the influences of the hidden curriculum, they will subtly but pervasively impose a tacit vision of citizenship. For example, reliance on a *single* "authoritative" text is likely to suppress key attributes of social reform and academic understanding, as will emphasis on recall of received "accepted" facts over student-initiated and -justified interpretations of events. One way or another, consciously or unconsciously, we will likely advance a particular rationale. For all of these reasons, we should be cautious about assuming that we can do it all, or that it doesn't much matter which vision or collection of attributes we judge to be most defensible. It should be stressed that the choice of a dominant purpose(s) should not be a whimsical personal preference. Rather it requires thoughtful and professional judgment based on a number of factors including the needs, best interests and rights of our students, their parents and of society, more broadly.

Developing our own clear sense of purpose is possible and desirable because in the present social studies climate of vague generalities, most curriculum frameworks, teaching approaches and learning resources can be interpreted and adapted to fit different purposes. Many teaching activities and materials—such as use of textbooks and primary documents, analysis of issues, field trips—are common to all four camps. These standard teaching approaches may be employed in different ways depending on the ultimate purpose for teaching social studies—for example, by varying the topics debated, the amount of deference to the authority of the textbook and the importance attached to students' wishes. This possibility of massaging teaching objectives, activities and resources to align with a particular purpose offers the most compelling reason for each of us to think clearly about the sort of citizen that ought to guide our social studies teaching. Every day in countless, often unconscious ways we shape students' development as members of society. If we are unclear about the direction, we will likely perpetuate the bland smorgasbord that has typified mission statements in social studies. In which case, we can hardly complain about a passive, unreflective and apathetic citizenry, since we may have nurtured this "vision" by default— by failing to infuse our teaching with a coherent direction. Each of us needs a clear and reasonable rationale, even if it differs from the teacher's rationale that students encountered the year before and will encounter the year after. In fact, a diversity of well-conceived rationales may be healthy. Doing things well even if the goals differ is preferable to consistently doing things in a tepid and diluted manner. Far fewer students will

be inspired or assisted by a social studies program that lacks clear focus and strong direction. To paraphrase a familiar proverb "Where there is no vision, programs perish."

ENDNOTES

[1] The conceptual framework for social studies that has had the most impact and the greatest longevity of any that have been offered is the one developed by Robert Barr, James Barth and Samuel Shermis (1977, 1978). Their typology which places citizenship as the ultimate goal of social studies consists of three traditions: citizenship transmission, social studies as social science and social studies taught as reflective inquiry. Other conceptual frameworks include the five-camp model of D. Brubaker, L. Simon and J. Williams (1977) and the seven program types of Max van Manen and Jim Parsons (1985).

Our four-rationale framework differs from the three traditions of the Barr et al. model in three ways. Our "social initiation" is a narrower notion than their "citizenship transmission." They include any form of transmission of a world view—one which may be a mainstream view or a rather esoteric view shared by a minority—as part of citizenship transmission. Following John Hass (1979) we limit "social initiation" to mainstream world views; we regard visions of society that are different from the mainstream view as "social reform." Following Jean Fair (1977) and Brubaker et al. (1977) we believe that "reflective inquiry" neglects an important tradition in social studies—the child-centred, personal fulfillment vision. We offer "personal development" to reflect this strand. Finally, following Suzanne Helburn (1977) we collapse the Barr et al. account of "reflective inquiry" with "social science" into what we call "academic understanding."

Brubaker et al. (1977) expand Barr et al.'s three traditions into five: social studies as knowledge of the past as a guide to good citizenship, social studies in the student centered tradition, social studies as reflective inquiry, social studies as structure of the disciplines, and social studies as socio-political involvement. Brubaker et al. add the two positions, social studies in the student centered tradition and social studies as socio-political involvement. They view the Barr et al. model as inadequate because it does not acknowledge the two camps into which progressive educators had split, the social problem and child centered orientations. Barr et al. acknowledge only the social problem camp in their reflective inquiry tradition. Brubaker et al. considered it necessary to acknowledge rationales based on social action as well.

van Manen and Parsons (1985) offer the only major Canadian attempt to categorize conceptions of social studies. These theorists set out seven program types: traditional subject matter program, student activity type program, structure of the discipline orientation, social reconstruction and reflective awareness, moral education and valuing processes, environmental education and social problems and Canada Studies and citizenship education. The traditional subject matter program type is built around the core subjects of history and geography. This program type is, of course, based on the same foundations as the citizenship transmission tradition in the Barr et al. So, too, the structure of the discipline program type is Barr et al.'s social studies taught as social sciences by another name. The same can be said for the van Manen and Parsons' student activity type program and Brubaker et al.'s social studies in the student centered tradition. van Manen and Parsons see four additional program types arising in the 1970s. The aim of the social reconstruction and reflective awareness program type "is the development of an active critical awareness on the part of all citizens to the need for social change toward a more just and equitable social world order" (p. 6). The moral education and valuing processes program type has at least two variations: values clarification intended to encourage students to choose their own coherent system of values and the moral reasoning approach intended to move children systematically up through a series of stages of moral development. The aim of the third program type, that of environmental education and social problems, is to help students develop "the ability to use a variety of knowledge sources and community resources in the examination of environmental issues" (p. 10). The Canada Studies and citizenship education program focuses on decision-making within a Canadian context. A major aim is to promote nationalistic goals. We believe that their typology conflates types of programs and rationales, accounting for a proliferation of conceptions of social studies.

[2] The structure of the discipline approach has been criticized on numerous counts (Fenton, 1991; Massialas, 1992; Dow, 1992). Criticisms include an over reliance on knowledge objectives and inquiry procedures from the social science disciplines, while ignoring the needs and interests of students and societal problems; materials which were too sophisticated for the students for whom they were intended; its failure to involve typical teachers in material development; ignorance of the hidden curriculum of gender, social class, ethnic and religious issues; the logistical complexity of many of the projects; and a failure to bridge the cultural gap between theory and the real world of teaching involving large classes, multiple preparations and often resistant students.

REFERENCES

Alberta Education. (1981). *1981 Alberta social studies curriculum*. Edmonton, AB: Author.

Barr, R., Barth, J.L. & Shermis, S.S. (1977). *Defining the social studies*. Arlington, VA: National Council for the Social Studies.

Barr, R., Barth, J.L. & Shermis, S.S. (1978). *The nature of the social studies*. Palm Springs, CA: ETC Publications.

British Columbia, Ministry of Education, Skills and Training. (1996a). *Social studies K to 7 integrated resource package, Review document*. Victoria, BC: Author.

British Columbia, Ministry of Education, Skills and Training. (1996b). *Social studies 8 to 10 integrated resource package, Review document*. Victoria, BC: Author.

Brubaker, D.L., Simon, L.H. & Williams, J.W. (1977). A conceptual framework for social studies curriculum and instruction. *Social Education, 41*, 201-205.

Bruner, J. (1960). *The process of education*. Cambridge, MA: Harvard University Press.

Bruner, J. (1971). *The process of education* revisited. *Phi Delta Kappan, 53*, 18-21.

Case, R. (1993). *Summary of the 1992 social studies needs assessment*. Victoria, BC: Queen's Printer.

Council of Ministers of Education, Canada. (1982). *Social studies: A survey of provincial curricula at the elementary and secondary levels*. Toronto: Author.

Department of Education, Alberta. (1935). *Programme of studies for the elementary school*. Edmonton, AB: Author.

Department of Education, Alberta. (1936), *Programme of studies for the elementary school*. Edmonton, AB: Author.

Department of Education, Alberta. (1941). *Programme of studies for the elementary school*. Edmonton, AB: Author.

Dougan, A.M. (1988). The search for a definition of the social studies: A historical overview. *The International Journal of Social Education 3*(3), 13-36.

Dow, P. (1992). Past as prologue: The legacy of Sputnik. *Social Studies, 83*, 164-171.

Dueck, K., Horvath, F. & Zelinski, V. (1977). Bev Prifit's class takes on the Calgary zoo. *One World, 17*, 7-8.

Fair, J. (1977). Comments of Jean Fair. In R. Barr, J.L. Barth & S.S. Shermis. *Defining the social studies* (pp. 106-109). Arlington, VA: National Council for the Social Studies.

Fenton, E. (1991). Reflections on the 'new social studies.' *Social Studies, 82*, 84-90.

Fitzgerald, F. (1979). *America revised: History schoolbooks in the twentieth century*. Toronto: Little Brown.

Haas, J.D. (1979). Social studies: Where have we been? Where are we going? *Social Studies, 70*, 147-154.

Helburn, S.W. (1977). Comments of Suzanne W. Helburn. In R. Barr, J.L. Barth & S.S. Shermis. *Defining the social studies* (pp. 110-113). Arlington, VA: National Council for the Social Studies.

Hirsch, E.D. (1988). *Cultural literacy: What every American needs to know*. New York: Vintage.

Jenness, D. (1990). *Making sense of social studies*. Toronto: Collier Macmillan Canada.

Leming, J.S. (1992). Ideological perspectives within the social studies profession: An empirical examination of the "two cultures" thesis. *Theory and Research in Social Education, 20*(3), 293-312.

Longstreet, W.S. (1985). Citizenship: The phantom core of social studies curriculum. *Theory and*

Research in Social Education, 13(2), 21-29.

Marker, G. & Mehlinger, H. (1992). Social studies. In P.W. Jackson (Ed.), *Handbook of research on curriculum* (pp. 830-851). Toronto: Maxwell Macmillan Canada.

Massialas, B.G. (1992). The 'new social studies': Retrospect and prospect. *Social Studies, 83*, 120-124.

McNeil, L. (1986). *Contradictions of control: School structure and school knowledge.* New York: Routledge and Kegan Paul.

MacQueen, K. (1997, June 30). Why Canada's young adults need a history lesson. *Vancouver Sun*, pp. A1, A2.

Milburn, G. (1976). The social studies curriculum in Canada: A survey of the published literature in the last decade. *Journal of Educational Thought, 10*, 212-224.

Moore, E. & Owen, E.E. (1966). *Teaching the subjects in the social studies: A handbook for teachers.* Toronto: Macmillan.

Nelson, J.R. (1980). The uncomfortable relationship between moral education and citizenship instruction. In R. Wilson & G. Schochet (Eds.), *Moral development and politics.* New York: Praeger.

Nelson, J.R. (1985). New criticism and social education. *Social Education, 49*, 368-371.

Newland, H.C. (1941). *Report of the supervisor of schools.* In *Thirty-sixth annual report of the Department of Education of the Province of Alberta.* Edmonton, AB: A Schnitka, King's Printer.

Newmann, F.M. (1975). *Education for citizen action: Challenge for secondary curriculum.* Berkeley, CA: McCutchan.

Osborne, K. (1984). A consummation devoutly to be wished: Social studies and general curriculum theory. In D.A. Roberts & J.O. Fritz (Eds.), *Curriculum Canada V: School subject research and curriculum/instruction theory.* Proceedings of the Fifth Invitational Conference of Curriculum Research of the C.S.S.E. Vancouver, BC: Centre for the Study of Curriculum and Instruction, University of British Columbia.

Osborne, K. (1991). *Teaching for democratic citizenship.* Toronto: Our Schools/Our Selves Education Foundation.

Osborne, K. (1996). Education is the best national insurance: Citizenship education in Canadian schools—past and present. *Canadian and International Education, 25*(2), 31-58.

Postman, N. (1979). *Teaching as a conserving activity.* New York: Delta Books.

Raths, L.E., Harmin, M. & Simon, S.B. (1966). *Values and teaching: Working with values in the classroom.* Columbus, OH: Charles E. Merrill.

Roth, A. (1991, April). Battle of the clamshell. *Report on Business Magazine*, pp. 40-43, 45-47.

Sears, A. (1994). Social studies as citizenship education in English Canada: A review of research. *Theory and Research in Social Education, 22*(1), 6-43.

Seixas, P. (1994). A discipline adrift in an "integrated" curriculum:The problem of history in British Columbia schools. *Canadian Journal of Education 19*(1), 99-107.

Seixas, P. (1997). The place of history within social studies. In I. Wright & A. Sears (Eds.), *Trends and issues in Canadian social studies* (pp. 116-129). Vancouver: Pacific Educational Press.

Shermis, S.S. (1982). A response to our critics: Reflective inquiry is not the same as social science. *Theory and Research in Social Education, 10*(1), 45-50.

Social Studies Advisory Committee, Faculty of Education, University of British Columbia. (1962). *History and geography teaching materials.* Vancouver: University of British Columbia.

Stanley W.B. (1981). The radical reconstructionist rationale for social education. *Theory and Research in Social Education, 8*, 55-79.

Stanley, W.B. (1986). Critical research. In C. Cornbleth (Ed.), *An invitation to research in social education* (pp. 78-90). Washington, DC: National Council for the Social Studies.

Thornton, S. J. (1991). Teacher as curricular-instructional gatekeeper in social studies. In J.P. Shaver (Ed.), *Handbook of research on social studies teaching and learning* (pp. 237-248). Toronto: Collier Macmillan Canada.

Tomkins G. (1985). The social studies in Canada. In Parsons, J., Milburn, G. & van Manen, M. (Eds.), *A Canadian social studies* (rev. ed.) (pp. 12-30). Edmonton, AB: University of Alberta.

van Manen, M. (1980). A concept of social critique. *The History and Social Science Teacher, 15*, 110-114.

van Manen, M. & Parsons, J. (1985). What are the social studies? In J. Parsons, G. Milburn & M. van Manen (Eds.), *A Canadian social studies* (rev. ed.) (pp. 2-11). Edmonton, AB: University of Alberta.

Werner, W. & Nixon, K. (1990). *The media and public issues: A guide for teaching critical mindedness.* London, ON: Althouse Press.

Wesley, E.B. (1937). *Teaching social studies in high schools.* Boston: D.C. Heath.

4

THE TEACHING OF HISTORY AND DEMOCRATIC CITIZENSHIP

KEN OSBORNE

I want to argue that history has an important contribution to make to the practice of democratic citizenship. In making this argument, I will examine, first, the nature and meaning of citizenship; second, the traditional linkage between history and citizenship; and, third, the ways in which a renewed approach to the teaching of history can help to produce a more democratic citizenship, both in theory and in practice, than we now know.

To say that history must contribute to democratic citizenship does not mean that history must be turned to narrowly political ends. It is another way of saying what Vaclav Havel recently wrote of schools:

> The role of the schools is not to create 'idiot specialists' to fill the special needs of different sectors of the national economy, but to develop the individual abilities of the students in a purposeful way, and to send out into life thoughtful people capable of thinking about the wider social, historical, and philosophical implications of their specialties. . . . The schools must also lead young people to become self-confident, participating citizens; if everyone doesn't take an interest in politics, it will become the domain of those least suited to it. (Havel, 1992, p. 12)

THE NATURE AND MEANING OF CITIZENSHIP

Citizenship is a notoriously vague word which means different things to different people. Its specific meaning takes its shape from the particular political and institutional context in which it is located. Education for citizenship, then, can have a misleading and even dangerous meaning. To some it indicates ideological indoctrination, the preparation of loyal servants of whatever regime is in power. To others, it means instilling the disposition to abide by and to help preserve the status quo.

Properly understood, however, it means neither ideological nor institutional conformity, and especially not when used in its democratic sense. As Derek Heater (1990) recently reminded us, it is an idea that has long historical roots, going back at least to Ancient Athens. In its contemporary form its most direct origins are to be found in the American and French Revolutions with their insistence that "the people" have the right and the authority to govern themselves. It is true that historically there were many exclusions from the people, including women, slaves, the poor, and others, but once the principle was established that the people were the only legitimate source of political power and authority, it became possible to argue just who constituted the people. In any event a clear conceptual distinction began to emerge between the newer concept of citizen and the older concept of subject.

This notion of the people carried a territorial connotation: the people were people of a particular sort living in a particular space, united by common attributes, responsibilities, values and aspirations. They were, in fact, or ought to be, a nation, and as a nation they considered themselves entitled to their own territorial and political unit, the nation-state. Such, at least, became the nineteenth century orthodoxy, which in turn became the orthodoxy of our own century. Nationalism, whatever its other failings, entrenched more solidly than ever before the concept of citizenship.

The connection between nationalism and citizenship which was so tightly forged in the nineteenth century must be loosened. We live in an age of international problems which demand international solutions.

Thus arose the essential ingredients of citizenship as the word is generally understood today: first, a sense of identity with some wider community, usually defined as the nation; second, a set of rights and entitlements, such as the right to vote and to be represented; and, third, a corresponding set of obligations, such as obedience to the law.

At the same time, citizenship is not a static entity. Its meaning changed and continues to change over time. It is in a process of constant definition. Its boundaries are always being tested, sometimes expanding and sometimes shrinking. Above all, it is closely connected with struggle. What we now take for granted as democratic citizenship rights were either won by subordinate groups in struggle against the dominant order of their day, or were yielded by the dominant order as a calculated response to a real or perceived crisis. It is a process that continues today and will persist into the future. This linkage between citizenship and struggle has important consequences for the teaching of history, but of this more later.

From its beginnings, citizenship has carried a certain democratic connotation. Citizens formed a community of equals who governed themselves, though it is true that they usually comprised only a small fraction of the total society of which they were a part. There were, however, always those who sought to give citizenship a broader social base. Their message entered mainstream political debate as a result of the American, French and Industrial Revolutions, when citizenship began to be linked with the concepts of popular sovereignty and equality of rights. The struggles of the nineteenth and twentieth centuries—for the vote, for the right to organize, for greater social equality and so on—were based on and gave further strength to a sense of citizens as people with powers and rights and with corresponding obligations. Citizens have a right to choose their governments, to make their voices heard, to play a role in politics, to enjoy certain social benefits and legal protections. At the same time, they are expected to obey the law, to pay their taxes, to play by the rules, and so on. However, the democratic aspects of citizenship are often limited and sometimes totally obstructed. Gender, class, race, ethnicity, income, age, property have all restricted the achievement and the exercise of citizenship rights and obligations.

By contrast, the central concept of democratic citizenship is its insistence that all citizens should be able to exercise their citizenship rights and obligations effectively and, therefore, that inequalities that frustrate this must be eliminated. To accomplish this there is an important place for education, though education alone will not be sufficient to the task. Even so, education can at least aim to give all people the knowledge, skills, and dispositions that will enable them to exercise their rights and obligations, and more generally to ensure that citizenship is not curtailed.

Beyond this, citizenship must not be defined only in national terms. The connection between nationalism and citizenship which was so tightly forged in the nineteenth century must be loosened. We live in an age of international problems which demand international solutions. They transcend not only national borders but the ability of national governments to deal with them. The proper balance between national and global thinking and action is a matter of debate, for we are not yet at a time when we can simply give our undivided loyalty to a global entity, if only because such an entity does not yet exist in any political sense. There can, however, be little doubt that we must think of citizenship in global as well as national terms. To speak of education for citizenship means producing citizens who can weigh their attachment to their country against their attachment to the planet and the human species.

More fundamentally, the attainment of democratic citizenship depends not only upon people learning how to exercise their rights and obligations but also upon institutional change. As theorists such as Philip Resnick (1984) and Carole Pateman (1970) have suggested, we must extend our definition of democracy beyond the idea of representation to that of participation. One can imagine various ways of doing this, but, however it is done, we must begin to think in terms of participatory democracy if democratic citizenship is to become a reality. We must also extend the practice of democracy beyond the conventionally political sphere. There is something profoundly contradictory, for example, in the fact that the workplace, where most people spend much of their lives, remains one of the most authoritarian places in contemporary life. If participatory democracy is to become a reality, it will need an educational foundation. Above all, to use C.B. Macpherson's words, it will mean "a change in people's consciousness (or unconsciousness) from seeing themselves and acting as essentially consumers, to seeing themselves and acting as exerters and enjoyers of the exertion and development of their capacities" (1977, p. 99). And here again, there is an obvious role for education and, more specifically, for history. We could, for example, perform a useful service for our students, and for democracy generally, by teaching them about the history of citizenship, both in theory and in practice (Marshall, 1977, 1981; Barbalet, 1988; Andrews, 1991; Heater, 1990; Beiner, 1994; Kymlicka, 1995).

HISTORY, CITIZENSHIP AND SCHOOLING

Compulsory schooling was a creation of the nation state. Despite the nationalist belief that nations were divine creations or somehow created themselves, it was soon realized that national spirit had to be created and maintained. Histories had to be written and taught; languages had to be formalised; literatures had to be established; minorities had to be assimilated; traditions had to be invented. Nationalism had to be instilled. Citizens had to be created. As Eugen Weber (1976) put it, peasants had to be turned into Frenchmen—and women presumably. In the words of a nineteenth century Italian nationalist, "We have made Italy; now we must make Italians" (Hobsbawm & Ranger, 1985, p. 267). In this process, schools were assigned a central role. Education became a crucial plank of nationalist policies everywhere. Here is how the Winnipeg School Board put it in 1914:

> On the school, more than upon any other agency will depend the quality and the nature of the citizenship of the future; on the way in which the school avails itself of its opportunities depends the extent to which Canadian traditions will be appropriate, Canadian national sentiments imbibed, and Canadian standards of living adopted by the next generation of the new races that are making their home in our midst. (School District of Winnipeg, 1914, p. 41)

For obvious reasons, history was assigned a prominent role in this educational enterprise. Along with literature, and supported by a panoply of school rituals and ceremonies, history was the major vehicle for the creation of national identity and patriotism. Anything that could be shown to contribute to the building of the nation was duly commemorated and described as good. Anything that did not was either condemned or ignored as irrelevant. This meant that Canadian history, for example, was seen largely as the building of the federation, with the consequent emphasis upon central Canada. It also meant that history was seen in very Whiggish terms. History was whatever shaped and led to the present. And, as one would expect, the present was seen as a desirable place to be.

History texts made it clear that nations were the work of exceptional individuals—larger than life explorers, heroic generals, far-sighted statesmen, intrepid pioneers. There would be an occasional reference to what might be called ordinary people but readers were then immediately whisked off into the world of the great and famous. Thus, Canadian students learned that Confed-

eration was the work of a handful of "fathers"; that the Canadian Pacific was built by William Van Home; that Québec was conquered by James Wolfe. And, of course, these great men were indeed men. Women rarely appeared in the pages of these texts and when they did it was usually doing what was regarded as women's work, such as teaching or nursing. Working people were similarly ignored. Native people were equally invisible and when they were described it usually was in ethnocentric or racist terms (McDiarmid & Pratt, 1971; Pratt, 1975; Osborne, 1980).

In other words, when the building of the nation was described, it was a particular type of nation that was envisaged. Here is how one text presented its ideal:

> in spite of the fact that government can do only what the people themselves pay for, there is the temptation to think that the more governments do, the more people should get, and that the citizen himself has little or no responsibility. . . . Democracies require from their people not merely obedience, but judgment, restraint, self-discipline and a spirit of cooperation. (Brown, 1946, pp. 647-648)

A popular textbook of the 1970's presented a broadly similar message, telling its student readers that "Canada was built and made prosperous by men who faced challenges with imagination, who rejected the notion of simple solutions." Indeed, it concluded, "Canadian history is reassuring in that Canadians have not been stampeded into rash action when faced by problems." (Herstein et al., 1970, pp. 2-4).

Overwhelmingly, the story of nation building was presented precisely as story, with all the authority of narrative. The impression was created not only that this was the way things happened but that they could have

---

History was the major vehicle for the creation of national identity and patriotism. Anything that could be shown to contribute to the building of the nation was duly commemorated and described as good. Anything that did not was either condemned or ignored as irrelevant.

---

happened in no other way. Nor was any scope allowed for historiography or interpretation. History was the story of what happened, plain and simple. From a student's viewpoint one could not do much with a story, or at least not with stories as presented in the textbooks, except to learn it and to learn from it, for the stories often carried a moral message. Even at their best, however, textbook narratives were not designed to be questioned. They were intended to entertain, to excite, but above all to instruct. Their very form reinforced the perception that history was a body of information to be learned. By and large it was something before which a student stood powerless.

This disempowering view of history was reinforced

by the dominant mode of teaching, which was largely examination-driven. Provincial examinations were standard practice until the 1960's and consisted almost exclusively of questions which relied only on factual recall. In response, teachers ensured their students were well drilled on the material that they expected to be on the examination. Obviously there were exceptions to this. There must have been adventurous teachers like Agnes Macphail who in the early 1900's

> abandoned much that she had been taught about rigid discipline and rote-learning of lessons in order

---

H.G. Wells argued that history teachers must take a good part of the blame for the First World War since it had resulted in large part from an excess of national and patriotic fervour on all sides, the result of the "poison called history" which had been taught in schools.

---

to arouse her students' interest in the world around and inside of themselves. She brought newspapers into the classroom, played games, and had heart-to-heart talks with the children about what they wanted to do with their lives. She became even more unorthodox in her teaching methods as she detested the school system's emphasis on exam preparation. She persuaded her board to subscribe to a magazine and daily newspaper for her classes to study. She also brought the books of Grey County native Nellie McClung into the classroom so that older children could share her reformist and feminist ideas. (Crowley, 1991, pp. 20-21)

Such teachers were the exception rather than the rule. The history teaching described by Hodgetts in 1968 in schools across the country was light years removed from Macphail's imaginative practice. The bleak and depressing picture presented in *What Culture? What Heritage?* is well known, though it is worth noting that Hodgetts himself assessed history teaching in terms of its contribution to the education of citizens. In doing so he found it sorely wanting, producing the very opposite of the goals to which it was ostensibly committed.

The conservative bias of history did not go unchallenged, especially between the wars. The Women's International League for Peace and Freedom criticized textbooks and curricula for overemphasizing militarism and patriotism (Boutilier, 1988; Socknat, 1989; Strong-Boag, 1989; Osborne, 1994a). The League of Nations Society called for a greater emphasis on international understanding. H.G. Wells added his powerful voice to the campaign to change history teaching, a question on which he declared himself to be a "fanatic." He argued that history teachers must take a good part of the blame for the First World War since it had resulted in large part from an excess of national and patriotic fervour on all sides, the result of the "poison called history" which had been taught in schools. Instead, Wells called for the abandonment of national and military history and its replacement by an emphasis on eco-

nomic, cultural and social history. He wanted history taught so that it showed the unfolding of a spirit of world community, leading in short order to the world state, and resulting in people identifying themselves not as national citizens, but as members of the human species (Wells, 1939; Osborne, 1991b).

Such criticisms were never more than skirmishes: history's main defences remained un-breached. By the 1950's history enjoyed a prominent place in the curricula of most provinces. And it was overwhelmingly traditional history, chronological, political and patriotic. During the 1960's, however, all this changed and history entered a period of marked decline (McLeod, 1982; Davis, 1995). This was the result not so much of attacks from without as disintegration from within, as history proved to have few public defenders, even among its own teachers. Admittedly, after the depressing revelations of *What Culture? What Heritage?* in 1968, there was not much to defend. Most people accepted the book's devastating criticisms of the state of history in the schools. Hodgetts intended it to be the launching pad for a renewed and revived history curriculum, but instead, history found itself challenged by the new inter-disciplinary subject known as Canadian Studies. Supported by the Canada Studies Foundation, and eventually by the provinces and then by the federal government, Canadian Studies became a major enterprise. What is intriguing in retrospect is its lack of attention to the systematic study of history. It resulted in much valuable and interesting work, but it was largely social scientific and inter-disciplinary in its approach. What was perhaps most striking of all was Hodgetts' own willingness to sanction a move away from history. In *What Culture? What Heritage?* he made a passionate and persuasive case for its centrality in any programme of civic education, especially in Canada. Ten years later, in 1978, with Paul Gallagher, then Director of the Canada Studies Foundation, Hodgetts wrote *Teaching Canada for the 80's*, an outline of the ideal Canadian Studies programme from Grade 1 to Grade 12 or 13. It had very little to say about history, concentrating instead on economics, politics and the environment (Hodgetts & Gallagher, 1978). It was as if Hodgetts had tried history and found it wanting, too frail a craft to carry the load he wanted to assign to it.

To a certain extent, the move away from history was given some credibility by researchers who used Piagetian theory and discovered that even high school students apparently did not understand history. Some researchers flatly said that students would never understand it, since they had not reached a level of cognitive development sufficiently sophisticated (Hallam, 1967). Today we have a clearer understanding of the limitations of this research and we are more optimistic about the capacity of students to understand history

(Egan, 1979; Booth, 1987; Shemilt, 1987), but in the 1970's the research did not help the cause of history.

Moreover, the discipline of history itself was becoming increasingly fragmented. New approaches to history brought immense gains in such fields as labour history, women's history, native history, ethnic history, educational history, and so on, but a price was paid, at least for schools, in the disintegration of any overall synthesis. Some of the new historical research found its way into the classroom but it became increasingly difficult, especially for hard-pressed teachers, to incorporate it into any wider framework. History tended to become a series of special topics held together, if at all, by the slenderest of organizing threads, and, though some historians bemoaned this lack of cohesion, few seemed willing to do anything about it (Bliss, 1991-92).

CITIZENSHIP EDUCATION TODAY

Paradoxically, at the same time that history was declining in status, interest in citizenship education—variously called civic or political education—was rising, in Canada and elsewhere (Osborne, 1984). Most of the new work in the field was inspired by political science rather than by history. It was intended to increase students' political awareness and sense of political efficacy. In the United States Newmann (1975) spoke of "environmental competence"; in England Crick, Heater, and others spoke of "political literacy" (Crick & Porter, 1978; Heater & Gillespie, 1981). Their programmes, and others like them, paid scant attention to history. They reflected the social scientist's concern with structure and function, not the historian's with development and change.

In Canada, this interest in citizenship education was reinforced by the rapid acceptance of multiculturalism as a guiding principle in education. In the space of only a few years Canadian schooling changed its emphasis. Having been originally created as instruments of cultural assimilation, in the 1970's schools celebrated cultural diversity (Troper, 1978). In the process the study of history suffered, as multiculturalism was studied through a range of interdisciplinary and integrated programmes. Historical topics were drawn on and historical episodes were used but only as a subordinate means to what was seen as a more important end.

By and large, many people seem to have abandoned the idea that a working knowledge of the history of one's own country and of the world of which it is a part is essential to effective citizenship, and especially so in the case of democratic citizenship. Despite this, there are some obvious connections between viable democratic citizenship and a reasonable knowledge of history.

The arguments for this proposition can be simply stated. First, a knowledge of history helps us become aware of the range of human behaviour, both good and bad, and to that extent helps to teach us what it means to be human. Second, it provides us with a sense of context and perspective for the consideration of contemporary phenomena; it teaches us to consider the long view, so to speak, so that we are less likely to be carried away by the enthusiasms of the moment. Third, it provides a sense of connectedness both with what has gone before us and what will come after us; it raises our loyalties and our preoccupations from the local and the immediate to the more global and long-term. Fourth, it also connects us with the long struggle by which human beings have sought to improve the human condition, thus enabling us to become the subjects not the objects of our own existence. Fifth, it helps us cultivate that habit of mind which is best described as constructive scepticism, both by giving us a stock of knowledge against which to test what we are tempted or persuaded to believe and by giving us the skills to distinguish a good argument from a bad one. And, sixth, history can be an endless source of interest and entertainment.

In short, the main advantage of history is that it enables us to think for ourselves about important issues bearing on the human condition. It makes it possible for us to see the world as it is (which means understanding how it came to be that way) and to see the world as it might be, while also helping us think about how to get from one state of affairs to the other. This is what makes the study of history an ideal preparation for democratic citizenship (Osborne, 1994b).

None of this means that the study of history consists of mere 'coverage' of subject matter. It was this examination-driven approach to history, with its determination to see that every fact was covered, whether or not it was understood, that killed students' interest in history in the first place, with the result that, like Russian soldiers towards the end of the First World War, they voted with their feet and abandoned what they saw as a hopeless and pointless task once they had a chance to make a choice. There is a long and complex debate among history teachers as to where best to draw the line between breadth and depth, and most of us have our own answer, but that there must be some appropriate combination there can be little doubt.

Curriculum developers have tried to solve this problem in various ways. In the 1960's Bruner (1960) and his followers unsuccessfully tried to identify the "structure" of history in order to make its teaching as effective as possible. Others spoke of "concepts" or "generalizations" (Morrisset, 1967). Fenton (1967) organized his programmes around what he called a "mode of inquiry." All were attempts to solve the problem of coverage. None was really appropriate to the nature of history as a form of knowledge. Structure, for example, as defined by Bruner, exists, if it exists anywhere, in the mind of the historian, not in the discipline of history. A mode of inquiry cannot properly be divorced from the subject to which it is to be applied. Whenever list of concepts or generalizations are produced as ways of organizing a history programme, they prove to be trite, vacuous, or highly debatable.

It is more useful to think of history as illuminating issues which persist in one form or another over time and which address important aspects of the human condition. This does not mean that we can plunder history for the "lessons" it teaches us, for it is seldom obvious what history teaches, or if indeed it teaches anything in the form of "lessons". As Peter Novick's (1988) study of the American historical profession reminded us, historians are no more sagacious or prudent than other people when they deal with matters outside their specialty. Nonetheless, a knowledge of history does throw light on the kinds of issues and problems that run throughout the attempts of human beings to gain control over their lives, individually and collectively. It is this that makes the study of history so important for the practice of democratic citizenship. It is also this that makes the selection of subject matter so important for it means that some forms of history are more important than others when it comes to deciding what should be taught. This does not mean that there is some authorized historical canon that all students must learn regardless of circumstance. It does mean, however, that the choice of subject matter cannot be totally idiosyncratic. Citizenship demands a common framework of knowledge, values and assumptions within which communication, debate and argument can take place.

All of which raises the difficult question of what or whose history should be taught. If history is to help citizens think about and act in their world, what do they need to know? Here the idea of history as illuminating important issues of human experience proves useful. It avoids the danger of compiling an encyclopaedic list of factual information which everyone is supposed to know, and thus tying the hands of teachers. Instead, it provides a sense of direction while allowing teachers, students and local communities to have some voice in the selection of specific content. The suggestion here is that the history curriculum should have two broad components: one which teaches students about the country in which they live, and one which teaches them about the world of which it is a part.

So far as the first is concerned, the chart on the following two pages is an attempt to describe what students ought to know about Canada. It should be emphasized that this is not intended to specify the nuts and bolts of a programme; nor is it at all intended to describe a particular course of study. It is, in fact, highly unlikely that a single year could do justice to what is being suggested here. Rather, the chart is intended to represent what students ought to be able to think about as a result of all their years of schooling. In practical terms, therefore, it calls for a degree of curriculum planning through the grade levels which is still the exception rather than the norm. It provides a framework within which such curriculum planning can take place. Here, then, is the knowledge of Canada which the study of history must develop if it is to contribute to democratic citizenship.

The ten statements are intended to describe what students should learn about Canada over the course of their schooling if they are to gain the knowledge necessary for the practice of democratic citizenship. They should serve as the basis for the kind of discussion that needs to take place at the local level so proper curriculum planning can ensure that history does in fact contribute to democratic citizenship. The statements deal with content, with what students should know. They derive from the conviction that any attempt to link history with citizenship must tackle the problem of content. At the same time, they try to avoid the danger of selecting content so rigidly that schools, teachers and students lose the freedom to devise programmes appropriate to their particular circumstances. This is why the statements take the form that they do, rather than listing such more obviously 'historical' topics as the War of 1812, Responsible Government, the Industrial Revolution, and so on. It must be recognized that when courses are organized in that way, there is a very real risk that teaching becomes a slog through the content, which is taught not because it serves some useful purpose, but simply because it is there. There is also the further risk that as teachers become more and more trapped in the teaching of content for its own sake, they become unable to make the connections between past and present that are vital if history is to contribute to democratic citizenship.

Nonetheless, even though the statements do not contain lists of historical content, conventionally defined, they are best taught and learned through history. Only in this way can the issues that they embody be properly understood. The important pedagogical task is to organise and teach history so that these issues emerge and are not swamped or lost sight of in the mass of historical detail. Though there is not a close fit, there is a broad similarity between what is being suggested here and the thematic approach to curriculum development described by Paul Bennett (1980).

If students are to be prepared for democratic citizenship they must learn not only about Canada but about the world of which it, and they, are a part. What, then, should they learn? As with the list of Canadian topics the chart, entitled "Knowledge of the world", (page 37) is an attempt to answer this question. It is based upon what appear to be the main characteristics of the world in which students will exercise their citizenship.

Like its Canadian counterpart, this list, though not stated in conventional historical terms, is best taught historically. This does not mean that each of the eight topics must be dealt with as a separate unit, each in its own historical context, but rather that the topics and themes should emerge from the history as it is taught. It is not difficult to see how history can be approached more or less chronologically but can still address important themes, as Ross Dunn (1989) has recently shown. He argues for an approach to world history that "takes the human community as a whole, rather than bounded cultures, as the primary field of study and that stresses in each era of the past the larger scale patterns of change that have brought the world to its present state of complexity and interdependence" (p. 220).

Perhaps the most important reason for approaching this task through history is that it is a powerful way of helping students to see themselves as part of a tradition, connected to those who have gone before them and to those who will come after. To quote Wells (1922): "Today, if life seems unadventurous and fragmentary and generally aimless it is largely because of this one thing. We have lost touch with history. We have ceased to see human affairs as one great epic unfolding. And only by the universal teaching of universal history can that epic quality be restored" (pp. 111-112). To put it another way, we must initiate students into what Michael Oakeshott once described as "the great conversation", that continuing debate about what it means to be human and what form of social life best promotes it. Without this sense of connectedness, citizenship is bound to be incomplete, and less humane and balanced than it must be if it is to be truly democratic.

An important task of this approach to history is to give students some idea of how human societies work. This might sound like a task for the anthropologist or the sociologist rather than the historian, but there is much to be learned from those social historians who see their task as depicting the total history of a given society. At the school level there is an important practical reason for tackling the job historically since this allows for the crucial dimension of story, anecdote and unfolding narrative which can be so powerful pedagogically. It makes possible the delineation of human personality and behaviour which is so important, both for pedagogy and for

---

KNOWLEDGE OF CANADA

1. *Canada is a country in which national unity cannot be taken for granted, It is officially bilingual, culturally diverse and subject to often severe centrifugal forces. Many of its various cultural groups are experiencing a new sense of identity.*

   Students should:
   a. know the variety of cultural groups that comprise Canada;
   b. know the major issues between Anglophone and Francophone Canada;
   c. know the history of English-French relations in Canada;
   d. be able to compare Canada with other multi-lingual countries;
   e. know about cultural ethnic and racial antagonisms past and present;
   f. know about the history and current situation of native people in Canada;
   g. understand the pros and cons of the various ideals of Canada e.g., unitary, bilingual, multicultural, sovereignty-association;
   h. examine the intersection of all these topics with issues of race, class and gender.

2. *Canada is characterized by strong feelings of regionalism, resulting from its history, geography and economic relationships.*

   Students should:
   a. know about the major regions of Canada;
   b. know about the different perceptions of Canada held in each region;
   c. know how regionalism has affected Canada historically;
   d. assess the varying interpretations of the role of regionalism in Canada;
   e. examine how all these topics intersect with issues of race, class and gender.

3. *Canada is exposed to powerful external forces, especially from the United States.*

   Students should:
   a. know the history of Canada-U.S. relations;
   b. know the current issues and relationships between Canada and the U.S.;
   c. know the various measures Canada has taken, past and present, to protect its national identity;
   d. assess the varying interpretations of the relationship between Canada and the U.S.;
   e. examine how all these topics intersect with issues of race, class and gender.

4. *Canada is an industrialized, technological and urbanized society, though to varying degrees in different regions.*

   Students should:
   a. know the history of industrial development, technology and urbanization in Canada;
   b. know the history of working people and organized labour in Canada;
   c. know about capitalism as an economic and cultural system, and about alternatives to it e.g., socialism, co-operativism;
   d. know about the environmental problems arising from industrial development;

e. know about and assess the measures undertaken and suggested to deal with these problems;

f. understand and assess the various analyses of industrial, technological society;

g. examine how all these topics intersect with issues of race, class and gender.

5. *Canada is a liberal parliamentary democracy, federally organized.*

Students should:

a. know the history and structure of Canada's political system;

b. compare Canada's political system with others;

c. understand how Canada's political system works in practice;

d. know the history of Canadian federalism and its current status;

e. be familiar with the various meanings of democracy;

f. understand the role that so-called ordinary people have played in Canada's history;

g. know about the major political problems facing Canada;

h. know the background and the current status of the constitutional debate and assess the positions taken in it;

i. examine how all these topics intersect with issues of race, class and gender.

6. *Canada has a mixed economy with inequities in the distribution of wealth and power.*

Students should:

a. understand how economic systems work;

b. know the history of economic development in Canada;

c. know about the distribution of wealth and power in Canada;

d. know about the extent and impact of poverty in Canada;

e. assess the various policies and proposals for dealing with current economic problems, including the distribution of wealth.

7. *Internationally, Canada is a middle power with a range of responsibilities and commitments.*

Students should:

a. know the nature of Canada's world position and its historical background;

b. know about Canada's role in the League of Nations, the United Nations, and other international organizations;

c. know about Canada's relationships with the developing world;

d. assess the position of Canada in world affairs and the possible directions it should take in the future;

e. examine how all these topics intersect with issues of race, class and gender.

8. *Canada is a society committed to the pursuit and implementation of human rights.*

Students should:

a. know about the historical development of human rights and their protection;

b. assess the strengths and weaknesses of existing formulations of human rights and of alternatives to them;

c. understand the provisions of the Constitution and the Charter of Rights and Freedoms;

d. know about violations of human rights in Canada, past and present;

e. be familiar with issues of racism and sexism, both in their historical context and in the present;

f. be personally committed to the observance of human rights.

9. *Canada has a rich artistic and cultural tradition.*

Students should:

a. know the main elements of the arts in Canada;

b. understand the role of the arts in society;

c. understand the issues facing the arts in Canada today;

d. acquire an interest in the arts;

e. examine the interaction between the arts and issues of race, class and gender.

10. *Canada is a country that frequently debates what kind of society it should be.*

Students should:

a. be familiar with the main elements of this debate;

b. be familiar with the main political philosophies and their historical development;

c. be familiar with the role of religion in Canadian society;

d. examine the intersection of all these topics with issues of race, class and gender;

e. form a personal assessment of the kind of society they think Canada should be.

KNOWLEDGE OF THE WORLD

1. *The world is increasingly interdependent and interconnected.*

    Students should:
    a. know how the world is interconnected e.g., through trade, alliances, technology;
    b. know how this interconnectedness has developed through time;
    c. know about the history and role of the United Nations and other international organizations;
    d. know about the history of nationalism and its role in the world today.

2. *The world is experiencing a serious disparity between developed and developing countries.*

    Students should:
    a. know the history of the expansion of European power throughout the world;
    b. know the history of imperialism, its rise and fall;
    c. understand the current links between the developed and developing world;
    d. understand the conditions of life in societies at varying stages of development;
    e. be familiar with the various definitions of and approaches to the idea of development;
    f. be familiar with the various policies and proposals for eliminating the gap between developed and developing countries.

3. *In the modern world war is still widely seen as an instrument of policy.*

    Students should:
    a. know the history of the major wars through history;
    b. understand what war means in human terms, for combatant and non-combatant, men and women, and so on;
    c. know about the history of the attempts to control or eliminate war;
    d. know the history of the nuclear issue since 1945.

4. *The world is paying increasing attention to questions of human rights.*

    Students should:
    a. know the major events and landmarks in the history of the struggle for human rights;
    b. understand the varying conceptions of human rights;
    c. know how these conceptions have changed through history;
    d. know the major episodes of violations of human rights through history;
    e. be familiar with contemporary issues of human rights, especially as related to issues of gender, race and class.

5. *The world continues to be shaped by varying social and political philosophies.*

    Students should:
    a. know the main 'isms' that have shaped the modern world e.g., capitalism, anarchism, fascism;
    b. understand the role of religion in society, past and present;
    c. be familiar with the range of theories of government e.g., democracy, absolutism.

6. *The world is increasingly influenced by technology.*

    Students should:
    a. understand the role of technology in human society;
    b. know the history of the Industrial Revolutions and their impact on transportation, communications, etc.;
    c. understand the various theories concerning the nature and impact of technology.

7. *The world is facing increasingly serious environmental problems.*

    Students should:
    a. know about the relationship between people and their environment at different time periods;
    b. understand the nature and scope of the problems facing the environment today;
    c. know the historical context of these threats;
    d. be familiar with the range of policies and proposals to cope with environmental problems.

8. *Many of the world's people live in inadequate conditions.*

    Students should:
    a. know how people have lived through history;
    b. be familiar with the range of human behaviour, both individual and societal, as shown through history;
    c. be familiar with the historical debate over the nature of the good life;
    d. know how people live in different parts of the world today;
    e. understand how people's lives can be affected by race, class and gender.

citizenship. It also helps students understand how different societies have worked over time, thus allowing not only for the portrayal of change but providing also for a rich and powerful basis for comparisons across different societies. In this regard, the Manitoba history curriculum (Manitoba Education and Training, 1985) offers a useful example. It provides for the examination of human societies (the Greeks, the Aztecs, the Chinese, medieval Europe, and so on) over time along these dimensions:

- how people meet their survival needs (e.g., for food, shelter, clothing, health and security);
- how people interact with their physical environment (e.g., how they are affected by climate, by resources (or lack of same), by landforms; and at the same time how they affect these geographic elements or cope with them);
- how people interact with others (e.g., through the family or kinship group, through social organizations);
- how people run their affairs (e.g., how they govern themselves, both at a very local level—a tribe or village—and at a larger scale level);
- how people go beyond their survival needs to secure a degree of comfort and ease;
- how people satisfy their non-material needs (e.g., their entertainment and recreation, their music, art and literature);
- how people explain and interpret their world, their sense of right and wrong, their values and beliefs, their religion.

This list of themes obviously offers a rich foundation for comparison across societies, especially if it is supplemented by another theme dealing with the question of how societies change, and deal with change. It provides an approach to history which gives students useful knowledge, which they can use to decipher the mysteries of the present and the future. It offers an empowering knowledge which students can use to understand and perhaps to change their world, rather than confronting them with a factual behemoth against which they feel understandably powerless.

A Question of Pedagogy

Any approach to history which is concerned with its contribution to democratic citizenship must take pedagogy into account. The lists of topics presented above cannot be considered in isolation from how they should be taught. They are not pronunciamentos for students to memorize. Rather, they are intended to be questions or issues or themes to be explored with the goal that students will arrive at their own personal positions concerning them, and in doing so will learn the necessary skills and dispositions that are as important to citizenship as is knowledge. Bernard Crick has usefully described these as "procedural values", which he sees as comprising, respect for evidence, for rationality, for justice and for tolerance (Crick & Porter, 1978). They will

be learned not only from explicit instruction but also from the example and the model that teachers provide in their daily conduct. It is this which, in part, makes the matter of how history is taught so important.

It is especially important in any consideration of teaching for democratic citizenship. Research into political socialization and political education has shown how powerfully teaching can affect students' sense of political competence. The so-called hidden curriculum can be more powerful than the actual curriculum which is prescribed. One day, for example I asked a grade eight student what he was learning in a particular class. As it turned out he was in a history class, but his answer to me was that he was learning to take notes from the overhead projector, which in fact was all that was happening in his class. In reality, he was learning a good deal more, not least the performance of a task which he did not particularly like and which he saw little point in doing but which he knew he should do cheerfully and to an acceptable standard. In a very real sense he was learning to be a good citizen, but a citizen of a specific kind.

I have written on the pedagogy topic elsewhere and here can present only some general conclusions (Osborne, 1984, 1991a). The main point is that democratic citizenship demands a pedagogy that emphasizes and examplifies the skills and values of critical awareness, participation, involvement and community which are central to its practice. Shor and Freire (1987) call it "liberatory pedagogy"; Giroux (1988), McLaren (1989) and others speak of "critical pedagogy"; Anyon (1981) calls it "transformative pedagogics". I prefer to think of it as teaching for democratic citizenship, which is a term which has the advantage of being easily understood, not least by democratic citizens themselves. Its main features can be broadly summarized as follows:

- Teachers have a clearly articulated and morally defensible view of education in its full social and political context;
- The material to be taught to students is worthwhile and important; it is worth knowing, especially in the context of democratic citizenship;
- The material to be taught is organized and presented as problems or issues to be investigated;
- Careful and deliberate attention is given to the teaching of thinking, not as set of isolated skills, but in the context of important knowledge;
- The material to be taught is connected with students' knowledge and experience but in such a way that it further expands them;
- Students are required to become active in their learning;
- Students are expected to share and build upon each other's ideas;
- Connections are established between the subject-matter in the classroom and the world outside the school;
- Classrooms are characterized by trust and

openness so that students find it easy to participate.

These nine principles have a good deal in common with some recent approaches to teaching, not least those to be found in feminist pedagogy and critical pedagogy. Their listing here is necessarily somewhat cryptic but they are more fully explained elsewhere (Osborne, 1991a). Without expanding on them here, it might be useful to provide an example of what they mean when applied to history, as described in the box below (left).

This approach nicely illustrates Mason's comment about relevance in teaching. In his words,

> Relevance is not a matter of adapting a subject to the apparent interests of a pupil or the apparent fashions of the moment. Relevance is achieved by assuming that a pupil or student has something to contribute to the subject. Relevance at its deepest has nothing to do with subject matter; it has to do with the status of the learner in relation to what is being learned. (Mason, 1977, p. 107)

And changing the status of learners from their largely desk-bound, worksheet completing, note copying status has a lot to do with democratic citizenship. It also makes both the teaching and the learning of history more interesting, more worthwhile and more rewarding. When taught in the ways outlined here, history can indeed fulfil its potential as the foundation of democratic citizenship.

TEACHING ABOUT THE GREEK CITY STATE

This example describes the task of teaching Grade 7 students about the Greek city state. Applying the principles listed above, and after having introduced the topic, the teacher began by asking students what they knew about hermits. They knew what hermits were, though it would not have mattered if they had not, for the teacher could easily have told them. The point of this opening was to get students talking about why so few people wanted to be hermits—preferring instead to live together in some sort of grouping. The teacher began this discussion by asking the students how many of them would like to be hermits and asking them to think of the advantages and disadvantages of living in some sort of community. This last point was supplemented with a request to students to think of as many types of community as they could. They responded well, coming up with a list that included towns, villages, tribes, clans, and so on. This in turn provided a springboard for students to discuss what characterized a community, what distinguished a community from, say, a rush hour crowd. Along the way the teacher raised such questions as whether the school was a community, or the neighbourhood, or any other local unit, including the significantly named community club. On the basis of all this discussion, the teacher then introduced the Greek city state, as yet another form of community. This concept of community then provided the glue that held everything together over the next several lessons as students learned about Athens and Sparta and various other aspects of Greek life. It ran through the lessons on Homer, on myth and religion, on the position of women and slaves, on education, warfare and citizenship, on the trial and execution of Socrates, and many other topics. As they worked, the students were not only learning about Ancient Greece, they were also learning about the idea of community. Equally important they were learning that they had a great deal to contribute to the topic, that their ideas counted for something, that there was a reason behind what they were being made to do, and that learning was an active, participatory affair. In other words, democratic citizenship was embedded in the teaching.

REFERENCES

Andrew, G. (Ed.) (1991). *Citizenship*. London: Lawrence & Wishart.

Anyon, J. (1981). Elementary schooling and distinctions of social class. *Interchange, 12*(1), 2-3.

Barbalet, J.M. (1988). *Citizenship*. Minneapolis: University of Minnesota Press.

Beiner, C. (Ed.). (1994). *Theorizing citizenship*. Albany, NY: SUNY Press.

Bennett, P. (1980). *Rediscovering Canadian history*. Toronto: Ontario Institute for Studies in Education.

Bliss, M. (1991-92). Privatizing the mind: The sundering of Canadian history, the sundering of Canada. *Journal of Canadian Studies, 26*(4), 5-17.

Booth, M. (1987). Ages and concepts: A critique of the Piagetian approach to history teaching. In C. Portal (Ed.), *The history curriculum for teachers* (pp. 22-38). Lewes: Falmer Press.

Boutilier, B. (1988). *Educating for peace and cooperation: The Women's International League for Peace and Freedom in Canada, 1919-1929*. Masters thesis, Carleton University, Ottawa.

Brown, G. (1946). *Building the Canadian nation*. Toronto: Dent.

Bruner, J.S. (1960). *The process of education*. Cambridge: Harvard University Press.

Crick, B. & Porter, A. (1978). *Political education and political literacy*. London: Longman.

Crowley, T. (1990). *Agnes Macphail and the politics of equality*. Toronto: James Lorimer.

Davis, B. (1995). *Whatever happened to high school history: Burying the political memory of youth, 1914-1945*. Toronto: Our Schools/Our Selves Education Foundation/James Lorimer.

Dunn, R. (1989). Central themes for world history. In P. Gagnon (Ed.), *Historical literacy: The case for history in American education*. Boston: Houghton Mifflin.

Egan, K. (1979). *Educational development*. New York: Oxford University Press.

Fenton, E. (1967). *The new social studies.* New York: Holt, Rinehart & Winston.

Giroux, H. (1988). *Schooling and the struggle for public life: Critical pedagogy in the modern age.* Minneapolis: University of Minnesota Press.

Hallam, R. (1967). Logical thinking in history. *Educational Review, 19,* 183-202.

Havel, V. (1992, June 25). A dream for Czechoslovakia. *New York Review of Books,* p. 12.

Heater, D.B. (1990). *Citizenship.* London: Longman.

Heater, D.B. & Gillespie, J. (Eds.). (1981). *Political education in flux.* London: Sage.

Herstein, H.H. *et al.,* (1970). *Challenge and survival: The history of Canada.* Toronto: Prentice Hall.

Hobsbawm, E. & Ranger, T. (Eds.). (1985). *The invention of tradition.* Cambridge, UK: Cambridge University Press.

Hodgetts, A.B. (1968). *What culture? What heritage?* Toronto: Ontario Institute for Studies in Education.

Hodgetts, A.B. & Gallagher, P. (1978). *Teaching Canada for the 80's.* Toronto: Ontario Institute for Studies in Education.

Kymlicka, W. (1995). *Multicultural citizenship.* Oxford, UK: Clarendon Press.

Macpherson, C.B. (1977). *The life and times of liberal democracy.* New York: Oxford University Press.

Manitoba Education and Training. (1985). *Social studies curriculum overview: K-12.* Winnipeg: Manitoba Education and Training.

Marshall, T.H. (1977). *Class, citizenship and social development.* Chicago: University of Chicago Press.

Marshall, T.H. (1981). *The right to welfare and other essays.* London: Heinemann.

Mason, E. (1977). 'A'-level History. *History Workshop Journal, 3,* 105-109.

McDiarmid, G. & Pratt, D. (1971). *Teaching prejudice.* Toronto: Ontario Institute for Studies in Education.

McLeod, R.C. (1982). History in Canadian secondary schools. *Canadian Historical Review, 53*(4), 573-585.

Morrissett, I. (Ed.). (1967). *Concepts and structure in the new social studies curricula.* New York: Holt, Rinehart & Winston.

Newmann, F. (1975). *Education for citizen action.* Berkeley, CA: McCutchan.

Novick, P. (1988) *That noble dream: The "objectivity question" and the American historical profession.* Cambridge, UK: Cambridge University Press.

Osborne, K.W. (1980). *"Hard-working, temperate and peaceable": The portrayal of workers in Canadian history textbooks.* (Education Monograph IV.) Winnipeg, MB: University of Manitoba.

Osborne, K.W. (1984). *Working papers in political education.* (Educational Monograph XII.) Winnipeg, MB: University of Manitoba.

Osborne, K.W. (1991a). *Teaching for democratic citizenship.* Toronto: Our Schools/Our Selves Education Foundation/James Lorimer.

Osborne, K.W. (1991b). H.G. Wells, education and catastrophe. *Journal of Educational Administration and Foundations, 6*(2), 17-38.

Osborne, K.W. (1994a). An early example of the analysis of history textbooks in Canada. *Canadian Social Studies, 29*(1), 21-25.

Osborne, K.W. (1994b). The teaching of history and democratic citizenship. In K.W. Osborne *In defence of history: Teaching the past and the meaning of democratic citizenship* (pp. 9-48). Toronto: Our Schools/Our Selves Education Foundation.

Pateman, C. (1970). *Participation and democratic theory.* Cambridge, UK: Cambridge University Press.

Pratt, D. (1975). The social role of school textbooks in Canada. In R.M. Pike & E. Zureik (Eds.), *Socialization and values in Canadian society* (pp. 100-126). Toronto: McClelland & Stewart.

Resnick, P. (1984). *Parliament versus people: An essay on democracy and Canadian political culture.* Vancouver: New Star Books.

School District of Winnipeg. (1914). *Annual Report.*

Shemilt, D. (1987) Adolescent ideas about evidence and methodology in history. In C. Portal (Ed.), *The history curriculum for teachers* (pp. 39-61). Lewes, UK: Falmer Press.

Shor, I. & Freire, P. (1987). *A pedagogy for liberation.* South Hadley, UK: Bergin & Garvey.

Socknat, T. (1989). For peace and freedom: Canadian feminists and the interwar peace campaign. In J. Williamson & D. Gorham (Eds.), *Up and doing: Canadian women and peace* (pp. 66-88). Toronto: The Women's Press.

Strong-Boag, V. (1989). Peace-making women 1919-1939. In R.R. Pierson (Ed.), *Women and peace.* London: Croom Helm

Troper, H. (1978). Nationalism and the history curriculum in Canada. *The History Teacher, 12*(1), 11-27.

Weber, E. (1978). *Peasants into Frenchmen: The modernization of rural France.* Stanford, CA: Stanford University Press.

Wells, H.G. (1922). *The salvaging of civilization.* New York: Macmillan.

Wells, H.G. (1939). The poison called history. In *Travels of a republican radical in search of hot water.* Harmondsworth, UK: Penguin.

— ✧ —

This article is a revised version of a presentation given to a conference of history teachers organized at the University of British Columbia in February, 1993, and subsequently published in 1995, in a much expanded version, as *The teaching of history and democratic citizenship.* Chap. in *In defence of history: Teaching the past and the meaning of democratic citizenship* (pp. 9-48). Toronto: Our Schools/Our Selves Education Foundation and James Lorimer.

5

GETTING INVOLVED IN THE LANDSCAPE: MAKING GEOGRAPHY COME ALIVE

IAN WRIGHT

Babies explore the spaces they occupy through sight, touch, taste, hearing and smell. Once they learn to crawl, they are off to discover what is behind the door or around the corner. As toddlers, they have to be restrained or placed in a stroller to curb their often enthusiastic explorations. When they learn to speak, they ask why the river, the store or the fire hydrant is where it is and how far is it to grandma's. But when they go to school, often they learn about their own community and about other places largely through vicarious, unconnected experiences. If they do go on field trips, their learning may be circumscribed because their teacher may have a narrow view of geography education; spontaneous exploration may be frowned upon because some teachers think they will lose control if they allow this. As students advance through the grades, they learn to draw and read maps, but they rarely use this knowledge to learn about new places. Mapping is often viewed as separate and distinct from learning about other aspects of geography and the classroom globe and world map are rarely referred to in other lessons. Many students are bored when learning about landforms and physical geography because they are taught as if all that mattered was learning to define and recognize capes, bays, glaciers and drumlins (an oval shaped hill occurring in previously glaciated areas). The maps they colour are often assessed on the basis of neatness and whether or not the cities and rivers are correctly labelled. They may learn about the relationships between the physical and social environments in a given space but they rarely connect this learning with what is going on in their own community or in the rest of the world. They learn mainly through visual means, rarely developing a *feel* for places through use of their other senses and use of their imagination. If they explore issues, geographic knowledge is often seen as irrelevant.

Students who have these sorts of experiences are not receiving a good geographic education. They do not appreciate geography because they view it as a collection of disconnected information and skills which have very little relevance to their lives. In contrast, students who receive a sound geographic education may come to love geography or, at least, come to appreciate what geography has to offer. They may go on field trips where they are encouraged to hypothesize why the river, store or fire hydrant is there and then carry out research in the field to ascertain the plausibility of their answers. They learn to create and interpret maps and use their skills in all relevant contexts—they view maps as a revealing source of geographic knowledge. They know that there are connections between landforms and climates and human activities. They can use this knowledge to explore problems such as predicting what will happen on the Indian sub-continent in the event of a drought, or the effects of global warming because they know something about world climate and trade patterns. They research problems of local and national interest—forestry, mining and agricultural practices, pollution and the extinction of wild life. They engage in simulated exercises involving the location of settlements. They use interactive CDs and download information from the Internet. And, not surprisingly, they often are interested in geography. They see that geography involves connected knowledge which is vital in understanding the world and resolving issues that affect the well-being of humans and the environment.

Different conceptions of geography education involve different teaching practices.[1] Teachers' conceptions of their subject, the goals they espouse, and the beliefs they have about learning and teaching influence what is taught and how it is taught. In the first example, geography is conceived as consisting of unrelated information and skills about physical geography taught in didactic ways. Students learn about mapping and landforms but rarely connect the two. They learn about particular areas of the world but do not connect what they learn about in one area to other areas or their own communities. Neither do they apply geographical knowledge to the exploration of issues. In the second example, students are taught using active learning methodologies about the two major facets of geography—the physical and the human, and the relationships between the two. They apply their knowledge to local and global issues.

In this article I outline some of the traditions of geography and how these apply to geography education. These traditions—the spatial, physical, area studies and earth science—find their counterparts in geography education in the themes outlined in the Geography Education Standards Project (1994, 34-35).[2] I then suggest how these traditions can be utilized to organize and teach geography. I close with suggestions for teaching about maps and for the use of direct and simulated experiences to make geography come alive for students.

CONCEPTIONS OF GEOGRAPHY AND GEOGRAPHY EDUCATION

The question "What is geography?" may seem to be a foolish one as surely everyone knows the answer. How else could there be curricula, textbooks and departments of geography in colleges and universities? But geography has an identity problem. Is it a physical science, a social science, part of the humanities, none of these, or all of these? As we will see, the answer we give will influence what we teach in the name of geography education.

Geography has characteristically been divided into four parts—called "traditions" by Pattison (1974). The most familiar component is the *spatial* tradition in which

the concern is with how things are arranged on the earth, for example, where the major mountain ranges, deserts and tropical forests are. Here the central medium of communication is the map, various types of which can display all such information concerning the physical nature of the earth. A second tradition, *human/land relationships* focuses on people's interactions with their physical environments, for example how agriculture changes the landscape and how the landscape influences agriculture. Here there is mingling of the physical and social sciences. In the *area studies* tradition, clearly defined spaces are studied in depth. Area studies involve the exploration of both large regions

---

The question "What is geography?" may seem to be a foolish one as surely everyone knows the answer. How else could there be curricula, textbooks and departments of geography in colleges and universities? But geography has an identity problem. Is it a physical science, a social science, part of the humanities, none of these, or all of these?

---

such as the Indian sub-continent and much smaller areas such as a city or a single farm. The emphases here can include the physical and social sciences along with the humanities. Finally, the *earth science* tradition is the focus for such physical science disciplines as mineralogy, glaciology and meteorology. Here students learn about the physical processes that shape the earth's surface. These four traditions make up "geo" (i.e., earth) "graphy" (i.e., describing)—the study of our earth. However, not all of these traditions have held equal prominence in geography education.

In Canada, the spatial tradition held sway when geography was taught in the public schools in English Canada in the 1800s (Tomkins, 1980) and it is still a powerful force in the teaching of geography. It has been complemented by the area studies approach but the translation of this approach into classroom practice has caused problems (Wolforth, 1983). A major problem with how area studies was taught in schools was that it created an impression of environmental determinism—where you lived *determined* who you were. Of course, our environments influence us, but they do not dictate what we become. A second problem with how area studies was taught arose because of the assumption that the more varied the terrains and climates, the more complex the culture—since cultures are a direct response to environmental factors. As a result some concluded that people who lived in areas with uniform terrain and climate were unlikely to develop sophisticated cultures because they had to make less effort to cope with their environment. Thus, Europeans, who had to cope with varied landscapes and climates, were superior to people in most of Africa who lived in fairly uniform environments. These racist views are no longer prevalent and area studies continue to be a focus in geography education. This area studies approach was complemented by "sample studies" in the 1960s. Here students undertook micro-studies of towns, cities and industries.

A contemporary approach which combines the area studies and human/land relationships traditions in geography education is to focus on relationships between people and their environments in a humanistic way. Many contemporary geographers are concerned with social problems of local and global relevance. Rather than merely describe relations, they ask evaluative questions about who should get what, where and how. For example, students who study international aid programs as part of their Geography 12 course in British Columbia research how food is distributed in countries where there is starvation and try to decide what policies Canada should adopt. Many environmental and global education programs implicitly use this social problems approach in which geography, science, economics and ethics are combined, and students learn about and often try to resolve problems of international, national and local significance.

Geography education in Canadian elementary and secondary schools reflects these varying traditions. In some provinces, there are separate geography curricula which address a variety of topics focussing, for the most part, on physical geography (the earth science and spatial traditions), and regional studies (the area studies and human/land traditions). In other provinces, geography is located within social studies curricula, sometimes appearing as discrete units on physical geography (typically utilizing the spatial tradition with some consideration of the earth/science one), or on the geography of Canada (typically from an area studies perspective) and other times integrated through interdisciplinary study of contemporary issues and focusing on the land/human and area studies traditions from a humanistic perspective.

However, as pointed out earlier, to teach geography in a holistic way will have to involve all the four traditions. Only by combining them will students be able to draw connections between the physical and human environments.

RATIONALES FOR GEOGRAPHY EDUCATION

There are a number of rationales that can be advanced for geography education.

- **Intrinsic value.** The study of geography can have intrinsic value. The places we know are imbued with meanings: the cornerstore where we regularly buy the newspaper, the house with the barking dog and the tree whose blossoms in the spring are a harbinger of better weather. The places we don't know often fascinate us and we want to find out more about them. We devour pictures in *National Geographic* and we visit other places because we want to see what is there. We want to discover something about our world and the marvels it contains. We are in awe when we see the Rockies, the Gaspe peninsula, a prairie sunset. We marvel at the pictures of the earth taken from space. The geography of places appeals to the human spirit.

- **Value for personal decision making.** Geography can have utilitarian value. Being able to read a map helps us plan trips and find our way around a city or a region. Having mental maps of places helps us locate places in the world and make some sense of them. For example, without knowing where Chernobyl is, I could have no idea of the magnitude of the nuclear disaster there and how it might affect

---

The places we know are imbued with meanings: the cornerstore where we regularly buy the newspaper, the house with the barking dog and the tree whose blossoms in the spring are a harbinger of better weather. The places we don't know often fascinate us and we want to find out more about them. We devour pictures in National Geographic and we visit other places because we want to see what is there.

---

me. Geography gives us a broader view of the world. Knowing about landforms, the location of the sun and weather patterns can help us choose where to buy a house, or locate a business. Geographic knowledge is also useful in a variety of occupations from urban planning, to agriculture, business, disease control, waste disposal and teaching.

- **Value for social decision making.** If we recognize that citizenship involves making decisions about matters of public policy, then a knowledge of geography is essential. How can one understand the consequences of Quebec separation without understanding its location in Canada? How can one comprehend First Nations peoples' land claims, or the effects of global warming, or the destruction of the Amazon rainforest without a knowledge of geography? By studying geography and learning how people live on the earth we can determine which arrangements work best. By studying the global consequences of our actions, we can begin to understand the interrelationships between people and their habitats. We can begin to care about the effects our actions have on others. Our ethnocentrism may diminish and our concern for human well-being can be fostered.

All three rationales pertain to the education of students; in particular, geography can contribute to the citizenship aims of social studies. Here the focus should be on helping students confront and try to resolve social issues which affect their communities, the country and the world.

ORGANIZING AND TEACHING THE GEOGRAPHY CURRICULUM

The four traditions of geography outlined above

provide a solid framework for geography education. The geography curriculum and the topics within it have to be arranged in such a way that the traditions are taught in an interrelated manner. It makes little sense to study physical geography without considering the effects of humans on landscapes and the effects of landscapes on humans. Neither does it seem advisable to study the problems of human settlements without considering the location of these (Winston, 1986, p. 48). Further, it would make little sense to consider broad economic, political, environmental or historical problems without taking into account the relevant geographical information. Geographical knowledge needs to be integrated into the other social sciences. Obvious areas are in the study of communities, cultures, social issues, economic systems and current events. In history, the location of empires, battles, historical sites and so on, all need to be found on maps. Past and present maps can be compared and the differences discussed and researched. Why did the Roman Empire "cover" so much of Europe and the Middle East? Why is this Empire not shown on later maps? Why did the boundaries of countries change? How did Canada's geography influence its historical development as a nation? In this way, we can avoid fragmenting geographical information and can integrate it with the other social sciences. We must also integrate the skills necessary to learn geographic information. These skills include the asking of geographic questions (identifying geographical issues and planning how to deal with them); acquiring geographic information from a variety of sources; organizing geographic information through maps, charts and graphs; analyzing geographic information by interpreting statistics, maps and other data sources to predict, hypothesize and evaluate; and answering geographic questions by developing generalizations and conclusions and by communicating them successfully (Geography Education Standards Project, 1994, pp. 41-44).

Below are four ways to organize instruction so that the major aims and traditions of geographic education are addressed in an integrated manner.

Study of a particular landscape

Landscape studies are indepth analyses of a specific place (e.g., a river delta, the local city/town centre). The place should preferably be one which can be studied through field work. Through meaningful activities, the key themes of geography can be introduced in a context that is relevant to students. For example, students could carry out an environmental assessment of an urban area by evaluating the appropriateness of the built environment, condition of the natural features, levels of noise, traffic density and pollution, ease of movement for people and vehicles, services available and overall attractiveness of the area.

Further suggestions for activities are found in the questions below which require knowledge of spatial relationships and human/land relationships. Answering these questions also involves application of geographical skills.

Study of an issue or problem

A second way to organize instruction is by focussing on an issue or problem that has significant geographic dimensions. These could include world problems such as global warming, the destruction of rain forests and the disposal of radioactive waste, or local problems of pollution and land use (e.g., Should a shopping mall be built in this location?). Problem solving and issue resolution provide an opportunity to develop many geographic skills including asking geographic questions, collecting, analyzing and presenting geographic information, and developing geographic generalizations. Further, it involves students in decision making. The model suggested on the next page is one way of structuring the study of an geography-related problem.

SAMPLE QUESTIONS WHEN STUDYING A LANDSCAPE

- What would you find on the site that is unlikely to be shown on a map of the area? If possible, create a map that depicts these features.
- How is this area different from where you live? from another area?
- Is this area useable for any of a range of purposes (e.g., as a factory site, to grow food, location of a park)?
- If you were going to build something here (e.g., house, factory, main road, park), where is the best place to put it? Why?
- What would you smell if you were on location? What are the sources of these smells?
- How could you improve this area environmentally? economically? aesthetically?
- Can you identify a particular landform feature (e.g., a cliff, a hill, a moraine)?
- What sorts of transportation networks can you identify?
- What did this area look like 100 years ago? Upon what did you base your conclusions?
- What do you think the area will look like in 10 years time? What clues can you offer for your prediction?
- What natural and human "hazards" can you find (e.g., erosion, flooding, fire)?
- How does the landscape influence the way people live?
- How have people changed the landscape? Which of these changes have been beneficial and which have not?

Study of regions

Another way to organize the curriculum is on the basis of regions. Rather than approaching this as a descriptive study of, say, the sub-Sahara, the Amazon rainforest, or the Canadian Shield, instruction can be organized around the concept of 'region.' Taking this approach, students might consider the questions such as: What would Canada look like if it was divided into regions based on the popularity of various kinds of pop music? Why would regions based on landforms make sense? To whom? Where does one draw a line to divide one region from another? These questions are intended to promote the realization that regions do not exist in the natural order of things, but rather are human constructions and that different people have different ideas about what constitutes a region.

Another way to organize a regional study is to divide the class into groups representing various landform regions. Each group would determine the benefits flowing from the region. Groups could establish their own criteria and then score their region based on these criteria. In a whole class session, each group would argue that their criteria were the most justifiable and argue for their region as contributing the most. Another idea is to create a model of the physical regions in a country, and then determine how these have shaped the historical development, settlement patterns, location of economic activity and the national culture(s). It is interesting for students to hypothesize, for example, how living in British Columbia influences people's perceptions of central Canada, especially about federal/provincial matters.

In a different vein, students might determine how a sustainable economy could be developed in a particular region. If this is likely to be an immense undertaking, the task could be limited to major natural resources. Students would be expected to obtain data about regions through a variety of sources—including E-Stat (the electronic data base produced by Statistics Canada)

Study of global systems

Many of the organizing ideas advanced by global educators involve teaching about global systems (Werner & Case, 1997). Systems include both physical (e.g., climate, glaciation) and human created ones (e.g., economic, social). The point of studying these is to focus on interrelationships. For instance, a topic could be organized around a particular product (e.g., oil, coffee), and the influences of global economic, climate and landform patterns could be ascertained. There could be a focus on a particular landform and the similarities and differences of similar landforms around the world could be studied. For instance, do people living in prairie regions in other than Canada, make use of the landscape in more or less sustainable ways. Could we improve the way we use our prairie landscape? By analyzing a particular phenomenon within the broader system, students can begin to see the often complex connections with other phenomena—for example, the destruction of the Amazon rain forest is linked to poverty levels in the region, the abundance of cheap clothing from certain countries is tied to the violation of women's human rights, and the provision of a water well and agricultural tools from Canada can reduce disease and improve the economic well-being of a village

---

MODEL FOR GEOGRAPHIC PROBLEM SOLVING

- *Identify the problem.* It will be easier to establish its importance and to draw connections with other aspects of the geography curriculum if the problem involves a large segment of the world's population, impacts a large area of the earth's surface either directly or indirectly, and requires several countries or international bodies to resolve.

- *Identify the site(s) of the problem.* In the context of a drought or earthquake the exact location in absolute and relative terms can be determined. With a crisis such as global warming, the location is impossible to determine so students should note the places that may create the majority of the pollutants which, in turn, create the warming conditions.

- *Describe the site(s).* Students research and identify the key features and conditions of the site(s), including human settlements, landforms, physical characteristics and human activities.

- *Determine the consequences of the problem.* Students explore both the intended and unintended consequences over the short and long term. For example, clear-cutting of forests creates jobs and is apparently less expensive than other methods of logging. However, there are unintended effects such as erosion. With problems such as droughts or floods, the consequences may have far-reaching effects in that crops grown in the area may no longer be available, leading to price increases and product shortages.

- *Research possible solutions.* Students collect information through library study and interviews and identify a wide range of possible solutions, and the benefits and shortcomings of each.

- *Decide on the most defensible solution.* Using a problem resolution or value analysis procedure invite students to deliberate on what would be the best course of action to pursue.

- *If feasible, take action.* To further enhance learning, students should, where feasible, act on their decision by writing letters to relevant organizations, publicizing their concerns through displays and letters to newspapers, and carrying out activities such as recycling cans and bottles, cleaning up streams and parks, and reducing their consumption of non-recyclable products.

in Africa, the villagers of which then provide food to other areas.

These four ways—study of particular sites, problems, regions, and systems—can be used to organize for instruction so that the major themes of geography education are addressed in an educationally sound manner. However, no amount of creativity in organizing geography instruction can compensate for poor pedagogy.

PEDAGOGY

Poor pedagogy is a major concern in geography education. Factors contributing to this state of affairs include lack of teacher training in geography and in teaching methods, absence of an educationally sound conception of geography and of a clear sense of purpose for teaching it. Also significant is inattention to the ways in which students construct their geographic understandings.

Students construct their geographic understandings on the basis of the incomplete information they possess and their level of cognitive development. Piaget reports on a six year old that he studied who believed that, "Mountains made themselves all alone. So that we can skate[3] (1971, p. 349)." Other young children interviewed by Piaget had their own explanations for physical phenomenon. Consider the following exchange about the creation of clouds:

> *Piaget:* And where does the steam for the clouds come from?
>
> *Student:* When you cook soup.
>
> *Piaget:* Does cooking soup make the clouds?
>
> *Student:* The steam goes out and it takes water with it. (Piaget, 1971, p. 303)

The strong egocentricity in young students' understanding of geography is illustrated by another child's comment, following a trip to London, that the Tower of London was "next to the ice-cream stall where we stopped" (Bailey, 1974, p. 29). This child's conception of location is very different from that of the conventional understanding. Children often do not know that water on a map is represented by the colour blue. Why should water be blue, and why should main roads on a map be coloured red when roads are either black asphalt or gray concrete? All children conceive of the world in their own ways and this is where geography teaching has to start—with what students believe about the earth and how they visualize space.

In this section on pedagogy, I focus on teaching about maps to illustrate how teachers can overcome student misconceptions to promote sound geographic understandings. I close with two general suggestions for effective geographic teaching—the use of direct experiences and simulations.

Teaching about maps

Considerable research has been carried out on children's mapping abilities (Milburn, 1980; see also Milburn's article in this collection) because maps are one of the key tools of geographers (they can show about 90 per cent of information about a given space). We know from Milburn's research that young children have difficulty in visualizing a physical space from a pilot's eye view. This involves a major feat of imagination. Young students often have difficulty appreciating that the map on the wall is from the "pilot's eye view" and that north is (usually) oriented to the ceiling. It is much better for students to have the map laid horizontally so that they have fewer problems in orienting themselves to the map. There are a number of activities to help elementary and secondary students make and use maps.

- **Scale and direction.** To help students begin to draw accurate maps, have them map, using appropriate symbols, their route to school, their classroom or the journey taken or the place lived in by a character in a story. Help them visualize from the bird's eye view by drawing objects from above and by viewing aerial photos of their community. Have them practice using different scales (one pace to one finger length) to draw maps and objects. At about grade three, introduce students to the compass and create simple orienteering activities around the school. Whereas elementary students would use the cardinal directions—north, south, east and west—at the secondary level students can use degrees to denote direction more specifically (e.g., N30°E), and to negotiate more complex orienteering routes.

- **Grid systems and latitude and longitude.** In about grade four, introduce students to latitude and longitude. To do this, use the globe and start with latitude as the Equator is clearly visible on the globe (where the two hemispheres are joined). Teach them that the parallels of latitude start at the Equator and go to the north poles where the latitude is 90 degrees north, and the south pole where the latitude is 90 degrees south. Have students locate where they are and find other places in the world that are on or close to their latitude. Help them discover where they would be if their latitude was in the other hemisphere. Ask them how they would indicate where they were if they were lost somewhere in the world. Ascertain the need for meridians of longitude by showing them that having only parallels of latitude as their position could result in a searcher having to travel around the entire world to find them. Once they have learned that longitude starts at Greenwich and ends at the International Date Line, students can use both coordinates to discover the location of places. Secondary school students can be more precise in their use of latitude and longitude by indicating the location of a given place using degrees, minutes and seconds or using other grids such as the Universal Transverse Mercator grid which is found on most topographical maps.

- **Elevation.** To help students interpret contour lines, let them draw contour maps of cones and pyramids, make models from the contour map of a hill and draw profiles from the contour map of a valley. This latter activity can be tackled by upper level elementary and beyond students.

Students could also be given contour maps along with photographs of the areas shown on the maps

such as PCGlobe and MacGlobe to create their own maps. At the same time, they should be taught that the information shown on maps is selective, that any world map is bound to be distorted (you cannot accurately depict the features on an oblate ellipsoid on a flat surface) and that maps can be used to de-

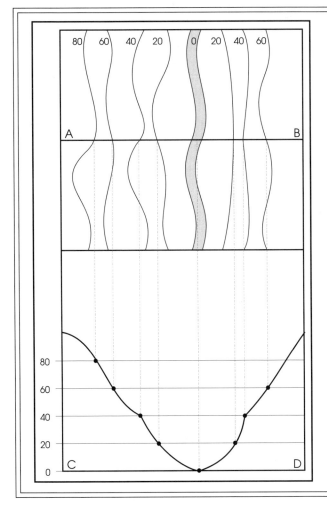

CONVERTING CONTOUR LINES TO CROSS-SECTIONAL VIEWS

This diagram shows how to translate contours from a map to a cross-sectional view of the terrain along a given line.

Instructions

Draw a section line A - B, and a parallel base line C - D. Draw parallel dotted lines to transfer to the base the points at which the contour lines (in this example at 20 meter intervals) intersect the section line. Mark off a vertical scale (in this example 20 cm equals 1 km) and plot points corresponding to the heights of the contour lines. Join the points with a smooth curve.

Contour Interval : 20 metres

Scale : 20 cm : 1 km

and asked to match them correctly.

- **Map interpretation.** Introduce students to a variety of maps by asking them to indicate the information they can glean about a particular place merely by using their atlases. Help students learn to read physical, demographic, economic, political, climatic and other types of maps, tables and charts by carefully leading them through the features of each. For example, on a map of sheep distribution clarify that one sheep on the map represents 10,000 sheep. As well, indicate that the location of the sheep is not exact, and the number of sheep is an approximation at the time the data were collected—by the time students see the map, the number could have changed drastically. Students can also be introduced to Landsat maps (see Kirman, 1991) and, at the secondary level, can use a variety of these to interpret landscapes. Students can also use computer programs

ceive (see, for example, *How to Lie with Maps* [Monmonier, 1991]).

- **Mental maps.** Being able to read maps created by others is only one aspect of mapping. Students have their own mental maps of places and these colour their perceptions. For instance, when students in Vancouver draw a freehand map of Canada, they often make the west far larger than it really is. Children in Halifax tend to show the east as being much larger than the west. When asked to draw world maps, students in both Europe and North America place Europe in the centre, students in Asia place their centre in Asia. These maps display their "world views," views which can have prejudicial effects. If Europe is seen as being at the centre of the world, then other places might be judged of less importance, and their peoples less worthy of consideration.

Other aspects besides maps are important for the

development of students' geographic understanding. Two teaching strategies that are particularly effective in making geography come alive are direct experiences and simulations.

Learning from direct experience

One of the best ways of studying a community is through field trips. I remember as a teacher in England, taking a group of inner-city students to the hills of Derbyshire. They had not seen countryside before, never climbed a hill, been in a cave, crossed a river on a log or hiked through bracken. They could have been told about such experiences or studied accounts of the area, but the real experience was far more meaningful.

On a field trip involving the study of a designated area, or on a traverse through differing areas, or from a vantage point, students could be given outline maps and draw, in their correct location, things they see. They can create their own maps using simple survey instruments. They can hypothesize why things are where they are and decide whether these locations are the most desirable. They can write about the feelings they have in a given place, list the smells and the sounds. They can "experience" the place.

Young students can feel the globe, run their fingers over 3-D maps, make their own globes from balloons, and their own landscapes from papier-mâché. Older students can create their own model communities, or build models to show how erosion changes a landscape.

And it is important for teachers, where possible, to visit the areas they are teaching about. Teaching about ancient Greece would be much richer after a visit to Athens or Olympia in that the teacher could bring to the teaching experience his/her personal reflections and photographs.

Learning through simulations

Simulations can be motivating and worthwhile learning experiences. Several are now on computer and others can be located in social studies journals. Wright (1995), includes a simulation involving the siting of an incinerator in a town. Each student is given a map of the town and becomes the owner of a designated property. A town meeting is held to determine the location of the incinerator. This game can be adapted for primary students by using a model of a community and having students choose a location for a playground or a shopping mall. A computer game suitable for elementary students is *CrossCountry Canada*. (Vincent, 1996). Playing the role of a truck driver, students learn about the geography of the area in which they are making deliveries. These experiences integrate the spatial, area and human themes of geography education, and all involve student decision making.

Concluding Remarks

In this article, I have tried to show how the traditions of geography have been and can be incorporated into geography education. Using these traditions as a basis for geography instruction would involve organizing curriculum and instruction in particular ways—around site specific studies, the resolution of problems and regional studies. In all cases, an emphasis is placed on relating geographic understandings both within the study of geography itself and within other social sciences. Only in this way can we avoid students perceiving geography as disconnected knowledge which has little relevance to their own lives. Geography has a great deal to offer in the education of the next generation. If we are to reap the benefits, then we must revitalize the teaching of geography in the schools.

Endnotes

[1] This is not meant to imply that teachers who had a narrow view of geographic education could not use active learning methods. However, the research literature does indicate that what was labeled "capes and bays" geography is usually taught using didactic methods.

[2] In the most recent conception of geography education advanced in *The National Geography Standards* (Geography Education Standards Project, 1994, pp. 34-35) geography is divided into the following themes:

- *The world in spatial terms*: use of maps and other ways of analyzing the spatial organization of people and places.
- *Places and regions*: knowing that people create regions and interpret them in various ways.
- *Physical systems*: understanding the physical processes that shape the earth and the distribution of ecosystems.
- *Human systems*: understanding the distribution of human populations, cultures, economic and settlement patterns, and how cooperation and conflict among people influence control of the earth's surface.
- *Environment and society*: understanding how people modify the environment, how these changes affect human systems, and the changes that occur in resource distribution.

[3] The student probably meant "ski" as people do not skate down mountains.

References

Bailey, P. (1974). *Teaching geography*. London: David and Charles.

Geography Education Standards Project. (1994). *Geography for life: National geography standards*. Washington, DC: National Geographic Research and Exploration.

Kirman, J. (1991). Elementary age children and remote sensing: Research from the Omega Project. *Canadian Social Studies*, 26(1), 17-19.

Milburn, D. (1980). Mapping in the early years of schooling. In R. Choquette, J. Wolforth & M. Villemure (Eds.), *Canadian geographical education* (pp. 71-88). Ottawa: University of Ottawa Press.

Monmonier, M. (1991). *How to lie with maps*. Chicago: University of Chicago Press.

Pattison, W. (1974). The four traditions of geography. *Journal of Geography, 63*, 211-216.

Piaget, J. (1971). *The child's conception of the world*. London: Routledge.

Tomkins, G. (1980). School geography in Canada: An historical perspective. In R. Choquette, J. Wolforth & M. Villemure (Eds.), *Canadian geographical education* (pp. 3-18). Ottawa: University of Ottawa Press.

Vincent, D. (1996). *Crosscountry Canada*. Burnaby, BC: Didatech Software.

Werner, W. & Case, R. (1997). Themes of global education. In A. Sears & I. Wright (Eds.), *Trends and issues in Canadian social studies* (pp. 176-194). Vancouver: Pacific Education Press.

Winston, B. (1986). Teaching and learning geography. In S. Wronski & D. Bragaw (Eds.), *Social studies and social sciences: A fifty-year perspective* (pp. 43-58). Washington, DC: National Council for the Social Studies.

Wolforth, J. (1983). Geography in social science education. In J. Parsons, G. Milburn & M. van Manen (Eds.), *A Canadian social studies* (pp. 70-82). Edmonton: Faculty of Education, University of Alberta.

Wright, I. (1995). *Elementary social studies: A practical approach*. Scarborough, ON: Nelson.

ADDITIONAL RESOURCES

Basaraborvich, Y., Coglon, J. & Mertz, D. (1992). My school game: A grade one game. *Canadian Social Studies, 26*(4), 170-171.

Burley, T. & Atkinson, G. (1986). Geographic skills: A research-based sequence for grades one to nine. *History and Social Science Teacher, 22*(2), 101-105.

Danzer, G. (1991). European cartography on the eve of the discoveries. *Social Education, 55*(5), 301-306.

Davis, U. (1981). *Canada, the world, and you*. Toronto: Gage.

Fernald, E. & Allen, R. (1990). Where is 'away'? A geographic concept. *Social Studies, 81*(1), 29-32.

Ford, L. (1986). Spotlight on geography. *Social Education, 50*, 16-17.

Kemball, W. (1980). *Canada and the world* (Book One). Toronto: Oxford University Press.

MacArthur, B., Magdalinski, J. & Smilar, R. (1992). The long haul: A grade five game. *Canadian Social Studies, 26*(3), 123-125.

Massey, D. & Shields, P. (1995). *Canada, its land and people*. Edmonton: Reidmore.

National Atlas Information Service. *Internet Link:* http://www-nais.ccm.emr.ca/

Natoli, S. (Ed.). (1994). *Strengthening geography in the social studies*. Bulletin No. 81. Washington, DC: National Council for the Social Studies.

Pickford, F., Granley, D., Christian R. & Roduta, P. (1994). Our school's paths and places: An introduction to maps. *Canadian Social Studies, 29*(1), 38-39.

Richburg, R. & Kreutzer, R. (1989). Understanding the ways things are by considering how they might be. *Social Studies, 80*, 107-109.

Swatridge, L. & Wright, I. (1995). *Canada: Exploring new directions*. Markham, ON: Fitzhenry and Whiteside.

Walford, R. (1969). *Games in geography*. London: Longmans.

6

The Anthropology of Everyday Life: Teaching Cultural Anthropology in Schools

Michael Ling

There are, often enough, two primary responses to anthropologists when they attempt to explain what they do. The first response is usually something like, "Oh yeah, I know about anthropology, *bones an' stuff*, right?". Once it is explained that, no, anthropology has a number of branches and that its major concern is with social or cultural aspects of human life, the response is often "that must be *interesting* . . . ", followed by an awkward pause, and occasionally accompanied by a furrowed, concerned brow, then ". . . any *jobs* in that sort of thing?".

I don't mean to make light of people's misperceptions about the discipline, nor their concern or even incredulity over its possible relevance or usefulness. This puzzlement has been an on-going dilemma for anthropology despite the efforts of many anthropologists to popularize the discipline, to make it more apparent how broad anthropology's interests can be and to show how pertinent it is to our everyday lives.

Anthropologists inquire into almost any domain imaginable, from fieldwork investigations into the ways of life of 'other', usually non-urban societies around the globe, to armchair inquiry into such things as the films, television and music of contemporary urban life. While anthropology may stereotypically be associated with National Geographic documentaries about lifeways *elsewhere*, teaching it in schools can introduce students to a way of looking at and considering *themselves* in their own society and, importantly, to recognize themselves as culture-bearers and culture-makers. We have tended to think of history and geography as the centerpieces of social studies, with disciplines such as anthropology considered either as peripheral or as too exotic, too removed from our lives to be included in curricula. But in its etymological roots, anthropology (from the Greek *anthropos* meaning 'human being') is fundamentally and simply concerned with the study of human beings in the broadest sense of the term, and so as a discipline it can be seen as a general way of looking at the world, one which can illuminate aspects of history, geography, politics, economics, language, the arts, along with numerous other disciplines.

The approach described in this article, one concerned with developing a perspective on "the anthropology of everyday life," is aimed at cultivating a sense of how we participate in, affirm, or even transgress cultural ways, but perhaps most importantly how in one way or another we 'make culture' in our daily lives. The wearing of certain kinds and styles of clothes in different social situations, our varying modes of speaking whether we are talking to professional associates, children or friends, the way we decorate our office spaces and our home spaces, are all expressions richly layered with cultural meaning and significance. Taught as a distinct subject, or as a component of a social studies curriculum, this approach to cultural anthropology can be seen as an over-view discipline able to integrate various subjects or topics. As a way of looking at the world, through inquisitive and critical lenses, it can help students see through or behind the norms and practices that shape their own lives, and the lives of peoples around the world.

But before proceeding with an outline of this perspective and two extended examples of how this may be developed with students, a few words about 'culture' since it is the core idea around which anthropology revolves. In fact, we might say that culture is to anthropology as the notions of time and space are to history and geography.

About the Notion of Culture

It has been commonly thought that *culture* is a set of unchanging, mysteriously-set-down-in-stone-from-the-deep-dark-past behaviours and practices. It is as though culture is a tool-box containing a fixed set of artifacts and customs that we inherit at birth. The problem with this view is that it overlooks the way groups, or individuals, and their habits change. If culture were simply a box of 'set things', then what do we do when our circumstances change and our particular set of tools cannot adequately respond to these changes? The fact that all societies can and do continually respond to environmental, social and technological change suggests that culture is not a static, unchanging set of practices and beliefs, but rather a very malleable one. And so, even if culture *can* be likened to a tool-box, it is one which constantly has its contents modified or replaced.

A further assumption in this 'box-of-culture' view is that people are locked into their cultural forms in ways that presumably prevent them from responding to or making use of 'other' cultural forms or expressions. But, again, if culture was just a set of features that one is encased in from birth, then how do we explain the fact that generally we can participate fairly freely in other cultural expressions, we can learn second, third and fourth languages, we can listen to, appreciate, learn and play forms of music that are not necessarily part of our 'culture of origin', and that we can even, to a certain extent, choose to 'live a culture' other than the one into which we were born.

It has become increasingly apparent as greater numbers of people from diverse cultural backgrounds come into on-going contact with each other that culture is fluid and changeable. One indication of the malleability of culture is the way that many peoples of the world have very quickly responded to and have made use of new technological innovations. The Inuit, for example, were incorrectly thought by many in the 1930s and '40s to live a static, unchanging existence. The introduction of the skidoo, however, was very quickly absorbed into the culture, made a part *of* the culture, in ways that some would now suggest are essential to their lives. Similarly, the introduction of cars or telephones in our grandparents' lives, television in our parents' lives, computers perhaps in our own, illustrate how new artifacts become part of our cultural landscape, so much so, that we often wonder how people ever did without them. Or more to the point, they become such an integral part of our day-to-day existence that they seem almost *invisible*—a 'natural' feature of our existence, we don't notice them as unique or novel in any way, they are just 'there' in our lives. We might even say that culture is effective as a force in our lives to the extent that it acquires this invisibility, or to the extent that we take the objects and ideas of culture for granted.

I should add, however, that material technologies are not in and of themselves culture, nor are they some measure of culturedness, they are simply artifacts—physical objects which may reveal much about a group when we look closely at how they are used by these people.

Culture, then, can be said to be the behaviours, habits, beliefs, expressions, artifacts and signs that a group, community or society creates to adapt to its physical and social environment. These notions of culture being *created* and *adaptive* are key aspects of a useful definition. They emphasize that we—collectively as social groups—'make it up as we go along', not without justification or rationale, but that we 'make culture' as a way of adapting to or modifying our worlds. What we do as biological and social beings is select what to *value* or *believe* in, and these selections are *relative* to the environment we are a part of. To get a sense of this, imagine ourselves being dropped into an unfamiliar environment, say a tropical rainforest. As we walk along we might ask ourselves: Is that snake there with the yellow head and green body dangerous? How about the

---

Culture, then, can be said to be the behaviours, habits, beliefs, expressions, artifacts and signs that a group, community or society creates to adapt to its physical and social environment.

---

one with the green head and the yellow body? Is that plant over there edible or will it poison me? That man coming toward me quickly with a knife at his side, how can I tell if he means to do me harm or help me? Or to take a less dramatic example, imagine being dropped into a foreign urban environment. Which way does the traffic flow? What in fact *are* the 'rules of the road'? What are the appropriate greeting behaviours between women and men, between women and women, between men and men? What are the rules around eating?

In its most basic sense culture helps to make things

somewhat predictable or less uncertain in a potentially very uncertain and even dangerous world. We learn to believe in certain things, for example, that particular snakes are to be avoided and to value certain behaviours, for example, that in some contexts it is entirely appropriate for men to link arms with one another while walking down a street, whereas in other contexts this is less acceptable. Societies communicate and reinforce these predictions by way of *social codes* or *cues*. These are the commonly defined behaviours, sounds, visual signs and signals which tell us something immediately about our worlds. They constitute the range of ways a society or community reinforces or expresses how it determines how we should look at the world, for example, through social roles, rules, myths, symbols, rituals, norms and habits. We internalize these codes and cues to such a degree that they become, as we often say, second nature, so much so that we are hardly aware that we 'decode' or interpret our environments every moment of the day (e.g., What codes and cues tell me that the person beside me in the elevator is standing a 'socially appropriate' distance from me? How did I come to learn that conversation between us is usually considered inappropriate, even if we are the only two people in the space, travelling up 20 floors together?).

Culture then can also be said to provide a screen or a lens through which we interpret and respond to the world, a so-called *world-view*, or as one theorist has put it: "culture is a society's way of constraining or narrowing your point of view" (Laughlin, 1990). Why do I feel it is inappropriate for me to burp loudly after a meal in a restaurant, and yet that it may be entirely appropriate in another context? Such are the ways a society, by way of culture, focusses or 'constrains' our view, so that we may tend to respond to 'other views' with resistance or even hostility. Put this way, it becomes easier to see that any cultural expression should be seen as a particular response to social and environmental circumstances. The current trend for body-piercing and tattooing is a cultural response—a set of codes or cues which communicate a range of ideas about the individual and their world. Perhaps, these practices signal the staking out or the reclaiming of an identity in the face of social pressures that render individuals invisible either by pushing them to the margins of the 'dominant society' because of economic disempowerment or by absorbing them into anonymity within the net of social conformity.

One of the most important conclusions of contemporary anthropology is that *any* cultural expression should always be considered in the context in which it is expressed. Which is to say, we need to be sensitive to the situation in which cultural values and beliefs are expressed instead of simply passing judgement on these expressions. This notion is expressed in the concept of *cultural relativity*, put simply, that all cultural expressions are relative to the context in which they exist. This isn't to say, as some have generalized it, that 'anything goes'—that we can never make warranted judgements about the ethical value of the actions of others. But what it does demand of us is that, for example, before dismissing the practice of tattooing or body-piercing as simply self-mutilation, and condemn it as inhuman or barbaric, we need first to understand the values and beliefs of that cultural community and, second, to look at our own forms of body decoration to determine whether or not we exhibit analogous behaviour. If we simply judge someone's practice of body-piercing as a perversion of *our* sense of how the body is to be treated, by not asking ourselves why this may have particular value or express a particular belief, we are ignoring what is meaningful and how it is meaningful to someone else,

---

In North America, for example, people typically bathe once a day, which is considered sufficient to maintain a socially acceptable measure of cleanliness. From a Japanese perspective, however, merely bathing once a day may be regarded as very unclean. Either perspective, seen from an ethnocentric point of view, would regard the other as inappropriate—either deficient or excessive cleanliness— missing the point that these behaviours are socially defined responses (or adaptations) to particular conditions.

---

missing out on possibly understanding another point of view, another world-view perhaps.

The need to see cultural expressions in relative terms is to guard against *ethnocentrism*, the mistaken belief that one's own world-view is *the* correct view of the world. What we ignore—one might say at our own peril—in being ethnocentric, in not seeing 'relatively', is that our own world-view is itself a particular construction, a set of adaptations to a particular social and physical environment. In North America, for example, people typically bathe once a day, which is considered sufficient to maintain a socially acceptable measure of cleanliness. From a Japanese perspective, however, merely bathing once a day may be regarded as very unclean. Either perspective, seen from an ethnocentric point of view, would regard the other as inappropriate—either deficient or excessive cleanliness—missing the point that these behaviours are socially defined responses (or adaptations) to particular conditions.

Closely related to ethnocentrism is the habit of *cultural stereotyping*, the tendency to see individuals and societies in simple, superficial and often negative ways. An anthropological lens encourages us to see beyond stereotypes, to see in fact, that stereotyping is based on partial, narrow and biased interpretations of cultural expressions which deny the validity, richness and nuances of people's personal and collective lives. An anthropological perspective requires that we be aware of the breadth and depth of cultural expressions in the world, and that one's own culture is but a specific instance of a pan-human and cross-cultural ability to interpret the world in diverse ways.

Anthropologists, among others, use the term *reflexivity* to describe this practice of reflecting on one's own social and cultural ways in light of others. The ability to be reflexive, we might say, is the ability to critically, reflectively engage with others and oneself—to be observant, aware, and to cultivate a habit of mind which is neither self-aggrandizing ("my culture is better than, more interesting, more valid than others"), nor self-denying ("my culture is not as rich, or as interesting, or as 'authentic' as others"), but self-aware. As a feature of anthropological practice reflexivity is essential. It emphasizes the 'relative' nature of culture, and encourages a sensitivity to the wide range of cultural expression.

To summarize the discussion thus far, I have made the following points about culture and cultural anthropology:

- Culture is not a single, concrete, unchanging entity. In fact, culture is not a 'thing' at all, but rather the label or name we give to the set of beliefs, values, behaviours and ways of living that any community of people expresses. Culture is *created* by people collectively as a way of *adapting* to social and environmental circumstances. Therefore, as circumstances change, so does culture.

- Culture is always *relative* to the circumstances in which it is created and exists. Cultures are ways of looking at the world, *world-views*, which are affirmed by *social codes* or *cues*, but no particular cultural world-view can necessarily be said to be better or more appropriate than another. The cultural *context* of any cultural expression must always be considered.

- Anthropology looks closely and critically at the 'taken-for-grantedness' of a world-view, and aims at making the beliefs and values of a culture, the social codes and cues, along with the reasons for them, more apparent. But importantly, an anthropological approach requires that we engage in this study *reflexively*, that is, by critically reflecting on our own cultural ways as a counter to the potential for superficial interpretations or stereotyping of other cultural ways.

These key points form the basis for an approach to teaching cultural anthropology which is known as the anthropology of everyday life.

The Anthropology of Everyday Life

Engaging in reflexive practice has made it apparent just how steeped we are in culture—in cultural expressions, codes and cues. As mentioned above, we are so infused with and by culture that much of it seems hidden or obscure to us. The anthropology of everyday

life aims to make these invisible codes and cues visible by making us more aware of how our habits, our identities, our roles, our rules, our taboos cause us to look at the world and interact with others in a certain way. Beyond this, however, the anthropology of everyday life points to the diversity of cultural expressions in the world, and seeks to understand the various contexts and foundations for these expressions.

Numerous writers have provided fascinating examinations of a variety of topics which are aimed at making the invisible aspects of culture and society visible. Witold Rybczynski, for example—an architect by profession—writes on the social meanings contained in how we construct our environments. His most notable book, *Home: A Short History of an Idea* (1986), traces the historical, cultural, economic and technological roots of our present-day North American notion of 'a home'. Henry Petrowski, a professor of civil engineering, uncovers the socio-cultural dimensions that underlie technologies and inventions. His books *The Pencil: A History of Design and Circumstance* (1990) and *The Evolution of*

What the anthropology of everyday life is involved with, then, is simply an examination of the seemingly commonplace, the usual, the taken-for-granted aspects (including objects, roles, attitudes and actions) of our everyday lives, revealing that there is often greater meaning in even the most simple cultural expression than we are sometimes aware of.

Useful Things (1992) entertainingly demonstrate the far-reaching implications and consequences for our lives of seemingly mundane artifacts.

Perhaps the most visible and broadly based exponent of an anthropology of everyday life approach is Margaret Visser, a Classical scholar by trade and a frequent commentator in various media. Her book *The Way We Are* (1995) is a collection of essays on the significance of commonplace cultural expressions such as the cross-cultural codes around the human tendency to blush, specific practices and rituals such as Valentine's Day, Thanksgiving and Christmas, and the hows and whys of the foods we choose to eat. (This last topic is dealt with in greater detail in two of her other books, *The Rituals of Dinner: The Origin, Evolution, Eccentricities and Meanings of Table Manners* (1991), and *Much Depends on Dinner* (1986).) Visser shows, for example, how Valentine's Day, originally a third-century Christian twist on a Roman fertility ritual, has been transformed over the centuries in Europe and North America into an occasion celebrating one's affection for lovers, family and friends. Interestingly, as it is adopted in other cultures now, it is taking on new and different forms, for example, in Japan, where the key ritual on Valentine's Day is for women to give gifts of chocolate to men. This has prompted the creation of a new reciprocal festival a month later, the appropriately named White Day, where men give gifts of white chocolate to women

(Visser, 1994, pp. 112-115). Examples like these illustrate the fluid nature of culture, the relative ease with which we can adopt and modify other cultural expressions, and the ways in which we construct meaning particular to our own cultural contexts.

What the anthropology of everyday life is involved with, then, is simply an examination of the seemingly commonplace, the usual, the taken-for-granted aspects (including objects, roles, attitudes and actions) of our everyday lives, revealing that there is often greater meaning in even the most simple cultural expression than we are sometimes aware of.

What we might especially keep in mind regarding this approach is that children and young adults are prime creators of and participants in culture. Young children are in the process of learning their society's ways, as are adolescents, who are also, often enough, deeply engaged in creations aimed at differentiating themselves from others. Furthermore, students are involved in two main cultural spheres: the cultural world of adults towards which they are being gradually guided, and the cultural world of children (there may well be numerous sub-cultural distinctions also, but for simplicity we might agree on these). In a very real sense they participate in these two cultures and see both the congruencies and incongruencies between them. Because of this they are potentially well-attuned and sensitive to the currents and turnings of culture, and so may be particularly well suited to and interested in investigating the worlds they inhabit.

Again, the main point to consider in the anthropology of everyday life approach is to develop awareness—critical, reflective awareness—of what, how and why we do what we do, along with how and why others do what they do. If students can see that their own cultural expressions and practices are shaped and reinforced by social circumstances, they may better appreciate the validity and context for other cultural ways around the world. The aim is not solely to help students identify the subtleties, idiosyncrasies and curiosities of culture, but to encourage informed, thoughtful interpretations of the world which, perhaps, may lead students to take concrete and considered action in the world with regard to cultural stereotyping, intolerance and insensitivity.

TEACHING THE ANTHROPOLOGY OF EVERYDAY LIFE

Teaching the anthropology of everyday life is to encourage students to examine as potential 'fieldwork' all aspects of their day-to-day lives, to see everything through a curious and critical lens, and to use themselves and their own lives as 'the field' being investigated. Cultural anthropology's main methodology or tool has been *participant observation*, a strategy of both

being an active participant in and a member of a community, while *also* being an observer of, or commentator on, culture. What we attempt to cultivate in the anthropology of everyday life is this sense of oneself as a participant observer. Even if we cannot travel to and live in distinctly different places, we can be participant observers in our own social settings. What follows are two activities aimed at developing this approach.

The Martian Anthropologist

In the mid-1950s an article entitled "Body Ritual Among the Nacirema" by Horace Miner (1956) was published in one of the key professional journals of anthropology. The article detailed the curious habits and lifeways of a people hitherto seemingly unknown to most North Americans, and to citizens of the United States in particular. Miner discussed among other things some of the bathroom and medical practices of 'the Nacirema' and how these practices reflected their cultural views about the body. The Nacirema, it turns out, are of course simply, 'American's (i.e., 'American'

By inverting the commonplace, and using the somewhat stilted language of a stereotype of a scholar, Miner held up a mirror to American lifeways so that his audience could see that their own cultural ways, their own world-views, could be seen (made visible) in precisely the same way that 'other' cultures had been.

---

spelled backwards), and what Miner very effectively and humourously managed to do was illustrate how *any* society's habits and practices reveal particular ways of looking at the world and the beings in it. By inverting the commonplace, and using a somewhat stilted scholarly tone, Miner held up a mirror to American lifeways so that his audience could see that their own cultural ways, their own world-views, could be seen (made visible) in precisely the same way that 'other' cultures had been.

In a Canadian version of the article, *Body Ritual of the Snaidanac*, for example, the author details how "a great deal of the Snaidanac's day is spent in ritual and ceremony. . . . the centre of this activity involves the human body; its appearance and health are vitally important for these people":

> While this is not unusual, the ceremony and philosophy concerning the body are unique. The fundamental belief behind their whole system of living appears to be that the human body is ugly and that its natural tendency is to decay and disease. As humans are trapped inside this ugly body, their only hope to avoid the decay and disease is religious ritual and ceremony. Every household had one or more shrines in their houses. . . . The most important place in the shrine is a box or chest which is built into the wall. In this chest, the natives keep their important charms

and magical potions. . . . Beneath the charm-box is a small font or basin. Each day every member of the family, one after the other, enters the shrine room, bows his or her head before the charm-box, mixes different sorts of holy water in the font and then proceeds with the brief rite similar to the Christian baptism. The holy waters come from the Water Temple of the community, where the priests hold elaborate ceremonies to make the liquid ritually pure. (source unknown)

Miner's article can be used as a model for students to think and write about some aspect of day-to-day life that they can look at in this way. I have used this strategy with high school students, but it can work with younger students, who may be very engaged by the chance to turn the adult world upside down.

I found it useful to frame the exercise around the question: What would such-and-such look like to a Martian anthropologist? In response, students have written about riding on an elevator (as a religious practice in which congregants meet periodically through the day in cubicles which ascend to the heavens and then return to the earth, reflecting their attempts to contact 'the Gods'), about laundromats (as sites for mating rituals), and the use of public telephones (as a medical therapy in which people attempt to effect a cure for ear and mouth troubles).

This is a good activity for adopting a different or 'foreign' perspective on some feature of life that we normally take for granted. As Miner demonstrated, often it is through an inversion of the norm that we see more clearly the constructed nature of our social habits and expressions. It humourously but very directly makes the point that, viewed from the perspective of someone who is not a member of a particular culture, any cultural expression can seem curious, strange, even silly. From the point of view of a professional anthropologist, this would be an example of how we tend to assume certain things and make incorrect judgements or conclusions from simple observations rather than what we might learn as participant observers.

One way to debrief this activity is to ask students as a class to list the judgements and conclusions the Martian observer made, and to identify what assumptions formed the basis for these. In this way, students are encouraged to see how stereotyping and biases are constructed (i.e., from partial knowledge and misunderstanding of cultural contexts). This point can be extended to examples of other cultural values or expressions—for example, the institution of 'sacred cows' in India, or the traditional culinary preference for raw meat among the Inuit of Canada's North. Invite students to examine in a more reflective way their own assumptions, preconceptions and judgements about

these practices and then to reflect on the bases for them. It is interesting to note, as the anthropologist Marvin Harris (1974) has pointed out, that the taboos around eating and mistreating cows among Hindus in India are based in a complex of interwoven ecological, social and historical circumstances. While Western observers, with different and very privileged agricultural techniques at their disposal, may see the taboos as "senseless", the practice helps maintain both social systems and ecosystems. The cows provide a fairly consistent source of nutrition especially for poorer people who live in deprived conditions, they provide field-plowing ca-

---

A Martian anthropologist's reading of the Hindu practice of revering cattle (or for that matter of the North American practice of revering cars) would presumably find it incomprehensible, and would interpret it only through it's own 'cultural lens'. A more reflexive reading, informed by the anthropology of everyday life, would see it in its broader environmental and social context.

---

pabilities (without having to resort to expensive and polluting automated machinery such as tractors, which in any case might be of little use in wet fields), and they are a source of both fertilizer and fuel (e.g., dried cattle dung is an effective alternative both to scarce wood and to expensive industrially-produced fuels like kerosene). Furthermore, the particular breed most used and revered, zebu cattle and oxen, are particularly well-suited to the physical environment, can survive on very little food or water and are resistant to a variety of diseases that other breeds are susceptible to in tropical climates.

Harris goes on to say that North Americans may be somewhat ignorant of what we consider sacred, or 'essential, unquestionable' parts of our existence:

> Automobiles and airplanes are faster than oxcarts, but they do not use energy more efficiently. In fact, more calories go up in useless heat and smoke during a single day of traffic jams in the United States than is wasted by all the cows of India during an entire year. The comparison is even less favorable when we consider the fact that the stalled vehicles are burning up irreplaceable reserves of petroleum that it took the earth tens of millions of years to accumulate. It you want to see a real sacred cow, go out and look at the family car. (Harris, 1974, p. 27)

A Martian anthropologist's reading of the Hindu practice of revering cattle (or for that matter of the North American practice of revering cars) would presumably find it incomprehensible, and would interpret it only through it's own 'cultural lens'. A more reflexive reading, informed by the anthropology of everyday life, would see it in its broader environmental and social context.

The Shrine Project

We tend to ignore the ways in which we invest seemingly common objects with meaning and significance. It is easy to point to the way someone in another society defines something as special or sacred, but harder to see these same impulses in ourselves. We are all familiar with formal, cultural shrines in which ideas of 'sacredness' or 'specialness' are expressed, usually in a religious or spiritual context. We are less aware of how we demarcate particular spaces or places within our *domestic* environments to express a similar, though more personal sense of specialness.

I often ask students to investigate the ways family members, friends or themselves collect and display objects that are special to them. Students should choose secular, non-religious collections so as to avoid offending anyone's beliefs and to get a sense of how we order and define our material worlds in other than formally socially sanctioned ways. Students have presented fascinating and insightful reports on "personal" shrines including their sister's/brother's poster collection of a band or film star; a wall of Jolt Cola pop cans which represented an expression of unique personal identity; the contents of a father's wallet; a husband's roll-top desk inherited from a relative; family photos and other artifacts on the top of a mother's/father's bedroom dresser; the cartoons, fortune-cookie messages and postcards on a family's refrigerator door; and even the pockets of a friend's favourite coat. The aim of the personal shrine is to help students see how we make aspects of the world special to us, which in turn reveals much about our personal values and beliefs. Sometimes these values and beliefs are mirrors of those of the society at large, sometimes they are in opposition to them, but in either case they represent a material expression of a world-view.

An effective way to reflect on the activity is to have students list what they see to be the values and beliefs expressed in these shrines and so, in effect, to attempt to construct the personal world-view depicted by these people through their shrines. Students should endeavour to identify what the elements of the shrine might mean both for the person and in the wider socio-cultural context. For example, empty Jolt Cola cans may be seen by society at large as simply garbage (though, hopefully, at least recyclable garbage), but for the maker of the Jolt Cola shrine, they expressed his distinct identity as a member of "punk and skateboard cultures" and his somewhat marginal relationship with society at large. Alternatively, the contents of the father's wallet comprised a shrine to his family and his working life. Both shrines represent in material form identifiable values and beliefs about self and society, and it is these features which student-anthropologists of everyday life help to elucidate.

The personal shrine activity can be extended by examining how people construct meanings for themselves in social groups and express this meaning in more socially formalized shrines and monuments. For example, students might look at a state or religious institution, say, the Canadian Houses of Parliament, a city hall, a war memorial, a temple or church, in an attempt to see how they express cultural values, beliefs and a sense of identity. A further step would be for students to examine the socially formalized shrines of cultures other their own, again with a sensitivity to the way the elements of the shrine express a cultural world-view, and in what ways this world-view and the values and beliefs it embraces can be seen as relative to the circumstances of the culture.

There are numerous other ways to engage students in the anthropology of everyday life. For example, ask students to compile a dictionary of slang or current jargon. Language is a key medium, if not *the* key medium, through which we define and communicate a world-view, and by which we differentiate ourselves from others. Alternatively, students could compile a list of cultural norms and then attempt to violate or transgress

---

What is important to recognize is that 'artifacts', and other less material or less obvious cultural expressions (e.g., words, manners, gestures, objects) are not just arbitrary 'things' in our worlds. They embody sets of ideas about how we perceive and act in our worlds. The exercise of identifying and unpacking the layers of meaning that surround everyday cultural expressions fosters student awareness of the many ways we create culture and how these creations construct a particular world-view.

---

a cultural norm and document the reactions of others, for example, talking spontaneously with strangers in an elevator, eating food with one's hands where usually one uses utensils, or using utensils with food usually eaten with one's hands. As teachers and responsible adults, of course, we must be very careful to discourage any actions which might result in harm or trouble befalling any students by discussing with them which norms are most appropriate and safe to violate. We would not want to condone an activity which might bring any degree of harm or undue discomfort to a student or unsuspecting, innocent culture-bearers.

What is important to recognize is that 'artifacts', and other less material or less obvious cultural expressions (e.g., words, manners, gestures, objects) are not just arbitrary 'things' in our worlds. They embody sets of ideas about how we perceive and act in our worlds. The exercise of identifying and unpacking the layers of meaning that surround everyday cultural expressions fosters student awareness of the many ways we create culture and how these creations construct a particular world-view.

A Final Word

Alexander Alland tells a wonderful story about his first fieldwork experience among the Abron in West Africa (1975, pp. ix-x). Being a keen, observant young anthropologist he paid close attention to every gesture, every expression that might reveal something subtle and significant about this culture. One day, while sitting by the village stream, he watched women fill their basins, gourds and pots with water. He noticed that the women would put either a fair-sized twig or a small branch in the filled container before setting it on their heads and walking back to the village. He was intrigued and mystified. Perhaps this was a symbolic social action, aimed at appeasing malevolent water spirits or maintaining social order in some way. He set about investigating this practice among the villagers, believing he was on the trail of something subtle and significant. As it turned out, however, the women's actions had a fairly simple, yet still intriguing, purpose. As we probably all have experienced, when carrying water in an open container the contents will slosh about creating a wave pattern. The more it sloshes, the greater the wave pattern, the greater the chance of losing water as it splashes over the sides of the container. The twig or piece of wood simply (and ingeniously) impeded the build-up of a wave pattern, thereby preventing the loss of water.

A lesson or caveat from this story is, of course, the need to be wary of considering our observations and interpretations as *the* 'final word' or as a complete, perfect explanation for any phenomenon. Also, it is important not to trivialize or exoticize anyone's life or cultural habits. We must help students acquire a sensitivity to and respect for the meanings that particular ways-of-living-and-being have for those who practice them. Furthermore, we are not attempting to 'get to the bottom' of cultural expressions, but rather to appreciate how any expression is rich with significance beyond what we might see at first glance with our cultural lenses. Anthropologist Clifford Geertz suggests that the desire to construct a simple, reductive explanation for any human expression could be characterized as "thin description" (1983). Anyone seriously interested in thinking about human beings from an anthropological point of view should endeavour for "thick description"—a multi-layered and nuanced description of a phenomenon, that resists reducing people's individual and social lives to easy categories and stereotypes, and sees the human capacity for culture in all its breadth and richness.

Living in a multicultural world, indeed as we become more aware that all of us in effect have a multicultural heritage of one form or another, as we travel and work more in different cultural milieus, as we encounter others with diverse and varied backgrounds, the anthropology of everyday life becomes a way of not simply cataloguing quirky bits of culture, but rather a way to engage in a conversation about how we make our worlds meaningful, about what it means to be human.

References

Alland, A. (1975). *When the spider danced*. New York: Basic Books.

Geertz, C. (1983). Thick description: Toward an interpretive theory of culture. In *Local knowledge* (pp. 3-30). New York: Basic Books.

Harris, M. (1978). *Cows, pigs, wars and witches: The riddles of culture*. New York: Vintage Books.

Laughlin, C., McManus, J. & d'Aquili, E. (1990). *Brain, symbol & experience*. Boston: New Science Library / Shambhala.

Miner, H. (1956). Body ritual of the Nacirema. *American Anthropologist*, 58(3), 503-507.

Petrowski, H. (1990). *The pencil: A history of design and circumstance*. New York: Alfred A. Knopf.

Petrowski, H. (1992). *The evolution of useful things*. New York: Random House.

Rybczynski, W. (1986). *Home: A short history of an idea*. Toronto: Penguin.

Visser, M. (1986). *Much depends on dinner*. Toronto: McClelland and Stewart.

Visser, M. (1991). *The rituals of dinner: The origins, evolution, eccentricities and meaning of table manners*. Toronto: HarperCollins.

Visser, M. (1995). *The way we are*. Toronto: Saturday Night / HarperPerennial.

Supplementary Reading

Barnes, N. (1992). The fabric of a student's life and thought: Practicing cultural anthropology in the classroom. *Anthropology and Education Quarterly*, 23, 145-159.

Brunvand, van J. (1981). *The vanishing hitchhiker: American urban legends and their meanings*. New York: W.W. Norton.

Brunvand, van J. (1984). *The choking doberman and other "new" urban legends*. New York: W.W. Norton.

Clifford, J. & Marcus, G. (Eds.). (1986). *Writing culture: The poetics and politics of ethnography*. Los Angeles: University of California Press.

Cove, J. (1987). *Shattered images: Dialogues and meditations on Tsimshian narratives*. Ottawa: Carleton University Press.

Farber, P., Provenzo, E. & Holm, G. (Eds.). (1994). *Schooling in light of the popular*. Albany: State University of New York Press.

Koziski, S. (1984). The standup comedian as anthropologist: Intentional culture critic. *Journal of Popular Culture*, 18(2), 57-75.

Marcus, G. & Fischer, M. (1986). *Anthropology as cultural critique: An experimental moment in the human sciences*. Chicago: University of Chicago Press.

Neal, A. (1985). Animism and totemism in popular culture. *Journal of Popular Culture*, 19(2), 15-24.

Pelissier, C. (1991). The anthropology of teaching and learning, *Annual Review of Anthropology*, 20, 75-95.

Radin, P. (1956/1972). *The trickster*. New York: Schocken Books.

— ✧ —

7

ARCHAEOLOGY IN SOCIAL STUDIES: AN INTEGRATED APPROACH

HEATHER DEVINE

Ask a student or a teacher what "archaeology" brings to mind and a variety of answers will be provided: Indiana Jones, the Atocha treasure, the pyramids of Egypt, the temples at Chichen Itza. But what about L'Anse Aux Meadows? And Head-Smashed-In Buffalo Jump? We rarely hear about archaeological sites in Canada; indeed one might think that no archaeological research is conducted here in Canada. We are even less inclined as educators to give it much prominence in our social studies programs. We perceive archaeology as an esoteric, even exotic, pastime having little to do with the real world.

Educators will argue that the demands of the core program are gradually eliminating instructional hours normally devoted to electives. They will note that they do not have the expertise to teach archaeology, and that there are few, if any, relevant instructional materials which lend themselves to integration with the core program. Finally, educators will introduce the issue of accountability and question the relevance of archaeology content when so many other topics need to be discussed in school. In short, teachers must have a strong case indeed to devote a week or two to the study of archaeology content.

ARCHAEOLOGY IN EDUCATION: A RATIONALE

Why study archaeology? Archaeology is often perceived as an esoteric discipline which, although fascinating, has little real utility in the modern world. How does archaeology contribute to our understanding of humanity?

First of all, archaeology satisfies innate curiosity about the past. We marvel at the pyramids and wonder how such an engineering achievement was possible. We argue about the origins of humankind, citing the Bible or Charles Darwin to support our views. We wonder whether people in the past shared the same hopes and fears, troubles and pleasures as people today. Archaeology helps to answer these questions by "putting a face" on ancient humanity through the evidence left behind.

Archaeology also serves an important historical function. It is our only means of charting the prehistoric past. Because the term "prehistory," loosely defined, means "before written records," we are totally dependent upon archaeological investigation for our knowledge of any ancient society that did not leave a written record of events. For indigenous peoples such as North American Indians, Australian Aborigines and African Bushmen, archaeological excavation is perhaps the only means of reconstructing the ancient (and more recent) roots of their cultures. The few existing historical records and oral accounts do not begin to provide a complete record of the aboriginal cultures that proliferated over thousands of years.

Archaeology serves yet another historical purpose. Not only does archaeological research provide prehistoric information, but it also serves to supplement and validate historical records we already have. Historical records cannot be viewed as totally accurate and complete depictions of life in the past. Historical records tend to document major events and the lives of prominent people. History is also inherently biased. The accuracy and completeness of any historical document is always influenced to some degrees by the personal values and interests of the writer, the social context in which the document is written, and the facts available to the writer at the time.

Archaeological research provides information concerning daily life in the past that historical accounts may exclude. In doing so, archaeological data serves to provide a "voice" to the ordinary people of long ago—the labouring classes, women, ethnic and racial minorities—all groups which, until recent years, have been largely underrepresented in historical literature and who have had little involvement in the writing of history.

ARCHAEOLOGY AS A SOCIAL STUDIES TOPIC

Archaeology can be a vehicle for the intrinsic instructional goals of social studies curricula. As a social studies topic, archaeology is a useful tool for achieving value, knowledge and skill objectives.

Archaeology is a social science. It studies culture in general and the evolution of cultural processes in particular. The study of past lifeways shows how these value systems change over time. Social science is nonjudgmental; we compare cultures not to determine the superiority of any one culture but to show how a variety of influences cause some lifeways to develop differently. In a multicultural society such as ours, understanding how diverse cultures develop helps us to understand why cultures conflict today.

Archaeology also fosters respect for our surroundings. Our physical environment is composed of both natural and man-made resources. Any discussion of the stewardship of our environment should stress that while we need to preserve non-renewable natural resources such as oil and gas for future generations, we must also strive to protect non-renewable heritage resources, whether they be historic buildings or archaeological sites. Archaeologists work to preserve our human past, and a learned appreciation and support of their activities not only helps to preserve our heritage but also stresses the importance of intrinsic values which contribute to the overall quality of life which we enjoy.

Few educators would support the notion that archae-

ology content is more important than the study of mathematics or science or history. Traditionally, archaeology is a rather minor topic area in social studies, and archaeology topics are taught to satisfy specific knowledge goals in the curriculum (e.g., to understand different methods of studying the past, as part of a study of native peoples). But all educators look for innovative, instructionally sound methods for motivating students and delivering core content. It is in this realm—the area of instructional technique—where the potential of archaeology content has largely been overlooked.

In classrooms across Canada, teachers are searching for ways to successfully incorporate a number of subject disciplines in a thematic context. Instructors are attempting to provide opportunities to master different

---

Archaeological data serves to provide a "voice" to the ordinary people of long ago—the labouring classes, women, ethnic and racial minorities—all groups which, until recent years, have been largely underrepresented in historical literature and who have had little involvement in the writing of history.

---

concepts and apply them to practical, real-world situations. Teachers want to promote qualitative instructional goals such as creativity and teamwork without sacrificing knowledge and skills. The multidisciplinary nature of archaeology implicitly satisfies all of these concerns and thus provides the strongest rationale for its inclusion in the curriculum.

An archaeology unit is an excellent way to foster inquiry skills, particularly those employed in the empirical and social sciences. Hypotheses are established and then tested through systematic excavation; conclusions are based on inferences derived from facts gleaned from excavation and historical, ethnographic and scientific information. Hypothesis formation and testing is an integral part of archaeological activity, and as a result archaeology is a useful tool for the development of thinking skills.

Archaeology activities also help in the delivery of mathematics and science content. Actual or simulated archaeological survey and excavation require students to utilize metric measurement, graphing and drawing to scale. Aspects of biology and geology—plant identification from pollen analysis, identification of animal bones, the study of soil formation and mineral analysis—can all be touched upon in an archaeology unit.

Language arts and fine arts can also be incorporated into the study of archaeology. Indeed, there are already some elementary language arts texts that incorporate units devoted to archaeological themes (e.g., the "Timespinners" unit in *Reading and How*, by McInnes, et al., 1985). The replicative experiments which are a part of archaeological research (e.g., pottery production, tool manufacture) serve equally well as a means of presenting hands-on activities in arts and crafts.

Archaeology is a participatory activity. Archaeological excavation requires active physical and mental commitment on the part of the students involved. Archaeological digging makes special demands on students in terms of stamina, precision and patience. Archaeology projects move pupils outside of the school and into the community. They compel the pupil to work cooperatively with classmates and members of the public. Most students, regardless of their academic potential, can derive a great deal of satisfaction from archaeology activities, and in doing so learn a surprising amount of material in a relatively painless fashion.

Activities in archaeology offer students a multidisciplinary approach to social investigation which is of benefit to both themselves and the community of which they are a part.

FIELD TRIPS

Field trip activities should be an integral part of any unit dealing with archaeology. Such visits could include trips to undeveloped archaeological sites on public or private land, excursions to archaeological digs in progress, or tours of historical interpretive centres and museums with an archaeological component (e.g., artifacts on display, archaeological features onsite).

Teachers must prepare in advance for field trips to archaeological sites, particularly undeveloped archaeological sites. Permission must be obtained from the landowner prior to taking students to archaeological sites on private property. The site should be visited in advance and the terrain and archaeological features noted. Then the instructor should prepare a structured field activity for students to complete during their visit to the site. Such an activity might consist of sketching rock art features, mapping tipi rings, burial mounds, or shell middens, or locating visible archaeological features (e.g., cellar depressions) using maps. Teachers are advised that often a visitor will not recognize archaeological features unless they know exactly what they are looking for. If instructors feel uncomfortable identifying and interpreting the archaeological features at a site, they might consider contacting a regional archaeologist or a member of a local archaeological society for assistance.

If students learn nothing else from a field visit, they should understand the need to protect archaeological sites. Students will benefit from a pre-visit discussion of the site and a review of basic archaeological terms. Students should also be advised of proper field etiquette. There should be no littering, no disturbance of livestock, and all gates must be closed after entering or exiting.

Do not, under any circumstances, excavate, disturb or remove artifacts from sites. If loose surface debris (e.g., bones, stone flakes, metal objects) is picked up and examined, it should be replaced in the exact location where it was found. What may seem to be a piece of loose garbage could be an important artifact. Archaeologists analyse artifacts on the basis of their original proximity to other artifacts at an archaeological site. Therefore it is essential that artifacts remain in as undisturbed a state as possible. In many provinces, surface collection of artifacts is illegal. Teachers are advised to consult the provincial laws governing historical resources for further information.

A trip to an archaeological dig in progess is always a useful experience. Sometimes it is difficult to visualize exactly what it is that archaeologists do. A field trip allows students to see first-hand the different steps involved in archaeological excavation and analysis. Occasionally there is also an opportunity to work as a volunteer excavator (see *Excavation Activity* below).

A "designated" archaeological or historical site is one which is administered by a municipal, provincial or federal body and one which has some degree of on-site interpretation, ranging from interpretive signage to a facility complete with exhibits and interpreters. If a designated archaeological site exists in your region, by all means take your class there. Most interpretive facilities offer school programming that complements topic areas covered in provincial curricula. If the facility has a strong archaeological component, hands-on activities such as archaeological dig simulations, prehistoric tool production, or artifact study may be offered. Often it is more convenient for the teacher to utilize these resources than to spend the time and money required to offer the same activities in the classroom setting. These facilities already have the necessary equipment, materials and trained staff to sponsor the activity.

Museum visits are also desirable, particularly if there are no archaeological or historic sites nearby. Many larger museums offer tours and hands-on activities for students. Younger pupils (K–3) may have the opportunity to handle artifacts in the context of a discovery room activity. Teachers are advised to contact local museums to determine what archaeological materials are available for examination. Some museums circulate outreach kits of facsimile artifacts.

EXCAVATION ACTIVITY

From time to time there are opportunities for students to work as volunteer labourers at archaeological sites. Some archaeological digs, such as those administered by the Toronto Board of Education Archaeological Resource Centre (Smardz, 1989) are run specifically for student participants. In most cases, however, student volunteers are accepted at archaeological digs on an *ad hoc* basis. Teachers should be aware that many archaeologists will not permit students under 18 years of age to excavate except under special circumstances. In most cases there are only one or two volunteer positions available for students, and the details must be cleared with the supervising archaeologist in advance. As with other field trip activities, student participants should be familiarized with the site, its history, the kinds of artifacts they are likely to encounter, etc. They should be advised on proper attire for excavation activity and prepare mentally for work on the dig. Archaeological excavation is often dirty and can be physically tiring. It can also be quite tedious. A person can excavate all day and not recover a single artifact. When artifacts are discovered, meticulous measurements and notes must be taken. Patience is a virtue in archaeological work.

Most archaeological excavation activity takes place in the late spring, summer and early autumn, depending on weather conditions. To find out about regional archaeological projects requiring volunteers, contact your local amateur archaeological society or provincial archaeological regulatory agency (see *Resources for Archaeology in Education*, below).

Do not attempt an excavation of an actual archaeological site unless it is under the supervision of a qualified archaeologist who has a permit for such work! This caution applies to survey and surface collection as well. If an excavation activity is desired, a simulated excavation can be planned and executed in the classroom setting. Or, students can visit an interpretive facility or museum that provides the opportunity to participate in simulated digs.

Often budget or time constraints prevent field trip excursions to archaeological sites. However, simulated excavation activities can be offered in the school setting. For instructions on planning simulated archaeological digs, contact interpretive facilities and museums with an archaeological program, regional archaeological resource management agencies, local amateur societies or anthropology publications geared to educators (see *Resources for Archaeology in Education*, below).

Some thoughts to keep in mind when planning a simulated dig:

- Plan your excavation well in advance. Choose artifacts with care, and place the items in your simulation unit according to the concepts you are teaching and the site you are creating.
- Whenever possible, use the tools used by archaeologists: trowels, line levels, tape measures, etc. All of these items are inexpensive and readily available at hardware stores.
- Stress precision in excavation. Make sure that students take accurate measurements of artifacts in the excavation unit before they are removed from the simulation unit, and that this information is recorded on an excavation form. Ensure that archaeological digging tools are used correctly and that artifacts are identified and analyzed using classification and inferencing skills.
- Keep in mind that a maximum of four students can work comfortably at a one metre by one metre unit an any given time. Have more that one unit available, and/or rotate students to ensure that all students have an opportunity to dig.

EXPERIMENTAL ARCHAEOLOGY

Archaeologists are interested in determining how artifacts were created and used because this information provides insights into aspects of technological development and diffusion. Experimental archaeology involves the researching of traditional techniques for tool construction and use and experimentation in the manufacture and utilization of tool replicas. Pottery construction, flintknapping (the process of chipping tools from stone), food processing, and weapons manufacture and use are all examples of experimental archaeology activities. Many of these activities, such as pottery manufacture and food processing, can be conducted successfully in the classroom setting. Other activities, such as flintknapping or weapon construction, can be potentially hazardous, and may not be appropriate for younger students. Do not attempt these activities with your students unless you are proficient yourself.

Archaeology, by its very nature, is a hands-on activity. . . .Too often students' sole experience with an artifact consists of passively peering at the item through the glass window of a museum case, where the object sits pristine and isolated, an object to be admired rather than understood.

Teachers should endeavor to incorporate at least one experimental activity in an archaeology unit. Archaeology, by its very nature, is a hands-on activity. Children find replicative experiments both challenging and enjoyable. More importantly, the use of reproduction artifacts for the recreation of traditional activities of the past serves to minimize the "museum mystique" surrounding artifacts. Quite often we forget that artifacts were not manufactured to be looked at, but were everyday items used and modified by ordinary people. Too often students' sole experience with an artifact consists of passively peering at the item through the glass window of a museum case, where the object sits pristine and isolated, an object to be admired rather than understood.

No matter how attractive the exhibit or how well written the display captions, a viewer is unlikely to recognise the skill and patience needed to manufacture and use artifacts from the past. But give a student the opportunity to attempt the traditional methods for manufacturing stone tools, making pemmican, baking bread or molding clay pots, and that individual is likely to re-think his or her notions of life in the past. It is not enough to identify artifacts from early times; what is important is to know how these objects came to be developed, how they were used and the impact of these objects on day-to-day survival in the distant past.

RESOURCES FOR ARCHAEOLOGY IN EDUCATION

The first step towards integrating archaeology activities into the social studies program is to identify a social studies concept compatible to archaeology content. Perhaps it is a general topic in Canadian history, such as the study of the western fur trade or early pioneer settlement. Or perhaps you would like to introduce students to the study of hunters and gatherers as part of an examination of culture. From there, you will want to focus on a more specific topic within the broader field to provide students with a case-study situation. Perhaps you will choose to study one particular hunter-gatherer group, or one specific pioneer community. Once you have narrowed your focus, your next task is to locate and compile resource materials. If you are studying a topic area featured in your social studies curriculum (e.g., Indian groups of Canada) most of the basic resources listed for the topic should provide you and your students with the background information required to research the topic in more detail. The bibliographical references provided at the end of the textbooks may also provide lists of books and films dealing with the archaeological aspects of the topic you have chosen.

The audiovisual and print materials produced through cultural organizations such as the National Geographic Society and the National Museums of Canada are worthy of note (See December 1988 issue of *The History and Social Science Teacher* for reviews of archaeology media—Ed.). Interpretive centres at federal and provincial historical sites sometimes provide printed material dealing with classroom-based archaeology activities as a service to schools which cannot take students to their facilities. University and college anthropology and classics departments may also have outreach materials of use to teachers. Periodicals such as *Equinox* and *The Beaver* print archaeology articles from time to time, as do many larger newspapers. Your school librarian will be able to assist you in compiling a classroom reference collection of suitable books.

However, many school libraries have only a limited number of references dealing with archaeology, particularly Canadian archaeology. Beware of pseudoscientific publications (e.g., *Chariots of the Gods*) which are erroneous interpretations of archaeological information. More useful and trustworthy sources of information are the provincial government bodies which deal with archaeological research and resource management.

WORKING WITH ARCHAEOLOGY: A FINAL NOTE

Regulations and fines do not prevent the destruction of archaeological sites. It is through public education that citizens learn the intrinsic value of our historic and prehistoric past. Archaeology in education, therefore, is essential to the investigation, interpretation and protection of Canada's archaeological heritage.

ARCHAELOGICAL AGENCIES

Each provincial and territorial government has an administrative body responsible for supervising archaeological research and protecting the archaeological resources in its jurisdiction. Most of these organizations have some form of outreach material available to members of the public, ranging from brochures and posters to videotapes and research reports. Teachers are advised that some of this material may not be suitable for utilization by younger students as the reading level can be fairly sophisticated and the content can be highly technical in nature. In most instances teachers will be required to review materials carefully and extract the information required to present archaeology content to students.

Teachers should also contact government archaeological agencies because these organizations maintain links with amateur archaeological societies, university archaeology department, and independent archaeological consultants—all useful sources of information should teachers need instructional materials, classroom speakers or in-service instructors.

Below are listed the addresses of each provincial and territorial archaeological resource agency. *[Editor: Some addresses have been updated.]*

Alberta
Public Education Officer
Archaeological Survey of Alberta
8820–112 St.
Edmonton, AB T6G 2P8

British Columbia
Director, Resource Management Branch
Ministry of Municipal Affairs,
Recreation and Culture
Parliament Buildings
Victoria, BC V8V 1X4

Manitoba
Staff Archaeologist, Historic Resources Branch
Dept. of Culture, Heritage and Recreation
3rd Floor, 117 Lombard Ave.
Winnipeg, MN R3B 0W3

New Brunswick
Provincial Archaeologist, Archaeology Unit
Dept. of Historical and Cultural Resources
Old Soldiers' Barracks
P.O. Box 6000
Fredericton, NB E3B 5H1

Archaelogical Agencies (cont'd.)

Newfoundland and Labrador
Resource Archaeologist
Historic Resources Division
Newfoundland Museum
283 Duckworth St.
St. John's, NF A1C 1G9

Northwest Territories
Senior Archaeologist, Archaeology Unit
Prince of Wales Northern Heritage Centre
Government of the N.W.T.
Yellowknife, NWT X1A 2L9

Nova Scotia
Education Section
Nova Scotia Museum
1747 Summer St.
Halifax, NS B3H 3A6

Ontario
Archaeology Unit, Heritage Branch
Ministry of Citizenship and Culture
2nd Floor, 77 Bloor St. West
Toronto, ON M4A 2R9
Archaeological Resource Centre
Danforth Technical School
840 Greenwood Ave., Room A4
Toronto, ON M4J 4B7

Prince Edward Island
Chairperson, Archaeological Advisory Board
c/o Extension Dept.
University of P.E.I.
550 University Ave.
Charlottetown, PEI C1A 4P3

Québec
Gouvernement du Québec
Ministère des Affaires culturelles
Direction général du patrimoine
Direction des services centraux
Bloc B—2e étage
225, Grande Allée Est
Québec, PQ G1R 5G5

Saskatchewan
Head, Archaeological Resource
Management Section
Heritage Resources Section
Saskatchewan Parks, Recreation, and Culture
1942 Hamilton St.
Regina, SK S4P 3V7

Yukon
Yukon Archaeologist, Heritage Branch
Dept. of Economic Development and Tourism
P.O. Box 2703
Whitehorse, Yukon Y1A 2C6

Archaeology in Education—Teacher References

Although there is a variety of resource materials available to teachers who wish to teach archaeology concepts, it may sometimes appear that there are few sources of information available for teachers interested in the curriculum planning aspects of archaeology education. Listed below are resources for teaching archaeology and anthropology in the school program.

Periodicals

Anthro. Notes

This publication, a National Museum of Natural History newsletter for teachers, is printed and distributed free-of-charge three times a year—fall, winter and spring. *Anthro. Notes* was originally part of the George Washington University/Smithsonian Institute Anthropology for Teachers Program funded by the National Science Foundation. To be added to the mailing list, write:

Anthro. Notes
c/o Ann Kaupp
Dept. of Anthropology
National Museum of Natural History
Stop 112, Smithsonian Institute
Washington, DC 20560 USA

Common Ground

This publication, subtitled *Archaeology and Ethnography in the Public Interest,* by the U.S. National Park Service, is published free-of-charge three times a year. To be added to the mailing list write:

Editor
Common Ground
National Park Service
Archaeology and Ethnography Program
P.O. Box 37127
Washington, DC 20013-7127 USA

Teaching Anthropology Newsletter

This publication, a Canadian version of *Anthro. Notes,* is published semi-annually and is distributed free-of-charge. To be added to the mailing list, contact:

Teaching Anthropology Newsletter
c/o Paul A. Erickson, Editor
Department of Anthropology
St. Mary's University
Halifax, NS B3H 3C3

Remnants

This newsletter is a publication of the English Heritage Education Service. While most of the content is designed to assist teachers in utilizing British historic sites, there is more general information on developing classroom activities to explore archaeology and history concepts. For more information, contact:

English Heritage Education Service
429 Oxford St.
London W1R 2HD, England

Archaeology and Education

This Canadian newsletter is published twice yearly, available by subscription from:

Archaeological Resource Centre
Danforth Technical School
840 Greenwood Ave.,
Room A4
Toronto, ON M4J 4B7

Archaeology and Public Education

This American newsletter is published four times yearly, available at a modest subscription cost from:

Society for American Archaeology
900 Second Street NE #12
Washington DC 20002-3557 USA

Teacher's Resource Packet—Anthropology

This resource package, available free-of-charge from the Smithsonian Institute, is full of useful reference items, including teacher-student activities and bibliographies of books and films. It can be obtained from the same source as *Anthro. Notes* (above).

OTHER READINGS AND RESOURCES

(1986). Practicing anthropology in precollege education. (Special issue). *Practicing Anthropology, 8*(3–4).

Ballard, R.D. (1988). *Exploring the Titanic.* Toronto: Madison Press (available through Scholastic).

Ballard, R.D. (1990). *The lost wreck of the Isis.* Toronto: Madison Press (available through Scholastic).

Bisel, S.C. (1990). *The secrets of Vesuvius.* Toronto: Madison Press (available through Scholastic).

Deetz, J. (1967). *Invitation to archaeology.* Garden City, NY: Natural History Press.

Dyer, J. (1983). *Teaching archaeology in schools.* Aylesbury, England: Shire Publications.

Falk, L. (1991). *Historical archaeology in global perspective.* Washington DC: Smithsonian Institute Press.

Fladmark, K.R. (1978). *A guide to basic archaeological field procedures.* (Publication #4). Burnaby, BC: Department of Archaeology, Simon Fraser University.

Green, E. (Ed.). (1984). *Ethics and values in archaeology.* New York. Free Press/Collier-Macmillan.

Holm, K.A. & Higgins, P.J. (Eds.). (1988). *Archaeology and education: A successful combination for precollegiate students.* Athens, GA: Anthropology Curriculum Project, University of Georgia.

Pitman-Gelles, B. (1981). *Museums, magic and children: Youth education in museums.* Washington, DC: Association of Science-Technology Centers.

Rollans, M. (1990). *A handbook for teaching archaeology in Saskatchewan schools.* Saskatoon, SK: Saskatchewan Research Council.

Smith, K.C. & McManamon, F.P. (Eds.). (1991). *Archeology and education: The classroom and beyond.* Washington DC: US Department of the Interior, National Park Service.

Stuart, G.E. & McManamon, F.P. (1996). *Archaeology and you.* Washington DC: Society for American Archaeology.

REFERENCES

McInnes, J., et al. (1985). *Reading and how.* Scarborough, ON: Nelson Canada.

Smardz, K.E. (1989). Educational archaeology: Toronto students dig into their past. *History and Social Science Teacher, 24*(3), 148–155.

This article, reprinted with permission of University of Toronto Press Incorporated, appeared originally in 1989 in *The History and Social Science Teacher, 24*(3), 140–147. Minor alterations to the original article have been made for stylistic and format purposes. We have supplemented the author's original list of teacher references and readings with additional, often more recent publications and with student resources. Some addresses have been undated. The organization of the resources has been modified slightly from the original.

Portions of this article were based on an earlier report prepared by the author entitled "Curriculum Development in Archaeology and Prohistory: A Needs Assessment in Social Studies Education" (Edmonton: Alberta Culture, Archaeological Survey of Alberta, 1985). The original resources listing was adapted by the author from a factsheet compiled by the author entitled "Alberta Archaeology in the Classroom: A Resource List for Teachers" (Edmonton: Archaeological Survey of Alberta, 1989).

8

Law-Related Education in Elementary and Secondary Schools

Margaret Ferguson

I can almost hear the groans of protest as teachers are assigned to read an article on the teaching of yet one more subject. In this case the subject is the study of law or, as it is more appropriately called, law-related education. Reactions to the teaching about law in elementary and secondary schools have been mixed. Over the last twenty years, many educators have become convinced that law-related education deserves a prominent place in the curriculum. Countless teachers promote law-related education without necessarily using this label. Others, especially at the secondary level, feel that "law" has no place in an already over-crowded curriculum. Among elementary teachers is a fear that this subject may be too complex for their students. But, perhaps, most teachers are unsure if or how extensively law belongs in the curriculum. The purpose of this article is to invite elementary and secondary teachers to learn and think about the role of law-related education, or LRE, in their teaching. I do this by considering six questions:

- What is law-related education?
- How did LRE develop?
- Why LRE?
- What are the approaches to LRE?
- Is LRE suitable for elementary students?
- Where does LRE fit in the secondary curriculum?

What Is Law-Related Education?

The term "law-related education" was coined in the United States and there has been some resistance to it in Canada. Although the preference is for a made-in-Canada term, suggestions such as "law-focused education," "law in the schools" or "legal education" have not met with universal approval. The term "legal studies" has some popularity in secondary schools but it connotes a certain style of teaching that may not be suitable with younger students. As a result, "law-related education" continues to be the best descriptor because it is broad.

There is a tendency to think of the study of law as the learning of a technical body of rules and procedures that lawyers acquire in law school and that adults learn on a piecemeal basis as they proceed through life. This is not the approach to teaching law that is recommended for elementary or secondary schools, partly because most teachers are ill-equipped for the task of disseminating such information, and also because it is not the most appropriate law-related content to teach in public schools. Laws are constantly changing, and they differ from province to province. It is too much to expect teachers to possess and convey accurate legal information about these many different areas of law. This is the reason why the term *law-related* developed: to distinguish the teaching *about* law in the schools from the teaching *of* laws to lawyers and other legal professionals. So too, it is important to keep in mind that law-related education is not necessarily a separate course of study. Although specific electives in law exist at the secondary level, and have since the 1940s, most teachers incorporate law-related topics into existing courses such as social studies, English/language arts, science, health, career and life management, ethics, Canadian studies, family studies and personal lifeskills. The infusion of law-related topics throughout the curriculum is especially appropriate when we remember that the law, itself, knows no subject boundaries: legal issues and disputes arise in all walks of life and the most important questions we face in society eventually make their way to the courts.

If law-related education is more than the transmission of technical information about laws, then what is it? As I see it, LRE is centrally concerned with examining the role law plays in our personal lives and in society. It is a course about law rather than a course on specific laws. Certainly, specific laws are studied from time to time, but the emphasis is on helping students gain the broader understanding of why we have laws, the sources of law, legal institutions and structures and other aspects of the foundations of law. The content of LRE is the ideas or concepts underlying the legal system, notions such as rights, responsibilities, authority and justice. LRE examines the values or beliefs embodied in our law, such as respect for property and human life. LRE involves developing basic citizenship skills—such as critical thinking and conflict resolution—to help students participate effectively in a legally-regulated world. LRE encourages active learning and the use of community resources and sites to gain a realistic look at the legal system in operation. Reducing cynicism, understanding the limitations of law and assuming some responsibility for making the legal system responsive to people's needs are important objectives for LRE.

How Did LRE Develop?

Law-related education developed in the United States in the late 1960s and early 1970s in response to several factors including the need to revitalize the mandatory civics courses. Although the teaching of civics has never assumed the same prominence in Canada, during the 1970s and throughout the 1980s there was a growing demand for better access to legal information and services. The message that "law belongs to the people" soon reached Canadian classrooms.

This call for the teaching about law in the schools came from many directions. Teachers and students who were influenced by the larger "access to justice" movement pushed for courses. Also, the providers of legal services realized that improved legal literacy of Canadians required a more systematic, sequential program of studies beginning at an early age. In 1977 Bora Laskin, Chief Justice of the Supreme Court of Canada, expressed his support for LRE:

> It's very important to have a citizenry which is socially literate and social literacy to me involves some appreciation of the legal system. It's just as important that our citizens have some appreciation of law as they should of English or French literature or Economics. I hope that our educational authorities will pay special attention to this. (cited in Norman, 1981, p. 10)

Two years later Ken Norman, Chief Commissioner of the Saskatchewan Human Rights Commission, implored social studies teachers to integrate law into their curriculum:

> I ask you to recognize that all components of a Social Studies curriculum have some application to the study of law. One simply cannot analyze any society from sociological, economic, social/geographical, historical, political, or anthropological perspectives without making reference to the legal system of that society. (1981, pp. 10-11)

By the early 1980s approximately 50,000 students were studying law in Ontario secondary schools and every province was either offering a law elective or planning to offer one. This explosion of legal interest, however, has been more of an unled mass movement than a planned educational development. Surveys of law-related courses across Canada indicate an eclectic pattern. Elective courses in law are frequently available to senior secondary students. Often these courses are offered by business education departments. Social studies courses abound in law-related content, especially studies of government and human rights. Law-related issues are also sprinkled throughout secondary courses such as "Man and Society," "Canadian Studies," "Ethics," "Career and Life Management" and "Family Studies." In English, students read novels and plays with law-related themes and study films with law-related content.

Why Law-Related Education?

A primary aim of schooling is to prepare students to become better individuals and better citizens. Law-related education has an important role to play in achieving this overall goal of public education. Hugh Kindred, a law professor at Dalhousie University who helped write Nova Scotia's high school law curriculum, expressed it this way:

> The infusion of law-related topics throughout the curriculum is especially appropriate when we remember that the law, itself, knows no subject boundaries: legal issues and disputes arise in all walks of life and the most important questions we face in society eventually make their way to the courts.

In a participatory democracy, it is vital that students learn about their rights and duties as citizens. Knowledge of the institutions that control the society is a prerequisite to intelligent democratic action. Since it is the law that organizes and supports these institutions, legal education is an obvious way for students to learn of them. In addition, it is important that students know not only their civic responsibilities, but also their freedom of action within the Canadian system of government. The measure of good citizenship is not inculcated conformity, but a healthy respect for the rights of others as well as one's own, and an allegiance to orderly processes, even in diversity. The character of law encourages such critical, yet constructive attitudes. Consequently its study will develop them in students, the next generation of Canadian citizens. (1979, p. 534)

As well, there is a profoundly practical reason for learning about the law; a reason which partly explains why secondary students are attracted to the subject. Law-related education is basic to survival in a world where law is already pervasive and likely to be even more so in the future. We marry, do business, govern, worship and even die according to law. Our written laws proliferate at a staggering rate. The federal government has enacted hundreds, if not thousands, of statutes and every province has approximately 500 statutes in place. We also have regulations appended to these statutes and they usually contain the procedural "nuts and bolts" that affect people. The regulations for each province number in the thousands. Add municipal bylaws to this list and it is easy to appreciate that the long arm of the law reaches into almost every aspect of our lives. Without some measure of understanding of the nature and scope of this influence, students' ability to function in society is likely to be impaired.

What Are the Approaches to Law-Related Education?

In a talk to Canadian educators, Isidore Starr (1989), one of the most respected leaders of law-related education in the United States, described three main approaches to LRE: conceptual, practical and participatory.

The conceptual approach

The conceptual approach examines central ideas such as liberty, justice and equality—so often mouthed and revered in schools. Starr was a secondary social studies teacher who went to night school to get his law degree. He discovered that the cases he was studying at law school could be adapted for classroom use and the benefits were many. He believed that students at any age could study these ideas if presented properly. Elementary teachers often use stories rather than court cases to provide the context for discussions of such important concepts as power, authority, privacy, responsibility and property. This approach focusses on broad principles and concepts and emphasizes critical thinking.

In studying criminal law from a conceptual approach secondary teachers might explore the extent to which "crime" is created by society. What is recognized as criminal depends on societal values. For example, if society pursued "suite crime"—illegal actions performed by white collar executives and others in fashionable surroundings—as vigorously as it prosecuted "street crime," the profile of the average criminal would be significantly different. In an often cited book, *The Rich Get Richer and the Poor Get Prison,* John Reiman argues that powerful social interest groups are responsible for severe harm to health and the environment and yet, according to him, are largely exempt from criminal prosecution (cited in Case & Baum, 1995, p. 123). Students might discuss the extent to which legislators have criminalized, or have failed to criminalize, certain actions because of political or economic motives. Students might also examine the concept of legal guilt—what the law requires in order to find a person guilty—as opposed to moral guilt. Also important is understanding the meaning and rationale for basic principles such as "innocent until proven guilty" and "proof beyond a reasonable doubt."

A key ingredient in the conceptual approach is to use real cases, or at least realistic case studies, to encourage students to wrestle critically with the facts, issues and arguments. Arriving at a decision that students can support with evidence replaces a search for the "right" answer. Outlined in the following box are suggested steps for involving students in a case study.

Case Study Method

- **Find the facts**. Who is involved? What happened? What is the complaint or charge? What facts are important?

- **Frame the issue(s)**. Usually the issue is posed in the form of a question: Was an assault committed? Was Mr. Jones wrongfully dismissed from his job?

- **Discuss the Arguments**. An issue will always generate at least two points of view. What are the arguments for and against? Which arguments are most persuasive? Why?

- **Reach a decision**. What did the court decide? Often teachers withhold the court's decision and ask each student to arrive at a decision. This is more difficult if students are working in groups and must reach a consensus. After students wrestle with the case, the court decision may be discussed.

- **Examining the reasoning**. Like students, judges disagree with each other. In cases heard by several judges a number of opinions may be expressed. Often one judge will write an opinion shared by the majority and those judges who disagree may write minority opinions. Invite students to do the same.

The practical approach

The practical approach, also known as the "street law" approach, explores immediate and personal problems that students currently face or are likely to face. This approach typically focuses on topics such as run-ins with the police, family disputes, leaving home, renting an apartment and buying a car. As to be expected it is a very popular approach with many secondary students. The most commonly addressed fields of law in a practical law approach are criminal law, juvenile law, consumer law, family law and landlord/tenant law. In studying criminal law from a practical law approach, a teacher—with assistance from a lawyer or police officer—might discuss student-posed questions such as:

- What are my rights if I'm stopped by the police?
- Do the police have the right to search my car for liquor?
- Can I be charged if I'm with friends who are smoking dope?
- What happens if I'm found guilty of . . . ?
- How do I find a lawyer?

The activity described in the box below offers a practical law strategy for sensitizing students to the diverse ways in which laws touch upon most aspects of their lives.

The participatory approach

There was a consensus among the early leaders in the LRE field that lecture-dominated teaching was to be avoided and, to the extent feasible, teachers and students should experience the law in an active, first-hand way. As a result, the participatory approach has had considerable support among LRE teachers. Favoured teaching methods include:

- mock trials, moot courts and legislative hearings
- visits to courts, legislatures and government agencies
- visits by judges, lawyers, police, legislators and corrections officers to classes
- police ride-alongs and visits to jails and prisons
- simulations and role-playing relating to jury selection, plea bargaining and police patrol

---

How Law Affects Our Lives

Prepare a fictional story with a title such as "A Day in the Life of Sally Jones." Construct the story so it represents an average day of a typical student. For example, the student will live in a certain type of dwelling, in a neighbourhood with other family members and, perhaps, some pets. Make it a school day. There may be after-school activities; older students may have jobs. Businesses may be visited. Goods may be purchased.

Invite students to identify instances where the law is involved. This can be done by a show of hands or as a written exercise. Expand on the instances identified during a large group discussion. Some laws that may be mentioned in the discussion are:

- *name*. Laws specify the surname a child can take. One's name is registered on the birth certificate which is a legal document. There is a legal procedure to follow for changing one's name.
- *address*. Do students live in a village, city or town? This designation is determined by law. There are zoning laws which specify what type of dwellings can be built in an area. The system of numbering homes and naming streets in municipalities is done according to law.
- *school*. Laws require children to attend school and these laws set the number of hours of instruction per day and per year. The law requires adults to pay taxes to support schools and sets out the rights and responsibilities of teachers and principals.
- *pets*. Municipalities have laws that affect the type of pet one can have, also whether or not a pet requires a license and a leash on public property. Cruelty to animals can be a criminal offence.
- *family*. Laws specify how marriage must take place, how people come to assume the rights and responsibilities of mother or father, under what conditions divorce can occur, when children can be removed from their home, who is entitled to inherit property when a family member dies and so on.
- *food*. Laws regulate the handling and packaging of food, what foods can be imported and exported, what businesses must do before they can sell food.
- *transportation*. Drivers and owners of vehicles have many laws to obey—licensing, insurance, highway traffic laws.
- *contracts*. Anytime goods are bought or sold, we are entering into a contract. To ensure that contracts are fair, we have a number of consumer protection laws.
- *money*. Laws establish what currency is legal tender in a country.
- *businesses*. The formation and operation of businesses is governed by law, including the rights and responsibilities of employers and employees.

Ask a lawyer to help in constructing the story and possibly with the class discussion. Many lawyers are willing to assist teachers and students.

- techniques of lobbying and skill in parliamentary procedure
- participating in election campaigns.

Attitudinal objectives are paramount in the participatory approach. Many students have negative attitudes towards the legal system, often gained from very limited experiences. Students who are exposed to different aspects of the legal system and to the perspectives of people who actually work in our legal system often acquire reduced feelings of frustration and alienation.

A participatory approach to the study of criminal law might begin with a visit to the local courthouse. Students might read the court docket where cases are listed, and note the kinds of offences people are accused of committing. They might sit in on a trial for a firsthand sense of court proceedings. They may talk with judges, crown prosecutors, defence lawyers, members of victim's rights organizations and former prisoners.

Most law-related programs in Canada combine all three approaches. There is value in each. The optimal combination depends largely on course objectives, student needs and teacher interests and knowledge. All of this should be guided by one's rationale for why law is a necessary part of the school curriculum in the first place.

Is LRE Suitable for Elementary Students?

Without doubt, LRE is suitable for elementary students. In fact, the elementary curriculum provides abundant opportunities to develop young students' law-related understandings and abilities. Elementary teachers commonly look to two sources when developing law-related lessons. The first is the many personal incidents that arise in the everyday life of teachers and their students, and the second is the rich law-related content found in children's literature.

Law in everyday experiences

The first place to look for everyday experiences as a source of LRE material is the classroom environment itself. Teachers often spend the first month of each school year creating a positive classroom climate. Establishing classroom rules and procedures is an integral part of this process and, in a way, is similar to deciding what laws will govern the people in a society. What process will the teacher follow? Will the classroom rules be set by the teacher in advance or will students be given an opportunity to make their own rules, perhaps during the now-popular classroom meetings? Will it be easier to enforce rules that students help make? How will the rules be enforced and can this be done by students or does the teacher have to act as police officer? Who decides the consequences and is it a good idea to have a number of options available so that the penalty can be adjusted to fit the offence? Is there need to clarify and interpret the rules as situations develop, and if some rules need changing, how is this to be done? Rule-making at the elementary level sets the foundation for discussions about law-making and teachers who value democratic principles will endeavour to involve students in the decisions affecting them. Rule-making is a major component of elementary law-related lessons.

Another major source of everyday law-related investigation has to do with the concept of justice or fairness. Elementary teachers frequently deal with questions about "what's fair." Adjudicating disagreements and managing conflict afford wonderful opportunities for law-related education: resolving disputes is a major function of law. Many schools have peer mediation programs where students in conflict, with the assistance of trained student mediators, learn to solve their differences without the intervention of teachers. The box below outlines the steps that a peer mediator might consider in assisting other students in resolving a dispute.

Considerations for Peer Mediators

- **Who is involved?** Make sure every person involved in the conflict is present. List their names, grades and homeroom teachers.

- **What happened?** Each student should be given a chance to say what happened without being interrupted or corrected by the others who are involved. You decide the order of speaking. Use active listening skills, asking open-ended questions to make sure you get as many facts as possible. After everyone has spoken, summarize the facts as you understand them. Does everyone agree this is what happened?

- **What is the real problem?** Help the students identify the issue that is causing the problem. Identifying feelings is often a first step (e.g., "I feel angry because . . ."). Each person has to listen very carefully to what the others are saying. The real issues are often hidden.

- **How can we fix the problem?** Encourage students to think of as many solutions as possible. Do not let them discard any solution until all the options are understood. What solution is acceptable to everyone? When an agreement is reached, make sure everyone understands it. Write down what was decided. The problem may happen again and the agreement may have to be changed.

Law in children's literature

Children's literature is another rich source of law-related elementary topics. Stories provide examples of good and bad leadership, of characters who display responsible and irresponsible behaviour, and of values (such as freedom, equality, justice and responsibility) that are considered so important in our society they become part of our law. Practically every story provides examples of how people resolve conflicts. If students focus on this topic, they learn that there are a number of ways to resolve disputes. With the author's help, students learn to make judgments about the effectiveness of each method. Some conflicts are expanded into mock trials such as those found in fairy tales or trial scenes (see Norton, 1992). The example below describes one educator's ideas for using *Peter Rabbit* to lay the foundations for larger understandings of law, justice and authority.

PETER RABBIT : A TALE OF TWO GATES

In an article entitled "A Tale of Two Gates," James Lengel (1984) suggests that children who learn to analyze stories such as *Peter Rabbit* are likely better able to analyze more complex incidents when they reach secondary school. According to this classic tale, Peter Rabbit lived with Flopsy, Mopsy, Cotton-Tail and his mother underneath the root of a very big fir tree. "Now, my dears," said old Mrs. Rabbit one morning, "you may go into the fields or down the lane, but don't go into Mr. McGregor's garden; your father had an accident there; he was put in a pie by Mrs. McGregor." Like most children's stories, *Peter Rabbit* sets out a problem of right and wrong, of making and breaking rules. Teachers can connect these personal, close-to-home conflicts with the larger law by asking:

- What kind of accident did father have?

- Was it fair for Mr. McGregor to punish father so harshly? What could have been a fairer punishment?

- What rule did Mrs. Rabbit make for her children?

- Did Mrs. Rabbit have the authority to make this rule? Why?

- What reasons did she have for making this rule?

- Is it a good rule? Why?

- Do you think the four children will obey? Why?

These questions introduce students to abstract concepts such as justice (fairness) and authority. In so doing, Peter Rabbit's "run-in" with Mr. McGregor and his garden gate lays an important foundation. Later at the secondary level, students might apply their understandings of authority and justice to analysing complex, real-life "gates" such as Watergate or Irangate.

WHERE DOES LRE FIT
IN THE SECONDARY CURRICULUM?

Many teachers at the secondary level feel pressured to cover material mandated by the curriculum and many doubt that they have either the time or expertise to teach about the law. These impressions may be espe-

cially warranted in reference to the street law approach. Most teachers are unlikely to possess the knowledge required to provide accurate and current advice about students' legal rights and responsibilities, and those teachers who have the requisite legal expertise may already be teaching the secondary elective courses in law. Where does this leave the more typical teacher who may have little background in law? I believe the answer may rest with the conceptual approach towards LRE. Regardless of their subject, secondary teachers are expected to improve students' abilities to solve problems and think critically about important ethical and social concerns. If one accepts that law offers a powerful model and context for reasoned decision making, then LRE has a place in all secondary classrooms. The question "Does Canada need a *Charter*?" is really a debate about the kind of society we want to live in, a debate that should continue long after students graduate. Opportunities to explore countless law-related issues exist in many courses as teachers discuss drugs, environmental protection, forensics, copyright, patents, computer abuse, child welfare, business fraud, employment standards and so on.

Arguably social studies teachers are in the best position to assume a leadership role in LRE. The content of social studies meshes easily with LRE and most teachers with a social studies or humanities background will be familiar with broad law-related concepts and principles such as fundamental rights, discrimination, freedom of expression. Since LRE ought not encourage the blind acceptance of all laws, even laws as important and powerful as the *Canadian Charter of Rights and Freedoms* can and should be examined with a critical eye. On the one hand, the *Charter* is designed to protect the fundamental rights and freedoms of minorities: the democratic principle of "majority rule" can result in injustice and abuse, and governments in Canada have not always wielded their power fairly as illustrated by the list, on the following page, of legally sanctioned discrimination. On the other hand, the *Charter* has its critics. The most frequently expressed objection is that the *Charter* is inconsistent with giving democracy a free rein. Many laws passed by governments have been set aside by judges because they do not conform to the *Charter*. Thus the *Charter* removes many important decisions from the democratically-elected political arena and places them in the closed arena of appointed officials. It is also argued that the *Charter* fosters excessive concern with individual rights and with the needs of special interest groups at the expense of the common good.

Social studies teachers are in a position to identify law-related content in other courses, and work with other teachers to ensure a coordinated approach within a school or district. For example, the historical context of the debate about Canada's need for a *Charter* could be introduced by a social studies teacher, taken up by the English teacher in the form of teaching about persuasive techniques and incorporated into a series of dramatic scenes or a mural by a fine arts teacher.

LEGALLY-SANCTIONED DISCRIMINATION IN CANADA

- In 1749, the British used black slaves to build the city of Halifax.

- In 1793, Upper Canada prohibited bringing new slaves to the province. Existing slaves remained slaves, although their children were to be freed upon reaching age 25.

- In 1885, the *Chinese Head Tax and Chinese Exclusion Act* imposed a special levy of $50 on all Chinese immigrants entering Canada. The tax was raised to $500 in 1903.

- In 1894, the municipality of the district of Surrey, British Columbia enacted a bylaw prohibiting the employment of Japanese and Chinese workers on city projects. (This bylaw was repealed in 1982.)

- In 1914, 376 Sikhs who had met the requirements for immigration to Canada were held on board their ship, *Komagata Maru*, for three months before they were forced back to sea.

- In the 1930's, the student who achieved the highest grade 12 academic standing in Alberta was denied the Social Credit government's annual prize because she was a native Indian.

- Between 1933 and 1945, when millions of European Jews were being persecuted by the Nazis, Canada accepted only 5,000 Jewish immigrants. (The U.S. admitted 40 times that number. Bolivia, which is a very small country, took almost three times the Canadian total.)

- In 1939, the Supreme Court ruled that a tavern which refused service to a black man had broken no law since, as a private business, the tavern could be run as its owner chose.

- Between 1943 and 1945, over 21,000 adults and children of Japanese ancestry were moved to internment camps, had their property confiscated and were expected to pay for their own upkeep. In contrast, Canadians of Italian and German origin were not interned even though Canada was at war with these countries.

- Not until 1947, could Chinese and East Indians vote in British Columbia elections. Canadians of Japanese ancestry could not vote until 1948.

- In 1954, the Prime Minister of Barbados, Grantley Adams, was denied a room in a Montreal hotel because of what the employee called "regulations."

- In the 1950's and 1960's, many tourist resorts in Ontario and Quebec refused accommodation to Jews and non-whites.

- Until 1960, native people could not vote in federal elections.

This list was developed by Case and Baum (1995, pp. 236-237).

CONCLUDING REMARKS

In my opening paragraph I invited teachers to think about the place of law-related education in the curriculum. As I tried to illustrate, abundant opportunities for LRE exist, at both elementary and secondary levels. And no single approach to LRE is required—teachers are encouraged to start small with an approach that best suits their purposes and abilities. There may be need for social studies educators to take a leadership role in promoting law-related education in the schools. It is no accident that key figures in the law-related movements in both the U.S. and Canada have been social studies teachers or educators with a background in the social sciences. Nevertheless, law-related opportunities and resources exist in virtually all subject areas. What do you think: Does LRE deserve a place in the curriculum and in your classroom? Can we do social studies well without a law-related component?

REFERENCES

Case, R. & Baum, D. (1995). *Thinking about law: An issues approach.* Toronto: IPI Publishing.

Kindred, H. (1979). Legal education in Canadian schools? *Dalhousie Law Journal*, 5(2), 534-542.

Lengel, J. (1984). A tale of two gates. *Update on Law-Related Education*, (Fall), 27-28.

Norton, J. (1992). The state vs. the Big Bad Wolf: A study of the justice system in the elementary school. *Social Studies and the Young Learner*, 5(1), 5-9.

Norman, K. (1981). Rights, responsibilities, and law in the schools. *Resource News*, 6(1), 10-11.

Starr, I. (1989). The law studies movement: A brief look at the past, the present and the future. In William Crawford (Ed.), *Law vs. learning: Examination for discovery* (pp. 11-15). Toronto: Canadian Law Information Council.

9

Global Education: It's Largely a Matter of Perspective

Roland Case

There has been considerable vagueness and uncertainty about the goals of global education. Whatever else it is, global education is not essentially about transmitting more information about the world. It is, I believe, centrally concerned with helping students view the world—and the events and people within the world—in a different light. This characterization of global education is often discussed in terms of developing a global perspective. Much has been written about the importance of promoting a global perspective beginning with Robert Hanvey's groundbreaking work, *An Attainable Global Perspective* (1976). I begin by explaining two dimensions of a global perspective and then I offer a rationale for it. I discuss briefly the content or *substantive* dimension of a global perspective. The main body of the paper looks at the nature and how to promote three traits comprising what I call the attitudinal or *perceptual* dimension of a global perspective.

What Is a Global Perspective?

A perspective implies a "point of view"—a vantage point from which, or a lens through which, observations occur, and an "object" of attention—an event, thing, person, place or state of affairs that is the focus of the observations. Thus an economic perspective (the point of view) would consider the financial costs and benefits of a proposed action (the object), while an ethical perspective would look at the morality of the action. A *global* perspective refers to a point of view or lens for viewing people, places and things around the world. I believe there are two dimensions of a global perspective:

- **substantive dimension**—the "object" or focus of a global perspective: the world events, states of affairs, places and things that global educators want students to understand. The substantive dimension refers to knowledge of people and places beyond students' own community and country, and knowledge of events and issues beyond the local and immediate.

- **perceptual dimension**—the "point of view" or lens of a global perspective: the habits of mind, values or attitudes from which we want students to perceive the world. The perceptual dimension, reflected in spatial metaphors such as narrow or broad, provincial or cosmopolitan, and parochial or far-reaching, describes a "global" mindset or outlook—a capacity to see the "whole picture" whether focussing on a local or an international matter. Nurturing the perceptual dimension of a global perspective requires developing the desired mental lenses through which the world is to be understood. As Louis Perinbaum (1989, p. 25) observes, global education is a way of looking at the world more than it is the accumulation of information about the world.

Unpacking global education involves specifying both the range of global phenomena to be explored (the objects—the substantive dimension) and the desired lenses through which this examination is to occur (the points of view—the perceptual dimension). Before elaborating on this two-dimensional account of a global perspective, I will explain why teachers should care about promoting a global perspective.

Why a Global Perspective?

The importance of attending to how students perceive the world can be illustrated by considering free-hand maps drawn by students from different countries. In a classic study, Thomas Saarinen (1973) compared sketch maps of the world created by high school students from four cities: Calgary (Canada), Helsinki (Finland), Makeni (Sierra Leone) and Tucson (USA). These sketches, which provide metaphorical pictures of students' images of their world, suggest how students' understandings are mediated by the lenses through which they view things. As might be expected, most students depicted their home country and home continent with a high degree of accuracy and detail, often locating them in the center of their map. This positioning of themselves at the centre of the world is symbolic of their outlook on the world. Typically, more distant continents were relegated to the "outer reaches" of the page and often reduced to vague blotches far smaller than their actual land masses warranted. These depictions symbolize the reduced levels of awareness of and significance attached to "foreign" countries. Curiously, isolated international features were exaggerated or rendered with unusual precision (e.g., Hawaii, the British Isles, the "boot" of Italy). For varying reasons, these "distant" features had particular significance for the map maker—perhaps, the student had visited the place, had relatives living there or had read about some event or place associated with that country. The aim in developing a global perspective is to expand and enrich students' perspectives, so that their views of the world are not ethnocentric, stereotypical or otherwise limited by a narrow or distorted point of view. If we neglect to nurture a "global" perspective students are likely to continue viewing the world narrowly through the lenses of their own interests, location and culture.

Much school instruction may fail to overcome—in fact, it may actually reinforce—students' parochial or distorted world views. For example, curriculum materials often promote what might be called a "food-costumes-customs" approach to other cultures—that is, the study of other cultures focusses on relatively superficial features of their life-styles. Exposing students to ethnic dishes and strange holiday practices is unlikely to promote an enlightened perspective on the lives and concerns of people in these "foreign" cultures (Zachariah, 1989). In my own well-intentioned attempts as an elementary teacher to interest students in other cultures I often featured the exotic and exceptional elements of these cultures. My approach had the undesirable effect of making these people more "alien" to some of my students. By attending to the bizarre, and to some extent trivial, cultural dimensions, I and other teachers may actually reinforce stereotypical perceptions (Schuncke, 1984, p. 249). Other forms of distortion are also commonplace. For example, students are likely to regard Africa and South America as primitive frontiers if their exposure to these continents is entirely in the context of subsistence living, genocide and deforestation. Many students are often surprised to learn of the existence of well-educated, affluent people living in modern African cities because their experiences have often been restricted to jungles and rural villages. So too, when poverty and under-development are discussed, students are likely to regard people from these countries with condescending paternalism unless students are also shown instances of local initiative and self-sufficiency (Mpanya, 1989). Unfortunately, until quite recently, treatment of Africa, South America and the Middle East in Canadian social studies curricula focussed predominantly on ancient (and now fallen) civilizations (Case, 1989, p. 6). The elementary social studies curriculum in at least one province still refers to the study of "primitive" cultures (British Columbia Ministry of Education, 1983, p. 40).

These types of lingering ethnocentric and stereotypical perceptions will not be resolved simply by teaching more about the world—merely having more information may not advance students' *understanding*. As I have suggested, much of what we notice and the interpretations we make depend upon the lenses though which we filter the raw data. Approaching a study with a parochial attitude is likely to confirm, not dispel, stereotypes and prejudice. We must attend directly to the perceptual lenses that colour students' global sense-making.

Promoting a global perspective is not an easy task. The conventional wisdom, as evidenced by the expanding horizon approach underlying social studies curriculum across North America, suggests that most elementary students are incapable of dealing with abstract concepts and with complex issues that are geographically remote from them. Fortunately, these long-standing assumptions about young students' in-

> The aim in developing a global perspective is to expand and enrich students' perspectives, so that their views of the world are not ethnocentric, stereotypical or otherwise limited by a narrow or distorted point of view.

ability to grasp complexity and remoteness have been discredited, both by academics (Egan, 1983; Roldao, 1992) and by practicing teachers. As a grade five teacher in Toronto explained, "I believe it is a mistake to think that children cannot identify with people and events on the other side of the world" (Willms, 1992, p. 15). This same teacher reported that at the beginning of the year her students "had no idea where India was or whether Africa was a country or a continent. They made comments about how 'primitive' these countries were and how poor people deserved to be poor because they didn't work hard enough." But these stereotypical attitudes changed as the year unfolded—for example, months later when discussing the Kenyan government's difficulty in protecting endangered wildlife, her students no longer automatically attributed lack of success to "incompetence or a lack of concern." Rather, they appreciated the dilemma posed by "the difficulties poor countries face in attempting to fund proper wildlife protection and the important role of cattle in the life of the Masai, whose animals compete with wildlife for grazing land" (p. 16). Others recommend the teaching of a global perspective to even younger students (cf. special global education theme issue of *Social Studies and the Young Learner*, 1994; Fountain, 1990). I have worked with a primary teacher who taught children aged five to eight years about the abstract notion of human rights, understood as a protection for those needs that are basic to all human beings (Chapman, 1991). This teacher concluded that progress will be slow and misunderstandings will persist, but "any effort to establish a primary classroom based on global, rather than parochial, concerns can only result in 'expanding' the 'horizons' of the students involved" (p. 66).

As I have tried to illustrate, global education ought to be an important concern for social studies teachers at all levels—we can and should begin nurturing an emergent global perspective with primary students.

WHAT COMPRISES THE SUBSTANTIVE DIMENSION?

As indicated above, the substantive dimension refers to the range of global topics about which people should be informed if their "world view" is to expand beyond a *perspective on the local* (i.e., understanding solely the events and workings of one's own community or country) to a *perspective on the global* (i.e., understanding the events and workings of the world). Although many writers have offered accounts of what I refer to as the substantive dimension, Willard Kniep (1986) and Robert Hanvey (1976) are the most widely cited. Amalgating their recommendations, it would appear that five topics ought to form the main objects of global study:

> Approaching a study with a parochial attitude is likely to confirm, not dispel, stereotypes and prejudice. We must attend directly to the perceptual lenses that colour students' global sense-making.

- **universal and cultural values and practices.** Hanvey uses the term "cross-culture awareness" to refer to knowledge and respect for the diversity of ideas and practices to be found in human societies around the world. Kniep emphasizes the importance of teaching about both commonality and diversity: teaching about *universal human values* which transcend group identity (e.g., equality, justice, liberty) and about *diverse cultural values* which define group membership and contribute to differing worldviews (e.g., values related to aesthetics, lifestyle, the environment).

- **global interconnections.** Kniep talks of "global systems" and Hanvey speaks of "global dynamics" to describe knowledge of the workings—the key features and mechanisms—of the interactive economic, political, ecological, social and technological systems operating worldwide.

- **present worldwide concerns and conditions.** Both writers identify the need to know about current and emerging global issues and problems —Hanvey calls it "state of the planet awareness." These persistent, transnational issues which span peace and security, economic development, environmental and human rights concerns include population growth, migration, poverty, natural resource use, science and technology, health and inter-nation and intra-nation conflict.

- **origins and past patterns of worldwide affairs.** Kniep stresses the importance of "global history"— seeing the historical evolution and roots of universal and diverse human values, of contemporary global systems and of prevailing global issues and problems.

- **alternative future directions in worldwide affairs.** Hanvey stresses the importance of "knowledge of alternatives"—also called "awareness of human choices"—learning of alternatives to the ways in which the world is currently run, including alternatives to unrestrained economic growth, current foreign aid and technical assistance policies and consumption patterns.

Although the substantive and perceptual dimensions intertwine, this list of topics identifies the content that these two prominent global educators see as the main focus for global education. In essence, they believe that students need to know that people across the world share some common values and differ in others, that events and forces in the world interconnect in powerful ways, that the world is facing a number of serious issues, and that these issues have deep historical roots and that humankind has the potential to alter the existing ways of "doing business."

I will now turn to the attitudes that must complement the study of these global topics.

What Comprises the Perceptual Dimension?

A major—possibly the key—challenge in developing a global perspective is to transform a *parochial perspective* (i.e., making sense of the world from a superficial, narrow, self-absorbed point of view) to a *broad-minded perspective* (i.e., making sense of the world from an "enlightened" point of view). There is little value in discussing alternative future directions, for example, if students are going to immediately dismiss these ideas because they don't suit students' immediate and possibly narrow interests. Hence the need to help students see things from a more "global" perspective. I believe it is useful in understanding both what is involved and how to promote it to characterize the perceptual dimension in terms of three lenses, or habits of mind: *open-mindedness, full-mindedness* and *fair-mindedness*.

Open-mindedness

As the term suggests, open-mindedness refers to a willingness to entertain new ideas and alternative ways of looking at people, places and events. Its opposite is closed mindedness—the unwillingness to consider or explore other ways of looking at things or the inability to see things as others might. Nurturing open-mindedness involves encouraging two traits:

- **recognize differences in points of view**. Students must realize that individuals will not always see the world the same way and develop the ability to see things from differing viewpoints.

- **entertain contrary positions**. Students need to accept the right of others to hold points of view that differ from one's own and to be willing to consider evidence or reasons for holding a contrary position.

Open-minded-ness is *the* crucial feature of the perceptual dimension. It identifies an openness to things that are unfamiliar or even strange to us. It involves more than understanding that people have different opinions on an issue—for example, some people are in favour of mandatory seat belts and others are against seat belts. It involves what Hanvey (1976, pp. 4-5) refers to as "perspective consciousness"—an awareness that each of us has a world view or "cognitive map" that is not universally shared by others and may be shaped by factors that we are unaware of and unable to control. Young students may need particular help in appreciating that there may be more ways to see an event than their own. Multiple points of view involves looking at issues from different disciplinary perspectives (e.g., seeing the economic, environmental and political implications) and also from different personal and cultural perspectives. In introducing point of view it may be useful to have students view and describe concrete objects from different physical locations. Sto-

ries also provide opportunities for students to take on a role and describe events and feelings from different characters' perspectives. When studying another culture, students should be encouraged to approach it from the point of view of an insider of that culture. Another strategy—a twist on the mental maps activity discussed earlier—is to invite students to draw mental maps from designated perspectives—say, from the point of view of someone living in their hometown, and then from the perspective of a group that students have been studying in class (Johnson, 1997). Students would be encouraged to depict on their maps the chracteristics of the world that would be most relevant to the people from whom the perspective is being taken—for example, Europe might be prominent on a map if many local immigrants had came from Europe, or Japan might be prominent if imported cars were popular.

Students may be open-minded with regard to some issues and not others, often depending on the degree of personal investment or familiarity with the points of view. For example, we are less likely to be open-minded when self-interest or deeply held values are at stake. The difficulty in seeing the other side was confirmed during a workshop I offered for New Brunswick social studies teachers at the height of the Canada-Spain conflict over turbot fishing off the coast of Eastern Canada. When I asked participants to list all the reasons why the Spanish were justified in their actions, one participant immediately exclaimed that they were no such reasons. Another participant demanded to know why I bothered with the justification *for* the Spanish actions. Although I personally believe that the Canadian government's actions were largely defensible (cf. Beesley & Rowe, 1995), unless I seriously consider the reasons for the Spanish position, I cannot have any confidence in the justification of my own position.

It is instructive to consider the reasons why the Spanish people were upset with Canada's dramatic confiscation of a Spanish fishing boat. After all, the Spanish have been fishing off the Grand Banks for 500 years. They were within international waters and there is a long-standing right to the "open seas." The fish quota that Spain was accused of ignoring was voluntary, and Spain had clearly indicated that it did not intend to comply with this quota. Finally, it is a gross exaggeration to blame Spanish fishers for the depleted stocks—an estimated 90 percent of the fish caught off the Grand Banks are caught within Canada's 200 mile limit. Relatively speaking, the Spanish catch of turbot stock was a minor part of the fish conservation problem (only 10 percent of the fish are caught outside the 200 mile limit where the Spanish were fishing). By learning about the basis for their claims, I was better able to appreciate the Spanish people's anger. As well, I may

> Students may be open-minded with regard to some issues and not others, often depending on the degree of personal investment or familiarity with the points of view.

qualify or soften my support for particular Canadian actions if I see some merit in the opposing side.

Teacher modelling is also an important way to encourage student open-mindedness (Torney-Purta, 1983). Modelling open-mindedness requires that teachers consistently and sincerely attempt to base their classroom comments and decisions on careful consideration of all sides, and show a willingness to change their minds or alter their plans whenever good reasons are presented.

Full-mindedness

Full-mindedness refers to the inclination to make up one's mind on the basis of adequate understanding of the whole story. Its opposite is simple mindedness—the penchant to leap to conclusions or to settle for simplistic or incomplete explanations. Promoting full-mindedness includes helping students develop the following traits:

- **anticipate complexity.** The inclination to look beyond simplistic accounts of complex issues, and to look for ramifications and interconnections and to see phenomena as part of a constellation of interrelated factors.

- **recognize stereotyping.** The ability to identify and dismiss portrayals of people or cultures that are superficial generalizations or objectifications (e.g., portraits of cultures or countries as quaint, eccentric, curiosity objects).

- **suspend judgment when warranted.** A willingness when dealing with complex matters to withhold coming to a firm conclusion until varying view points, and the evidence for them, have been considered.

Anticipation of complexity involves fostering student skepticism of explanations that fail to consider with sufficient imagination the range of interacting factors and consequences of most global events—it is a call to resist seeing events in the world as isolated and localized. Although it is inevitable and often desirable that global issues be simplified somewhat, it is important to discourage superficial or naive views (e.g., black-and-white accounts and definitive lists of *the* causes of events). If students are not alerted to, or if they refuse to accept, the messy reality of many of our enduring global predicaments, they will be satisfied with crude and simplistic responses to problems. Simplified solutions, however, are unlikely to succeed—world famine will not be resolved by producing more food (we already produce enough food to feed everyone) and we will not eliminate poverty merely by creating more jobs (many people considered to be below the poverty line are fully employed or are not capable of working). Unless students anticipate the ramifications of a course of action, they are less likely to advocate proposals that accommodate adequately the interconnected nature of many global situations. A case in point is the so-called

green revolution that failed to accommodate the social, psychological, financial and agricultural implications of abandoning supposedly unsophisticated farming practices.

Educators can discourage simple-mindedness by stressing the interrelated factors involved in most global events and the inevitability of ramifications for most actions. For example, solutions to global population problems should be discussed in the context of competing social and religious pressures, such as parents' reliance on their children to supplement family incomes and to provide for old-age security, and deep-rooted religious beliefs and cultural values. Young students can be introduced to the complexity of events by having them trace the myriad consequences of a single action (e.g., the effects of an environmental change) or the range of factors that have influenced an event (e.g., all the people and countries that contributed to the breakfast eaten that morning). Fostering student appreciation of global complexity may require replacing superficial exploration of many topics with fewer, but more in-depth, case studies. In general, teachers who model an appreciation of the complexity of most issues are likely to promote student acquisition of this attribute (Newmann, 1991, p. 330).

Stereotyping occurs when global educators, however well-intentioned, focus on the quaint or exotic features of a culture.

Recognition of stereotyping refers to developing students' ability to identify the inadequacy of accounts of people, cultures or nations that are limited to a narrow range of characteristics (i.e., important features of the group are ignored) or that depict little or no diversity within them (i.e., differences within the group are ignored). Unlike the previously discussed element of complexity, which focusses on explaining events with appropriate intricacy, resisting stereotyping involves describing groups of people with sufficient diversity. For example, a Polish academic complained to me about the tendency in the West to talk about Eastern Europe as if it were a single entity; he warned that in communicating with this region we must attend to the diversity within and among countries. Similarly, the crude treatment of African culture in many social studies textbooks fails to do justice to the fundamental differences among African cultures and to their richness (Beckett & Darling, 1988, pp. 2-3). As was mentioned earlier, stereotyping occurs when global educators, however well-intentioned, focus on the quaint or exotic features of a culture. For example, curriculum resources regularly stereotype Egypt as a museum or curiosity piece—as the land of pyramids and sphinxes.

In addition to cultural stereotyping, a particularly relevant form of stereotyping is the inclination to focus on "we-they" dualisms. Casting issues as "our country against other countries" is stereotyping whenever it disguises mutual international interest in supposedly national concerns. Similarly, dualisms among international sectors (e.g., north-south, east-west, developed-developing countries) involve stereotyping whenever the interests of all countries in a bloc are reduced to the interests of the bloc and set in opposition to the interests of other blocs. The problems with these dualisms are their tendencies to ignore the cross-boundary similarities and shared interests in many problems (e.g., Eastern Europeans are likely as concerned about cancer as are North Americans) and to polarize camps on issues when divisions are not warranted (e.g., ending the nuclear arms race was a goal shared by people on both sides of the Iron Curtain). Of course, we can go to the opposite extreme by exaggerating the extent to which our interests are shared by all nations and peoples.

Recognizing stereotypes is important because unflattering stereotypes of people, cultures or nations are often deliberately encouraged. For example, creating hostile stereotypical images of people from an opposing country is often used to fuel widespread hatred against an enemy (Silverstein, 1989). Even in situations where the motives are benign, the effects of stereotyping are often undesirable. Condescending and paternalistic attitudes toward people in developing countries may be a function partly of our stereotypical images of these people (Werner, Connors, Aoki & Dahlie, 1977, p. 33). Building students' resistance to stereotypical accounts decreases their inclination to dehumanize or marginalize groups, because students see these groups as having a full range of human attributes. In other words, we should try to inoculate students against accepting portrayals of foreigners "as cardboard characters in a stilted puppet play" (Zachariah, 1989, p. 51). On a positive note, we can develop students' resistance to stereotyping by increasing their appreciation of the similarities and shared interests among people, and by combating tendencies to paint international issues in black-and-white terms.

The previously mentioned strategies for promoting appreciation of global complexity are appropriate for encouraging appreciation of global diversity: gross generalizations about people and nations should be discouraged, and examples of differences *within* cultural and national groups should be provided. Although more extensive study of fewer cultures or nations may be preferred to the relatively superficial study of many peoples, we must guard against stereotypical impressions encouraged when a heterogeneous entity, say Africa or aboriginal peoples, is considered exclusively in the context of one sample, say Nigeria or the Haida. As a general rule, we should avoid presenting only the dominant images of a country or people (e.g., avoid dealing exclusively with the poverty in Africa, and with the civility in Japan).

Being open-minded also implies having a tendency to suspend making firm judgments when evidence is inconclusive or when a thorough examination of the issue has not been carried out. As the Scottish philosopher David Hume observed, a wise person proportions his or her belief to the evidence. Teachers can encourage full-mindedness in their students by not always having the answer and by being comfortable with uncertainty—that is, being satisfied with tentative conclusions until full review of complex issues can be carried out.

Fair-mindedness

Fair-mindedness refers to the inclination to give a fair hearing to alternative points of view—to judge matters on the basis of their own merits, and not simply in terms of our own interests and preferences. Its opposites are bias and self absorption. Promoting fair-mindedness includes encouraging a willingness and ability to:

- **empathize with others.** To place oneself in the role or predicament of others or at least to imagine issues from the perspectives of other persons or groups.
- **overcome bias.** To resist imposing the interests or perspective of one's own group over those of other countries or peoples.

The ability to empathize does not imply that we must agree with the positions taken by others or be supportive in all cases—it requires solely that we try to understand in a vivid way what others think and how they feel.

The ability to empathize does not imply that we must agree with the positions taken by others or be supportive in all cases—it requires solely that we try to understand in a vivid way what others think and how they feel. Empathy is not the same as open-mindedness, although the two are interrelated. Empathy presupposes an openness to ways different from our own, but it goes further than openness, in that empathy requires that we "feel" the other person's predicament. The rationale for promoting empathy stems from the fact that merely learning more about other people or countries may not increase students' appreciation of what these people's life is really like. However, the inclination to empathize with others is not identical with promoting unqualified acceptance of others—a sensitive exposure to certain practices may legitimately redouble students' sense of another's oddness or unreasonableness. Thus, promoting empathy is not tantamount to encouraging moral relativism—students may still judge that certain practices are undesirable or unappealing. However, as the common expression suggests, no one should criticize another until they have walked in his or her shoes.

Bias refers to an unwarranted or unfair preference for one's interests or affiliations. It was reflected in contrasting descriptions of British and Iraqi actions provided by the British press at the height of the Persian Gulf War. More specifically, British forces were described as "cautious" and "loyal," and Iraqi troops as "cowardly" and "blindly obedient;" British sorties were "first strikes" and "preemptive" while Iraqi initiatives were "sneak missile attacks" and "without provocation" ("Mad Dogs and Englishmen," 1991). These accounts are prejudiced even if we all agree that Iraq deserved condemnation for provoking the war, because otherwise identical actions were judged differently merely because of which side performed them.

There are three forms of bias that are particularly relevant for global education:

- **ethnocentrism.** This refers to the view that one's own cultural group is superior to all others. It is not necessarily ethnocentric to prefer most features of North American life to customs and practices in other cultures; rather, it is ethnocentric to judge them better simply because they are our ways. Unless students are able to see the merits of other cultures, the study of other cultures will simply fuel the belief that our ways are the best and the others are inferior. As Jenness (1990) remarked in his extensive review of the history of social studies in the United States, some educators are concerned that "the world studies program may well turn out to be a fatter photo album, ethnocentrically selected and arranged" (p. 412).
- **national fanaticism.** This refers to a refusal to impartially assess policies and events involving our own country or to recognize that on some occasions national best interests, as opposed to the interests of other countries or people, should not be paramount.
- **presentism.** This refers to a preoccupation with the interests and well-being of current generations to the exclusion of the interests of persons yet to be born into the world. In other words, the felt urgency of our immediate needs and desires may preclude our fair-minded consideration of others' future needs. Concern with this form of bias underlies much criticism about our inadequate sensitivity to the long-term environmental consequences of national policies and consumer decisions.

Encouraging fair-mindedness is not inconsistent with promoting patriotism, cultural pride and concern for present problems. Fair-mindedness is in opposition to blind patriotism, unreasoning devotion and excessive preoccupation with present concerns. Although fostering national interests is an appropriate and desirable component of global education, attention to our own national interests must not obscure any moral obligations we have to the global community. It would be morally wrong not to have some sensitivity to the rights of others in the global community. And as I implied by the discussion of the Canada-Spain conflict over turbot fishing, when making decisions that affect others, fairness requires that we make judgments only after a balanced examination of opposing positions.

To encourage fair-mindedness, students should regularly be expected to explore and defend positions from different points of view, especially from perspectives that are not personally held by them. For students who have difficulty in being fair-minded, teachers may try "challenging" their thinking in non-threatening ways by presenting opposing reasons and by looking for inconsistencies in their attitudes. More likely, however, reasoning with students will not be sufficient. Students may benefit from exposure to evocative situations where they can "feel" for themselves the power and merit of other perspectives. There are at least three sources of these sorts of visceral experiences:

- **vicarious experiences** where students come to live the lives of others through films and stories. There are many collections of films (Full Frame, 1993; National Film Board, 1988, 1992, 1993; Public Affairs Branch, 1988) and stories about other countries and cultures (Lickteig & Danielson, 1995; Stewig, 1992; UNICEF, n.d.); many of which are written or produced by people from other countries (cf. Walker, 1989);
- **simulated experiences** where students act out through role play or in some other type of simulation activity the predicaments of others;
- **first-hand experiences** where students encounter in "real-life" meaningful contexts—through field trips, guest speakers, exchanges, pen pals, social action projects—the humanness and points of view of others.

Experiences such as these—whether brought about by reading a story, participating in a simulation or experiencing things first hand—help to evoke students' sensitivities to points of view that they might otherwise downplay or ignore.

CONCLUSION

In this article I have attempted to make four points: (1) illustrate the importance of helping students approach the study of their world from a more "global" perspective, (2) explain five main areas of the substantive—or content—dimension of this perspective, (3) explain three key traits of the perceptual—or attitudinal—dimension and (4) suggest ways in which the perceptual dimension may be nurtured—through direct instruction, teacher modelling and "experiential" activities. Although my focus is social studies, it is apparent that promoting a global perspective should not be limited exclusively to this subject, nor should it be an occasional add-on that occurs within a designated global education unit. Rather, efforts to promote a global perspective can and should be infused throughout the curriculum.

REFERENCES

Beckett, K. & Darling, L. (1988). *The view of the world portrayed in social studies textbooks.* (Occasional paper #13. Explorations in Development/Global Education). Vancouver: Research and Development in Global Studies, University of British Columbia.

Beesley, J.A. & Rowe, M. (1995, May 24). Why Canada

was right in the turbot fight. *The Vancouver Sun,* p. A15.

British Columbia Ministry of Education. (1983). *Social studies curriculum guide: Grade one - grade seven.* Victoria, BC: Author.

Case, R. (1989). *Global perspective or tunnel vision? The mandated view of the world in Canadian social studies curricula.* (Occasional paper #23. Explorations in Development/Global Education). Vancouver: Research and Development in Global Studies, University of British Columbia.

Chapman, M.S. (1991). *Nurturing a global perspective among primary students, using Chilean arpilleras.* Unpublished Masters of Education thesis, Simon Fraser University.

Egan, K. (1983.). Social studies and the erosion of education. *Curriculum Inquiry, 13*(2), 145-214.

Fountain S. (1990). *Learning together: Global education age 4-7.* London: World Wildlife Fund.

Full Frame. (1993). *The big picture: Film and video for global education.* Toronto: Author.

Hanvey, R.G. (1976). *An attainable global perspective.* New York: Global Perspectives in Education.

Jenness, D. (1990). *Making sense of social studies.* New York: Macmillan.

Johnson, C. (1997). *Expressing a global perspective: Experiences in a Mexican classroom.* Unpublished paper.

Kniep, W.M. (1986). Defining a global education by its content. *Social Education, 50,* 437-446.

Lickteig, M.J. & Danielson, K.E. (1995). Use children's books to link cultures of the world. *Social Studies, 86*(2), 69-73.

Mad Dogs and Englishmen, *Manchester Guardian,* (1991, February 22), p. 36.

Mpanya, M. (1989). *The image of Africa: PVO materials.* Paper prepared for Africa Partnership Project, InterAction, New York City, December 1989.

National Film Board. (1988). *Focus on Canada: A film and video resource handbook for secondary level social studies.* Montreal: Author.

National Film Board. (1992). *NFB green video guide.* Montreal: Author.

National Film Board. (1993). *Face-to-face video guide: Video resources for race relations training and education.* Montreal: Author.

Newmann, F.M. (1991). Promoting higher order thinking in social studies: Overview of a study of 16 high school departments. *Theory and Research in Social Education, 19,* 324-340.

Perinbaum, L. (1989). A new frontier for teachers. *Alberta Teachers' Association Magazine, 69,* 23-25.

Public Affairs Branch. (1988). *Insight: International development film catalogue.* Hull, PQ: Canadian International Development Agency.

Roldao, M. (1992). *The concept of concrete thinking in curriculum for early education: A critical examination.* Unpublished doctoral dissertation, Faculty of Education, Simon Fraser University.

Saarinen, T.F. (1973). Student views of the world. In R. M. Downs & D. Stea (Eds.), *Images and environment: Cognitive mapping and spatial behavior* (pp. 148-161). Chicago: Aldine.

Schuncke, G.M. (1984). Global awareness and younger children: Beginning the process. *Social Studies, 75,* 248-251.

Silverstein, B. (1989). Enemy images: The psychology of U.S. attitudes and cognitions regarding the Soviet Union. *American Psychologist, 44,* 903-913.

Social Studies and the Young Learner. (1994, March/April). Special theme: Global perspective in a new world.

Stewig, J.W. (1992). Using children's books as a bridge to other cultures. *Social Studies, 83*(1), 36-40.

Torney-Purta, J.V. (1983). Psychological perspectives on enhancing civic education through education of teachers. *Journal of Teacher Education, 34,* 30-34.

UNICEF. (n.d.) *Children's literature: Springboard to understanding the developing world* (A curriculum guide intended for grade three to eight). Toronto: Development Education Committee, UNICEF.

Walker S. (1989). *Stories from the rest of the world: 1989.* Saint Paul, MN: Graywolf Press.

Werner, W., Connors, B., Aoki, T. & Dahlie, J. (1977). *Whose culture? Whose heritage? Ethnicity within Canadian social studies curricula.* Vancouver: Centre for the Study of Curriculum and Instruction, University of British Columbia.

Willms, J. (1992). The children next door: Bringing the global neighbourhood into the classroom. *Orbit, 23*(1), 14-16.

Zachariah, M. (1989). Linking global education with multicultural education. *Alberta Teachers' Association Magazine, 69,* 48-51.

—— ✧ ——

This article is a revision of a 1995 article, "Nurturing a Global Perspective in Elementary Students" published in R. Fowler and I. Wright (Ed.), *Thinking Globally about Social Studies Education* (pp. 19-34). Vancouver: Research and Development in Global Studies, University of British Columbia. It draws to some extent on a 1993 article, "Key Elements of a Global Perspective" published in *Social Education, 57*(6), 318-325.

10

ESTABLISHING OBJECTIVES FOR A MULTICULTURAL PROGRAM

JOHN W. FRIESEN

The rapid rise of interest in multiculturalism in Canada may be regarded with both joy and apprehension. It is encouraging to witness the many efforts that are being undertaken by the various segments of society to foster tolerance and understanding (i.e., ethnic clubs, schools, governmental agencies, etc.) but along with the proliferation of programs and activities comes a justifiable concern about the development and articulation of appropriate philosophical assumptions as a basis for such action. Consider some of the ways in which multicultural efforts have been launched (i.e., adjustments in school curricula and teacher training, community exchange programs, governmental grant programs, media productions, conferences intended to raise awareness and to build bridges, and race relations courses in such institutions as police departments, schools and community organizations). Often these efforts have been initiated because the idea is popular, not because the initiators have a grasp of relevant ground principles.

There are several very basic factors to consider in establishing programs intended either to encourage interaction between members of different ethnic backgrounds or to heighten awareness of cultural differences. These include the selection of resources, designing objectives, obtaining commitment from participants, determining program structure, evaluation and the role of the leaders or practitioners. Because the formulation of justifiable objectives is so important, that discussion will take up the bulk of this paper and the other components mentioned will be dealt with briefly at the end. The objectives identified here are not necessarily mutually exclusive but the order in which they are presented reflects an increasing intensity of importance.

DETERMINING PROGRAM OBJECTIVES

In educational circles it goes without saying that any undertaking must have clear goals about what is to be accomplished and what the outcomes might be. Individuals and organizations not familiar with the rudiments of good pedagogy, however, may plunge into what might seem to be a good enterprise without taking cognizance of what the effects might be. This does not mean that educators should not also be establishing appropriate objectives, and this discussion is an attempt to illustrate some of the possible avenues with regard to multicultural pursuits.

Objective one: Celebrations (food—fairs—festivals)

Although the emphasis on multiculturalism in Canada is of relatively recent origin, research efforts in the field have been annotated as early as 1960 (Van Til, 1960). The official announcement of Canada's seriousness about the concept came just over a decade ago in the form of the federal government's adoption of the official multicultural policy in 1972. The first activities included an acknowledgement of cultural diversity through food fairs, promotion of ethnic celebrations and exchanges and other rather light-hearted efforts. Even today agencies like the Secretary of State office and provincial departments like the Cultural Heritage Branch in Alberta foster these activities by assisting with funding. Many cities have initiated festivals that accentuate cultural uniqueness, for example, Winnipeg's Folkorama which has been duplicated in many other of the larger urban centres.

> As a form of entertainment or just a "night on the town" these cultural celebrations are hard to beat. As a form of attitude development in the sense of building lasting relationships or encouraging mutual empathy for personal heritage they accomplish little.

Participating in a cultural celebration can be a very enjoyable experience. The food is good and frequently exotic, the displays reveal hours of painstaking efforts in terms of crafts, and many of the programs of song and dance encourage participation on the part of the audience. As a form of entertainment or just a "night on the town" these celebrations are hard to beat. As a form of attitude development in the sense of building lasting relationships or encouraging mutual empathy for personal heritage they accomplish little. They may still be justified as an awareness building effort but when the festivity is over chances that oblivion to cultural diversity will resume are probably quite high.

A local school that practices a variation of this emphasis attempts to emphasize cultural diversity by featuring a different ethnic "special day" every week of the school year. Care is taken to reflect the ethnic makeup of the community when this is done and the result is a school-wide "theming" situation in which each classroom reflects on the particular celebration for a short time during the week. A general bulletin board display is also featured. Illustrative special days would include these:

- Chinese New Year, January or February of the 1st moon
- Czechoslovakian Memorial Day, 3rd Sunday of April
- Danish Constitution Day, June 5
- Irish St. Patrick's Day, March 17
- Japanese Hana-Matsuri (Flower Festival), April 8
- Pakistani National Day, (Birth of the Prophet Mohammed) March 23,
- Russian Day of Mourning, May 10
- Ukrainian Independence Day and Unification Day, January 22

Celebrating someone else's heritage can be a mutually rewarding experience on a temporary basis, but unless care is taken to make the happening more than a light-hearted occasion void of any deeper psychological bonding, it is doubtful that the activity may be considered very effective in terms of lasting benefits.

Objective two: Curiosity quest

One of life's entertaining moments may be experienced at a zoo in observing a group of people watching a pair of baboons. This doesn't mean that the baboons are not entertaining, for indeed they are, but witnessing one's fellow homosapiens is a special kind of entertainment, not entirely void of a little embarrassment. Many members of the ethnic community feel that such a "museum" approach to ethnicity is an insult to the integrity of their heritage, especially when any unique custom or role is reacted to with more than a normal expression of surprise or discovery. When attempting to set up a field trip to visit the newly established Holdeman Mennonite school near Calgary a few years ago, I was informed by members of their school board that while they would be happy to exchange ideas with university students, they saw no particular benefit in their visiting a classroom as observers. "It would only interrupt our students," I was informed, "and it would provide the visitors with no more than a typical experience in the sense of watching any group of children functioning in any classroom." They were right, of course, and we undertook the visit on the grounds they outlined.

Much of our information about cultural eccentricities in the public sense has been perpetrated by the *National Geographic Magazine* model in which various cultures are sympathetically and politely portrayed, often in a barebreasted fashion if they are women but not if they are white women! Whose imagination is not stirred by an article describing how little Vietnamese girls are taught that they are inferior to males or that the Japanese family that "bathes together, stays together" because allegedly they do it in the nude in a family tub!

Some educators mistakenly play to the curious side of life when they suggest that a certain pupil in class belongs to what is implied to be a bit of an atypical group. Native students in our university have told me many times how much they dislike being identified in a class because of their cultural background and being expected to speak with great wisdom about some aspect of their history or value system. If the truth were known, many of them, like us, *live* their culture without intending to report on it in a formal sense at a given time.

The Alberta Government's Settlement Services Department (1984) recently prepared a series of "Newcomer Books" comprising information about housing, money, schooling, the job market, etc., intended to be of help to new immigrants to the country. Much of the information is so matter-of-fact that it would be taken for granted by the average citizen. When I showed the collection of ten books to a fourth year university class several students inquired as to where they might obtain them, because they felt the books contained information they should have. The incident suggested to me that if every native-born citizen could step back and evaluate Canadian culture from a truly objective stance (if such could be attained), it might well be concluded that our way of life has its own curious elements.

It is a well-established fact that the social sciences have demonstrated that there are often greater differences between individuals *within* any racial or cultural group than there are *between* such groups (Over-street, 1962). The implication of this finding is that there are more similarities among individuals than there are differences. Moreover, if cultural differences are ferreted out for special attention, we may not be sure that we have identified the most *important* differences between people. Also, forming an atmosphere of unusuality or curiosity about such differences disallows the bonding effect that is helpful to mutual growth. Thus an emphasis on fulfilling common needs (i.e., the need to be accepted, appreciated and encouraged) is a much better way to proceed.

Objective three: Contribution counting

In 1969 the Federal Government committed a gaffe when they released their White Paper on Native Affairs in Canada (Chrétien, 1969). The chiefs of Alberta's forty-four Indian bands were quick to voice their objections in the form of their Red Paper, objecting most strongly, perhaps, to the government's suggestion that Indian lands be turned over to local ownership, but also to the patronizing tone of the White Paper which suggested that Canadians develop a "positive recognition of the unique contributions of Indian culture to Canadian society." The Native view was that their contribution should have been obvious. After all, had they not occupied the country for several thousand years without the aid of their invaders? Did their contribution require a special mention?

There is a corollary observation to be made here, however, and this is with regard to the *correct* delineation of ethnic contributions to Canadian life. Although historians of the past have sometimes misrepresented the exact role which the various cultures have played in the formation of this nation or how their lifestyles have affected various aspects of it, today the scene is different. There are, in fact, many ethnic histories being written by minority group members themselves. Is their version closer to the truth or do they yield to the temptation to embellish the facts a bit in the interests of balancing the account?

A teaching approach that encourages the contribution counting approach is to highlight individuals of particular ethnic backgrounds when studying the various school subjects. In science, for example, students could study black inventors or doctors, in math they could concentrate on selected ethnic concepts of time (e.g., calendars) and in physical education they could participate in various forms of cultural games. Again, there may be advantages in this approach, but if exercised to the exclusion of other approaches, they may stress the matter of ethnic origin disproportionately.

When denoting contributions it might be better to emphasize the positive elements of a culture rather than dwelling on the negative; at least this is a good starting point. One classroom teacher has class members put up pictures of themselves at the beginning of the year (either self-portraits or photographs), with an accompanying sheet of paper on which each member of the class may write a positive comment about the individual. Participants may sign their names if they feel so inclined. At the end of the exercise the students are asked to introduce a classmate according to the information written about them. The class then discusses how they felt about the experiment in terms of having had all those nice things said about them. Of course, the activity has an element of "unreality" about it, but student evaluations indicate that it is a very uplifting experience for them. Perhaps a similar approach could be adopted for the study of ethnic history and culture, at least as an initial step.

Objective four: Case studies

The fact that Canada is a pluralist nation suggests that there is ample opportunity to examine a variety of lifestyles in one setting. The approach to such a study is really not complicated if one adopts the tack that most immigrant groups, for example, have a lot in common. Several aspects of such a study might include examining their arrival in Canada in terms of (i) making a living, (ii) establishing home life, (iii) social adjustment—getting along with others, (iv) selection of location in Canada (e.g., rural or urban) also later migrations within the country, and (v) assimilation process in terms of intermarriage, language and religious retention. By selecting even a few such examples, one can easily see similarities among the groups and draw parallels to contemporary life. When studied in everyday terms an appreciation of common humanness may develop. The approach also includes these advantages:

- It reflects the reality of Canadian society;

- It allows minority group members an opportunity to learn about their own backgrounds and thus respect and support them;

- It helps students to become aware of and sensitive to the meaning of cultural diversity in Canada; and

> When denoting contributions it might be better to emphasize the positive elements of a culture rather than dwelling on the negative; at least this is a good starting point.

- It presents examples of cultural diversity in a meaningful and personalized manner.

A project devised by a Calgary high school teacher endorses the study of Canadian subcultures via representative individuals of national fame. Students are requested to write a biographical sketch of well-known Canadians in terms of their ethnic origins. Questions to be answered orient the assignment toward the study of a people, not an individual: (i) What was the country of their origin? (ii) Where is that country? (iii) What was the major reason for these people to leave their country? (iv) In what parts of Canada did these people settle? (v) What kinds of jobs did they take up? and (vi) Do a brief biographical sketch of representative persons, such as:

- Bruno Gerussi, Italian television star
- Louis Riel, Métis leader
- David Suzuki, Japanese media star
- John Ware, Black rancher
- Peter Verigin, Doukhobor leader
- Harry Freedman, Jewish leader

Objective five: Consciousness raising

Studying a culture in some depth gets one beyond the food-festivities level of intrigue and allows for the development of understanding and perhaps appreciation. The study must be undertaken in accordance with the principles of objective yet sympathetic research, however, for merely to "cover material" without relating it to known practicalities will benefit little. The same holds true for other activities like conducting field trips; maximum benefits like changing attitudes can only occur if the visitors and those being visited are brought together under certain conditions. As Ahmed Ijaz (1982) has pointed out, effective intergroup contact can be maximized if the following principles are operant:

- The interacting individuals should be of equal status;
- There should be an obvious support of inter-ethnic contact by persons or institutions in authority;
- Contact should occur on a personal basis over a fair length of time rather than on a casual basis or only once;
- The contact situation should provide interdependent activities and common goals that can only be reached by the cooperation of all members of the group; and
- The contact should be pleasant and rewarding.

The process of consciousness raising must begin in one's immediate environment where opportunities are often easily overlooked. George Bancroft's (1979) study of immigrant teachers suggests that even in schools involved in developing multicultural programs there is a tendency for staff to overlook talent available within their own circles. When such individuals *are* approached, however, and their experience is tapped, some interesting events may be inaugurated. In one situation a teacher from another country, for example, had his students establish contact with his former students back home and now they correspond.

The purposes of attempting to draw attention to cultural differences in a sensitive and meaningful way will include these foci:

- Presenting alternative cultural explanations for normative behaviour by presenting indepth explanations representative of various ethnic groups;
- Developing sensitivity to the concerns of particular ethnic communities; and
- Investigating stereotypes and the reasons for their development in particular forms.

While the literature on stereotypes is rapidly mounting (Cauthen, Robinson & Krauss, 1971), one of the most intriguing aspects of the phenomenon has to do with the origins of particularized concepts of individuals and groups. Often when people examine the reasons why they hold certain views they better understand them and may even subject them to possible amendation. For classroom purposes a variety of relevant discussion techniques may be employed: (i) brainstorming, (ii) Phillips 66, a technique that consists of selecting six group members to organize themselves by selecting a leader and a recording secretary and solving a problem in six minutes, (iii) tutorial groups in which several individuals study a situation and act in a leadership capacity to the rest of the class, (iv) a task group which is assigned a particular problem to investigate, (v) role-playing, (vi) an inquiry group which acts on a situation by emphasizing the acquisition of new facts, and (vii) problem solving group (Orlich, *et al.*, 1980, pp. 255–265).

Objective six: Communication

One of the requirements of good communication is to be sensitive to the vagaries of each situation. An exercise that demonstrates the difficulties of achieving this in a group setting is to ask the group members to pair off in twos, engage in a conversation about something that happened during the day and then close their eyes and review what transpired in terms of three questions: (i) what was your partner wearing? (ii) what color are his/her eyes? and (iii) describe his/her face in some detail. Of course, few individuals will score 100% on the exercise, but it will illustrate the extent to which we sometimes overlook rather important aspects of the communicating process (Tiedt & Tiedt, 1979, pp. 47–48).

Multicultural activities based on effective communication basically involve the following characteristics:

- Group members interact positively with each other;
- The processes undertaken serve to enable members to conceive of themselves as worthwhile human beings;
- The environment created operationalizes a philosophy of human rights;

- The environment is process oriented rather than product oriented;
- Allowance is made for the fact of varying learning and communicating styles of different cultural backgrounds.[1]

Establishing rapport as a means to good communication can often be accomplished through relatively agenda-free tasks such as the one recommended by the Mennonite Newcomer Services of Edmonton. It consists of making garden plots available to newcomer families who may learn the art in Canadian style by working in partnership with a Canadian colleague. Working together on such a simple task allows for the development of friendship on a relatively meaningful plane. When communication is maximized, people are accepted as individuals regardless of their peculiar characteristics such as race, creed, color or beliefs. Drawing attention to specific traits such as culture often overshadows the process of meaningful human interaction which can penetrate or overlook differences in taste, perception or ideology.

An interesting parable that emphasizes the uniqueness of individual perception goes like this:

> One day Soshi was walking on the bank of a river with a friend. "How delightfully the fishes are enjoying themselves in the water," Soshi exclaimed. His friend spoke to him thus: "You are not a fish; how do you know that the fishes are enjoying themselves?" "You are not myself," returned Soshi, "How do you know that I do not know that the fishes are enjoying themselves?" (Tiedt & Tiedt, 1979, p. 45)

Learning to appreciate individual differences, it seems, is not an uncomplicated task.

Objective seven: Caring

The increasing humanization of education has brought about significant changes in the way in which the individual pupil is regarded. One of the emerging concepts to crystalize is that of self-esteem which is currently conceptualized by educators as a kind of gauge by which to measure success. Students who have a positive image of themselves do better in school and teachers who conceive of their own contributions in a positive way similarly affect the success rate of their students. The impact of these findings suggests that a wholesome school atmosphere is a significant factor in enhancing learning and the result has been to view the teacher-student relationship in a much more humanistic manner.

Group dynamics that foster enhanced human relationships include these characteristics:

- Accepting the individual as a person regardless of his/her sex, age, physical characteristics, mannerisms, etc.;
- Encouraging the individual to see his/her background, heritage and personality as an asset;
- Assisting the individual to perceive of his/her background and heritage as worthy of making a contribution; in the language of Nathaniel Hawthorne, "Every individual has a place to fill in the world, and is important in some respect, whether he chooses to be so or not."
- Accepting the individual who functions in a bicultural sphere on the terms that he/she perceives his/her two environments to require of him/her.

Methods by which self-esteem may be developed to a higher plane vary from such exercises as having a child write a paragraph about himself and having it presented to his peers in a positive way to the more sophisticated method of utilizing a sociogram to determine where class members stand in relation to each other and then arranging their interactions so that every individual has an opportunity to experience acceptance by others and in turn by himself. That privilege by very definition is the right of every Canadian.

Multicultural programs can mistakenly play to the drummer of cultural differences to the extent that human similarities are overlooked. Common to us all is the need for acceptance and appreciation and the need to know that at least some of our efforts make a difference in the world in which we move. When that kind of caring is the primary focus of multicultural program building, our efforts will develop on a sound footing. The goal of acceptance/understanding has no equal in the human enterprise.

Corollary Challenges

As indicated earlier the determination of objectives is an important aspect of program development but there are also other factors to take into account. First is the matter of identifying available resources and while this search will include identifying spokespersons from various ethnic communities and locating sites to be visited, etc., one should not overlook the resources in one's own institution or community. The makeup of Canadian society is such that resource persons having ethnically relevant backgrounds or experience that can enhance a multicultural program are probably in the immediate vicinity of any planning group. It will require only a little groundwork to locate them.

A second concern has to do with obtaining a commitment from participants in a multicultural effort. As is the case with any innovation, fear of the unknown often provokes uncertainty about its possible benefits. Some of the more common objections to such a program have been identified by John Kehoe of the University of British Columbia:

> We don't have any racial problems in our school so we don't need programmes that deal with problems that don't exist. . . . We don't teach about ethnic groups because we don't have any ethnic minorities attending our schools. . . . We don't have the neces-

sary materials for multicultural education. . . . If you encourage multiculturalism you threaten national unity. (Kehoe, 1984, pp. 5-7)

There is an effective response to each of the above objections and these should best be offered in a spirit that allays fears, develops communication and builds confidence. In addition to community confidence, however, it will also be essential in a school setting to cultivate the approval of the administration, one's colleagues, and students who will be involved. The latter group may well be a part of the process of determining objectives and planning the exact nature of the enterprise.

A third concern is structuring the program. Time-wise, the activities could comprise a single day or a singular activity like a field trip. Alternately, the length of the program could even be stretched to a full six weeks of study or comprise an entire curriculum unit. Whatever route is chosen, a few practical considerations may be relevant.

- If a case study of an ethnic group is selected, be sure to get your facts straight about their culture. Select only reliable sources which may be validated either by contacting known multicultural leaders, librarians or members of the ethnic community to be studied. The same holds true for a field trip; pre-trip input should be based on accurate and sensitive information.

- In ethnic studies, emphasize the similarities of people rather than accentuating their differences. This may build a sense of commonality with the group being studied.

- Avoid the insensitive approaches of condescension, paternalism, dishonest praise, prejudice and discrimination (Wood, 1983, p. 82).

- Bear in mind that all cultures change and vary within themselves and thus the information you may have accumulated with respect to a particular group may not exactly coincide with what you later experience. The fact is that Canadian ethnic communities are on the move and the processes of assimilation and adaptation are very much active. The positive side of this phenomenon is that even an adjustment in perception is part of the enrichment of a multicultural activity.

- Multiculturalism thrives best through the development of a total atmosphere, which is an atmosphere of acceptance. Where the emphasis on differences is undertaken, it should be accomplished as a means of enrichment or as an opportunity for blossoming on the part of those who may be involved.

A final concern relates to evaluation. One way to accomplish this would be through a kind of pre and post testing arrangement if an appropriate instrument can be obtained. Alternately, several individuals may be appointed to act as interviewers and reporters to maintain contact with participants throughout the event or program and thus gather information developmentally for a final report.

ROLE OF THE PRACTITIONER

Several very basic principles for functioning as a leader or facilitator in a multicultural enterprise have emerged as the field has developed:

- Bear in mind that the initiation of a successful program does not automatically guarantee significant changes anywhere else in the community. By establishing workable humanistic principles in the classroom, one does not necessarily set world standards; also the opportunity to influence a group of participants in a positive pattern for a relatively short duration does not guarantee that the impressions gained will be long-standing.

- Be prepared to make mistakes. Even efforts with the best of intentions may be misunderstood, particularly when varying culture perspectives are involved. Still, the process will be worthwhile.

- Consider a multicultural program very much an activity that allows for learning from human experience. Making too many expectations of a program that is designed to produce the maximum in terms of acceptance and understanding is unrealistic. Life will still go on.

- Develop a kind of philosophical-mindedness that when you have done your homework "everything will turn out alright in the end." If you believe in human acceptance, act on it, even if not everyone catches the same vision that you do. Keep in mind that even red-necks must have something about them you can learn to love.

- Be real, not a phoney. When Harry Wolcott (1967) taught school in a Kwakiutl village school on Vancouver Island, he discovered very quickly that he was not a Kwakiutl and he was not expected to be one. He had values of his own and he was expected to reveal them and perhaps even to share them on occasion. Seeking to cover up one's own convictions or beliefs or pretending to have none makes one less than a human being, a phoney. Multiculturalism, if it accomplishes nothing else, must achieve the goal that "it's O.K. to be me." If the practitioner personally falls short of that goal there is little he can do for someone else in promoting understanding.

ENDNOTE
[1] See Fred Carnew (1984) for a discussion of the research basis for Native learning style differences.

REFERENCES
Bancroft, G. (1979). *They come from abroad*. Toronto: Guidance Centre.

Carnew, F. (1984). Toward policy in native education.

Multicultural Education Journal, 1(2), 4–18.

Cauthen, N.R., Robinson, I.E. & Krauss, H.H. (1971). Stereotypes: A review of the literature, 1926–1968. *Journal of Social Psychology, 84*, 103–125.

Chrétien, J. (1969). Statement of the government of Canada on Indian policy, published under the authority of the Minister of Indian Affairs and Northern Development, Ottawa.

Ijaz, M.A. (1982, February). Can we change our students' racial attitudes? *Orbit*, 19–21.

Kehoe, J. (1984). *A handbook for enhancing the multicultural climate of the school.* Vancouver: Wedge Publications.

Orlich, D.C. et al. (1980). *Teaching strategies: A guide to better instruction*, Toronto: D.C. Heath.

Overstreet, H. (1962). Some contributions of science to the easing of group tensions. In M.L. Barron (Ed.), *American minorities: A textbook of readings in intergroup relations* (pp. 513–518). New York: Alfred A. Knopf.

Settlement Services, Department of Manpower. (1984). *Newcomer* series. Edmonton: Government of Alberta.

Tiedt, P.L. & Tiedt, I.M. (1979). *Multicultural teaching: A handbook of activities, information and resources.* Boston: Allyn and Bacon.

Van Til, W., Ed. (1960). Intercultural education. In *The encyclopedia of education research* (pp. 718–728). New York: Macmillan.

Wolcott, H.F. (1967). *A Kwakiutl village and school.* New York: Holt, Rinehart and Winston.

Wood, D. (1983). *Cultural heritage . . . Your neighbourhood.* Edmonton: Alberta Educational Communications Corporation.

SUPPLEMENTARY READINGS

(1983). *The History and Social Science Teacher, 19* (Multicultural feature issue).

(1991/92). *Educational Leadership, 49* (Multicultural education theme).

(1997, January/February). *The Social Studies, 88* (Citizenship and Multicultural education themes.)

Aboud, F. (1985). *Children and prejudice.* Oxford: Blackwell.

Banks, J.A. (1994). *An introduction to multicultural education.* Boston: Allyn and Bacon

Banks, J.A. & Banks, C.A.M. (Eds.). (1989). *Multicultural education: Issues and perspectives.* Boston: Allyn and Bacon.

Bennett, C.J. (1995). *Comprehensive multicultural education: Theory and practice.* Boston: Allyn and Bacon.

Ladson-Billings, G. (1992). The multicultural mission: Unity *and* diversity. *Social Education, 56*(5), 308-311.

Moodley, K.A. (1995). Multicultural education in Canada: Historical development and current status. In J. Banks & C.A.M. Banks (Eds.), *Handbook of research on multicultural education* (pp. 801-820). New York: Macmillan.

NCSS Task Force on Ethnic Studies Curriculum Guidelines. (1992). Curriculum guidelines for multicultural education. *Social Education, 56*(5), 274-294.

Osborne, Ken. (1993). Multiculturalism under the miscroscope. *Manitoba Social Science Teacher, 20*(2), 14-19.

Shapson, S. & D'Oyley, V. (Eds.). (1984). *Bilingual and multicultural education: Canadian perspectives.* Avon, England: Multicultural Matters.

This article, reprinted with the permission of University of Toronto Press Incorporated, appeared originally in 1985 in *History and Social Science Teacher, 21*(1), 32–38. Minor alterations to the original article have been made for stylistic and format purposes.

11

ENVIRONMENTAL LITERACY FROM A GLOBAL PERSPECTIVE

MILTON MCCLAREN

The admonition to act locally and think globally has become a slogan of the environmental movement. Many environmental educators and environmentalists have taken an interest in global environmental problems such as world climate change caused by greenhouse gasses, the loss of biological diversity, and atmospheric ozone depletion. Similarly, those interested in the domain of global education have also connected thought and action, as in the title of the 1991 ASCD Yearbook, *Global Education: From Thought to Action* (Tye, 1991). That monograph employed the definition of global education from Hanvey (1976):

> Global education involves learning about those problems and issues that cut across national boundaries, and about the interconnectedness of systems—ecological, cultural, economic, political and technological. Global education involves perspective taking—seeing things through the eyes and minds of others—and it means the realization that while individuals and groups may view life differently, they also have common needs and wants. (Hanvey, cited in Tye, 1991, p. 5)

Many environmental problems are of global scale and their understanding and solution requires both local actions and global cooperation. The biophysical world has always been an integrated system of systems. Humans, especially in the eras of industrial nationalism, colonialism, and imperialism drew arbitrary boundaries across this seamless fabric and defended those boundaries with fanatical passion, forgetting in the process the ultimately interconnected nature of the earth. However, the development of nuclear weapons, world transportation, world-wide communication systems, global economics, and the growing evidence of global environmental changes induced by human activities have reminded humankind that not only are we dependent on, and part of, the natural system, but we are also all ultimately involved in the lives of other people.

In some cases environmentalists' global concerns appear to focus on blaming the less-developed world for overpopulation and habitat destruction. But even more sophisticated accounts sometimes reveal limited understanding of indigenous knowledge and values, cultural diversity, and the real causes of environmental degradation. Environmental education must develop greater sophistication by fostering global thinking about environmental issues and personal actions.

Elsewhere, I have described environmental literacy as comprising 10 factors or dimensions of thinking and understanding (McClaren, 1989). This definition or conceptual framework for nurturing environmental literacy has been used quite widely in the development of environmental education curriculum materials (e.g., McClaren [1995], *Water Stewardship: A Guide for Teachers, Students and Community Groups*; McClaren & Kristjanson [1993], *Global Change and Canadians: A Guide for Teachers*; and McClaren, Samples & Hammond [1993–1995], the *Connections* series). Although global perspectives are implicit in it, my (1989) framework was not connected clearly to the concerns of global education. This essay emphasizes the relationship between a global perspective and the elements of environmental literacy.

To begin, it may be useful to consider what a global environmental perspective is. I would suggest that a global perspective entails having an understanding of the planet as a set of interconnected biogeochemical systems (a global ecosystem) coupled with an appreciation of the diversity of the human population. To appreciate human diversity is to recognize not only the fact but also the importance and value of that diversity. While biological species are being eliminated through human activities, many cultural species are also vanishing under the onslaughts of globalized commerce and communication. To some, the new world order is a pathway to peace and prosperity. To others, it entails an enormous loss of cultural diversity and with it a decline in the richness and depth of human understanding. From a biologist's point of view, cultures have developed within ecological contexts—ecology and culture have coevolved. Human culture is not outside of nature but an intrinsic element in it. The challenge for global education is to foster a global perspective that celebrates both uniqueness of and commonality across cultures while reconciling humankind with the natural world. This conception echoes, albeit in somewhat different language, Case's (1993) proposal that a global perspective entails a substantive dimension and a perceptual dimension, the first being focussed on the more objective aspects of the workings of the world and its cultures, and the second on the valuative, metaphoric elements of a global view.

How may the elements of environmental literacy be viewed from a global perspective?

ELEMENTS OF ENVIRONMENTAL LITERACY

The ability to think about systems

The development of environmental literacy requires seeing the world systemically, understanding where things come from, where they go, and how energy and materials are transformed in planetary cycles. Systems thinking also means recognizing that as world commerce becomes a reality, consumptive behaviours and life-style choices in one part of the planet may have powerful consequences in other locales. From a global perspective, environmental literacy means thinking

An apparently innocuous personal life-style choice can have a serious effect on both wildlife and humans in other parts of the world, and ultimately on ourselves.

about the impact of personal life-style choices on a world scale. This sort of systems thinking requires quite a bit of knowledge. A good example is sun-grown versus shade-grown coffee. Because of the recent popularity of coffee houses and espresso bars in North America, world demand for coffee has escalated. Traditional agriculturalists grow coffee in small plantings in the shade of larger trees, often wild trees. The larger trees not only provide shade, they also provide habitat for many species of birds. Unfortunately, to meet rising coffee demands, large plantations of coffee plants are being established using new sun-tolerant varieties. The new varieties yield more beans and are easily harvested by machines, but the large shade trees are removed, destroying bird habitat in the process. Moreover, shade coffee was often raised by peasant growers on small, hand-picked plots. The larger sun plantings are created through land assembly by large-scale landowners; small farmers are displaced to make way for the large farms. Extending the links in the chain further we may discover that the number of song bird species in North America is decreasing, much to the dismay of birders and wildlife managers in Canada and the United States. One reason may be that the winter habitat of some of these birds has been destroyed to make way for coffee plantations. Thus, an apparently innocuous personal life-style choice can have a serious effect on both wildlife and humans in other parts of the world, and ultimately on ourselves. Systems thinking at the global level requires asking questions not only about local inputs and outputs but also about potential impacts at the source of the resource, or the point of consumption of the product, no matter how far apart the two may be.

The ability to think in time: To forecast, to think ahead, and to plan

With systems thinking we also need to introduce the concept of thinking about time factors in environmental and human processes. We need to nurture the capacity to think beyond the here and now. Years later, today's quick and convenient "fixes" often turn out to cause serious environmental problems. On a global scale this problem is illustrated by the production and distribution of CFC's (chlorofluorocarbons) and their subsequent destruction of upper atmospheric ozone. CFC's were first developed as human-synthesized compounds in the 1920s. One of their advantages was great chemical stability (a reason, for example, for their use in fire extinguishers). Because people in the 1920s did not have the advantage of having a global perspective on the dynamics of the atmosphere or climate, they did not appreciate that this very durable molecule could survive to be transported both vertically, into the stratosphere, and horizontally, towards the polar regions. It can take five years for a CFC molecule to find its way into the upper atmosphere. Once there, a single CFC molecule can catalyze the destruction of many thousands of ozone molecules. CFC is also stable enough to survive in the atmosphere long enough to be transported horizontally from the industrialized northern hemisphere, where most CFC's are made, across the equator and southward to the south polar vortex, where conditions in the late southern winter and early spring are ideal for the destruction of ozone. This is why the most striking examples of ozone depletion in the stratosphere have been recorded above the South Pole, even though there are no CFC sources at or near the polar continent. Because ozone is a crucial shield against incoming ultraviolet (UV) solar radiation, its destruction can increase ground-level UV, with possible health consequences for humans and death of or damage to plants and animals. For many decades we produced and used CFC's. They appeared to be wonder-compounds, perfect examples of the benefits of modern chemistry. Now, even if we were to stop all CFC production immediately and remove and destroy all existing CFC's, we would still have ozone destruction for years to come. The problem has ecological momentum. It took time to create and it will take more time to eliminate. It is also of global importance.

Many of earth's systems operate on a global time scale. Global environmental thinking requires us to consider not only the immediate but also the long-term, future costs and benefits of our actions. A key element of the concept of sustainability is that actions in the present should not result in limited options and degraded environments for future generations. The concept needs to be extended through global thinking. For example, developed nations still sell banned pesticides to Third World countries, where they will cause future problems. Developed nations also export toxic wastes to poorer regions for long-term storage, knowing that these chemicals will not be safely contained or handled and may even be stolen for black-market sale. Some affluent nations would rather ship potential hazards elsewhere, to places where poverty makes immediate profit more influential than possible future catastrophes. By doing so these nations may safeguard their own future generations at the expense of those in less fortunate regions. These practices are hardly compatible with global sustainability.

The ability to think critically about value issues

Almost all modern problems, environmental or otherwise, have elements rooted in human value systems. Global society is pluralistic and multicultural. Whereas all humans have common needs, which they share with other life forms, the ways these needs are met, as well as ideas about the quality of life, are shaped by widely different values in different cultural and socioeconomic groups. One must consider the different value perspec-

Because each Canadian may consume 14 times more energy in a year than a typical person on the Indian subcontinent, in qualitative terms this changes the population of Canada from 28 million to 392 million, at least when the ecological footprint of the average Canadian is considered.

tives at work around an environmental issue before making judgments or advocating solutions. Thus, for instance, the problem of species loss would seem to have very little to do with the status and education of women in less-developed nations. In some cultures, however, women are the active farmers and land stewards—yet environmental education efforts have often been directed at men who appear to be in leadership positions. When environmental education about deforestation or land management is delivered by women, for women, the results are more significant because the women actually make day-to-day, local decisions in those areas. In some parts of southeast Asia, for example, women have played major roles in reforestation, with consequences for habitat enhancement and soil and water conservation. Without understanding cultural value structures, it is easy to judge erroneously and to advance impractical or even harmful strategies. Developing environmental literacy within a global perspective requires learning enough about other cultures to understand their value systems and the possible environmental consequences of those values.

The ability to separate number, quantity, quality and value

Many people in the modern world are confused about the differences among the terms number, quantity, quality and value (Bateson, 1979). Some people assume that bigger, faster or more expensive is better. We equate the possession of many material possessions or a lot of money with higher moral authority and a high-quality life. Many people have considerable difficulty recognizing that although the population of Canada is numerically less than that of India or the People's Republic of China, what really matters in global environmental terms is not numbers but the consumer patterns of the individuals and communities the numbers represent. Rees (1992) has proposed the concept of the ecological footprint as a more accurate way of representing the impact on the earth of various life styles. Thus, because each Canadian may consume 14 times more energy in a year than a typical person on the Indian subcontinent, in qualitative terms this changes the population of Canada from 28 million to 392 million, at least when the ecological footprint of the average Canadian is considered. (The calculation of ecological footprint is actually more complicated than represented here, but the idea is illustrated by this example.)

One of the most important benefits of global education for environmental education is to develop increased understanding of different criteria for quality and value and of different ways of thinking about number, quantity, quality and value relationships. The environmental ethics of the tribal peoples of the South African deserts, of Australian aborigines and of the Mohawk First Nations are quite different from each other and from those of many industrialized urban people. Concepts of waste, use, species' rights, place, space and number all vary widely from culture to culture. When one culture appreciates the views of another, that culture is often prompted to reflect on its own values, concepts of quality, and relationships with the natural world. What modern cities' inhabitants value may seem totally valueless to a rain forest dweller. Sustainable development has been advocated as a means of reconciling economic activities with wise stewardship of the environment. At the core of the concept of sustainability is a set of values about consumption and ethical environmental behaviour. The concept is not simply a mechanistic policy formulation: almost certainly, sustainability cannot be attained simply by extending the developed world's life styles and environmental behaviours to the rest of the planet's peoples—by bringing them "up" to our standard. What will likely be required is the development of new perspectives on consumption, ownership, needs and wants. Knowledge about other cultures, living in other environmental contexts, and about their ways of living with each other and the land can enrich our thinking about sustainability and stewardship.

The ability to distinguish between the map and the territory

We are surrounded by high-quality representations of the world. We have photos in full colour, videos, stereos, models, CD's and simulations. Although these can be very useful in helping us to appreciate other environments and cultures, we may become so fond of our maps that we forget that they are not entirely faithful representations of how things actually are.

Many of our notions about the environment, such as about the nature of tropical or temperate old-growth forests, are elaborate stereotypes. In addition, many of our views of the world's other cultures are also stereotypes. In the developed world many people view the inhabitants of less-developed nations, especially very poor ones, as being universally sad, malnourished and poverty stricken, to say nothing of illiterate and ignorant. The stereotype of lazy, unenergetic and unambitious tropic dwellers is also still alive and well, as any glance at advertisements for holidays in sunny climes will reveal. The problem with these stereotypes, as with all stereotypes, is that they impoverish or misdirect thinking. Misconceptions result about where our culture fits into the world and about how we might solve our problems and take advantage of our opportunities. Opportunities for first-hand experiences through travel and communication have never been greater. Ironically, the power of virtual worlds, elaborate maps made according to unrevealed principles and concepts, has also

never been greater. Environmental education and global education need to be primarily empirical if they are to invite first-hand, reflective encounters with the natural, cultural and economic worlds. Environmental and global education require critical thinking to reveal the stereotypes underlying many representations of reality. As was remarked in a recent article in *The Economist*, "Virtual reality isn't."

The ability to move from awareness, to knowledge, to action

Writers in environmental education recognize the need to have people take personal actions that help solve environmental problems. The popular saying "Think Globally, Act Locally" might more appropriately be phrased "Think and act locally with the globe in mind." Many educators and curriculum designers understand poorly the link between awareness, knowledge and action. It is important to understand that knowledge, and certainly information, carries no automatic set of instructions for conversion into appropriate actions. Many a young scientist learns the hard way that no matter how much data he or she gathers, the data alone makes no decisions. Furthermore, some things can be learned only through action itself. Thus, a class may learn about water pollution and how to test for water quality. It may become aware of problems in a local creek. But, if the class decides to act on the problems, its members move into new territory, territory in which they will confront the need for tools and the requirement to act politically to be able to communicate with and influence various community groups. From these experiences they will gain powerful new understandings, most of which are available only by taking action. By continually disconnecting the cycle of learning from action we have removed from schooling some of the most important resources for educational development.

> Effective action on global environmental problems such as greenhouse gas emissions will have to result from millions of locally taken, personal actions.

The problem of learning to take appropriate action takes on new dimensions when viewed from a global perspective. Many of the best-known environmental success stories resulted from individuals or groups with extensive local knowledge working with great focus on a local project. Many well-known environmentalists and environmental philosophers, including Thoreau and Leopold, drew inspiration for their writings from special places of great personal significance. In a world in which many people move constantly and have little time to really absorb what is happening in a particular locale, the understanding and commitment necessary for sustained, effective action may never develop. The global traveller may have few roots anywhere. Furthermore, it is easy to be overwhelmed by the sheer variety and complexity of different cultures and settings. Effective action on global environmental problems such as greenhouse gas emissions will have to result from millions of locally taken, personal actions. Internationally, people from different cultural and national groups will have to develop the skills in communication and negotiation required for international agreements and frameworks that can nurture and give legitimacy to local action. To simultaneously develop both a sense of attachment and connection to a local, personally significant environment and a sense of global connectedness is a challenge for global environmental education.

The ability to work cooperatively with other people

No modern environmental problem can be solved by a single person. Many environmental issues are complex; they will require international cooperation as well as cooperation among neighbours in local communities. Effective skills in group processes and communication and the ability to apply them in a variety of cultural, political and economic contexts will be very important. Many specialists will have to work in interdisciplinary and cross-cultural teams. These teams will have to learn to solicit and employ citizen participation. Experts alone cannot solve environmental problems. Thus, cooperative learning, on local, regional, national and global scales, is critically important here. In the work of international environmental research and international peacekeeping we find excellent illustrations of this element of environmental literacy from a global perspective. However, the failure (or limited success) of the recent Berlin conference on greenhouse gas emissions demonstrates the urgent need for nations to learn how to cooperate and resolve conflicts in ways that result in win:win as opposed to win:lose scenarios. As long as representatives of less-developed nations believe the developed world expects their countries to pay for greenhouse restrictions, we are unlikely to make progress on this issue. The Cod War on the Grand Banks of the Atlantic will not be the last conflict over fisheries resources. If we are to avoid serious economic or even military sanctions, we will have to develop the skills of negotiation and communication essential for cooperative international problem solving and action. Schools customarily employ teaching models that require debate, role playing, and other simulations of real-life decision making. To incorporate a global perspective, students will need to apply knowledge about other nations' positions to these simulations so that they can gain the insights possible by viewing a common environmental problem from within unfamiliar roles.

The capacity to develop an aesthetic response to the environment

Many people become concerned about the environment when they first notice a degradation in the quality of their own lives—for instance, when their favourite trout-fishing stream no longer produces fish and becomes laden with pollution or silted up, or when they notice that the air they breathe no longer smells fresh, even after a spring rain, or when the sun seems to be continuously filtered through a screen of haze. Other people become aware of the shoddy quality of urban development, of housing tracts where unit after unit marches across the landscape without a break for green space or park land, of malls built more for the convenience of cars than people, or of the loss of heritage buildings. When people have a sense of loss, of eroded quality or of poor design and thoughtless planning, they are often responding as much to aesthetic dimensions of their life experiences as to scientific or economic facts.

Aesthetics and values are close relatives. Different communities, political units and cultures have different standards of aesthetics. Many fields have been greatly enriched in the aesthetic realm by cross-fertilization from one culture to another. We can learn much about the problems of agricultural practice, architecture, land-use planning, water stewardship and other environmental fields if we recognize their aesthetic dimensions and appreciate how societies in other places and times have addressed them. Again, it is essential for environmental education and international policy making to recognize that one culture's view of beauty may be quite distant from another's. Even within a single nation's boundaries, different cultures and socioeconomic units have different perspectives on nature and on the beauty and value of natural places. Hence, no consideration of the environment, whether built or natural, can be complete without contemplation of its aesthetics and of the responses these awaken in us. Such consideration will be larger and richer if informed by multicultural and multinational awareness. Reflection on experiences in environmental and cross-cultural education is a powerful tool for awakening aesthetic perception and developing understanding. Knapp (1992) has provided useful instructional ideas to help teachers systematically foster reflection.

A basic set of concepts and facts plus the ability to learn new ones and to unlearn the old

There are concepts to be learned, and useful facts to be recalled, in the course of developing environmental literacy and global understanding. Ecological principles and concepts are important organizers for experiences in the environment and provide insights applicable to critical thinking about environmental issues. Students need to understand biological and geological cycles, bioenergetics, food and energy relationships, and concepts such as adaptation and diversity. It has been said that the first photographs of the whole earth from space changed the way humans saw themselves in relation to the planet and to each other. That change in world view has great transformative power (Lovelock, 1979). At a scientific level it has impelled the current thrust of

> The recent Berlin conference on greenhouse gas emissions demonstrates the urgent need for nations to learn how to cooperate and resolve conflicts in ways that result in win:win as opposed to win:lose scenarios.

research to understand global systems and global changes. At a cultural level it has caused us to rethink the status of national boundaries and the nature of national security. Of all the new understandings required of humankind today, the ability to think of the world as one unit may be the most important. It requires us to ask more interesting questions, and to rethink old assumptions. In terms of a global cultural perspective, we are just beginning to appreciate how different and how similar humans are. We are simultaneously challenged and fascinated by human commonalities and diversities. This struggle between fear and delight, attraction and repulsion, love and hate will likely continue well into the next century. Enhanced global trade and commerce, global communications systems and world travel can powerfully contribute to the solution of human environmental and social problems, but the insights these bring will not always be pleasant. I suspect that the really interesting learnings and conversations across cultures around the globe are yet to come. Our relationships to each other and the environment will often be their focus. There is new knowledge under the sun and new ways of thinking about the world. Global education and environmental education share a commitment to nurturing both the acquisition of new knowledge and the development of new ways of thinking. If learning is seen as an act of intellectual construction, it sometimes requires deconstructing old knowledge schemes and changing old habits of mind. This is particularly important in the context of adult education. Information alone is not sufficient. People will need both time and effective assistance if they are to work through the significance of global and environmental thinking for themselves.

The capacity to use skills in eight processes: knowing, enquiring, acting, judging, opening, imagining, connecting and valuing

The skillful application of an "ecosystem" of processes is essential to effective intelligence. These processes apply not only to environmental education, but to all forms of education. To develop them fully, curricula need to be designed to systematically attend to them during students' development in the course of schooling. All need not receive equal emphasis at all times, but all need emphasis during some phases of learning. All are equally important. There is no universally appropriate, logical sequence for their use in all contexts. In some situations, students may begin with their awareness of a problem or opportunity (*opening*). In others, taking stock of what is known and developing strategies for finding out more is of central importance (*knowing* and *enquiring*). In still other situations, starting with value positions (*valuing*) may be most useful. By encountering a variety of educational problems and by learning in a variety of contexts, through a number of teaching models, students can develop proficiency in these processes, which may be focussed on issues of global, regional or local importance and scale. Thinking globally and environmentally requires their

application. Like any skills they can be enhanced through regular application and guided practice.

CLOSING THOUGHTS

Environmental educators and global educators often feel unrepresented on the curricular agenda, especially in secondary schools where traditional academic subjects such as English, physics, chemistry and history have high status or where subjects like computer science, technology, applied skills and business have won position because they are seen as having economic and vocational relevance. Global education and environmental education are not really subjects or courses to be added to the already crowded curriculum. They are ways of thinking about the curriculum: "global education calls for the infusion of a global perspective into all curriculum areas" (Tye, 1991, p. 5). They represent a basis for creating lively conversations among the traditional and the more recent disciplines and fields of study. Unfortunately, they can also suffer from a sort of tragedy of the common at the curricular level: that which belongs to every field, in effect, belongs to no field, and has no place. Curricular decisions in schools are often turf struggles and battles for status, resources, staff, and time. Trans- or metadisciplines such as global education and environmental education can easily get short shrift in these struggles. Moreover, because global education and environmental education are inherently radical in the sense that they invite reconsideration of the givens in our culture, of the fundamental assumptions, they also threaten many who see them as challenging the *status quo* they think schools should reinforce or inculcate. There is no easy answer to this problem. Global and environmental educators can make progress by practising some of their own ideas—including rather than excluding, inviting creative problem solving, developing win:win situations—and by helping more and more people to become excited by the richness their perspectives offer. In speaking about the Gaia Hypothesis, Lovelock (1979) once remarked that it was not really important whether the hypothesis was true or not; what was important was that it permitted a new or different look at familiar subjects and concepts, and raised interesting questions which could lead to novel investigations. The same might well be said by way of explaining the need to include global and environmental education in the contemporary curriculum.

REFERENCES

A survey of the Internet: The accidental superhighway. (1995, July). *The Economist*.

Bateson, G. (1979). *Mind and nature: A necessary unity*. New York: E. P. Dutton.

Case, R. (1993). Key elements of a global perspective. *Social Education, 57*(6), 318–325.

Hanvey, R. (1976). *An attainable global perspective*. New York: Global Perspectives in Education.

Knapp, C.E. (1992). *Lasting lessons: A teacher's guide to reflecting on experience*. Charleston, WV: ERIC

Clearinghouse on Rural Education and Small Schools.

Lovelock, J.E. (1979). *Gaia: A new look at life on earth*. Oxford: Oxford University Press.

McClaren, M. (1989). Environmental literacy: A critical element of a liberal education for the 21st Century. *Alces, 25*, 168–171.

McClaren, M. (1995). *Water stewardship: A guide for teachers, students, and community groups*. Victoria, BC: Ministry of Environment, Lands, and Parks.

McClaren, M. & Fulton, K. (in press). *A thematic approach to learning about global change*. Ottawa: Royal Society of Canada.

McClaren, M., & Kristjanson, E.K. (1993). *Global change and Canadians: A teachers guide*. Ottawa: Canadian Global Change Program of the Royal Society of Canada.

McClaren, M., Samples, R. & Hammond, B. (1993–1995). *Connections* (A series of books for students and teachers). Toronto: Ginn Publishing.

Ress, W.E. (1992). Ecological footprints and appropriated carrying capacity: What urban economics leaves out. *Environment and Urbanisation, 4*(2), 121–130.

Tye, K.A. (Ed.). (1991). *Global education: From thought to action*. Alexandria, VA: Association for Supervision and Curriculum Development.

This article, which is reprinted with permission, appeared originally in 1995 in G. Sniveley and A. MacKinnon (Eds.), *Thinking Globally About Mathematics and Science Education* (pp. 11-24). Vancouver: Research and Development in Global Studies, University of British Columbia. Minor alterations to the original article have been made for stylistic and format purposes.

12

MOVE OVER BUSTER: WOMEN AND SOCIAL STUDIES

JANE TURNER

PENNEY CLARK

In *The Descent of Woman*, a wonderfully entertaining book about human evolution, Elaine Morgan (1980) challenges the predominant theory by examining it from a female perspective. She arrives at a very different picture than the traditional masculine tale of how human beings evolved from apes.

Morgan begins with the same questions asked by other scientists. What happened to the apes during the twelve million year period of drought called the Pliocene? Why did our ape-ancestors become bi-pedal? How did they start using weapons? Why did the naked ape become naked? How did our sex life become so involved and confusing? Her research reveals a markedly different story than described in the classic rendition, *Naked Apes: A Zoologist's Study of the Human Animal* by Desmond Morris (1969).

Morgan explains that Morris and others posit that apes descended from the receding forests during the Pliocene and ventured into the grasslands to look for food. In order to see across the veldt they stood up, picked up weapons and ran after their prey on two legs. Because they were often away on the hunt for long periods of time, it became necessary to pair bond so that men could have women to come home to. Sex would have to be more complicated so that the pair bond would last a lifetime.

Morgan has numerous problems with the male-focussed version of the story of evolution. For instance, if men lost their body hair so that they would not overheat while on the hunt, why did women, who did not engage in the hunt, lose more hair? Why would apes stand up on two legs to run if using four was faster? How did apes become such skilled tool users? The answers, according to Morgan, as to how apes evolved into pre-humans lie in the ocean.

With no trees left to offer protection from the carnivores that stalked her, the female ape and baby would have to find another place of refuge. Because she had bi-pedal capability, she could wade into the waters of the ocean and wait out her hunter in relative safety. Most of the animals at the ocean's edge were "slower, smaller and more timid than she was herself" (Morgan, 1980, p. 19). Having a hairy body was a distinct disadvantage however, so the hair receded and was replaced by a layer of subcutaneous fat which kept her warm in the water. It was often difficult to see because of the glare of light off the ocean's surface, so body signals were not much help to communicate with others in the group. Vocal noises carried nicely over water, however. It was a distinct disadvantage to remain on all fours as it often led to drowning, so there was constant reinforcement for standing on two legs. Food was readily available, if she was able to crack open the shells that protected many of the food sources. A plethora of stones and slow moving edible objects created the right environment for the weapon user to evolve. Caves, readily available at the sea shore, provided a good place to store food so it would not be carried away by the tides, thus beginning a cave-dwelling habitat culture.

Morgan builds the story of a marine environment evolution piece by piece. She details examples of other marine mammals that are similar to humans, where no other mammalian similarity exists. Her evolutionary history, based on women's biology, makes a convincing case that descriptions of the world based solely on a male viewpoint, might radically change if approached from another perspective.

Morgan's reinterpretation of evolution raises a more general, fundamental question: If this story can be so completely reconfigured by approaching it from a woman's perspective what else would change when gender is taken into consideration? More particularly, how might taking gender into consideration affect social studies curriculum and instruction?

Morgan's reinterpretation of evolution raises a more general, fundamental question: If this story can be so completely reconfigured by approaching it from a woman's perspective what else would change when gender is taken into consideration? More particularly, how might taking gender into consideration affect social studies curriculum and instruction? Will our explanations of events and our selection of what to focus upon change if we look at events through the perspective and interests of other women? Several theorists offer approaches for including women in the study of history (Thompson Tetreault, 1987; McIntosh, 1983). Building on this work, we offer a three-tiered model of levels of inclusion of women in the history component of the social studies curriculum. We begin with the minimalist level of inclusion—what we call *an exclusive male focus*— and then move to *a supplemented male focus* and finally we consider *a gender-balanced focus*.

AN EXCLUSIVE MALE FOCUS

We refer to the minimalist level of inclusion of women as an exclusive male focus. This male world view consists of the story of male accomplishments, experiences and visions of what is important. Women are subsumed within this view of men. It is simply assumed that the experiences of males represent the experiences of all humankind. There is no recognition that women might be considered separately, as a group with its own accomplishments, experiences and visions or that their experiences can be intertwined with the experiences of men to form a holistic narrative. Women are generally absent from curricula and textbooks developed from this perspective. The few women who find their way in tend to be either queens or saints (Clark, 1995). Such women are included because they acted in the public sphere. The criteria for inclusion focus on occupations and activities that mattered to and were dominated by

men. They were "great" women on the same scale and by the same criteria as the "great" men who are included.

A junior high school textbook, *Patterns of Civilization, Volume I,* (Beers, 1983) offers a typical example of this focus. This text has a historical scope and sequence of over fifteen hundred years of European history and includes chapters on the "golden ages" of China, India and Japan. It contains only thirteen references to specific women in its index and no general reference heading for women. The few women who are included in the text—women such as Catherine the Great, Elizabeth the First and Queen Isabella of Spain—are those who would fit into the category of "great women"; those whose political, economic or military power shaped events in the same way that great men's have.

The presentation of Joan of Arc, the only woman appearing in the text who was not a member of the aristocracy or ruling class is informative. In her picture (p. 91) she is dressed in armour, holding a sword, long hair tucked behind her head. She looks like a male and is presented as a noteworthy historical character because of her male-like soldierly role in the Hundred Years War. There is no attempt to describe Joan as representative of the female gender. She is important because her actions are similar to other males. She fights for King and country, actions that are valued and emphasized in the traditional male-dominated historical canon.

A SUPPLEMENTED MALE FOCUS

History at the supplemented male focus stage retains the traditional male-based framework of the first stage. However, an effort is made to include more women by adding them along the way. This approach was a response to concerns expressed beginning in the late 1960s and 1970s regarding the absence of women in textbooks. These concerns precipitated textbook studies, first of basal readers and then of texts authorized for use in other curriculum areas. As a result of these studies, every province established criteria for authorizing texts for use in schools. Textbook publishers were obliged to include women, in what has been referred to as an 'add-women-and-stir' approach. This is achieved in several ways. Women who would have been included in the supplemented male focus continue to be included. These are the women who were prominent in the public arena of history such as Joan of Arc and Eleanor of Aquitane. Women who were famous only because they were married to prominent men, such as Amelia Douglas, wife of Sir James Douglas, first premier of British

Columbia, are included as well. Also in the text are "ordinary" women who took the time to record their day-to-day experiences; women such as Susanna Moodie and Catherine Parr Traill, early settlers in Upper Canada. Women's movements such as the struggle for suffrage and the temperance movement are also included. Even anonymous women find their way into the texts. For instance, the caption under a photograph in a secondary text on government says "This working woman . . . is protected against sexual discrimination in Canadian society" (p. 154).

Information about these women often appears in sidebars adjacent to the content of the main text. They seem to be added on to meet text adoption criteria, but do not enter into the main flow of the narrative.

Not surprisingly, this approach has been referred to disparagingly as "Filler feminism" (Lerner, Nagai & Rothman, 1995). It is deficient is several ways. Although women do appear in the texts, it is as afterthoughts to the male domination of history. In a secondary text, *Towards Tomorrow* (Morton, 1988), Emily Carr, an artist important for her depictions of First Nations life on the west coast of Canada, is referred to only in a caption along side one of her paintings, and in a sentence about Canadian nationalists encouraging Canadian culture Nellie McClung, who fought for women's rights, through her writings, offers contemporary Canadians an opportunity to understand the social, political and economic challenges faced by Prairie families at the turn of this century. McClung is not listed in the index of the text, but there is a picture of her in a section entitled, "How the War Changed Canada" where it is noted that McClung and other suffragists helped women gain the vote. Imagine the outcry of historians if Lord Durham and his report, the document that instituted responsible government for some men in Canada, was not listed in the text index and relegated to a single caption under a picture placed in the margins. Students would understand that this person and his accomplishments were really just a footnote in the important events of history. So too will be their impressions of Nellie McClung and women's suffrage. Agnes MacPhail, Canada's first female Member of Parliament shares two sentences in the text with the leader of her political party. It seems they "held yet another view. They wished Canada to disarm, renounce war and set an example to the world" (p. 98). No further information is available in the text about women's involvement and leadership in the peace movement, or about Agnes MacPhail herself, for that matter.

Women's participation in World War II is noted in this text. Two photographs portray women's participation. One shows a woman working in a nose-cone of an airplane with the caption, "As during the first World War, women took over jobs for men fighting on the front" (p. 113). As with Joan of Arc women are portrayed as important because they are replacements for men. A second picture shows women at a flight training school in Quebec, but the focus is on two young women wearing skirts, legs crossed and leaning towards each other so their heads are touching and their hands clasped. They seem to be sharing some girlish secret from the smile on one's face as she listens to her friend (p. 120). The seriousness of women's contribution to the military effort seems to be negated by the visual image presented. In no way would any of these pictures call into question traditionally held assumptions about women's role in society. This portrayal of women's activities during World War II supports the more general observation that textbooks recreate conservative or established visions of the world

The seriousness of women's contribution to the military effort seems to be negated by the visual image presented. In no way would any of these pictures call into question traditionally held assumptions about women's role in society. This portrayal of women activities during World War II supports the more general observation that textbooks recreate conservative or established visions of the world (Baldwin & Baldwin, 1992). No attempt is made to revise the record of history so that women's actions, thoughts and feelings are represented.

(Baldwin & Baldwin, 1992). No attempt is made to revise the record of history so that women's actions, thoughts and feelings are represented.

While the depiction of women has broadened, it is still very limited since most women did not participate directly in the political, military and economic events considered key from the traditional male view. Nel Noddings (1992) has argued that this approach is demeaning to women and trivializing to history because women are included in curriculum materials for achievements which would not be acknowledged if males had done them. She refers to "curriculum makers dig[ging] around in dusty archives to see if there was some female participant in an important political conference whose name can now be included in texts—even though most of the male participants will still be unnamed" (p. 231).

Noddings also points out that women have done things of great importance that have not been acknowledged because they were done by women and their deeds were not the kind recognized by traditional "malestream" history. Noddings uses the example of Emily Greene Balch, who received the Nobel Peace Prize in 1946, and yet her name is not mentioned in a major encyclopedia published in the 1950s. However, Generals Pershing and Patton are each recognized with about a column of print and a photograph. In a late seventies edition, the same encyclopedia recognizes Belch with a few lines, while giving Pershing and Patton the same recognition as previously. Noddings' concludes that Balch was included only because she was a woman and women now have to be included. "I do not believe that she is included because historians and curriculum makers have awakened to the importance of peace studies or because they now recognize the significance of work that women have found central to their lives" (p. 231).

A Gender-balanced Focus

This final level is more a goal than a reality. That goal is a synthesis which recognizes both male and female perspectives and activities. This is history from a human rather than merely a male perspective.

Although a history where women's interests, activities and achievements are treated as equal in importance to men's is the ultimate goal, this does not preclude histories based exclusively on women. These are necessary to fill a void created by mainstream history textbooks which focus mainly on the accomplishments of men. For instance, in the Yukon, a book called *Our Land Too: Women of Canada and the Northwest 1860-1914* (Moore, 1992), was recently written for use with the grade ten curriculum to address the gender gap in the history textbook currently in use. This book was not intended to replace the existing text, but rather to balance it. This text should have an important place in classrooms in the Yukon, at least until balanced history textbooks have been written.

In the same vein, the photograph and text on page 103, reproduced from *British Columbia Heritage*, is an example of efforts to show the experiences and contributions of women to the Cariboo Gold Rush, an historical event which is commonly considered to be male dominated. Again, such efforts are not intended to replace curriculum materials currently in use, but to address their gaps related to depiction of women. If these gaps are not addressed, the story remains incomplete.

Another effort to redress the imbalance is a new periodization of Canadian history based on technological, economic, social and political dimensions of women's experience (Prentice, Bourne, Cuthbert Brandt, Light, Mitchinson & Black, 1988). These feminist historians identify the following as turning points in Canadian women's history:

- the transition from a pre-industrial to an industrial society in the mid-nineteenth century. This signalled an end to family economies and resulted in the development of industries which were, in time, to employ many women outside the home.

- the achievement of prohibition and suffrage, two major goals of the first wave of the women's movement in Canada.

- the beginning of the massive entry of married women into the paid labour force, which occurred during World War II. Women began to spend a greater part of their lives working outside the home, thus making marriage a less definite transition than it had once been. (p. 13)

In a gender-balanced curriculum, historical events and movements, previously ignored in social studies curricula, would come to the fore. As an example, curricula would focus not just on war (fought primarily by men) but on peace movements (organized primarily by women). Students might examine the activities of individual activists for peace, as well as the activities of such organizations as the Women's International League for Peace and Freedom. Noddings (1992) suggests that the motives of those who make curriculum be questioned in this regard. She asks, "Why are peace and peace-making so clearly undervalued in traditional historical accounts? Has the association of women with peace aggravated the under-valuation?" (p. 232).

Separate spheres have been suggested by historians, including many feminist historians to explain the neglect of women by mainstream histories. If men occupy the public space and significant history is about politics, economics and war (public events), then obviously men will be the subject of political, military and economic history. Women, on the other hand, occupy the private sphere of domestic and family life. Social histories which make reference to domesticity and family organization would of course deal with women.

Separate spheres have been suggested by historians, including many feminist historians to explain the neglect of women by mainstream histories. If men occupy the public space and significant history is about politics, economics and war (public events), then obviously men will be the subject of political, military and economic history. Women, on the other hand, occupy the private sphere of domestic and family life. Social histories which make reference to domesticity and family organization would of course deal with women. There are important gaps in our historical understanding because the important work of women has been traditionally overlooked; the public sphere has been highlighted at the expense of the private. Histories that focus on the efforts and activities of women would fill in the gaps in our historical knowledge. Finding out what happened in the more typically female private sphere enlightens us all about the whole pattern of human development.

It is interesting to note that a focus on the private sphere not only reveals women's domestic work in the home itself (although this is not to be taken lightly), but also the work which women have done behind-the-scenes of important political events. Gail Cuthbert Brandt (1992) reminds us of the importance of the background of social events at the Charlottetown and Que-

BREAKING NEW GROUND: WOMEN IN THE CARIBOO GOLD RUSH

The "Hurdies" in Barkerville   BC Archives 95344

When asked to conjure up images of the Cariboo Gold Rush one automatically thinks of men camping by the river, living off the land and dreaming of fortune. This image, though true for some, completely ignores women's presence. Women were a vital part of the social and economic life of the Cariboo.

Women involved in the gold rush enjoyed independence and authority—two characteristics neither readily available nor socially acceptable in the south. In the Cariboo, women were less tied to social roles and more able to pursue a variety of occupations. The high point appears to have been in 1869, when twelve women were listed as businesswomen in their own right in the Business Directory. These women were responsible for running hotels, saloons, restaurants and laundries in Barkerville and surrounding area. Others shared business ownership with their husbands. Left on their own while their spouses tried to strike it rich, these women were fully capable of overseeing the day to day business affairs. Janet Morris set up her first boarding house in 1862 and later established the Pioneer Hotel in Camerontown and the Hotel de Fife on Lightning Creek. Mary Clunes ran a boarding house and sponsored several balls.

Women entrepreneurs were also found in Cariboo saloons. Known as Hurdies, the "Hurdy-Gurdy Girls" would dance, for a fee, with the miners. Arriving in Barkerville in 1865, the women charged $1.00 a dance and provided the miners with fun and companionship. The shop owners and saloon keepers were not as taken by [sic] with the Hurdies, jealous of the amount of money the dancers were able to make. The editor of the Sentinel newspaper saw it differently. He felt the Hurdies really earned their money as their style of dancing was very vigorous and involved the men tossing the women up in the air. While most of the Hurdies left the Cariboo as the rush slowed down, others remained and married Barkerville merchants.

Though women were more able to enjoy economic freedom in the Cariboo, the society was still male dominated. Male violence was a fact of life for many women, especially the Native and Chinese women. Court records show that miners used liquor to take advantage of Native women, sometimes causing their deaths. Similar incidents are evident in the Chinese community.

Some women, however, were able to seek redress in the court. In June 1865 Florence Bennet charged William Williams with breaking into her house and "putting her in great bodily feat." Found guilty, William was required to pay damages and keep the peace for six months. In December 1870, Full Moon, a Native woman, charged W.D. Moses with assault. He was fined $15.00, $4.00 of which were given to Full Moon to compensate for her town clothes. Several Chinese women, led by Mrs. Mowey, sought the aid of the court to protect them from extortion; in 1872 Soo Lang was sentenced to two years imprisonment for having attempted to exact illegal licence fees from several Chinese women.

Bringing to light the history of women's participation in the Cariboo Gold Rush gives us new images of that time. We are able to see women breaking out of the frail and quiet Victorian stereotype, becoming individuals in their own right. Janet Morris, Full Moon and Mrs. Mowey are examples of these proud and strong women of the Cariboo.

British Columbia Heritage, *October 1993. Reprinted with permission. Information for the article was originally taken from Van Kirk (1992).*

bec Conferences, prior to Confederation. It was the women who organized the balls, dinners and excursions, creating the congenial atmosphere which ultimately lead to a coming together of disparate political views, resulting in the forming of the nation. As she says, "While we cannot reconstruct the dinner conversation, there is little doubt that the women's social graces were pressed into service to help forge new political alliances. Their influence . . . was considerable" (p. 8). Cuthbert Brandt also reminds us of the importance of Anne Brown, wife of George Brown, who has been credited as a Mother of Confederation because she was able to influence Brown's attitude as a sworn enemy of John A. Macdonald and help him to see the benefits of Confederation.

However, a focus on separate spheres of activity does not provide a panacea. This approach may solidify inequities. Mary Kay Thompson Tetreault (1987) points out that the separate spheres argument often perpetuates stereotypically appropriate male and female behaviours and activities. For example, not all women support peace initiatives and many men are not war mongers. As well, notions of public and private spheres can legitimize inequality, subordinating the private sphere to the public. Paid work, valued more highly than unpaid labour in Western society, exemplifies the secondary position of private sphere activities. The dichotomy of private and public is also a fairly modern, middle class construct. Many women have never had the luxury of participating solely in the private sphere. Before the Industrial Revolution, the home and the family unit were often the site for all work. Also, economic realities prevent many contemporary women from working solely in the private sphere.

Finally, the public and private spheres are not as clearly delineated as once thought. Thatcher Ulrich's (1990) history of Martha Ballard, a seventeenth century midwife in New England, connects the private activities of a homemaker and midwife and the public, political, economic and legal events of the time. Thatcher Ulrich also shows how Martha Ballard participated in both the public and private spheres through the diversity of her economic life. Martha contributed to the family's economic well-being in several ways, including domestic tasks and her duties as a midwife, as well as her participation in a family business. With this example, Thatcher Ulrich disrupts the notion of rigid, separate spheres of men and women's work existing in binary opposition to one another. Critical analysis shows the private sphere merging with the public one.

Martha Ballard shows the mythology of the notion that there is a "timeless permanence in binary gender representations" (Scott, 1988, p. 43). The social institution of marriage and the organization of the household economy are neither fixed nor predisposing of gender roles. The roles which Martha Ballard and the other women of her community assumed partly emerged through their kinship systems, but also developed through their personal inclinations and talents, social

and political positions and their chronological ages.

The work of Thatcher Ulrich shows that the division between private and public is not so clear-cut. From the evidence available through Martha Ballard's diary, women did participate in the public sphere of the New England town of Hallowell in the seventeenth century. They were an integral part of the economy, in production, consumption and trade. They were part of the community life, through small scale politics and large scale economics. The impact of women in the town of Hallowell went well beyond the household boundaries.

IDEAS FOR INCORPORATING WOMEN IN SOCIAL STUDIES

Given that women are still not seen as an important presence in social studies curricula and textbooks, we need to consider ways of including women in historical accounts and acknowledging their experiences, thoughts and contributions. We conclude this article with a few suggestions for doing this. Some of these ideas are level-two inclusions—the supplemented focus—but others contribute towards a gender-balanced focus.

- **Biographies**. Below is a list of 100 Canadian women from which students could choose women to investigate.

Maude Abbott	Beryl Fox
Rosalie Abella	Celia Franca
Kate Aitken	Sylvie Frechette
Doris Anderson	Barbara Frum
Margaret Atwood	Nancy Green
Elizabeth Bagshaw	Raines
James (Miranda) Barry	Anne Hebert
Veronize Beliveau	Marion Hilliard
Marilyn Bell	Cora Hind
Martha Louise Black	Abby Hoffman
Roberta Bondar	Adelaide Hoodless
Marguerite Bourgeoys	Frances Ann Hopkins
Rosemary Brown	Pauline Jewett
June Callwood	Pauline Johnson
Anne Cameron	Diane
Iona Campagnola	Jones-Konihowski
Kim Campbell	Karen Kain
Maria Campbell	Joy Kogawa
Pat Carney	Minna Keene
Emily Carr	K.D. Lang
Adrienne Clarkson	Silken Laumann
Camille Claudelle	Judy LaMarsh
Anne Cools	Margaret Laurence
Sheila Copps	Monique Leyrac
Nellie Cournoyea	Dorothy Livesay
Marie de L'Incarnation	Flora MacDonald
Alice Desjardins	Agnes Macphail
Celine Dion	Nellie McClung
Amelia Douglas	Pauline McGibbon
Dionne Quintuplets	Grace McGinnis
Nicola Everton	Hannah McIntosh
Sylvia Fedoruk	Sarah McLachlan
Maureen Forrester	Audrey McLaughlin

Rita McNeil	Deborah Robinson
Helen Gregory Magill	Gabrielle Roy
Karen Magnussen	Laura Sabia
Jeanne Manae	Buffy Sainte-Marie
Clara Brett Martin	Jeanne Sauvé
Joni Mitchell	Catherine Schubert
Lucy Maud Montgomery	Pat Schulz
Susanna Moodie	Barbara Anne Scott
Anne Mortifee	Laura Secord
Alice Munroe	Shawandithit
Emily Murphy	Carol Shields
Anne Murray	Elizabeth Simcoe
Madeleine Parent	Marlene
Irene Parlby	Stewart-Strait
Catherine Parr	Emily Stowe
Traill	Jenny Trout
Julie Payette	Charlotte Whitton
Mary Pickford	Alice Wilson
Manon Rhéame	Bertha Wilson

Each student could choose a woman and write a biography complete with photograph, or, in the case of historical figures who predated photography, a drawing of how the student imagines the person might have looked. Categories of information might include: childhood, education, career choices, family life, personal characteristics, highlights in her life, setbacks and achievements. Variations on the biography are to complete a job application form or resumé on the part of the individual chosen, or compose an obituary. If these options are chosen, students should be given samples so that they can become familiar with commonly used formats.

- **Memoirs**. Students could conduct research on a female family member who is no longer alive. Sources could be other family members who could relate their memories of the individual, friends of the individual, the individual's tombstone, as well as family memorabilia such as letters, journal entries, recipes, photographs and the family bible (where people often record important family dates). Students should then write a memoir using the information they have obtained.

- **Textbook analysis**. Ask students to analyze a textbook to assess its portrayal of women. They should consider omissions as well as the way women are portrayed when present. Here are sample questions:

  - Are women visible both in the pictures and the written content of the text?

  - Are they present in numbers which seem reasonable considering the content of the text? (For instance, a text on military history could reasonably be expected to depict few women.)

  - Are women and girls shown in a variety of roles (e.g., wife, mother, worker in the paid labour force, friend, neighbour)?

  - Are women shown as contributing in important ways to their community, their employer, their family?

  - Are females of all ages depicted?

  - Are females and males shown in mutually supportive relationships?

- **Supplementary textbook passages**. Ask students to take a passage from a history textbook which omits women and rewrite it as it might have been written if the authors had taken women's perspectives and contributions into account. Examples include a war, European exploration of North America from the perspective of native women or life in a medieval castle from the perspective of a female serf.

- **Surveys**. Acquaint students with the fact that surveys of Canadian households reveal that women engage in far more housework and childcare duties than do men, regardless of whether the women work in the paid labour force. Suggest that they keep track for one week of all duties performed in their household and by whom. Remind them that some household duties are not actually performed on the premises. These would include grocery shopping, banking and purchases of other household items. Once the information is gathered it could be shared among family members and discussed.

- **Gender analysis**. Ask students to analyze a passage from a history textbook for its gendered perspective. For example, concepts such as politics, economics, security and citizenship rights may mean very different things to females and males. Textbooks traditionally approach such concepts from a stereotypically male-gender perspective. For instance, the term *security* is often used in the context of protection of national boundaries. When women discuss issues of security, they often do so in the context of personal, family and community security. Have students substitute new information that would address the topic from the other-gendered perspective. Once the analysis is completed, ask them to evaluate the differences that arise from these perspectives.

- **Women's perspectives**. Many parts of the curriculum are open to inclusion of women's history. Ask students to find topics that lend themselves to inclusion such as: labour history, the Industrial Revolution; or any social/cultural history segments, such as daily life in the Middle Ages or in an Iroquois village, immigration, improvements to democratic rights or media literacy. When including women's history, incorporate the data in ways that demonstrate to the students that this information is as important as the information about men. One way to ensure this sense of importance is to make it part of the understandings that are assessed.

FINAL THOUGHTS

It is time for privileged men to move over and make room for the marginalized, most specifically, women.

Noddings' observation that, "Women have done things of great importance that go unrecognized because they were done by women and because the focus of their efforts has not been the focus of political history" (1992, p. 231) should become a guiding principle in social studies.

Women's stories are being researched and written. Academic historians are including gender in their conceptions of history. The work that has been done and is being extended by those in the academic community needs to be included in school social studies. It isn't just for the sake of fairness and equity that we encourage their inclusion, although that is a sufficient argument when one considers that at least half of the students in social studies classrooms are females who might find their own stories fascinating. It is imperative that we expand our horizons beyond the world according to man in the interests of understanding the world we inhabit and that which we inherited. We can no longer accept half the story.

REFERENCES

Baldwin, P. & Baldwin, D. (1992). The portrayal of women in classroom textbooks. *Canadian Social Studies, 26*(3), 110-114.

Bartlett, B., Craig, R. & Sass, G. (1989). *Towards tommorrow: Canada in a changing world, government.* Toronto: Harcourt, Brace, Jovanovich.

Beers, B.F. (1983). *Patterns of civilization, Vol. I.* Scarborough, ON: Prentice-Hall.

Clark, P. (1995). *'Take it away, youth!' Visions of Canadian identity in British Columbia social studies textbooks, 1925-1989.* Unpublished doctoral dissertation, University of British Columbia.

Cuthbert Brandt, G. (1992). National unity and the politics of political history. *Journal of the Canadian Historical Association, 3,* 3-11.

Dresden Grambs, J. (1987). Commentary: Resistance to women's scholarship in the social studies. *Social Education, 52*(3), 228.

Lerner, R., Nagai, A.K. & Rothman, S. (1995). *Molding the good citizen: The politics of high school history texts.* Westport, CT: Praeger.

McIntosh, P. (1983). *Interactive phases of curricular revision: A feminist perspective.* Working Paper #124. Wellesley, MA: Wellesley College Center for Research on Women.

Moore, C. (1992). *Our land too: Women of Canada and the Northwest 1860-1914.* Whitehorse: Govt. of the Yukon.

Morgan, E. (1980). *The descent of woman.* Scarborough House, NY: Stein and Day.

Morris, D. (1967). *The naked ape.* London: Cape.

Morris, D. (1988). *Towards tomorrow: Canada in a changing world, history.* Toronto: Harcourt, Brace, Jovanovich.

Noddings, N. (1992). Social studies and feminism. *Theory and Research in Social Education, 20*(3), 230-241.

Prentice, A., Bourne, P., Cuthbert Brandt, G., Light, B.,

Mitchinson, W. & Black, N. (1988). *Canadian women: A history.* Toronto: Harcourt Brace Jovanovich.

Scott, J. (1988). Gender: A useful category of historical analysis. In *Gender and the politics of history* (pp. 28-50). New York: Columbia University Press.

Seixas, P. (1993). Parallel crises: History and the social studies curriculum in the USA. *Journal of Curriculum Studies, 25*(3), 235-250.

Staff. (1993, October). Breaking new ground: Women in the Cariboo gold rush. *British Columbia Heritage,* p. 3.

Thompson Tetreault, M.K. (1987). Rethinking women, gender, and the social studies. *Social Education, 53*(1), 170-178.

Thatcher Ulrich, L. (1990). *A midwife's tale: The life of Martha Ballard based on her diary, 1785-1812.* New York: Vintage.

Van Kirk, S. (1992). A vital presence: Women in the Cariboo gold rush, 1862-1875. In G. Creese & V. Strong-Boag (Eds.), *British Columbia reconsidered: Essays on women,* (pp. 21-37). Vancouver: Press Gang.

SUPPLEMENTARY READINGS

Belenky, M., Clinchy, B., Goldberger, N. & Tarule, J. (1986). *Women's ways of knowing.* New York: Basic Books.

Corrective Collective. (1974). *Never done: Three centuries of women's work in Canada.* Toronto: Canadian Women's Educational Press.

Creese, G. & Strong-Boag, V. (Eds.). (1992). *British Columbia reconsidered: Essays on women.* Vancouver: Press Gang.

Crocco, M.S. (1997). Making time for women's history. . .When your survey course is already filled to overflowing. *Social Education, 61*(1), 32-37.

Gaskell, J. & McLaren, A. (1987). *Women and education: A Canadian perspective.* Calgary: Detselig.

Gaskell, J., McLaren, A. & Novogrodsky, M. (1989). *Claiming an education: Feminism and Canadian schools.* Toronto: Our Schools/Our Selves Education Foundation.

Gaskell, J. & Willinsky, J. (1996). *Gender informs the curriculum: From enrichment to transformation.* New York: Teachers College Press.

Gibson, E. (Ed.). (1997). Theme issue: Women's issues in social studies. *Canadian Social Studies, 31*(2).

Holt, E. (1990). *Remember the ladies: Women in the curriculum.* ERIC Clearinghouse for Social Studies Education Digest, EDO-SO-90-2.

Klein, S. (Ed.). (1985). *Handbook for achieving sex equity in education.* Baltimore, MD: John Hopkins University.

Kirman, J. (1990). Women's rights in Canada: A sample unit using biographies and autobiographies for teaching history chronologically. *Social Education, 54,* 39-44.

McDowell, L. (1988). Coming in from the dark: Feminist research in geography. In J. Eyles (Ed.), *Research in human geography,* (pp. 155-173). Oxford: Basil Blackwell.

Nemiroff, G.H. (Ed.). (1987). *Women and men: Interdis-*

ciplinary readings on gender. Montreal: Fitzhenry & Whiteside.

Nodding, N. (1992). The gender issue. *Educational Leadership, 49*(4), 65-70.

Pratt, G. (1993). Feminist geographies. In R.J. Johnston, D. Gregory, D.M. Smith (Eds.), *Dictionary of human geography* (3rd. ed.). Oxford: Blackwell.

Stevens, A.M. & McDowell, L. (1978). Filling in the picture: Resources for teaching about women in Canada. *History and Social Science Teacher, 14*(1), 7-14.

Strong-Boag, V. (1988). *The new day recalled: Lives of girls and women in English Canada, 1919-1939.* Toronto: Copp Clark Pitman.

Strong-Boag, V. & Fellman, A.C. (Eds.). (1991). *Rethinking Canada: The promise of women's history* (2nd ed.). Toronto: Copp Clark Pitman.

Strong-Boag, V. (1990). Writing about women. In J. Schultz (Ed.), *Writing about Canada: A handbook for modern Canadian history* (pp. 175-200). Scarborough, ON: Prentice-Hall.

Theme issue. (1989). *History and Social Science Teacher, 25*(1).

ADDITIONAL RESOURCES

Memoirs, Autobiographies and Biographies

Berton, L.B. (1954). *I married the Klondike.* Toronto: Little, Brown.

Campbell, M. (1973). *Halfbreed.* Toronto: McClelland and Stewart.

(1974-1992). *The Canadians Series.* Toronto: Fitzhenry & Whiteside.

Kate Aitken	*Lucy Maude Montgomery*
Emily Carr	*Emily Murphy*
Marion Hilliard	*Catherine Schubert*
E. Cora Hind	*Laura Secord*
Nellie McClung	*Elizabeth Semcoe*
Aimee Semple McPherson	*Emily Stowe*

Carpenter, J. (1977). *Fifty-dollar bride.* Sidney, BC. Gray Publishing.

Carr, E. (1966). *Growing pains.* Toronto: Clarke Irwin.

Chong, D. (1994). *The concubine's children.* Toronto: Penguin.

Cosgrain, T. (1972). *A woman in a man's world.* Toronto: McClelland and Stewart.

Goudie, E. (1973). *Woman of Labrador.* Toronto: Peter Martin Associates.

Jameson, A.B. (1932/1965). *Winter studies and summer rambles in Canada.* Toronto: McClelland and Stewart.

LaMarsh, J. (1968). *Memoirs of a bird in a gilded cage.* Toronto: McClelland and Stewart.

Langton, A. (1950). *A gentlewoman in Upper Canada.* Toronto: Clarke Irwin.

Maynard, F.B. (1973). *Raisins and almonds.* Markham, ON: Paperjacks.

McClung, N. (1965). *The stream runs fast: My own story.* Toronto: Thomas Allen and Son.

Moodie, S. (1852/1962). *Roughing it in the bush.* Toronto: McClelland and Stewart.

Tippett, M. (1994). *Emily Carr: A biography.* Toronto: Stoddart.

Traill, C.P. (1926/1971). *The backwoods of Canada.* Toronto: McClelland and Stewart.

National Film Board Films

And we knew how to dance: Women in World War I. Twelve Canadian women, aged between 86 and 101, recall their entry into munitions factories and farm labour.

Attention: Women at work! A documentary about four women in nontraditional jobs.

Black mother, black daughter. An exploration of the lives and experiences of Black women in Nova Scotia.

The burning times. An in-depth look at the witch-hunts that swept through Europe a few hundred years ago.

Canada's first woman MP. A biographical study of Agnes Campbell MacPhail, Canada's first woman Member of Parliament. This is an abridged version of *The lady from Grey County.*

Doctor, lawyer, Indian chief. An exploration of the crucial roles native women have played historically in their cultures. The focus is on five native women across Canada.

Doctor woman: The life and times of Dr. Elizabeth Bagshaw. A biographical study of Dr. Bagshaw, one of the first female doctors in Canada.

Great grant mother. An examination of the contributions of women to the settlement of the Canadian West.

A love affair with politics: A portrait of Marion Dewar. An examination of the political career of Marion Dewar, mayor of Ottawa for seven years.

Media & society: Images of women. An exploration of the relationship between media images and the way women see themselves and are defined by others.

Moment of light. A depiction of Evelyn Hart, one of the world's greatest interpreters of classical ballet.

Non-traditional jobs for women. Three films dealing with an apprentice engineer (*Pretend you're wearing a barrel*), a railroad "yardman" (*She's a railroader*) and an independent drywall contractor (*Laila*).

No way! Not me! Rosemary Brown, feminist, activist and former NDP member in British Columbia deals with the topic of female poverty.

Prairie women. An examination of rural prairie women in the interwar period, who organized around such issues as better health care, access to birth control, improved legal rights for women and peace and disarmament.

Women and work. An examination of the workplace today from a female perspective in a series of four videos: *A balancing act, Careers to discover, The glass ceiling* and *A web not a ladder.*

13

Peace Education: Politics in the Classroom?

Susan Hargraves

Paper cranes fill school corridors. Students write to world leaders asking them to ban nuclear weapons. Others make placards bearing anti-nuclear slogans and participate in mock protest marches through the local community. Feeling uncomfortable? You're not alone.

In the early 1980's, an increasingly popular peace movement gained the attention of many elementary and secondary educators all over North America. Working independently and in groups, both with and without school district support, many teachers began to raise the issue of nuclear war and its prevention in their classrooms. This movement grew out of a sense of urgency, fueled by the belief that nuclear war was imminent. The Bulletin of the Atomic Scientists regularly published a picture of a clock which indicated just how close the world was to nuclear war. During this period, the clock reached "two minutes to midnight." The movement also grew out of a sense of increasing alarm, as young people all over the world reported fear and hopelessness regarding their future. An almost evangelical fervor marked much of the resulting classroom activity. Not surprisingly, so did controversy.

Early Controversy over Peace Education

"Propaganda!" "Advocacy!" "Indoctrination!" These were some of the criticisms leveled at peace educators in the early 1980's. In an article titled "Terrorizing Children," two critics complained

> nuclear curricula, presumably designed to ease a child's anxiety, in fact introduce him [sic] to fears he has probably not entertained, and exacerbate any that he has. The child is provided with false or misleading political information which makes national policy seem capricious or malevolent or irrational. He is on the one hand taught virtues of helplessness, on the other recruited to the propaganda purposes of the teacher. (Adelson & Finn, 1985, p. 35)

As these comments suggest, at the heart of the controversy was whether or not peace and nuclear war-related issues belonged in the classroom, and if so, how could they be taught in a non-harmful and non-politicized manner. While most people agreed that nuclear war was to be avoided, there was no consensus as to how that was to be achieved. Some believed the very presence of nuclear weapons invited war, while others believed the opposite. The problem for teachers was how to reconcile these competing perspectives and to present age-appropriate, reliable information to students. Some of the resulting educational efforts have been delivered with more enthusiasm than finesse. These failings, however, can reasonably be attributed to the growing pains associated with the beginnings of any new field, especially given the urgency of this issue at the time.

In this article I step back from the heyday of the early 1980's to trace peace education's development from its origins after World War II to the present. In so doing I address the confusing and sometimes conflicting definitions and understandings of peace education. As well I distinguish between the content focus of peace education and the mind-sets that should underlie any investigation in this field. Using classroom examples I illustrate how teachers can responsibly develop these mind-sets in their students so that they may view and act differently on the world stage, for instance, in supporting peace efforts in war torn countries and using non-violent ways to settle disputes in the home and school.

ORIGINS AND DEFINITIONS OF PEACE EDUCATION

While peace education became a popular movement in the early 1980's, it originated earlier at the end of World War II and the establishment of the United Nations. The preamble to the UNESCO (United Nations Educational, Social and Cultural Organization) charter states the goal of peace education at this time: "since wars begin in the minds of men [sic], it is in the minds of men that the foundations of peace must be constructed." Initially the purpose of peace education was to prevent war. In the early 1980's the goal had become even more specific—to prevent nuclear war. Since the early 1980's, peace education has shifted from an exclusive preoccupation with the nuclear issue towards a wider range of social and environmental concerns. Like other burgeoning fields, peace education has matured since its early days.

The current focus is on individuals to create peace in the world first through their own actions and interpersonal relationships. Conflict resolution and peer mediation have become central to the peace education curricula of the 1990's. This shift in focus is largely the result of increased interpersonal violence. It is widely known that youth violence is on the increase in the United States where "Gunfire kills 15 individuals under the age of 19 daily" and "the homicide rate among teenage males (15-19 years) more than doubled between 1985 and 1991" according to Johnson and Johnson (1995, p. 2). In Canada between 1986 and 1991 the number of juveniles (12-17 years) charged with violent crimes increased from 9,300 to 18,800, or 102% (MacDougall, 1993, p. 2). It is unclear whether this represents an increase in violence or in the reporting of violence. Although no hard data exist regarding violence in Canadian schools, teachers in surveys regularly report a high level of concern. In recent years, teachers of younger and younger children now also report violent behaviour as a concern.

A 1993 Envirionics Research Poll reported that Canadians ranked school violence first before academic standards, as the issue of greatest educational concern (91% Favour Testing, Poll Shows, 1993, p. A8).

Further fuelling the impetus for peace education is a deepening awareness of more subtle forms of violence in schools and in communities. Particular attention is being paid to the phenomenon of bullying. It is not clear if the incidence of bullying is on the rise, or not. This is due in part to the under-reporting by victims, as well as the carefully hidden behaviour of most bullies. Estroff Marano observed that, "bullying inhabits a covert kids-only world—right under the noses of adults" (1995, p. 62). Teachers and administrators often claim that bullying does not happen in their schools. Parents rarely hear about incidents when their kids are victimized. Quite a different picture emerges, however, when students are given the opportunity to report their experiences anonymously (Olewus, 1989).

Since the early 1980's, peace education has shifted from an exclusive preoccupation with the nuclear issue towards a wider range of social and environmental concerns. . . . The current focus is on individuals to create peace in the world first through their own actions and interpersonal relationships.

In a dramatic and provocative study, Debra Pepler of York University took over 52 hours of videotape on Toronto school playgrounds. She documented over 400 episodes of bullying including a 37 continuous minute incident of kicking and punching that took place in a playground while supervisors were close at hand (Estroff Marano, 1995, p. 65). At one point during a videotaped episode a supervisor checks to see that everything is okay and all three children, including the victim, report that they are just playing. Nevertheless, victims often report deep scarring that can have long-lasting consequences from such incidences. Schools have not yet fully recognized the seriousness of this problem, nor how to deal with it. This is very much a growing edge of peace education in the nineties.

Long-time peace educator, Betty Reardon (1988, p. xii) believes that comprehensive peace education has a place at every level of schooling, and in every subject area and should operate in all spheres of informal or lifelong education. According to Reardon, peace education is global education in that it relates to all human interactions on and with the earth. According to this definition, there is very little education that is *not* peace education.

Although the intent of Reardon's definition of peace

education is to "open a door widely" so that many may enter, I suspect that it has the opposite effect. Educators who are not deterred outright by such an enormous and awesome task may stumble while trying to address the overarching and unfocussed content.

Other writers define peace education as one of four components of global education, along with environmental, human rights and development education (Greig, Selby & Pike, 1987). These authors distinguish between broad and narrow foci for each of these areas of study. Narrowly focussed, each field remains relatively distinct:

> A purely local or biological approach to environmental education, for instance, has little or nothing in common with studying poverty in the 'Third World' (narrowly focussed development education) or with studying war and disarmament (narrowly focussed peace education). (Greig, Pike & Selby, 1987, p. 29)

Conversely, when broadly focussed each of the four 'educations' converge. For example, conflict of any kind, whether interpersonal or international, often arises over the distribution or sharing of limited resources. This is true for siblings fighting over a toy and for nations fighting over oil fields or fishing rights.

This distinction between a broad and narrow focus sets a helpful overall picture or context for peace education, illustrating both the areas of overlap with related areas of study and places where peace education stands alone.

In the interests of further clarifying the notion of peace education it is helpful to borrow a distinction between the substantive and perceptual elements of a "global perspective" (Case, 1991). The "substantive" element refers to knowledge about people, places, events and issues beyond student's own communities and country, and includes knowledge of global systems, international events, world cultures and global geography. The "perceptual" element may be described metaphorically as the "lens" through which the substantive elements are viewed. As such it includes one's point of view—the matrix of concepts, orientations, values, sensibilities and attitudes through which students perceive the world. This distinction may be applied to peace education.

SUBSTANTIVE ASPECTS OF PEACE EDUCATION

The "substantive" dimension within peace education focusses mainly on knowledge about the root causes and elimination of violence in its various forms. Violence includes overt acts resulting from unresolved conflict as well as the more subtle forms inherent in the structures of a relationship or of a society, known as "systemic violence." At the heart of this concept is the interrelationship of violence, aggression, inequity and injustice within and between systems, which is characterized by conflict and may operate at any level: personal/local, national/global and so on.

At the level of broad focus, topics may include any area where conflict arises: economic sustainability and development; self-determination, human rights and international aid to name a few.

At the level of narrow focus, peace education is concentrated on themes such as conflict resolution, community building and violence prevention. Until recently these topics have been covered by elementary teachers as aspects of classroom management and by secondary teachers in guidance and health courses. This has begun to change somewhat. In the last ten years, there has been a proliferation of programs promoting social skills, conflict resolution, violence prevention and peer mediation.[1] Despite a lack of systematic measurement of the effectiveness of such programs schools and teachers are embracing them in increasing numbers.

This is due in part to a growing need, as violence becomes a day to day reality in schools. Substantive peace education has at its core promoting knowledge about violence in all its forms. As vast a task as all this represents, peace education would fall short of fulfilling its goals if it stopped here. In addition to knowledge, peace education also seeks to influence attitudes and values through the perceptual mode.

PERCEPTUAL ASPECTS OF PEACE EDUCATION

The perceptual aspect refers to a way of approaching and considering information in a global and interdependent world. It is the lens through which information is viewed. Depending on the lens that is used, the information may remain distant and irrelevant or unused.

Put more boldly, unless teachers understand the perceptual dimension of peace education, they run the risk of wasting their time. With violence prevention programs, for example, a frequent lament is that while students know "all the steps" and can "go through the motions" of resolving a conflict, they often choose not to act peacefully on their own. Without a shift in mindset, without looking at things differently, mastery of all the excellent information and techniques will make no difference. In fact, the desired ends may be subverted as students recognize the "formulas" of resolving conflict or community building and throw up barriers of resistance.

In describing the perceptual aspect of peace education five mind-sets are useful.[2] They are:

- perspective consciousness
- systems thinking
- complexity orientation
- responsibility focus
- action orientation

Although somewhat discrete, these mind-sets overlap and exist in a kind of dynamic tension with one another.

Each mind-set will be discussed separately. In each case a rationale for the mind-set will be provided, skills necessary to its development will be discussed and activities which have been useful in helping students develop the mind-set will be described. The classroom examples are most often drawn from conflict resolution, community building and violence prevention curricula and frequently have application to more than one mind-set. For example, an activity listed in "Developing Complexity Orientation" may also be appropriate in "Developing Perspective Consciousness."

These mind-sets are more than ideals or attitudes to be achieved. Within each is a set of developmental tasks and skills that can be learned, even by very young children. Studies with young children show that many appear to learn systems-thinking remarkably quickly (Roberts, 1978, 1983). This is not to say that the skills and strategies are fully articulated and refined. There is still much work to be done in developing strategies that achieve identified goals.

Developing perspective consciousness

Perspective consciousness is a term used by Hanvey (1987) in his well-known work on global education. He defines it as an "awareness that each of us has a worldview or 'cognitive map' that is not universally shared by others and may be shaped by factors we are unaware of and unable to control" (p. 85). It is this awareness that forms the foundation of all conflict reso-

lution. I add to Hanvey's concept the practice of perspective-taking or empathy because this mind-set can only be achieved when one has stood in another's shoes and seen the world through another's eyes.

How does one achieve an awareness that how I see the world is different from how others see it and that doesn't necessarily make you wrong and me right? Furthermore, is it developmentally appropriate, or even possible, for even very young children to do so? Or, stated another way, isn't it appropriate for young children to be egocentric? What role does empathy play in developing this mind-set? In order to be aware of others' perspectives, is it necessary to stand in their shoes?

While we may start out placing ourselves at the center of the universe, it is both possible and desirable to move beyond that view and to do so early in life. In conflict situations, much of the heat is generated by an inability to appreciate another point of view. Conversely, resolution is greatly facilitated when disputants can understand that there is more than one perspective on a given issue. This paves the way for more than one "right" answer.

The central skills in developing perspective consciousness are empathy building, suspending judgment (the ability to listen to a contrary point of view in an accepting, not dismissive frame of mind) and good communication (particularly listening and questioning).

PERSPECTIVE CONSCIOUSNESS ACTIVITIES

- **Retelling the story**

  An activity that is enjoyed by students of all ages is to take a familiar story, usually a folk or fairy tale, and have them retell it from a different point of view. While this may seem an appropriate elementary activity, secondary students enjoy and benefit fom it too. A published example of this is *The True Story of the Three Little Pigs by A. Wolf* as told by John Scieczka (1989) in which the wolf tells quite a different story from the familiar one. Students can rewrite other familiar stories, changing them as required by the shift in point of view. This activity also works well as a role play or drama. Older students can apply this strategy beyond literature to factual accounts of events in the news or in history. A grid can be developed to classify how various individuals might view an event or issue differently.

- **Adversarial roles**[3]

  In conflict scenarios it is useful to have adversaries role play each other. If emotions are running high, this is best done by separating students and working with each independently. This technique has proven very effective in breaking conflict deadlocks.

  Students are most successful using this technique when they have had prior experience role-playing conflict scenarios that don't involve them personally. Without the emotional heat of a real conflict, students are better able to acquire new skills. Teachers can generate a list of typical conflicts (e.g., someone took another student's book without asking, a student is being excluded by former friends) or students can anonymously write their own list of typical conflicts at home or school. A simple, two person conflict is chosen. In pairs, each take a role and play it for two or three minutes. The teacher then calls, "Switch roles" and the students take on the role of the other character. The goal of this exercise is not necessarily to resolve the conflict, but rather to experience the change in perspective that accompanies a changed role. The experience can be de-briefed by inviting comments from students about how it felt to take on the role of their adversary and what they learned from it.

  This technique works well also in helping students appreciate the complexity of a controversial issue. Instead of taking on one role, students take on many different roles related to the same issue. This can be

---

done using a cooperative learning model with a jig-saw format. Students become "experts" in a certain point of view, present their case, then assume another, somewhat contrary point of view. This activity works particularly well with secondary students, but can be adapted for elementary.

- **The believing game**

  A powerful tool for building perspective-consciousness, developed by Educators for Social Responsibility (ESR), is called "The Believing Game" (Elbow, 1983). This has been used extensively with secondary students, but skilled elementary teachers can adapt it for younger students. It is not, however, an introductory level activity. It should be preceded by experience in identifying one's own, then others' points of view.

  The typical process for playing the game is to have a representative (real or role-played) present an *unpopular* view to a class, such as banning the eating of meat or advocating nuclear war. Prior to this, students outline their contrary belief by making a list of twenty reasons for eating meat or eliminating nuclear weapons, for example. Students are asked *temporarily* to suspend their beliefs and embrace the speaker's ideas. They do this by silencing any disagreement "inside their heads" and by asking questions that would help them accept this different point of view. Examples of these questions might be: "Tell me more about how you came to that decision/belief" or "Help me understand why you believe x" or "Can you tell me more about your experiences or background that have led you to this conclusion?" As this questioning continues, students "affirm" those parts of the belief that they can now accept. For example, they might say something like, "I can accept that having a strong disincentive for using nuclear weapons is necessary to keeping peace." At the same time they may be silencing internal voices of disbelief, such as, "But using nuclear weapons as a disincentive may lead to accidental nuclear war." A technique for silencing voices of doubt is to have students imagine doubts as logs floating down a river; when doubts appear, let them float by. Little by little, the class identifies what they are able to "believe."

  After the presentation and question-answer sessions are concluded the experience is de-briefed in two parts. The first part de-briefs the process by asking questions such as, "What was that like for you?' or "What was difficult for you?" or "What surprised you in that experience?" A key question at this point is to ask how students' thinking has changed as a result of this activity. It is important to note that this process can cause anxiety for students, because it asks them to move outside the security of familiar and comfortable beliefs. The more deeply held the belief, the greater the potential for anxiety. Sensitive de-briefing of the process is essential.

  The second part of the de-briefing is equally important. This is the place where students now disagree with what they have heard. It is helpful if the class has previously articulated their contrary beliefs in some detail before beginning "The Believing Game." At this point the list of reasons which students had generated initially would be reviewed and changes made. If the "game" has been successful, students will want to modify their reasons. This does not necessarily mean that they will have completely changed their minds and adopted the opposing point of view. Instead, what is hoped for is that their reasons for believing whatever position they choose will be better ones, based on a deeper appreciation of the competing tensions in this issue.

Developing systems thinking

Systems thinking has been described as "a discipline for seeing wholes" (Senge, 1990, p. 68). It is a movement away from reductionist, simplistic cause-effect linking to seeing patterns, structures and interrelationships. In the practice of conflict resolution it builds on perspective consciousness by allowing for shared problem-ownership rather than an adversarial "us vs. them" orientation. It also provides a way to see a problem as something more than simply the actions of an adversary, but rather the interweaving of a variety of factors and circumstances.

Senge (1990) said it best: "Living systems have integrity. Their character depends on the whole" (p. 66). When we try to reduce living, dynamic entities into their component parts, we not only lose something in the process, we lose everything. As Senge points out, "Dividing an elephant in half does not produce two small elephants" (p. 66). What we have instead is a mess. To understand system—whether we're talking about the workings of government, the growth of democracy or a conflict between two individuals—we need to look beyond linear chain-reactions to a dynamic whole with patterns of interrelationship, rather than snapshots frozen in time.

The basic skills involved in systems thinking include seeing interrelationships where actions influence one another (represented by a cycle or systems-loop) and finding patterns over time (cycles and series of connected cycles). Using the arms race as an example, Senge suggests that its causes lie not in competing political ideologies, "but in a way of thinking both sides have shared" (p. 70). He describes how the Americans looked at Soviet arms, perceived a threat and built up U.S. arms. The Soviets did the same in reverse. Each blamed the other's arms build up as the cause of the arms race.

Senge suggests that they were caught in a cycle of escalating aggression, where each moved further and further from its goal of decreased threat. This can be illustrated by taking each of the straight lines that represent the isolated, cause-effect thinking of both the Americans and Soviets and interrelating them as reflected in the circle on the right.

The core skills of systems thinking involves finding patterns, connections and relationships between events or persons which may have been viewed in isolation. Flow charts, systems loops and web charts are graphic ways to represent this approach.

In interpersonal conflicts, children and adults often identify the cause as something the other party said or did. A systems thinking approach to conflict resolution changes that. To paraphrase Senge, your enemy is not to blame. You and the cause of your problems are part of the same system: "The cure lies in your relationship with your enemy" (p. 67). The cartoon character Pogo went one step further when he said, "We have seen the enemy and he is us."

THE ARMS BUILD-UP CYCLE

USSR arms itself

Need to build USSR arms

Threat to Americans

Threat to Soviets

Need to build US arms

US arms itself

SYSTEMS THINKING ACTIVITIES

• **Breaking the cycle - Elementary**

A strategy similar to Senge's cycle is helpful in getting elementary children to see their actions as part of a dynamic set of interacting factors. Begin with a chalk or flannel board and a set of cards with masking tape on the back. Have students generate a list of typical interpersonal conflicts they experience with their peers. Be ready to provide examples of your own if students are unable to think of any (e.g., someone took someone else's book, pencil, lunch, seat, best friend and so on). Place cards at the top of three columns with the following headings, "Feel," "Think," "Do." Using one of the examples, ask students in turn what they might feel, think and do in response. For example, if someone takes your book you might *feel* "angry," *think* "I'm going to get even" and *do* something to hurt them as much or a little more. Write their responses on cards and place them under the appropriate heading. Ask them next to speculate what the other person will feel, think and do in response. Again write these on the appropriate cards, placing them under the appropriate headings. Students may be quite concrete in their descriptions, for instance, "I'll break his pencil," rather than "I'll get even." Work with their statements to repeat the pattern as long as interest as high. Then ask if anyone can see a pattern. Work toward generic descriptions. Write those headings on cards and ask if anyone can put the cards in a loop or circle instead of a line. You will end up with something like this:

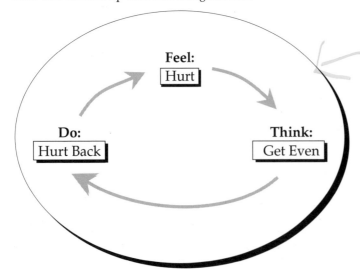

Feel: Hurt

Think: Get Even

Do: Hurt Back

Label this a Conflict Escalation Cycle and explain that it is a pattern that fits many escalating conflicts. Students can then use the model to develop examples with their own conflicts. These may be invented or drawn from their own experience.

To break the cycle, ask children what they could do to change the pattern and de-escalate conflict, or improve the situation. It might be helpful to characterize the previous pattern as an "enemies" cycle and this one as a "friends" cycle. In other words ask the students to imagine that the person who took the initial action is their best friend, rather than someone they don't like. In that case, what might they feel if she took their book. They might feel mildly annoyed, or curious about why she took it without asking first and they might think, "Oh well, I guess she had a good reason, I think I'll ask her."

Work with students to create concrete examples of de-escalating conflict scenarios. They will need external guidance in extended practice before they are able to do this independently, because it runs counter to much of their experience and the dominant themes in the media. Once children have mastered these two cycles they may apply them to situations beyond their personal experience—stories they are reading, movies they have seen or current events they have collected from the newspaper. Additionally, once the notion of a reinforcing loop is understood they can develop other examples such as the food chain, the precipitation cycle, developing physical fitness and so on. This simple first step is foundational to its use in more sophisticated and complex extensions.

- **Breaking the cycle - Secondary**

As a starting point secondary teachers may choose an escalating conflict drawn from historical events (e.g., the FLQ Crisis, the start of W.W.I, the end of the Cold War) or contemporary dilemmas (e.g. Hutu-Tutsi conflict in Africa, indigenous people's struggle for self-determination) and illustrate the system as it is or was, then experiment with breaking the cycle by changing single events (e.g., sending in a peacekeeping force, military intervention or economic aid). The goal is to see how breaking the cycle can change a negative dynamic into a positive one, in much the same way as Soviet president Gorbachev did by behaving very differently from his predecessors and interrupting the cycle of the arms race. The success of this activity comes from the graphic representation of the information. As such it may be useful to have secondary students work with cards they can manipulate before they write the cycles on paper.

- **Wooly thinking**[4]

A simple, but effective way to illustrate the notion of a system is easily conducted with a group of students and a ball of wool (it should be quite large, and works best if it is multi-colored). Have students sit in a circle. Hold a discussion which involves all students in the classroom. The topic could be related to a unit under study, to classroom life (e.g., criteria for a project, questions to ask a guest) or life outside the classroom (e.g., favorite movies, if I won the Lottery). The teacher begins the discussion, holding the ball of wool and passing it to the first speaker, while still holding onto the end of the wool. The speaker holds the ball of wool while speaking, then passes it to the next speaker while still holding onto the wool, keeping the piece of wool between the teacher and the first speaker taut. This process continues back and forth across the circle for the duration of the discussion. At the end of the time, a web has been woven that connects all members of the group. It will be random, in accordance with the discussion. It will also be beautiful; a work of art. Students can make observations about their connections and the pattern created. They can draw parallels between interactions in this system and others with which they are familiar (e.g., hockey teams, their family, the food chain). The concrete representation provided by the web can be very useful in helping students understand more abstract systems.

Developing complexity orientation

Complexity orientation refers to an expectation that issues (whether of conflict, international development, desertification or municipal politics) are often more complex than they first appear, especially as presented by a strong advocate or opponent. This orientation encourages us to de-polarize issues; to move beyond simplistic either/or, black and white perspectives. Case describes it as "a skepticism about accepting simple explanations in the first place" (1993, p.12). This orientation allows students to move beyond stereotypes and overgeneralizations about people or cultures.

It is often said, "things are rarely as they seem." This is particularly true in conflict situations. Complexity orientation seeks to develop in students an attitude or habit that allows them to suspend judgment when first encountering a new idea, opposing viewpoint or person from a different cultural background so that they may appreciate this new information or person with authenticity, not caricature.

Developing complexity in one's thinking may be done through conversation or through more traditional forms of investigation. In conversation, the skills of good communication apply: listening (including active listening), making eye contact (where culturally appropriate), maintaining open body language and asking open-ended questions. Asking questions is itself an art requiring practice and refinement.

In deriving information from sources other than conversation, the tools of good information analysis apply, including finding information in a variety of sources, detecting bias, identifying assumptions, separating fact from opinion and formulating good research questions.

COMPLEXITY ORIENTATION ACTIVITIES

- **Exploring assumptions[5]**

A successful technique for promoting complexity orientation is to begin an inquiry by posing three simple questions:

- What do I know for sure about x?
- What do I think I know?
- How can I find out more?

Early primary students studying families might begin with a webbing activity asking first, "What do we know for sure about families? Children typically respond, "They all have moms and dads." Teacher records response. Someone else says, "My dad doesn't live with us, so my family is just my mom and my sister and I." Debate probably ensues. Teacher underlines initial response, noting that we're now uncertain that families have moms and dads. The teacher then asks, "How can we find out?" The children make suggestions, which form the next steps in the inquiry. And so the process continues. Starting with assumptions drawn from the children, the teacher presents examples and challenges that complicate the issue. Pupils revise assumptions based on new information, proceed to gather more information and break down stereotypes in the process.

This simple technique teaches children that issues are rarely as simple as they first appear. They also learn that their perspective is probably insufficient to paint a full and accurate picture; they need the perspectives of others to fully understand the issue. This process also serves to validate the individual's point of view, communicating that each voice needs to be heard. In this gentle way young children learn to challenge assumptions and to beware of their own biases.

With older students a more sophisticated approach suggests the following questions:

- How do we know what we know?
- Whose facts are these?
- What biases are inherent here?
- What assumptions underlie this position?
- What is it about the individual who holds these views that has contributed to this position?
- What is it about me that makes me sympathetic/antagonistic to these views?
- What are the economic, social, cultural, historical or environmental factors that are pertinent here?
- What are the interests behind the position?

Whereas elementary students began with a familiar concept like "families," secondary students may apply these questions to more complex concepts such as human rights, self-determination, sustainable development or global citizenship. They can begin by defining these terms from their own understanding, then look to other sources to amplify their view. In making such comparisons, it is desirable to choose examples that represent various points of view, not polar opposites. In complicating thinking, the goal is to move beyond oversimplification, a black and white view of issues. A rule of thumb is to have students seek out three to five different points of view on any given issue. They may use a variety of sources including print and non-print materials.

- **On a continuum**

Students choose a controversial issue (e.g., logging in old growth forests, year-round schooling, corporal punishment, assisted suicide, legalization of marijuana) and identify its polarities. This may be done graphically by placing opposing views at either end of a continuum (e.g., suicide is always wrong; suicide is always right). Students then determine other points of view that fall between the two extremes and place them on the continuum appropriately (e.g., suicide may be right under certain circumstances). Beneath each position students identify the supporting values, assumptions, beliefs and experiences. This is what is known as the "interests" behind the position.[6] Identifying the interests is a powerful tool that greatly facilitates resolution; it does so by complicating the issue. In so doing, it allows disputants to identify more than simply their oppositional views and to find areas of agreement or "common ground."[7]

- **Anger mountain**[8]

  In anger management lessons it is common to represent anger as a mountain. Students then learn about the escalating and de-escalating phases of an angry episode in terms of climbing and descending the mountain (e.g., the triggering event, mild discomfort, building anger, rage and so on). They learn to gauge points at which they can problem-solve, need to cool down or back off. In teaching for complexity, it is helpful to create the understanding that anger is usually a secondary emotion. Most children and many adults can recognize and identify their anger, but are unaware of the strong feeling(s) which preceded it. One way to build this understanding is to have students draw "anger mountain," then create and label layers of strata underneath the surface. These layers represent the emotions which are behind the anger; often hurt or pain. With older students, it may be useful to talk of the "mask" of anger, which hides deeper, more subtle feelings. They can list the other feelings they have in addition to anger or they can draw a picture of a mask and symbolically represent the other feelings behind the mask.

Developing responsibility focus

Responsibility focus is a mind-set that says, "What is my part in this and what can I do about it?" In conflict situations it subverts the tendency to find someone else to blame and then solve the problem by prescribing for the "other" a solution. In psychological terms, this mind-set can also be described as an "internal locus of control." In other words "an individual perceives that he causes his own outcomes" (Curwin & Mendler, 1988, p. 29). These authors conclude, "The degree of responsibility we take for our actions is directly related to our locus of control. The more internal we are, the more responsible" (p. 29). Conversely, individuals who blame circumstances, people or events beyond their control for the course of their lives are said to have an "external locus of control." These people experience life as something that happens to them. An example of this outlook is described in the following anecdote:

> A friend once told me the story of a little boy he coached in Little League, who after dropping three fly balls in right field, threw down his glove and marched into the dugout. "No one can catch a ball in that darn field," he said. (cited in Senge, 1990, p. 19)

Responsibility focus builds on the notion of interconnectedness and acknowledges that what I think, say or do affects me and the world I inhabit. It looks for ways that individuals can have impact, both in their closest relationships and in the world at large.

Students may possess vast amounts of knowledge about peace and elimination of violence—its essential nature, conditions required to achieve it both personally and globally, likely obstacles and how they can be overcome—and may have been trained in all the relevant methodologies such as anger management, conflict resolution, negotiation, mediation, community building and more, and yet do nothing to achieve a more peaceful and harmonious world. If they have well-developed, extensive knowledge and skills, yet believe that problems are "out-there" for someone else to solve, little will have been accomplished. Achieving a responsibility focus is to see oneself as powerful, in control and able to have an impact and serves to pave the way toward peace and elimination of violence.

Community building (Peck, 1987) activities provide effective ways for students to learn responsibility. Nash (1986) describes the process and its results this way,

> It means inviting students into the process by which the community is shaped, challenging them to think about what it means to be a responsible member of the group. If you feel controlled by others and have to accept living by their orders or rules, you have no need to control yourself. But if you are included in solving the problems of living in community and shaping the rules, you need to exercise more self-control because you are being treated as a responsible person. Instead of trying to beat the system, students become part of the system they are helping to create. (p. 26)

Ultimately, the only way to teach children responsibility is to give them opportunities to be responsible. Although this sounds like a truism, surprisingly few adults are comfortable with or skilled at giving young people significant amounts of responsibility, although they often endorse the need for teaching children to be responsible. It is safer and easier to hold the controls oneself, than to share them with students. Providing students with opportunities to make choices and be responsible also means allowing them to experience the consequences of their actions.[9] This can be especially difficult for some adults. Involved are self-management skills and community building strategies. Sheldon Berman of ESR describes classroom communities require the following conditions:

- Respect and tolerance for differences are norms.
- All members share in the decision-making process.
- Learning is a cooperative process.
- Conflicts are used as teaching moments.
- Fear and force are not used as instructional or disciplinary strategies.
- People listen to, acknowledge and care for others.
- There is a sense of a larger purpose and a connection to the larger world.

RESPONSIBILITY FOCUS ACTIVITIES

- **Classroom and school meetings**

There are many models of classroom meetings or school councils in which students of all ages learn to share power and responsibility appropriate to the age and experience of the group. The "pioneer" of classroom meetings is William Glasser. In *Schools Without Failure* (1969) he describes the process and types of classroom meetings in some detail.

These can be powerful and effective depending on the degree to which they are genuine rather than token experiences. One notable example is the Student Advisory Council (SAC) in a United States elementary school district (Shaheen, 1989). In this model three student delegates (two elected representatives and one chosen to ensure wide representation of both positive and negative leaders, as well as balance) and one visitor from each of the classes at a given grade level meet with the school principal, Director of Elementary Education and, when necessary, other district administrators to identify and solve problems. Visitors rotate through the meetings so that over the course of the year all students attend at least one SAC meeting. It is made clear that the delegates are not there to represent only their own opinions, but rather to outline the concerns of the class, so that "when all four people from each classroom walk through the door for a SAC meeting, it is as if all of their classmates and teacher walked in with them" (p. 362). Anyone in the school or in the community can bring a problem to SAC. Typical problems include improvements needed in the lunch program, bathrooms, buses and general building problems such as no intercom or unsynchronized clocks in the old building. All grades one through five in South Orangetown schools, Blauvelt, New York have SAC's. These councils allow the children to take ownership of their school and be and feel empowered to take responsibility. Students new to these schools reportedly see very real differences, and say things like, "Here the children want to be friends rather than fight. Here teachers and aides try to help solve kids' problems rather than ignoring fighting and teasing. At this school there is more caring."

The councils are only one of several structures used to create this climate. Two others that are mentioned in Shaheen's article are: Due Process Boards at grades three to five where students who feel they have been treated unfairly meet with a group of peers, principal and Director of Education at lunch time for a hearing; and Theodore Fair Bear, a large teddy bear who is a kind of school mascot who watches over everyone ensuring that they are fair to one another.

In many ways it is easier to achieve this kind of democratic model with elementary students because of their innate desire to please, tendency to defer to adult authority and strong concern for fairness. With the onset of puberty, young people often become fiercely independent, challenging of authority and more interested in their peers than in the adults in their lives. These adolescent traits are all the more reason to provide structure and guidance in sharing responsibility and power. For many students, school has become the only place where they are able to develop a sense of belonging and caring. The efforts to create community in secondary and elementary classrooms can have impact far beyond schools.

- **Inner/outer scenarios**

Using the concept of locus of control, have secondary students examine situations involving individuals with an internal locus of control problem. Initially have them write the scenario from the point of view of an external locus of control. Scenarios might be chosen from course materials (e.g., characters in history or current events) or from their own lives. For example, in a study of black civil rights in the U.S. students might write about Rosa Parks, first with an external locus of control, sitting at the back of the bus, as blacks were required to do in the American South prior to the 1960's. Students would then re-write the story as it eventually happened with Rosa Parks with an internal locus of control refusing to sit at the back of the bus, and in so doing starting a protest movement that resulted not only in blacks being allowed to sit anywhere on the bus, but also in the securing of other civil rights for black people everywhere.

- **Charter of rights and responsibilities**

Early in the year students in classrooms of all ages can participate in an activity to identify expectations for how the classroom should operate if it is to be a positive place for learning. One way to structure this activity is to develop a list of "rights and (corresponding) responsibilities" for students and teachers. A team of Greater Victoria School District students, teachers and administrators developed such a list for the district. Among other principles, they determined that students have a right to an education that is relevant to their social and intellectual development and a corresponding responsibility to take ownership of their education by being active and involved in their own learning. This list is posted in every elementary classroom or copied into every secondary student's book, referred to often and amended when necessary. In this way, students are encouraged to develop a responsibility focus mind-set that puts them in charge of their own lives.

Developing action orientation

Action-orientation describes an expectation to move beyond words and ideas to do something about a problem. It asks not, "What *might* I do about this?" but "What *will* I do about it?" This mind-set exists in dynamic tension with the complexity orientation. The expectation of complexity might imply that one waits to get the whole picture before opinions are formed and action may be undertaken. Whereas the action-orientation demands that I act on the information I have, knowing that I may be wrong and allowing for the option of changing my mind. This does not imply that one acts on impulse. There is a need to analyze a situation and gather relevant information before one acts. However, one must be prepared to act even in the face of uncertainty.

This mind-set seeks to replace apathy with action. It attempts to counter the "someone else will take care of it" approach with "what can I do to help?" It builds on the notion of personal and social responsibility by taking the next step. In so doing, it counteracts the "unintended" curriculum which inadvertently accompanies much of the teaching and learning in schools that suggests it is enough to *know* about an issue and it is not necessary to *do something* about it. In fact, all of a student's learning in social studies is preparation for this step. Teachers can help students begin to take steps toward active citizenship and to apply the knowledge and understandings gained through their academic study by engaging them in action-oriented activities. The skills involved in developing an action orientation are learning to take a stand (i.e., going public with one's beliefs), changing positions as more information comes to light and acting in the face of uncertainty.

ACTION ORIENTATION ACTIVITIES

- **Life choices map**

  Taking action may be hypothetical or actual. Students need practice in rehearsing or trying out different possible actions before they take real action. This may be done in simulations, role plays or written exercises. In the Life Choices Map students make themselves the object of the exercise, take a character from their studies or create an entirely fictitious character. They then work through various real or possible actions (choices) and predict the effects. In studying the French Revolution, students might consider the life of Louis XVI. They could make a map of his rule through to his death and they could then add to the map alternate choices at certain points (e.g., allowing the Three Estates to have one person one vote from the beginning; reducing the extravagance of the court, using military intervention against challengers early on, successfully fleeing to Vienna) and speculate how these alternatives might have changed the outcome. The object of this type of exercise is to demonstrate the relationship between actions and their consequences, and to help students break out of their willingness to "accept their fate." This activity is similar to a "decision-tree" where students look at issues and graphically represent decisions, alternatives and their consequences (Merryfield & Remy, 1995, p. 33). For example, students may consider the invasion of Kuwait by Iraq, and outline the alternatives facing the international community at that time. Both activities effectively illustrate the relationship between actions and consequences; the Life Choices Map is a more personalized approach, intended to bring the student one step closer to individual action.

- **Human graph**

  Students need a great deal of practice in taking action especially in front of their peers. Many are inclined to take a passive or noncommittal stance. One excellent technique for breaking the passivity habit is the Human Graph (Bellanca & Fogarty, 1990) also known as Taking a Stand. Place a line of masking tape from one end of the classroom to the other, or posts signs around the room that say "Strongly Agree" at one end and "Strongly Disagree" at the other. Identify the mid-point or neutral place in the middle. Students are then asked to "take a stand" on a given statement (e.g., Marie Antoinette deserved to be executed, the voting age should be 14, ten year olds should set their own bedtime). Students can discuss their reasons for the stand they have taken. Class activities are then conducted which give students new information on the topic. The graph is repeated and students are encouraged to reconsider their stand, based on the new information received. Teachers can facilitate this movement by speaking personally about how their thinking and beliefs have changed over time (e.g., "I used to think thirty was old, but now fifty seems young.") Emphasize the importance of staying open to receive new information, and to the possibility that beliefs may ultimately be proven wrong.

- **Community projects**

  Students also need to move beyond rehearsal and take actions that are real. Teachers need to be careful here to choose developmentally appropriate topics and tasks. It is also important to check with school or district administration if issues are politically sensitive or present a challenge to community standards. With elementary children it is often helpful to let parents know what you are doing. Careful selection of projects is necessary to ensure success. (See Clark, "All Talk and No Action?" in this volume.)

Actions can be at the classroom, school or community level. Projects that promote habits of cooperation or service to others are particularly recommended. The best projects will be those that fit the students' interests and the needs about which they feel most strongly. Activities that teachers have chosen include: establishing a student peacemakers club, where students are trained to help others mediate and resolve playground conflicts; setting up a buddy system for students new to the school; reducing the use of paper in school; collecting used books and school supplies to send to schools in India; fund-raising for aid to places in crisis such as Bosnia or Zaire.

Teachers need to understand the subtle complexities of projects undertaken and to anticipate the major consequences before embarking on a project. However support is available to help teachers assess appropriate actions. Agencies which promote international development—CIDA (Canadian International Development Agency), the International Red Cross, Oxfam, Doctors Without Borders—and organizations which work at a community level—food banks, women's shelters, animal shelters, free stores—are often in the best position to understand the complexities of the issues and to provide assistance.

While undertaking social action projects implies some risk, the many benefits make such projects worthwhile. Not only do students often look back on such projects as highlights of their school life, they also take the first and possibly pivotal steps to becoming active participants in their world. This is to achieve the ultimate goal of social studies education—participatory citizenship.

CONCLUSION

My goal has been to provide an overview of peace education, how it has been implemented historically and what it looks like in contemporary classrooms. My emphasis has been on developing five mind-sets which provide overlapping tools for looking at peace, conflict and violence. These mind-sets endeavour to move students from a detached, dispassionate analysis to one that facilitates involvement and responsibility. In short, these mind-sets attempt to bridge the gap between analysis and action. In so doing, the goal of building a more cooperative, peaceful world may be furthered.

While these mind-sets are central to the goals of social studies education, they are not exclusive to this subject. In fact, the goals of peace education permeate all aspects of the curriculum and have as much to do with the way classrooms function as with any single course of study. Peace education has moved beyond concerns about avoidance of war to "an approach to learning which will help students develop the skills, knowledge and creativity they need to live peacefully in an interdependent and increasingly complex world" (Clarke, 1991, p. 7). Is it political? It can be, when it addresses highly controversial social issues involving students in direct social action—and many educators believe that schools have a role to play in these areas. There is also an immense domain of peace education that is not controversial. It involves the development of knowledge, skills and attitudes to live and work together cooperatively, embracing differences and resolving disputes in non-violent, respectful ways. It ought to be as central to education as the "3R's."

ENDNOTES

[1] Very few violence prevention programmes have collected systematic information about their effectiveness. One exception to this generalization is the *Second Step* program developed by the Committee for Children of Seattle. It is a violence prevention program aimed at kindergarten to grade 8 students that has a thorough research base which suggests positive results. It differs from other social skills programs in its primary emphasis on the development of empathy in addition to other anger management and problem-solving skills. Another exception is the *Child Development Program* in San Ramon, California. It is a school which promotes caring and responsibility in children through a focus on five major areas: cooperation, understanding others, highlighting core values, helping and developmental discipline. Programs are thoroughly monitored and scrutinized. It has won many prestigious awards for its work and is becoming internationally known.

[2] In Case's (1995) schema, the perceptual aspect of a global perspective contains three cognitive lenses: open-mindedness, full-mindedness and fair-mindedness. This model includes all of Case's components, with some differences and additions.

[3] Adapted from *Creative Conflict Resolution* (Kreidler, 1984).

[4] It is difficult to identify the origins of this activity. It became something of a symbol in the anti-nuclear movement. In an early example, a group of women in Vermont called the "Spinsters" staged a piece of "guerilla theatre" using a variation on this theme (Reid, 1982). With thousands of yards of colored yarns and string, the Spinsters wove a web between trees at the entrance to the Yankee Nuclear Power Plant in Vernon, Vermont in March 1980. Before long, police came and cut the web down. The women began weaving again immediately. This process continued over the course of a week. In the words of the Spinster's pamphlet, the purpose of the web was to "entangle the powers that bury our children" by "reweaving the web of life" (p. 290). It is symbolic of the interconnectedness of all life and in contrast to the threat posed by nuclear accidents. This scene was repeated often in anti-nuclear protests.

[5] Adapted from workshop presentations through *Edu-*

cators for Social Responsibility (ESR), Cambridge, MA.

[6] For detailed explanation and illustration of this fundamental conflict resolution concept, see *Getting to Yes, Negotiating Agreement Without Giving In* by Roger Fisher and William Ury (1981).

[7] In systems thinking terms, this is a "high-leverage" (offers greatest chance for positive impact) place for intervention. In conflict situations, most people intervene where they feel the greatest stress, which is typically a place of "low-leverage" or little impact. Often this is the point where people are dealing with symptoms, making improvements in the short-term, but making things worse in the long-run.

[8] Adapted from workshops presented in the Conflict Resolution Program of the *Justice Institute of British Columbia.*

[9] Authors Richard Curwin and Alan Mendler in *Discipline With Dignity* (1988) suggest that in the past we have given too much control to students. They speculate that there may be a tendency now to overreact and take all of the controls back. What they propose instead, is a systematic process of providing increasing responsibility to students based on their developmental readiness.

REFERENCES

Adelson, J. & Finn Jr., C.E. (1985). Terrorizing children. *Commentary*, 29-36.

Bellanca, J. & Fogarty, R. (1990). *Blueprint for thinking in the cooperative classroom.* Arlington Heights, IL: Skylight.

Belland, K. (1986, 1990, 1992, 1996). *Second step: A violence prevention curriculum.* Seattle, WA: Committee for Children.

Case, R. (1995). Nurturing a global perspective in elementary students. In R. Fowler & I. Wright (Eds.), *Thinking globally about social studies education* (pp. 20-34). Vancouver: Research and Development in Global Studies, University of British Columbia.

Case, R. (1991). Key elements of a global perspective. *Social Education, 57*(6), 318-325.

City of Victoria. (1995). *Report of task force on violence prevention.* Victoria, BC: Author.

Clarke, P. (1991). The problem with social studies. *Teacher, 4*(3), 7.

Curwin, R.L. & Mendler, A.N. (1988). *Discipline with dignity.* Alexandria,VA: Association for Supervision and Curriculum Development.

Elbow, P. (1983, April). *Critical thinking is not enough.* Delivered as the Reninger Lecture at the University of Northern Iowa, Cedar Falls.

Estroff Marano, H. (1995). Big. Bad. Bully. *Psychology Today, 22*(6), 50-82.

Fisher, R. & Ury, W. (1981). *Getting to yes, negotiating agreement without giving in.* New York: Penguin.

Glasser, W. (1969). *Schools without failure.* New York: Harper and Row.

Greig, S., Pike, G. & Selby, D. (1987). *Earthrights: Education as if the planet really mattered.* London: Kagan Page.

Hanvey, R.G. (1987). An attainable global perspective. In W.M. Kniep (Ed.), *Next steps in global education: A handbook for curriculum development* (pp. 83-109). New York: American Forum.

Johnson, D.W. & Johnson R. (1995) *Reducing school violence through conflict resolution.* Alexandria, VA: Association for Supervision and Curriculum Development.

Kreidler, W. (1984). *Creative conflict resolution.* Glenview, IL: Scott, Foresman.

MacDougall, J. (1995). *Violence in the schools.* Toronto: Canadian Education Association.

Nash, A. (1986, Fall). Combating anarchy in the middle school. *Independent School, 66,* 25-32.

91% Favour testing, poll shows. (1993, May 29). *Toronto Star,* p. A8.

Olewus, D. (1989). Bully/victim problems among schoolchildren: Basic facts and effects of a school-based intervention program. In K. Rubin & D. Pepler (Eds.), *The development and treatment of childhood aggression* (pp. 411-448). Hillsdale, NJ: Erlbaum.

Peck, M. S. (1987). *The different drum: Community making and peace.* New York: Simon and Schuster.

Reardon, B. (1988). *Comprehensive peace education.* New York: Teacher's College Press.

Reid, C. (1982). Reweaving the web of life. In P. McAllister, (Ed.), *Reweaving the web of life, feminism and nonviolence* (pp. 289-294). Philadelphia, PA: New Society.

Roberts, N. (1978, April). Teaching dynamic feedback systems: An elementary view. *Management Science,* 836-843.

Roberts, N. (1983, January/February). Testing the world with simulations. *Classroom Computer News, 28.*

Scieczka, J. (1989). *The true story of the three little pigs by A. Wolf.* New York: Scholastic

Senge, P. (1990). *The fifth discipline: The art and practice of the learning organization.* New York: Doubleday.

Shaheen, J.C. (1989). Participatory citizenship in the elementary grades. *Social Education, 53*(6), 361-363.

— ✧ —

14

FORMS OF DIMENSION-BASED STRANDS

TODD A. HORTON

The original intent of social studies, as its name implies, was to engage students in studying society. The point of these studies is to prepare students to live and participate productively and effectively within society. If we take seriously the challenge of preparing "complete" citizens, then we need a way of articulating the scope—the areas of knowledge and range of competencies—the subject ought to promote. As well, we need some idea of the sequence in which these should be introduced.

In an earlier article in this collection, "Elements of a Coherent Social Studies Program," Case suggests that developing a vision for the subject requires understanding three basic features: the underlying rationales for social studies, the goals that social studies will promote in order to further the rationale and the strands around which the subject matter is organized to promote the desired goals. It is the latter of this trio of considerations which is the focus of this article—specifically, dimension-based strands.

Dimension-based strands are organizational approaches to the scope and sequence of the social studies curriculum that derive from significant facets of the social and physical world. They organize the study of society into multidisciplinary parts—for example, our various roles as citizens or the major cultural or physical realms of the world—and promote understandings, abilities and values associated with these dimensions. Other models or strands articulate and organize the content and skills of social studies around the social science disciplines (e.g., history, geography, anthropology, law) or around the pressing concerns of our age (e.g., environmental education, peace education, human rights education, multicultural education). According to proponents of dimension-based strands the social sciences are a somewhat narrow and confining way of studying the world—the world does not organize itself according to discrete disciplines and many aspects of becoming a citizen, such as learning to solve personal problems, do not fall within any discipline. The limitation of concern-based strands is that they focus on the priority issues of the day but may neglect less urgent but nonetheless important aspects of citizenship, such as knowing the services available in one's community or learning to accept one's duties as a parent or employee. Proponents of dimension-based strands claim that social studies is more understandable and meaningful to students when organized around the commonplace dimensions of the world. As well, social and physical dimensions provide a more systematic way of articulating the entire range of studies of society that students should undertake. Four types or forms of dimension-based strands are most commonly discussed:

- **expanding horizons**—the study of society beginning with the child's immediate milieu and expanding through space and time (e.g., self and family—> community—> province or region—> nation—> world);
- **social roles**—the study of society organized around common roles that people occupy in their lives (e.g., worker, family member, citizen, consumer);
- **development studies**—the study of society built upon the tracing through time of common phenomena (e.g., parliamentary democracy, technology, revolution, energy, medicine);
- **regional or area studies**—the study of society organized around geo-political regions (e.g., North America, Pacific Rim, the Middle East).

In this article, I explore these four forms of dimension-based strands as potentially worthwhile organizing approaches for social studies. As well, I illustrate how they might be operationalized in the curriculum and discuss criticisms associated with each form of dimension-based strand.

EXPANDING HORIZON MODEL

The prevailing dimension-based strand in social studies, especially at the elementary level, is the ex- panding horizons approach. Based upon Hanna's "expanding communities" (1963), and alternatively known as "expanding environments," its basic premise is that the immediate and concrete world of the child should be the initial focus of exposure to social studies, followed by an "expansion" out toward more abstract concepts as the child matures. As illustrated below, in the expanding horizons model students learn about the self, family and community in the primary grades, and as they grow older, they are introduced gradually to more abstract topics such as the province or region, the nation and, finally, the world.

This curricular approach is closely linked to Piagetian development stage theory, and the belief that children are most familiar with their immediate environment and that their frames of reference are confined to it. As Chapin and Messick (1989) state, "children usually learn better about real things and life around them than about abstract topics that they cannot see or feel" (p. 23).

The merit of this approach is thought to rest in its evolving nature. By beginning with the child and the family, teachers can facilitate children's exploration of their own lives—the persons and things most important to themselves. Students learn to examine and question their individual needs and preferences. Social skills

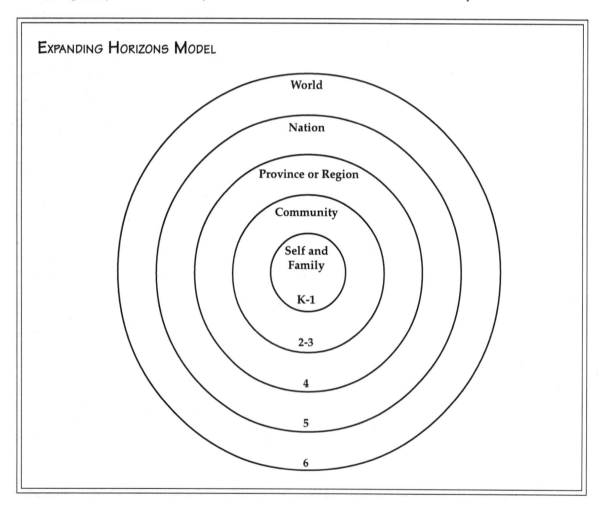

EXPANDING HORIZONS MODEL

World

Nation

Province or Region

Community

Self and Family

K-1

2-3

4

5

6

are introduced to help children understand that, though they have worth as individuals, they must also learn to interact as a member of a collective. Using all of their senses, children experience their favourite pets, learn to play cooperative games with their friends, explore vegetables their father encourages them to eat and observe flowers in their garden. Thus, learning is both an intellectual and experiential activity.

Advocates of this approach point to the fact that abstract concepts such as *time* and *place* can be gradually introduced in the early grades and solidified in familiar context. For example, the study of the neighbourhood in grade three might involve looking at different types of housing and how and why they have changed over the years (time), or possible routes one might take to get to various community sites such as churches, community centres or shopping malls (place). The concepts acquired through exploration of students' own lives and their local environments serve as building blocks for subsequent study of the more abstract and remote dimensions of the world. By the time students reach the upper elementary grades, they are more fully prepared to move beyond their immediate place and time into an interdisciplinary study of a more distant—temporal and spatial—world. Teachers can take individual concepts such as the province or the nation and study them in depth. Each concept builds on the foundations of those from the previous grade, while foreshadowing subsequent ones.

The scope of the expanding horizons model has been the subject of extensive criticism and, despite the merits discussed above, many teachers and theorists have expressed concern about its underlying assumptions. (Egan's criticism of the expanding horizon approach is found in "Resisting the Erosion of Education" in this volume.) Especially controversial is the premise that children are most familiar with their immediate environment and that their frames of reference are confined to it. Many believe that public media, especially television, introduce children to other places and times and familiarize them with other cultures and approaches to life at very young ages. It is not uncommon to find young children who are aware of Hercules, pirates, pioneer life and Mars. All may be beyond their "immediate" environments or "direct" life experiences but are very much a part of their frames of reference and areas of interest.

Criticisms have also been directed at the sequence of the expanding horizons model. It has been criticized for being grade bound: topics often are isolated from related topics because they do not match the grade-level theme (Baskerville & Sesow, 1976). For example, while studying about their province in grade four, teachers tend not to discuss content concerning Canada as a whole as this is seen to be the purview of the grade five curriculum. Similarly, discussions of local communities often ignore comparisons with communities in other parts of the country or world. Thus, relationships be-

tween topics are often overlooked in an effort "not to get ahead of ourselves." Joyce and Alleman-Brooks (1981) criticize the model's failure to provide for the teaching of issues of immediate concern to children. Others have questioned the model's philosophical grounding in developmental psychology (Akenson, 1989). Children learn to mentally manage complex concepts such as past, present and future, imaginary and real, and near and far away, at a very young age and there is little to suggest that young students cannot also grasp concepts such as the province, nation and the world or explore the family and community outside their immediate environment. Still others question the need to sequence topics from smallest to largest on an age-grade basis, stating that the notion of a 'region' is as abstract a concept as 'nation' (Welton & Mallan, 1992). Despite these criticisms, expanding horizons continues to be the model of choice in Canadian and American elementary social studies curricula.

SOCIAL ROLES MODEL

Another dimension-based strand that has been experimented with in schools is the social roles model. Created under the auspices of the Social Science Education Consortium in 1978, it was a direct result of the New Social Studies movement efforts to revitalize the social studies. The rationale of the social roles model is that social studies can contribute more fully to the development of effective participants in society by focussing on who we are, what we do and how these roles interact. This K-12 curriculum was organized around seven roles that people perform throughout their lives: citizen, worker, consumer, family member, friend, member of social groups and self. At each grade-level students would explore aspects of each of the seven roles.

Proponents of the social roles model claim that in comparison to other models, this design is more relevant and motivating for students because the seven social roles are taught within the context of students' experiences. It seeks to not only prepare students for political participation, but also for the economic and social realities of work, the family and the marketplace. It integrates other curricular areas such as language arts, mathematics, economics, business education, while sharing responsibilities with career-education specialists, guidance counselors and community leaders. In the boxes on the following pages is an outline (adapted from Superka & Hawke, 1980) explaining the definition, competencies and teacher responsibilities of each of these social roles.

Although the social roles model has been praised for its blending of various curricular orientations into a coherent conception of social studies, it has also been challenged. Critics believe that it does not clarify the role of citizen sufficiently, nor does it indicate its level of importance in social studies. Issues related to the role of citizen such as understanding political systems and structures and general knowledge of the country ap-

EXPLANATION OF SOCIAL ROLES MODEL

Role	Definition	Competencies	Teacher Responsibilities
Citizen	Relationships between individuals and political entities (e.g., the state, government agencies and political organizations). Organized efforts to influence public policy.	Voting, obeying just laws, challenging unjust laws, paying taxes, participation in political parties, studying public issues, advocating positions on public policy questions, working for volunteer organizations and holding public office.	Within history, geography, political science, economics and other disciplines, educators must not only identify topics or concepts related to the citizen role but also determine which of these are most essential to that role. Help students understand the inter-relationship between the citizen role and the other social roles.
Worker	The type of employment chosen and engaged in by a person. The relationship between the enhancement of the individual through work and the productive contribution each person makes to the betterment of society.	Acquiring knowledge about careers and such occupation-related skills as identifying information related to job openings, preparing job applications, interviewing for jobs, performing basic computation and effective communication.	Help develop decision-making skills and constructive attitudes toward work. Provide students with awareness of careers directly related to the social sciences (e.g., urban planner, government administrator). Help students reflect on their work related-experiences. Provide students with knowledge concerning the role of the worker in national society and the world (e.g., labour unions, trade policies, women in the work force). Help students analyze and discuss the inter-relationships between the worker role and other social roles.
Consumer	Persons who buy and use the goods and services produced by workers.	Understanding consumer law, supply and demand, consumer protection, inflation, money and credit, boycotts, energy, the environment, international trade.	Help students understand this role in the context of the national economic, political and social systems and to appreciate the global interdependence of consumers. Provide students with the conceptual tools for adapting to future changes. Provide historical, economic and political perspectives of the consumer role. Help students understand the inter-relationship between the consumer role and other social roles.
Family Member	Persons "related" by birth, marriage, adoption and emotional affinity who reside together and consider themselves part of a family unit.	Understanding the responsibilities of child-care, caring for the elderly, assigning duties and sharing facilities in the home, entertaining visitors and providing various forms of support to other family members.	Drawing on psychology, sociology, history, anthropology and economics, help students understand and deal with parent-child relationships, sibling relationships, the rights and responsibilities of parents and children, changing family roles, the family as an institution, the future of the family, marriage and courtship, diverse types of families in Canada and throughout the world. Help students understand the inter-relationship between the role of the family member and other social roles.

Role	Definition	Competencies	Teacher Responsibilities
Friend	Persons to whom we are not related in the "family" sense but whom we choose to associate with because of common interests and a developed sense of trust, affection, understanding and acceptance.	A variety of competencies based upon the type of friendship and the levels of commonalty, trust, affection and acceptance that has developed. Generally, the traits valued by all humanity such as trustworthiness, honesty and "appropriate" levels of openness are held in very high regard.	Help students understand the evolutionary nature of friendship, how to make and keep friends, dealing with friendship-related conflicts, the changing nature of friendships throughout life, the importance of friendship in society. Help students understand the inter-relationship between friends and other social roles.
Member of Social Groups	Membership in three types of groups: • those determined by birth (e.g., gender, race, age cohort); • those such as religious groups, ethnic groups or socio-economic groups into which persons may be born but from which they may move; • those chosen by an individual.	An awareness of group responsibilities, rules and norms. Reconcile individual understanding with society's general perceptions and expectations and change as necessary.	Help students understand prescribed expectations and norms associated with membership. Make students aware of the existence and nature of different types of groups, analyze particular affiliations with groups, make conscious individual decisions about the extent of participation in groups and the overall impact of groups to the nation and the world. Help students understand the inter-relationship between being a member of a social group and other social roles.
Self	A psychological and sociological "sense of identity" or awareness of oneself.	Engage in activities that help us define who we are (and who we are not), and develop positive feelings about ourselves.	Provide learning experiences to help students understand how the other social roles influence a sense of identity and self-esteem. In particular, programs and activities focussed on how multicultural and sex-role awareness contribute to the development of identity. Together with other subject areas, social studies should help students be aware of and feel positive about their own thoughts, feelings, beliefs and values. Values clarification, moral development and other approaches from psychology and sociology can be used to achieve this objective.

pear to be sacrificed or "downgraded" in an effort to make the individual the focus of social studies. Others feel that the social roles model assumes the universality of these seven roles and that, though they may be applicable to a western industrial society in the late twentieth-century, they are not applicable to many subsistence-level economies found in the world today, nor will they necessarily be the social roles that will dominate the lives of people in the future (Helburn, 1980). It is also not clear how the model will avoid tedious repetition if the seven roles are addressed at every grade level.

Despite the prospect of igniting student interest in exploring their own lives and the intricately connected roles they perform in society, the social roles model has not found its way into many social studies classrooms. Teachers, along with administrators and academics, have left this dimension-based strand on the sidelines as a loosely defined, largely untried possibility.

DEVELOPMENT STUDIES MODEL

A third form of dimension-based strand is development studies. Development studies is based upon the premise that the roots or historical development of everyday concepts should be the organizing focus of social studies. Concepts such as parliamentary democracy, dentistry, technology, transportation or racism are traced backwards in time from their present-day in students' lives through in-depth multidisciplinary investigation to the historical roots of the phenomenon. These investigations provide opportunities to learn about history, geography, political science, anthropology and the other social science disciplines. Thus, broader social studies understandings emerge *through* these investigations. For example, a teacher might choose to examine the concept of "democracy" and have students begin investigating the evolution of democracy from its current Canadian context (touching upon issues of accountability and representative government), through the struggle for universal suffrage in Canada and elsewhere (touching upon notions of racial, gender and class discrimination), moving through the emergence of democratic traditions and institutions in European nations, to its Western roots in the direct democracy practices and philosophies of ancient Athens. Younger students might trace developments in writing implements from the current electronic forms to the earliest stone tablets.

Fundamental to the development studies model is the understanding that ideas, practices and inventions change through time and these changes have an impact upon the development of contemporary society. Each action and inaction impacts upon another. The purpose of development studies is to help students understand that persons and events discussed in the classroom are not isolated bits of history or trivia, but parts of a continuous flow of change running through time. The unique historical feature of the development studies approach is its start with the familiar contemporary experience and its peeling back of the changes as students look further and further into the past.

Despite this, development studies has not escaped criticism. Concerns have been raised that because this model attempts to examine core concepts through people and events it "tends to embrace long periods of historical time often resulting in a kind of 'Cook's Tour'" (Lomas, 1990). The feeling is that in an effort to cover several concepts teachers move about history rapidly and fail to provide the appropriate context that would promote understanding of the time and place. As well, there is the concern that many concepts are centred around 'things' and run the danger of not giving 'people' sufficient prominence in the classroom. A related criticism of this model stems from the tendency to delve so 'deeply' into a few notions. It is thought that considerable time may be spent on trivial and often isolated topics, resulting in a program that lacks sufficient breadth.

Development studies has rarely been used as the organizing model for the teaching of social studies.

REGIONAL OR AREA STUDIES MODEL

Regional or area studies is an approach to the teaching of social studies that has been popular in schools for over a century. Although still widely used at the secondary level, elements of regional and area studies have been incorporated into the expanding horizons model for elementary students. Based upon the premise that the world is too large a unit to examine as a whole, it is divided up into geo-political units for more manageable study. Regions may take the shape of countries, as in the case of studies focussing on Mexico, France and Kenya; or continents or grouped around a defining concept which gives the area cohesiveness, as in the case of the Deep South, the Middle East and the South Pacific.

Proponents of this model enjoy the possibility of a multidisciplinary approach that allows students to acquire in-depth understanding of a region. For example, the Canadian north could be explored through anthropological topics such as the evolution of aboriginal governments, historical topics such as the search for the Northwest Passage and geographic topics, such as the relationship between culture and climate. Others view this as an approach that helps students understand that regions have identified common features as such; the notion that all regions have elements in their history, geography, politics, economics and culture that bind their peoples together, giving rise to a sense of identity. Regions are both people and place, and the two intermingle to develop the whole; one does not exist without the other.

Although regional and area studies has its supporters, it also has its detractors. Critics claim that by dividing up the world into small geo-political portions, the relationships among people and places are not as evident. Regions do not exist in isolation from one another but are in a constant state of interaction and reciprocal influence. The division according to regions means that certain global events (e.g., the Pacific, European and African arenas for World War II) and global phenomena (e.g., global warming) may not be treated in their full context. There is also concern that a regional studies approach may lead to selective choosing of only those places that are illustrative of certain elements (e.g., white, affluent, English speaking), while others are neglected. This has been the criticism levelled at programs that continue to be Eurocentric to the exclusion of people and places in Africa, Asia, Latin America and other areas. Whatever the concerns levelled at regional or area studies, its simplicity has helped it remain a prominent organizational model in social studies.

CONCLUSION

The four forms of dimension-based strands discussed in this article are models, each with its own benefits and drawbacks. Rarely will any one of them be the sole model chosen by teachers or curriculum developers, for no one model will likely suit all educational needs, nor emphasize all aspects of the subject that are deemed important. Recognize that the choice of one strand does not preclude adopting elements of the others. The challenge facing teachers and curriculum developers is not to select *the* correct manner of organizing

a social studies program but to ensure that whatever choices are made are done so on the basis of informed and thoughtful consideration. In the box below are a number of criteria that may help in deciding which approach or mix of approaches including discipline-based, concern-based and dimension-based strands will be most suitable.

Keeping these criteria in mind increases the likelihood that the resulting program will be structured in a manner that serves the requirements of both teacher and students and that optimizes the potential of social studies as a relevant and valuable subject.

REFERENCES

Akenson, J.E. (1989). The expanding environments and elementary education: A critical perspective. *Theory and Research in Social Education, 17*(1), 33-52.

Baskerville, R.A. & Sesow, F.W. (1976). In defense of Hanna and the expanding communities approach to social studies. *Theory and Research in Social Education, 4*(1), 20-32.

Chapin, J.R. & Messick, R.G. (1989). *Elementary social studies*. New York: Longman.

Hanna, P.R. (1963). Revising the social studies: What is needed. *Social Education, 27*, 190-196.

Helburn, S.W. (1980). Reactions. *Social Education, 44*, 592, 652-653.

Joyce, W.W. & Alleman-Brooks, J.E. (1982). The child's world. *Social Education, 46*, 538-541.

Lomas, T. (1990). *Teaching and assessing historical understanding*. London: Historical Association.

Parker, W.C. (1991). *Renewing the social studies curriculum*. Alexandria, VA: Association for Supervision and Curriculum Development.

Superka, D.P. & Hawke, S. (1980). Social roles: A focus for social studies in the 1980s. *Social Education, 44*, 577-585.

Welton, D. & Mallan, J. (1992). *Children and their world* (4th ed.). Boston: Houghton Mifflin.

CRITERIA FOR ADOPTING SCOPE AND SEQUENCE

- Promotes the goals and rationale for the program
- Designates content for each grade
- Recognizes that learning is cumulative
- Reflects a balance of local, national and global content
- Reflects a balance of past, present and future content
- Emphasizes concepts and generalizations from history and the social sciences
- Promotes integration of skills and knowledge
- Promotes integration of content across subject areas
- Promotes use of diverse teaching methods and instructional materials
- Is consistent with current research pertaining to how children learn
- Is consistent with current scholarship in the disciplines
- Promotes transfer of knowledge and skills to life
- Has the potential to challenge and excite students

Adapted from a more extensive set of criteria published by the National Council for the Social Studies (cited in Parker, 1991 p. 67).

15

Resisting the Erosion of Education: A Case for Disciplines in Social Studies

Kieran Egan

The social studies curriculum does not work. It does not work conceptually, and it is not work ing in practice. Conceptually, it lacks the logical and psychological principles necessary to give it a coherent structure. In practice, surveys consistently show it to be the least popular subject with students, and show, among school leavers and college freshmen, massive ignorance of even its most basic subject matter.

My purpose in this article is to discuss three ideas which seem to have had a profound influence in making the social studies curriculum what it is. The best known exposition of these ideas can be found in the writings of John Dewey, particularly in his *Democracy and Education*. The degree to which his writings have had a causal influence on the curriculum, and the steps whereby that influence might have been felt, are not my concern here. Rather, his writings are referred to because they embody the set of ideas which find a realization in the present social studies curriculum, and which provide what theoretical basis it has.

The social studies curriculum does not work. It does not work conceptually, and it is not working in practice.

There has been much debate about how far, or even whether, Dewey's ideas have been put into practice, and how far practices which claim Dewey as their theoretical source are in fact reasonable interpretations of his words. In some cases the interpreters seem to have added their own words to Dewey's, or even replaced his with theirs, retaining only the influence attaching to his name. The "expanding horizons" form of curriculum (that is, beginning study with the material of the child's immediate environment and gradually expanding the topics to things more distant), for example, is sometimes associated with Dewey's writings; at other times it is claimed to have nothing to do with Dewey's ideas, deriving rather from some principles of developmental psychology. Whatever the historical case about the development of the present general form of the social studies curriculum, it seems to me clear that the theoretical justification for this general form is nowhere else as adequately and systematically laid out as in *Democracy and Education*. Even if the present form has in fact been brought about by atheoretical piecemeal tinkering, nevertheless a theoretical justification for that form is available in Dewey's writing. And, of course, tinkering is never atheoretical—even if theory is not conscious, it informs presuppositions which determine curriculum decisions. In what follows, then, my criticism of the general form of the social studies curriculum is aimed at those of Dewey's ideas which support it. If some readers want to claim that the ideas are not his but are some interpreter's, then they will have to show that the words Dewey uses mean something different from what I take them to mean. When discussing "expanding horizons," for example, I mean by that precisely what the quotations from Dewey suggest.

I will discuss Dewey's interpretation of the truism that one must begin all teaching and learning from the child's everyday experience, from what the child already knows best, and work gradually outward from that, and will consider how that idea has provided the most powerful principle giving form to the social studies curriculum. I will discuss Dewey's distinction between "natural" and "formal" learning, and see how that is influential in determining further aspects of the curriculum structure and dominant methods of teaching in social studies. I will also look at Dewey's distinction between what I will call socializing and educating, and note how that has a most general and pervasive influence on thinking about the proper content and purpose of the social studies curriculum.

In each case I will criticize Dewey's interpretations and distinctions. My aim is not to construct a compelling argument against Dewey's overall thesis in *Democracy and Education*, even if I could. Rather, I focus on those parts of it which provide some of the fundamental ideas on which the present social studies curriculum stands, with the intention of showing the frailty of those foundations. So I am going to begin by sketching two, connected, arguments: first, if we want our students to become critical thinkers about their present social experience we should teach about things like Ancient Greece, the Medieval Papacy, Chinese society during the Ming dynasty, the rise and fall of the Dutch empire rather than about the material of their local environments; second, that if we focus on Canada we will produce ignorance, boredom and, at best, Canadian myths, none of which will contribute to helping students become critical thinkers about their present social experience. A third argument is that young children can much more easily learn academic history than they can learn the current content of the early grades of the social studies curriculum.

SOCIALIZING AND EDUCATING: OUR PAST VS. HISTORY

The term social studies began to appear in the early part of this century. It was associated with child-centered ideas about educating, which in turn were associated with interdisciplinary forms of curriculum organizing. If our focus is on "the needs of children" and how they make sense of things, we might conclude that disciplinary distinctions are largely insignificant. Thus any study of what John Dewey calls "the associated life of man" (1916/1966, p. 211) should be considered all of a piece, not divided into separate disciplines taught in different ways at different times. "While geography emphasizes the physical side and history the social, these are only emphases in a common topic" (p. 211)—they are simply "two phases of the same living whole" (p. 218). Thus history and geography, on being absorbed into social studies, were seen as radiating out from the student in temporal and spacial dimensions, providing wider contexts to enrich understanding of the students' immediate social experience. This became common in Canada by the 1930's and 1940's. Once in this yoke with social studies, history and geography increasingly lost their disciplinary autonomy and were made to serve as agents in the general socializing purpose of social studies. Their aim in socializing, that is to say, was to focus on the students' present social experience, and help to explain it. This aim provided a criterion whereby one could decide what history was most "relevant."

Events which most profoundly affected present social circumstances were thus selected, and events remote in time, place and causal connection with the present, omitted. In socializing, our concern is to make

---

In socializing, our concern is to make the student familiar with present social conditions and future trends. Thus in a social studies curriculum whose purpose is very largely the socialization of students, the study of the Medieval Papacy has to compete for teaching time with topics like law, racism, sexism, consumerism, environmental pollution, local government and so on. As far as socialization is concerned, the Medieval Papacy is clearly a non-starter in this field.

---

the student familiar with present social conditions and future trends. Thus in a social studies curriculum whose purpose is very largely the socialization of students, the study of the Medieval Papacy has to compete for teaching time with topics like law, racism, sexism, consumerism, environmental pollution, local government and so on. As far as socialization is concerned, the Medieval Papacy is clearly a non-starter in this field.

But when history becomes an agent of socialization, it begins to develop a different aim from that which distinguishes history as an academic discipline. The aim of history as an academic discipline is to come to understand the past in its own terms, in its uniqueness, for its own sake and the sake of the pleasure of such understanding. Initiation of students into this understanding, in however fragmentary and incomplete a way, and in providing them with some taste of the pleasure—which is proper to such understanding, is an educational task. It isn't easy, of course. If it were, anyone could do it and teachers wouldn't have a claim on professional status. But it is worthwhile. It is very important that we distinguish this aim, and the teaching activities which will bring children towards it, from the aim of socializing and its use of the past. In socializing, we do not aim to bring children to an understanding of the past for its own sake, but rather we use the past in order to focus on the present.

Most generally one might distinguish the aims of socializing and educating by saying that the former aims to make people more alike while the latter aims to make them more distinct. A successful program of socialization will lead to people sharing attitudes and values, and images of their nation. Such common attitudes, values and images are seen as necessary for a society to exist. When politicians express their concerns about what the schools should achieve, we tend to see precisely a set of socialization aims; attitudes, values and images of the province and country that are considered appropriate or necessary for good citizenship. Socializing uses of the past tend to concentrate on what Michael Oakshott calls "a glimpse of the current myth of the history of the nation" (1970, p. 63).

"Myth" here is not the same as lies. Rather, it is used in the sense of that which *organizes our affective responses*. Such a myth of the history of the nation is not concerned simply to present a picture of what happened, but is concerned with involving our emotions with the picture. In teaching about conflicts with the United States, for example, one does not, in socializing, seek to present such knowledge for its own sake. It is a potent part of establishing a sense of Canada's distinct identity. It is not enough that Canadian children learn about the events and the characters. Clearly they are to approve of certain events and ambitions and disapprove of others, and they are to identify with certain sentiments and characters. The socializing purpose would not be met if most Canadian children regretted the fact that Canada had not been absorbed into the United States. In looking at any of the key events in Canada/ U.S. conflicts we tend to celebrate those which enhanced Canadian autonomy and to regret those which reduced it. Students in American schools studying the same events would have them fitted into the myth of the history of their nation differently. The fitting of them into a particular pattern is the means whereby we attach emotions to them; and it is this emotion-laden pattern which is what is meant by myth.

This socializing use of the past, this telling of a national story, is different from the study of history. It is not different in that it is false and simplistic whereas history is true and complex—there can be as many errors and falsehoods and simplifications in historical narratives as in a myth of a nation's history. (Though it should be noted that the telling of a national story more easily falls into falsehood. If the prime purpose is to "body forth" the current myth of the nation's history, it will often be possible to present the myth more powerfully and dramatically by leaving out bits here, inventing bits there, exaggerating the villainy or heroism of this character or of that nation. This form of falsifica-

tion is far from uncommon in our textbooks, though probably less common than in American textbooks where the myths are more fully developed.) The uses of the past are different in their purpose and methods and in the way the mind works in learning or discovering the one or the other.

However carefully we present "our story"—the current myth of the history of Canada—we are selecting according to a principle which heightens the significance and inevitability of the present. This is a much more subtle perversion of history than outright falsification. If we focus everything towards the present, significance is determined by how far any event can be shown to have contributed to present conditions. Thus huge chunks of the past are condemned to "irrelevance"

If we focus everything towards the present, significance is determined by how far any event can be shown to have contributed to present conditions. Thus huge chunks of the past are condemned to "irrelevance" by this criterion. Yet, of the variety of things which make up the present, much is trivial, random and insignificant in any more general account of human history.

---

by this criterion. Yet, of the variety of things which make up the present, much is trivial, random and insignificant in any more general account of human history. What happens in presenting "our story," in using the past to focus on our present, is to exaggerate the present and the value of present circumstances and institutions. It represents the whole significant history of the world as having the purpose of bringing about the present conditions which we experience. This does not encourage—a prominent aim of social studies—critical reflection on the present; rather it encourages a sense of awe and respect before conditions and institutions which the massive drama of history has brought about. It gives them an improper sense of inevitability, of necessity.

The study of history is different from this primarily in that it does not seek to tell a story which is focussed on the present. Nor does it seek to tell "our" story. The past is not seen as a drama in which we associate with one side against another; we do not focus especially on our ancestors, our religious faction, our nation or on our heroes and heroines. In the study of history we are concerned simply with what happened. The struggle of humanity, the causal roles of blind chance and iron necessity, are everywhere evident. We don't look to history for practical lessons, but for human understanding, for an enrichment of human meanings: it is an expansion of our experience. We can learn from it discipline in making sense of human experience generally and in making sense of our own experience, but not in the sense sought by social studies. In contrast with social studies, where the students' experience is the focus of attention and where the students' opinions are elicited and valued, the study of history teaches that students' opinions are irrelevant, what they think about the past does not matter. What matters is what happened, what someone else's opinion was, what other people thought. It helps us to treat our own experience with the objectivity we learn to bring to that of others. Social studies tends towards narcissism; history takes the students' attention away from themselves.

My purpose here is to argue that typical statements of aims for social studies tend towards contradiction. The focus on students' immediate social experience is in conflict with the aim to teach them to be critical thinkers about their society. If one wants to teach a measure of objectivity and an ability to think critically about events and institutions one should focus on teaching academic history. If one wants a compliant citizenry who accept the institutions and conditions around them as somewhat sacred, as greater and finer than any that exist elsewhere (or, if one prefers, as worse than others), as the product and purpose of the historical drama, then one should continue the socializing use of the past which is at present a central feature of social studies in North America.

The distinction between socializing and educating is hard to draw precisely, but it is, I think, one which everyone recognizes, at least at its extremes. The crux of the distinction, it seems to me, is the aim. The aim of socializing is to bring people to share certain values, ideas, skills or whatever, and the criteria that determine which values, ideas, skills or whatever, should be included in the curriculum are the shifting criteria of utility to present or anticipated future social experience. The aim of education is the expansion and refinement of individual understanding, and the criteria which determine what range of studies should be included in the curriculum to bring about such understanding are relatively stable criteria of disciplined knowledge.

PREREQUISITES TO MATURE UNDERSTANDING

I am trying to make the unlikely argument that detailed study of the Medieval Papacy will probably contribute more towards the avowed aims of the social studies curriculum than will a focus on issues in students' present social experience. In order to make the argument it will be useful to ask the reader to reflect on when in his or her own experience the social issues which we would all agree are now vital became meaningful. How old were you when you began to *appreciate* the *meaning* of racism, of the law, of levels of government? How old were you when the concept "society" became meaningful? These are difficult questions to answer because we may well have had a conditioned response to, say, racism at an early age, and its meaning accumulated gradually at times, took on sudden dimensions and insights at other times and so on. But appreciating the meaning of racism, which is what we want our social studies curriculum to teach, is quite different from a conditioned response. Also we

probably learned a definition of the word "society" when we were quite young, but we should be able to recall when the word became a meaningful concept, fitting together with other concepts, with knowledge of a range of particular events and with various experiences.

In all these cases, for nearly all of us, the answer to these questions will be "in adulthood." We appreciated the meaning of the very general and complex concept "society" only when we were adults. Indeed, frequently the things about society and the issues of our social experience that we most eagerly want to introduce into the curriculum are those whose meaning we have most recently come to appreciate. Thus consumerism, sexism, the law, environmental pollution and so on, are impelled into the curriculum by adults who have relatively recently learned to appreciate the crucial importance of these elements in their common social experience.

What we reflect on too little is what knowledge and what experience was necessary to make those issues meaningful for us. If our understanding of their meaning is based upon a lot of background knowledge, upon realizing the responsibilities of citizenship, upon a concept of society that is complex, and upon the psychological developments that follow years of talking and working and travelling and so on, we must ask how can we communicate those meanings to the, by definition, immature who do not yet have the necessary prerequisite knowledge, concepts or experiences. Now one can push this too far and suggest some absolute inability of students to grasp these concepts and the issues that are made meaningful by them. On the other hand—and I am claiming much more commonly—one can forget and underestimate what experience and knowledge were necessary in our own cases before those issues became meaningful.

Well, of course, we don't expect students to develop right away a fully mature concept of society, or appreciation of the meaning of the social issues around them. We begin with developing the prerequisites to that ap-

---

I am trying to make the unlikely argument that detailed study of the Medieval Papacy will probably contribute more towards the avowed aims of the social studies curriculum than will a focus on issues in students' present social experience.

---

preciation. The argument here is about what those prerequisites are.

The common answer is that those prerequisites are initially an introduction of the issue, information, discussions, maybe films, etc.—the usual array of teacherly ingenuity in initiating the student into a partially new understanding of some issue. My argument is that the best product of this approach—which is what is embodied in our present curriculum—is myths. The worst is bored incomprehension. And the commonest is probably a mixture of the two.

The meaning of the social issues of our time derives in part from an understanding of their history and, perhaps in more important part, from an understanding of the movement of blind chance and iron necessity in their stately and brutal dance through time. A flowery phrase perhaps, but a crucially important point. The meaning of the social issues of our time cannot be approached directly. Without a context, not merely of surrounding facts, but more importantly of developed human meanings, such issues can be grasped by the immature only in a mythic way. So students will be at the mercy of any trendy and trivial notion that floats by. Their opinions will be conditioned and predictable. They will be merely socialized to a point of view, an attitude; they will not be educated.

It is one of those paradoxes of our experience that the most immediate things are those we come to know and appreciate last. Often among the last people we come to know are our parents. We do not discover the world by knowing first what surrounds us and gradually working outwards. Like so much of the underlying theory of the social studies curriculum, that is exactly the opposite of our experience. Why do we insist on an "expanding horizons" model for the early grades, and as far as we can in secondary, when none of us has come to an understanding of the world that way? We need only reflect on our experience to see the falseness of that idea. Why do we ignore the simple truths of our experience when drawing up, or revising, social studies curricula?

If we want students to be able to reflect critically on their social experience we must concentrate on developing not a superficial acquaintance with the issues, but the more important prerequisite grasp of meanings in human events that can come most efficiently from the study of history. The choice before us is simple. We can teach "irrelevant" history in order that as adults our students will be able to think critically about their society, or we can directly teach about the issues of society before the concept "society" has become meaningful, and so generate myths, leaving students conditioned and socialized, at best. The content of the curriculum is not a trivial matter. It does matter what is in grade six and what in grade nine and so on. The curriculum is the sequence of building *meanings* of prerequisite knowledge and understanding, layer on layer, that can lead to the fullest understanding possible in our circumstances. If the sequence of curriculum content cannot be seen to follow from some clear educational theory then we are in trouble. The curriculum is treated like a ladder onto whose steps bits and pieces can be tacked, and be moved about if too many people complain and be put somewhere else. Sensible curricula are embodiments of ideas. When there are hardly any ideas, the curriculum is jumbled.

> There is only one idea evident in the typical structure of the social studies curriculum. That idea is summed up in the term "expanding horizons."

What Children Know First and Best

A final point that needs to be made against prevailing presuppositions is that young children would find it much easier to learn academic history than about the content of their immediate social experience. The early ideas about child development which have survived in the general form of the elementary social studies curriculum (and which have been reinforced by some interpretations of Piaget's theory) suggested that young children have not yet achieved the conceptual development which would allow them to make sense of history (Hallam, 1969). Those ideas about child development also have been taken to support the belief that, during those early years, children can readily elaborate the concepts which impinge on them in their immediate social experience—homes, families, communities, etc.

I have already argued that the appreciation of the meanings of immediate social experience is among the things that we learn only in adulthood. In a developmental sequence from early childhood to adulthood they come among the last things we learn. It remains, then, to argue that history can be grasped in a meaningful way by very young children in, say, grades one to six. While I will argue here that this is possible, a further point I wish to stress is that for the development of a mature appreciation of the meanings of social experience the kind of early understanding of history I will touch on below is a prerequisite. That is, the introduction of academic history into the elementary curriculum in place of the present content of social studies is *necessary* to developing towards the mature appreciation we are aiming for—for all children, not just for the very brightest.

There is only one idea evident in the typical structure of the social studies curriculum. That idea is summed up in the term "expanding horizons." The source of this idea in curriculum thinking seems to lie in a mixture of "child-centered," early developmental psychology and some confusion about the truism that one must work from the known to the unknown. Dewey gave these ideas their definitive form, observing, for example:

> It is a cardinal precept of the newer school of education that the beginning of instruction shall be made with the experience learners already have; that this experience and the capacities that have been developed during its course provide the starting point for all further learning. (1938/1963, p. 74)

He adds that there should be "orderly development towards expansion and organization of subject matter through growth of experience" and that it is "essential that the new objects and events be related intellectually to those of earlier experiences, and this means that there be some advance made in conscious articulation of facts and ideas" (1938/1963, pp. 74, 75).

When this is translated into content for the social studies curriculum, we get that familiar focus on the local knowledge and experience which children are assumed to bring with them to schools. They begin from this. So we study families, neighborhoods, then larger communities, then interactions among communities and so on "outward," expanding children's knowledge along lines of content associations from what they know and experience in their daily lives. One problem with this lone organizing principle is that it begins to lose its determining force by about grade six, once children have made contact with other "culture realms" of the world. By then, however—I will argue—quite enough *erosion of education* has already taken place.

Within this gradual movement out from the local and immediate, one apparent anomaly—a kind of hiccup in the smooth flow—is the typical study of the form of life of one or more aboriginal society. The rationale for this within the expanding horizons model is again given by Dewey. Such a study is a part of the gradual expansion towards understanding the complexity of students' present societies:

> Recourse to the primitive may furnish the fundamental elements of the present situation in immensely simplified form. It is like unraveling a cloth so complex and close to the eyes that its scheme cannot be seen, until the larger coarser features of the pattern appear . . . and by seeing how these were solved in the earlier days of the human race, form some conception of the long road which has had to be traveled, and of the successive inventions by which the race has been brought forward in culture. (Dewey, 1916/1966, p. 215)

Throughout the social studies curriculum, students must always work from something within their immediate experience. Dewey puts it: "What is here insisted upon is the necessity of an actual empirical situation as the initiating phase of thought" (p. 153). This principle is to apply not only to young children:

> Even for older students, the social sciences would be less abstract and formal if they were dealt with less as sciences (less as formulated bodies of knowledge) and more in their direct subject-matter as that is found in the daily life of the social groups in which the student shares. (p. 201)

Given such an interpretation of the truism, it seems to follow easily that "The true starting point of history is always some present situation with its problems," and "local or home geography is the natural starting point" (pp. 214, 212).

A connected principle which informs the structure of the social studies curriculum is expressed by Dewey as:

> The knowledge which comes first to persons, and that remains most deeply ingrained, is knowledge of how to do; how to walk, talk, read, write, skate, ride a bicycle, and so on indefinitely. (p. 185)

Dewey, in drawing up what has been the theoretical blueprint for the social studies curriculum in North America—a blueprint whose general form and character, and rhetoric, have remained virtually unchanged for the past three quarters of a century—claims that he has based it on what he calls the "psychological principle." That is, his curriculum plan derives not from some logical analysis of subject matter, but from an observation of how children learn. Thus in drawing up our social studies curriculum, we must expand from "actual empirical situations" (p. 153); we must establish a "progressive order, using the factors first acquired as means of gaining insight into what is more complicated" (p. 20); we must root all subject matter "in the daily life of the social groups in which the student shares" (p. 201). "Before teaching can safely enter upon conveying facts and ideas through the media of signs, schooling must provide genuine situations in which personal participation brings home the import of the material and the problems which it conveys" (p. 233); and he assures us that, "recognition of the natural course of development . . . always sets out with situations which involve learning by doing" (p. 184).

One effect of all this has been to banish history from the elementary social studies curriculum, and to provide only the sketchiest glance at "our story." If one has to begin always from actual empirical situations it will be difficult, and a very long road, to get to Ancient Greece—unless, that is, one trivializes it to a look at how ancient Greek houses were different from and similar to our houses. But Sophocles, Thucydides and Socrates didn't live and die to tell our children that.

Before children can walk or talk, before they can skate or ride a bicycle, they know love and hate, joy and fear, good and bad, power and powerlessness, and the rhythms of expectation and satisfaction, of hope and disappointment.

Bertrand Russell, after his first disastrous experiment in organizing a school, observed that the first task of education is to destroy the tyranny of the local and immediate over the child's imagination. The social studies curriculum (not T.V.) is the main instrument in Canada for doing the opposite. We must begin then with the basic "psychological principle" which Dewey articulated, and which has so profoundly influenced the form of the social studies curriculum, and see whether it is true.

It is, of course, a truism that children must begin from what they know and build on that. But it is a very complex truism, early expounded in Plato's *Meno*. What has been lost between Plato and Dewey is a sense of the subtlety of the dilemma. Dewey constantly interprets what children know first and best in gross terms of the content of their experience. What alternative is there?

Before children can walk or talk, before they can skate or ride a bicycle, they know love and hate, joy and fear, good and bad, power and powerlessness, and the rhythms of expectation and satisfaction, of hope and disappointment. They know love and hate, good and bad, better and more profoundly than they ever know even how to walk or ride a bicycle. Children who never learn to walk or talk or read or skate know love and fear, expectation and satisfaction, hope and disappointment.

The knowledge which comes first to persons and remains most deeply ingrained is not knowledge of "how to do;" it is the fundamental emotional categories upon which we learn increasingly to make sense of anything in the universe and in human experience. It does not, then, follow that "primary or initial subject matter always exists as matter of an active doing, involving the use of the body and the handling of material" (Dewey, 1916/1966, p. 184). It does not follow, then, that the only access children can have to the world and wider human experience is through lines of gradually expanding content associations from their local environments and immediate experiences. Those environments and experiences provide not only restricted exposure to particular knowledge, they provide fundamental categories for making sense of the world—and children can have direct meaningful access to anything which can be organized within those categories.

What is at issue here is not whether children know better how to walk and ride a bicycle than they know love and hate, hope and disappointment. These represent quite different kinds of "knowledge," and attempting a comparison of them as kinds of knowledge even would be a bit odd. Two points seem worth making here, however. First, the above suggests at least that there is an alternative way of interpreting the truism and that this alternative interpretation is sensible.

The second point is that if our concern in education is with understanding the world and experience and the growth of knowledge about these, our beginning seems more sensibly based on children's knowledge of the most fundamental categories of thought whereby these are made meaningful, rather than on their ability to walk and skate. These latter, it might also be noted, are "knowledge" only in an extended sense of the word—we would more usually call them skills or abilities. We say we know how to skate, but such knowledge is subconscious. If we attempt to deal with it consciously we begin to stumble and fall over. This again suggests a poor foundation for a process which is concerned with the development of conscious understanding of the world and experience.

If one considers what most engages children's minds it is surely stories about monsters, witches, dragons, knights and princesses in distant times and places, rather than the subject-matter, however actively engaged, of families, local environments and communities. Children clearly do not have to be led from their everyday reality by a process of expanding horizons till they gain access to talking animals in bizarre places and strange times. It is clear that children have direct access to their curious imaginary realms. Indeed, they have much easier access to these than to the content of their everyday world when it is treated as "subject-matter." Why should this be so? One reason is that fairy tales are organized on those fundamental moral and emotional categories which are the things children know first and best. Such tales embody struggles between good and bad, the brave and the cowardly; they give content to love and hate, fear and security.

My purpose here has been to show that the sole organizing principle evident in the present social studies curriculum is based on a highly dubious interpretation of what children know best. That is, the logical form of the "expanding horizons" curriculum seems to be based on a psychological error. Children do not know how to walk or skate better or earlier or in a more real way, than they know love and fear; and, anyway, observations about how well they know how to walk or skate are somewhat beside the educational point. In enunciating his "psychological principle," then, Dewey articulates something which is far from the self-evident truth it has commonly been taken to be, and is anyway not the central observation to make about children's minds if one's focus of interest is their education.

Two other observations might be made about the elementary social studies curriculum. First, it seems intent on teaching children things which they will learn anyway from their everyday experience of the world. If there are any twenty year olds who do not understand about the structure of neighborhoods, it is not because they were not taught it properly in grade one or two. Second, the social studies curriculum most eloquently expresses a contempt for children's intelligence.

It is almost as if adults assume that because children know so little they must also be stupid and unable to learn much. Consequently they are given as a central part of their elementary education a curriculum that is almost entirely vacuous and where not vacuous, trivial.

Children come to school already knowing the most profound things human beings have to learn. They know good and bad, love and hate, power and oppression, joy and fear and so on. They are—it is apparently

> If one considers what most engages children's minds it is surely stories about monsters, witches, dragons, knights and princesses in distant times and places, rather than the subject-matter, however actively engaged, of families, local environments and communities.

our nature—eager to make sense of the world around them using these intellectual tools. In learning more about the world, these tools, or concepts, become more sophisticated and refined. But they are there when children arrive at school in simple yet powerful forms. They can use them to understand Greek history as they use them to understand their own experiences of struggling for autonomy against oppression, of greed and generosity, of courage and cowardice, of chance happenings and causal sequences. And in using them to learn, say, Greek history, they are also expanding and refining the tools or concepts they have available with which to make sense of the world. An elementary social studies curriculum which is largely filled with the superficial features of their local environments and immediate experience largely ignores the most powerful tools with which children can make sense of their world.

The imaginative grappling with the world which is engaged by using these fundamental tools in learning is simply passed over in the present social studies curriculum. It is no wonder that by grade six or seven these children have such difficulty learning history. The tools by which they could make sense of it have been largely ignored, and anyway, when history is presented it typically is not organized in terms of the fundamental emotional concepts by which children would have access to it. What is lost in all this is the development of those intellectual tools which best enable children to make sense of human experience. The expanding horizons social studies curriculum may thus be seen, paradoxically again, as an instrument which helps to alienate children from their social experience.

CONCLUSION

Dewey resolved the duality between natural and formal learning by seeking to collapse the latter to the former; he avoided the duality we have suggested between socializing and education by largely collapsing the latter to the former and calling the result "education." Now clearly this simplifies matters somewhat, but while Dewey frequently writes about the importance of what we have called educational activities, he nowhere provides a criterion for selecting them for the curriculum that can compete with the criterion drawn from what we have called socializing activities.

Despite Dewey's discussion of the intrinsic value of certain educational activities, and the overall aim to liberate the child from the local and immediate, the general effect of his constant tying of all studies to empirical experience and social activity seems to be, in social studies at least, a curriculum that remains in thrall to the local, the provincial, the narrow. His rhetoric stresses the means of escape; his criteria for choosing a curriculum keeps the child's imagination tied to the present and the local. Given the above distinction, I would want to retitle Dewey's celebrated book, *Socialization for Democracy.* In it he has little to say about education; it is a book about socializing. And given that he has largely collapsed education to socializing it seems to me—not to put too fine a point on it—that *Democracy and Education* has been one of the most powerfully influential anti-educational forces on North American schools.

My argument runs counter to what is generally *presupposed* about history and social studies and so may be rejected not so much on the grounds that there is something wrong with the argument as such but simply on the grounds that it is crazy. It is generally presupposed that if one wants children and students to know more about their immediate social experience one should spend more time teaching about it. The problem with this presupposition, I have argued, is that it ignores the nature of our social experience.

Knowledge of human experience is not the same kind of stuff as knowledge of physics. It is not a matter of learning more or less secure theories and the facts which support them. Knowledge of human experience comes through an understanding and appreciation of meanings. Sympathy with human motives, a sense of the complexity of intermingled chance and necessity in human events, a knowledge of human passions, fears, ambitions and so on, provide our access to those *meanings*. The dialectical interconnection between everyday experience and the events of history can help build children's and students' understanding of those meanings. There is no direct and immediate access to these meanings. It is folly to assume that without a disciplined understanding of human events, such as the study of history can provide, one can directly initiate children and students into an enriched understanding of the meanings of their own social experience.

So what should we do? First, get clear on the differences between socializing and educating. We should revise the social studies curriculum out of existence and introduce a new kind of history curriculum (such as is outlined in Egan, 1997). We should attend more sensitively to what are prerequisites to developing a meaningful understanding of our social experience, and erradicate in this process those activities associated with values clarification, attitude formation, much of what passes for inquiry or discovery learning, and the rest of the fashionable panoply of socializing and myth-encouraging practices that erode education in our schools.

REFERENCES

Dewey, J. (1916/1966). *Democracy and education.* New York: Free Press.

Dewey, J. (1938/1963). *Experience and education.* New York: Collier Books.

Egan, K. (1979). *Educational development.* New York: Oxford University Press.

Egan, K. (1997). *The educated mind: How cognitive tools shape our understanding.* Chicago: University of Chicago Press.

Hallam, R. (1969). Piaget and the teaching of history. *Educational Researcher, 12,* 3-12.

Oakshott, M. (1970). Education: The engagement and its frustration. *Proceedings of the Philosophy of Education Society of Great Britain* (pp. 43-76). Oxford: Blackwell.

SECTION TWO :

ENDS AND MEANS

▶ CONTENT KNOWLEDGE

▶ CRITICAL THINKING

▶ INFORMATION GATHERING AND REPORTING

▶ PERSONAL AND SOCIAL VALUES

▶ INDIVIDUAL AND COLLECTIVE ACTION

16

Beyond Inert Facts and Concepts: Teaching for Understanding

Roland Case

If the mind of the child when learning, remains merely passive, merely receiving knowledge as a vessel receives water which is poured into it, little good can be expected to accrue. It is as if food were introduced into the stomach which there is no room to digest or assimilate, and which will therefore be rejected from the system, or like a useless and oppressive load upon its energies.

Report on a System of Public Education
for Upper Canada
Egerton Ryerson (1847, p. 58)

As sure as the fall turns to winter and Wimbledon follows the French Open, there will be newspaper reports of students' lack of knowledge of basic Canadian facts accompanied by a call to teach more Canadian content. One recent report decried "a shocking lack of knowledge of the country's background" (Harris Burgess, 1997) and another handed Canadian youth a "failing grade in history" claiming that high school graduates were "ignorant of the lessons and achievements of the past" (MacQueen, 1997). What are we to conclude from these consistently poor results. Should we spend more time on factual knowledge in social studies? Should we adopt a back-to-basics approach to teaching facts? I think not on both counts for the reason Egerton Ryerson expressed 150 years ago. As his opening quote implies, perhaps the problem is not that students were never "taught" that, for example, Sir John A. Macdonald was the first Canadian prime minister and that Confederation occurred in 1867, but that the ways in which they were taught contributed to many students forgetting these facts. Consider the following remark by an American high school student on the amount of material covered in his social studies courses:

> Much of the time it is total skim, it's very bad. In one course we covered 2,000 years. Every week we were assigned to cover a 30-page chapter. We had 30 dates a week to memorize. The pity of it is that now I don't remember any of them. (cited in Parker, 1989, p. 41)

There is an even more fundamental issue about what and how we should teach, one that arises from the difference between *remembering* historical information—factual recall—and *understanding* historical events. Students may not remember exactly when Confederation occurred or that the awakening of Quebec nationalism in the 1960s is called the "Quiet Revolution" yet they may nevertheless have some understanding of the significance and key features of these events. Clearly, those understandings are more important than recall of the date and the label. Unfortunately, many public reports calling for more content fail to make this distinction clear. It is even more crucial that as social studies teachers we not overlook this distinction.

In this article I explore how we might teach social studies content—both factual knowledge and concepts—in ways that foster understanding rather than mere recall of information. My reference in the title of this article to *inert* facts and concepts comes from Alfred North Whitehead's famous book, *The Aims of Education* (1929/1967), where he suggests that "the central problem of all education" is in preventing knowledge from becoming inert (p. 5). By inert, Whitehead means "ideas that are merely received into the mind without being utilized, or tested, or thrown into fresh combination" (p. 1). Harvard educational psychologist David Perkins (1993) defines inert knowledge as "knowledge that learners retrieve to answer the quiz question, but that does not contribute to their endeavors and insights in real complex situations" (p. 90).

Calling attention to the need to see our task as engendering understanding, not transmitting information, has been a persistent theme in social studies. John Dewey wrote in his influential book, *How We Think*, that "the aim often seems to be—especially in such a subject as geography—to make the pupil what has been called a 'cyclopedia of useless information'" (cited in Hare, 1994, p. 72). In 1960 Shirley Engle warned of a "ground-covering fetish" by which he meant the practice of "learning and holding in memory, enforced by drill, large amounts of more or less isolated descriptive material" (p. 302). More recently, Walter Parker (1989) urged that learning not be seen as "the warehousing of facts" but as the "progressive construction of understandings" and teaching not be the "telling of fact" but the leading of a construction project where the teacher acts as a contractor—not actually building the house but contracting to students the sorts of labour that will culminate in their building of a house (p. 41).

These admonitions to engage students in thinking about and with the content of the curriculum are easier said than done. Numerous challenges must be identified, understood and thoughtfully addressed. I begin first with issues and suggestions for teaching factual information in ways that promote factual understanding and then consider the teaching of concepts in ways that promote conceptual understanding. But before proceeding further let me clear up some key terminology:

- *Factual information* is found in descriptive claims about the way the world is and why it is this way. These include what in social studies are typically called 'facts' and 'generalizations.' Facts are descriptive statements about a singular event, object or person, such as "Mount Everest is the highest peak in the world" and "John A. Macdonald was Canada's first prime minister." Generalizations are broad statements that encompass a range of occurences, objects or people, such as "Early European exploration of North America was motivated by the desire for economic and political gain" and "Natural resources have dominated Canada's economic and social development."

- *Conceptual information* is found in statements about the meanings of words such as "A community is an interacting group of individuals with common bonds" and "Justice means getting what one deserves." These statements differ from factual statements because even if a bona fide community never actually existed the statement about communities is true by definition. The word 'concept' is used ambiguously in social studies by some to refer to generalizations (because conceptual statements typically apply broadly) and by others to refer to the ideas or meanings captured by words such as 'justice,' 'table' and 'community.' I use 'concept' exclusively in this latter sense.

And finally, what of the concept 'understanding'? What does it mean to understand as opposed merely to possess (or recall) information about something? Three attributes seem especially significant:

- *Understanding implies basic comprehension of information.* Understanding a fact or concept is not mere patter off the lips in response to a stock question or a request to rehash a rotely memorized definition. At the least understanding implies that students can thoughtfully rephrase the answer in their own words. Richard Lederer (1987) has compiled an amusing "history" of the world from comments by students who apparently so poorly understood what was taught that they have got their facts wrong. His report of students' account of ancient Rome is as follows:

    Eventually the Romans conquered the Greeks. History calls people Romans because they never stayed in one place very long. At Roman banquets, the guests wore garlics in their hair. Julius Caesar extinguished himself on the battle fields of Gaul. The Ides of March murdered him because they thought he was going to be made king. Nero was a cruel tyranny who would torture his poor subjects by playing the fiddle to them.

Hilda Taba used the phrase "the rattle of empty wagons" to refer to students who had learned to use the labels for concepts without grasping their mean-

More recently, Walter Parker (1989) urged that learning not be seen as "the warehousing of facts" but as the "progressive construction of understandings" and teaching not be the "telling of fact" but the leading of a construction project where the teacher acts as a contractor—not actually building the house but contracting to students the sorts of labour that will culminate in their building of a house (p. 41).

ing (Parker, 1988). The "rattle of empty wagons" resonated with me when I heard of a recent episode in a social studies class on free trade and protectionism. Students were assembling impressive-looking lists of the reasons for each side when a visitor to the class asked one student what 'protectionism' meant? The student was taken aback and then responded," Oh, it's like when you install an alarm system in your car." If this was offered as a literal example of the concept, I wonder how well the student really knew what he was attempting to justify with the long list of reasons he had just assembled.

- *Understanding implies appreciation of significance and interconnection.* Remembering that Confederation occurred in 1867 is not the same as understanding this fact. The latter requires to some extent that students know the significance of this event and how it fits into the larger historical picture. Imagine asking students: Which is the more important event in Canada's development as a nation—Confederation or the first basketball game? We would have little confidence that students really understand Confederation if they chose the first basketball game. This is because we would doubt that they correctly appreciated the magnitude of the implications of each event. Imagine also asking: What is the relation between Canadian sovereignty and Confederation? If students could not see any connection we again might doubt that they understood Confederation, since they seem to have little appreciation of the constellation of ideas that interconnect with the specific event or phenomenon. For this reason, amassing of discrete facts and concepts add little to understanding since it is the inter-relationships that are central.

- *Understanding implies some grasp of the warrants for the claim.* A final aspect of understanding is the need to appreciate, to some extent at least, what kind of evidence is required in deciding whether one should accept or reject a proposed statement. Imagine students are told that certain statements in their textbook are thought to be false, say, that Confederation was not in 1867 or that early European exploration of North America was not motivated by the desire for economic and political gain. If students had no idea whatsoever what might count as supporting or refuting evidence for these claims then we might wonder how well they understood what these claims signify.

Our task, if we are concerned to promote factual and conceptual understanding, is to help students comprehend, connect and seek justification for the information they receive.

TEACHING FOR FACTUAL UNDERSTANDING

There are countless suggestions that might be made about teaching factual knowledge in ways that increase students' understanding of the content. Much can be said about presenting (or packaging) information in ways that will appeal to and engage students. In this article I explore various suggestions clustered around two other general themes:

- Getting students to "work" the content
- Sampling not covering content.

Working the content

According to Whitehead information remains inert if students do not utilize, test or re-interpret the ideas. In other words, students must, in some fashion, "work" the ideas they encounter—they must put the knowledge into use. Answering straightforward recall questions after reading a text and or taking down notes verbatim while listening to a lecture are merely acts of receiving transmitted information. Students are working the content only when they start to think about the material—that is, they begin to make judgments about or with it. As Parker notes "thinking is how people learn" (1988, p. 70). This certainly does not mean that it is inappropriate to transmit information—we must transmit information to our students. The point is that passing on information—including *covering* the Crusades and *doing* Egypt—is not the heart of our task. This is merely a means to an end. Our real objective must be to enable students and get them in the habit of thinking about key ideas learned about these topics.

Answering straightforward recall questions after reading a text and or taking down notes verbatim while listening to a lecture are merely acts of receiving transmitted information. Students are working the content only when they start to think about the material—that is, they begin to make judgments about or with it.

The need for students to continually think about the content is crucial. It is not sufficient to "front-end load" considerable content and at a point near the end of a unit or term invite students to reflect on the ideas they had heard and read about. As Ryerson's metaphor suggests, information that has been passively acquired is not digested in a way that makes it available for future use. It ceases to be—because it never was—food for thought. For this reason we must find ongoing ways to involve students in thinking as they learn, so that they will, in fact, learn. I will discuss three avenues for inviting students to work the content:

- interrogate the text
- reframe the material
- solve the problem.

Interrogate the text

Perhaps the most obvious way to invite students to work the content is by making the "text" problematic, either by raising doubts about its content and/or about its source. Too often information contained in textbooks and other learning resources is presented to students as noncontroversial fact. This information is simply accepted as given. Rarely are students asked to question the adequacy, objectivity and completeness of the content. We can and should invite students to "interrogate the text" in several ways:

- **Competing accounts**. Provide competing accounts of an event, situation or issue and have students decide for themselves which account, if any, is to be believed. The failure of most textbooks to consistently provide alternative accounts is perhaps the most limiting factor in getting students to work information from these sources. We need regularly to supplement one-sided accounts—whether in textbooks or in lecture notes—with opposing perspectives. Even young students can be engaged in this enterprise by, for example, having them consider two accounts of the same schoolyard encounter or read competing versions of what should be done to make their neighbourhood a better place.

- **Single problematic account**. Provide a single account of an event, situation or issue, but assist students in acquiring the analytic tools to call into question whether or not the account is to be believed. Notions such as stereotyping, or gender, class and national bias offer tools for getting students to assess their textbooks and other materials. The example in the box at the bottom of this page illustrates how a single text, in this case an account of Simon Fraser's descent down the Fraser River, can be made problematic by assisting students in seeing alternative inferences to those put forth by the author.

- **Problematic source**. Provide students with analytic tools to call into question the very source of the text. Students might, for example, use the following criteria to judge the credibility of various documents:
  - Is it a first-hand account or is it an account based on second-hand information?
  - Does the author have an obvious bias?
  - Does the author have a solid reputation?
  - Is the person well informed on the topic?
  - Is the report offered as a truthful account (or is it a fictional or embellished account)?

Reframe the material

A second way to invite students to work the content is to require that they provide an original synthesis of the ideas presented. Unlike the first approach, which makes the content problematic, this approach assumes that the content is credible and invites students to reframe the content by setting it in a different context or frame of reference.

- **From a different perspective**. One way to reframe content is to have students rewrite an account from the perspective or point of view of others than those in the original text, for example, by describing how a geographer as opposed to an economist, or a logger as opposed to an environmentalist, or a king as opposed to a peasant, would look upon relevant issues. Eric Bonfield, a humanities teacher in Surrey,

---

EXCERPT FROM THE DESCENT OF THE FRASER RIVER

On May 28, 1808 Simon Fraser led twenty-three men to find a route from the interior of British Columbia to the Pacific Ocean along a river which Fraser imagined to be the Columbia River. Day after day they encountered obstacles as they paddled down the river. The river was a continuous series of rapids and the carrying places were extremely dangerous or very long. The places where they had to carry their canoes to get around the rapids were so rough that a pair of moccasins was worn to shreds in one day. Fraser decided the First Nations people he had met were correct in saying that the river was not passable for canoes. So Fraser and his men set out on foot, carrying packs weighing eighty pounds each. In his diary, Fraser wrote that they experienced "a good deal of fatigue and disagreeable walking" but he and his men continued on their journey.

The above paragraph is the opening to an abridged account of *The Descent of the Fraser River* by Malcolm G. Parks. It portrays Simon Fraser's exploration down the Fraser River in 1808. The passage can be treated as a non-controversial account of an historical event or be made problematic by helping students see the difference between descriptions of *directly observed events*—what someone would actually see or hear if they were a fly on the wall at the time—and the *inferences* that the author or a reader might draw from these events. For example, it is stated that "The route was so rough that a pair of moccasins was worn to shreds in one day of portaging." The wearing out of a pair of moccasins in one day is the directly observable fact. The author's implied inference seems to be that Fraser and his men were determined, preserving and willing to endure danger and great sacrifice. We could speculate about other inferences that might be drawn from this same event. Perhaps the moccasins wore out because they were of an inferior quality, in which case Fraser, or whoever outfitted the expedition, may have been incompetent. Alternatively, the moccasins may have worn out because Fraser and his men were not careful when portaging, in which case they might be clumsy, inept wilderness trekkers who very not good at navigating portages. The task for students would be to read the entire passage and find additional sources to determine which inferences were most plausible given the available directly observable facts. (A full version of this account and an accompanying lesson plan is contained in my article in this collection titled "Course, Unit and Lesson Planning.")

British Columbia, frequently invites his students to construct hypothetical conversations between famous historical and contemporary characters.

- **In another genre**. Students can be invited to represent their understandings of a body of information in another medium (e.g., in story board or schematic form) or in symbolic form. Metaphors offer an intriguing way of reframing content. For example, students might be asked to offer an overarching metaphor to explain a phenomenon they have just studied. If taken seriously this task involves considerable reflection since metaphors should be unexpected, offer insight into the phenomenon and draw both the creator and the audience into investigating the connections between the compared items. Alternatively, students might assess the adequacy of supplied metaphors—for example, when studying about revolutions or the media, students might examine the following metaphors: "A revolution is an exploding volcano" or "Television is chewing gum for the mind."

- **To a new situation**. Another way to reframe content is to have students apply information supplied in one context to a novel situation. Vancouver teacher Rob Sandhu has his students apply insights from their study of the Industrial Revolution in England in the late eighteenth century to current developments in Thailand. In another lesson, students decide which political philosopher—Thomas Hobbes or John Locke—has the more useful advice to offer for modern governments.

- **Apply an analytic framework**. Another approach is to provide a model or framework which students use to analyze a body of information. For example, the box below offers a four-step model for analyzing the progression of revolutions. Students might be asked to determine whether or not the French Revolution is consistent with this model, or to consider a current emerging crisis and determine which stage has been reached.

Solve the problem

A third approach to encouraging students to work the content is by resolving a problem or settling a dispute that makes use of the information presented. A simple but effective example of creating a problem to engage students in thinking about content arose in the context of an elementary teaching resource on Weyburn, Saskatchewan. The resource consisted largely of worksheets requiring textbook retrieval of information about the local climate, services, geography and so on. What would otherwise have been mere transmission of information became an invitation to work this information by posing the following problem:

> Your mother is about to be transferred to either Weyburn, Saskatchewan or Prince George, British Columbia. She asks you to gather information and offer her your advice in deciding which would be a better place to live for your family.

Sampling not covering content

It should be obvious that if students are to work the content they will be unable to cover as much of the curricular terrain as they would otherwise do if they dealt with everything in a more passive, less probing manner. The pressure to cover content remains one of the enduring impediments to successful social studies teaching. A high school student offered the following telling metaphor on the amount of material covered in his social studies courses: "sometimes these classes can be like trying to take a drink from an open fire hydrant" (cited in Leming, 1994, p. 105).

The perceived need to cover large quantities of material may arise to some extent from a belief that our job as social studies teachers is to transmit information about the world. One of my objectives for this article is to encourage teachers to see promoting understanding

---

MODEL FOR ANALYZING REVOLUTION

Stage	Characteristics
Preliminary	Class antagonisms, government inefficiency, inept ruler, intellectuals transfer loyalty, economic upgrade, failure of force.
First Stage	Financial breakdown, government protests increase, dramatic events (such as storming the Bastille), moderates attain power, honeymoon period.
Crisis Stage	Radicals take control, moderates driven from office, civil war, foreign war, centralization of power in a revolutionary council, council dominated by strongman.
Recovery Stage	Slow, uneven return to quieter times, ruled by tyrant, radicals repressed, moderates gain amnesty, aggressive nationalism, return to normalcy as country gains strength.

This analytic model, developed initially by Crane Brinton in 1965, has been adapted for classroom use by Bob Benoit and Joseph Braun (1988).

as our crucial task. This would mean that we need not "get through" the textbook or feel that good teaching requires "covering" every topic in a unit. We would be wise to side with Whitehead (1929/1967) who urged "What you teach, teach thoroughly" (p. 2).

The key to balancing the quantity of information with the quality of understanding may lie in the advice offered by Hilda Taba. She believed that "coverage" of topics was impossible—there was always too much to cover. Instead teachers should "sample" rather than survey the content. Thus the important question for Taba was not *"how many* facts, but *which* facts we want students to think about" (Fraenkel, 1992, p. 174). John Dewey talked of "generative knowledge"—knowledge that had rich ramifications in the lives of learners (Perkins, 1993, p. 90). Generative knowledge consists of conceptual and factual insights that apply across many circumstances. Is it important, for example, that student study all the major early Canadian explorers or is it sufficient that they consider one or two explorers and come to appreciate the extent to which personal, economic and cultural motives drove early exploration? Is it imperative that students study all the major inventions and effects of the Industrial Revolution or is it sufficient that students come away with a few broad understandings, grounded in specific instances, of the way, for example, technology transformed (for the better and for the worse) almost every aspect of British society. These broader insights which span cultures and time periods are the sorts of generative understandings that we ought to emphasize.

Before leaving this point, it is useful to consider one of the reasons why broad surveys of topics may be desirable. It is thought that devoting considerable amounts of time on in-depth studies means that students are in danger of acquiring very narrowly circumscribed understandings. This potential shortcoming can be mitigated using a sampling approach. The notion of a geological survey of the surface of an area followed by more probing exploration at carefully selected sites is an apt metaphor for the sampling of topics. Students may receive via mini-lectures, films or fact sheets highly condensed overviews of a period or culture, which then set a context for more focussed case studies of particularly promising issues. Another strategy is to divide topics among groups of students who pursue areas in some depth and then share their findings with their classmates, thereby broadening the scope of everyone's understanding.

TEACHING FOR CONCEPTUAL UNDERSTANDING

Concepts are the neglected content dimension in social studies. While, generally speaking, we may devote too much attention to factual information, we are guilty of devoting very little attention to teaching concepts, and when we do teach a concept it often amounts to little more than providing a definition of the word. This is unfortunate because concepts are powerful determinants of perception. Concepts provide the intellectual categories or lenses through which we organize and make sense of the world. The simplest way to illustrate this point is to draw attention to the drawing on this page. What do you see? People will typically answer "a rabbit," "a duck," "a puppet" or some other creature. These answers arise only because we possess the concepts 'rabbit,' duck' and 'puppet.' If we did not have these concepts we would not see them in the drawing. Hence the difference, when looking at the drawing, between seeing undefined markings and seeing representations of objects is the possession of relevant concepts. Concepts actually shape what we see. It is this reason which helps to explain the Chinese proverb that "We see what is behind our eyes." If our students do not have, for example, the concepts 'injustice' and 'rights' they will not see injustice in a situation where one person's rights are being violated. The example of Simon Fraser discussed earlier presupposes that students can distinguish the concepts of 'directly observable fact' and 'inference' otherwise they will not appreciate that a statement such as "Fraser bravely rode the river" is not an incontrovertible fact but an interpretation inferred from the facts. Similarly, without the concepts of 'need' and 'want' younger students will not recognize an important difference between their basic entitlements to liquids and food, as opposed to their desires for soft drinks and ice cream.

References to students possessing or not possessing a concept is potentially misleading since this may imply that concepts are either/or—either students understand the concept or they do not. In many cases students will have an incomplete or distorted sense of a concept, which in some cases is worse than if they didn't have any conception whatsoever of the words. For example, many students believe the opposite of 'democracy' to be 'communism.' Since most student believe that democracy is a good thing, this means that communism must be a bad thing. Communism may or may not be

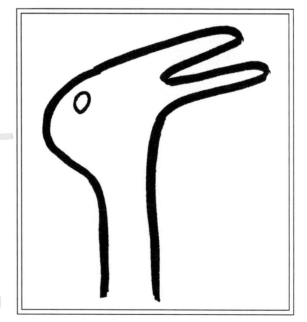

Key elementary concepts

beliefs	cultural relativism
belonging	democracy
causality (cause/effect)	division of labour
change	economic growth
choices	ecosystem
citizenship	empire
community	ethnic group
conflict	ethnocentrism
cooperation	feudalism
culture	freedom
discrimination	free enterprise
diversity	goods and services
environment	historical empathy
equality	ideology
fact	industrialization
fairness/justice	institution
families	interest group
identity	market economy
interaction	mass communication
interdependence	mass production
leadership	mixed economy
loyalty	monopoly
multiculturalism	multiculturalism
nation	national debt
needs	national deficit
neighbours	nationalism
neighbourhood	perspective
peace	progress
personal power	pluralism
province	power
respect	presentism
responsibilities	propaganda
rights	protectionism
safety	quality of life
self-worth/self-esteem	race
time	region
tradition/custom	revolution
wants	scarcity
values	security
	sexism
	social class
Key secondary concepts	social contract
acculturation	socialization
adaptation	society
affirmative action	state
assimilation	status
authority	sustainable
balance of power	development
bias/prejudice	technology
capitalism	terrorism
citizen	tradition
civilization	unilateral
colonialism	violence
conformity	

undesirable, but it is not inherently undemocratic, as many students' conceptual confusion leads them to believe. But notice they will *see* communism in this light because of a conceptual confusion between economic systems (e.g., capitalism, communism) and political systems (e.g., democracy, dictatorship).

The metaphor of concepts as intellectual lenses is especially apt in that some individual's glasses or eyesight are not well focussed—they see the world in a blurred sometimes incorrect form. The possession of rather crude concepts means that things are often lumped into vague dichotomous categories such as "awesome" and "gross" or "fun" and "boring." Our task then is not solely to introduce students to new concepts in social studies, but also to continually refine their conceptual understandings so that our students learn to see the social world in increasingly discriminating ways.

There are many concepts for students to acquire in social studies. They are typically divided into two categories: *concrete concepts* which refer to tangible objects such as mountain, ocean, valley, map and globe, and *abstract concepts* such as justice, time, culture and discrimination.

Because of the volume of concepts to be taught in social studies, it is important to be selective. There is no point in teaching a concept merely because it is found in the curriculum or textbook. Students may already have a good grasp of the idea. For instance, most primary students will have some understanding of family before they begin to work with it in social studies. They will have lived in a family of one type or another for about six years. They don't need to be taught the obvious features of families. Rather, they may need experiences such as looking at pictures, reading stories and talking with other children which will help them to see that some families are different from the ones they are familiar with (e.g., they may have only one parent living in the home), but they are nevertheless families. Our efforts should be directed towards extending and deepening understanding and in correcting misperceptions of familiar concepts. As well we should introduce students to unfamiliar concepts that might have significant generative potential. The box on this page illustrates a range of abstract concepts commonly found in elementary and secondary social studies curricula.

Promoting conceptual understanding

Being able to offer a definition of a word is not the same as understanding the concept. For example, a 'rule' might be defined as a principle or regulation that governs conduct. Knowing this does not exhaust what we would want students to understand about rules. Definitions offer at best the bare bones of a concept. There are many nuances and connotations associated with the notion of rules that might be important in enriching students' understanding of the concept. One such attribute is the negative connotation that many students associate with rules, namely that rules are restrictive and that they prevent individuals from doing what they want to do. We might teach students that rules do not only prohibit actions; they often enable and protect actions. For example, the rules of a game enable us to play the game: if there was no rule that a goal is scored when a puck crosses the goal line, we could not play hockey. Even rules that prohibit actions, typically do so in order to enable others to do certain things. For example, we can safely cross a street only because there are rules that stop cars from proceeding on a red light. Rather than simply offer a definition of a word, promoting conceptual understanding involves teaching the attributes or features that govern the application of the concept. As the American philosopher William James said, "A word is a summary of what to look for" (cited in Parker & Perez, 1987, p. 164). The attributes of a concept describe what the objects or events covered by the word will possess. We recognize certain geographic objects as, for example, rivers or ponds only because we know the attributes each is to exhibit (e.g., one flows, the other does not).

Identify key attributes

A first step in teaching a concept is to identify the key attributes that we want students to learn. It is generally unwise to attempt to teach all attributes of a concept at any one time. Better to begin by teaching particular attributes that students most need to understand.

Conceptual attributes are sometimes differentiated according to *essential* and *non-essential* attributes. The latter category is itself often divided into two sub-categories—*typical* and *non-typical* attributes.

- Essential attributes are features that are necessary for the correct use of the concept. For example, having three sides is an essential attribute of the concept 'triangle.' An essential attribute of the concept 'rule' is that it regulates actions.

- Non-essential attributes refer to all other attributes of a concept. They include typical attributes which are features that are often associated with the concept and may be helpful in understanding it but are not necessarily present in all cases. For example, "mountains are (often) very high" and "mountains may have snow" are typical but non-essential attributes. Typical attributes of 'rules' are that they often involve punishment or negative consequences if broken, and that they often prohibit or prevent action but may also protect or permit action. Another typical attribute of rules is that they are often written down. Non-typical attributes are features that are completely irrelevant to understanding the concept.

It may be the case that teaching students about typical features is an important as teaching them about essential features. But students must understand that a typical attribute need not always be present for the concept to apply.

Listed in the following box are several attributes for randomly selected concepts in social studies. They are

SAMPLE ATTRIBUTES

Concept	Attributes
bias	• is an unfair preference or prejudice that colours observations or conclusions • is a predisposition to praise or blame without sufficient evidence • too many forms: ethnocentrism, sexism, racism, presentism, anthrocentrism
change	• affects virtually all things • may be brought about by humans or by nature • may be negative or positive • may be gradual or dramatic
culture	• is human's response to nature • is rarely static; changes over time • refers to many different aspects of a society (i.e., language, religion, customs, laws, art, music) • is more than costumes, clothing and food • shapes in powerful ways our beliefs and values
needs	• needs are requirements for adequate functioning • needs may be psychological or physical • some needs are common, others are unique to certain individuals
perspective	• orients what we see and how we see things • can be physical or mental • may be narrow or broad, empathic or closed, chauvinistic or fair-minded

suggestive of the key understandings (both essential and typical attributes) that we would want students to acquire about each of these concepts.

Teach the key attributes

Four strategies are especially helpful in promoting conceptual understanding. Illustrations of each strategy are found in the box on the following page—Teaching Concrete Concepts—and in the box on the succeeding page—Teaching Abstract Concepts.

- **Provide an opportunity to "experience" the concept**. Whether it is a concrete or an abstract concept it is important for students to "experience" the concept. With concrete concepts, this may occur by having actual physical objects or pictures, as opposed to merely referring to examples. In the case of abstract concepts it is often more difficult but even more necessary to provide students with an opportunity to "experience" key attributes of the concept. In teaching about perspective, for example, we might involve students in describing objects from different physical locations (e.g., crawl underneath the desk, stand to one side). Simulations may also be effective. For example, to introduce the notion that rules serve positive purposes involve students in a game with constantly changing rules and watch as they come to realize the problems that arise when we don't have rules to rely upon.

- **Consider exemplars of the concept.** Concepts are learned by coming to understand the range of application or scope of the concept. Thus it is important to provide or have students generate multiple illuminating examples of the diverse uses of the concept. In teaching concrete concepts such as 'desert' young students need to see numerous examples of

TEACHING CONCRETE CONCEPTS

Concrete concepts are most easily taught by providing students with a wide range of pictures or actual objects that are exemplars and non-exemplars of the concept. The point is to help students recognize the essential, typical and non-typical attributes of the concept. With younger students it may be sufficient to have them distinguish essential and non-essential attributes as suggested by the chart for teaching the concept 'desert.' We might walk students through the attributes and illustrate them with exemplars and non-exemplars. Alternatively, as suggested by the chart for teaching the concept 'globe,' we might list the attributes and ask students to categorize the attributes and support their decisions with reference to exemplars and non-exemplars. An even more open-ended approach is to provide students with a set of pictures or objects and a blank chart for them to complete by generating and classifying attributes. Students might also be asked to locate their own exemplars and non-exemplars and produce a definition of the concept.

THE CONCEPT 'DESERT'

Attributes	essential attribute	non-essential attribute	Exemplars and non-exemplars
is very hot	√		glacier (non-example)
few human beings		√	desert settlements (example)
has no plants		√	cactus, oasis (non-examples)
has very little rainfall	√		tropical rain forest (non-example)
is inhabited by camels		√	Baja Desert (non-example)

THE CONCEPT 'GLOBE'

Attributes	essential attribute	typical attribute	non-typical attribute	Exemplars and non-exemplars
is round (spherical)				
is made of plastic				
is the size of a basketball				
has smooth surface				
shows geographic detail				
varies in colour				

These examples are adapted from Dueck (1979).

TEACHING ABSTRACT CONCEPTS

Abstract concepts are usually more difficult to teach than concrete concepts. The chart below lists seven strategies and their specific applications to the teaching of two concepts—'rules' at the elementary level and 'perspective' at the secondary level. All seven strategies would rarely be used at any one time, and the first four strategies are, generally speaking, the most useful.

Teaching ideas	'rules'	'perspective'
Experiential introduction	Play a "rotten rules" game to teach about the value of consistent rules. Without any introduction, throw an inflated balloon among the class. Students will automatically react by hitting the balloon back and forth. As students play, capriciously assign points for highest, lowest, hair colour, type of clothing of the hitter and so on. Be inconsistent—take off points for the same action or characteristic for which students earlier received a point.	• Show footage of an incident (e.g., hockey game/ J.F. Kennedy shooting) taken from different camera angles. • Have students describe or draw objects from different physical locations (e.g., crawl under the desk, stand to one side). • Offer documents of a specific event in early Canadian history from British, French and First Nations view points.
Definition	Share the following definition with students: a rule is a principle or regulation governing conduct.	Share the following definition with students: a perspective is a mental or physical outlook or point of view.
Exemplars	Ask students to identify why the following are examples of 'rules': • There is no running allowed in the school hallway. • The first person to cross the finish line wins the race. • Every sentence must end with either a period, a question mark or an exclamation point.	Explore different types of perspectives: • *physical perspectives:* on top of mountain, from bottom of valley; • *biased perspectives:* ethnocentrism, sexism, racism, presentism; • *discipline-based perspectives:* economic, political, ethical, artistic; • *social class-based perspectives:* ruling class, middle class, lower class.
Non-exemplars	Ask students to identify why the following are not examples of 'rules': • I don't like it when people run in the school hallway. • I came first in the race.	Distinguish between an opinion (i.e., a particular position on an issue or question) and a perspective (i.e., the orientation from which the position arises—biased, open-minded, etc.).
Etymology	The origin of 'rule' is "regula"—a straight stick or pattern.	The origin of 'perspective' refers to an optical instrument for viewing objects.
Synonyms and antonyms	Explore the following synonyms: • laws and regulations.	Explore the following synonyms: • point of view and orientation.
Derivative words	Discuss words that are related to or derivatives of 'rules': • to rule—to control, guide or govern; • a ruler [straight edge]—a device for guiding the drawing of lines; • unruly—uncontrolled.	Discuss words that are related to or derivatives of 'perspective': • perception; • periscope; • keeping things "in perspective".

the range of deserts that exist. So too with abstract concepts. The key is to find exemplars that highlight the attributes to be taught.

- **Consider non-exemplars of the concept.** Equally important in coming to understand a concept is knowing the limits or boundaries beyond which the concept does *not* apply. For this reason, non-exemplars are very useful. Non-exemplars are not simply any non-examples of the concept, rather they are closely related non-examples—instances that are frequently confused with the concept or, at least, are very similar, but different in important respects. Consider the difference between an opinion and a perspective. An opinion is a non-exemplar of a perspective—having an opinion on an issue is not the same as having a perspective on an issue. Opinions originate from perspectives; members of a group may have different opinions even though they look at the issue from the same perspective (e.g., cultural geographers disagree on a given theory) or similar opinions from different perspectives (e.g., Canada and US see eye-to-eye on free trade). Thus it might be helpful for students to recognize that opinion statements such as "I support capital punishment" and "I disapprove of capital punishment" do not indicate a perspective, whereas statements such as "Morally speaking, capital punishment is indefensible" and "As a victim of crime, I am in favour of capital punishment" do reveal a perspective from which the opinion is offered.

- **Provide or generate a definition.** Although on their own definitions do not capture all the attributes of a concept, providing or having students create a definition (especially if they have explored exemplars and non-exemplars) contributes to their conceptual understanding.

Other strategies which may be useful in teaching the attributes of some concepts include the following:

- **Explore the etymology of the word.** Etymology refers to the root origin of a word. Sometimes this origin provides a clue as to an essential attribute of the concept as illustrated by the etymology of 'perspective' which refers to an optical instrument for looking at objects.

- **Examine synonyms and antonyms.** Often synonyms and antonyms are helpful because students may be more familiar with these other words and, consequently, drawing attention to these words reinforces students' understanding of the concept under investigation.

- **Compare derivative words.** Derivative words are words that come from the same stem as the concept under investigation. It is interesting, for example, to compare the notion of a ruler (i.e., a straight edge) with the concept of a rule: a ruler is a physical device for guiding the making of lines, whereas a rule is a verbal device for guiding our actions.

Assess for conceptual understanding

Numerous strategies can be used to assess how well students have understood the conceptual attributes:

- Provide students with original examples and non-examples and ask students if they are instances of the concept:

  Are the following examples of rules?
  — No one is allowed to use my radio without my permission.
  — Many people vote in federal elections.

- Ask students to come up with their own original examples of the concept:

  Give two examples of a family rule or a school rule.
  What perspectives might we use to examine chalk? the Industrial Revolution?

- Answer students to address questions about specific attributes:

  Do all rules forbid action and are all rules written down?
  Give an example of a rule which prohibits and a rule which enables.

- Ask students to distinguish non-examples from examples:

  Explain in your own words the difference between a request and a rule. Give examples of each.
  Explain in your own words the difference between an opinion on an issue and a perspective taken on an issue. Give examples of each.

- Ask students to apply the concept in an assignment:

  Write a letter about [some historical or contemporary issue] from a particular perspective (e.g., Archie Bunker, Ralph Nader).
  Describe a classroom or historical incident from the perspectives of three different participants.

Conclusion

The focus of this article is on teaching content knowledge—both factual and conceptual—in ways that foster understanding. I have argued that knowledge acquisition is not a matter of transmitting bits of information and vocabulary to students. Superficial "coverage" of information or acquisition of facts for their own sake is not worthwhile—if for no other reason than it appears that much of it is forgotten almost as soon as it is taught. Our primary task is not to present learners with prepackaged information for mental storage but to facilitate, in meaningful contexts, the comprehending, questioning and making use of relevant facts and concepts. I suggest in promoting factual understanding that we engage our students in working the content of the curriculum, and this necessarily means sampling across topics in order to allow for in-depth study. In promoting conceptual understanding I emphasize the importance of identifying the key attributes for selected concepts and teaching these largely through direct experiences and the use of exemplars and non-exemplars.

For those who may feel overwhelmed by the range of factors and options in promoting factual and conceptual understanding, let me close with a brief, practical application of the key ideas found in this article. Let us propose teaching for understanding about a current event, say for example, a local strike by municipal employees. We might ask two questions in deciding how to address this topic:

- What are the concepts and body of facts that are key to understanding this dispute?
- How will students best acquire and work with these ideas?

In response to the first question, students require at least a passing acquaintance with the history of labour/management struggles and with the rationale for unions. Concepts such as 'strike,' 'collective bargaining,' 'essential services' and 'respecting a picket line' seem to be essential. And, of course, students need to know the particulars of union and management positions on the dispute. Students might acquire and work with these ideas in a variety of ways, including the following:

- After hearing a brief lecture on labour history, students create a cartoon capturing the essential elements of this struggle as seen through union and management eyes, including opposing perspectives on collective bargaining and strikes.
- Drawing from a collection of newspaper articles or from interviews with local representatives, students prepare, in their own words, a summary chart for each side listing (a) the key bargaining issues, (b) evidence supporting each position and (c) possible counter-arguments.
- In a simulated sidewalk encounter, groups of students alternate role playing each of the parties affected by the job action (e.g., striking employee, management representative, sympathetic citizen, unsupportive business person).
- Adopting the stance of an impartial arbitrator, students propose and defend a fair and lasting resolution to the dispute.

Although there is much to consider in thoughtfully promoting students' understanding of social studies content, as I hope this example indicates, we can make satisfying progress by exercising a modicum of creativity, focussing on the essential facts and concepts, and setting tasks which require that students engage with the information.

REFERENCES

Benoit, B. & Braun, J.A. Jr. (1988). Teaching Brinton's model for analyzing revolution. *Social Education, 52*(6), 447-449.

Dueck, K.G. (1979). Teaching concepts: From theory to Practice. *History and Social Science Teacher, 14*(2), 103-112.

Engle, S.H. (1960). Decision making: The heart of social studies instruction. *Social Education, 34*(8), 301-306.

Fraenkel, J.R. (1992). Hilda Taba's contributions to social education. *Social Education, 56*(3), 172-178.

Hare, W. (1994). Content and criticism: The aims of schooling. In J. Tooley (Ed.), *Papers of the annual conference of the Philosophy of Education Society of Great Britain* (pp. 72-89). Oxford: New College, University of Oxford.

Harris Burgess, J. (1997, January 4). Low marks in Canadian history. *Globe and Mail.*

Lederer, R. (1987). Student bloopers. *Language Quarterly.*

Leming, J.S. (1994). Drinking from a fire hydrant. *Theory and Research in Social Education, 22*(1), 96-106.

MacQueen, K. (1997, June 30). Why Canada's young adults need a history lesson. *Vancouver Sun*, pp. A1, A2.

Parker, W. (1988). Thinking to learn concepts. *Social Studies, 79*(2), 70-73.

Parker, W. (1989). How to help students learn history and geography. *Educational Leadership, 47*(3), 39-43.

Parker, W. & Perez, S.A. (1987). Beyond the rattle of empty wagons. *Social Education, (51)*3, 164-165.

Parks, M.G. (illustrated by C.W. Jefferys). (undated). The descent of the Fraser River. In *Discoverers and Explorers in Canada—1763-1911* (Portfolio II #4). Toronto: Imperial Oil Ltd.

Perkins, D. (1993). The connected curriculum. *Educational Leadership, 51*(2), 90-91.

Ryerson, E. (1847). *Report on a system of public education for Upper Canada*. Montreal: Lovell and Gibson.

Whitehead, A.N. (1929/1967). *The aims of education and other essays*. New York: Free Press.

— ✧ —

17

CHILDREN IN SPACE AND TIME

DENNIS MILBURN

As children grow and develop they constantly receive information which they sort and classify so that they may come to know the world around them. This drawing together of information into a pattern of thoughts, speech and action results in the formation of concepts. In this article, I will discuss two of these concepts: the concepts of space and time.

We all acquire these concepts in some measure, though they are more highly developed in some people than in others. From the very earliest years a child looks at the world by organizing space and the arrangement of objects in space. Children organize time not only in the conventional sense or for the convenience of day-to-day living, but also more abstractly by projecting thoughts ahead and reflecting on what has passed. In concrete terms, the development of both is a necessary feature of school life and, in the simplest form, we can see these concepts applied in the case of geographical space and historical time. Children do not come to school with these concepts firmly established. Several factors occur in the early years of schooling which may help children move towards understanding time and space in their own conception of the world.

SPACE

The acquisition of the concept of space is more than the ability to estimate distance or draw in perspective or judge how far to throw a ball. As children develop, the acquisition of spatial concepts becomes an extremely complex operation. At school this process can be seen in holding a pencil, drawing a circle, writing one's name, painting a picture, tying shoe laces, climbing the monkey bars or threading one's way through the classroom without falling over. All such activities demand a physical control not only of objects but also the manipulation of "spatial data." This development is not merely the result of periods of instruction from parent or teacher. The construction of internal sorting criteria is greatly dependent on practical activity and experience.

If we analyze activities which children do in the early grades we may conclude something about how children acquire the frames of reference by which they can coordinate space. The coordinates which make up this framework may appear to adults, at first glance, to be relatively simple. They may be such features as an understanding of what is vertical and what is horizontal, or knowing what is meant by right, or left, in front, or behind. These concepts must be learned (Russell, 1956). All of us have had problems at some time with right and left and have seen children move slowly and painfully to master such an understanding. We cannot take such apparently simple things for granted. Children not only reason differently than adults but they have quite different world views (Piaget, 1950). At times children seem to acquire philosophies as if by magic. For example, children at a very young age will act upon an hypothesis of "fairness" though they are not able to describe this moral precept.

In his *Psychology and Perception* Vernon (1962) states that each of us have a series of body axes by which we can understand ourselves in space and which help us coordinate space. As has been previously mentioned, an understanding of what is vertical and what is horizontal is a coordinate children gain early in life. An even more difficult coordinate is an understanding of right and left, and still more difficult is a perception of depth or distance. Children need these understandings to coordinate themselves in space. Space to a child is a kind of all-enveloping container made up of a network of sights and objects which need to be sorted using consistent criteria.

Often teachers tell children that vertical lines are lines which go up and down and horizontal lines are lines which go across. However, when the lines join to make angles or to construct the shape of an object, a further explanation of horizontal and vertical is necessary. Is a door a vertical line? Is a door two vertical lines and two horizontal lines? Many children will not be able to transfer the idea of vertical or horizontal from what they *see* to what they draw. For example in Figures 1 and 2 we see two first grade drawings of a teacher standing at the chalkboard. The teacher is wearing clothing with a pattern of vertical stripes. One child has drawn the stripes correctly, the other has turned the stripes in space and made them horizontal. As far as the second child is concerned the clothing is striped, whether the stripes are vertical or horizontal is immaterial.

[Editor's Note: A section of the original article has been removed here. This section discussed the development of children's understanding of right and left and their categorization of space according to topological properties (e.g., proximity, order and enclosure) and aspects of Euclidean geometry (e.g., angles, parallelism and distance). One figure depicting student work has been removed. The remaining figures have been renumbered accordingly.]

Since maps, and particularly local maps, show the space things take up on the ground, it is important for children to be able to draw objects from above. Piaget places the ability to do this around the age of eight, though other authorities disagree and place this ability even later. Normally, in their early years, children will "map" any object pictographically. That is, they will draw houses on their sides, they will place on maps things which are impermanent (e.g., cars, dogs). They

will, in essence, draw a picture. If we wish to ask children to attempt to draw things from above it is necessary to use a phrase such as "Draw a bird's eye view." However, this may lead to questions such as How high is the bird flying? (In one case, a child drew a lawn with a worm in the middle, this being considered as a suitable answer to the question, Draw a bird's eye view.) To draw a "pilot's eye view" may be a more useful approach. However, young children have difficulty drawing "from above" even in the simplest situation. *[Editor's Note: A brief section giving specific examples of grade one students' inability to draw from a pilot's eye view was removed here. It included two figures depicting student work. The remaining figures have been renumbered accordingly.]* First grade children could not draw a bottle from above. Almost all children drew bottles as seen from the side. This reinforces the ideas of Piaget who claims that children will draw objects from their own point of view. It is a comparatively late stage of development which allows them to draw all objects uniformly from a "pilot's eye view."

The developmental nature of such cognitive processes, as stressed by Piaget, can be observed by analyzing drawings or maps on a topic such as *My route to school*. As an added factor, some of the examples given of *My route to school* were drawn by children from Chile. The progression through the various stages of development was similar to the stages which North American children pass through.

Figure 3 shows the work of a six year old Chilean boy. He places himself in space by recording the various turns he has to make to get from home to school. The fact that he places his school near his house is subordinate to the mental path he has traced in his mind and recorded. Of further interest is that questioning revealed that the only road the child traversed was "Sebastial Elcano" which ran by his home. Other turns marked are within the school's gates and grounds. The reason for this is problematical. It may be that the turns in space within the grounds of the school are well known. In any case these turns bring the child to the end of his journey, relatively close to his starting point. This is not an uncommon feature in children's drawings of their route to school and it could be said that they are conditioned by the size of the paper they are using. They may start in one corner, draw around the edge of the paper and reach their destination at a point on the paper convenient to them.

Figure 4 is a map by a seven year old boy in which he has attempted to coordinate space, or perhaps more simply, to organize a journey in proportion. The first part of the journey is well drawn, there is both a traffic

First grade children could not draw a bottle from above. Almost all children drew bottles as seen from the side. This reinforces the ideas of Piaget who claims that children will draw objects from their own point of view. It is a comparatively late stage of development which allows them to draw all objects uniformly from a "pilot's eye view."

Figure 1

Figure 2

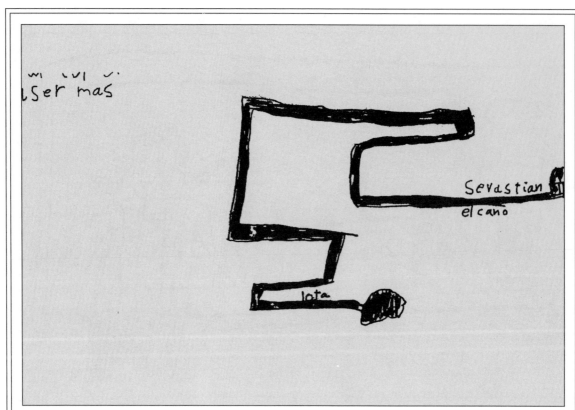

Figure 3

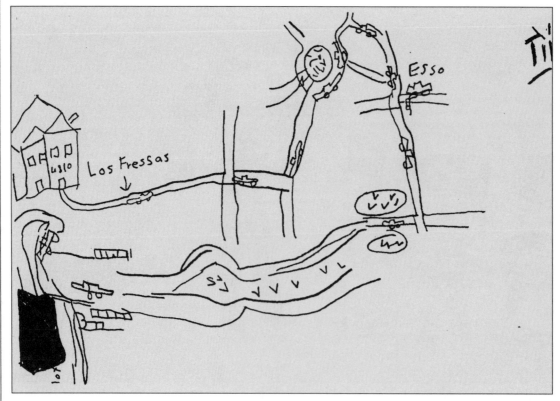

Figure 4

"island" and a gas station to serve as points of reference. Then, near two pools and a river, the route becomes discontinuous and disjointed, returning to greater accuracy near the school in the bottom left hand corner. Such discontinuity is a common feature in the development of a child's ability to organize space. Space is organized in "sections." Those parts which have been well observed are drawn in detail. Other sections of the route are drawn less precisely (for example, a long straight road may be foreshortened). Sections of the journey will be well drawn when the child has found a need to concentrate on detail. Recreating this type of journey in a representational form is complex and, as J. and S. Sauvy (1974) remark, "Dimensions are not respected."

We must also take into account, as has been mentioned, that the child is limited by the confines of the paper. Adults behave in the same way when drawing maps on subjects such as "How to find my house." They begin with panache, but as they begin to fill the paper, the relative scale alters. Their drawings become cramped and over-detailed.

In the classroom this problem may be overcome by giving an additional sheet (or sheets) of paper so that the journey may be continued. If this is done the scale has some chance of remaining constant.

Figure 5 is a drawing by an eight year old Chilean girl. The frame of reference is the street "block." Names are added as further pointers and a route is shown to assist the "reader." The journey travelled has apparently been formalized in the child's mind. Houses and poplar trees are still drawn in profile and, since the original drawing was brightly coloured, serve more for decoration than accuracy. However, this is an accurate representation of a journey.

Figure 6 shows a nine year old boy's reduction of his journey in a map of stark simplicity. In this case the boy's route to school represents a long cycle ride, and the mental map is therefore of greater complexity. At the age of nine, however, the child is also progressing, by normal developmental stages, to be able to draw his map from a pilot's eye view. His map is consistent in technique and contains no extraneous or impermanent details.

Finally Figure 7 shows the map of an eight year old from Vancouver, Canada. Like her Chilean counterparts she draws some objects pictographically, though the organization of data in space is fairly accurate. However, there is a further complication because this child wishes to show slopes. The apparent curves in the roads are in fact gradients, and in the bottom left hand corner a flight of steps climbs a steep wooded incline.

Though such children's maps may appear to be a comparatively simple exercise, the children have been asked to do a number of tasks at once. They have been asked to observe, to recall their observations, to plot the data and to construct techniques for doing so. They have been asked to give points of reference with rea-

Figure 5

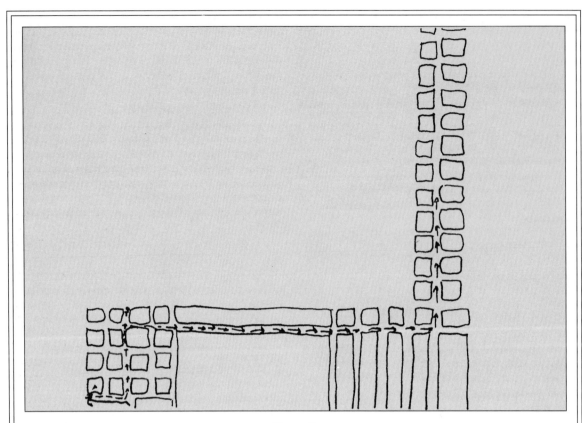

Figure 6

Figure 7

sonable accuracy and, most difficult of all, to coordinate space in representational form.

The growth and development of the concept of space in the three year span from six to nine is marked, as a comparison of the figures will indicate. There is, however, no strict adherence to chronological age in the development of spatial concepts, except in the ability to shift to a pilot's eye view in the seven to nine year old age range.

An exercise such as *My route to school* probably calls for a more abstract level of thought than, for example, reconstructing the same exercise using toys as models. In toy play there is a more active control of the environment and the process of trial and error gives the exercise a more flexible nature. Blaut and Stea (1974) have indicated that children as young as the age of three can produce reasonable mental maps using toy play. They postulate that initial exercises carried out in pre-school or kindergarten classes can allow formal map learning to begin at the age of school entrance, and not in the intermediate grades. However, the examples given in the previous figures reflect the infinite variety of ways in which children could draw their route to school. Children can, and do, invoke fantasy; they note objects which are impermanent; their eidetic imagery is extremely selective; and in the end they may become tired or frustrated and simply bring the exercise to a hurried closure.

A number of conclusions may be drawn from such responses from children. Not only is a developmental pattern clearly in evidence, but there is a considerable amount of input which the child draws from his or her own perception of the environment. This internal activity, which can be technically called "spatial cognition," can only take place if satisfactory frames of reference have been created and can be called upon to solve spatial problems. When we ask students to "Draw a map to show X" we are asking the child to represent ideas in a factual and visible manner.

The developmental understanding of maps is clearly seen to contradict any instructional pattern which demands that the child draw a map of a province, complete with rivers and towns. Children may draw such maps accurately, but the maps may also be meaningless to the child. For this reason many children's introduction to maps through world maps or national maps may be an unsatisfactory exercise for both children and teacher. Most children have simply not developed an adequate concept of space to understand this type of aerial distribution. There is no reason, for example, why young people should "know" that the blue on a map or the blue areas on a globe usually represent water.

Neither can they be expected to know that the continents are the "shapes" we concentrate on. While adults who look at a world map may well have some concept of the shape of the major continents, young children have none. To many children under the age of seven, world maps appear merely as a colourful pattern. It is important, therefore, to reflect how dangerous it is to refer glibly to "the basic skills of mapping."

The first steps in spatial cognition appear to be the building up of frames of reference. However, as experience and awareness grow, these frames of reference are complemented by the development of cognitive maps. A cognitive map is not necessarily a map in the traditional sense. It is a scheme within our mind which has the functions of the familiar map, but does not necessarily have the physical properties of such a graphic model.

Cognitive maps are in our mind when we respond to advertisements such as "Come to sunny Florida," or "Would you like to get away from it all?" Cognitive maps are, in a sense, an interpretation of the real world and are assembled in a highly individual manner from known data. For example, when a motorist gets stuck in a traffic jam, he may use his cognitive awareness of the route which he travels to attempt to by-pass the obstruction. At this time the motorist is calling upon his experience and attempting to interpret what he knows.

Saarinen (1969), in his work on students' views of the world, shows that school children depend very much on "centrality" (1969). For example, African children in the secondary school will tend to place Africa in the centre of their world map, while their knowledge of the other continents remains fairly vague and the shapes they draw of them indeterminate. He also gives an example of a map of North America drawn by an American teenager in which he clearly labels Florida as "North and South Vietnam." Whether or not the student was conditioned by the fact that he had frequently heard that Vietnam was in "South East Asia" (i.e., in the South East), or whether he thought of Vietnam as a peninsula, as is Florida, is not known.

Some mental leap is needed in the classroom between the conjuring up of spatial information which, as it were, lies within our heads and transferring that information into a visible and representational form. There appears to be a great difference between actual spatial perception and the ability to record spatial perceptions. The analogy is somewhat akin to the ability of a child to explain a concept verbally, and the ability of the child to be accurate in any verbal explanation. An example of this can be seen in a five-year-old child's definition of "sharing." This concept is difficult to ver-

Many children's introduction to maps through world maps or national maps may be an unsatisfactory exercise for both children and teacher. Most children have simply not developed an adequate concept of space to understand this type of aerial distribution.

balize, yet the child made a reasonable definition, adequate to his stage of development, when he defined sharing as meaning "He can have it when I have finished with it." While this is not a dictionary definition of sharing, it is a definition which the child can operate and can represent by speech.

Research has shown that children pass through various stages both of seeing and drawing objects from a highly egocentric point of view. Children move from the house drawn from the side, for example, to the more difficult task of organizing data in space. Here they encounter the projective element, when a child needs to assume an entirely different position, and move ultimately from a two dimensional viewpoint to a pilot's eye view. Such movement is not controlled by the cultural environment, since it has been shown that children in different countries go through the same stages. There does appear to be some order or transformation from one state to another. We know from working with children that their ideas, impressions and mental structures do not atrophy but continue to change constantly, just as concepts do not remain fixed but are enlarged or altered as new information is assimilated. Children's concepts of space may vary widely, but they are concepts which develop internally and individually and are valid referents for the children concerned. All children attempt to fashion an orderly model of the universe through various encounters with experience.

Time

"Time" may first appear a more concrete and manageable factor than the concept of space. Time, as we know it, is measured in seconds, minutes, hours, days, weeks, months, years and centuries. Yet the concept of time is projective even in a personal sense, since we all interpret time in a highly individual manner. Measured time can become, in fact, a restraint on our actions.

Benjamin Franklin said "Do not squander time, for that's the stuff life is made of." Young children, however, find time in the adult sense to be supremely unimportant. Events are important, time is not. After five minutes of a car journey parents often hear the question "Are we nearly there?" Young children are concerned with the present and find it difficult to categorize the past into a rational and orderly manner. An adult may say, "When I was on my holidays last year," whereas a child will say, "When I was on my holidays." To project into the future is difficult for us all. "Soon" is a relative term for young children and to project a verbal statement indicating that an event is "in a few weeks" or "next month" is most often meaningless.

In their early days of school children will attempt to learn to tell the time. Exercises with, for example, play-clocks are a common feature in kindergarten and first grade. Nevertheless, time is still related to events. The number of hours in a day is mainly a convenient way for adults to timetable their lives. We therefore see that in teaching children, time will be linked with known events. They will be taught "At three o'clock we go home," or "I go to bed at eight." Some authorities say that the first point in time which a child comes to understand is bed-time, and few would argue that children become reasonably prescient in anticipating events which affect them.

Once at school children assimilate events of the day and the events of the days of the week very quickly. From this they learn to "name" time in hours or days. However, children have more difficulty understanding the concept of a year or any greater span of time. Many children must wonder why during most months we count to 30 or 31 and then start again, except for the fact that those numbers grade imperceptibly into the next month. Our own acceptance of days and months is a direct result of a socially imposed pattern. We do not question the pattern and may see this pattern as immutable. Children can only begin to recognize the passage of time by identifying a number of discrete points which they then begin to put in some form of order. Passages of time between these points will remain extremely unclear throughout life. In our early years we cannot envisage time ahead, and as adults we telescope what has passed into isolated and discontinuous incidents. Nevertheless, some points in time remain crucial for children.

> Many children must wonder why during most months we count to 30 or 31 and then start again, except for the fact that those numbers grade imperceptibly into the next month. Our own acceptance of days and months is a direct result of a socially imposed pattern. We do not question the pattern and may see this pattern as immutable.

A child's birthday is usually the most important event of the year for children in our Western type of society. There is no doubt that a child's knowledge and appreciation of time heightens as his birthday approaches. The word soon becomes next week, then two days from now and, ultimately, tomorrow. There is also little doubt that a year's chart showing "our birthdays" is one of the most useful ways of introducing children to the didactic fact that there are twelve months in a year.

After the factor of the birthday, Christmas is the next most important event. Using these events, children can begin to see the passage of time through events which are important to them. That is, they follow a normal pattern of intellectual growth in that they approach time through utilizing concepts which are adequate to their disparate stages of development. They can, in essence, "perform" in a time frame which is credible to them.

In this sense, the sorting of cards which have symbols on them to illustrate festivals (for example, a card with a heart on it to denote St. Valentine's Day) is a useful exercise to place these festivals in order, and to give meaning to the words "before" and "after." To start from the card marked "My birthday" is one approach, while another common approach is to start with a card which denotes Christmas. However, even though the order of events can be learned fairly quickly, there is still little awareness of the passage of time.

Indeed, adults find the passage of time difficult to display if they are faced with a practical exercise. An experiment which illustrates the difficulties of adults in assessing historical time asks a group of adults to write down a historical event on a card. It is not necessary to know the date. They then take turns arranging the cards in chronological order for each new card may reorganize chronological time. Two main features emerge from this experiment. First, in the construction

---

The ideas of horizontal and vertical become reference points to assist in the organization of space. Similarly, events, both for children and adults, become reference points in the organization of time. A knowledge of historical time, therefore, may occur through the acquisition of disparate "events" which are then put in order. We see again in this activity the aspect of sorting and classifying which is a fundamental part of concept formation.

---

of such a time scale it is noticeable that the scale becomes structured after the first person has laid down the first card. In general, people will use the first cards as a starting point in the same way as a child uses a card for My birthday as a point of reference and subsequently places all the cards relative to the first card, using the basic logic of before and after.

The "spread" of cards (i.e., in physical space) on the time scale only becomes relative to historical time when a card has to be moved to place another card between them. Thus, for example, if someone has laid down a card marked "Henry the Eighth, Dissolution of the Monasteries," and next to it a card is placed marked, "Death of Queen Elizabeth," a subsequent card which may have noted "The Spanish Armada" then must be placed between the "Henry the Eighth" card and the "Queen Elizabeth" card. This action usually prompts adults to attempt physically to spread the cards out "in time" though in the early part of the experiment they merely place the cards in some sort of historical order. Thus we see that adults, themselves, have a concept of time and perhaps an idea of the spread of historical time. In general, however, this concept remains very sketchy throughout adult life. Adults will probably know that "The Greeks came *before* the Romans," though they will have little idea of the amount of space (or time) that these civilizations would take up on a time scale. Historical time must, of necessity, be selective. The facts,

as points of reference known and understood by adults, will be a viable basis for understanding chronology.

It has been stated that space concepts depend partly on those frames of reference which help to assimilate the acquisition of a Euclidean network. The ideas of horizontal and vertical become reference points to assist in the organization of space. Similarly, *events*, both for children and adults, become reference points in the organization of time. A knowledge of historical time, therefore, may occur through the acquisition of disparate "events" which are then put in order. We see again in this activity the aspect of sorting and classifying which is a fundamental part of concept formation. Historical events may be kaleidoscopic, but in order to make some sense out of them we must attempt to put them in some type of order. Certainly the chronological method of teaching history is not the only method of teaching history; there are a number of other methods of "order." What we are discussing here is the method or methods by which children can move towards their own concept of both personal time and historical time.

Research evidence suggests that children can manipulate and understand, as well as adults, those broad sweeps of time as, for example, geological time (Milburn, 1966). Children between nine to fourteen years old seem to be able to assimilate a basic premise like "Mountains rise and fall, climates change," more easily than adults. They can use the names of geological eras correctly, and with understanding.

Thus, children who have been discussing the geological time scale can say with understanding that the deserts of the Permian and Triassic periods were eventually drowned by the Jurassic and Cretaceous seas. Children at this age are not inhibited by attempting to understand geological periods in years, as are adults. Adults will constantly ask "How many years ago were there swamps in existence which eventually turned into coal?" To say in response that the coal measure swamps of the Carboniferous period occurred approximately 300,000,000 years ago has really very little meaning. If, however, one has studied the broad sweep of geological periods from the Pre-Cambrian period to the present day, the point that coal measure swamps existed in the late Paleozoic era at least places this period in relation to other events.

This exercise in geological time illustrates an important stage in the acquisition of the concept. Children, here, are putting events in order and understanding the grand sweep of temporal succession. In this example, we see that to children successive events constitute series: "x" comes before "y" and "x" and "y" before "z." The research of Piaget (Piaget & Inhelder, 1956) suggests that the concept of seriations is mastered by the age of seven or eight.

However, one aspect of the conception of time extends beyond seriation. This concept is the factor of duration. This concept attempts to classify time by setting one "piece" of time against another. Here we need to establish some form of classification that time span "A" is longer than "B," and that "A" is relative to "B," and that "A" and "B" are relative both to "C" and to each other.

The factors of succession and duration need to be coordinated so that time can be classified by both the event and the span of that event. Children are quick to point out that someone is younger than they are. However, if questioned they may say he is younger because "he is smaller." In other words they have an idea of seriation but not of duration. Similarly, children may understand that events happened "before" the time span between the events. This attribute is built up slowly and it is not until the age of 9 to 10 years that phrases such as "still four days to wait," or "I was there last month" acquire significant meaning. We may all reflect that our concept of the duration of time becomes insignificant when we relate it to periods of sleep. Between falling asleep and waking, time apparently ceases to exist. The understanding of time is, therefore, a highly personal attribute. Time "words" are acquired with varying degrees of understanding and before and after may present the same amount of difficulty to a six year old "five centuries ago" presents to an adult.

Both time and space concepts are acquired by experience with the world around and by the development of frames of reference. The establishment of the coordinates which make up the frames of reference start early in the life of a child and are not necessarily "taught" (Milburn, 1980). In teaching, the danger is perhaps to start too far along the conceptual path. We often assume that facts must be self-evident as mentioned in the case of assuming that a child must surely know that the blue expanse on a map represents lakes, seas or oceans (Milburn, 1972). Not only may a child not understand this, there may also be a lack of understanding of what lakes, seas and oceans actually *are*. The internal system of coordinates is reinforced by the specific understanding implied through verbal definitions. This accords with the fact that, as most concepts are represented by verbal symbolism, an understanding of words is a visible sign that concept acquisition is taking place. Space and time are in themselves difficult concepts to explain and all people differ in the extent and manner in which these concepts are understood. Nevertheless, the input of experience transmitted through perception, memory and even imagination ultimately lead to generalized conclusions by which we judge the world around us and attempt to understand both the past and the future.

REFERENCES

Blaut, J.M. & Stea, D. (1974). Mapping at the age of three. *Journal of Geography, 73*(7), 5-9.

Milburn, D. (1966). *A first book of geology.* Oxford: Blackwell.

Milburn, D. (1972). Children's vocabulary. In N.J. Graves (Ed.), *New movements in the study and teaching of geography* (pp. 107-120). London: Temple Smith.

Milburn, D. (1980). Mapping in the early years of schooling. In R. Choguette, J. Wolforth & M. Villemure (Eds.), *Canadian geographical education* (pp. 71-87). Ottawa: University of Ottawa Press.

Piaget, J. (1964). *The psychology of intelligence.* London: Routledge & Paul.

Piaget, J. & Inhelder, B. (1963). *The child's conception of space.* London: Routledge & Paul.

Russell, D.H. (1956). *Children's thinking.* Boston: Ginn.

Saarinen, T. (1969). *Perception of environment.* Commission on College Geography, Resource Paper No. 5, Washington, DC: Association of American Geographers.

Sauvy, J. & Sauvy, S. (1974). *The child's discovery of space.* Harmondsworth: Penguin.

Vernon, M.D. (1962). *Psychology and perception.* Harmondsworth: Pelican.

— ✧ —

This article, which is reproduced with permission, appeared originally in 1985 as "Children in Time and Space" in J. Parsons, G. Milburn, & M. van Manen (Eds.), *A Canadian Social Studies* (2nd ed.) (pp. 120-141). Edmonton: University of Alberta. As indicated, two brief sections have been removed in the article. In addition, minor alterations have been made for stylistic and format purposes.

18

Making Sense of the Past in a Multicultural Classroom

Peter Seixas

Teachers across Canada are confronting classrooms full of students more diverse in their back grounds, capabilities and expectations, than they can remember. At first, this diversity may be encountered as an impediment to teaching. But, to their credit, teachers have generally asked themselves how they might harness diversity for enhanced learning. Nowhere are there greater possibilities than in the history classroom.

Yet these possibilities are not obvious. As long as history is conceived of as a set of given facts to be learned, then the fewer facts that students know in common when they arrive at the classroom door, the more basic must be the teacher's starting point. If, however, we have a different notion of what it means to learn history, then new opportunities do indeed open up.

In the past decade considerable attention has been directed towards a "constructivist" view of learning. Rather than seeing learning as the accumulation of facts, constructivism suggests that we learn by making sense of new phenomena in light of our existing beliefs and thought patterns. Constructivism thus asks teachers to pay close attention to 1) the beliefs and assumptions that students bring to the classroom and 2) how they supplement, modify and even reject those initial stances in the face of new experience, arguments and information. Constructivism as an approach to teaching and learning history thus requires that teachers become conscious of the structures of their students' historical understanding. Students' beliefs about the nature of history will shape their understandings (and misunderstandings) of particular phenomena. Thus, teachers need to ask questions such as: What do students consider to be historically *significant*? What do they accept as *evidence* for a historical argument? What kinds of *moral judgements* do they make of historical actors far removed from the cultural milieux of the late twentieth century? Who or what do they believe is *responsible for historical change*? and Do they make deep and unstated *assumptions about historical progress or decline*? Students in a multicultural classroom—indeed, in any classroom—will very likely entertain diverse beliefs on each of these questions. Constructivist history teaching thus becomes both far more complex and far more meaningful than simply presenting new layers of facts for students to accumulate in memory.

This article will take up the challenge suggested by the title: how to help students from diverse backgrounds make richer sense of the past. It will do so by examining the ideas—collected through interviews—of five high school students with widely divergent background knowledge and experiences, five students who, collectively, can be viewed as a microcosm of a multicultural history classroom. What does the past mean to each of them? How do they start to construct an understanding of their own lives in time? As we answer these questions for each of these students as an individual, we can begin to think about the possibilities for their exploring the meaning of the past *together*, and what kinds of teaching might help them to do so.

Two decades ago, the families of these five students had very little in common. They were scattered around the world, in North and South America, in south and east Asia, and in Europe. They inherited different belief systems, rooted in widely divergent cultures and traditions. They had experienced different events of the twentieth century; and even where they had experienced the "same" event (like World War II, for example), their relations to it were radically different. The families' traditions, beliefs and experiences were not irrelevant to their children's understanding of the past. Indeed, family stories, along with holidays, films and memorials, provide some of the most basic frameworks of collective memory. Yet today these five students find themselves in the same grade 11 classroom in a large, workingclass, urban, Canadian school, where more than 75 percent of the students speak English as a second language. How does their "school" history intersect with their collective memories? What are the disjunctions between school and family as sources of historical knowledge? And how might we restructure the teaching of history in order to make more meaningful bridges among the belief systems which jostle (or bypass) each other in the multicultural classroom? In order to answer these questions, we need to look closely at students' differing historical understandings.

How does their "school" history intersect with their collective memories? What are the disjunctions between school and family as sources of historical knowledge? And how might we restructure the teaching of history in order to make more meaningful bridges among the belief systems which jostle (or bypass) each other in the multicultural classroom?

PEDRO: AN INTEGRATED WORLD OF HISTORICAL THINKING

Pedro was enthusiastic about his social studies classes. Pedro's historical thinking was rooted, nevertheless, more in his family's immigration experience than in school subject matter. Since the age of seven, he had attended a weekly Portuguese school which incorporated Portuguese history and culture into language classes. His family's background thus provided a scaffold on which Pedro organized a relatively rich store of historical information, including material from his school classes.

Pedro: In the past, right, there was more like family unity and so right now, everything is—like people aren't home as much, but they're all doing stuff. Then

there's also like morality, like back then like people's words meant something. . . ."

Interviewer: Where do you think you got the idea . . . that there was more family unity in the past and that . . . there was a clear sense of morality? Did you study that in a social studies class?

Pedro: No. Like I was born in Portugal. I really like it there. . . when I went there, there's this one whole town . . . everybody knows everybody, you know, there's big families. I remember when I was there that I'd go and help my uncle in the field. We'd help people, and then in return . . . there'd be, you know, kind of like a party, you know, they helped us . . . We didn't have a tractor and then this other person had a tractor but they needed help with their potatoes so we'd help them with that and they helped us.

Drawing on his family experience, Pedro applied this almost classical statement of sociological ideal types to his school study of Canadian history, recalling early Scottish settlement in Nova Scotia: "They set up their own village, like the whole family just came over and nothing really changed. . . . gradually things began to change [later] because of urbanization." Pedro constructed meaning in history by implicitly shaping a broad historical narrative which worked equally well to make sense of his family experience and his understanding of early Canada: in this case, a sense of increasing social fragmentation, alienation and moral decline as a consequence of urbanization.

Moral dilemmas also framed his sense of his family's participation in twentieth century history. His father had been in the Portuguese army: "He was in the African War in the 60s and . . . he was kind of bitter about it. He said, 'I lost a year of my life fighting.'" Pedro explained further that his father "didn't really believe in that." With the sensitive subject of the Portuguese army in Africa, he was careful not to "bring anything that's unpleasant." Nevertheless, in casual conversation, he had learned of the conflict and his father's participation. From his family, then, Pedro did have some sense of the moral issues involved in colonial conflict.

In spite of a range of historical knowledge, a powerful metaphor supplied by the family's immigration to Canada, and a disposition to find patterns and relationships in history, Pedro did not articulate a clear basis for historical knowledge. Asked to compare information gathered from an oral interview with that from books, he made this insufficiently critical statement: "I find that the interview is more interesting because you know what they're saying is true, right, and like . . . from books, it's coming from like other people. Most of this is true, right, but some details you can't be too sure." He mistook the engagement of the oral history interview for the "truth" of the information which his informant had provided. With more systematic examination of primary sources in a formal learning environment, he might have been able to draw a more nuanced distinction between the analysis of primary sources and the use of secondary historical accounts.

In balance, however, the interviews with Pedro suggest a student for whom school history had been a success. His interest in historical detail and historical patterns gave him the disposition needed to integrate seamlessly the historical material from social studies, Portuguese school and family experience. He was the only one among the five students to do so.

ANITA: TWO WORLDS OF HISTORICAL THINKING

The history which Anita learned in school provided her with a framework for historical understanding, yet her own ethnic and family background—important aspects of her identity—remained largely outside its purview. She was born in Canada but both her parents immigrated from India. Articulate and outspoken, Anita claimed, like Pedro, that social studies was one of her favourite subjects; she has received a "B" in it for the past two years.

Unlike Pedro, much of her own construction of history was dominated by content from her recent school history courses. She believed that technology, the industrial revolution and World War I were some of the most significant developments in history. Improvements in technology were offset by the problems of "pollution and ozone layers and all that stuff." She also expressed concern about changes in levels of individual and social violence. Anita's historically significant issues were thus a combination of contemporary concerns read backwards and material from social studies classes.

Despite her involvement with school history, Anita did not necessarily take her school textbooks as models of objective truth.

Anita: . . . most of where we get our information is from textbooks. But then again those are written from somebody's point of view, too.

Interviewer: You're telling me that . . . whatever story I make up and write down in a book and I call . . . history, is that just as good as anyone else?

Anita: It is your point of view, right? It's just like in our history book now, that's their point of view that we're learning about. . . . then there are teachers that tell us things. Like they get their information basically from the same resources, like all the books and everything, but everybody has their own point of view. Nobody really knows what happened. You have to be there.

Somewhat like Pedro, Anita came back consistently to the phrase, "you have to be there," in order to establish the truth of what happened. This was particularly important to her, because, although she was aware of

the problem of point of view of secondary historical sources, she could not articulate rules within which the secondary account must function.

Interviewer: So essentially, you don't believe, when you read a history book, you think, this is just like another novel, this is just another story.

Anita: No, I know some of it is true. . . . But I'm sure it's got some of their own point of view in it. Like the basic facts are probably true, like there was a World War I, and this is what it involved and this was the result. But then there's some stuff that could be thrown in it, right? You get the basic picture of what was happening, but you never know the whole story.

This was a balanced—if extremely underdeveloped—account of the problem of historical knowledge. She was confident that much of the story we receive about the past is true, and that somehow, we work towards the unattainable goal of getting "the whole story." She had avoided two possible stances which would seriously impede her ability to develop further genuine historical knowledge: blind belief in whatever the textbook or teacher says, and thorough skepticism which holds that there is no way of knowing anything about the past.

Little of Anita's picture of historical time seemed to be rooted in her family stories or ethnic identity during the initial interview. Before my second interview with her, Anita talked with her uncle about his experiences as an eight-year old boy during the fighting between India and Pakistan in the late 1940s. Of what she learned, she observed, ". . . you don't get this out of the books. . . . the feeling, I never used to know why the

It was clear that the historical world of her own ethnic group, one which was clearly important for her identity . . . had not been explored in school. Her historical understanding remained, in part, untapped potential.

Moslems and Hindus fought so much. I always was wondering what do they have against each other. . . ." One danger for Anita was that she had found someone who was actually "there" and she seemed to have dropped the critical stance with which she approached secondary historical accounts. The problem was exacerbated because the information came from a respected relative. In response to a question of whether she found any of his story unbelievable, she responded, "I just learned a lot about, like I never knew anything hardly about India or anything about the history or anything." Though school history had been important to her, it had not provided her with the means to approach this source critically.

Anita was embarrassed about her ignorance about India. She recounted her experience in a video store specializing in East Indian videos.

The guy there, he's always bugging me . . . asking me questions about school. . . . I really did not know much about [Gandhi], all that I know was that he had something to do with independence, that's all I knew about him. . . . And he goes I am really ashamed for you. He totally embarrassed me there.

After the discussion with her uncle, she resolved to return and tell him what she knew. Thus, the acquisition of more knowledge led to feeling more confident vis-a-vis her own ethnic community. This story led to rumination on the positive nature of her ethnic identification.

Anita's social studies classes had been a success for her. From the subjects explored in school, she had constructed a sense of past events which was directly meaningful to her. Nevertheless, it was clear that the historical world of her own ethnic group, one which was clearly important for her identity as indicated in the second interview, had not been explored in school. Her historical understanding remained, in part, untapped potential.

CARMEN: A WORLD OUT OF CONTROL

Carmen was a recent immigrant from Hong Kong with some difficulty with the English language. She generally received "C"s in social studies, one of her least favourite subjects. She had been in an English-as-a-second-language (ESL) class the previous year, and had not been exposed to any of the Canadian history that students in the regular grade 10 class had experienced.

In contrast to Anita, who could deal with her relative factual ignorance through a basic sense of the possibility of significance and evidence, and the use of empathy, agency and moral judgment, Carmen could not. Her lack of basic historical knowledge made it difficult for her to build the initial scaffold for more learning. Asked what significant events shaped the present, she responded: "World war . . ."

Interviewer: . . .what's so important about wars?

Carmen: That's probably the only thing that anybody knows about.

She was one of the few students who could not articulate (in English) even a rudimentary rationale for choosing significant events.

She found it similarly difficult to articulate what might count as acceptable historical evidence on which to make judgments in history. She had seen a movie about the Japanese taking "slaves" from China and doing some medical tests. This led her, she said, to think that the country of Japan was bad.

Carmen: This is a very secret thing, nobody knows it, but somebody took the pictures.

Interviewer: . . . When you see a movie like that, how do you know that they're telling the truth?

Carmen: Because my grandma, she lived in Japan for a few years.

Her Chinese grandmother had been married to a Japanese man whom she eventually divorced. The family feud and the film reinforced each other, but Carmen failed to comprehend that the portrayal of the Japanese could be viewed critically, or that it might be understood in the context of ongoing fighting between Chinese and Japanese in the twentieth century.

While she had formed judgments about the Japanese, she did so using an intellectual framework which doubted all evidence, which despaired of ever knowing the truth. In response to Anita's doubts about textbooks being written from particular points of view, Carmen observed more starkly, "Yeah, maybe they lie or something. We don't know."

In a discussion of Hitler, Carmen tried to establish her moral bearings.

Carmen: . . . how about some people think of he's a hero?

Anita: Who thinks he's a hero?

Carmen: Many friends of mine, they said that he's a hero . . . he did a lot of stuff that maybe are very great, I don't know.

Anita: Where was this? in Germany?

Interviewer: Yes.

It seemed that Carmen's friends admired Hitler's ability to act. She described this with phrases such as that he had a "very, very good will to do it," that he wanted "to control something," and "to rule the whole world, he has a mind inside himself." She could not explain, however, her Chinese friends' admiration for a white supremacist. Nor did she know enough of even the basics of recent history to relate Hitler's international aggression to that of Japan, against which she spoke vehemently.

Carmen seemed unable to organize the fragments of historical information which have drifted her way into a meaningful framework. There are no rules of evidence. Nothing is to be believed, but some things have to be.

Carmen seemed unable to organize the fragments of historical information which have drifted her way into a meaningful framework. There are no rules of evidence. Nothing is to be believed, but some things have to be. Hitler is a hero—perhaps—simply because he tried to act in a world in which it is so hard to know anything or do anything. Awful things happen, because some people (the Japanese) are awful, but their actions are a secret. But the secret is on a film in public theatres. Carmen did feel empathy for the victims of atrocity stories, but history is basically out of control and unknowable.

For her interview, Carmen interviewed a friend of her father's, who had been in Hong Kong during the attack by Japan, largely confirming her earlier sense of the Japanese. She juxtaposed their high level of technological development with their brutal conduct of war, and expressed shock at their inhumanity—"maybe the Japanese are really weird."

Yet Carmen did not think that they could be discussed in school classes, because of the effect that they would have on Japanese students. She saw no way of bringing the content of her family's historical experience into the more public realm of the school, because of the hatred and antagonism which remained from the past. Nor was their any broader analytic framework — methodological or theoretical—which could encompass these divisive ethnic histories and make them a part of a common discussion, a common curriculum in a multicultural classroom. If she had had a more solid structure for assembling historical knowledge, bringing this discussion to the school classroom might not have been so unthinkable. Instead, the interview with a family friend provided new examples of the private prejudices with which Carmen entered the classroom.

ADAM: ALIENATION

School history had failed Adam almost as thoroughly as it had Carmen. But otherwise their circumstances were very different. In class, Adam, a Canadian-born Caucasian, appeared withdrawn and removed, his eyes half-closed during much of the lesson. His grades had been only marginally passing over the past two years. On the other hand, he had one of the more developed historical frameworks among all of the students. Asked about the discrepancy, he explained, ". . . it's just the way that class works and the teachers. It's just like I don't play their game right now." This alienation from the structures of schooling was reflected in his intellectual stance towards official versions of national history, as well. But while he felt alienated from the structures of power, he had a way of understanding them which put him in a very different situation from Carmen.

Like Carmen, Adam thought that "wars" were the most significant aspect of history (a recently completed oral history assignment on the theme of war should be seen as part of the context for this prevalent response among the sample.) Unlike her, he was clear as to why: "It's the most drastic of the disagreeing," and they usually led to "solutions," or major world political rearrangements. He could not remember a war which he had studied in a school class; he claimed to have learned about wars from documentaries on television, but, as became clear in the second interview, he had also had many discussions with his father, a Vietnam veteran, about the experience of war.

Adam brought a critical approach to all historical accounts. His views were articulated with an example from the United States' intervention in Vietnam: "They usually have a real reason and front story of why they're doing it, right, and so what will be recorded in history books is their story, unless you look into their [the other] side which hardly anyone does." He cited further examples of the United States acting in its self-interest while providing a protective screen of biased interpretation, in the Persian Gulf, in Panama and in other post-Vietnam interventions. He continued to hold onto the theoretical possibility—and the actual rarity—of objective history.

> Like if they [historians] do it right and get both sides and try to make a realistic thing . . . [they could succeed.] . . . Of course, like say English historians, they're not going to say that . . . the [English] government was wrong. . . . Of course, they're going to make the enemy look bad. . . .

He suggested another strategy for dealing with the claims of national leaders, "to look back at their own past deeds to determine how credible their word is." One could, he proposed, assume a certain consistency in a nation's foreign policy. If its leaders offered a rationale for particular actions inconsistent with the nation's previous history, there were grounds for suspicion. The problem for Adam was not that historical evidence is impossible to read, but that national self-interest leads to a deliberate skewing of interpretations. His thinking about the evaluation of historical sources thus went several steps beyond Anita's "you have to be there." Underneath his conception of evidence and interpretation was a moral condemnation of powerful nations, the winners of wars who use their power to impose their own interpretations of events on others.

Adam did not despair of ever knowing historical truth: he knew it was possible, but on the other hand, the truth was not available without digging beneath the official presentation of events. . . . His school social studies classes had not engaged in this project, and so his most creative historical thinking took place in settings and on subjects removed from the classroom.

Adam talked with his father about his experiences in Vietnam. In his own assessment of his father's account, he continued to be most interested in the process of historical interpretation, the selection of facts for the sake of a story which would somehow protect the interests of the teller. He did not condemn his father, however: ". . . like I can tell parts that he skips because he's sensitive about some things. . . ." He remarked that his father and his compatriots "basically . . . all arrived [in Vietnam] not knowing anything about where they were or what was going on."

Adam did not despair of ever knowing historical truth: he knew it was possible, but on the other hand, the truth was not available without digging beneath the official presentation of events. And what made this effort worthwhile was a moral task of exposing those who wielded power. His school social studies classes had not engaged in this project, and so his most creative historical thinking took place in settings and on subjects removed from the classroom.

ROBERTO: FAMILY STORY AS A TEMPLATE FOR HISTORY

Roberto was the child of Chilean parents who emigrated with their young children shortly after the 1973 coup. He enjoyed watching documentaries on public television (over the protests of other members of his family), and claimed that World War II was particularly significant in shaping today's world. But, to a degree more striking than for most other students, his family had experienced a key historical event which shaped their stories of the past, and provided Roberto with a direct link to historical events filled with personal meaning. Repeatedly he referred to Salvador Allende and the coup as a major historical event in his picture of the past. He did not know a lot about the remainder of the history of Chile. Nor was there much overlap with topics studied in social studies classes: "we haven't really touched upon topics . . . about stuff like military regimes." Nevertheless, the coup provided a focus for his interest in history and a means to understand his place in it.

Like Adam, he recognized that history is complicated, and that in coming to historical understanding, one has to consider the problem of perspective. In Central America, "they've been fighting for a long time. . . . Panama . . . got taken over by the States. . . . It was better for the States because you know they've got the Canal and everything . . ." but he questioned whether this represented progress for Central Americans themselves. Here he put a new twist on a familiar refrain: "I guess you have to be there to know like from the people's point of view." The value of the primary source (i.e., being there) would be to give insight into "the people's point of view" as opposed to the point of view of the United States.

Because of his family's experience, the possibility of there being different perspectives on a historical event empowered him, and gave him a way to understand the complexity of historical conflict, rather than debilitating his historical judgment, as it did for Carmen. The Chilean coup, as he understood it, was about people who were motivated to act for clearly identifiable reasons. His general model for historical agency was drawn from the story of the coup: "I don't think [things in history] change by accident. There's been mostly a group of people or something or a force trying to do something to change it, like sometimes for the better and sometimes for the worse."

Progress was linked to the efforts of real people. Furthermore, some people were good and some were bad? "I think like—this is like coming back to me, my home country—because I'm from Chile and what my uncles and what my dad have told me, stuff about Allende, that was the president, like a lot of my uncles had been tortured and stuff, right, and friends of my mom's and of my uncles had been killed." Perspectives might differ, but there was no question about the place of his family in history and the judgments he was willing to render on different historical actors.

On the other hand, Roberto's social studies classes had never provided him with an opportunity to explore "that kind of stuff about my country." And thus, he had found only rare opportunities to apply in social studies the strong framework he had constructed from his family's history and experiences.

Roberto's social studies classes had never provided him with an opportunity to explore "that kind of stuff about my country." And thus, he had found only rare opportunities to apply in social studies the strong framework he had constructed from his family's history and experiences.

CONCLUSIONS

The students in this sample identified plausible areas of significance in history, but other than for Anita and Pedro, these themes and events generally bore little correspondence to what they studied in social studies classes. Despite real potential, the students' own historical belief systems rarely intersected with the themes taken up by their textbooks and teachers. Families, television and popular culture in general, provided sources for much of their thinking about the past. Family experiences, in particular, had shaped the underlying processes through which students established historical facts, assessed historical interpretations and hypothesized about historical patterns. The lens of family experience was crucial in Adam's critical skepticism towards official statements, in Roberto's understanding of the perspective of "the people" and in Carmen's understanding of the Japanese.

Most students understood that secondary interpretations and media reports were coloured by the position of the authors. They were less able to articulate a means of analyzing primary sources, and expressed willingness to accept the testimony of eyewitnesses uncritically. Nevertheless, Adam and Roberto each articulated some insights into the special problems or value of primary sources.

Family stories and family experiences had a profound impact on how many of these students understood the past. Unfortunately, their social studies classes have generally neglected these sources of historical understanding. How might we, in the schools, mend this gap?

In order to engage diverse family stories, teachers have to provide a common ground, with common rules of evidence and interpretation, explicitly taught. Without them, students have no means of assessing the multiplicity of myths and distortions which they encounter. With the guidance of a teacher, these students could examine, together, the recollections of a war veteran, the memories of a refugee, the dramatization of a TV chronicle and the construction of a museum exhibit. The teacher might juxtapose these sources with contemporary newspaper accounts, excerpts from historians' writings and textbook passages covering the same events. In such a history workshop, over time, students could come to understand the mutability of history and the problems of interpretation. With a teacher's expert guidance in learning to read each source critically, they might no longer accept the eyewitness' recollection *or* the textbook as a simple window on the past, but to regard each as an important piece of the historical puzzle. In the history workshop, they would understand that historical knowledge must be constructed critically from these accounts.

As the place where students from diverse backgrounds work out a common framework of historical methodology, the school history workshop would be a place where private and personal meanings drawn from stories of the past emerge in a broader, more systematically critical setting. In this setting students would examine family stories and build upon them. They might begin to understand the impact of people like themselves in shaping the world they are coming to know. In this setting, students could see the relationship of the soldier who "wasted a year of his life" fighting for Portugal in Africa to the American who "arrived in Vietnam not knowing what was going on." Students might examine historical challenges to human rights, and thus start to make comparisons between Japanese treatment of prisoners of war, Pinochet's repressive regime in Chile and the treatment of Japanese-Canadians during World War II. The experience of immigration might provide the basis for exploring the discontinuities between traditional, agricultural societies and a dynamic, urban-oriented capitalism, and the effects and responses of the people who lived through the changes.

Attending to students' prior historical knowledge, rooted in their families, communities and popular culture, school history might enable students to 1) critique their prior knowledge, 2) extend their prior knowledge, and 3) understand the relationships of their family and community stories to those of other groups in the population.

These five students' historical understandings and historical deficits thus suggest directions for reform in the way we teach history in the schools. First, we need to provide explicit attention to historical method, using the critical reading of varied sources of evidence to show students the possibilities and limits of historical interpretation. Second, we need to help students articulate their underlying ideas of historical significance, historical agency, and progress and decline. What do students see as important, historically? What are their grounds for such views? Who or what is responsible for historical change? What counts for them as historical progress? Only by making explicit their underlying assumptions about these questions, can students begin to deal with—and possibly change—their ideas about how history actually works. In the give and take of the multicultural classroom, they should also begin to understand how their potentially disparate perspectives are related to each other. Far from exacerbating ethnic tensions, such multicultural historical education would provide a common public forum for the discussion of divergent historical views and experiences. Indeed, these discussions, if well chosen, have the potential to set crucial contemporary questions of political morality, social activism and progress into their necessary historical contexts, not only for recent immigrants but for all Canadian students.

Supplementary Readings

Of the following books and articles, Gardner defines the general orientation of constructivism as a product of the "cognitive revolution" in educational psychology. Holt, Seixas, Shemilt and Wineburg use research to examine what this orientation means for doing history with children and adolescents. Bliss, Ignatieff and Lowenthal offer impassioned—and very different—assessments of the impact of historical understanding and the lack of it, on contemporary society. Levstik and Barton provide the only "how to" handbook, deeply informed by the new research. This list only scratches the surface of a fast-growing body of literature.

Bliss, M. (1991, Winter). History/Canada/Fragmented. *University of Toronto Magazine*, 6-11.

Gardner, H. (1991). *The unschooled mind: How children think and how schools should teach.* New York: Basic Books.

Holt, T. (1990). *Thinking historically: Narrative, imagination, and understanding.* New York: College Entrance Examination Board.

Ignatieff, M. (1993). *Blood and belonging: Journeys into the new nationalism.* Toronto: Viking.

Levstik, L.S. and K. Barton (1997). *Doing history: Investigating with children in elementary and middle schools.* Mahwah, NJ: Lawrence Erlbaum Associates.

Lowenthal, D. (1996). *Possessed by the past: Heritage and the spoils of history.* New York: Free Press.

Seixas, P. (1997). Mapping the terrain of historical significance. *Social Education, 61*(1), 22-27.

Seixas, P. (1996). Conceptualizing the growth of historical understanding. In D. Olson & N. Torrance (Eds.), *Education and human development* (pp. 765-783). London: Blackwell.

Shemilt, D. (1987). Adolescent ideas about evidence and methodology in history. In C. Portal (Ed.), *The history curriculum for teachers* (pp. 39-61). London: Falmer.

Wineburg, S.S. (1991). On the reading of historical

texts: Notes on the breach between school and academy. *American Educational Research Journal, 28* (3), 495-519.

— ✧ —

The interviews upon which this article draws were conducted in 1991. The author conducted two interviews of approximately one hour each, with each student. The research was originally reported in 1993 in "Historical Understanding Among Adolescents in a Multicultural Setting," *Curriculum Inquiry,* 23(3), 301-327, of which this article is a highly condensed version.

19

Principles of an Ethic of Critical Thinking

Alan Sears

Jim Parsons

A disciple is not above his teacher, but everyone when he is fully taught will be like his teacher.

—Jesus Christ, Luke 6:40 (R.S.V.)

In 1989 James Leming published a provocative article titled, "The Two Cultures of Social Studies Education," in which he claimed there was a wide gap within the teaching of social studies between theorists (mostly university professors) and practitioners (teachers). According to Leming, for over seventy years academics in social studies have emphasized a more radical issues-centred, critical thinking approach to social studies, whereas social studies practitioners have remained more conservative and focussed on knowledge acquisition. Leming characterizes the two approaches to social studies as rival "cultures," each with their own "body of customary beliefs, values and practices, constituting a distinct complex of tradition" (1989, p. 404). He contends that the gap is divisive: "Little dialogue, if any, exists between the two cultures; distrust and lack of respect are obvious. Stagnation and decreasing public credibility plague social studies education" (p. 405). While other writers use less forceful language, it is widely recognized that a theory-practice gap exists and that social studies education suffers because of it. Although Leming was writing about the situation in the United States, considerable evidence suggests a similar gap in Canadian social studies education, where theorists advocate an active and questioning citizenry while the transmission view of education dominates our classrooms (Sears & Hughes, 1996).

In this article we explore the nature of this division and identify two dichotomies that explain its persistence—the "content vs. process" and the "strategy vs. ethic" dichotomies. We then propose a remedy, suggesting the need to nurture in educators at all levels acceptance of five principles of, what we refer to as, an ethic of critical thinking.

Content vs. Process

An essential feature of the competing cultures within social studies is suggested in the title of Devon Metzger's (1985) article, "Process Versus Content: The Lost Illusion." This division between process and content is one dimension of a split between those who view social studies as a vehicle to develop critical thinking and those who view it, in the words of Keith McLeod (1989), as a vehicle "to teach the requisite culture" (p. 6).

John Dewey and many modern writers believe that a "critical" dimension is essential to a democratic society. If democracy is to survive, it needs citizens who function in a critical and participatory mode—what Benjamin Barber (1989) calls "strong citizenship" (p. 355). It is not enough that citizens vote. They must be thoroughly informed about issues, persistent in questioning leaders, and actively constructing and implementing solutions to societal problems. The biblical mandate for this action is to be both "hearers and doers" of the Word. Fundamental to this orientation is what Shirley Engle and Anna Ochoa (1988) refer to as "counter socialization," which they describe as emphasizing "independent thinking and responsible social criticism" (p. 30).

Why such a radical view of active social studies? One of the most basic answers to this question centres on the notion of 'freedom' itself. Writers as diverse as the Brazilian Paulo Freire (1970, 1971) and Canadian political scientist Edwin Webking (1989) argue that a citizenry without the ability to think critically can be exploited and marginalized even in a democracy.

While theorists highlight the central role of social studies as preparation of a critical citizenry, the "real world" concern of most social studies teachers is the content of the curriculum (Leming, 1989, p. 407). According to Metzger (1985), "content has dominated and will likely continue to dominate high school social studies education" (p. 115).

Webking warns that democracy has become equated with commercial and industrial processes, in which the end is the facilitation of business and commercial transactions. In such a society, people are in danger of becoming merely the means of achieving this commercial end—their ability to pursue their own life plans and, indeed, their very dignity as humans are diminished.

While theorists highlight the central role of social studies as preparation of a critical citizenry, the "real world" concern of most social studies teachers is the content of the curriculum (Leming, 1989, p. 407). According to Metzger (1985), "content has dominated and will likely continue to dominate high school social studies education" (p. 115). In contrast to the counter socializing role for social studies proposed by theorists such as Engle and Ochoa, numerous studies indicate that most classroom teachers view social studies as a vehicle to socialize and to prepare students to conform to existing social structures (Leming, 1989). According to these studies many teachers avoid addressing issues and value questions, and many resist using any sources of information other than the textbook. In the everyday world of social studies teachers, "covering content" typically requires reliance on a singular, authoritative point of view—that found in the textbook.

The pressure on teachers to cover the content stems partly from external forces such as school administrators, parents and impending examinations. Administrators and parents often feel that textbook knowledge is safer and certainly more "objective" than unsanctified knowledge. Even students, who have been encouraged to memorize, are more comfortable doing what they have always done. And, almost everyone accepts the notion of "additive intelligence": a person who knows more "stuff" is more intelligent than a person who knows less. The motivation to emphasize content in social studies may also come from internal sources. In one study, teachers who do not emphasize critical thinking reported that most of the pressure to cover content came from within themselves (Onosko, 1989). Over and above any external pressure, these teachers personally believed that expansive content ought to be covered. On the other hand, teachers who stressed critical thinking in their classrooms, generally speaking, worked hard to ensure that the modest outside pressure to cover content did not deter them from their principal task, the development of students' critical thinking abilities. Another explanation for teachers' preference for content is that the critical thinking road is not an easy one. Inquiry is more demanding to teach than facts. It requires more work and preparation. And not everyone is comfortable with discussion and argument—they are louder than memorization and they require more time. As well, critical thinking may be controversial.

For all of these reasons, including the additional practical obstacles and resistance from administrators, parents and students, many classroom teachers are likely to adopt the seemingly easier and less problematic focus on teaching content. Unless, of course, they are extremely committed to critical thinking.

STRATEGY VS. ETHIC

A second explanation for the gap between the academic discourse and classroom actuality is the tendency for many practitioners to view critical thinking as a teaching strategy. In his article, "The Path Not Taken: Dewey's Model of Inquiry," Laurel Tanner (1988) argues that modern interpreters of Dewey have missed his essential point. Critical thinking must be more than simply following a sequence of steps in addressing an abstract mental exercise. It must involve students in real, felt problems. Tanner points out that "critical thinking has gone the canned and packaged way" (p. 472). In other words, curriculum developers and textbook authors have reduced critical thinking to a strategy, a series of steps or planned exercises that can be executed by a trained practitioner, the teacher. While teachers need coherent and workable strategies for implementing a thinking curriculum, strategies alone are not enough to alter the traditional content focus of the social studies classroom. Critical thinking is not essentially a matter of teaching and learning strategies.

Viewing critical thinking largely as a teaching strategy disguises the crux of what it means to promote this goal. Teaching strategies have both up-sides and down-sides. On the plus side, they reduce the teaching experience to relatively simple and easy to understand activities. Unfortunately a "strategy approach" to anything, including critical thinking, casts teachers as implementers of a set system. In the words of Ted Aoki (1989), this reduces a teacher to a "technical practitioner" (p. 18). Teachers need to understand their teaching "not only as a mode of doing but also as a mode of being with others" (p. 18). Consequently, teachers committed to critical thinking need to embody this ethic in their own dealings with students—it cannot simply be a matter of technique. As James MacDonald (1988) writes: "after many frustrating years, I have realized that if one wishes to influence others' ideas and perspectives, one must literally embody these ideas and perspectives" (p. 162).

When explaining the lack of critical thinking in many classrooms, it is significant that the embodiment of a critical spirit has been conspicuously absent in many teachers' own education, including in their own university courses (Engle, 1986; Engle & Ochoa, 1988; Metzger, 1985). Engle (1986) writes:

> For reasons I have never fully understood, most history professors completely change their colors when they step out of their role as research scholars and take on the mantle of "herr" professor. As scholars, they hold truth in great tenuousness; they are not all of one mind; their disciplines are hotbeds of controversy; they are forever correcting one another's errors. But once they have laid aside their research eyeshades and donned the teaching robes, they become authorities whose mission is considered to be the transmission of their superior knowledge to students. Teachers, and this includes many college professors, either find it too arduous a task, or possibly inappropriate, to share with students the problems and questions in the field. Teachers are poorly prepared by their own education to confront the controversy and uncertainty that is the real bone and sinew of scholarship. They are poorly prepared to help students learn the skills of social criticism that are so important to democracy. One reason that the new social studies floundered is that it had limited access to teacher preparation. (p. 21)

Promoting critical thinking at any level is not simply a matter of implementing a few strategies from a pedagogical cookbook—rather it is a way of life in the classroom. Viewing critical thinking as a teaching method only, used in much the same way as an overhead projector, mistakes technique for ethic. To fully support critical thinking, educators must commit to an ethical stance—to a way of living in and addressing the world that places a premium on helping students make up their own mind. Teachers (and students) must regard critical thinking as an ethic—as a philosophy or system of fundamental beliefs about how to act. Only those educators committed in this way to a social stud-

ies program that supports critical thinking will presevere in the face of the considerable obstacles.

AN ETHIC OF CRITICAL THINKING

What does it mean to be committed to an ethic of critical thinking? An ethic always involves considered action. It is personal and thoughtful. It is chosen among other, often easier alternatives. Most importantly, an ethic cannot and should not be imposed on someone. As with any ethic or philosophical position, it consists of or is based on acceptance of basic principles for acting. As a way of better understanding what is required to promote critical thinking, we offer five principles of an ethic of critical thinking and suggest how these principles may be "worked out" within a classroom. These principles could be divided up differently and given different names, but we believe that each has a unique and important focus.

- Knowledge is not fixed, but always subject to re-examination and change.
- There is no question which cannot, or should not, be asked.
- Awareness of, and empathy for, alternative world views is essential.
- There is need of tolerance for ambiguity.
- There is need of a sceptical attitude towards text.

We believe that without a profound personal commitment to these principles and the resolve to embody them in one's teaching, a critical social studies will not become a reality in the classroom.

Knowledge is not fixed, but always subject to re-examination and change

Like Gradgrind, Charles Dickens' prototypical teacher in *Hard Times*, school is often a place for learning "the facts, the facts, and the facts." Some teachers and students regard these "facts" as permanent unchanging truths. Facts acquire almost a mythological status—they are passed down, from generation to generation, often without question. Unfortunately, this mindset not only stifles critical thinking before it starts, but is misleading.

So-called "objective" facts are often subjective, and rock-hard knowledge frequently crumbles given the test of time. Social scientists regularly point out how an event can be, and is, interpreted differently by different people—according to their ideological background. The term 'freedom', for example, did not mean the same thing on different sides of the Berlin Wall. And, there are numerous examples of once solid scientific or historical facts being shaken by the tremors created by new evidence. One of the more exciting instances is the newly-advanced theories about dinosaurs. The field of paleontology has recently been turned upside down by evidence indicating that dinosaurs were probably warm blooded, relatively intelligent and more like birds than the reptiles they have long been thought to have been. Similarly, historians assumed for years following World

War II that Winston Churchill had blundered by sending British troops to defend Greece from a Nazi invasion in the spring of 1941. Greece was lost and many British troops were killed or captured. It was only later, after the revelation of sensitive intelligence material that had been kept secret for years, that scholars discovered that Churchill had information about the planned German invasion of the Soviet Union that spring. His decision to aid Greece was not primarily to save that country, but to delay the German invasion of Russia, an objective which was accomplished (Stevenson, 1976).

So-called "objective" facts are often subjective, and rock-hard knowledge frequently crumbles given the test of time. Social scientists regularly point out how an event can be, and is, interpreted differently by different people—according to their ideological background.

There are countless more examples of "established facts" which have been challenged by new evidence. Students need to confront and study such examples. Only then are they encouraged to view contemporary "facts" with healthy scepticism. Scepticism is often thought of as negative, and often confused with cynicism. Scepticism is a healthy beginning step to academic rigour. To be sceptical is to learn to consider, to think for oneself. Nor is scepticism alienating. True alienation comes when one is separated from the truth, and is powerless to distinguish what should be believed from that which does not warrant our belief.

Teachers need to be constantly mindful of the tenuous nature of knowledge within social studies and to communicate this tenuousness to their students. This does not happen often enough. As Metzger (1985) laments, "I can only surmise that many social scientists, as teachers, lose sight of their own origins as they travel from the library to the classroom" (p. 117).

There is no question which cannot, or should not, be asked

The proposal that all questions be entertained may seem radical, yet asking questions even those about our basic assumptions is at the core of critical thinking. Dewey (1916) argued that "an undesirable society . . . is one which internally and externally sets up barriers to free intercourse and communication of experience" (p. 99). Freire (1971) calls for "a continuous dynamic questioning of culture. If we do not do this, culture becomes static in the form of myths. We would thus fall into an elitist situation which would be no longer liberating or humanizing" (p. 226). Engle and Ochoa (1988) urge that "citizens of a democracy must be allowed room for doubt, even of their most cherished beliefs" (p. 11).

Despite the insistence of conservatives such as E.D. Hirsch (1988) that schools inculcate cultural norms and a "civil religion," it is incumbent upon teachers as educators "to make—and to help others to make—problematic the mythical power of the slogans which

domesticate us" (Freire, 1971, p. 226). To do this, teachers must present materials and explore circumstances which will cause students—in appropriate and responsible ways—to examine and raise questions about the fundamental assumptions of their society. It is important here to emphasize, as do Engle and Ochoa (1988) that:

counter socialization does not necessarily imply a rejection of what has been learned earlier in life. Rather, it calls for a thoughtful assessment through which individuals can read their own conclusions as they face an unknown future where traditional values will undoubtedly warrant reexamination. (p. 31)

While the phrase "No pain, no gain" hardly applies, it is important before they commit to critical thinking, for teachers to recognize the inherent difficulties. Radical questioning is seldom comfortable for either teachers or students. Rigorous discussion of fundamental beliefs often frightens those who hold these principles strongly or who witness the discussion. There is the fear that a younger generation may reject those principles held most passionately by adults. However, if a fundamental belief is to be held strongly, it must be rigorously considered. If there is no chance that it might be considered and then rejected, there can be no academic rigour or true critique in any discussion. Certainly, rejection of core beliefs is possible. But, teachers must offer students the chance to grow intellectually. It is instructive to consider that the strongest steel is subjected to the hottest flame—anything worth believing is worth subjecting to critical scrutiny.

This commitment to examine fundamental beliefs presents teachers with an additional challenge. Teachers must be prepared to have students question the very structures of their classes. Scarier yet, they should actually encourage students to do this. Our experience suggests that students are as anxious about questioning structures as their teachers are in having them do it. Although students are excited by the process, because they often see questioning as necessary to growth, they are often nervous—the enterprise strips away the cosy comfort of the established structure of the school or classroom. It is sometimes easier to follow along than it is to make tough decisions and assume responsibility for these decisions. Students, like most humans, often remain in chosen bondage, blaming others for their plight. It is a less authentic way to live; but, it is easier. The kind of inner turmoil that questioning creates is often the catalyst for very productive thinking. The problem is, it often hurts.

Awareness of, and empathy for, alternative world views is essential

None of us can escape our backgrounds, nor should we want to. We cannot approach an issue from a truly neutral position. Our genetic and cultural background, combined with our personal experiences, give us a perspective through which we see the world. This perspective should be cause for celebration, not fear. Without this organizing frame for our experiences, we would be unable to make sense of things that happens to us. We view, for example, certain events as instances of justice or injustice only because we have the idea that people are entitled to certain rights. Similarly, because many do not regard animals as possessing the same rights as humans they will view identical actions applied to both humans and animals in significantly different lights. We are ideological humans, and our ideology helps us relate to all that we see. We are, in this respect, what we have learned.

Although none of us can ever completely escape our perspective, becoming aware of what it is and how it differs from the perspectives of others is essential to critical thinking. In the past, social studies was dominated by a western orientation which espoused a worldview held by many in the mainstream of Canadian culture. Every world map in school had North America at its centre; every history book offered a history of the world according to a white (male) western vision of how things were and ought to be. Although this western view helped in understanding history, because it was offered as *the* correct view of the world, it offended and marginalized people with other perspectives. The recent explosion of interest in "global education" challenges the appropriateness of a single dominant orientation. As Case (1995) points out "global education is not essentially about transmitting more information about the world", but "centrally concerned with helping students view the world—and the events and people within the world—in a different light" (p. 19).

Central to critical thinking is understanding conceptions of the world that differ from our own. In an increasingly pluralistic society many different voices exist within Canadian classrooms. Students need to be brought into significant contact with people, texts and artforms which view the world from perspectives different from theirs. It is no longer adequate merely to read accounts written by westerners about other parts of the world and other peoples. Students need to listen to other people speak through their own text, art or personal voice, and teachers need to emphasize the importance of "real" listening, which means seeking to understand. As Barber (1989) writes:

> I will listen means to the strong democrat not that I will scan my adversary's position for weaknesses and potential trade-offs, nor even that I will tolerantly permit him to say whatever he chooses. It means, rather, I will put myself in his place, I will try to understand, I will strain to hear what makes us alive. (p. 356)

To embody this principle of respect for alternative views, educators at all levels need to learn to listen to students, to value what they have to say. Often real listening allows us to discover that we share much with the speaker. We also need to learn to listen in order to learn how to tolerate silence. Silence in classroom is often misconstrued as wasted time; on the contrary, it is essential to perspective taking: "One measure of healthy political talk is the amount of silence it encourages, for silence is the precious medium in which reflection is nurtured and empathy can grow" (Barber, 1989, p. 356).

In addition to the need for cross-cultural perspectives, critical thinking requires cross-disciplinary insights. Western society is enamoured with scientific rationality, and has discounted ways of knowing that are considered to be less rational. As one writer notes: "Technological rationality refers to the dominant mind set of our culture" (MacDonald, 1988, p. 165). There has been within social studies generally and the critical thinking movement particularly an emphasis on the scientific method as practiced by social scientists. But the scientific method, if there ever was such a thing, is reductionist—any study of problems or issues is reduced to an empirical analytic process. As Ted Aoki (1989) points out, the empirical analytic approach is, in itself, inadequate for thinking about issues, because "multifold indeed are the ways in which people relate to the world" (p. 12).

The study of social problems requires interdisciplinary materials from a number of perspectives. Engle and Ochoa remind us that ethical issues are involved in most questions in social studies:

> since models for thinking about questions of good and bad are more likely to be found in the humanities than in the social sciences, selections from literature, art, music, religion, philosophy, and journalism would be utilized alongside and on a par with selections from the social sciences and history in the thoughtful study of any topic, episode, or problem. (1988, pp. 128-129)

There is need of tolerance for ambiguity

Real world problems seldom have tidy, final solutions. Typically they involve "profound uncertainty" because of the need to accommodate complex and conflicting interests, the lack of conclusive knowledge on most matters, and the fact that most public problems are never finally resolved (Newmann, 1989, p. 358). Unfortunately, schools do not do a good job of promoting tolerance for the ambiguity of real-life.

Generally speaking, the educational system is geared to teaching "the facts" and testing for "the right answer." Engle and Ochoa (1988) suggest that the social studies reforms of the 1960s and 1970s failed largely because "teachers were unprepared to deal with materials that led to no correct and final answers" (p. 102). The old social studies curriculum had one distinct advantage—it was based on readily identifiable, carved-in-stone answers and solutions. Critical social studies has one big problem—reflection and action about real issues rarely produce one, permanent resolution. If critical social studies is going to work in schools everyone involved needs to build tolerance for ambiguity. This is especially true for students. Teachers, parents and administrators are not the only ones who are uncomfortable when there are no "right" answers. For all their struggle with authority, students are the most like fish out of water without a concrete structure. Our experience with students suggests that they are, in terms of the traditional system, the ones who are the most uncomfortable with change and the least likely to want it. Many of these students do well in a system where learning the "right" answer is required. These are the rules they know. When these rules are changed, they are disoriented. It is hard to face the idea that there may not be

If critical social studies is going to work in schools everyone involved needs to build tolerance for ambiguity. This is especially true for students. Teachers, parents and administrators are not the only ones who are uncomfortable when there are no "right" answers.

someone somewhere who knows if their answer is the right one. Teachers need to keep raising questions about students' sure answers, working to build a tolerance for ambiguity. Some students who are satisfied that they have sufficiently answered the question will react badly in the face of probing. Nevertheless, there is need to continue to sensitively raise questions, gently point out inconsistencies, and encourage further reflection. This is the critical way. Somewhat surprisingly, "weaker," less academic students sometimes fare better in this more ambiguous environment. They are more accustomed to questioning authority; they rarely had the right answer anyway, so they may be more willing to speculate; they are more likely to be comfortable with the possibility that they may not be right; and they find great comfort in a system where their answers are not always criticized.

Teachers are often encouraged to bring about closure—that is, to bring every lesson and topic to a final, testable conclusion. Unfortunately, closure does not operate very neatly in the real world. To seek to provide closure prematurely encourages a tendency to be rigid and simplistic. Issues have innumerable sides. Each needs to be considered, While some resolution may be achieved, these issues are seldom finally resolved. The propensity of social studies teachers to cover large amounts of material is detrimental to a full examination of issues. Social studies classes should allow for in-depth looks at a relatively small number of issues and be flexible enough to permit digressions when questions prove more complex or interesting than anticipated. Students need to be encouraged to seek out alternative courses and solutions for issues. An interesting format to foster realistic assessment of alternatives is to organize a public hearing where "outside" groups are invited to respond to positions that students have taken on contemporary issues. Students might then realize that real issues rarely have solutions that

satisfy everyone or that are without "costs".

There is need of a sceptical attitude towards text

Textbooks stifle critical inquiry when they are treated as unquestioned authorities. Typically teachers afford text an honoured and weighty stature: "As students we all quickly learned that the material between two hard covers was sacrosanct" (Metzger, 1985, p. 116). While the printed word is extremely important, no text ought to go unquestioned or be regarded as containing definitive information about a topic. School textbooks are particularly suspect. Many are produced for their marketability, not for their intellectual accuracy. The rise of public groups with vested interests scrutinizing texts (Engle & Ochoa, 1988), the political and economic agendas of publishing companies (Apple, 1988), and the desire of school personnel to cover a lot of material and avoid controversy have led to the publishing of texts that give an "oversimplified and misleading interpretation of human events" (Engle & Ochoa, 1988, p. 52). Textbooks are political, too, because they reflect the world view of the status quo: history is taught "primarily from a military and political perspective" (Metzger, 1985, p. 116), "overt propaganda [is] passed off as facts" (Engle & Ochoa, 1988, p. 52). Political scientist Marshall Conley argues (1989) that "textbooks, at least in Canada, are incorrigibly hierarchic and deferential in their sympathies" (p. 146).

The use of textbooks as sole sources of information has great appeal for teachers and administrators. It makes planning easier, avoids issues that might disturb the community, and emphasizes factual information which is easy to grade. If thinking is to be encouraged, textbook versions of "the facts" need to be supplemented and challenged:

> We should deliberately help students to experience different versions of a human event and to look for and question the assumptions that underlie a particular version. In short, textbook expositions should be questioned and criticized and students should be helped to develop the skills of criticism. Students should not be punished with failing grades for quarreling with the text. (Engle & Ochoa, 1988, p. 59)

School textbooks, themselves, provide potentially wonderful opportunities for students to exercise their critical vision. One of the most profound experiences I (Sears) had as an undergraduate history student was when a professor required our class to read both a Soviet and American eye witness account of the Soviet invasion of Hungary in 1956. I still remember the sense of revelation when I realized that two observers of the same event could report it so differently. My attitude toward the written word has been different ever since. Students need to be confronted with alternate views to those put forth in their textbooks.

CONCLUSION

There has long been a disparity between social studies as conceived by theorists and as practiced by teachers. The academic community has tended to emphasize critical thinking, while the professionals in the field have stressed content acquisition. In this article we offered our explanation for this theory-practice gap. Although teachers have been exposed to critical thinking, we believe that they have not, by and large, adopted it as an ethic. When faced with the difficulties of implementing a critical social studies in their classrooms, teachers who are not ethically committed to the process are pushed to choose a "safer" and less problematic content-centred approach. Critical thinking as an ethic implies several fundamental principles that cannot be learned, but must be experienced. It is incumbent on teachers at all levels to embody an ethic of critical thinking in their own teaching if they seriously expect to prepare thoughtful, independent-minded citizens.

REFERENCES

Aoki, T. (1989). *Layered understandings of curriculum and pedagogy: Challenges to curriculum developers.* Paper presented at symposium sponsored by the Alberta Teachers' Association, Edmonton, March 4, 1989.

Apple, M.W. (1988). The culture and commerce of the textbook. In W. Pinar (Ed.), *Contemporary curriculum discourses* (pp. 223-242). Scotsdale, AZ: Gorsuch Scarisbrick Publishers.

Barber, B.R. (1989). Public talk and civic action: Education for participation in a strong democracy. *Social Education, 53*(6), 355-356.

Case, R. (1995). Nurturing a global perspective in elementary students. In R. Fowler & I. Wright (Eds.), *Thinking globally about social studies education* (pp. 19-34). Vancouver: Centre for the Study of Curriculum and Instruction, University of British Columbia.

Conley, M.W. (1989). Theories and attitudes towards political education. In K. McLeod (Ed.), *Canada and citizenship education* (pp. 137-156). Toronto: Canadian Education Association.

Dewey, J. (1916). *Democracy and education.* New York: Macmillan.

Engle, S. (1986). Late night thoughts about the new social studies. *Social Education, 50*(1), 20-22.

Engle, S. & Ochoa, A. (1988). *Education for democratic citizenship: Decision making in the social studies.* New York: Teachers College Press.

Freire, P. (1970). *Pedagogy of the oppressed.* New York: Herder and Herder.

Freire, P. (1971). A few notions about the word 'conscientization'. *HardCheese, 1,* 23-28.

Hirsch, E.D. Jr. (1988). *Cultural literacy: What every American needs to know.* New York: Vintage Books.

Leming, J. (1989). The two cultures of social studies education. *Social Education, 53*(6), 404-408.

MacDonald, J.B. (1988). Curriculum consciousness and social change. In W. Pinar (Ed.), *Contemporary curriculum discourses* (pp. 156-174). Scotsdale, AZ: Gorsuch Scarisbrick Publishers.

McLeod, K.A. (1989). Exploring citizenship education: Education for citizenship. In K. McLeod (Ed.), *Canada and citizenship education* (pp. 5-17). Toronto: Canadian Education Association.

Metzger, D.J. (1985). Process versus content: The lost illusion. *Social Studies, 76*(3), 115-120.

Newmann, F.M. (1989). Reflective civic participation. *Social Education, 53*(6), 357-360.

Onosko, J. (1989). Comparing teachers' thinking about promoting students' thinking. *Theory and Research in Social Education, 17*(3), 174-195.

Sears, A. & Hughes, A. (1996). Citizenship education and current educational reform. *Canadian Journal of Education, 21*(2), 123-142.

Stevenson, W. (1976). *A man called intrepid: The secret war.* New York: Ballantine Books.

Tanner, L.N. (1988). The path not taken: Dewey's model of inquiry. *Curriculum Inquiry, 18*(4), 471-479.

Webking, E. (1989). The Charter and the teaching of human rights and citizenship. In K. McLeod (Ed.), *Canada and citizenship education* (pp. 73-82). Toronto: Canadian Education Association.

This is a revised version of a longer article published originally in 1991 as " Towards Critical Thinking as an Ethic" in *Theory and Research in Social Education, 19*(1), 45-68.

20

TAKING SERIOUSLY THE TEACHING OF CRITICAL THINKING

Roland Case
Ian Wright

THE STATE OF AFFAIRS IN SOCIAL STUDIES

Teaching students to think well has been a goal of social studies since the inception of the subject in 1916. At that time, the U.S. National Education Association identified promoting "good judgment" in making decisions as a central element of social studies (Barr, Barth & Shermis, 1977). This notion of "good judgment" mirrors contemporary accounts of critical thinking. In the intervening years, the call to improve students' thinking in social studies has been made countless times. Few educators—teachers and teacher educators alike—oppose the idea of getting students to think more critically.

Yet the rhetoric outstrips practice. There is a rather depressing irony: thinking critically is much valued and yet inadequately addressed in classrooms. This dichotomy was recognized in the *1942 Yearbook for the National Council for the Social Studies* which observed that American social studies teachers had "accepted critical thinking in principle without bothering to define the term precisely or to do much by way of direct instruction to see this goal was achieved" (Anderson, cited in Parker, 1991, p. 345). Fifty-years later, in his introduction to a special issue on higher order thinking, the editor of *Theory and Research in Social Education* remarked that as long as he could remember critical thinking had been a goal of social studies, yet with a few notable exceptions it had remained just that—a goal and not a classroom reality (Fraenkel, 1991, p. 323). Or, as Parker puts it, the teaching of thinking in social studies remains "more wish than practice" (1991, p. 354). Research in the U.S. supports these observations. For example, Su's (1990) study, based on interviews with 112 educators, found that although teachers stated that they valued critical thinking they did not implement it in their classrooms. Similarly, in her study of a three-year project to foster critical thinking in social studies, McKee (1988) found that teachers spent only four percent of class time on reasoning activities.

This predicament appears to extend to Canadian schools. A survey of over 1,700 elementary and secondary teachers of social studies in British Columbia (Case, 1993) found that almost 88 percent supported the teaching of critical thinking (79 percent judged it to be a major emphasis in their teaching), yet the 1989 provincial assessment involving social studies teachers of over 100,000 British Columbia students in grades 4, 7 and 10 concluded that: "The relative lack of teaching strategies which support the development of critical thinking, particularly at the secondary level, suggest that students are not being supported in the development of critical thinking" (Bognar & Cassidy, 1991, p. 82).

At the risk of being trite, taking seriously the challenge of teaching students to think critically is long overdue. Many of the studies cited above identify factors responsible for this depressing state of affairs. The explanations often focus on a lack of pre-service and in-service preparation both in critical thinking and in the teaching of critical thinking, a paucity of suitable teaching methodology and resources, and the demands of too much curricular content to cover. We agree that these factors are crucial to the problem, but believe there is a more fundamental impediment, namely widespread confusion or, at least, "haziness" about (1) what critical thinking really means and (2) what is involved in promoting it (Bognar et al., 1991, p. 105; Fraenkel, 1991, p. 323; Parker, 1991, p. 345). Little will be gained by altering training, resources and curriculum if teacher educators, curriculum developers and classroom teachers remain unclear about what this would require. Before we can begin to turn the tide of neglect, educators need a richer, more concrete understanding of critical thinking and of how it is promoted.

We propose to characterize the prevailing views on the nature and pedagogy of critical thinking, and point up their inadequacies. In the process, we lay the foundations for what we regard as a more promising understanding of and approach to teaching students to think critically.

The Nature of Critical Thinking

According to the prevailing view—and by "prevailing" we mean what is typically found in professional journals and student textbooks—learning to think critically is widely viewed as mastery of a series of discrete skills or operations which can be generalized across a variety of contexts. These generic operations often include interpreting, predicting, analyzing, evaluating and so on. This view is frequently predicated on a distinction between knowledge, skills and attitudes. Since

matter of the curriculum (or in the textbook) has been covered. Notice how consistently, despite the rhetoric about its centrality and importance, critical thinking activities are attached to the end of a chapter or a unit.

Not only does this positioning relegate critical thinking to a low status, but it reinforces the dangerous impression that critical thinking is a task that is undertaken from time to time, *if* time permits. To illustrate why critical thinking should not be identified with a particular set of tasks, consider the lists below. On the left-hand side is a list of tasks or operations, and on the right-hand side is a list of qualities or characteristics.

task/operation	*quality/characteristic*
• interpreting a passage	• superficially or in-depth
• writing a report	• discerningly or blindly
• predicting a result	• rashly or cautiously
• preparing a talk	• carefully or hurriedly
• analysing an issue	• seriously or frivolously

As we see it, the prevailing view would locate critical thinking in the left-hand column, as a label for a range of activities or operations that students undertake—if students are interpreting, analyzing or evaluating they are, by definition, "doing" critical thinking. We believe this to be a serious mistake—critical thinking is more appropriately located in the right-hand list, as a label for a set of qualities or characteristics that may or may not be present in virtually any task students undertake. Just as students may read a passage slowly or quickly, or superficially or in-depth, so too they can read a passage in a critically thoughtful way, or not. This point applies equally to analyzing, predicting and evaluating. The mere fact that someone is analysing an issue does not mean that they are doing it critically. In fact, the consequences of our collective failure to teach critical thinking are student analyses that fail to detect dubious assumptions, contain many fallacious and unsupported statements, and reveal close-minded, prejudicial attitudes.

Since critical thinking is seen to fall with the skill domain of educational objectives, the teaching of knowledge is separated from the teaching of critical thinking which, perhaps, explains why many teachers complain that critical thinking detracts from teaching content. As a result, . . . critical thinking is overlooked or downplayed, becoming an add-on or an enhancement if and when the subject matter of the curriculum (or in the textbook) has been covered.

---

critical thinking is seen to fall with the skill domain of educational objectives, the teaching of knowledge is separated from the teaching of critical thinking which, perhaps, explains why some teachers complain that critical thinking detracts from teaching content. As a result, when pressured to teach the content—judged by many teachers to be the core of the curriculum—critical thinking is overlooked or downplayed, becoming an add-on or an enhancement *if and when* the subject

We believe that critical thinking refers to the thinking through of any "problematic" situation where the thinker seeks to make a judgment about what it would be sensible or reasonable to believe or do. The need to reach reasoned judgments—to think critically—arises in countless kinds of situations from problem solving, decision making, issue analysis, inquiry and other so-called "processes," to reading, writing, speaking and listening. All of these are occasions for critical thinking, since there is limited value in undertaking these tasks in an uncritical manner. Thus critical thinking is not usefully viewed as a unique type of operation or "process," but as a particular set of qualities of thinking regardless of the task or operation. This emphasis on the quality of thinking focusses teachers' attention on the crucial dimension in promoting critical thinking. Students develop as critical thinkers as their judgments come to embody the qualities of good thinking. Thus, in deciding whether or not students' cooperative planning of a field trip was critically thoughtful we would consider, among other qualities, the accuracy and adequacy of their ideas, the extent to which they seriously considered the ideas of others, and the degree of respect they showed for the ideas of those with whom they disagree.

The implications of conceptualizing critical thinking as a quality, not an activity, are profound. Critical thinking need not be treated as an "add-on" activity, but as an orientation that guides any task students undertake, including such "rote" tasks as taking notes and reading the textbook. Students can be encouraged to think critically as they learn to take notes by making the task problematic. Consider the following scenario: "Suppose the premier has asked for concise notes on the day's front page news. Your notes must be less than one-half page in length, focus on the important issues and clearly summarize the main points." In responding in a critical thoughtful manner to this task, students must judge what to report on the basis of importance, coverage of main points and conciseness. So too, the learning of content can and should be approached in a critically thoughtful manner. For example, in a teaching resource building on our model (Case, Daniels & Schwartz, 1996), students are invited to critique the opening page of a popular grade nine textbook which offers the following account of the Battle of Bunker Hill: "The heroic stand of American patriots in this battle inspired the colonists in their struggle for independence" (Beers, 1983, p. 1). To complete the task, students first identify those words which suggest a pro-American bias in the statement (e.g., "heroic," "inspired"), then students recast the sentence in a blatantly pro-British bent, and finally they rewrite the account from a more fair-minded perspective. In the process, content (and the textbook) is made problematic, as opposed to being transmitted as non controversial facts to be accepted unquestioningly. To do otherwise is to discourage a "critical" disposition in students.

This last point raises a final major deficiency in the prevailing view of critical thinking. By identifying critical thinking as a skill, distinct not only from knowledge but from also attitudes, we overlook the crucial role of attitudes in the formation of critical thinkers. Developing the dispositions of a careful and conscientious thinker are crucial—no amount of "skill" will overcome the limitations of closed-minded, prejudicial thinking. This omission is particularly alarming since the desired attitudes are unlikely to develop through occasional exercises—they typically require more sus-

tained and concerted attention. All of this highlights the inadequacy of the add-on, discrete activity view of critical thinking.

Let us now look more closely at the prevailing view of how critical thinking is to be developed.

THE PEDAGOGY OF CRITICAL THINKING

In effect, the prevailing view of the way to promote thinking is to provide students with opportunities to practice thinking. This assumption, that the mere practicing of thinking will improve student's critical competence, is replete in social studies textbooks. Rarely do we find textbooks that do more in their so-called critical thinking sections than pose questions or present items (e.g., a picture or a passage) for students to consider. Of course, students need opportunities to think, but the mere practice may do very little to help them get better at what they do. Of what value in becoming a better thinker is there in asking students to assess the pro and con arguments on an issue if they are profoundly unaware of the standards they should use in critiquing competing pieces of evidence? Ironically, it may be counter productive to present such tasks without instruction since they may reinforce bad habits, such as closed-mindedness, ethnocentrism and hasty generalizations. Thinking critically is, in effect, responding thoughtfully to a particular challenge by making appropriate use of intellectual resources—or what we call "intellectual tools." In this respect, arriving at a thoughtful answer is akin to constructing a house. Repeated attempts at either endeavour are unlikely to be fruitful unless the "builder" possesses the requisite tools—in one case, the appropriate cutting and mending tools (e.g., saw- and hammer-like devices) and, in the other case, the relevant critical concepts, standards of good reasoning and dispositions of thoughtful reflection. Proponents of a "pedagogy of practice" have been deaf to the calls of notable writers (e.g., Paul, n.d.; Lipman, 1992) to provide students with the standards of reasoning and other requisite intellectual resources. Only as students acquire these tools do they learn to competently think through the tasks that teachers put before them.

Even when some "tools" of critical thought are introduced in curriculum materials, they are typically inadequate and crudely done. Standards of good thinking, if mentioned at all, are often described in the vaguest of terms, for example, "Decide if this interpretation is reasonable? or "Judge whether or not the argument is logical?" Terms such as "reasonable" and "logical" offer little direction to someone who does not already have a clear grasp of sound thinking. Dull tools make

> By identifying critical thinking as a skill, distinct not only from knowledge but from also attitudes, we overlook the crucial role of attitudes in the formation of critical thinkers. Developing the dispositions of a careful and conscientious thinker are crucial—no amount of "skill" will overcome the limitations of closed-minded, prejudicial thinking.

for dull distinctions. Providing the requisite tools demands a more careful unpacking of the implied standards of good reasoning. For example, students need to learn that reasonable may be judged in terms of consistency with the body of relevant and credible evidence. In mastering these concepts, students will need help in learning to distinguish relevant from irrelevant reasons, and to recognize and apply the more specific criteria for assessing credibility.

A final common impediment to promoting critical thinking stems from the tasks or questions put to students. Many "thinking" assignments may not actually invite critical judgment. Requests such as "Which option do you like the most?" and "Take a position for or against this issue." may simply illicit students' ruminations about their tastes or prejudices, but not require that students critically assess these matters. In addition, many "higher-order" questions pose unhelpfully vague challenges. For example, social studies teachers are frequently urged to provide two or more competing accounts of a historical event and invite students to write their own history. Yet the tools for critically addressing this task are profoundly contextual. At least, three underlying issues may be at stake, each requiring different tools. Perhaps, the "problematic" issue is the credibility of the authors of the documents. In this case students need to employ criteria for judging appeals to authority (e.g., the author has studied the topic, is a recognized expert in the field, is not in a position of bias). Alternatively, the issue may hinge on the reliability of individual observations described in the documents. If so, students need to employ criteria for assessing observational accounts (e.g., the observer is not in conflict of interest, is functioning at a moder-

ate level of emotional arousal, has a reputation for being honest and correct, has no preconceived notions of how the observation will turn out, made the report close to the time of observing). Or, the underlying issue may be a matter of deciding upon the most plausible inferences based on the body of accepted facts. This requires that students be able to distinguish inferences from direct observations, and learn to assess inferences for their consistency with the body of evidence. Our experience is that many professional resources—especially those recommending generic problem solving or decision making models—neglect the significant differences in requisite tools that vary with the type of problem or decision that students confront.

In response to the prevailing pedagogy of critical thinking we recommend that teachers work on three fronts:[1]

- directly and systematically teaching, in context, the range of intellectual tools, that include background knowledge, criteria for judgment, critical thinking vocabulary, thinking strategies and habits of mind;

- scrutinizing the questions and tasks asked of students to ensure that students frequently engage with bona fide critical challenges—e.g. rich invitations to think critically;

- developing communities of thinkers where critical reflection is valued and reinforced by infusing expectations and routines to think critically in every aspect of students' school lives.

These three fronts are depicted in the following graphic and described in-depth in the three succeeding parts of this article.

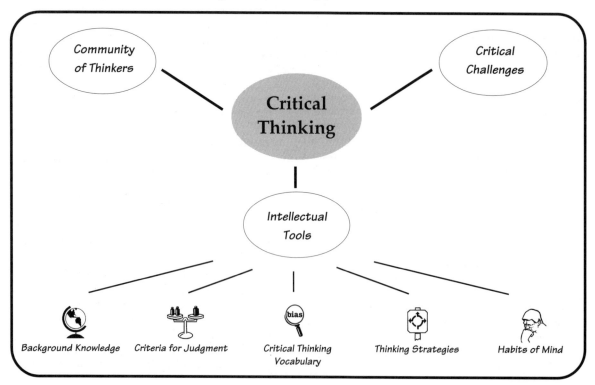

TEACHING THE INTELLECTUAL TOOLS

Neither the hand nor the mind alone would amount to much without aids and tools to perfect them.

— Francis Bacon
Novum Organum (1623)

In this second part we describe five types of intellectual resources or "tools" for thinking:

- possession of relevant *background knowledge*—the information about a topic that is required for thoughtful reflection;

- understanding of appropriate *criteria for judgment*—the criteria or grounds for deciding which of the alternatives is the most sensible or appropriate;

- possession of key *critical thinking vocabulary*—the range of concepts and distinctions that are helpful when thinking critically;

- fluency with relevant *thinking strategies*—the repertoire of strategies, heuristics, organizing devices, models and "tricks" that may be useful when thinking through a critical thinking problem;

- possession of essential *habits of mind*—the values and habits of a careful and conscientious thinker.

Background knowledge

The most obvious and basic "tool" for critical thinking is background knowledge. Students cannot think critically about a topic if they know nothing about it. In fact, expecting students to speculate on matters about which they know very little may have the undesirable consequence of encouraging ill-informed conclusions. Because the requisite background knowledge will depend on the particular problem under consideration, there is no set list of information in a subject area that students must acquire. Rather background knowledge is best understood in the context of particular questions or tasks—by identifying what students would need to know about in order to make a well-informed judgment on the matter before them.

Criteria for judgment

Critical thinking is essentially a matter of judging the reasonableness of alternatives. Necessarily, all judgments are based on criteria of some sort or another. For example, people will judge a movie as "good" because it was funny or because it moved them emotionally—these are the criteria for their assessment of movies. Although we will not always share identical criteria when judging something, students need help in thinking more carefully about the criteria to use when judging various alternatives and when judging the adequacy of their own reasoning. As was suggested earlier, when interpreting historical documents, students may need to apply the criteria for judging the reliability of an observation statement. A reasoned judgment cannot competently be made without these criteria. Some of the criteria that are particularly relevant are general criteria of good reasoning. These include accuracy, reliability, logical coherence, weight of evidence, clarity,

precision and relevancy. It is not essential that critical thinkers be able to name these standards, but they must be able to apply them appropriately in judging the reasoning and actions of others and in monitoring their own thinking and acting.

Critical thinking vocabulary

Critical thinking is possible only if we have a vocabulary or set of concepts that permits us to make important distinctions among the different kinds of issues and thinking tasks facing us. When interpreting historical documents, for example, students need to be able to distinguish the concepts of "direct observation" and "inference." Possession of these concepts is not essentially a matter of acquiring "correct" terminology, but a matter of understanding key distinctions that facilitate thinking critically about, in this case, interpretive matters. Other key critical thinking vocabulary includes:

- cause and effect;
- factual, value and conceptual (definitional) statements;
- premise and conclusion;
- points of view (e.g., moral, aesthetic, environmental);
- necessary and sufficient conditions;
- deduction and induction.

Thinking strategies

Although critical thinking is never simply a matter of following certain procedures or steps, there are strategies or heuristics that are useful for guiding performance of thinking tasks. The most useful strategies tend to be those designed to guide thinking in particular areas or domains of knowledge. For example, making lists of the reasons for and against a value position may help many in deciding which side of an issue to support. Because of differences among students, some strategies will be more or less helpful to individual students. Examples of simple, but nevertheless potentially helpful, strategies include:

- when struggling or blocked, stand back from a situation to get the total picture;
- talk through a problem or confusing issue with another person;
- double check responses before deciding that the task is completed;
- use models, metaphors, drawings and symbols to simplify problems;
- use various graphic organizers (e.g., webbing diagrams, Euler circles, "T" charts) to represent information;
- before deciding on a course of action that affects others, put oneself in their position and imagine how they might feel about the situation.

Habits of mind

Being able to apply relevant criteria and strategies is of little significance in promoting critical thinking unless students also have certain habits of mind. Without, for instance, the disposition to be careful and critical in approaching particular tasks, students are unlikely to be successful. Developing each student's resolve to think critically is vital if schools are to foster critical thinking. These habits, commitments and sensitivities include such things as:

- *open-mindedness*—willingness to withhold judgment and seek new evidence or points of view when existing evidence is inadequate or contentious, and willingness to consider evidence against one's view and to revise one's view should the evidence warrant it;

- *fair-mindedness*—willingness to give fair consideration to alternative points of view and commitment to open, critical discussion of theories, practices and policies where all views are given a fair hearing);

- *independent-mindedness*—the willingness and personal strength to stand up for one's firmly held beliefs;

- *an inquiring or "critical" attitude*—an inclination to question the clarity and support for claims or actions;

- *respect for high quality products and performances*—appreciation of good design and effective performance;

- *an intellectual work ethic*—a commitment to carrying out relevant thinking tasks in a competent manner.

Although these tools are not generic—different kinds of each of the five types of tools will typically be required when thinking through any given critical challenge—over time students can develop a repertoire of tools which will empower them to critically address a wide range of problematic situations. To illustrate this point, the charts on the following pages list the specific tools (of all five types) that secondary students might be expected to develop in order to address in a critically thoughtful manner three common social studies tasks: interpreting data, analysing issues and presenting information.

INFUSING CRITICAL CHALLENGES
Critical challenges are the tasks or questions that provide the impetus and context for critical thinking.

If students are to improve in their ability to think critically they require numerous opportunities to think through problematic situations. Critical challenges may be extended assignments (e.g., undertaking case studies or class debates, producing elaborate displays or reports on controversial issues, and designing, administering and analyzing the results of surveys). They may also be very focussed tasks that take a few minutes only to work through (e.g., generating a few criteria to use in deciding which picture in the textbook is more representative of the historical period, or which of several possible titles of a student essay is the best). The use of critical challenges does not imply a particular pedagogical style, what is sometimes called an issue- or problem-centred approach. Critical challenges can be used

with any approach to teaching: activity centres, textbook-based programs, cooperative groupings, self-directed study and so on, provided students are encouraged and assisted in assessing the reasonableness of what they are hearing, seeing or doing. The teacher's job, regardless of the form of question or task, is to ensure that these approaches represent rich invitations to think critically.

Earlier we discussed weaknesses in many so-called thinking assignments put to students. In this part, we explore four criteria for judging a good critical challenge:

- Does the question or task require judgment?
- Will the challenge be meaningful to students?
- Is the challenge embedded in the core of the curriculum?
- Is the challenge focussed so as to limit the requisite tools?

Does the question or task require judgment?
Critical thinking occurs only in the context of a problematic situation. If an answer is simply there, waiting to be found, or if any and all answers are acceptable then there is no invitation to think critically. A question or task is a critical challenge only if it invites students to assess the reasonableness of plausible options or alternative conclusions—the assignment must require more than retrieval of information, rote application of a strategy or mere assertion of a preference.

One impediment to promoting critical thinking is the difficulty in distinguishing when a question or task explicitly invites critical thinking and when it does not. Critical challenges can be distinguished from two other types of questions—what we refer to as "Where's Waldo?" and "All answers are valid" questions.

- **"Where's Waldo?" questions.** This type of question requires the identification or retrieval of information. The label for these questions is based on a series of children's picture books called *Where's Waldo?* The books consist of sets of pictures containing hundreds of figures only one of whom is Waldo. Children are challenged to locate Waldo among the maze of other individuals in each picture. Although the correct answer can be very difficult, it is not a critical challenge because the task involves locating a pre-established, non-contentious answer. Often questions such as "What were the major causes of World War II?" and "How does electricity work?" may simply be Where's Waldo questions if students are expected to retrieve the answers from their class notes, their textbooks, the library or from memory.

- **"All answers are valid" questions.** This type of question invites students to offer their opinions on matter where their answers are essentially personal preferences or mere guesses. Questions such as "Who is your favourite character in this period?", "What do you like best about Canada?" and "What will the world be like in two hundred years from

TOOLS FOR INTERPRETING SOCIAL SCIENCE DATA

Background knowledge

Understands that documents can be read beyond their surface meaning.

Has knowledge of the range of symbols used in maps and other graphic representations.

Understands that interpretations may be from different perspectives or lenses (e.g., from feminist perspective, employer/employee perspective).

Understands that the past is often different from the present in many subtle and undetected ways.

Criteria for judgment

Is familiar with the following criteria:

- justifies interpretations in light of consistency with other evidence in text with other known beliefs and theory;
- recognizes ambiguity and vagueness;
- recognizes bias.

Judges the reliability of observations in light of the following criteria:

- first-hand and not hearsay;
- good access to event;
- no conflict of interest;
- is corroborated;
- is representative coverage of situation/population.

Judges the credibility of an authority in light of the following criteria:

- no conflict of interest;
- has solid reputation;
- is well-informed about the topic;
- there is general agreement among experts;
- used proper methods to research topic.

Vocabulary

Understands the following concepts:

- inference and direct observation;
- cause and effect;
- point of view;
- bias;
- stereotype;
- hypothesis;
- primary and secondary source;
- degrees, minutes, seconds;
- types of scale (i.e., RF, stated, linear);
- global position index—six-figure coordinates;
- impartial versus neutral.
- cause versus correlation;
- deconstruction;
- propoganda;

Can distinguish the following forms of bias:

- Eurocentricism;
- egocentricism;
- national chauvinism,
- cultural chauvinism;
- presentism;
- anthrocentricism.

Strategies

Looks to identify author's purpose or hidden intentions.

Summarizes ideas in one's own words.

Sequences or translates information into various forms to assist in interpretation.

Habits of mind

Does not take everything at face value—is inclined to question when warranted.

Is willing to consider alternative points of view/interpretations.

Is willing to evaluate information when it is important to do so.

Withholds reaching a conclusion when the evidence is inconclusive.

Has historical empathy—the capacity to place oneself in the minds and times of historical persons.

TOOLS FOR PRESENTING INFORMATION

Background knowledge	Criteria for judgment	Vocabulary	Strategies	Habits of mind
Has a basic understanding of the following forms of presentation: • various types of graphic displays (e.g., collages, murals, overheads); • small and large group presentation approaches (e.g., debates, lectures); • the mechanics of formal written presentations (e.g., titles and headings, report structure); • the principles and techniques in making short video presentations. Understands that presentations serve different purposes (e.g., create awareness, inform, persuade). Has some knowledge of audience needs and how to respond to different audiences. Can present on same topic from significantly different perspectives (e.g., victim/advocate) and for different purposes (to promote, to critique, to inform). Knows the elements and principles of a formal debate.	Is familiar with the following criteria: • presentation is interesting and appropriate to the audience; • oral and visual communication is clear and accurate—does not distort the information; • presentation is thoughtfully sequenced; • topic is focussed and keeps to the point; • medium is suitable for the message; • integrates various media within a presentation.	Understands the following concept: • media as "representation;" • media as "construction."	Generates titles and sub-headings to classify / organize information. Uses rehearsal techniques and mock-ups to prepare presentations. Develops appropriate outlines to sequence presentations. Prepares speaking notes and other aides to support a presentation. Uses graphics (e.g., timelines, charts, graphs) to present information. Carefully edits written reports. Makes use of relevant and illustrative examples in oral and written communication. Uses accepted bibliographic style to reference sources of ideas. Uses recognized techniques of persuasion (e.g., focus on the positive, appeal to authoritative figures).	Considers needs of the audience. Is flexible in adjusting presentation as needed. Takes pride in preparing quality work. Is willing to engage respectfully in group discussion.

TOOLS FOR ANALYSING SOCIAL ISSUES

Background knowledge

Has substantive knowledge about the issue at hand.

Has some knowledge of the types of concerns that should be considered when defending a position on a social/ethical issue.

Criteria for judgment

Is familiar with the following criteria:

- avoids ambiguous language;
- supports arguments with reasons;
- uses evidence and examples to substantiate reasons;
- fairly considers all reasonable alternatives/perspectives;
- judges whether an explanation is oversimplified;
- judges whether the evidence is sufficient to establish the claim.

Avoids most basic informal fallacies:

- ad hominem;
- false appeal to tradition;
- false appeal to popularity;
- false dichotomy;
- slippery slope;
- straw person;
- begging the question;
- false appeal to authority;
- vagueness.

Vocabulary

Understands the following concepts:

- assumption;
- justification and evidence;
- argument, premise and conclusion;
- factual and value claims;
- generalization;
- pro and con;
- justice/fairness;
- eyewitness;
- fallacy;
- generalization and overgeneralization;
- unstated assumptions;
- truth, validity and soundness;
- deductive and inductive reasoning.

Strategies

Thinks of counter-arguments.

Creates pro and con charts.

Uses role taking to understand other perspectives.

Can follow a complex issue analysis model:

- define the issue and explain why it is important;
- research and explain all major pro and con arguments;
- evaluate the comparative strength of competing reasons;
- formulate a defensible position that considers the interests of all who are affected;
- offer counter-arguments in defence of position.

Uses diagrams to trace structure of arguments.

Habits of mind

Is willing to tackle an issue.

Is open to points of view other than one's own—especially those that are counter to one's own position.

Is fair-minded—will judge ideas on their merits and not simply enforce personal interests and biases.

Is independent minded—resists the pressures to adopt and espouse opinions merely because they are popular.

Has an intellectual work ethic—is committed to thinking in a thorough and careful manner.

Is tentative in one's belief until there is sufficient evidence to warrant a more definitive position.

now?" are not likely to be critical challenges because almost no answer could be said to be unacceptable. Who is to say that a student should like the heroine more than the villain in a historical episode? Or that someone can be faulted for liking Canada best for its cold or rainy weather?

Both "Where's Waldo?" and "All answers are valid" questions are valuable questions to ask of students. Our sole point in drawing attention to them is to make it clear that they are not critical challenges—these two types of questions do not explicitly invite critical reflection.

There is a further feature of posing critical challenges that deserves explanation. The point can be made by distinguishing *reasoned judgments* from what may be called *rationalized judgments*:

- A rationalized judgment is a position that is supported after the fact with reasons why it could be justifiable. These reasons may simply be excuses—attempts to justify a position that has not been arrived at through careful, open-minded scrutiny. A rationalized judgment occurs when students leap to conclusions or reiterate positions that they have heard others put forward, and then after making the judgment think of reasons to support it.

- A reasoned judgment is a criteria-based (or reason-driven) position. It is a position that is defended because it meets the perceived requirements of a thoughtful answer.

Although we cannot guarantee which type of judgment students will make, there are ways of posing critical challenges that are more explicitly invitations for reasoned judgment:

- specify (some or all of) the criteria for judgment that students are to use in defending their answer (e.g., Provide an interpretation of this cartoon that is plausible, comprehensive and insightful);

- expect student to demonstrate that they have considered alternative positions (e.g., Argue with conviction both sides of the issue: Should Quebec separate from the rest of Canada?).

Will the challenge be meaningful to students?

Thinking critically is not an amusing mental game to be played, but an important feature of daily life. If students view a challenge as irrelevant and unimportant they are unlike to engage seriously in the activity and, over time, are likely to regard critical thinking as a boring or trivial exercise. Consequently critical challenges should arise within meaningful contexts. Often these contexts are real-life, but they need not be. It is sufficient that the thinker see the challenge to be interesting or stimulating (to some extent at least) and that

the context provide an adequate grounding for deciding what would be reasonable. Critical challenges are likely to engage students to the extent that the challenges:

- create dissonance with students' pre-existing beliefs;
- involve real (or, at least, realistic) problems;
- have an obvious connection with a contemporary event, the local community or a personal concern of students;
- provide a sufficiently rich context so that students can get fully into the situation;
- when feasible, are chosen or suggested by students themselves.

Is the challenge embedded in the core of the curriculum?

As we have emphasized, critical thinking should not be an add-on, nor should it interrupt the pursuit of other curricular goals. Rather, we should encourage students to think critically about matters that are at the very core of the curriculum. The key to infusing critical thinking into the curriculum is to recast the core elements of the subject matter in the form of critical challenges. In this way students confront the material in the context of thinking critically about it, and not merely as a matter of retrieving information. For example, instead of asking students to learn "the five causes" of World War II invite them to judge which of a list of influences is the most significant factor in the outbreak of the war.

> The key to infusing critical thinking into the curriculum is to recast the core elements of the subject matter in the form of critical challenges. In this way students confront the material in the context of thinking critically about it, and not merely as a matter of retrieving information.

Critical challenges can be embedded into ongoing activities by connecting or infusing a challenge into the topic under consideration, for example, by focussing on a statement or picture in a textbook, on an event in a story or one that happened in the community, or on students' questions. Critical challenges need not be large scale undertakings, since these kinds of challenges may take considerable time. Although in-depth challenges are valuable, there are many opportunities to pose challenges "in passing."

Is the challenge focussed so as to limit the requisite tools?

We have stressed the role of "tools" in dealing competently with critical challenges. If students lack crucial background knowledge or are unaware of relevant criteria, and if they do not acquire these tools as they address the challenge, then the value of posing challenges may be lost. Students are less likely to develop their ability to think critically if they are fumbling in the dark. For this reason, it is important to anticipate the tools required by a challenge and to compensate for those tools that are not already in students' repertoires:

- provide instruction (e.g., teach any new concepts, introduce thinking strategies that students might use);
- provide support materials (e.g., supplement background knowledge by including a data sheet or referring to pages in the textbook);
- offer reminders (e.g., encourage students to attend to specific habits of mind).

One way to increase the likelihood that students will already possess, or will be able to acquire, all the requisite tools is to narrow the focus of the challenge or "make it compact." Critical challenges must be sufficiently delimited so that students do not require encyclopedic background knowledge in order to do a competent job. For example, instead of asking "Assess the legacy of the Enlightenment thinkers"—a task that could fill volumes—it may be better to pose a more focussed challenge: "Based on the following two documents and your own knowledge, which Enlightenment philosopher— Hobbes or Locke—offers the more realistic theory of government for modern society?"

The chart on the following page offers sample prompts for critical questions and tasks, with accompanying examples.

BUILDING A COMMUNITY OF THINKERS

A community of thinkers is a collection of individuals interacting in mutually supportive ways to nurture critical reflection.

If we are serious about critical thinking we must establish the conditions that are likely to nurture the required attributes. This involves infusing expectations and opportunities to think critically in all our students' school lives. If classroom and school routines do not consistently reinforce thoughtful reflection, then little or no lasting gains can be expected from occasional lessons on critical thinking. This point was affirmed by studies of the effects of educational programs on developing respect for others. Various researchers have found that the specifics of the curriculum have a marginal impact on this key attitude—the classroom climate is the determining factor (cf., Daniels & Case, 1992, pp. 19-23). If teachers solicit and value student opinions, and provide a healthy forum for student dialogue, then students are more likely to come to respect other's opinions.

Generally speaking, in promoting critical thinking the influence of the hidden curriculum—the latent norms and subtle messages that powerfully affect what students actually learn—has been underestimated or overlooked. Consider, for example, the tendency of many people to cast issues in dichotomous terms—as black or white, and right or wrong. This attitude is reinforced by the traditional classroom debate that has been the paradigm format for engaging students in issue discussion. In a two-sided debate the objective is to prove that the opposing side is without merit by refuting, belittling or ignoring opposing arguments. There is a tacit prohibition against changing one's mind part way through the debate. Crossing to the other side is like crossing the floor of the House of Commons—both are seen as betrayals. Increasingly teachers are replacing this adversarial, closed-minded format with more open-ended discussions where students are encouraged to see the merits of all sides and to recast binary options as extreme positions along a continuum. To facilitate this approach, class discussions may be configured in a "U" shape—students with polar views (either strongly agreeing or strongly disagreeing) locate themselves at either end, and students with mixed opinions sit along the rounded part. At varying stages in the discussion students are encouraged to move physically along the "U" as their intellectual position on the issue changes. In this way, less dogmatic attitudes are reinforced

Building a community of thinkers is vital for, at least, two reasons. First, critical thinking is not a set of abilities that one uses from time to time, such as learning how to cook or how to play basketball. Critical thinking is a way of approaching almost everything that one encounters. This mindset will not develop if classroom routines transmit inconsistent messages or fail to reinforce this expectation. Second, the classic image of the isolated thinker is a misleading one; we should not expect to be able to think through all of our "problems" by ourselves. Rather we should actively develop, supplement and test our ideas in conjunction with others— to put our heads together. But many students may be unwilling or unable to contribute to and benefit from collaborative reflection. Perhaps, they do not listen very well, or they cannot accept any form of criticism, or they do not know how to monitor what they say, or they have no confidence in their ability to add to the discussion. Students will acquire these tools only through participation as a member in a community of thinkers.

Nurturing the appropriate climate is an orientation that pervades all of our actions. We can transform our classrooms into communities of thinkers by working in the following ways:

- setting appropriate classroom expectations;
- implementing appropriate classroom routines and activities;
- personally modeling the attributes of a good critical thinker;
- employing effective group questioning techniques;
- developing the tools for student participation in a reflective community.

Classroom expectations

Teachers' expectations of their students are often self-fulfilling. Specific expectations that support a community of thinkers are:

- students are expected to make up their own minds— not simply take someone's word for things;
- students and teachers are expected as a matter of

Critical question prompts	Example of question
Who is more "x"?	• Whose suggestion for solving the problem is more realistic?
	• Who was the greater explorer—Vancouver or Cook?
Judge the character	• Is Simon Fraser a hero or a rogue?
Defend an interpretation	• What is the cartoonist really saying in this drawing?
Settle the dispute	• Should this recreational site be developed?
	• Your mother has been informed that she is being transferred to either Weyburn, Saskatchewan, or Prince George, British Columbia. She asks you to gather information and offer her your advice in deciding which would be a better place to live for your family.
Is this really an "x ?"	• Is the term "Quiet Revolution" an oxymoron?
"The best of" award	• Which of the civilizations studied this semester has made the most significant political contribution to our society?
What's wrong with this?	• Has the author provided a fair and full account of what actually happened?

Critical task prompts	Example of task
Rewrite from point of view	• After reading a pro-European version of Simon Fraser's descent down the Fraser River, write a fair-minded account of what happened on this trip.
	• In 1876, *The Yorkshire Post* referred to the charge of the Light Brigade during the Battle of Balaclava as "That glorious blunder of which all Englishmen are justifiably proud." Write two editorials—one that supports this statement, and another that refutes it.
Make a memo	• Write a letter of reference on behalf of Thomas More to Henry VIII.
Apply in realistic context	• The premier has asked for concise notes on the day's front page news. Your notes must be less than one-half page in length, focus on the important issues and clearly summarize the main points.
Create a masterpiece	• Create a poster-size advertisement to discourage fellow students from smoking, effectively employing the techniques of persuasion without distorting the evidence.

course to provide reasons or examples in support of their observations, conclusions and behaviour;

- students and teacher are expected to seriously consider other perspectives on a issue and alternative approaches to a problem before reaching a firm conclusion;

- all persons are to be treated respectfully by everyone, even if their ideas are wrong or silly;

- disputes about ideas are encouraged, but they must never be directed personally or be mean-spirited;

- it is not acceptable merely to criticize and complain—the pros of a position should always be examined as should possible solutions to problems;

- the insincere use of critical techniques to show off or to be contrary is not tolerated (this does not mean that there is no place for well-intentioned devil's advocacy).

Classroom routines and activities

A community of thinkers can be supported by building into the daily classroom operation various routines and activities that habituate students to particular frames of mind. Some of the routines that support a critical community are:

- the vocabulary of critical thinking is used as a matter of course in classroom discussion (e.g., Asking "What can you infer from this picture about the individual's state of mind?" "What assumptions are you making?");

- assignments, including those that are for marks, consistently contain a non-trivial commitment to thinking critically;

- students regularly scrutinize textbooks, news articles and reports, and other "reputable" sources of information for bias, stereotyping, overgeneralization and inaccuracy;

- student ideas and suggestions are regularly considered and (when appropriate) accepted in setting assignments, establishing rules for the class and establishing criteria for evaluation;

- thoughtfully supported, insightful or empathic responses (even if flawed) are to be valued more than merely correctly recalled responses;

- students regularly explore and defend positions from particular points of view, especially from perspectives that are not personally held by them;

- students regularly identify and defend criteria to evaluate their classroom behaviour and work, and then apply these criteria to themselves and their peers;

- the conditions for thoughtful reflection are respected—students are given adequate time to reflect and provided with the tools to address their tasks critically (e.g., students should not be expected merely to guess).

Teacher modelling

It has been said "Example is not the best way to influence people, it's the only way" (reported in Norman, 1989, p. 27). This principle applies to critical thinking. If we want our students to be good critical thinkers we must model these attributes ourselves. We may want to consider being a role model in the ways suggested below:

- not being dogmatic and not always having the answer—living with ambiguity—being satisfied with tentative conclusions until full review of complex issues can be carried out;

- sincerely attempting to base all comments and decisions on careful and fair-minded consideration of all sides;

- be willing (if asked) to provide "good" reasons for our decisions and actions (This does not mean that every time any student asks for a justification that the lesson must be interrupted);

- being careful to avoid making gross generalizations and stereotypical comments about individuals and groups, and seeking to expose stereotypes in books, pictures, films and other learning resources;

- being willing to change our mind or alter our plans when good reasons are presented;

- always acknowledging the existence of different positions on an issue (e.g., looking at events from different cultural, gender and class perspectives);

- not being cynical—adopting, instead, a realistic but questioning attitude toward the world.

Questioning techniques

We can support a community of thinkers by being effective questioners. We must pose questions that go beyond recall or retrieval of information by inviting students to make reasoned judgments. We can further support critical thinking by consistently responding to student comments using non-threatening probing techniques such as those listed below (Saskatchewan Education, 1988, p. 34):

Seeking greater clarity
- Could you give me an example?
- Is your point "this" or "this"?

Probing for assumptions
- You seem to be assuming that . . .
- Is this always the case?

Probing for reasons and evidence
- Is there reason to doubt this evidence?
- How could we find out if this is true?

Exploring alternative perspectives
- How might other groups respond?
- What would people who disagree with your position say?

Probing consequences or implications
- What effect would this have?
- If this were the case, what else must also be true?

Tools for community participation

Just as students are taught to be good citizens, so too students need to be taught how to be effective contributors to and beneficiaries of a community of thinkers. Many of the tools employed in individual reflection apply here, however other tools are uniquely employed in collaborative deliberation. Some of these tools are suggested below.

Background knowledge
- knowledge that individuals may see things in significantly different ways;
- knowledge of how individuals are likely to react in various situations;

Criteria for judgment
- ensuring one's comments are relevant to the discussion (on topic);
- ensuring one's comments are expressed in a manner that will be clear to everyone;

Critical thinking vocabulary
- unanimous, consensus, minority positions;

Thinking strategies
- group management strategies such as taking turns, assigning cooperative roles, active listening and keeping a speaker's list;
- strategies for critiquing in a non-threatening manner including putting the comment in the form of a question, preceding comment with a caveat or preceding comment with positive remarks;
- strategies for presenting information in group settings including limiting comments to a few points, speaking from notes and connecting remarks to previous speaker's comments.

Habits of mind
- independent-minded—willingness to stand up for firmly held beliefs;
- sensitivity to others—attention to the feelings of others;
- self-monitoring—attention to how one's actions are affecting the group.

CONCLUDING REMARKS

We are optimistic that the current state of affairs can be improved. As we have tried to illustrate the prevailing view does little in the way of teaching for thinking. In this article we hope to combat the prevailing view by clarifying the nature of critical thinking and how to effectively promote critical thinking in social studies. Of course, greater clarity is not enough—extensive training, resources and curriculum revision are required—but it represents a necessary and promising first step in taking seriously a challenge raised consistently since the very beginning of social studies.

ENDNOTE

1 This account of the three fronts of critical thinking is based on the work of Bailin, Case, Coombs and Daniels (1993, 1994).

REFERENCES

Allen, R. (1975). *Values education series*. Evanston, IL: McDougal, Little.

Bailin, S., Case, R., Coombs, J. & Daniels, L. (1993, September). A conception of critical thinking for curriculum, instruction and assessment. Unpublished report to Examinations Branch, Ministry of Education, Victoria, British Columbia.

Bailin, S., Case, R., Coombs, J. & Daniels, L. (1994). A conception of critical thinking for curriculum, instruction and assessment. *Horizon, 32*(1), 5-16.

Barr, D., Barth, J. & Shermis, S. (1977). *Defining the social studies*. Arlington, VA: National Council for the Social Studies.

Beer, B.F. (1983). *Patterns of civilization* (Volume 2). Scarborough, ON: Prentice-Hall.

Bognar, C., Cassidy, C., Lewis, W. & Manley-Casimir, M. (1991). *Social studies in British Columbia: Technical report of the 1989 social studies assessment*. Victoria, BC: Ministry of Education.

Case, R. (1993). *Summary of the 1992 social studies needs assessment*. Victoria, BC: Queen's Printer.

Case, R., Daniels, L. & Schwartz P. (Eds.). (1996). *Critical challenges in social studies for junior high students*. Burnaby, BC: Field Relations, Faculty of Education, Simon Fraser University.

Daniels, L. & Case, R. (1992, June). *Charter literacy and the administration of justice*. Final report for the Department of Justice Canada, Ottawa, Ontario.

Engle, S. (1960). Decision-making: The heart of Social Studies. *Social Education, 24*(7), 301-309.

Evans, W. & Applegate, J. (1982). *Making rational decisions*. Salt Lake City, UT: Prodec.

Fraenkel, J. (1991). Editorial. *Theory and Research in Social Education, 19*(4), 323-325.

Hullfish, G. & Smith, P. (1961). *Reflective thinking: The method of education*. New York: Dodd, Mead.

Lipman, M. (1992). Criteria and judgment in critical thinking. *Inquiry, 9*(2), 3-4.

Massialas, B. & Cox, C. (1966). *Inquiry in social studies*. San Francisco: McGraw-Hill.

McKee. S. (1988). Impediments to implementing critical thinking. *Social Education, 52*(6), 444-446.

McPeck, J. (1981). *Critical thinking and education*. New York: St. Martins.

Norman, P. (1989). *The self-directed learning contract: A guide for learners and teachers*. Burnaby, BC: Faculty of Education, Simon Fraser University.

Parker, W. (1991). Achieving thinking and decision-making objectives in social studies. In J. Shaver (Ed.), *Handbook of research on social studies teaching and learning* (pp. 345-356). Toronto: Collier Macmillan,

Paul, R. (no date). *Using intellectual standards in the elements of thought*. Unpublished paper, Center Critical Thinking and Moral Critique, Sonoma State University, California.

Saskatchewan Education. (1988). *Understanding the common essential learnings: A handbook for teachers.* Regina, SK: Author.

Shaver, J. & Larkins, A. (1973). *The Analysis of Public Issues Program.* Boston: Allyn and Bacon.

Su, Zhixin. (1990). Exploring the moral socialization of teacher candidates. *Oxford Review of Education, 16*(3), 367-391.

This article, which is reprinted here with the permission of the publisher, was first published in Fall 1997 in *Canadian Social Studies*. Minor alterations have been made for clarity and stylistic purposes.

21

Escaping the Typical Report Trap: Learning to Conduct Research Effectively

Penney Clark

Does this scenario sound familiar? We assign students a research report on some topic, perhaps on a famous person, or ancient Greece or pioneers. Students head for the library and grab from the shelf the first three sources they can find. They copy the first paragraph from the first source, the second paragraph from the second source and so on until their report meets the minimum required word count. Come presentation time students troop one by one to the front of the class to read their reports in a low, monotone voice. Seemingly, they understand little of their contents since they can't answer questions based on the information they've just read. And judging from follow-up questions from other students, the rest of the class either wasn't listening or simply didn't understand the presentation.

What can we do in social studies to avoid this dismal, yet all-too-common, scenario? One place to begin our escape from this fruitless, time-consuming trap is to clarify why we engage students in conducting research and preparing reports. Is it primarily so students can learn about famous people, ancient Greece or pioneers? While acquiring information may be one of our objectives, there are faster, more efficient ways to achieve this end. Presumably the more important purpose is to develop students' ability to independently conduct research on any topic. As the above scenario suggests, there is much we need to do to help students in this regard.

In this article, I present a seven-step model for helping students, at both the elementary and secondary levels, learn how to carry out and present research. The secret to success is to devote as much, or more, attention to teaching about the process of conducting research as to the final report. Teacher and teacher-librarian guidance along the way is crucial. We should not send students off unaided to the library, research assignment clutched in their hands, and expect them to present a well written, original and thoroughly researched report on the due date. We can make the complex task of conducting and reporting on research an interesting and educationally useful experience for students by implementing strategies such as those described in the following model:

- select and focus a topic
- formulate guiding questions
- identify information sources
- extract information from sources
- record and organize information
- synthesize information into an effective presentation format
- assess—by teacher, self and peer—at each stage of the research project.

SELECTING AND FOCUSSING A TOPIC

The first steps in successful research projects are the thoughtful selection of a topic and the narrowing of the topic to manageable proportions.

Selecting a topic

Three interrelated considerations are relevant when choosing a topic:

- **curricular importance**. Student research, because it can involve a variety of resources and perspectives, provides an opportunity to develop richer understanding of curriculum content than would be achieved by using a single textbook. However, research is more time consuming and, therefore, topics should be selected carefully for their relevance to the broader content goals of the curriculum. This may mean that research questions should go beyond asking for mere summaries of information by inviting students to take a position or reach conclusions arising from their research.

- **availablity of resources**. The choice of topic should depend on the resources readily available to students. If the only accessible reference is an encyclopedia, then we should not be suprised that students produce bland reports. Teacher-librarians can be a great help in locating resources with diverse perspectives and rich detail. They will often reserve materials so that they are available to students when needed. If school resources are limited, teacher-librarians can also assist by borrowing outside resources on a shortterm basis.

- **student interest**. Research projects provide opportunities for students to explore areas of individual interest. As such, they can have powerful motivational value if students care about the topic. Allowing students a say in the selection of topics is one way to increase the likelihood of student interest. Another means is for the teacher to stimulate interest in topics by raising provocative questions and issues that students might expect to encounter.

Focussing the topic

Research projects are unmanageable if the scope is too grand or vague. Since students often have trouble zeroing in on a topic they will need assistance in articulating the scope of their research. Before directing students to choose their own topic, it may be helpful to model with the entire class the focussing strategy described in the box on this page.

These narrower topics then become the focus for individual research projects. After modeling this procedure with the entire class on a topic unconnected to the theme(s) of the actual research project, have students (individually or in small groups) engage in a similar process when selecting their own topics. Students may want to consult with friends and family and to scan the textbook or other resources for help in generating the list of categories and topics. Before allowing students to proceed with their research, check their topic choices to ensure that they are not too broad.

FOCUSSING A RESEARCH TOPIC

Begin with a broad general theme, such as "European Exploration of North America," and brainstorm as a class a list of categories within this theme. The list might contain the following:

- colonization of New France
- Native and European interaction
- British-French rivalry
- famous explorers
- the fur trade

Then select one of these categories and generate more specific topics that fall within its scope. For instance, narrower topics under the heading "Fur Trade" may include the following:

- fur forts
- routes of the fur trade
- the daily life of a voyageur
- beaver hats and fur fashion
- Native peoples and the fur trade

FORMULATING GUIDING QUESTIONS

It is often helpful in giving even greater focus and purpose to a research project to have students frame questions that they will endeavour to answer in their report. In generating meaningful guiding questions it often helps to start with what students already know about their topic, and then move to what is unknown.

Starting with what students know

Students are often pleased to discover that they already know quite a bit about a topic. Getting students to record, at the outset, what they know about their topic encourages them to connect prior and newly-acquired information. One caution is that all of the prior information which students "know" may not be correct. It can be recorded anyway. Then, as they gather new information, they can check their original list for accuracy.

One way to generate and record what is already known is through webbing. Ask students to think of everything they can that links to the key words or ideas contained in their topic. Webbing encourages the free flow of ideas since students make any links that come to mind, rather than fitting information into predetermined slots. (See "Web of Prior Information About Fur Forts" on the following page.)

Moving to the unknown

Once students have reviewed what they already know about the topic, they can turn their attention to what more they would like to know. If students are interested in a topic, there will be many questions. By listing and then organizing these questions, students are aided in zeroing in on the most important and interesting aspects of the topic.

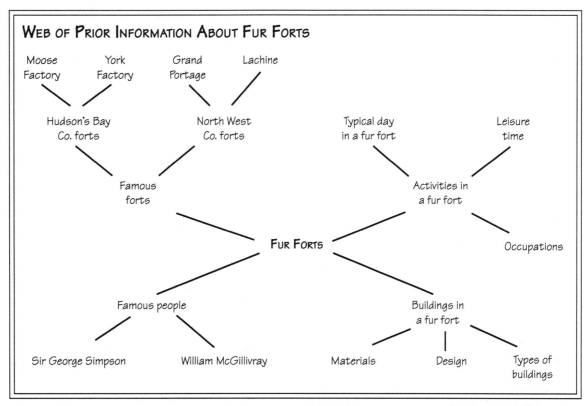

WEB OF PRIOR INFORMATION ABOUT FUR FORTS

Moose Factory — York Factory — Grand Portage — Lachine

Hudson's Bay Co. forts

North West Co. forts

Typical day in a fur fort

Leisure time

Famous forts

Activities in a fur fort

FUR FORTS

Occupations

Famous people

Buildings in a fur fort

Sir George Simpson

William McGillivray

Materials

Design

Types of buildings

One way of implementing this approach is to list student questions about a topic on chart paper and then cut up the paper so that each question is on a separate piece. Either as a whole class or in smaller groups, students can then sort the questions into categories and develop one general question for each category. As the chart "Student Questions About Fur Forts" shows, the topic "Fur Forts" might elicit eight specific questions that could be grouped under three general questions.

A variation of this approach that can be used to help primary students generate and cluster specific questions is to ask every student to write on an index card a question about the chosen topic. Arrange students in a large circle and invite one student to place his or her card on the floor in the centre. If anyone else thinks they have a question which could be grouped with the first one, they should place their card in line just below the first card and explain why it belongs there. When all questions have been clustered in this mannner, students can choose a general question from those in each group, or formulate a new question, which subsumes the specific questions on the index cards.

Armed with a few general questions (that summarize the many specific questions they have), students

---

STUDENT QUESTIONS ABOUT FUR FORTS

Brainstormed questions

- Were there schools in the forts?
- What did people do if they didn't take part in the fur trade?
- Was life hard or easy for people living in the forts?
- Did women live in fur forts?

- When did fur forts stop being used?
- What happened to the fur forts?

- What did people in a fur fort eat?
- How did they obtain food?

General questions

What was it like to live in a fur fort?

What happened to the fur forts, and when?

What food sources were available to people living in a fur fort?

are able to use information sources more effectively. With a clear focus for reading, students have less difficulty separating relevant from less relevant information. Otherwise, they will often assume that, if the author considered it important enough to mention, it must be important enough to include in their notes. With questions in mind, students can scan for answers, rather than reading every word and constantly wondering what they should be looking for.

IDENTIFYING INFORMATION SOURCES

A third step in conducting research is to help students learn how to identify relevant and reliable information sources. Possible information sources are infinite. It may be useful to brainstorm specific possibilities as a group before students begin their research. If this is not feasible because individual projects are too varied, encourage students to brainstorm individual lists. Information sources can include print, people and places, as well as audio-visual materials and computer resources.

Print materials can include encyclopedias and other reference books, magazines, almanacs, nonfiction trade books and literature. These materials can be found in libraries. In addition, print information can be found in so-called "fugitive" materials. These are materials which are not meant to be long-lasting because they are frequently updated. Many of them are not found in libraries. This category of print material includes pamphlets and bulletins published by advocacy groups (e.g., environmental organizations), government departments and agencies (e.g., tourist bureaus) and private corporations (e.g., travel agencies). People possibilities are endless. Places might include historic sites, museums, parks, zoos and resource centres of various kinds. Audio-visual sources include pictures, slides, filmstrips, videotapes, films, and laserdiscs. Audio-visual material can be a particularly useful information source for less capable readers. The Internet and CD-ROMs are other valuable sources of data.

After generating possible information sources, encourage students to think about which sources are the most promising to consult. We can develop this critical spirit with young students by presenting them with a pair of resources and asking them to explain which would be the better source to consult, given the question we want answered (e.g., "If we want to know what 'voyageur' means should we consult a newspaper or a dictionary?" and "If we want to know what voyageurs do should we consult an encyclopedia or a dictionary?"). With older students, ask more complex, open-ended questions (e.g., "List five information sources about Native people's role in the fur trade. Comment on potential biases or selectivity in each source.").

Identifying information sources is an area where the teacher-librarian can be of particular assistance, both in terms of arranging for appropriate resources to be available to students, and in helping students locate those resources most useful to them.

EXTRACTING INFORMATION FROM SOURCES

The next step in conducting research is to find the desired information in the source. In order to effectively and efficiently extract this information students need to be competent in the use of such tools for locating information as tables of contents, indices, guide words and computer menus. It should not be assumed that all students are adept at using these information retrieval tools—especially in the area of electronic sources.

This is yet another step in which the teacher-librarian can be of assistance. Some teachers and teacher-librarians team-teach research skills. Preparation work is cut in half when the teacher and teacher-librarian each prepare a lesson on a specific skill (e.g., using a table of contents or an index) and teach that lesson to one-half the class and then to the other.

RECORDING AND ORGANIZING INFORMATION

The next step is to record and organize information in a form that will be of use in completing a report. This step, too, requires specific teaching. Four examples of strategies for helping students record and organize information are described below: partner talk, guiding question folders, notetaking columns and data charts.

Partner talk

Partner talk is a strategy for organizing information that relies heavily on extended discussion prior to any written recording. Before beginning to write their reports each student explains to a partner their topic and the information they have found about each of the guiding questions. This approach can be used even if students in each pair have different topics.

CARRYING OUT A PARTNER TALK

- Students work in pairs. Each partner tells the other what he or she already knows about the topic. The partners ask each other questions.
- Individually, partners find a resource book and read relevant sections.
- Partners return and relate the new information they found.
- Partners question one another to find out what additional information is required.
- Partners return to the resources used previously or to new resources to answer these additional questions.
- Partners share answers. Repeat previous steps until all needed information has been gathered.
- Students prepare their reports.

This idea is from Ann McIntyre, a teacher-librarian in Edmonton Public Schools.

Guiding question folders

Students write each of their general questions at the top of a separate sheet of paper. An additional, final sheet is given the title, "Bibliography." All sheets are kept in a folder. As students conduct their research, they record information on the appropriate sheet, always remembering to record the source on the Bibliography page. When students write their first draft, the information they need is organized for them. Below is described a way of adapting this procedure for a group report with primary students.

USING A GUIDING QUESTION FOLDER WITH PRIMARY STUDENTS

- Brainstorm with the students information already known about the topic. List these "facts" on strips of cardboard and place them in a pocket chart for easy reference.

- List the questions students have about the topic. Choose three or four key questions.

- Write each key question at the top of a sheet of chart paper. Have students print each question at the top of their own sheets of paper. Add a sheet called "Book List," where the books used as information sources are listed.

- Read aloud all or parts of the books chosen as information sources. Encourage students to draw information from the pictures as well as from the words. Students are to raise their hands any time one of their questions is answered. Record answers in note form on the appropriate piece of chart paper. Students can print the answer on their papers as well. As they listen, they can also check the validity of the information they already knew. They may find some of their information is incorrect. If a "fact" is incorrect, discard the card on which it is written. If correct, tape the card to the appropriate sheet of chart paper.

- Students generate and print on chart paper statements based on the information gathered. The information from each page will form one paragraph of the report.

- Choose a title for the report.

- Have students copy the report for themselves and illustrate it.

Notetaking columns

Notetaking columns are sheets of paper with a line down the middle. List the guiding question headings on separate sheets as in the guiding question folder strategy. Draw a vertical line down the middle of each page. Students use the left-hand column to jot down information from the reference source. In the right-hand column, students restate that information in their own words.

Data charts

Data charts are an effective format for recording information. The limited space provided means that students are required to record in point form; the framework encourages use of several information sources; and, since only a few questions or topics are listed, they must be major ones.

Until everyone is comfortable with the format, it is a good idea to use data charts as a class, rather than individually. Group practice "runs" should focus on topics unrelated to those students will be exploring for their individual projects. (See "Data Chart: Peru" on the following page.)

USING A DATA CHART

- Prepare a blank data chart on an overhead transparency and individual charts for every student. Ask students to record information on their individual sheets as the information is recorded on the overhead transparency.

- Identify and record a title for the research topic.

- Generate numerous questions. Invite students to discuss which of these questions are the most important or interesting. List four or five major questions in the first column of the chart.

- In the second column, record what students already know in response to each question.

- Provide students with the titles of two or three brief sources which they will use as information sources. Record the titles of the sources at the top of the remaining columns. So students do not become bogged down in any one source, choose sources that are brief. Sources such as a picture or a poem are useful, not only because they are brief, but also because they illustrate the variety of information sources that students should consider.

- Read or show the first source to students. Have students share information from this source that answers any of the questions asked in column one. Decide, as a class, on the best and briefest response to each question. Record each response in point form.

- Repeat this procedure with all other sources.

- Working together as a class, develop a summary response statement for each question.

SYNTHESIZING AND PRESENTING INFORMATION

The most common methods of synthesizing and presenting research information are written reports and oral presentations. I discuss how to make these two common formats more effective and I suggest alternative ways of synthesizing and presenting information.

Strategies for written reports

- **Explain to a colleague.** Have students explain their topics to other students, using their notes as a guide. This helps them to practise expanding their notes into sentences and to sequence their information logically. In addition, questions asked by other students may indicate information gaps that need to be addressed. (This approach is similar to Partner Talk except that students work from notes. Partner Talk is oral until the final step.)

- **Draft without notes.** It can be useful to have students write the first draft of the report without reference to their notes. This encourages students to think carefully about what they are writing and helps them to make the report their own. They can return to their notes for their second draft.
- **Selective efforts.** Polished written reports require several drafts, each of which must be edited. However, it may not be necessary to take every report

through to final polished product. It may be better to allow each student to choose from among the reports assigned over the given year which will receive the extra effort. These are the ones which will receive the professional looking laminated cover and be displayed publicly.

- **Writing from a point of view.** Students can represent what they have learned from their research from a particular point of view. It is more interesting for students to write—and for the teacher to read—a letter from a settler on the Canadian prairies to relatives in the Ukraine, than a straightforward description of life on a prairie homestead. Or how about a

DATA CHART: PERU

Our general questions	What we already know	Source:	Source:	Source:
#1. What is the land like?				
#2. What are the major ethnic groups?				
#3. What are the major industries?				
#4. What do people do in their leisure time?				
#5. What roles do women play in this society?				

Summary statement—Ques. #1 _____

_____

Summary statement—Ques. #2 _____

_____

Summary statement—Ques. #3 _____

_____

Summary statement—Ques. #4 _____

_____

Summary statement—Ques. #5 _____

_____

society columnist description of the glittering social events which accompanied the Charlottetown Conference of 1864?

This type of writing is often referred to as RAFT writing—ROLE, AUDIENCE, FORMAT, TOPIC. Students write in *role* (e.g., from the point of view of a world leader, journalist, pioneer, inventor, a famous person in history), to a particular *audience* (e.g., to newspaper readers, a relative, prospective employers, television viewers), using a particular *format* (e.g., newspaper editorial, poem, letter, journal entry, telephone conversation, rap song), on a particular *topic*.

The depth of understanding of the subject need not be diminished when students use an unusual format. In fact, it must often be greater in order to make the writing ring true. For instance, it would be more challenging for students to write entries in Sir John A. Macdonald's journal during the Pacific Scandal crisis than a straightforward account of the crisis. It is one thing to simply describe events and quite another to present them from the perspective of one of the key players. To write entries in Macdonald's journal, students must add to their knowledge of events an understanding of how Macdonald would feel about them, how he saw his role and how he viewed the role of others.

It is important to offer students the opportunity to display their reports in prominent locations. The teacher-librarian can be helpful in this regard since the school library is a very appropriate choice for garnering public recognition for students' efforts.

Strategies for oral reports

- **Using visual aids.** Visual aids help make the presentation more interesting to the audience. Some students, who are not aural learners, have difficulty listening for any length of time to an oral delivery of information. Visuals also provide memory cues to guide the oral delivery. Visual aids help make the presenter feel more at ease. As a presenter, it can be comforting to know that the eyes of the audience will not be directed at you for the duration of the presentation. In addition, pointing to a picture or map gives presenters something to do with their hands, which can lessen nervousness.

- **Synthesizing another student's report.** To encourage students to listen carefully when others are presenting their reports, it is useful to ask students to take notes. One approach is to ask each student to use his or her notes to write a summary of another student's report. The example is from a grade three class, where students made oral presentations on a topic of their choice. (See "Summary of Emily's Talk" on this page.)

There is no rule that says oral reports must be made by one student standing in front of a group of 30 others. Here are two other approaches to try:

- **Rotating presentations.** Speakers are placed at different spots around the room and small groups of students rotate from one speaker to the next. It is not essential, in this format, that every student hear every other student's presentation. This approach has several advantages over the whole class/one-speaker-at-a-time method. First, it is far less intimidating for a student speaker to make a presentation to a small group than to the entire class. Second, the speaker has the opportunity to repeat the speech several times, gaining confidence and improving delivery with each presentation. Third, members of the audience may be more attentive in this format because they are not forced to sit in one place for long periods of time. Also, they have more opportunity to ask questions because there are fewer questioners.

- **Co-operative group presentations.** In this approach, a group of students work together to make the presentation, each focusing on a particular aspect of the topic. One student might serve as moderator, introducing the topic and panelists, calling on questioners and keeping things running smoothly. This approach is helpful to the speakers. They can assist one another with difficult questions asked by the au-

---

SUMMARY OF EMILY'S TALK

By Laura Brown

If you want to know anything about anesthetics just ask Emily.

Anesthetics are drugs that make it possible for operations and other medical treatment to be carried out painlessly. Anesthetics are made from laughing gas. Horace Well invented anesthetics.

A long time ago even the most minor operation was quite painful because back then they didn't have anesthetics.

The main anesthesias are local and general. A general anesthetic is when you get a needle put through your vein.

A local anesthetic is when they don't put you to sleep such as when the dentist puts a needle through your gum when you have a filling.

The other anesthetic is when some ointment is swabbed on with a Q-tip or a cotton ball to numb the feeling in a certain area. The method called inhalation is when the doctor gives you gas through a mask.

This example of a summary done by a grade three student at Caulfeild Elementary in West Vancouver is reprinted with Laura's permission, and that of her teacher, Vivian Brighten, and her mother, Wendy Pitt-Brooke.

dience and the burden of response does not fall on the shoulders of a single individual. In addition, they have an opportunity to develop group participation skills such as co-operating with, and listening to, others and taking responsibility for contributing to discussions.

Note that students should not simply be thrust into a cooperative project without assisting them in developing the tools they will need for effective cooperation. These would include the willingness and ability to listen carefully to others in the group, willingness to await one's turn to speak, and to share materials.

Alternative reporting formats

As suggested above, there are many alternatives to formal oral and written reports. The chart on this page ("Alternative Reporting Ideas") lists a number of suggestions, any of which can be approached in various ways. For instance, a timeline may consist entirely of words, it may be illustrated or it may be represented "live." Pat Shields (1996) suggests that, in a "living timeline" format, students prepare role plays using costumes and props, on historical figures, either fictional or real, that they have researched. The role plays are presented in chronological order so viewers can see how perspectives changed over time.

ASSESSING STUDENT RESEARCH

It is potentially misleading to place assessment at the end of this model, since assessment should not be viewed as the last step in a research project, but should be seen as an ongoing part of the entire process. Three principles are key to effective assessment of student research projects:

- generate and share assessment criteria prior to completion of any assignment;
- assess research procedures in addition to products;
- include self-assessment and peer-assessment.

Prior setting of criteria

Set out, or better yet negotiate, the assessment criteria for students at the very outset of the project or at the beginning of each stage of the process. This way, there are fewer surprises. Assessment is less menacing for students if they know from the outset how their work will be assessed and if they have had some say in establishing the basis for assessment. Encourage students to use the criteria to assess their own work before presenting it for teacher assessment.

The sample criteria on the following page ("Assessing Oral Presentations") could be handed out to students when they start preparing for an oral presentation. Note that the criteria in this example, other than those listed under "Delivery," would also be applicable to a written report. For most written reports, a section dealing with writing mechanics would be added.

Assess both procedure and product

All aspects of the research process can and should be assessed, starting with students' ability to focus their topics and frame guiding questions, through the effective use of data charts, to the quality of the final written, oral and visual products. Assessing along the way makes the task less massive for the teacher and provides students with ongoing feedback, which reduces the likelihood that mistakes made early on in the process will scuttle the entire project.

The form "Research Project Feedback" on the next page lists sample assessment criteria for each step in the research model described in this article. Teachers could use a form such as this one to make notes along the way regarding each student's ability to meet the criteria.

Include self- and peer-assessment

Self-assessment and peer-assessment should be part of every research project because they provide students with more, and more immediate, feedback than a teacher can possibly provide. Students will need to be helped to learn how to provide constructive feedback to others—this, in itself, is a valuable learning experi-ence. Students need to think about and learn ways of making comments in a positive and sensitive manner (e.g., precede any concerns with several positive features, put forth concerns in the form of a query or issue to think about). An example of a joint assessment sheet for use by student and teacher in assessing a poster presentation is found on page 205.

Parting Comment

Throughout the article I have pointed to the value of making maximal use of teacher-librarians. They can be very helpful in many ways, including identifying appropriate resources in the school resource centre, obtaining other resources from outside sources, designing activities which require resource centre support, instructing students in skills needed to work through the research process and providing a public venue for displaying finished reports. The most "dramatic" example of co-operative planning and teaching between a classroom teacher and a teacher-librarian I have heard involved a grade two class researching dragons. Under the guidance of their teacher and the teacher-librarian, students had examined portrayals of dragons in literature, determined the characteristics of dragons and then

---

ASSESSING ORAL PRESENTATIONS

	Excellent	Good	Adequate	Inadequate
Content • is accurate • covers major points • is sufficiently detailed • is interesting				
Organization • begins with effective introduction • is arranged in logical sequence • has an effective closure				
Delivery • is easily heard • looks at audience • uses expressive speaking voice				
Visual aids • effectively illustrate key points • are clear • are visually appealing				

Comments _____

_____

_____

RESEARCH PROJECT FEEDBACK

Topic _____   Name _____

SKILLS	COMMENTS
Topic • is worth pursuing • is narrow enough to be manageable	
Guiding questions • are relevant to topic • adequately summarize specific questions	
Information sources • are relevant to topic • provide reliable information	
Extracting information • Students can use appropriate locator aids (e.g., index, table of contents, guide words, computerized directory to library resources)	
Recording and organizing information • notes are brief • notes are well organized • notes cover important points related to topic • notes are drawn from several sources • notes are expressed in student's own words	
Presenting information • written drafts have been carefully editted and corrected • presentations are appropriate for audience and topic • visuals are thoughtfully designed and constructed • written and oral reports are thoughtfully sequenced • reporting (in any form) clearly and accurately presents the collected information	

SELF AND TEACHER ASSESSMENT OF A POSTER

	Self rating				Teacher rating			
	very good	*good*	*satis-factory*	*poor*	*very good*	*good*	*satis-factory*	*poor*
content/message is important								
content/message is clear								
well laid out/designed								
effective use of medium								
visually appealing								

formulated three questions they would ask a dragon if they happened to meet one. As students were discussing possible questions, a dragon (the grade six teacher) burst into the classroom and attempted to kidnap their teacher. Of course, she was eventually saved by St. George (the custodian). But, true to form, the librarian played a key role in keeping the dragon from being ripped apart by students until St. George could arrive. This life-saving gesture was necessary because St. George had been momentarily delayed by a custodial emergency, and these grade two students were determined to protect their beloved teacher. The now subdued dragon turned out to be meek and mild, and only too happy to be interviewed. And, of course, forever grateful for the services of the teacher-librarian.

REFERENCES
Shields, P. (1996). Experiencing and learning through simulations and projects. *Canadian Social Studies, 30*(3), 142-143.

22

THE SOURCE METHOD TO TEACH SOCIAL STUDIES

HARRY DHAND

Teaching and learning with the raw materials of history and current events is the source method. Students use the historian's and social scientist's investigative skills to analyze, question, interpret, draw inferences, synthesize and evaluate data sources.

The source method is gaining in popularity for several reasons. First, the use of sources appropriately fits the inquiry approach. Second, the easy access to sources through Xerography. Publications such as *Jackdaw Series*, (published by Clark, Irwin) and *Canadian Scrapbook Series* (published by Prentice-Hall) have also played a significant role in popularizing the use of sources (Halloran, 1972, p. 5).

Sources provide insights into events or personalities and can explain a point of view not amplified by the textbooks. Sources provide different points of view and pose many exciting questions to the young readers (Sheahan and Quinn, 1970, p. 40). Through the use of sources students develop historian's skills such as detecting bias, establishing authenticity, validity, reliability, and frame of reference of the source. The utility of the source method helps develop critical thinking skills and analytic ability among students. Because events of the past become more relevant and meaningful to students, sources arouse students' curiosity. Students are able to envision the era and this encourages questions about it.

HISTORIOGRAPHY AS A TEACHING DEVICE

With the source method, historiography is used as a teaching device. Historiography includes the processes through which history is made and understood. It deals with the writing, tools, skills, techniques and methods of the historian and with the understanding of the content of history (Gawronski, 1969, p. 53).

Historians seek the truth. They follow methodological analyses of how multitudes of facts are related, why certain events happened as they did, with what consequences, and how those consequences affect us today and in the future. Historiography contributes to critical thinking. Students develop analytic and investigative skills by studying the way historians question, decide what is fact, draw inferences, develop hypotheses, make generalizations, place interpretations on events, record data, compile reliable evidence and distinguish between valid and artificial conclusions. Recent research indicates that historiographical study can develop higher order thinking skills (Green, 1990). "Historians have a heavy responsibility not merely to teach people substantive historical truths but also to teach them how to think historically" (Fischer, 1970, p. 316). Secondary teachers of social studies and history have a professional responsibility to teach meaningful social studies and to teach students how to think historically and critically and to get them into the habit of doing it (Commager & Muessig, 1980, p. 119).

Students realize through the study and careful examination of documents that errors exist in the reporting of historical events because of biases and different frames of reference. Moreover, the interpretations of certain historical events are difficult to understand today because of our different values and attitudes. Although we use old documents, records, and sources, we tend to interpret and evaluate them with today's perspective rather than from the light of their era. This also helps students to recognize their own biases and those of their contemporaries, as well as the biases and frame of reference of the historian. All these experiences help students to develop their own philosophy of history. They are, therefore, less likely to become passive recipients of others' conclusions and more likely to become active and critical participants in the theater of history.

Historical mindedness and perspective are developed through the use of sources of history. This helps students to develop a frame of reference with a more balanced and comprehensive outlook. The world view and historical mindedness are enhanced when students learn and practice the skills of the historian. Those skills and historical concepts should be introduced as early as possible in the _____ school and continued through high _____

SELECTI_____

_____ be
_____ at
_____ r

or _____
teri _____ d
seco _____

Pr _____ direct
record _____ om the
past. In _____ make the
study of _____ source is an
indirect r _____ ng, a primary source
usually da _____ e of an event and a secondary
source generally dates from later times.

RECOMMENDATIONS BASED ON RESEARCH

After a comprehensive review of the research on the use of documents or sources in developing historical understanding and the process of historical inquiry, Dhand (1989) made a number of recommendations to practicing teachers. My recommendations include the following:

- The teacher should be knowledgeable in the area of inquiry teaching and should directly teach the historian's investigative skills.
- Historical sources or documents should be used and tested at different grade levels and with different ability levels to obtain a useful set for the teacher's individual purposes.
- Sources should be used with different units of study. Add variety whenever possible.
- Teachers should be alert to the possible effects of sources and documents on the affective domain. Thus the use of sources and documents in values education should be considered.
- When teaching with sources and documents, the teacher must know prior to the session precisely what to do. Therefore, the teacher should make a detailed lesson plan.
- A clearly defined method of teaching and content must be used.
- All sources and documents must be checked for reading and comprehension difficulties. Any prerequisites to understanding must be covered prior to using the source.
- Guide questions prepared by the teacher and given to the students are a useful evaluation tool.
- Anecdotal records should be kept for each student as they are a useful indication of student interest and understanding.
- Time should be allotted for oral discussion and questions.
- Sources and documents should never be used in isolation from other instructional devices. In terms of comprehension, the best results were found when the use of sources and documents was combined with other methods.
- Sources and documents must be logically and pedagogically fitted into the topic being studied.
- Sources and documents must be carefully selected in light of students' level of understanding and significance to the topic being studied.
- A series of related sources and documents should be used as opposed to a single source used in isolation.
- Sources and documents of a controversial nature are preferred, Sources that portray personalities rather than objects seem to be more interesting to students.
- Reading levels of the students should be constantly assessed to assure comprehension of the material.
- It is a good strategy to have students working in groups with sources and documents. When groups of students read enough sources together, are provided with well-planned questions and with examples relating to their own lives, there is a better understanding of the material.

- Finally, excessive use of sources should be avoided. They can become boring and exhaustive for both teachers and students.

SAMPLE ACTIVITIES

These exercises or activities are meant to be illustrative only and teachers may wish to modify the procedures to suit their classroom conditions. The major purpose of these types of activities is that they seek to develop the historian's or social scientist's skills and historical attitudes.

Teachers and students should define and discuss the significance of terms related to sources and source method in historical and social inquiry such as: Fact, opinion, objectivity, frame of reference, bias, climate of opinion (spirit of the time—Zeitgeist) reliability, validity, propaganda, subtle bias, value judgments, mind set, primary source, secondary source, tertiary source, processing of information, hypothesis, data (evidence), perspective, historical mindedness, drawing inferences, and the process of inquiry.

Detecting bias in sources

- **Exercise I**

You are a judge in the court. The following case of a fight between Johnny and Doug comes before you. You have to make a decision based on the evidence presented.

1. *Johnny's father's testimony*: This big boy was hitting my boy. John hit him in the face and made this boy's nose bleed. Johnny did the right thing.

A question is asked. "Would you believe it?" "No." "Why?" "Because he is Johnny's father. We cannot believe the testimony because of Johnny's father's frame of reference."

2. *Doug's father's testimony*: Doug knocked that wicked kid down with one punch as the other kid started the fight.

"Would you believe Doug's father's testimony?" "No, because of his frame of reference."

3. *A neighbor's testimony* (who has seen the fight): The two boys were fighting. Johnny hit Doug. Doug's nose began to bleed. Doug punched Johnny and he fell down on the ground.

"Would you believe her?" "She is likely to be more objective due to her frame of reference." "Is she a primary or secondary source?" "How do you decide?" 'You have to keep two principles in mind—proximity to events and processing."

4. There are other discussion questions:

Is the witness reliable? What degree of faith can you put in his or her testimony? Is the testimony valid or relevant to the case in point? Does the witness have a bias? Have you examined other witnesses or sources? Is the witness competent? (Lee, Ellenwood & Little, 1973, p. 76). Has the witness contradicted himself or herself? Are there contradictions between or among other witnesses or sources? Are there similarities between or among different witnesses or sources? Can you distinguish between facts and inferences? Have you checked the language for emotionally charged words? Identify adjectives that indicate exaggeration or bias such as big and wicked. Are there value judgments? Compare and contrast the testimonies of two witnesses. Examine any other problems related to bias (Dhand, 1990, p. 64).

The above questions are useful guidelines for analyzing the source and for detecting bias in the source. Students must determine the author's point of view, reliability and validity of each statement (Pusey, 1984, p. 210).

- **Exercise II**

For detecting bias in the newspapers, the teacher can develop a number of examples and hands-on practice exercises. A few examples are presented here (Kirman 1992).

1. Divide the class into groups of four. Each student is a member of an editorial board for a daily newspaper. They can choose their own editor. Give each editorial board 15 stories of international, national, and local significance. There is room for up to five stories on the front page of the newspaper. Let each editorial board select the stories that can be printed on the front page.

2. Students can actually prepare the front page of a newspaper.

3. Many more items such as bias through crowd count and statistics can be added.

4. In the debriefing, each editorial board could discuss the reasons for selecting the stories of selection. A discussion could also zero in on detection of bias and source control. A similar strategy can be developed for the analysis of other media.

The exercise shows the bias of the editorial board:

- through selection and omission
- through placement of the story
- by headlines
- through inserting photos, captions and camera angles
- through the use of titles and names
- by word selection and connotation

- **Exercise III**

Anne Medina (1991) in her speech to the English Teachers of Saskatchewan gave a few examples of subtle bias. The examples given below pertain to the coverage of the Gulf War 1991 by the Western media:

- They have a war machine. We have an army, navy and air force.
- They have censorship. We have reporting guidelines.

- They have propaganda. We have press briefings.
- They are cowardly. We are cautious.
- Their missiles cause civilian casualties. Our missiles cause collateral damage.

(*They* and *Their* refer to Iraq and *We* and *Our* refer to the Western world and the allies in the Gulf War 1991.)

These pairs of statements can be used as an exercise to detect bias in the sources of information. Students should examine the techniques of propaganda used by the author in a subtle way. Students can also examine the problems usually associated with bias, perspective, and prejudice (Dhand, 1989, p. 124).

Differentiating sources

- **Exercise IV**

One principle that can be used to differentiate a primary source from a secondary source is proximity to events or how far removed the source was from the events. The following exercise will clarify the principle:

> Last Friday morning while walking along the University Bridge, John Whitehead witnessed the terrible car crash and pileup. He went home and told his father-in-law and mother-in-law about the accident. In the evening, John went out to the movie. The *Saskatoon Star* correspondent called to find out about the accident. John's mother-in-law talked to the correspondent. Based on her description of the accident, the correspondent wrote the story. The local news editor made some changes and the proofreader made some corrections. Next day, the story appeared in the newspaper. Is the newspaper story a primary or secondary source?

In the debriefing discussion, a number of questions are raised about the distance from events, and the degree of processing, the author's assumptions and values.

- **Exercise V**

Another principle that is used to distinguish between a primary source and a secondary source of information is the processing: through how many hands the information has gone. This exercise helps clarify how the evidence or information changes when passed from one person to another:

> Our friends Judy and Bob Anderson visited Jamaica last year. They were robbed while staying in Apartment No. 29, 895 Carlson Blvd., Murphy Gardens, Kingston. The following articles were taken: a Panasonic radio cassette, a Sony Walkman, two Citizen watches, two rings and $729.00 (US Dollars).

Steps

1. Ask eight students to go out of the classroom. They should be numbered from one to eight.
2. Give copies of the above robbery story to the rest of the class. They should carefully read the description of the robbery.
3. First student (No. 1) outside the classroom is told the description (the story) of the robbery in a whisper. He whispers it No. 2. She whispers it to No. 3, and so on. This is done individually.
4. First student (No. 1) is called in the class. He tells the story. Then Nos. 2, 3, 4, 5, 6, 7 and 8 enter the room one at a time and tell the story, turn by turn, as they heard the story from the student ahead of them. The class should be asked to write any changes in each retelling of the story. Students should be asked to try not to laugh or comment during the eight retellings of the story.
5. In the debriefing discussion, students analyze changes in each retelling of the story. Many things in the story will change by the time it is told the eighth time. Another variation of the exercise is that each one in the class retells the story. Then it could be retold 25 times. Discussion could also focus on the historians' and the social scientists' task of finding the truth about the past events, on historiography, types of sources, and processing (Glassman, et al., 1979, p. 31). This exercise can also be used to focus on listening skills and communication distortion.

- **Exercise VI**

This is an exercise in differentiating between primary and secondary sources. The distinction between primary and secondary sources is frequently a narrow one. Using the chart on the following page, the students check either the primary or secondary source and give an appropriate explanation in the remarks column.

A large number of other sources can be profitably used with appropriate examples to make history come alive for students. The variety is almost infinite; for example: census records, business and telephone directories, reminiscences, oral histories, maps, real estate abstracts, deeds, charters, treaties, newspapers and other media, pamphlets, statistical data, chronicles, annals, notes and private journals (Ryan & Ellis, 1974, p. 50), poems, textbooks, magazine articles, lectures, almanacs, cartoons, photographs, directories, business files, homestead files and records of harvests.

The teacher should emphasize that at times some of the items can be used as either primary or secondary sources. I have tried to distinguish between primary and secondary sources for instructional purposes. Ultimately, this distinction becomes somewhat artificial since the interconnected and interrelated use of primary and secondary sources is fundamental to historical inquiry (Cantor & Schneider, 1967, p. 4).

	Primary	Secondary
Advertisement	X	

Explanatory Remarks: Usually secondary source, but there are exceptions. For instance, if one wants to compare the price of a loaf of bread in 1867, and that of today, one could use the ad of Montreal Bakery from *The Gazette* of those days and Saskatoon Bakery price given in the *Star Phoenix* of today. In this example, the ads are used as primary sources of information.

	Primary	Secondary
Atlases	X	

Explanatory Remarks: Usually they are primary sources but in special circumstances they could be secondary. For example, after the Sino-Indian War 1962, the border dispute case was presented in the United Nations. The United Nations asked for atlases from both countries to verify the McMahan Line. Chinese atlases showed the disputed territory as part of China and Indian atlases showed the same territory as part of India. British atlases printed before 1947 were summoned for verification.

	Primary	Secondary
Census Reports	X	

Explanatory Remarks: Unless they are rigged.

	Primary	Secondary
Diaries	X	

Explanatory Remarks: Usually they are primary sources unless fake like Hitler's diary a few years ago.

	Primary	Secondary
Paintings	X	

Explanatory Remarks: Usually primary unless they are fake.

Using conflicting sources

• **Exercise VII**

How would you deal with an event if only two conflicting pieces of evidence on that event were available?

> It is the year 4592 A.D. You are a member of a team of historians and social scientists who are trying to reconstruct what happened in the Gulf War 1991. Because of previous nuclear obliteration most of the evidence was destroyed. Only two pieces of conflicting evidence are left. One is the news report on the Gulf War in *The New York Times* and the other is a written copy of the speech made by Saddam Hussein, the then President of Iraq, on the Iraqi War. How would you decide as a historian what happened in the Gulf War 1991?

Historians and social scientists might examine the points on which both sources agree that might be closer to the truth. Other factors they might discuss are the terms of reference of both sources, assumptions and values of the authors, their sense of history,

development of ideology and other conditions existing at those times. Students could also examine the historians' methods of determining the accuracy of the sources.

Evaluating sources

• **Exercise VIII**

This is an exercise in evaluating sources of information. Students should rank order the sources given below according to their reliability from 1 for the most reliable source in each item, to 3 for the least reliable in each item:

Item I: *The status of nuclear development in Iraq after the Gulf War 1991*

❑ A report by the Iraqi government

❑ A UN team's official report after their final visit

❑ An Israeli newspaper's lead story

Item II: *Canada's participation in the Gulf War 1991*

❑ A movie just released in the theaters on the Gulf War 1991

❑ The diary of the general in charge of Canadian forces in the Gulf

❑ American (US) newspaper reports on the Gulf War

Item III: *Current living conditions in China*

❑ CBC documentary just released

❑ Chinese government documentary just released

❑ Memoirs of Mao Tsetung

Item IV: *Devastation caused by the atomic bombs on Hiroshima 1945*

❑ A novel set in Hiroshima in which the major character saves a number of lives

❑ The memoirs of the bomber pilot written in the 1980s

❑ A documentary film prepared by a neutral country from the available photographs and interviews of the survivors

Item V: *The description of the Hungarian Revolution of 1956*

❑ The coverage of the Hungarian Revolution of 1956 by Pravda

❑ The smuggled report of a correspondent of a neutral country

❑ *Time* magazine report

Item VI: *The living conditions of the Cubans as gathered through*

❑ The current cartoons from the newspapers

❑ Paintings painted by Cuban artists

❑ A visit by a team of journalists to Cuba

There are no 100% accurate answers in the rankings. In the debriefing session and discussion following the exercise, students concentrate on the reasons for putting greater faith in one source than the other, the frame of reference of the source, the ability to tell the truth (reliability), and the authenticity of the source. Assessment of the accuracy of facts, objectivity and validity of the source could also be discussed.

CONCLUSION

The use of historical sources and documents is an excellent way to teach students to think critically and historically. Teachers are urged to teach the skills of the historian such as detecting bias, establishing validity and reliability of the source, and evaluating sources. With its potential influence on learning through inquiry, the source method could become a powerful instrument in history and social studies classrooms.

REFERENCES

Ballard, M. (Ed.) (1970). *New movements in the study and teaching of history*. Bloomington, IN: Indiana University Press.

Cantor, N.F. & Schneider, R.I. (1967). *How to study history*. Arlington Heights, IL: AHM.

Commager, H.S. & Muessig, R.H. (1980). *The study and teaching of history*. Columbus, OH: Charles E. Merrill.

Dhand, H. (1989). *A handbook for teachers: Research in teaching of the social studies*. New Delhi: Ashish Publishing House, 8/81, Punjabi Bagh.

Dhand, H. (1990). *Techniques of teaching*. New Delhi: Ashish Publishing House, 8/81, Punjabi Bagh.

Fischer, D.H. (1970). *Historian's fallacies: Toward a logic of historical thought*. New York: Harper & Row.

Gawronski, D.V. (1969). *History: Meaning and method*. Glenview, IL: Scott, Foresman.

Glassman, M. et al. (1979). *Cooperation and community life*. Saskatoon, SK: Cooperative College of Canada.

Green, R.P. Jr. (1990). Religion and politics in 19th century America: Historiography as a teaching resource? *Social Education, 54*, 294–297.

Halloran, F.M. (1972). *A critical investigation of the theory proposing the use of documents in the teaching of history in selected works of five Canadian authors, and of the practice which those works recommend*. Unpublished master's thesis, University of Toronto, Toronto.

Kirman, J.M. (1992). Using newspapers to study media bias. *Social Education, 56*, 47–51.

Lee, J.R., Ellenwood, S.E. & Little, T.H. (1973). *Teaching social studies in the secondary school*. New York: Collier Macmillan.

Medina, A. (1991, March). Speech to the Saskatchewan English Teachers Association Annual Convention at Saskatoon, Saskatchewan.

Pusey, S.M. (1984). Sleuths in the classroom. *Social Education 48*, 209–211.

Ryan, F.L. & Ellis, A.K. (1974). *Instructional implications of inquiry*. Englewood Cliffs, NJ: Prentice-Hall.

Sheahan, S. & Quinn, G. (1970). Using documents to teach Canadian history. *Canadian Journal of History and Social Science, 6*, 40–47.

— ✧ —

This article, reprinted with permission of University of Toronto Press Incorporated, appeared originally in 1992 in *Canadian Social Studies*, 26(4), 165-169. Minor alterations to the original article have been made for stylistic and format purposes.

23

"In Their Own Voices and In Their Own Times": Exploring Social History Through Oral Narrative

Tony F. Arruda

The histories many of us read in school, if they dealt with individuals at all, usually involved middle- or upper-class white males. Constructed from traditional and official sources or from the writings of privileged observers, such histories reflected deep social class, gender, racial and ethnic biases. After all, until well into the nineteenth century, only a small fraction of society was literate and an even smaller fragment privileged enough to warrant careful preservation of their commentaries in archives. As students, of course, we remained largely oblivious to the selective stories being told. Meanwhile, the escapades of captains and kings often failed to ignite our imaginations and contributed heavily to our boredom with social studies.

In the 1960s, a movement towards writing social history (uncovering stories of everyday life, social groups and classes in the past) began to bring to centre stage the voices of people who typically lived and died without leaving behind them much of a written record of their lives. The result is that oral history (i.e., the collection of oral reminiscences, testimonies or commentaries) which traditionally was a maligned, often shunned stepchild of academic history, has over the last thirty years injected substance and sparkle into history, a subject that for many of us, and I among them, was too often an overly-sober discipline saturated with dates, unknown figures and abstract events.

Oral history has produced some of the most enticing recent social histories of marginalized, "ordinary" and silent groups including blacks, women, workers, immigrants, aboriginal peoples, teachers, as well as children and youth, including First Nations children in residential schools.[2] These histories represent not only a shift in perspective toward "history from the bottom-up" and a new focus upon "ordinary people," but also a shift in methodology toward a tendency for historians to speak to subjects themselves in order to find out what life was like for them in the twentieth century. Such practice has helped to dispel the conventional view that historians prefer their people safely dead.

Only after being led to read some relatively new social histories of childhood and of immigrant groups did I become captivated by history. Here for the first time were histories that spoke to me. Stories of the Portuguese in Canada, for example, excited me if only because they validated my own experiences as an immigrant child within a Portuguese-Canadian family. I found myself nodding while reading these historical accounts—not nodding off to sleep but in agreement with what I was reading. The subject was relevant. And if I disagreed with what I read, I did so with the conviction of lived experience. I was engaged. These histories set my own and other immigrants' lives within the context of a large drama: human migration for economic and political reasons, inevitable cultural conflict in the host country, forces tending toward assimilation, forces tending toward alienation and so on.

Sadly, despite this shift toward oral testimony in social histories of ordinary people, there has yet to be a corresponding shift toward the use of oral history in social studies classrooms. As we will see, some teachers direct students to take up meaningful projects which involve interviewing parents, relatives and others in the community about their past (or present) lives. Generally, however, the oral narratives of "common," "ordinary" and "silent" folk are still not a significant part of the mainstream social studies curriculum.

JUSTIFICATION FOR USE OF ORAL NARRATIVES

I believe that social history should be more widely incorporated in the social studies classroom to generate a more inclusive and engaging curriculum and that oral history is a powerful tool facilitating that process. To begin with, if we consider social studies to include sociological, anthropological and psychological understandings of society, we must incorporate one of the most basic and useful tools of social science, talking to individuals about their actual lives and perspectives, in the social studies classroom. In contrast to the static nature of traditional written sources such as biographies, diaries, newspapers, police reports, census data and reporter interviews, oral history offers two-way communication with living subjects who can correct, clarify, rephrase and amplify their testimony.

A second and I believe crucial reason for the use of oral history is that existing non-oral sources may not reflect the uniqueness of individuals nor their local communities. The rapidity of demographic change in urban schools, for example, calls for more culturally-inclusive historical sources. In multicultural school settings where students of non-British and non-French backgrounds form the bulk of student populations, oral history is a means of supplementing textbooks with non-Western history and culture.

The current ethnic composition in many Canadian schools requires that social studies embrace twentieth-century and particularly post-World War Two immigration into Canada and the development of immigrant communities as key features of recent Canadian history. Whether immigrant, or Canadian-born to immigrant parents, students might create oral histories of family settlement or community development jointly with a parent or relatives. This simple enterprise may validate events highly significant to the family history which would otherwise have been passed over in the formal history curriculum. In one such case, students in Portuguese heritage language classes in Toronto worked with the local Portuguese-Canadian community to produce a volume entitled, *No Tempo dos Nossos Avos* [*In Our Grandparents' Time*] (Lopes & Lopes, 1991).

Besides furnishing content knowledge about cultural groups and historical events, the very process of creating oral and life histories, as *No Tempo dos Nossos Avos* illustrates, may positively influence students' relationships with relatives as well as their personal identity and self-esteem. Unlike textbooks, which by their nature can never represent the diverse voices of "our" past and present, oral and life histories allow students to investigate their own paths to the past. The most culturally-sensitive text cannot properly represent all cultures, let alone address the gender, class and other divisions within a single cultural group.

In a recent study of Portuguese-Canadian adolescence, a well-educated Canadian-born woman who had integrated quite successfully into Canadian youth culture admitted she nonetheless sometimes felt alienated in Canada. She remembered "being ripped off" as a teenager, feeling "disconnected" without an extended family in Canada. In her words,

> I'm constantly explaining that I'm Portuguese and I have a lot of family in Portugal—my grandparents are there, quite a few of my aunts and uncles, cousins. And I really have a desire to link with them somewhat and I am more interested now in the Portuguese culture than I was when I was growing up—there's a part of me that is missing that sense of culture. It was almost so much becoming Canadian that a part of me is really lacking that, not having that culture . . . I have this need to want to connect . . . learn a little bit more about it . . . it's the sense of identity, I think, and a sense of having been different and not having been in the main[stream]. . . . I don't want it to be that my sense of family starts here, starts with me, or starts with my parents. . . . I want to know that I'm one of a long generation of people. (Arruda, 1993, p. 20)

Schools which shift oral history projects closer to the heart of the curriculum truly "walk the talk" of Canada as a multicultural country, and espouse ethnicity as an esteemed characteristic of Canadian heritage.

A third justification for oral history is that, by its very nature, it demands student activity of the sort long prescribed by educators such as John Dewey or Edwin Fenton. Oral history projects of various lengths have been suggested in social studies curriculum journals (Sutherland, 1959, 1970; Mehaffy, 1984; Sears & Bidlake, 1991), are encouraged in activities sections of textbooks, and in at least a few pages of social studies curriculum and instructional methods textbooks (Ellis, 1991; Wright, 1995). Oral history assignments and projects certainly engage fundamental pedagogical understandings that learning requires "relevance," "active participation" and is both an individual and group process (Ministry of Education, British Columbia, 1994, p. 1). Whatever the problems a more personalized history might pose for students' historical understanding, helping "make" stories engages and extends students' prior knowledge and is worth doing for pleasure and its own sake.

Oral History Projects

Oral history generates knowledge and perspectives unavailable in other sources because it recovers the lived experiences, thoughts and emotions of ordinary and otherwise silent participants in history (most of us). Thus, acting in the manner of popular or academic historians, students should be speaking to living subjects themselves: people they know, relatives or neighbours, "invisible" people who might never rise to public view. Using the life history approach, and guided by advice in the literature, students might enquire about individuals' childhood and youth, their lives in the family, in their neighbourhoods, at school, in paid and unpaid work, their friendships and so on. Students who are apprehensive about a formal, structured interview might simply arrange to audio-tape an individual reminiscing aloud while leafing through an old photograph album. This strategy also allows students to select an enticing event or detail for further exploration. Alternatively, students might frame an entire interview with a single question: "What was it like to go to a rural school? What work did you do as a girl (boy)? Why did you become a nurse (factory worker)? Or, can you tell me what logging on the coast was like in the fifties? What was it like being in the union down on the waterfront?

Under careful guidance, oral projects may become central, not peripheral, parts of an experiential or critical curriculum, especially if they place students face-to-face with people whose lives have been altered by historical events.

Innovative teachers have asked students to undertake oral history projects of varying degrees of intensity and sophistication and with very good results. When teachers are asked to consider how oral history might enhance the curriculum, many first think of incorporating it within units on the Depression, the Second World War or the Holocaust. One of my student teachers invited a survivor of the Holocaust from the local community, an advisor to the film, *Schindler's List*, to speak to a grade eight English class integrating the *Diary of Anne Frank* with a short unit on World War Two. For years, grade eleven students at Sturgeon Creek Regional Secondary School in Winnipeg invited world war veterans into the school around Remembrance Day in order to interview them about their war-time experiences. Often, the point of such endeavours is not to foster "useful" knowledge or skills, but to enable learners to develop "an experiential dimension of consciousness of the past" (Pratt, 1983, pp. 23-24).

Under careful guidance, oral projects may become central, not peripheral, parts of an experiential or critical curriculum, especially if they place students face-to-face with people whose lives have been altered by historical events. In a project led by two history professors, for example, seventeen ninth grade students in Long Island spent a semester taping and transcribing stories of thirty-six women who had lived through World War Two. Students discovered how a watershed event such as a war caused "gaps" in home and industry, thus changing notions of "women's work" and the meaning of women's "independence." The project culminated in a publication entitled, "What Did You Do in the War, Grandma?" Students and interviewees then participated in two public forums moderated by the historians. Such elaborate efforts contribute weight and importance to the stories of ordinary people.

Oral history ventures, especially with younger children, may take the form of simple storytelling assignments. Several sets of grade six students at the Talmud Torah Vancouver Jewish elementary school, for example, have over several years conducted short interviews with a relative about a single memory from their childhood. Their assignment was outlined on a single page and required, in total, about an hour and a half of class time. The stories were taped and transcribed by students and then photocopied, assembled and bound by their two teachers. Booklets entitled *Mi Dor L'Dor* [*From Generation to Generation*], were offered as surprise gifts to parents and grandparents at Chanukah. Some of the stories are sketchy and consist of only a few sentences. One story, for example, barely outlines a Jewish woman's memory of her childhood encounter with Arabs in Southern France. Another story, "The Left Turn," also minimalist, only hints at the drama faced by a Jewish family escaping Czechoslovakia in 1968. Under a teacher's guidance, these stories might be developed further, serving as a springboard for classroom discussion or further enquiry. For example, "The Left Turn," copied here in its entirety, could be a catalyst for discussions of immigration, government and social change.

Hi, my name is Andy Vizer. My son [Roy Vizer] asked me to tell a story about my past. I come from Czechoslovakia, which has changed a lot since my childhood.

In 1968 we went on a vacation which was when Russia took over. We were out of Czechoslovakia and then we were allowed to go back. We drove home and came to a turn. The road to the right went back to Czechoslovakia, the other, left to another country called Austria. We ended up not going home. We took the left turn that eventually led me to Canada in the next month or so. (Talmud Torah Jewish School, 1991, p. 2)

The diversity of the stories arising out of this project surprised the teachers. Students and teachers found out for themselves the heterogeneity within the ethnic category, "Jewish." The open-ended assignment allowed students to interview people of different ages and social strata whose stories originated in diverse places across the globe, including Israel, Poland, Germany, Russia, Africa and Chile, as well as communities across Canada.

A more extensive and very successful oral history project, the Tatla Lake School Heritage Project, was launched in 1986. Under the direction of their teacher, Ann Piper, seven students at Tatla Lake Elementary-Junior Secondary School conducted interviews with long time local residents of the Chilcotin region of British Columbia. Their stories along with historical photographs were compiled in a publication, *Hoofprints in History*. Among personal narratives of settlement, wildlife encounters and ranch life, we get glimpses of ordinary individuals managing in tough circumstances: a woman raising five children on a ranch after her husband passed away; or local residents, without government assistance, bulldozing Bella Coola's only road link to the rest of British Columbia. The publications succeed as "class assignments," *and* they fill a gap in written history, something Piper addressed in the preface of the first volume:

> Our written history is sparse in the extreme, yet we all have heard a lifetime of stories worth remembering but unrecorded. It was our hope that at the same time as we were learning about those earlier times and practicing our English skills, we might also contribute something to the written record of our area. (Schneider et al., 1986, p. vii)

Hoofprints in History has not achieved the renown of *Foxfire*, the student-produced quarterly of "cultural journalism" which focussed upon the history and traditions of a rural area in the state of Georgia (Mehaffy, 1984). Nonetheless, by 1991, the series had grown to five volumes and sold thousands of copies, disseminating the history of a unique area of British Columbia across the province and beyond.

In an innovative attempt to serve the needs of both students and lonely seniors, Amy Hughes, teacher at Lord Byng Secondary School in Vancouver, worked out a semester-long "life review project" in conjunction with two coordinators of a local intermediate care facility. Over the course of three months, twenty-four students opened a cross-generational dialogue through a series of life history interviews with select individuals in the home. In the following excerpts, students incorporated details that would "best illuminate" residents' personal histories into "creative non-fiction" stories. These were "returned" to the subjects before being entered into the highly polished student publication, *Snapshots of a Generation* (Residents of Yaletown House and the students of Lord Byng High School, 1994). Jason Crawford, one of the students, learned something of the plight of thousands of child emigrants sent to labour in Canada decades earlier from listening to the life of John Brady:

> These young people were deprived of the rights that we take for granted. John is a lesson to all Canadians that we must guard our human rights to dignity and self-respect.

> Born January 1, 1910 in Ireland, the earliest thing that John Brady can remember is being four-years-old in a home with other orphans in Birmingham,

England. Only six short years later this child was sent by the Catholic Immigration Society to a farm in Chapleau, Quebec. The farmer, Mr. McCauley, was seventy-five-years-old and his wife was sixty-eight, and both were too old to manage the farm on their own.

> "I had never seen a farm let alone a cow. I was in charge of doing all the chores and going to school. I was only ten-years-old and was working dawn until dusk in this strange place," John said. (Residents of Yaletown House et al., 1994, pp. 25-26)

Strong bonds developed between some students and residents as illustrated by the writing of Karen Minami about Catherine Clark:

> As I look around her room, I notice the colourful drawings of beautiful flowers which she spends hours carefully drawing with intricate detail. I have one of these drawings in my own room. It is displayed on my desk to help inspire me, just as Catherine Clark does. Perhaps it is her positivity or her wisdom. Maybe it is her faith or her patience. Whatever quality it is, Cathy inspires me deeply. (Residents of Yaletown House et al., 1994, p. 20)

When students undertake an oral history project, as "historians," they give voice, space and legitimacy to someone else's life and perspective. With guidance from their teacher, students may come to understand that history is created, that history is influenced by one's perspective, indeed, that they are writing but *a* history, *one* account of things.

ROLE OF TEACHERS

Teachers play a critical role in these projects from their inception to the production, preservation and distribution of the histories. There are many practical considerations to weigh, especially in larger projects, including the scale and cost of the project, the support of school administration and community, and the altered student-teacher relationship (Mehaffy, 1984). Teachers must guide students in forming hypotheses and help them develop structured, semi-structured or open interview schedules. They should raise the matter of gaining subjects' consent and the responsibility to return the history to the subject in some manner. They will need to help students establish workable parameters for the study, guiding them as they practise interviews, decide upon interview length, determine whether it should be taped or captured on video and whether to make partial or full transcriptions.

Teachers should encourage students to contextualize the oral narratives. They should instruct students to hunt for one or more of a variety of primary sources frequently found lying dormant in closets and attics. These would include such things as diaries, letters, newspaper clippings, old magazines and catalogues, old school books, household family and business account books including rent and bill payments, programmes, certificates, membership cards, picture post-cards and, of course, those valuable old photographs.

Additionally, teachers will want to help students establish the form in which the information will be displayed and preserved, whether on a poster, or within an essay, photo-essay, book of biographical sketches, audio- or video-tape library, or in some experimental form. A relatively-new multi-media source available on CD-ROM, *True North-Arrivals* (1995), featuring the written text, voice and photographs of real immigrants, is an exciting preview of the form such oral history projects might assume as CD-ROMs become easier to author.[3]

Once stories are transcribed, teachers of language arts, social studies, English or integrated studies classes could encourage further interdisciplinary work within response journals or other formats. Secondary students, for example, might attempt to categorize the types of stories people tell, or identify recurring plots and thematic "saturation points" in aggregate stories (Bertaux, 1981).

At some point, teachers should lead students, especially those in secondary grades, to consider the resulting histories as "joint-narratives" (Polkinghorne, 1988). Students must understand that oral (or other) historians, like journalists, psychologists and sociologists are hardly neutral. Both through the questions they ask and those they forget to ask, and through their very presence, they help shape the emerging story.

CAUTIONS

I will now raise five general cautions about undertaking oral history projects in social studies classrooms.

- Teachers have to be sensitive to the potential problems associated with doing family histories. Some relatives may not want a particular story to go public. Asking students to do a family tree may be perceived by an abandoned single parent as a problematic if not outrageous task. For these and other reasons, teachers must provide students with choices including the option to interview a non-relative or pairing up with another student to interview a single respondent.

- Although students may embark upon an oral history assignment primarily to discover how and why people acted in a particular time and place, teachers should encourage students to comb for underlying historical events and details in stories that might otherwise be regarded by students as "trivia, intriguing at best, boring at worst" (Helmrich, 1989, p. 313). Although recent research suggests students may be more capable of handling history in general than was once thought, students may not be as critical of nar-

rative sources as we would like them to be (Downey & Levstik, 1988, pp. 340-341).

Through discussion and use of supplementary resources, teachers can assist students in placing individual lives within their larger social and economic context. While stories of ordinary life may teach students about how people made choices and faced consequences, I am particularly concerned that students not overplay the role of human agency in history. Teachers must contextualize oral history projects within a broader curriculum. They must not allow students to underestimate social, economic, political and ideological forces behind imperialism, slavery, world conflict and poverty and their limiting effects on people's choices.

> *Through discussion and use of supplementary resources, teachers can assist students in placing individual lives within their larger social and economic context.*

- Teachers and students must consider the problems of memory and its reliability (Sutherland, 1992). Having students prepare a variety of well-informed questions (or "levers") will help respondents lift into consciousness a rich array of details tightly clustered about important episodes (Thompson, 1978, p. 167). However, students need to be reminded that memories are more useful in gaining impressions of the past rather than providing exact facts and figures. Because memories are recalled and recast over and over again in association with contemporary perspectives, adult reminiscences may overlook many details that were important to respondents years earlier. One valuable lesson secondary students should learn is to treat oral testimony as they would other sources and seek corroborating evidence, including that provided by other respondents.

- Students investigating their own paths to the past must recognize that their Canadian "ethnic" communities are not classic ethnic cultures as might appear in the homeland. They are dispersed made-in-Canada immigrant cultures whose social institutions and social practices reflect, at least in part, a minority culture's adaptation to the influences of a dominant culture. Furthermore, social cleavages develop within an immigrant cultural group owing to social and economic class differences, and gender, as well as date of arrival in Canada. Contrary to Hansen's Law of Third Generation Return (i.e., what the grandparent chose to forget, the grandchild now wishes to remember), young members of the second- and third-generation ethnic groups may feel little affinity, even scorn, for the history of their group. If adolescents fear stigmatization by peers, some may be embarrassed, even mortified, by student presentations of oral histories which reveal the practices of other members of their group.

Teachers should also know that teaching "about" another culture does not always overturn stereotypes. Exposing students to cases of historical discrimination against Chinese, Japanese, East Indians and aboriginal peoples may diminish empathy for victims. In one instance, the practice led some students to conclude that the solution to discriminatory actions was to restrict immigration of certain racial and ethnic groups into Canada (Kehoe, 1978).

As "filiopietism" (essentially the glorification of one's own immigrant group), has marred some social histories, students must be alert to the possibility that some members of a community will deliver ahistorical and rosy accounts of life in Canada. Depending upon their grade level, students might begin to "interrogate" the oral testimonies of relatives, and particularly those of the politicized notables and "respected elders" of a community.

- Teachers may lack the necessary perspective, even content knowledge, to guide students to appropriate outcomes. Neither elementary school teachers (who frequently have not majored in social sciences), nor secondary school history specialists are necessarily authorities on such things as all cultural backgrounds, interviewing strategies or the ethical problems of oral history research. A basic framework teachers can provide their students (besides learning to listen and respect respondents' stories), is one in which students look for common life experiences, but do not overlook variability within class, gender, ethnic and "race" categories (Stasiulus, 1990; Arruda, 1993).

CONCLUDING REMARKS

I have not provided a comprehensive how-to-do-it approach to employing oral narratives in the classroom. Dozens of articles and books exist on how to undertake a range of oral history projects, for example, Donald Ritchie's comprehensive yet practical guide, *Doing Oral History* (1995). Rather, I emphasized with a few illustrations the substantive and therapeutic results that are possible when students, teachers, families and communities act in concert on an oral history project. I have pointed out that traditional historical sources often overlook ordinary individuals and local circumstances. I have argued that in an intensely pluralistic society, we must generate new sources which can help overcome long-standing cultural stereotypes. As Jack Kehoe pointed out in a recent address, "every grade 6 textbook that has ever been written has somebody in China bent over in a rice paddy planting or picking rice. Every grade 6 textbook" (1992, p. 8). When we approach ordinary individuals to talk about their lives, we are certain to flesh out new realities. If we fail to talk to ordinary people, a huge part of human experience vanishes without record.

Understandably, calls to re-orient the social studies curriculum frustrate many teachers who are already juggling overwhelming curriculum choice and time constraints. Yet, oral history must not be perceived as one more add-on, something we do for a week before getting back to the burdensome curriculum. It must not remain at the edges of curriculum as things to be done time-permitting. Typically in social studies students gain the impression that history is about events that happened "back then" and to unknown individuals. As far as academic sociologists, anthropologists and historians are concerned, ordinary *people* in their families, at school, at work, in church, in communities, in conflict or at leisure are the very subject matter. Why should this not be so for students?

The approach of speaking to living subjects fits well with relevant "experiential" education. It engages children in a span of time that is more easily grasped than classical or medieval eras. Depending upon ability, grade level and teacher interest and expertise, children can attempt some comparisons with the distant past. Children can also gain insights into the lives of their peers and their parents through an oral history project. As Sari Weintraub, teacher at the Talmud Torah Jewish School reminded me, normally, "Kids don't ask their parents these kinds of questions" and "Who asks those sorts of questions on a playground?" How many of us now wish we had spent but a single hour of those years of social studies undertaking real homework, interviewing and taping a loved relative who has now passed away? Sadly, the cogency of such action only makes sense as we ourselves move through the life course as learners begin to take the past more seriously and begin to frame past lives with new questions. As teachers, however, we can help instill in our students the sense that the past is worth preserving, that it can be preserved, and that they as "ordinary" people do in fact help make history. An oral history project is a perfect opportunity to make this point clear to them.

I will conclude with the most recent challenge to academic historians as launched recently by Canadian historian, Paul Axelrod:

> Historians who are able to paint *both* the broad canvas (social structure) *and* the individual portraits (human experience and responses) will especially advance the historiographical art, as will those scholars who are best able to hear their subjects in their own voices and in their own times. (1996, p. 38)

Many teachers have yet to concentrate on having students "paint" portraits of ordinary historical actors. Those already engaging students in the venture of making social history with the voices of ordinary people might now consider the second part of Axelrod's prescription. The challenge for these teachers is to consider how far they can encourage students to place ordinary individuals accurately within the larger picture of their own times.

Oral history must not be perceived as one more add-on, something we do for a week before getting back to the burdensome curriculum.

ENDNOTES

1 The quote "In Their Own Voices and in Their Own Times" in the title is taken from Axelrod (1996, p. 38).

2 For a focus upon immigrant women, see Franca Iacovetta (1986); for children, see Joy Parr (1980), Neil Sutherland (1990), as well as his forthcoming book; for aboriginal children in schools, see Celia Haig-Brown (1988); for children and teachers in their historical settings, see Jean Barman et al. (1995).

3 Ten modules for Windows or MacIntosh are available: Africans, Chinese, English, French, Indian, Irish, Italian, Japanese, Polish and Ukrainians.

REFERENCES

Arruda, A.F. (1993). Expanding the view: growing up in Portuguese-Canadian families, 1962-80. *Canadian Ethnic Studies, 25*(3), 8-25.

Axelrod, P. (1996). Historical writing and Canadian education from the 1970s to the 1990s. *History of Education Quarterly, 36*(1), 19-38.

Barman, J., Sutherland, N. & Wilson, J.D. (Eds). (1995). *Children, teachers, schools in the history of British Columbia.* Calgary, AB: Detselig.

Bertaux, D. (Ed.). (1981). *Biography and society: The life-history approach in the social sciences.* Beverly Hills, CA: Sage.

Downey, M.T. & Levstik, L.S. (1988). Teaching and learning history: The research base. *Social Education, 52*(5), 336-342.

Ellis, A. K. (1991). *Teaching and learning elementary social studies.* Needham Heights, MA: Allyn and Bacon.

Haig-Brown, C. (1988). *Resistance and renewal: Surviving the Indian residential school.* Vancouver: Tillacum Library.

Helmrich, J.E. (1989). The curricular validity of local history: Surface events and underlying values. *Social Education, 53*(5), 310-313.

Iacovetta, F. (1986). From Contadina to Worker. In J.R. Burnet (Ed.), *Looking into my sister's eyes: An exploration in women's history* (pp. 195-222). Toronto: Multicultural History Society of Ontario.

Kehoe, J. (1978). Multiculturalism: The difficulty of unpredictable strategies. (Appendix I). In J. Kehoe (Ed.), *Ethnic prejudice and the role of the school.* (pp. 2-10). Unpublished manuscript.

Kehoe, J. (1992). Multicultural education in the 90's: Where do we go from here? *Perspectives, 24*(2), 4-10.

Lopes, J.M. & Lopes, M. (1991). The collection of social histories in the Portuguese Heritage Language Program. *Canadian Modern Language Review, La Revus canadienne des langues vivantes. 47*(4), 708-711.

Mehaffy, G.L. (1984). Creating a Foxfire-concept magazine: Some preliminary considerations. *Social Studies, 75,* 13-17.

Ministry of Education, British Columbia. (1994). *The kindergarten to grade 12 education plan.* Victoria, BC: Author.

Parr, J. (1980). *Labouring children.* London: Croom-Helm.

Polkinghorne, D. (1988). *Narrative knowing and the human sciences.* Albany, NY: SUNY Press.

Pratt, D. (1983, June). History in schools: Reflections on curriculum priorities. Unpublished paper delivered at Canadian Historical Association, Vancouver, BC.

Residents of Yaletown House & the students of Lord Byng High School. (1994). *Snapshots of a generation: The Life Review Project.* Vancouver: Yaletown House Society.

Ritchie, D.A. (1995). *Doing oral history.* New York: Twayne.

Schneider, S. with Thompson, M., Harris, T., Proctor, A., Mueller, C., Self, A. & Dowd, S.O. (1986). *Hoofprints in history: Tales of the Chilcotin past.* Tatla Lake, BC: Tatla Lake School Heritage Project.

Sears, A. & Bidlake, G. (1991). A senior citizens' tea: A connecting point for oral history in the elementary school social studies. *Social Studies, 82*(4), 133-35.

Stasiulus, D.K. (1990). Theorizing connections: Gender, race, ethnicity and class. In P. Li (Ed.), *Race and ethnic relations in Canada* (pp. 269-305). Toronto: Oxford University Press.

Sutherland, N. (1959). History brought to life. *BC Teacher, 39*(3), 144-145.

Sutherland, N. (1970). *When Grandma and Grandpa were kids.* Toronto: Gage.

Sutherland, N. (1990). "We always had things to do": The paid and unpaid work of anglophone children between the 1920s and 1960s. *Labour/Le Travail, 25,* 105-141.

Sutherland, N. (1992). When you listen to the winds of childhood, how much can you believe? *Curriculum Inquiry, 22*(3), 235-255.

Talmud Torah Jewish School. (1991). *Mi dor l'dor: From generation to generation.* Vancouver: Grade six students with the assistance of their teachers, C. Leisen and S. Weintraub.

Thompson, P. (1978). *The voice of the past: Oral history.* Oxford: Oxford University Press.

True North—Arrivals. (1995). CD-ROM. Whitby, ON: McGraw-Hill Ryerson.

Wood, L.P. (1994). "What did you do in the war, Grandma?" An oral history of Rhode Island women during World War II. *Social Education, 58*(2), 92-93.

Wright, I. (1995). *Elementary social studies: A practical approach* (4th ed.). Toronto: Nelson Canada.

SUPPLEMENTARY READINGS

Dunaway, D.K. & Baun, W.K. (1996). *Oral history: An interdisciplinary anthology.* Walnut Creek, CA: AltaMira Press.

Hickey, M. (1991). "And then what happened, Grandpa?": Oral history projects in the elementary classroom. *Social Education, 55*(4), 216-217.

Gluck, S.B. & Patai, D. (1991). *Women's words: The feminist practice of oral history.* New York: Routledge.

Grele, R.J. with Terkel, S., Vansina, J., Tedlock, D., Benison, S. & Harris, A.K. (1991). *Envelopes of sound: The art of oral history* (2nd ed.). New York: Praeger.

Olmedo, I.M. (1996). Creating contexts for studying history with students learning English. *Social Studies, 87*(1), 39-43.

Seixas, P. (1993). Historical understanding among adolescents in a multicultural setting. *Curriculum Inquiry, 23*(3), 301-327.

Singer, A. (1994). Reflections on multiculturalism. *Phi Delta Kappan, 76*(4), 284-288.

Steel, D.J. & Taylor, L. (1973). *Family history in schools.* London: Phillimore.

Wigginton, E. (Ed.). (1972). *The Foxfire book.* Garden City, NY: Doubleday.

Wigginton, E. (1988). The Foxfire phenomenon. *English Journal, 77,* 35-8.

Wigginton, E. (1989). Foxfire grows up. *Harvard Educational Review, 59*(1), 24-49.

This article is based upon "Speaking with the Subject: When Students Undertake Oral History," a paper delivered at the Curriculum as Narrative/Narrative as Curriculum Conference, University of British Columbia, May 1996. The author would like to thank Peter Seixas for his comments on that paper.

24

Using Interviews in Social Studies

Alan Sears

All teachers wish to stimulate student enthusiasm for learning in social studies. When students become truly engaged in a project, they take off in unexpected directions, producing work that is vastly superior to their customary levels of achievement. The reward for teachers is knowing that the project made a difference. Involving students in interviews with interesting people from outside their ordinary realm of experience is one way to engage students' interest in social studies.

The interview is relevant in many situations, from the study of historical events to the examination of contemporary social issues. As Francis Kazemek (1985) points out, this technique is versatile: "The interview/oral history format can be used in some manner with all people and by all elementary and secondary students to help them become more proficient language users and more sensitive members of the community" (p. 212). In this article I discuss several occasions where I have successfully used interviews with social studies students, and I describe the benefits and provide suggestions for implementing these kinds of projects.

Interview Projects

I first used interviews as part of a local history project with grade six students. A colleague and I had developed a history curriculum using source documents, cemetery visits and architectural studies. Our students made great progress in learning to "read" both written and three-dimensional sources. The one element we felt was missing was the collection of historical information directly from seniors. In order to get students and seniors together, we devised the concept of a senior citizens' tea. We invited local seniors to our school for an afternoon of refreshments and entertainment provided by the students, followed by an opportunity for students to individually interview seniors on predetermined topics. The interviews went extremely well and student enthusiasm, reflected in the quality of the reports they wrote after the interviews, convinced us that we were on to a good thing. The tea became an annual event (Sears & Bidlake, 1991).

I also used an interview project with a class of grade 10 students who were enrolled in a modified program. We were studying the economy in a Maritime Studies course, and the text described people working in various occupations in different sectors of the economy. The descriptions focused on such topics as responsibilities, qualifications, working conditions, hours, pay and job satisfaction. After developing questions on these topics, students were assigned to interview a non-relative, who was working full-time. I had not planned on having students share their reports with anyone except myself, but they were of such high quality that we spent several class periods discussing the various occupations covered. I then passed the reports on to other Maritime Studies teachers in the school to share with their classes. The quality of the work from a class labelled as slow learners impressed me and the other teachers.

The interview assignments that I most enjoyed reading were produced by students enrolled in a grade 11 Modern History course. I had been struggling to make the turmoil of the 20th century more real for them and

Initially, many students are nervous and uncertain about conducting interviews. . . . Eventually, most students become excited about sharing their discoveries both orally and in writing.

decided to assign students the task of interviewing someone who had been involved in an international conflict. Students were to find an individual who met one of the following criteria:

- A veteran of the armed forces who had served in the First or Second World War, in an area of conflict such as Korea or with a Canadian peacekeeping mission. The person may have served in the Canadian armed forces or those of another country.

- A civilian who had lived in a war or occupation zone such as Holland during the Second World War, in Britain during the blitz or in Vietnam during the more recent conflict in that country.

The purpose of the interview was to foster an intimate personal view of modern conflict. Students were to inquire into the individual's views on the causes of conflict, the morality of it, the actual events, the areas involved, the strategies and equipment used, and the effects and consequences. The interviews consisted of a minimum of 25 questions, some of which were made up in class. After the interviews were completed, the information was presented in a formal essay.

Prior to assigning the interview task, I contacted the local branch of the Royal Canadian Legion and arranged for volunteers to be interviewed in the event that some students were unable to find their own interviewees. Out of 60 students, only 14 needed this help.

The quality of the final assignments was exceptional and the range of topics covered was fascinating. I had been afraid that students would get a rather narrow view of conflict from completing their own interviews, but this problem was avoided by having students share information and insights with the rest of the class. Interviewees ranged from a woman whose war-time role in the British Home Army involved gassing rabbit warrens to prevent the pests from eating much needed produce, to a man who spent four years as a prisoner of war in Japan.

These are only a few examples of how interviews might be used to enrich social studies instruction. Possible topics are almost limitless, and include collecting information on contemporary issues and exposing students in an in-depth way to people of different cultural or ethnic backgrounds (see, for example, Sears, 1989, 1991).

BENEFITS

The most obvious benefit, as mentioned above, is the motivational effect of these assignments. Initially, many students are nervous and uncertain about conducting interviews, but with very few exceptions, the process goes much better than they expect. Eventually, most students become excited about sharing their discoveries both orally and in writing. Rives Carroll (1985), who carried out an interview project in Washington, DC, found that it gripped students in a way that other projects had not: "For each child, this was a period of self-discovery. Stories about their ancestors, which were full of adventure, hardships, and courage, built pride and respect. Students realized history was alive all around them" (p. 151). Kazemek (1985) argues that part of the motivational value springs from the inherent love of storytelling that is basic to humanity. This love is reflected in the many parables, folktales and legends that are part of most cultures.

An extensive range of language skills is employed throughout the interview process: students converse with one another to develop questions, they interact with interviewees using both "participant" and "spectator" modes of language (Lubarsky, 1987, p. 522), they analyse and edit the information they collect and, finally, they present it in written form. Karen Jorgensen-Esmaili and Rosalind Sarah (1986) point out that the social participation, communication and inquiry skills developed go beyond those of most traditional language assignments as students formulate, ask and orally respond to questions in a realistic social setting. Perhaps the factor that most influences language and social development is the need to use their skills in a situation that, unlike most school assignments, is connected to life outside the school. As Kazemek (1985) points out, interviews allows students to use language in a "purposeful and imaginative way" (p. 212).

Assigning student essays based on interviews avoids the age-old trap of plagiarism (usually unintended) that many students fall into when asked to write a report. Other aspects of student writing can also be improved using interviews. If students carefully structure their interview questions around key topics, information is collected in a systematic way that lends itself to producing well-structured papers. In the projects described earlier, student enthusiasm was also evident in the lively, descriptive prose they produced and, like Kathleen Turner (1985), I found the resulting papers "among the most enjoyable and rewarding assignments I've encountered" (p. 353).

Shirley Engle and Anna Ochoa (1988) argue that an effective social studies curriculum must make use of data collected from diverse sources that could not possibly be encompassed in a single textbook (p. 128). An interview assignment recognizes the value of alternative sources of information and lessens reliance on teacher-delivered information. Students appreciate that they are contributing unique and relevant information to their peers, and this realization, in itself, has motivational value.

A further benefit of this type of assignment, given the mix of abilities in most classrooms, is its suitability for all levels of students (Kazemek, 1985). It can be used effectively at various grade levels and by students of varying ability levels in the same grade. Students who have difficulty gathering information from written sources are given an opportunity to shine, and effective use of tape recorders can ease the burden of note taking.

The relationships which students develop with other people in their community is perhaps the most significant benefit of these projects. Students learn to appreciate varying perspectives, develop awareness of the breadth of resources in the community and acquire a deeper understanding of interrelationships in communication (Turner, 1985, p. 353). As a result of the senior citizens' tea described earlier, my grade six students gained new insights into the lives, experiences and attitudes of senior citizens. This lesson contributed significantly towards breaking down students' long held, rather negative stereotypes. As well, the seniors became involved in the children's lives and, indeed, the life of the whole school in a positive and enriching way. All these projects fostered the kind of positive and substantial relationship between the school and the community which social studies educators since Dewey have advocated.

PROCEDURES

Richard Daly (1983) identifies several interview formats ranging from very structured, entirely pre-scripted questioning to unstructured, largely spontaneous questioning. He suggests that *informal case histories,* which are semi-structured interviews, are most appropriate for classroom use since they provide clear structure while allowing for flexibility and interchange. Daly identifies three types of informal case history interviews relevant for school use:

- the *autobiographical* approach which concentrates on the subject's life story in whole or in part;
- the *biographical* approach which deals with the life story of another person known to the subject;
- the *topical* approach which examines a topic familiar to the subject.

Regardless of which interview type a teacher uses, Kazemek's (1985) four stages are a useful guide in implementing an interview project:

- setting up the interview;
- preparing students;
- conducting the interview;
- working with the information.

Setting up the interview

The first, and most obvious, step is to decide on the interview topic. This may be dictated to some extent by the curriculum; but, as Kazemek (1985) points out, possible topics are extensive, including early childhood, school days, parents, children, community, first (and subsequent) jobs, hard times, war, politics, specific historical events, religious practices and customs, crafts and hobbies, folktales, jokes, music and food (p. 214).

One factor in deciding upon a topic is availability of suitable persons to interview. Teachers may need to do background leg-work, as I did, in writing to the Legion, to ensure that sufficient interviewees were available. Another consideration is bringing together students and the people to be interviewed. In many cases students can make their own contacts, but where younger children are involved, teachers may have to play a greater role. One way to facilitate contact is to bring interviewees to the school, as we did through the senior citizens' tea. This strategy avoids the problem of students visiting homes of people whom they do not know well.

Preparing students

Almost inevitably students will be nervous when assigned an interview. This nervousness can be alleviated somewhat by sound preparation for the interview process itself, background knowledge on the topic, and practice with interviewing techniques. Students will feel more comfortable during the interview and be better

---

The relationships which students develop with other people in their community is perhaps the most significant benefit of these projects. Students learn to appreciate varying perspectives, develop awareness of the breadth of resources in the community and acquire a deeper understanding of interrelationships in communication.

---

able to respond spontaneously when unexpected information comes up, if they have read about and discussed the topic beforehand. Students can be prepared for the interview itself by discussing as a class the set of guidelines for effective interviewing outlined on the following page, "Suggestions for Effective Interviews."

Finally, giving students an opportunity to practise interviews with peers, parents or other familiar and non-threatening individuals will bolster their confidence and hone their skills. Kazemek (1985) recommends practising in triads, with one student playing the role of interviewer, one the interviewee and the third an observer to provide feedback about the interview.

Conducting the interview

Many key elements to consider in conducting the interview are listed in the "Suggestions for Effective Interviews," but a couple of additional points should be emphasized. It is important for students to locate themselves in a comfortable setting where the interview will not be disturbed. To help in probing and clarifying interviewee responses it is may be advisable for students to bring, in addition to a clearly written list of their specific questions, a short list of stock questions that they might use as prompts (e.g., Could you give me an example of . . . ? Could you say more about . . . ?). A related point, is the need to encourage students to deviate from their prepared questions if unexpected and interesting information comes to light, as it will in most cases. Alan Wieder (1984) suggests that "the best questions develop with the story" (p. 72).

Working with the information

After the interviews have been conducted students move into the more traditional activity of preparing a written report. This involves reviewng the transcript to select important information and organizing that information. If the interview questions have been well structured, a natural plan for the paper may already be present. If not, teachers may need to help students identify and sequence broad categories for the information they have and fit the specific points into those categories. Once the basic structure or outline is present, writing can begin. Depending on the quality of work produced and the teacher's objectives, students may be asked to submit an initial draft for editing. After the final paper is written, a copy should be shared with the interviewee, who will no doubt be interested. An exciting finale to such a project is to "publish" a compilation of the papers, to be placed in school and local libraries and sold (at a nominal fee to recover costs) to students and other interested persons. This distribution of student work to a wider audience gives it added significance and becomes a motivational factor for future assignments.

CONCLUSION

Interview projects can enhance many aspects of a social studies curriculum, including content acquisition, skill development and attitude formation. Interviewing has long been recognized as a legitimate method of gathering information by historians and social scientists and it is time for its wider use by teachers. As Daly (1983) points out, perhaps the most important reason to use interviews is reflected in the high levels of student achievement resulting from this activity:

> Oral history is a methodology, a process, or a procedure which can be used by teachers as a way to reveal some interesting truth about the subject matter or content they teach every day. More importantly perhaps, it can be used as a learning activity to stimulate students to higher levels of performance in the classroom. (p. 10)

Using interviews is certainly consistent with the vision of powerful social studies teaching advocated by the National Council for Social Studies (1994) which emphasizes active, integrative learning that builds connections between school work and the world outside of school.

REFERENCES

Carroll, R. (1985). Exploring the history of neighbourhood: A community project. *Social Studies, 76*(4), 150-154.

Daly, R.F. (1983). Oral history: Its background, definition, and interview types. *ERIC* document ED237380.

Engle, S. & Ochoa A. (1988). *Education for democratic*

citizenship: Decision making in the social studies.
New York: Teachers College Press.

Jorgensen-Esmaili, K. & Rosalind, S. (1986).
Intergenerational interviews. *Social Education,*
50(4), 288-290.

Kazemek, F.E. (1985). Stories of our lives: Interviews
and oral histories for language development.
Journal of Reading, 29(3), 211-218.

Lubarsky, N. (1987). A glance at the past, a glimpse of
the future. *Journal of Reading, 30*(6), 520-529.

Sears, A. (1989). Ben Johnson and social studies
teaching: Classroom use of current social issues.
History and Social Science Teacher, 24(3), 158-161.

Sears, A. (1991). Cultural pairing: Widening the
cultural horizons of prospective teachers.
Multiculturalism/Multiculturalisme, 13(3), 10-15.

Sears, A. & Bidlake, G. (1991). The senior citizens tea:
A commencing point for oral history. *Social Studies,*
84(4), 133-135.

Turner, K.J. (1985). Oral history: A window on the
past for communications students. *Communication-*
Education, 34(4), 352-353.

Wieder, A. (1984). Oral history in the classroom: An
exploratory essay. *Social Studies, 75*(2), 71-74.

This is an updated and revised version of a 1990 article,
"Enriching Social Studies with Interviews," *History and*
Social ScienceTeacher, 25(2), 95-98.

25

Integrating Computer Technology in Social Studies: Possibilities and Pitfalls

Susan E. Gibson

Canadian educators are experiencing increased pressure to incorporate computer technology in their classrooms. Recent provincial and federal initiatives and newly developed school-based plans have made classroom availability and use of technology a high priority. Expanded educational use of computer technology through computer programs, data bases and the Internet is widely accepted as both inevitable and necessary.

Novice and experienced computer users alike may be overwhelmed by the prospects of this challenge. Feelings of inadequacy are exascerbated by an expanding glut of flashy computer programs and rapid innovations in electronic technologies. Understandably, questions of how, when and where to use computers as teaching and learning tools are foremost on the minds of many social studies teachers.

Significantly, Postman (1992) warns us that technology can be "both friend and enemy" (p. xii). Educators need to understand both the educational possibilities and problems of this technology if they are to get beyond the hype and rhetoric of computer use in their classrooms. In this article, I synthesize some of what is known about the influence of computers on teaching and learning. Represented here are the views of teachers, parents, students and researchers. Most of the studies cited were undertaken within the last decade; many were carried out in social studies classrooms. Based on these findings, suggestions are offered to encourage teachers to reflect on the computer as an educational tool and consider how to maximize its benefits in their social studies teaching. I also provide specific computer resources that social studies teachers may find useful in their teaching.

Possibilities Afforded by Computer Technology

Computer technology affords numerous possibilities for enhancing learning and teaching, including increased learner motivation, wider and easier access to "authentic" information, enhanced individualization of learning, more active involvement in learning, increased collaboration with other learners, expanded ways of communicating learning and increased productivity.

Enhanced learner motivation

A widely acknowledged effect of computer use in schools is the excitement about learning it generates (Gibson & Hart, 1996). Although many children have home computers, the novelty of computers does not seem to be wearing off (Dwyer, 1994). Computers have been found to be more engaging and interesting to students than textbooks, even though, in most cases, students learn the same information from either source

(Mitchell-Powell, 1995). Students are also motivated to explore ideas further using the computer (Morden, 1994). The computer's facility in creating polished-looking products is immediately gratifying and builds student confidence in their writing abilities (Held et al., 1991). The tracking of students' progress and responses through computer games, simulations and drill-and-practice offer on-going feedback that is encouraging to many learners (Morden, 1994). Computers are seen as personally relevant to students of all ages and their use promotes attitudes that support life-long learning (Held, Newsom & Peiffer, 1991).

Increased access to information

Computers are touted as the most efficient way of dealing with the so-called information explosion. They provide teachers and students with quicker and easier access to extensive and current information (Gibson & Hart, 1996). Through use of computers, students can learn to manage information rather than to memorize it (Wiburg, 1991). As well, computer use has been found to increase the amount of information acquired by students (Peck & Dorricott, 1994).

Perceived authenticity

Information gathered from the computer is seen to be connected to "real" local, national and global issues (Wilson & Marsh, 1995). Students also have the advantage of gaining first-hand knowledge of other cultures through, for example, direct e-mail "conversations" (Peck & Dorricott, 1994). This exposure to first-hand information may overcome many students' insular view of the world (Morden, 1994). As well, information acquired through direct data gathering is more personally relevant to children than retrieving information from a prepackaged book (Peck & Dorricott, 1994). The fact that students recognize that computers are likely to be a part of their future employment lends authenticity to their work (Means & Olson, 1994).

Increased individualization

Information on the computer is presented in a variety of forms (e.g., in graphs, pictures, text) and through a variety of modalities (e.g., auditory, visual). These features mean that computers accommodate different learning styles (Wiburg, 1991) and enable students to develop their own unique strengths by accessing information through their preferred modality (Wade, 1995).

The ability to work at one's own pace using the computer and to explore areas of personal interest promotes a more individualized approach to learning social studies. Computers can give students greater responsibility for their own learning by providing opportunities to choose what to investigate. These opportunites to determine the direction for their learning encourage independence and initiative (Peck & Dorricott, 1994). The resultant sense of empowerment may lead to ehanced learner confidence.

Expanded interactions

Computers may encourage students to become more actively involved in their learning by allowing for student control of the information accessed. For example, computer simulations allow students to direct and vicariously experience varied events. This more active involvement alters student-teacher interactions: the teacher need no longer be the primary dispenser of information, but rather can become a facilitator of students' explorations (Budin, 1991).

Opportunities for collaboration

Computers have been found to positively influence classroom learning environments. Computer technology can promote a more meaningful "workshop" atmosphere in which children work together and share ideas (Held et al., 1991). Collaboration between learners is further enhanced when students work cooperatively on tasks (Dwyer, 1994). Learning with and from others is rapidly expanding beyond the classroom walls as e-mail and Internet resources facilitate contact with other children in classrooms around the world. Teachers, too, can collaborate via technology with colleagues both locally and globally as they plan and share suggestions for computer use.

Expanded representation of ideas

Students are provided with multiple ways of representing their ideas with the assistance of a computer. Computers offer exciting possibilities to design multimedia presentations that demonstrate learning, rather than relying on a paper and pencil format (Gibson & Hart, 1996). These presentations can be shared with others, both in their own classroom, as well as beyond the classroom (Fisher, Wilmore & Howell, 1994).

Increased productivity

Computers have been found to enhance student products. In an eight-year study of classrooms from kindergarten to grade 12, Dwyer (1994) found a 10% to 15% improvement in achievement scores among regular computer users, as well as 30% gains in student productivity. The enhanced professional quality of the products adds to this sense of greater productivity (Means & Olson, 1994). The word processing capacity of computers eliminates some of the frustrations of writing and enables some children to express their ideas in writing (Edinger, 1994). Consequently, students write more and with greater fluidity (Dwyer, 1994). Not only can students become more productive through use of computers, but teachers can become more efficient because of easier and quicker access to information and resources (Gibson & Hart, 1995; Nugent, 1993). For example, access to video clips and slide shows through CD-ROM encyclopedia programs can reduce the difficulties of ordering film and video materials. Teachers also claim to be able to cover larger amounts of material in less time using the computer (Schug, 1988).

Pitfalls in Computer Use

Despite the positive influences attributed to computers, there are concerns about the influence of computer technology on teaching and learning. These include the fear that essential reading, writing, research and critical thinking skills will not be learned as effectively as they should be through the use of technology; and that students' understanding is compromised without direct concrete experience. As well, there are social and emotional concerns relating to increased isolation of computer users, decreased opportunity for developing social skills and gender exclusion because of the competitiveness that the technology may encourage.

Mindless fact gathering

Although students have access to an abundance of information through the computer, questions remain about the kind of information which is being accessed, what is being done with it, and whether or not it is overwhelming for students. A secondary social studies teacher I spoke with had recently assessed student computer-generated projects. She found that while her students had presented "the facts" using various graphic formats they had not made any judgments or drawn any conclusions from the information they had gathered. Without instruction in how to critically examine and make informed choices about the material, information gathering can become a mindless exercise in which quantity of material overrides quality of insight (Ragsdale, 1991). This sort of fact-gathering exercise does little to promote historical thinking and understanding (Yeager & Morris, 1995).

Ragsdale (1991) cautions further that while computers may be good at generating factual information, they often fail to convey the context and the broader perspective that thoughtful learning requires. Timely historical anecdotes and explanations by the teacher are especially important to helping children develop historical understanding (Nugent, 1993).

Poor curriculum coverage

There is concern that the curriculum is distorted or misrepresented when mediated through computer programs by reducing the curriculum to "content coverage" (Held et al. 1991; Gibson & Hart, 1996) and by omitting key curricular objectives and adding new ones (Fisher et al., 1994). For example, Means and Olson (1994) found the computer programs they examined "covered a very narrow slice of a subject domain and were often a poor match with curriculum guidelines or teacher preferences" (p. 16). Nugent (1993) discovered that "instructional outcomes from a student activity are influenced by the goals and tasks which are included and omitted in the computer program" (p. 9). When considering the applicability of computers in teaching and learning, teachers should first consider the curriculum and then seek ways to integrate technology so that it meets these curricular needs (Budin, 1991).

Reduced reading development

Despite the potential for increased student motivation and productivity, questions remain about what students are missing as a result of computer use. One concern focusses on reduced development of reading skills. Although computers offer visual and auditory representations of information, much of the visual stimulation is pictorial in nature. Text inserts in computer progarms tend to be short, particularly at the elementary grade levels. Many computer programs provide text inserts in audio format as well, so students need not "read" to find information (Gibson & Hart, 1996). Television has already predisposed children to fast-paced, visual stimulation. It is feared that students are less interested in concentrating on the written word for prolonged periods of time. This may eventually result in an unwillingness to "curl up with a good book," if such a disposition is not nurtured in the classroom and the home (Gibson & Hart, 1996). Even when more substantial text inserts are provided, the limited portion of a document available on a computer screen at any one time is problematic. Not being able to access the entire document with ease may increase students difficulty in learning to follow a complex series of events and thoughts (Nugent, 1993).

Diminished writing skills

While the computer may encourage student writing, the polished look of computer-generated products may create "psychological" resistance to producing more refined work. Students may lose interest in completing all stages of effective writing—in particular the rough draft stage—if their "first draft" is already a polished-looking product. As well, the limiting view afforded by the computer screen may discourage students from reading their entire piece to check the flow of ideas. As a result, teachers claim that increasingly they encounter student work that is disjointed and lacking in cohesion. There needs to be continued emphasis on the pre-writing stage where students are encouraged to capture their ideas in note form and think about them before writing the report (Gibson & Hart, 1996).

Neglected research skills

Computers have been touted as an effective tool for facilitating research, but questions remain about what constitutes computer research and how that research is carried out. Research can be a form of "guided discovery" where the teacher, acting as a facilitator, has a critical role to play; alternatively, research may solely be "free exploration" on the students' part (Ragsdale, 1991). The abundance of sources to access on the computer can easily side-track students into spending a great deal of time off task (Gibson & Hart, 1996). The mere cutting and pasting of information from Internet websites, for example, does little to promote the ability to synthesize, sequence and analyze information. As well, there is the moral issue of copying and laying claim to others' words. Research skills need to be carefully taught and monitored to ensure that students develop proficiency. Yeager and Morris (1995) recommend using "productive" software which encourages children to organize and analyze the information collected so they develop effective research skills.

Need for critical thinking

Another area of concern is the development of critical thinking. Students, in particular, tend to accept the computer as an authority and view the information accessed as the "Truth." There is a inclination to view the computer as a neutral conduit (Ragsdale, 1991). Students need to be taught to recognize that information from a computer represents a particular viewpoint, as does a textbook or any other resource. They need to be encouraged to think critically when using the computer, just as they would when making judgments about other resource materials used in the classroom. Lengel (1987) encourages teachers to ensure students are taught how to draw reasonable conclusions from data, see several points of view, and distinguish warranted from unwarranted opinion as they interact with computer technology.

The use of the Internet raises important ethical reasons for teaching students to be critical of computer sources (Adams & Hamm, 1988). Students need to be taught that some information available is inappropriate (i.e., pornographic sites) and in some cases inaccurate (i.e., hate propaganda sites), and therefore should not be accessed.

Ragsdale (1991) cautions further that the ability to use the computer does not necessarily equate to understanding. "Training people so they will have the knowledge to use a tool is not the same as educating them so that they will have the wisdom to apply the tool" (Ragsdale, 1991, p. 161). Postman (1992) argues further that students need to be encouraged to think about the technologies they are using and their consequences, in order to become technologically literate.

Absence of real-life experience

It has been acknowledged that one of the more powerful advantages of computer use in learning is that information can be presented in highly visual and auditory formats which appeal to students' varied learning styles. However, one of the more commonly accepted principles of learning is that real-life, tactile experience is an important foundation to learning. Firsthand, multi-sensory experiences provide the basis on which to build more abstract learning, such as that offered by the computer. Even those computer programs offering experiences such as simulated field trips and virtual reality cannot promote the same learning and deep understanding that comes from the real-life experience. Many educators believe, for example, that understanding our human relationship to the physical environment can only come through direct experience with that environment.

Reduced direct interaction

A further concern arising from the possibility of extensive reliance on computers is the potential isolation from other humans. Computer conversations on e-mail and the Internet are often touted as a way of overcoming shyness and expressing oneself without inhibition. Mitchell-Powell (1995) suggests, however, that these "conversations" are limited by both language and cultural barriers. As well, while such "conversations" may entice the more non-conversant to interact, they do little to develop those social skills which require face-to-face conversation and direct human interaction (Ragsdale, 1991). The importance of human interaction to learning cannot be underestimated for such things as giving encouragement, considering feelings, making judgments and increasing one's sense of self worth (Budin, 1991). The non-verbal signals accompanying face-to-face conversation help to convey what is meant and felt by the speaker. Learning to be sensitive to these non-verbal clues is an important aspect of students' social development.

Having students work cooperatively on computer projects is one way of countering this problem of isolation. However, children need to be taught how to apply cooperative learning strategies to their work with the technology (Held et al., 1991). If not, increased competitiveness over who controls the computer can result, with more reticent students being pushed aside. For example, Fisher et al. (1994) found that student power relations changed while using the computer resulting in increased student disagreement and conflict. A teacher working with a computer pilot project discovered that the girls in her grade five class were more resistant than were boys to using computers, especially if it meant competing with the boys (Gibson & Hart, 1996).

SUGGESTIONS FOR SOUND COMPUTER USE

Arguments in favour of computer use and cautions about their use in teaching and learning abound. However, since computer technology is a fact of life in elementary and secondary schooling, the important question to ask is not whether or not computers should be used, but rather how they can best be used to enhance teaching and learning. I offer several suggestions to help teachers decide upon the nature and extent of computer technology in their teaching.

Become more knowledgeable

Regardless of the particular approach to computer technology a teacher adopts, it is important that teachers make conscious and informed decisions about how, when and where to use computers. The reaching of sound decisions on these matters requires that teachers be skilled in the operation of basic computer technologies and knowledgeable about computer resources. Because of constant technological developments, teachers must continually upgrade their computer knowledge and skills. One avenue is to take advantage of the variety of computer workshops and training programs offered in their local area. Many school boards, private companies community colleges and universities hold after-school or weekend training sessions. Provincial and local conferences on technology provide additional opportunities for updating. On-line tutorials and self-help books are also available with most computer programs. Journals such as *The Computing Teacher* and *Computers in the Schools* offer countless practical ideas and descriptions of current developments in the computer field.

Using Computers to Compare Canada's Regions and People

Initially, the class could brainstorm a list of subtopics to investigate. These might include climate, resources, industries, occupations, population, cities, landscape and interesting facts. The class could be divided into groups representing each of the different regions. The challenge for each group is to prepare a multimedia production designed to "sell" their particular region to an audience of their peers. Teacher instruction in writing and in critical thinking could be interspersed at various stages throughout the project work as needed.

Students could begin data retrieval by accessing information to support each of the subtopics from a number of sources. The digitized resources suggested below should be used in conjunction with other print and non-print resources. CD-ROM programs, such as *Adventure Canada* (Mac), *Canada Geograph* (Mac) and *Canada's Regions and Resources* (IBM/Mac) provide images, video, text, narration and music about Canada. Computerized simulations such as *Cross Country Canada* (Mac) in which the user takes on the role of a truck driver delivering goods to different parts of Canada or *The Yukon Trail* (Mac) where the user re-enacts life as a prospector during the Yukon gold rush, provide a more interactive experience for students. Electronic encyclopedias are another excellent digitized resource. Some of the more user-friendly ones for elementary students are *Microsoft Encarta* (IBM), *Compton's Interactive Encyclopedia* (IBM), the *New Grolier Multimedia Encyclopedia* (Mac), *PC Globe* (IBM/Mac) and the *New Canadian Encyclopedia Plus* (IBM/Mac).

The Internet provides a wealth of excellent websites about Canada for both students and teachers. *The Canadian Kids Page* (http://www.onramp.ca/~cankids) provides an opportunity to meet other Canadian kids, see other Canadian classrooms and get to know Canada better. E-mail penpal opportunities are also available through this website. The *Virtual Tourist* website (http://www/tourist.com/vt) allows children to take virtual trips through any country in the world, including Canada, by simply highlighting their choice on a world map. *Canada's SchoolNet* (http://schoolnet.carleton.ca) provides teachers with background information and activity ideas relating to various subject areas, including social studies.

Data collected from these various sources could be recorded, organized and stored initially in a word processing program such as *ClarisWorks* (IBM) or *Microsoft Works* (Mac). A spreadsheet or database program, found in both *ClarisWorks* and *Microsoft Works*, could be used to organize and tally comparative information on Canada's regions. Using computers in this fashion teaches children their value as not only information retrieval tools, but also as organizing and synthesizing devices.

Once the data have been collected, organized and synthesized, the next step is to encourage students to create a multimedia presentation about their region. A hypercard program such as *HyperStudio* (Mac) allows children to create "stacks" of text information on a wide variety of topics, to incorporate pictures and sound into these stacks and to connect these "stacks" to one another using "buttons" in order to produce a cohesive final product. Pictures, maps and graphs can easily be incorporated and a "slide show" can be produced. An LCD (Liquid Crystal Display) or a Smartboard device attached to a classroom computer would allow students to present their computerized product to the whole class.

Networking with other teachers is an effective way of becoming more familiar with the many possibilities that computers afford. Collaborative projects between novice users and more skilled users can make early classroom experiences with technology less threatening. It is also very useful to share lesson plans, units and projects—both the successful and less productive ones.

Develop a personal vision

Teachers should take the time to develop their own personal vision of instruction using computer technology (Held et al., 1991). As Budin (1991) suggests, "If we want students to grow up to be autonomous and creative thinkers and citizens, their teachers need to model autonomy and creativity in their use of curriculum and technology" (p. 21). Dwyer (1994) claims this creativity in thinking about computer use may require some teachers to "undo" their current thinking about teaching and learning. Dwyer, Ringstaff and Sandholtz (1991), for example, suggest that to be effective in their use of technology teachers will need to shift their views of learning from "knowledge instruction" to "knowledge construction." This implies a shift from the view of teacher as holder and transmitter of knowledge to students as constructors of their own knowledge.

Clarifying their own purposes and goals for using computers as learning tools is central to each teacher's development of a personal vision. When thinking about these goals and purposes, teachers should be mindful of the possibilities and cautions discussed earlier. It may also be helpful for social studies teachers to consider the following questions:

- What is most important for my students to know and be able to do in social studies?
- What role can computers play in promoting these important goals?

- How can I ensure maximum benefit from computers in my social studies teaching?
- What can I do to enhance my students' learning while they are using the computer?
- What should the roles and responsibilities of my students as computer users be?

Maximize the benefits

Studies have found that the most frequent instructional uses of computers have traditionally been for word processing, game playing, and performing drill and practice exercises (King, 1994/95; Woodrow, 1991). Teachers should look beyond this limited view of technological use in teaching. Programs that challenge children to design, create and collaborate, rather than simply "play," offer the greatest potential for overcoming some of the previously mentioned concerns (Dwyer et al., 1991).

One of the more user-friendly ways of enhancing reading, writing, research and thinking skills with computer technology is through the use of hypercard programs. As an illustration, the box describing a computer-supported project (page 231) might be undertaken during an elementary social studies unit on Canada's regions and people. Projects similar to this one can be initiated for numerous social studies topics across the grade levels. Using diverse computer resources in this fashion increases student confidence in their use of the computer as a multipurpose tool, while encouraging them to be innovative. Seasoned computer users could investigate other hypertext programs that allow for greater variety of design options.

Reflect on successes and problems

A final piece of advice for teachers who are both beginning and experienced computer users is to take the time to reflect on the successes and problems encountered with the particular approaches used. An openness to refining existing approaches and trying new ones is crucial if teachers are to make rich use of the educational possibilities for computer technology. Sharing these successes and failures with others can help to build a community of computer users from which to glean new ideas.

Concluding Comments

The inclusion of computer technology throughout the entire schooling experience is a given, and teachers need to prepare themselves for this responsibility. A first step in meeting this challenge is to be mindful of the different ways in which learning can either be enhanced or impeded by the use of computers. This article has attempted to raise some of these considerations for social studies teachers

Before closing, one final observation about the "technological revolution." Despite the fears expressed by some educators of computer technology displacing teachers, Postman (1992) assures us that the very nature of education guarantees that the human teacher will continue to have an important role in teaching and learning. Technology cannot replace teachers' intimate knowledge of their students, teachers' creativity and their ability to provide the emotional support that is a crucial element of teaching (Peck & Dorricott, 1994). Consequently, computing should always be seen as a tool. Regardless of how extensively teachers use computer technology in their classrooms, the emphasis—first and foremost—must still be on good teaching.

References

Adams, D. & Hamm, M. (1988). Video technology and moral development. *Social Studies, 79*(2), 81-83.

Budin, H. (1991). Technology and the teacher's role. *Computers in the Schools, 8*(1/2/3), 15-26.

Dwyer, D. (1994). Apple classrooms of tomorrow: What we've learned. *Educational Leadership, 51*(7), 4-10.

Dwyer, D., Ringstaff, C. & Sandholtz, J. (1991). Changes in teachers' beliefs and practices in technology-rich classrooms. *Educational Leadership, 48*(8), 45-52.

Edinger, M. (1994). Empowering young writers with technology. *Educational Leadership, 51*(7), 58-60.

Fisher, C., Wilmore, F. & Howell, R. (1994). Classroom technology and the new pedagogy. *Journal of Computing in Childhood Education, 5*(2), 119-129.

Geiger, P. (1994). Beyond bells and whistles. *American School Board Journal, 181*(3), 41-44.

Gibson, S. & Hart, S. (1996). *Project E.L.I.T.E.: A case study of elementary teachers' perspectives on the use of computers for teaching social studies.* Paper presented at the International Council of Psychologists Annual Convention. Banff, Alberta.

Gooler, D. (1995). Perspectives: Technology as content in social studies curricula for young learners. *Social Studies and the Young Learner, 7*(3), 27-30.

Held, C., Newsom, J. & Peiffer, M. (1991). The integrated technology classroom: An experiment in restructuring elementary school instruction. *The Computing Teacher, 18*(6), 21-23.

Jones, I. (1994). The effect of a word processor on the written composition of second-grade pupils. *Computers in the Schools, 11*(2), 43-54.

King, J. (1994/95). Fear or frustration? Students' attitudes toward computers and school. *Journal of Research on Computing in Education, 27*(2), 154-169.

Lengel, J. (1987). Thinking skills, social studies, and computers. *Social Studies, 78*(1), 13-16.

Means, B. & Olson, K. (1994). The link between technology and authentic learning. *Educational Leadership, 51*(7), 15-18.

Mitchell-Powell, B. (1995). More than just a pretty interface: Access, content and relevance in computer technology. *Social Studies and the Young Learner, 7*(3), 11-13.

Morden, D. (1994). Crossroads to the world. *Educational Leadership, 51*(7), 36-38.

Nugent, S. (1993). *Teachers' reactions to an instructional resource disk.* Unpublished Master's Thesis, University of Alberta, Edmonton.

Peck, K. & Dorricott, C. (1994). Why use technology? *Educational Leadership, 51*(7), 11-14.

Postman, N. (1992). *Technopoly: The surrender of culture to technology.* New York: Alfred A. Knopf.

Ragsdale, R. (1991). Effective computing in education: Teachers, tools and training. *Education and Computing, 7,* 157-166.

Schug, M. (1988). What do social studies teachers say about using computers? *Social Studies, 86*(3), 112-115.

Wade, R. (1995) Redefining instructional materials. *Social Studies and the Young Learner, 7*(3), 17-18.

Wiburg, K. (1991). Teaching teachers about technology. *Computers in the Schools, 8*(1/2/3), 115-129.

Wilson, E. & Marsh, G. (1995). Social studies and the Internet revolution. *Social Education, 59*(4), 198-202.

Woodrow, J. (1991). Teachers' perceptions of computer needs. *Journal of Research on Computing in Education, 23*(4), 475-493.

Yeager, E. & Morris, J. (1995). History and computers: The views from selected social studies journals. *Social Studies, 86*(3), 105-112.

ADDITIONAL RESOURCES

World Wide Web

Use Netscape to locate the following websites:

African National Congress
- http://www.anc.org.za/index.html
  Events in South Africa

Ask ERIC
- gopher://ericir.syr.edu:70/1/
  A variety of educational topics

Canadiana
- http://www.cgi.c.cmu.eduf.web/unofficial/Canadiana/README.html
  This is all about Canada, including maps, games, atlases, quizes, trivia and a museum.

Canadian Government
- http://info.ic.gc.ca/opengov/
  Canadian governments departments & their functions

Canadian Heritage Project
- http://heritage.excite.sfu.ca/
  Bronfman CRB Heritage Project

Canadian Kids' Home Page
- http://www.onramp.ca/~lowens/107kids.htm
  Information for Canadian students

CBC News Headlines
- http.//radioworks.cbc.ca/radio/programs/news/headline-news/
  News headlines, updated hourly

Economics Resources for K-12 Teachers
- http://ecedweb.unomaha.edu/teach.html

Egyptian Educational Site
- http://pharos.bu.edu/Egypt

Favourite Education Places on the Web
- http://www.clp.berkeley.edu/CLP/education.html
  Links to useful education sites

Governments of the World
- http://info.ic.gc.ca/opengov/world.html
  Governments of nations around the world

Helping Your Child Learn History
- http://www.edgov/pubs/parents/history/index/html
  Lessons and activities for parents and teachers in teaching social studies for children age 4-11

History/Social Studies Web for K-12
- http://www.execpc.com/~dboals/boals.html
  Many ideas for locating and thinking critically about social studies Internet resources

NATO
- http://www.af.mil/nato-www.html
  Current information about North Atlantic Treaty Organization

National Atlas Information Service
- http://www-nais.ccm.emr.ca/
  Canadian Centre for Mapping

Online Educator
- http://www.cris.com/~felixg/OE/index.shtml
  Articles of interest to teachers, updated weekly

SchoolNet
- http://schoolnet.ca/lang-soc/
  The social studies page on Canada's most popular educational web site

Statistics Canada
- http://www.statcan.ca
  Links to current statistics on immense range of topics

Teachers Helping Teachers
- http://www.pacificanet.net/~mandel/SocialStudies.html
  Formed by a group of teachers; provides the most popular lesson plans for K-12

Top Ten Educational Sites
- http://shasta-co.k12.ca.us/www/telementors/mentor5.html
  Many links around the Web, updated monthly

Tour of Parliament
- http://www.cisti.nrc.ca/programs/pio/intro.html
  Tour of Canadian parliament buildings

WebMuseum
- http://www.cnam.fr/louvre/
  Paintings from the Louvre

What Do Maps Show?
- http://info.er.usgs.gov/education/teacher/what-do-maps-show/index.html
  Lesson plans on map reading (Grades 3-5)

Where on the Globe is Roger?
- http://www.gsn.org/gsn/proj/rog/index/html
  Learn about history, culture and geography as Roger drives his truck, Bubba, from continent to continent

World Safari
- http://www.supersurf.com/fun.html
  Every month this website visits a different country

World War I
- http://www.lib.byu.edu/~rdh/wwi/
  World War I document archive

World War II
- http://www.webcom.com/~jbd/ww2.html
  Day-to-day account of World War II. American perspective

Print Resources

(1997). A new view of the world: Using technology in social studies education (Theme issues). *Social Education, 61*(3), 147-172.

Courtois, M. & Bauer, W. (1995, November/December). Cool tools for searching the web. *Online,* 15-32.

Courtois, M. (1996, May/June). Cool tools for web searching. An update. *Online,* 29-36.

Schrock, K. (1996). It must be true. I found it on the Internet. *Technology Connection, 3*(5), 12-14.

Tate, M. & Alexander, J. (1996). Teaching critical evaluation skills for world wide web resources. *Computers in Libraries, 16*(10), 49-54.

Vockell, E. & Brown, W. (1992). *The computer in the social studies curriculum.* Toronto: Mitchell McGraw-Hill

— ✦ —

26

NURTURING PERSONAL AND SOCIAL VALUES

We are all citizens of one world, we are all of one blood. To hate a man because he was born in another country, because he speaks a different language, or because he takes a different view on this subject or that, is a great folly. Desist, I implore you, for we are all equally human.

—Johann Comenius
17th Century educational reformer

ROLAND CASE

One of the most important, yet deeply controversial goals in social studies is the teaching of values. On the one hand, many believe that becoming educated is not simply, or even essentially, a matter of acquiring a body of knowledge. Equally important is the nurturing of personal and social values that will guide our decisions and actions in just and productive ways. By personal values I mean the values that individuals hold about themselves—values such as self-esteem, integrity, personal responsibility for one's actions and pride in one's work. Social values refer to the values that we hold about others and about society generally, including national pride, commitment to justice, respect for law, respect for the environment and a cooperative and empathic attitude. Social studies particularly is seen by many as providing an important opportunity to promote the fundamental values that society requires of its citizens. However, despite the centrality to citizenship of values education—also referred to as character education (cf. Burrett & Rusnak, 1993)—there is considerable controversy. The dominant historical objections to the teaching of values in schools revolve around three issues:

- *Should we nurture values?*—Should values be taught in schools? Or should schools be value free?
- *What values should we nurture and who decides?*—What values are to be promoted in schools? Who selects and defines these values, and on what basis?
- *How should values be nurtured?*—What methods can and should teachers use to promote values in a manner that respects the rights of students and parents?

In this article I deal mainly with the third question by exploring three overlapping approaches to promoting personal and social values. But before doing so, I discuss the first two questions more briefly.

SHOULD WE NURTURE VALUES?

In some respects the question whether or not we should teach values in school is a moot point. Schools cannot be value free and teachers cannot avoid promoting values. The fact that we praise children for being honest, thoughtful and punctual signals the embedded values in our schools. Every time we permit or prohibit certain behaviour we implicitly promote certain values over others (e.g., school rules against fighting or throwing rocks attest to our valuing of individual well-being and protection of property). These rules and countless others like them inevitably affect the values that students develop.

Whether educators want to or not, inevitably, through either the explicit curriculum or the "hidden curriculum"—the implicit norms and values that are promoted, often unintentionally, through the way we run our schools and conduct our classes—we influence student attitudes and values. For example, if we mark student work for neatness or praise them for asking inquiring questions, we are encouraging students to act in these ways; if we do not reinforce neatness or an inquiring attitude we are implicitly telling students that they are not valued. This is true for everything we do (or do not do) in school. The only real choice teachers have about promoting values is whether our influence will be largely hidden and inadvertent or explicit and systematic.

In an interesting article, Daniel Duke (1978) illustrates how schools may affect students' attitudes in unintended and undesirable ways. He suggests that many students may develop a cynical attitude towards our legal system because of common school practices. We can appreciate the hidden lessons schools teach students about the fairness of our system of laws by contrasting the espoused civic ideals with the regulatory practices that actually operate in many schools. Duke concludes that it is difficult for students to develop respect for law and for principled behaviour if their experiences in school, which is the first and most extensive public institution young citizens encounter, consistently reinforce the opposite.

The box at the bottom of this page contrasts the rhetoric about the rule of law with the practices that Duke believes actually operate in many schools.

Ultimately, decisions about value issues—including whether or not schools should intentionally teach values—should be subjected to rational scrutiny. Teachers must thoughtfully assess the pros and cons before making their decision. The box on the following page lists competing reasons for and against the intentional teaching of values in schools. It is interesting to note, at least according to this list, that the majority of objections to intentionally teaching values are not against the idea *per se*, but are concerns about which values to promote and how to do so responsibly. These are the issues to which we now turn.

What Values Should We Nurture?

There are no simple answers for determining the values to be intentionally promoted in schools. Nevertheless it is useful to consider the degree of consensus about the value. (This is by no means the only criterion for deciding which values, it is merely a promising starting point.) On one end of the spectrum are values (especially very general values) that are widely acknowledged as acceptable or even highly desirable attributes of citizens. Honesty, pride in one's work, concern for the well-being of others, respect for the property of others are examples of values that would likely have broad public support. A justification for including these values in the public education curriculum derives from the notion of *parentis locus*—the notion that schools must, to some extent, take up the role and act on behalf of parents. Promoting certain values can be seen as an extension of the type of upbringing that reasonable parents would want for their children. As was suggested in the 1931 Hadow Report: "What a wise and good parent would desire for his [or her] children, a national educational system must desire for all children" (cited in Cassidy, 1994).

In the box on page 238 are listed the sorts of per-

What Schools "Teach" about Our Legal System

We tell students . . .	• that we live in a society based on democratic principles.
Yet, often in schools . . .	• school rules tend to be determined by those least subject to their application.
We tell students . . .	• that all people are to be treated equally before the law.
Yet, often in schools . . .	• many teachers fail to enforce school rules consistently.
We tell students . . .	• that the punishment should be reasonable and that it should fit the crime.
Yet, often in schools . . .	• the consequences for disobeying school rules frequently lack logical relationships to the offences. For example, the punishment for skipping classes is often suspension from school.
We tell students . . .	• that society is committed to safeguarding the rights of individuals against abuse by the state.
Yet, often in schools . . .	• students have few options if they disagree with a claim brought against them by school authorities.
We tell students . . .	• that no one is above the law.
Yet, often in schools . . .	• teachers frequently fail to model the rule-governed behaviour they expect of their students.

SHOULD SCHOOLS INTENTIONALLY PROMOTE VALUES?

Reasons for

- Teaching about values is part of the school's mandate. Official rationales for public education typically refer to the need to develop the values of productive citizenship. For example, the stated purpose of the British Columbia school system includes promoting the "attitudes needed to contribute to a healthy society and a prosperous and sustainable economy" (Ministry of Education, British Columbia, 1993). The Ontario Ministry of Education (1986, p. 6) identifies numerous values in its goal statement, including self-worth, respect for the environment and "values related to personal, ethical or religious beliefs and to the common welfare of society."

- Teaching values is a precondition for many other objectives in the curriculum: knowledge and skills cannot be developed without accompanying value components. For example, students will learn little without self-esteem, curiosity and open-mindedness. Students will be unable to work cooperatively unless they have some respect for the feelings of others, are willing to play by the rules and so on.

- Many important values need attention, and schools have a significant, perhaps unique, opportunity to make a difference. If racism and discrimination are promoted within some families, how will these undesirable—and in some cases illegal—values be countered if not by the educational system?

Reasons against

- Values promoted in schools may conflict with values held by individual parents, local communities or society more generally.

- Students may be indoctrinated into accepting values that are essentially individual in nature (i.e. teachers may fail to respect individual student's freedom of conscience and right to personal inclinations).

- Despite their best intentions, it is feared that schools will do a poor job of promoting values (e.g., instead of teaching about equality, schools may unintentionally promote condescending attitudes towards various cultural or racial groups).

- Values often raise extremely sensitive issues that may profoundly upset students.

- Because values may be controversial, actively promoting values may, in certain circumstances, present a professional risk for the teacher (e.g., the teacher may become embroiled in controversy).

sonal and social values which seem indispensable for healthy human existence and which would likely be broadly supported. (No doubt some may object to my suggestions or insist on adding other essential values.) Promoting these values (at least in general terms) is unlikely to conflict with broadly-held parental or community values (although, from time to time, individual parents and community members may not share them). This "consensus" list may serve as the starting point for identifying the values to be nurtured in schools.

At the other end of the spectrum are personal and social values that are profoundly controversial—particularly value positions or attitudes on specific issues such as abortion, same-sex parenting, affirmative action and capital punishment. In these cases, since society generally is sharply divided, teachers should assume that there may not be a single most acceptable position—well-informed, thoughtful people may not share the same values. In these cases, if the issue is to be raised (and it may be that in many communities some value questions are too controversial to be raised in school), the objective should not be to promote a specific value

position, but rather to encourage students to the extent feasible to make up their own minds after thoughtful consideration of the issues. The teachers' responsibility would be act in a respectful and fair manner, seeking to instill appreciation of the need for sensitivity when dealing with divisive issues and to facilitate students' gathering and assessing information pro and con before reaching a resolution to the issue for themselves. Notice that a fair manner may not mean that teachers devote identical attention to all sides. If students are already well aware of one side, it may be necessary to spend more effort helping them see other sides of the issue. But it should be clear that we are not favouring a side *because* it reflects our own position, but to ensure that students see all important viewpoints. Because students may be unduly influenced by their teachers, it is important to consider under what conditions teachers should withhold their own personal positions from students.

Many values are largely matters of personal inclination, such as dictates of religious conscience, life choices, political affiliations and personal aspirations. In schools which are committed to cultural and political pluralism it is inappropriate to espouse or favour the values of one religious or political ideology over those of others. Consequently, it would be inappropriate, for example, as then Vice President George Bush did, to encourage schools to teach about the law so as "to combat criticism of our representative government (reported in American Bar Association, 1982, p. 1). As Ken Osborne notes, "a well- informed, democratic and interested citizen need not be supportive of government policies" (1982, p. 59). In these situations, since there are no agreed-upon "correct" values (nor should there be), the teacher's role is to encourage students to explore and clarify these values for themselves. Although teachers should not presume which conclusions students will reach about these values, there may be considerable merit in providing students with opportunities to examine their own belief systems.

SUGGESTED CONSENSUS VALUES

Personal values
- acceptance of self, realization of one's own worth
- integrity and frankness with self
- sense of hopefulness for the future
- willingness for adventure; sense of mission
- desire to make a productive contribution
- curiosity, interest in learning
- respect for work well done
- appreciation of beauty in art and in the environment
- pride in family and ethnic background
- concern for personal hygiene and health
- self-disciplined/self-directed
- independent-mindedness (courage of one's convictions)

Social values
- respect for the dignity and worth of every human being
- commitment to equal opportunity for all
- tolerant, patient and kind
- desire for justice for all
- acceptance of social responsibility
- commitment to free thought, expression and worship
- commitment to peaceful resolution of problems
- respect for privacy
- national pride
- environmental stewardship
- fair-minded
- concern for well-being of animals
- respect for the rule of law

This list is drawn largely from the values advocated fifty years ago by a social studies curriculum committee from Dalton Schools in New York City, cited by Ralph Tyler in his classic book on curriculum design (1949, pp. 92-93).

The commitment to encourage students to make up their own minds on non-consensual values reduces concern about indoctrinating or imposing personal beliefs and, if communicated to parents, may alleviate suspicion and opposition. However, some issues deeply divide communities and taking the open-minded view may not satisfy everyone. Our dilemma is, on the one hand, a responsibility to develop students' ability to engage with and resolve value issues in non-violent, thoughtful ways and, on the other hand, a responsibility to respect within limits parental rights to raise their children as they see fit. Ultimately, these decisions are matters of *professional* judgment—of deciding what is most defensible in light of the needs and rights of the individuals and groups that educators have a responsibility to serve. It is not sufficient justification that I happen personally to value it. The more contested or individualistic the value, the more sensitive and vigilant teachers must be both about empowering students to thoughtfully make up their own minds and about parents' right to be informed of and to direct their children's education.

Merely because some values may be inappropriate in schools and other values, if addressed at all, must be handled with extreme sensitivity, does not mean that there are no values about which consensus among reasonable people could be reached. I believe there are many such personal and social values which are essential components of any social studies curriculum. And there may be many other values which, if taught appropriately, have a legitimate place in public education.

HOW SHOULD VALUES BE NURTURED?

So much has been written on teaching about values that it is hard to get a handle on this topic.[1] For our purposes, I believe it useful to focus on three broad approaches: (1) creating classroom and school environments that reinforce desired values, (2) facilitating direct "emotional" experiences that evoke desired sensitivities and (3) engaging students in thoughtful deliberation about their values. Although they will be discussed separately, these approaches overlap and should be mutually supportive.

Creating reinforcing environments

Values do not develop in a vacuum. In fact, they are more likely to be nurtured by the subtle, yet pervasive, influences operating within a social environment than they are by short-lived instructional techniques. The literature on the hidden curriculum attests to the power of environmental conditions in supporting or inhibiting the acquisition of attitudes. For example, the tone or atmosphere in a classroom is overwhelmingly cited as a primary factor in developing social attitudes (Leming, 1991; Patrick & Hoge, 1991). Studies reported by Judith Torney-Purta (1983) indicate that the particular content of the curriculum is less influential in developing students' political attitudes than is establishing a classroom climate where students feel free and have opportunities to express their opinions. Teacher behaviour is especially important in signalling to students what really counts. Teachers who are open-minded are more likely to foster these attributes in their students. So too, teachers who sincerely demonstrate their empathy for others are more likely to nurture empathic tendencies in their students. There may be no more effective strategy to promote values than by sincerely and consistently communicating to students through our actions that certain values matter. Examples of teacher behaviour, expectations and activities which reinforce concern for others are suggested in the following box.[2]

REINFORCING CONCERN FOR OTHERS

Student expectations and activities

- a code of rules or principles of behaviour towards fellow students is clearly articulated and closely enforced;
- verbal or physical abuse of students by students is as unacceptable as verbal or physical abuse of teachers by students;
- good deeds by students are acknowledged;
- students are frequently engaged in role reversals where they are asked to think of how others might feel in various situations;
- students are frequently asked to express why they care or do not care about events or people that may seem removed from their lives;
- student are invited to participate in projects where they do something positive for others.

Teacher modelling

- the teacher refrains from "put downs" and sarcasm, and treats students (and colleagues) with the utmost respect and deference;
- the teacher acknowledges the error, and attempts to redress the action if he/she treats a student unfairly;
- the teacher undertakes random acts of kindness;
- the teacher is seen by students to be a caring person with compassion for their concerns and difficulties.

Facilitating direct experiences

A second approach to nurturing personal and social values is to provide opportunities for students to "feel" the effect of caring for these values. Unlike a reinforcing environment, whose goal is to gradually habituate students to particular frames of mind, the point of direct experiences is to provide students with opportunities to vividly and emphatically encounter for themselves the power and merit of certain ways of being. Often these experiences will open students' minds and hearts to perspectives that they would otherwise miss or downplay. There are at least three types of direct experiences that nurture values: vicarious, simulated and first-hand experiences.

- **vicarious experiences**. To live vicariously is to encounter life through the experiences of another. Film and literature—both fiction and non-fiction—are especially effective in this regard. Vicarious experiences allow students to "live" the lives of others and in so doing experience the power of feeling and caring about matters that may otherwise be foreign or remote. At a recent conference Susan Inman, a teacher at Windermere Secondary School in Vancouver, talked of the power of having her students view the National Film Board video, *Where the Spirit Lives*. Prior to viewing this moving film about the plight and courage of First Nations students in residential schools, several of her students had shown indifference, perhaps even callousness, to First Nations people. The video personalized—put a profoundly human face to—what were previously stereotypical images. As a result, her students' sensitivity to the feelings and concerns of First Nations individuals was greatly enhanced. Personally, I remember as an elementary student being profoundly moved by an historical novel about the Jesuit martyr Isaac Jogues. Although I have since tempered my feelings towards these missionaries I have never lost my sense of admiration for individuals who are so committed to a principle that they are willing to endure great hardship and sacrifice.[3]

- **simulated and role-play experiences**. Drama, role play and other simulations allow students to adopt and act out the actions or predicaments of others. One of the most famous examples of a simulated experience was described in the award-winning documentary, *The Eye of the Storm* (Peters, 1987). In an effort to help her grade three students appreciate the consequences of bigotry, Jane Elliott began without announcing it to discriminate against the blue-eyed children in her class, and the next day she discriminated against the brown-eyed children. Students were moved by the unfairness of this simulated prejudice. In a follow-up documentary, *A Class Divided*, filmed almost fifteen years after the simulation, the students in Elliot's class described the profound influence that this earlier experience had in shaping their values.

- **first-hand experiences**. Powerful evocative experiences need not be second-hand, students can encounter value-nurturing situations in "real-life" contexts—through guest speakers, field trips, student exchanges, pen pals and social action projects. A powerful guest speaker can do much to change student attitudes. Certainly many of my early stereotypical attitudes towards ethnic and racial groups were exploded when I first encountered articulate and impassioned individuals from these groups. Social action projects can also be powerful value-nurturing experiences. As Mary-Wynne Ashford (1995) reports in her article, "Youth Actions for the Planet," involvement in environmental and humanitarian projects can counter the global hopelessness prevalent among many students.

To further illustrate the power of direct experiences, imagine the effect of the activity—The Eporuvians Come to Call—described in the box on this page in helping students empathize with what others may feel about perceived inequities. An Australia Broadcasting Corporation (1986) film titled *Babakiueria*—a phonetic spelling of "barbecue area"—offers a similar reversal perspective of Aboriginal explorers discovering a group of white inhabitants of a campground.

Experiences such as these—whether brought about vicariously, through simulation or in first-hand encounters—help to evoke students' sensitivities to important values. The point is *not* to manipulate students into a particular perspective, but to ensure that students, who may be self-absorbed, experience other predicaments and feelings.

Promoting thoughtful deliberation

The third approach to values education encourages students to think about their values. On its own, this approach will rarely be sufficient to induce values and, perhaps, may not be the best first step in promoting value change. However, we are in danger of manipulating and indoctrinating students if, at some point, we do not encourage them to reflect on the implications and significance of their values. Eventually, students must thoughtfully make up their own minds. Generally speaking, the deliberative approach has two strands:

- **values clarification** where the objective is to help students *clarify* the values that they hold and the implications of these values for other aspects of their lives;

THE EPORUVIANS COME TO CALL

The following three scenarios are intended to evoke empathy for the historical treatment of First Nations people. The teacher reads a scene and allows students time to reflect (and write) about their thoughts before proceeding to the next scene.

Imagine . . .

Scene 1: You're playing in your backyard when a group of odd-looking men dressed in strange clothes walk into your yard. They look dirty and hungry, and are shouting and gesturing in a strange language. They try hard to communicate with you, but you can't understand them. You can tell, though, that what they are saying is very important.

Not knowing what else to do, and because they look hungry, you invite them into your house and give them some cake and tea. Soon, you are able to communicate with them using hand signals and gestures. You still don't know what they want, but you begin to understand that they are from a faraway land called Eporue. They really like your town and they want to stay here.

- How would you feel? Scared? Flattered? Angry? Friendly? Annoyed? Curious? Excited?
- What would you do? Would you help them out? Ask them to leave?

Scene 2: Imagine that you welcome the Eporuvians. After all, you want to be helpful, and they seem so lost. You let them stay in your house, and you keep feeding them. You show them around the town and introduce them to your friends. However, you begin to notice that they have a disagreeable habit of taking your things. All in all, they don't seem very considerate. You begin to wonder whether making friends with them was such a good idea, after all. You also start to wonder if these house guests will ever leave.

After a while, you begin to realize that they want to keep living in your house and taking your things. In fact, they think that they own the place—and the land it's on, too. They stick the Eporuvian flag in the ground, and claim your yard for their leader.

- What would you do? Would you organize your friends to drive them out? Try to reason with them? Trick them into leaving? Give up and be friends?
- How would you feel? Scared? Angry? Puzzled? Disappointed?

Scene 3: By now, they don't bother talking to you much anymore, except when they want something from you. They bring their relatives—and lots of other Eporuvians—to live in your town. Eventually, they tell you and your family to leave, and give you a broken-down shack to live in, with no yard, no running water and lots of other people crowded into it (who have all been forced off *their* land, as well).

You never get your land back. For 200 years, the story of how the Eporuvians forced you off your land is handed down from generation to generation. You tell your children, who tell their children, and so on, for ten generations.

- How will your descendants feel about the Eporuvians? Would you call them heroes or villains?
- If you were a descendant of the Eporuvians, how would you feel about what happened? Would you feel any responsibility to extend friendship to these people?

The Eporuvian role play was developed by Anne Hill, an elementary teacher in Terrace, British Columbia.

- **values analysis** which proposes a more critical examination of student values, where students *assess* the adequacy of the reasoning behind their value positions.

Of the two strands, primary students would be most likely to engage in values clarification, as values analysis requires a more sophisticated ability to reason.

Values clarification

Louis Raths, Merrill Harmin and Sidney Simon (1966) are the best known proponents of the values clarification approach, although many others have espoused this approach and it is widely evident in current educational practice. The underlying premise of the values clarification approach is that individuals experience dissonance as a result of their being unclear, confused or uncommitted to their values. Since values are seen to be an intensely personal and emotional matter, the teacher's role is to help students overcome this dissonance by inviting them to clarify and affirm their own values. This approach identifies three features of a sincerely-held value:

- **choosing**. Individuals must choose their values by considering the implications of a range of alternatives, without pressure or influence from others.
- **prizing**. Once chosen, individuals should cherish—be happy with the choice—and be willing to publicly affirm the value.
- **acting**. Individuals should act consistently to re-affirm and strengthen their commitment to the value.

The teacher's primary responsibility is to encourage students to clarify their own values for themselves. Teachers facilitate this by organizing activities that stimulate students to think about their values, and by providing occasions for students to publicly affirm, celebrate and act on them. In helping students clarify, teachers might ask questions which invite students to identify their values, to think about the personal meaning and implications, and to consider the consistency of their words and deeds through the use of clarifying questions such as the following:

- Is this something you value?
- How did you feel when it happened?
- What are some good things about it?
- Have you thought much about it?
- Where does this idea lead? What are its consequences?
- Do you *do* anything about it?
- Is what you have just said consistent with . . . . [a previous action or comment]?

Other clarifying activities include inviting students to rank order alternatives or locate values on a continuum; and to reflect on and discuss provocative statements, problems or issues posed by the teacher. Concurrent with activities to clarify values would be opportunities to publicly affirm and act on them. A classic values clarification activity (described in the boxes on the following pages) is to create a personal coat of arms whereby students symbolically represent and share their most cherished values.[4]

Values analysis

Unlike the values clarification approach where the focus in on students' personally *clarifying* their choices through reflection and action, the focus of values analysis is on students *critically examining* their value assumptions and reasoning. This latter approach believes that on their own students may not always see the gaps or inadequacies in their thinking and that students may actually hold discriminatory or prejudicial attitudes. In fact, the values clarification approach has been fiercely criticized for promoting a non-critical relativistic view of morality. As long as students are consistent and willing to act on them, the values clarification approach would find these values acceptable. Value analysis believes that some values may be unreasonable and, even if students sincerely held them, they should be helped in seeing their limitations. This is especially important with social or ethical values—the values we hold towards others. Although the values analysis and value clarification approaches both respect the importance of students making up their own minds on the basis of thoughtful consideration, the value analysis approach wants to *teach* students to think critically about their values, especially their ethical values. These values are seen to be far less private a matter than is presumed by the values clarification approach.

The Association for Values Education and Research (AVER) operating out of the University of British Columbia is a prominent advocate of the value analysis approach. Its work provides a structure to help teachers and students reflect more critically on their values. The AVER (1978, 1991) approach is based on a reconstruction of the logic of value reasoning into three elements:

- **the value judgment**: a statement about what the person judges to be desirable/undesirable or what ought, or ought not, to be (e.g., "school is horrible" or "school ought to be illegal");
- **the factual evidence to support the judgment**: a descriptive or factual statement of what actually is, was or is likely to be, which is seen to be relevant to the judgment taken (e.g., "I have to work hard in school");
- **the implied or underlying value principle**: the more general value position which the person has implicitly accepted by virtue of the factual reason offered (e.g., "Situations that force people to work hard are horrible—or ought to be made illegal").

When students offer and defend a position on a value issue (say, whether it is wrong to tell a "white lie" or on their attitude to accepting more immigrants into Canada), their reasoning can be reconstructed, using these elements into deductive arguments, consisting of a major premise (*the implied value principle*), a minor premise (*the factual evidence*) and the conclusion (*the value*

PERSONAL COAT OF ARMS

A popular values clarification project is for students to create a personal coat of arms that symbolically represents the values that each holds dear. The project integrates well with social studies units on knights and chivalry, First Nations peoples, patriotism and nationalism, cultural heritage, personal growth and self esteem. The undertaking can be more or less ambitious, but since the purpose is to help students identify and celebrate their own values, there is merit in taking the time to ensure the project fosters self-discovery and personal pride.

- **Creating context.** Introduce the project by drawing attention to the historical and contemporary uses of coats of arms and heraldry (e.g., First Nations, medieval and contemporary nobility, national flags, university and family crests). Explain that many citizens treat their national flag with great reverence because it is a symbol of their motherland—they may be outraged when people burn or trample on the flag, soldiers carry the flag into battle as a symbol of what they are fighting to protect. Desecrating a flag or other personal crest shows disrespect or scorn for that person's or group's most cherished values. Ask students to consider for a moment the values they would "give their all" to promote or protect.

- **Identifying the values.** Depending upon the time available and student level, the coat of arms may contain one or two panels only, although they usually contain between four and six panels, each representing a different value. An outline of a coat of arms (such as the one represented on the right) may be provided to students, either as a working copy (i.e., as a proto-type for a poster-signed design that they will eventually create) or as the final copy of their coat of arms. Typically, the teacher establishes the number of panels and the themes (although it need not be so directed). The following are common themes for panels:

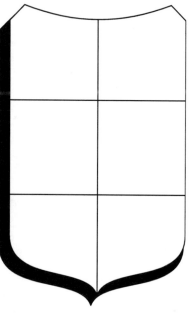

  - most cherished family characteristic or event;
  - most cherished ethnic/cultural characteristic or event;
  - most cherished national characteristic or event;
  - most cherished personal character trait(s);
  - most cherished character trait(s) sought in one's friends;
  - most significant personal accomplishment(s) to date;
  - personal motto or guiding principle;
  - most significant personal aspiration(s);
  - most significant contribution(s) one could make to one's friends or family
  - most significant contribution(s) one could make to the world at large;
  - what one would hope to be remembered by—one's epitaph.

  Selection of the themes should be guided by the specific goals of the project— for example, if increased cross-cultural awareness is an objective, then the first and second values on the above list would be especially relevant.

- **Exploring the values.** Once the themes have been established, students should then be encouraged and *assisted* in thoughtfully exploring what this would mean for them personally. Again, depending on the specific themes, students might be assigned one or more of the following tasks:
  - interview a relative about their family or ethnic background;
  - read about individuals who exhibit character traits that they admire;
  - as a class, brainstorm a list of character traits or life goals and rank-order their priorities;
  - think about what they would do if they had one year to live and were guaranteed success in whatever they attempted;
  - discuss with others who know them well what is seen to be their strengths and ambitions.

- **Representing one's values.** Although words may be appropriate in some panels (e.g., a personal motto or epitaph) the coat of arms' impact lies in its symbolic representation. Depending upon student level, simple drawings, photographs or magazine pictures on regular-sized paper may suffice. Alternatively students might be asked to create a shield-sized poster. Regardless of size, the effect is more powerful if students spend time exploring different types of symbols, including corporate logos (e.g., the Nike "swish" represents the wing of the goddess Victory—"victory" in Italian is *nike*) and national flags and crests (e.g., the dramatic rising sun in the Imperial Japanese flag, the olive branches of peace caressing the globe in the United Nations flag). It is especially valuable to point out the symbolism in each design (e.g., a dove symbolizes peace, lions symbolize courage). The significance of particular colours may also be explored (e.g., white symbolizes purity, red symbolizes life). Encourage students to create original or adapted representations, and not rely exclusively on well-established symbols. Some students may be embarrassed about their inability to draw. This can be mitigated by downplaying the artistic element (including not assigning marks for technical merit) and by allowing pictures, computer graphics and even "commission renderings" by fellow artists in the class.

- **Celebrating the values.** Since a primary purpose of the project is to publicly affirm students' values, it is important that there be an opportunity to share and celebrate the coats of arms. (Student should not be required to participate if they do not wish to). There are several ways in which this might be done:
  - each person explains his or her coat of arms to other students in a small group, to the whole class or in a gallery walk;
  - the class might interpret the symbolism in each coat of arms and guess what it means before having the creator explain it to them;
  - the coats of arms may be displayed around the classroom or in the school hallway or library for others to admire.

  However displayed it is important that students feel safe about sharing their deeply-held values and are encouraged to feel pride in their representations and in the values they symbolize.

judgment). For example, a student might offer the following judgment on the desirability of increased immigration quotas: "It's stupid for the Canadian government to increase immigration levels." When asked to provide factual evidence to support this conclusion, the student might respond: "The more new immigrants we accept, the more current residents are out of work." The implied value principle that the student must accept if the reasoning is to be valid is that: "The Canadian government should not adopt policies that cause unemployment among Canadian residents." This reasoning can be roughly translated into the following syllogism:

Major premise (implied value principle):
The government should not adopt polices that cause unemployment among Canadian residents.

Minor premise (factual evidence):
Increasing immigration quotas causes unemployment among Canadian residents.

Conclusion (value judgment):
Therefore the government should not increase immigration quotas.

The purpose of reconstructing value reasoning in this way is to provide teachers with three points at which to help student thinking critically about their views. Students can be taught to query whether or not: (1) the major premise (implied value principle) is acceptable, (2) the minor premise (factual evidence) is factually true, and (3) the conclusion (value judgment) follows from the premises, especially when all of the reasons are considered.

The unique contribution of the AVER approach is the "tests" or challenges that students and teachers can apply in assessing the acceptability of the implied value principle. University of British Columbia professor Jerrold Coombs (1980) has identified four ways to challenge our principles: (1) assess an implied principle for consistency with other basic values held by the individual; (2) assess the consequences of adopting the principle for everyone involved; (3) assess the consequences of adopting the principle in other relevant situations; and (4) assess the cumulative consequences of adopting the principle in repeated instances.

- **consistency with other basic values**. An obvious test of the acceptability of an implied principle is whether or not it is consistent with other more basic tenets in one's own value system. It would not be justifiable to accept a principle that was inconsistent with one's fundamental values. For example, if I believed it wrong to discriminate against people on the basis of race, then I would be inconsistent in accepting a principle which suggested that white immigrants be given priority. Similarly if I believe that the lives of people ought to be placed above money, then I would not be consistent in rejecting refugees whose lives were in danger, merely to save tax dollars.

- **consequences for everyone involved**. A second way to evaluate the acceptability of the implied principle is by assessing the consequences of adopting the principle for all of the people likely to be affected, especially those who are likely to be most significantly affected. Students should take on these others' perspectives and ask: "How would I feel if I were in someone else's shoes? Would I judge the principle to be fair from that perspective?" If I would find the implied principle unfair if I were in someone else's position, then that is a reason for not finding the principle acceptable. Even young children use this test when they say: "How would you like it if I did that to you?"

- **consequences in other relevant situations**. A third way to test an implied principle is to consider the consequences in other similar situations. If applying the implied principle in these situations would be undesirable then this is a reason for rejecting or at least modifying the principle. Consider, for example, the implied principle that it is always wrong to tell a lie. It would be appropriate to imagine other situations where telling a lie might be justified. Suppose I were living in Nazi Germany during World War II. Would I consider it wrong to lie to soldiers who asked if there were any Jewish people living in my house? If I think I am justified in lying in this situation then I should modify my implied principle to something like, "it is wrong to lie unless to protect someone's life." It would then be useful to imagine situations which were not a matter of saving a life where I would still consider it acceptable to lie. The point of the test is to explore other situations where the same principle might apply to determine if I can accept the consequences of adopting the principle in these situations. If not then, the principle needs to be modified or rejected.

- **consequences for repeated instances.** A final way in which to test the acceptability of an implied principle is by supposing repeated instances of this type of situation were to occur. If the consequences of re-peated applications are unacceptable, with no rational way to justify allowing only some instances of the act, then fairness requires preventing everyone from acting in that way. For example, although it may not be particularly undesirable for one person to walk across grass in a park or to throw a cigarette butt on the ground, the effect of everyone doing it is to ruin the grass or create horrible litter. The philosopher Marcus Singer (1958, p. 162) refers to this as the generalization argument: "if the consequences of everyone's acting in a certain way would be undesirable, then no one has the right to act in that way without a reason or justification."

Each test would need to be explained to students, perhaps introduced one at a time. Students need to learn when a test is likely to be relevant, perhaps by having students apply a particular test to a list of principles that have been supplied to them.[5]

To illustrate the power of the AVER approach in helping students think more critically about their value positions, the boxes following outline a seven-step model for value analysis applied to the issue of Canada's immigration quotas.

REASONING ABOUT CANADA'S IMMIGRATION QUOTAS

- **Identify and clarify the issue under discussion.** Before getting too far into a topic, students need to be precise about the issue before them. For example, is the dispute over the criteria for selecting new immigrants or the size of annual quotas of immigrants allowed into Canada? Students would need to understand that Canada sets quotas for three classes of immigrants: (1) *refugees* who are fleeing from political oppression or from desperate conditions; (2) *family immigrants* who are applying to be reunited with their relatives and (3) *independent immigrants* who have no political or family claims; many of whom are wealthy applicants willing to invest in Canadian businesses.

- **Generate possible factual reasons supporting both pro and con.** Once an issue is clarified, students should consider the reasons, pro and con. It is important that the reasons be framed as factual or descriptive statements (i.e., what actually is, was or is likely to happen). Individually or as a class, students may list pro reasons down one column and con reasons down the other column, as illustrated below.

Issue: **Should Canada increase its immigrant quotas for:**

- refugees?
- family class immigrants?
- independent immigrants?

Pro	*Con*
• many immigrants may be in desperate economic need;	• many Canadians may feel invaded by more immigrants;
• many immigrants may need protection from war and political prosecution;	• many immigrants take advantage of the system;
• increased immigration adds to the population size of Canada;	• immigrants drain money from other Canadians through increased need for social programs;
• increased immigration results in enriched lives and lifestyle for many new immigrants;	• increased immigration leads to overcrowding in some areas;
• many immigrants bring talents and human resources that benefit Canada;	• increased immigration drives the minimum wage down;
• immigrants provide a pool of workers to fill low paid jobs that may otherwise go unfilled;	• increased immigration discourages integration of ethnic groups into mainstream society;

- increased immigration unites separated families;
- increased immigration adds to the cultural diversity of Canada.

- increased immigration fuels racial/ethnic tensions in Canada;
- increased immigration leads to higher house prices;
- increased immigration will lead to the European culture becoming a minority in Canada.

- **Investigate the accuracy of the factual claims offered.** Students should be discouraged from accepting at face value the factual reasons they offer. Often students will have little evidence for their beliefs and in some cases their beliefs may be inaccurate or only partly true. For example, it is not obvious that increasing immigration drains money away from current residents. One of the government's motives for increased immigration is economic—it is seen to provide a larger consumer base of support for domestic industries and businesses. As well, it is more economical to accept into Canada immigrants who have already been trained, say, as medical doctors or computer analysts, than it is to educate them domestically. After seeking evidence for all the suggested reasons, students should, where appropriate, modify or reject suggested reasons. For example, the claim that immigrants drain money may be found to be clearly false in the case of independent immigrants, or the suggestion that increased immigration leads to higher house prices may be false in the case of refugees.

- **Test the acceptability of each implied principle.** Students would be expected, for each factual reason that is thought to be true, to identify the implied value principle by reconstructing the logic of their reasoning into a deductive argument. For example, the principle implied by the argument that many Canadians may feel invaded by increased immigration is something like the following: The government should not adopt policies that cause Canadian residents to feel a sense of invasion. Students would then apply one or more of the principle tests discussed earlier to each of the implied principles. Principles found to be unacceptable should be modified or rejected. Three of the "tests" are useful in assessing the acceptability of the above-mentioned principle:

  — *consequences for everyone involved.* Students should endeavour to put themselves in the position of someone whose parents live in another country, but who cannot immigrate because other Canadian residents feel somewhat invaded. Or, put themselves in the position of someone who is in danger of being tortured in their home country if their application for refugee status is rejected because some Canadian residents may feel invaded. Would students still think it fair to accept this principle if they were in these peoples' predicaments? If not, then the principle should be modified or rejected.

  — *consequences in other relevant situations.* Students should endeavour to think of a different government policy that they support, but which many people might find invasive. Perhaps the issue is mandatory seat belts. Would students be willing to give up on the policy merely because many Canadians feel their freedom is invaded by having to wear seat belts? If not, then they do not accept the principle that merely because people feel invaded policies should be scrapped.

  — *consequences for repeated instances.* Students should consider the general consequences of scrapping government policies simply because many people may feel invaded. Would governments be able to act at all if this principle was accepted? Few, if any, policies do not threaten some group, including limits on speeding, gun control, smoke-free areas, minimum wage and anti-discrimination laws. The consequence of the implied principle, if accepted, might be that governments could never implement any policy.

- **Weigh all remaining (valid) reasons pro and con.** The next step, after having eliminated all the reasons that are unwarranted because of unacceptable implied principles, is to assess the collective weight of the remaining pro and con reasons. This involves deciding the importance of the values underlying each reason (the implied principles) and the extent to which each position affects these values. For example, students must consider whether or not a relatively modest loss of economic benefit to current residents should be given priority over the life-and-death protection afforded to political refugees whose lives may be in danger.

- **Present and defend a judgment on the issue.** Finally students should determine their own stand on the issue. This may be a simple "for" or "against" position, but more often it will be a qualified or modified stance. For example, students might decide that immigration quotas should be increased in some areas and decreased in other areas, or that quotas should be increased across the board provided immigrant fraud is reduced. Students would be expected to demonstrate how their position is the stronger alternative and how it attempts to accommodate the valid concerns stemming from the opposing perspective.

As I hope this discussion of the AVER approach indicates, there is need to teach students how to think critically about their values. Although there are multiple approaches to values education—classroom environment, direct experiences and values clarification—ultimately, teachers must encourage students to reflect critically on their values, especially on their social or ethical values—those pertaining to how others are to be treated.

Concluding Remarks

I want to close this article on values education with a plea for two virtues: sensitivity and perseverance. Although we should be sensitive to our students in all that we do, there is particular need for caution when dealing with values. Not only are values rife with controversy, they are deeply tied to students' feelings. We have a special responsibility to enter into this domain with the greatest of sensitivity for our students.

The consequences of a failure in this regard were demonstrated to me while visiting a high school in New York City several years ago. I had been invited to observe a lesson involving an abbreviated version of the personal coat of arms activity (which I described earlier in this article). The teacher opened the lesson by sharing a personal coat of arms he had done. It was sketched in pencil on a regular sheet of paper and, consequently, was not readily visible to students. He explained to the class the four panels on his coat of arms and assigned students to develop their own. The values they were to represent were an aspect from their cultural background, their favourite food, their favourite activity and the epitaph they would like for their headstone. Their coats of arms were to be drawn on a photocopied sheet of regular paper which he handed out. Students were given a few minutes only to think about and sketch a symbol to represent each value. A male student asked if he could complete the activity at home. He was told to finish it before the end of class, otherwise he might lose the sheet. The student then volunteered to come back after school to complete the assignment, whereupon the teacher suggested that if he just got down to work immediately he would be finished in no time. With 15 minutes remaining in the period, the teacher randomly divided the class into groups of four. Students were to explain their coat of arms to the other three members of their group. In one group, I noticed the sole female student being ignored by the other three male group members. She sat there for the entire time, with her coat of arms in her slightly outstretched arms, waiting to be invited by the others to explain her cherished values. This "values" lesson was not sensitively handled. The young woman's self-esteem was damaged that day. The male student who wanted to take his coat of arms home to do a proper job learned that "getting it done" was the main thing. And the personal pride of everyone in the class was diminished by having their values treated in such a slapdash fashion and trivialized by such banal categories.

And now a point about perseverance. In talking about the slow pace of significant educational change, Ralph Tyler likens teachers' efforts to the effect that dripping water has upon a stone: "In a day or week or a month there is no appreciable change in the stone, but over a period of years definite erosion is noted. Correspondingly, by the cumulation of educational experiences profound changes are brought about in the learner" (1969, p. 83). Clearly we must take the long view on nurturing personal and social values. It requires incremental, collective effort—no one teacher can do it quickly or on her own. Each of us is responsible for doing our small part to promote the values that will guide students in thinking and acting as responsible human beings and citizens. Arguably, there is no goal more important than this for social studies educators.

Endnotes

[1] For a comprehensive exposition of approaches to values education see *Values Education Sourcebook: Conceptual Approaches, Methods, Analyses and an Annotated Bibliography* (Social Science Education Consortium, 1976).

[2] Suggestions for creating classroom environments that reinforce attitudes of thoughtfulness are discussed in article #20, "Taking Seriously the Teaching of Critical Thinking", by Roland Case and Ian Wright.

[3] The use of literature to evoke powerful feelings is discussed in article #36, "Promoting the Aesthetic Experience: Responding to Literature in Social Studies", by Roberta McKay.

[4] An extensive set of other lesson ideas using the values clarification approach can be found in Simon, Howe and Kerschenhaum (1972).

[5] Suggested activities for introducing principle testing are described more fully in the AVER teaching materials (1978, 1991).

References

American Bar Association. (1982). What's happening in law-related education? *LRE Report, 3*(3), 1-6.

Ashford, M-W. (1995). Youth actions for the planet. In R. Fowler & I. Wright (Eds.), *Thinking globally about social studies education* (pp. 75-90). Vancouver: Research and Development in Global Studies, University of British Columbia.

Association for Values Education and Research. (1978). *Prejudice.* Toronto: OISE Press.

Association for Values Education and Research. (1991). *Peace: In pursuit of security, prosperity, and social justice.* Toronto: OISE Press.

Burrett, K. & Rusnak, T. (1993). *Integrated character education.* (Fastback #351). Bloomington, IN: Phi Delta Kappa Educational Foundation.

Cassidy, W. (1994, May). An examination of caring and compassion in social studies education. Unpublished paper, Simon Fraser University, Burnaby, British Columbia.

Coombs, J.R. (1980). Validating moral judgments by principle testing. In D. Cochrane & M. Manley-Casimir (Eds.), *Practical dimensions of moral education* (pp. 30-55). New York: Praeger.

Duke, D.L. (1978). Looking at the school as a rule-governed organization. *Journal of Research and Development in Education, 11*(4), 116-126.

Leming, J.S. (1991). Teacher characteristics and social education. In J. Shaver (Ed.), *Handbook of research on social studies teaching and learning* (pp. 222-236). New York: Macmillan.

Ministry of Education, British Columbia. (1993). *The Intermediate Program: Grades 4 to 10.* Victoria, BC: Queen's Printer.

Ministry of Education, Ontario. (1986*). Curriculum guideline: History and contemporary studies (Part A).* Toronto: Author.

Osborne, K. (1982). Civics, citizenship and politics: Political education in the schools. *Teacher Education, 20,* 58-72.

Patrick, J.J. & Hoge, J.D. (1991). Teaching government, civics and law. In J. Shaver (Ed.), *Handbook on research on social studies teaching and learning* (pp. 427-436). New York: Macmillan.

Peters, W. (1987). *A class divided: Then and now.* New Haven, CT: Yale University Press.

Raths, L.E., Harmin, M. & Simon, S.B. (1966). *Values and teaching: Working with values in the classroom.* Columbus, OH: Merrill.

Simon, S.B., Howe, L. & Kerschenhaum, H. (1972). *Values clarification: A handbook of practical strategies for teachers and students.* New York: Hart.

Singer, M.G. (1958). Moral rules and principles. In A.I. Meldon (Ed.), *Essays in moral philosophy* (pp. 160-197). Seattle, WA: University of Washington Press.

Social Science Education Consortium. (1976). *Values education sourcebook: Conceptual approaches, methods, analyses and an annotated bibliography.* Boulder, CO: Author.

Torney-Purta, J. (1983). Psychological perspectives on enhancing civic education through the education of teachers. *Journal of Teacher Education, 34,* 3-34.

Tyler, R. (1969). *Basic principles of curriculum and instruction.* Chicago: University of Chicago Press.

— ✧ —

This article is a considerably expanded account of ideas found in a 1996 paper "Promoting 'Global' Attitudes" in *Canadian Social Studies, 30*(4), 174-177.

27

TEACHING FOR HOPE

WALT WERNER

One cannot live in this media-rich culture without feeling some unease about the future. Weekly we encounter disturbing images of urgent proportions. A litany of enormous challenges—including poverty and famine, human rights abuses and repression, desertification and ecological stress, social chaos and international debts—confronts our increasingly interdependent world. After Lebanon, Cambodia and Ireland came Ethiopia, Sudan, Bosnia and Rwanda, and we have come to expect that a list of similar place names will continue. Systemic interactions among diverse problems are overwhelming in their complexity and ambiguity, and this leads to uncertainties. According to the Club of Rome,

> Never in the course of history has humankind been faced with so many threats and dangers . . . the causes and consequences of which form an inextricable maze. . . . Individuals feel helpless, caught, as it were, between the rise of previously unknown perils on the one hand, and an incapacity to answer the complex problems in time and to attack the roots of evil, not just its consequences, on the other hand. (King & Schneider, 1991, pp. 127, 128)

Even though this barrage of bad news leaves us psychologically fatigued, we still need to rationalize the realities of what we see and hear, because no matter what our politics, we want a better future (Kennedy, 1993; Roche, 1993).

For children, though, pictures of a broken world speak directly to their own future. Implied is their tomorrow. Whether this realization occurs in a dramatic moment of insight or slowly awakens as a vague awareness, the consequence can be uncertainty about the future or, even worse, some loss of hope.

Classrooms are unwitting partners in this loss. It begins when youth encounter texts and images that imply a deeply problematic future. Through classroom projects, video and print resources, and discussions of current events, students glean bits of information from which they construct their personal views, often of a crisis-ridden and confusing world created by adults who seem unwilling or unable to change it. "Youngsters piece together these fragments in a jumbled patchwork of mixed perceptions that make them anxious," observed Van Ornum (1984, p. 16); "The world is not safe. If adults are scared and helpless, what chance do kids have?" When unchecked, these feelings lead over time to insecurity or cynicism about the prospects for individual and collective futures.

Such outcomes, however, are educationally unacceptable because schools are in the business of strengthening realistic hope in the future. Let me illustrate with an event from a grade ten social studies class. Groups were organized around research projects related to a number of global issues. I thought they were learning well to sort through controversial problems when a

---

She simply wanted to study the shells, as she said, "because they're beautiful." I suddenly realized that here was a sixteen year old whose sense of future was threatened.

---

young woman quietly informed me that she would rather drop out of her study group and do an individual project on cowry shells. When asked what social or economic issues were represented by these natural artifacts, she replied that she was not aware of any issues nor was she interested. She simply wanted to study the shells, as she said, "because they're beautiful." I suddenly realized that here was a sixteen year old whose sense of future was threatened. The cumulative effect of my "ambulance chasing" pedagogy was a sense of helplessness, a feeling that the range and complexity of issues were too difficult to understand, let alone solve. My focus on problems left her with a deepening uncertainty.

Anyone who is a teacher is necessarily an optimist. Our working with young people represents a commitment to the future. We are teaching for hope. But what does it mean to have hope? Many years ago Philip Phenix reminded educators that "Hope is the mainspring of human existence." This is no idle slogan, for as he explained, "conscious life is a continual projection into the future. . . . Without hope, there is no incentive for learning, for the impulse to learn presupposes confidence in the possibility of improving one's existence" (1974, p. 123). Essential to hope is a knowledgeable and reflective confidence in the future and a willingness to engage it. The future, whether one's own or that of a larger group, is seen as open, having possibilities rather than foreclosed or predetermined. This belief entails confidence that current problems and worrisome trends can be addressed in response to care and effort, that good planning and strategic action taken today can have significant consequences. In short, hope expresses itself as a "Yes" to tomorrow.

How can youth's sense of hope for the future be strengthened through classrooms? Part of the answer lies in the important roles that *emotion, information, vision* and *efficacy* have in young people's coming to understand the problems and complexities of their larger world. Through a teacher's sensitive use of these four avenues, hope can be encouraged during discussions about global issues.

EMOTION
Honest treatment of subject matter, whether in the humanities or sciences, will at times give rise to emotionally loaded concerns and questions about the future. For decades educators have known that harm to learn-

ing does not necessarily come from material that evokes emotion (Jones, 1970, pp. 69-86). Any learning that is memorable and important is also emotion-full. Expressions of feeling—such as surprise, anger, wonder, uncertainty, awe, consternation, commitment—engage the interest and imagination of students, extend their involvement with the subject matter, and imbue the curriculum with the kind of personal significance that impels rather than hinders learning.

There is an emotion, however, that is not a friend of learning: anxious students do not perform well. Anxiety about the future rests on feelings of helplessness and isolation in the face of threatening prospects (Jones, 1970). And when children are unwilling to talk freely about topics that engender this sense of aloneness and hopelessness, their uninformed imaginations give rise to misperceptions of issues that can further reinforce anxiety (Stackhouse, 1991).

How can the study of global problems and issues help youth feel less anxious about the future, less helpless about the prospects for change, and less alone in their imaginations? That students feel threatened by questions about the future needs to be dealt with rather than avoided. Classroom discussions, when sensitively directed by the teacher, can counter anxiety. For example:

- watch for *signs of anxiety*, and seek ways to ameliorate this feeling and to promote a sense of community and efficacy. Indicators of a loss of hope can be varied. For example, off-hand comments or jokes during conversations about world problems may indicate fear, confusion, resignation or anger; these refusals to discuss issues seriously may be masking deeper ambivalences. Expressions of apathy or lack of interest—such as protesting the topic, disengagement from discussion, incomplete or poorly done projects—may also be attempts to protect oneself.

- take seriously the *sentiments* about anxiety or hopelessness that children express during discussions of current events and issues. Help them articulate the reasons for these attitudes, and where appropriate, provide counter examples and new information that challenges narrow or unsubstantiated beliefs.

- focus discussions not only on the informational content of issues, but also on their *emotional content*. How do students feel about the issue? Emotions have to be shared—listened to and discussed—in order to be understood and harnessed for learning. As concerns are expressed, children realize that they are not alone in their imaginations about the future; there are broader communities of concern embracing people around the earth.

INFORMATION
Shielding children from global problems cannot be a solution to preserving their sense of hope. Purging the curriculum of topics that raise concerns for young peo-

ple, or focusing discussion only on 'safe' areas, are not options except for making classrooms more sterile places. As Van Ornum suggests, "Today's young people, for better or worse, are savvy and cynical. Old before their time, they know a dodge when they see one" (1984, p. 3). They already know from television that many people lead wretched lives because of environmental degradation, armed conflicts and poverty, and that some adults are not hopeful about change (Kaplan, 1994). But if children hear little acknowledgment of these realities, they conclude that educators either do not care or are not being honest; neither case instills confidence in learning about global issues. The perceived dark side of the world calls for information rather than silence.

Thoughtful discussion of information is essential, though, because a source of hopelessness can be misinformation, misunderstood information or a lack of information about the nature and extent of a problem. Any defensible belief in the future has to include, among other things, an adequate knowledge—a realistic understanding and honest appraisal—of what is the situation. Herein lies a responsibility of educators to ensure that students have accurate and balanced input when discussing global issues, and to check whether the inferences drawn from classroom conversations and other texts are reasonable. Sketchy or inaccurate 'facts', as well as hearsay, casual comments and a neglect of context, can lead to unwarranted conclusions, over generalizations or false impressions of what the future might be like (Jickling, 1994).

If we want students to develop a reasoned hope in the future, then during classroom discussions:

- probe for *inferences* that children hold about the future. Are these inferences warranted by the best information at hand? Could their *conclusions* lead to unfounded fears or unrealistic expectations? Uninformed or misinformed fears and confidences both constitute naiveté.

- provide greater awareness of the broad range of *institutions* dedicated to gathering and disseminating reliable information about issues, and of the many groups that use this information to lobby governments for new policies or changed laws. This research and development work is premised on a strong confidence in the future.

> "Where there is no vision," says an ancient proverb, "people perish". . . . Rich imagination is the stuff of hope.

Emphasis in the classroom upon inert information—often packaged as worksheets and end-of-chapter questions—only provides youth with disconnected 'facts' about the state of their world. Unless meaningful connections among these isolated bits and pieces are forged, the picture of the larger world may make little sense beyond a bewildering array of problems. Hope falters when the content learned by students does not lead to better understanding.

VISION

Hope cannot rest only upon an understanding of what is or will be the case (information), but also upon imagined alternatives and how these may be achieved (vision). "Where there is no vision," says an ancient proverb, "people perish." It is not enough to want a "better world" without articulating what this might mean: What are one's priorities for an improved world, and how could they be achieved? Alternative futures are defined as we "name" them through goals, plans and policies. Problem-solving calls for a willingness to project outcomes and to choose from among competing scenarios. Rich imagination is the stuff of hope. But imagination withers whenever young people are treated as less than mindful agents through unimaginative pedagogy.

Children's hope is strengthened as their imaginations are engaged in understanding and "making" their world:

- introduce *visionary concepts* that define alternatives for the future. Some examples are "sustainable environment," "respect for the rule of international law," "the commons," and "human rights." That these concepts may be controversial does not disqualify them from classrooms, but highlights the fact that they represent important values for envisioning the future.

- discuss why the world community has forged institutions that embody and implement *collective visions* for the future. Examples include the world court and international law, as well as the many other agencies and covenants of the United Nations (Department of Foreign Affairs and International Trade, 1994).

- give students opportunities to define and share *personal visions* for the future. Imagination is clarified and enlarged as it is challenged in a context of alternatives (Boulding, 1995; Korten, 1995). Not only do the visual and performing arts offer multiple modes for expressing doubts and hopes about the future, but also through "writing and sharing stories, creating images, and participating in roleplays, we can simulate events as though we are already in the future. Our objective in such visualizations is not to predict the future, but to perceive potential futures in the here-and-now and to conceptualize what it will take to get there from here" (Bryant, 1995, p. 40). Visions can be created and shared through various avenues, including poetry, music, drama, dance, story, drawing and painting.

Hope is never fostered when students' own creative envisioning of desirable futures is disallowed, when information about the world is treated as a given to be received rather than reimagined. Youth need to theorize about possibilities.

EFFICACY

A concern that youth express when they begin to recognize the extent of world problems is why adults are not solving them. This query is not about more information on specific government policies and projects, but more deeply about how the world of adults works. It is an attempt to understand the kind of world in which they live: is it a world in which adults do not care about problems that occur elsewhere? where adults do not know what to do? or where adults care more about present interests than consequences for the future? Some of children's deepest fears about abandonment are here tapped (Hevesi, 1990). They seek assurances that adults can be trusted to protect the new generation's future. No wonder they become apprehensive.

Our goal is to encourage the development of those abilities and dispositions that allow young people to engage in appropriate personal, social and political action. Hope is indistinguishable from a belief that individuals and groups influence and shape their futures through action. A strong sense of personal efficacy is a driving force behind any achievement. Without it there is little open-mindedness to new ideas, willingness to reflect on one's own plans, or motivation and confidence in becoming proactive. To paraphrase Saul Alinsky, "There can be no darker or more devastating tragedy than the death of people's faith in themselves and in their power to direct their future. Denial of the opportunity for participation is the denial of human dignity. . . ." Students need to understand why they are not powerless to make a contribution at some level.

Fostering efficacy is not an add-on to studies of global issues, but should be part and parcel of the ongoing discussions:

- focus on the world-wide extent of *agencies, partnerships* and *networks* engaged in problem solving. Young people are not aware of the range of groups—whether governments, international institutions, non-governmental organizations, grassroots community initiatives, or the private sector—committed to action and what they are doing. The important understanding here is that the difficulties facing our interdependent globe are being worked on by many people in various ways.

- infuse *good news stories* about the successes that individuals, groups and institutions are having in their actions. Elicit examples of actions that have been and are being taken to solve problems. Valuable experience and skills have been gained over the past decades, and considerable progress was achieved in areas such as health, agriculture and social justice (Canadian International Development Agency, 1987). The purpose for introducing positive examples is to provide a balanced and honest, not utopian, view of the gains that are made locally and internationally.

- encourage discussion of *personal actions* that could be taken at home and in the school or community. The complexity of issues and problems does not preclude consideration of meaningful action: What can I personally do? Is there collective action that we should plan? Depending upon the age and circumstances of students, activities may involve letter writing, changing one's consumer habits, attending a seminar for further information, joining the work of a community organization, or forming a school club. Appropriate action is not only a way to apply what is learned, but also a means for understanding issues better and strengthening efficacy.

Curricula and classrooms are largely organized around and for passivity. Often students are taught political incapacity rather than efficacy through the large amounts of inert knowledge they are given. They learn inadvertently that "doing schoolwork" is not meant to be "real work" that has any direct impact on (or even relevance for) larger issues. This is why discussions about efficacy are so important for undercutting learned helplessness.

CONCLUSION

Classroom discussions of global issues may increase student anxieties about the future. This is why educators need to reflect on the roles that emotion, information, vision and efficacy may have in shaping young people's beliefs about their tomorrow. I am not advocating that we put a light and happy face on the world. Youth already have a sense of dark crises on the horizon, but these realities need not imply despair. Hope requires a careful understanding of issues, and the development of reasoned visions and a realistic sense of efficacy. It is then that the sobering images on TV screens and the problems they imply can be seen with possibility.

Let me conclude with a personal anecdote. Late one night I heard my son who was in grade one at the time call from his room. I turned on the light and noticed that he had been crying. "When I grow up," he announced, "there will be no more wilderness." Whatever he meant by "wilderness" was not as important at this point as his expression of a threatened personal future. This loss of hope had started earlier in the day during a classroom discussion about stresses on ecosystems around the world, followed that evening by a television documentary on the loss of wilderness in Western Canada. Because he lacked adequate information and the necessary conceptual tools to appraise the issues, what little understanding he gained from these two events led to a confused and anxious inference about his own future. I assured him that, although wilderness was indeed under serious threat in places, many groups of concerned people just like him were working to protect ecosystems through new policies and laws, and that there were things that he and I could do as well. Over the next few days we sought new information, shared our visions and explored ways to enhance efficacy.

REFERENCES

Boulding, E. (1995). Why imagine the future? *In Context. A Journal of Hope, Sustainability, and Change, 40,* 50.

Bryant, B. (1995). Rehearsing the future. *In Context. A Journal of Hope, Sustainability, and Change, 40,* 39-50.

Canadian International Development Agency. (1987). *Sharing our future. Canadian international development assistance.* Hull: Minister of Supply and Services Canada.

Department of Foreign Affairs and International Trade. (1994). *Canadian reference guide to the United Nations.* Hull: Minister of Supply and Services Canada.

Hevesi, D. (1990, May 22). N.Y. children feel both fearful, guilty about the homeless. *The Globe and Mail,* p. A19.

Jones, R. (1970). *Fantasy and feeling in education.* New York: Harper Colophon Books.

Jickling, B. (1994). Studying sustainable development: Problems and possibilities. *Canadian Journal of Education, 19*(3), 231-240.

Kaplan, R. (1994). The coming anarchy. *The Atlantic Monthly,* February, 44-76.

Kennedy, P. (1993). *Preparing for the twenty-first century.* New York: Random.

King, A. & Schneider, B. (1991). *The first global revolution: A report by the Council of the Club of Rome.* New York: Pantheon.

Korten, D. (1995). A new day's coming. *In Context. A Journal of Hope, Sustainability, and Change, 40,* 14-18.

Phenix, P. (1974). Transcendence and the curriculum. In E. Eisner & E. Vallence (Eds.), *Conflicting conceptions of curriculum* (pp. 117-132). Berkeley, CA: McCutchan.

Roche, D. (1993). The new world order: Justice in international relations. *Global Education, 1*(1), 31-38.

Shuman, M. (1994). *Towards a global village. International community development initiatives.* London: Pluto Press.

Stackhouse, J. (1991, October 18). There's method in the misery. *The Globe and Mail,* pp. A1, A4.

Van Ornum, W. (1984). *Talking to children about nuclear war.* New York: Continuum.

— ✧ —

This article, which is reprinted with permission, appeared originally in 1995 in R. Fowler and I. Wright (Eds.), *Thinking globally about social studies education* (pp. 51-60). Vancouver: Research and Development in Global Studies, University of British Columbia.

28

Activism in Social Studies: The Chamberlin-Glassford Exchange

Chuck Chamberlin
Larry Glassford

This article contains three papers:
an intial essay by Chamberlin,
a response by Glassford and
a rebuttal by Chamberlin.

Citizenship as the Goal of Social Studies: Passive Knower or Active Doer?

Chuck Chamberlin

An Edmonton grade four class had been studying Alberta's forestry industry for over two months when their teacher asked her students whether they thought the new pulp mill proposals being announced were a good idea. To help them make an informed decision, Monique helped set up a chart listing some of the consequences of building the mills or not. Finally, students wrote letters to Premier Getty, Forestry Minister Fjordbotten and news media telling about their decisions and reasons. The class received a reply from Getty, and CBC-TV came out to the school and interviewed students, then showed a clip on their 6:00 news.

This was particularly interesting because Alberta's social studies curriculum states that "Responsible citizenship is the ultimate goal of social studies." This is defined as follows:

Responsible citizenship includes:

- understanding the role, rights and responsibility of a citizen in a democratic society and a citizen in a global community
- participating constructively in the democratic process by making rational decisions
- respecting the dignity and worth of self and others. (Alberta Education, 1989, p. 1)

The responsible citizen needs to participate constructively, then, and the curriculum underscores this by including a model for decision making that ends with:

- Take action (if feasible and desirable).
- What can we do? Do it.
- Was that a good thing to do? Why or why not?
- Was this a good way to answer our problem? Why or why not? (p. 8)

This good citizen presented to us in the Alberta social studies curriculum is very much like these grade four students. They had done months of research, knew a great deal about the environmental, economic, health, aesthetic and recreational consequences of starting up more pulp mills and *used* their knowledge to make an informed decision on the issue. Most teachers would stop there, feeling that social studies time should be used for learning about the world, not helping students take action to make the world a better place. That raises the question of whether the traditional knowledge building role of social studies is adequate to develop responsible citizens who not only understand the roles, rights and responsibilities of citizens in a democratic society, but also participate constructively in the democratic process.

If schools are to prepare actively participating citizens, they need to be concerned about the development of a strong sense of political efficacy, or a belief that it can make a difference if you all get together and write letters to the premier, the minister of forestry and the media. Unless students believe their efforts will be effective, all the knowledge in the world is unlikely to lead them to be responsible citizens who participate constructively. Monique began providing experience for her students in taking action, and in getting used to the role of exerting influence on public issues and decisions. Perhaps she made some progress, as half of her students answered Yes when asked "If a school rule was unfair, do you think you could do anything to get it changed?" Perhaps the effect of working together as a class had some influence on their answers, as nine of those eleven students who answered Yes then explained

that the school authorities were completely virtuous that they couldn't even conceive of there being unfair school rules. One wonders how much encouragement they have been given over their five years of schooling to think critically, examine alternatives or take responsibility for making independent judgments. It seems more likely that obedience, passivity, compliance and respect for authority have been a heavy emphasis at home and in school.

Five other students who answered No said, "They won't listen," or "You can't fight rules." One wonders what experiences have led to this cynicism about attempts to influence people in authority.

These students were also asked four questions about their likely success in influencing other levels of government; the results are shown in Table 1.

Such low levels of expected success in exerting influence are discouraging in a country that prides itself on being a democratic society where political participation is essential. How did these students come to hold such pessimistic views? Perhaps they have been sub-

TABLE 1	% Agree	% Disagree	% Don't Know
If I wanted to, I could get someone in the city government to listen to what I want.	36	36	23
When I grow up I believe I will have a fair chance of influencing people in government.	45	9	45
If I joined together with others, we could cause some rules and laws to be changed.	32	55	14
If people would quit complaining and get active, they could change what the government does.*	55	18	27
Mean: % 42			

* These, and the items in Tables 2 and 3, come from an instrument developed by Dr. John Seymour, University of Manitoba.

they could get other kids to help work for change. Typical was the student who wrote, "I think I could because I would get a group together and go talk to [the principal] about it." Other students said they would "go for a petition" or more forcefully, "get a lot of kids and all tell the teachers and force them to change the rules," or "if all the students got together they could just stay home until the principal will forget the rule." Perhaps the sense of community solidarity and strong sense of political efficacy indicated in these statements reflects the experience of a whole class writing letters and appearing on TV to attempt to exert influence on a social issue, an experience planned and provided by their teacher.

It is instructive to also examine the reasons given by the 11 students who said No, they didn't think they could do anything to change an unfair school rule. Three said the school rules were good ones, in the best interests of the safety and security of all, and shouldn't be changed. These students were so strongly convinced

jected to such a heavy emphasis on obedience, politeness, respect for authority, and hard work that it seems wrong to expect to stand up and speak out. Some evidence for that conclusion is found in students' answers to the items in Table 2.

Vastly higher percentages of these nine to ten-year-olds agreed with the importance of obedience, good manners, loyalty, hard work and respect for Canada's institutions than agreed with likely success in influencing government. These attitudes and self-concepts are not innate, but are learned, and schools must be part of that learning process. However, these students are not nearly so likely to learn that part of their responsibility as citizen is to stand up for what they believe in, and speak out to try and make our society a better place for all of us to live in. Note the much lower percentages of agreement with these items as shown in Table 3.

It may well be that most of these children have had nine to ten years of home life emphasizing obedience not assertiveness, conformity not creative thought, re-

TABLE 2

	% Agree	% Disagree	% Don't Know
A good citizen obeys the law.	86	0	14
A good citizen is always polite.	55	23	27
A good citizen is loyal to his or her family.	86	4	14
A good citizen works hard.	77	4	18
A good citizen has good table manners.	68	14	18
A good citizen studies hard in school.	86	4	09
A good citizen keeps up with what is happening in the world.	77	9	14
A good citizen stands up when O Canada is played.	73	9	18
A good citizen shows respect for a funeral.	86	0	14
			Mean: % 78

spect not equality, acceptance not critical reflection. It may well be that their five years of schooling has mostly reinforced those home attitudes. Indeed, it seems likely that for most of these students' school lives they've been encouraged to *know* about the world, but not to *act* on it. Embedded in this role of only knowing but not acting is a hidden curriculum of passivity, not active citizenship.

Newmann (1975) has argued that teaching students to be passive knowers rather than active doers defeats the key principle of democratic government, consent of the governed. Central to Newmann's argument is the ethical importance of equality, based on the moral premise that every human being is entitled to respect and dignity. Dignity, Newmann asserts, is possible only

upper-status, wealthy, white, middle-aged citizens taking a 'conservative' stand on such issues as welfare" (p. 50). Further, Newmann reports, government leaders in the Verba and Nie study

> were more responsive to active than to inactive citizens. That is, they were more aware of the activists' views, tended to share those views, and spent more of their efforts trying to implement them. Views of the inactive citizens were not as consistently known, shared, or pursued by government leaders. (pp. 53–54)

Newmann's solution is to develop skills, predispositions and self-concepts needed for active participation in public affairs by all citizens, not just those who have developed a strong sense of political efficacy from

TABLE 3

	% Agree	% Disagree	% Don't Know
A good citizen joins a political party.	27	27	45
A good citizen tells others what he or she thinks about political problems.	55	9	32
A good citizen tries to change things in the government.	32	45	23
A good citizen gets other people to vote in elections.	55	23	27
A good citizen works to get politicians to do what he or she wants them to do.	9	50	41
			Mean: % 36

if the claims and interests of each person are treated impartially, which, in turn requires that society be organized so that power is distributed as equally as possible through rights to participate in periodic selection of leaders and direct participation to affect the outcome of specific issues. This emphasis on equal access to power minimizes the chance that equal rights can be violated. Newmann concludes, however, that the consent ideal is not being realized, and that "education is, in part, responsible for its failure" (p. 46). He cites Verba and Nie's study, indicating that: 11% of citizens are extremely politically active and 47% are relatively inactive, and that "high participators are over-whelmingly

seeing their upper SES parents exert power and influence. Programs that stop short at reflectively inquiring into issues and making decisions on them offer a version of citizenship that models knowing and deciding, but not acting: passivity. Hence education for knowledge rather than for action would seem to still bear responsibility for the failure of the consent principle and the continued inequality revealed in elite domination of political affairs.

Wood (1984) also has argued the case for a conception of active citizenship rather than the "passive knower-decider." Wood advocates participatory democracy, where citizens take "direct action on social issues—

picketing, protesting, democratic takeovers" (p. 226) as necessary if the hidden curriculum of the school is to change from one that promotes working-class passivity to one that nurtures a sense of political efficacy among all classes. Wood suggests we learn from theorists such as Apple the school's social role, namely

> that schools teach a limited, very limited vision of democracy. . . . Removing from the curriculum any mention of citizen action or resistance, schools seem to limit our vision of democracy to an occasional trip to the ballot box. Gone is the active participant, enter the passive consumer. (pp. 224–225)

An Alternative Model of Citizenship Education

Wood's activist conception of citizenship was built into the provincial curriculum in Alberta, during the decade 1978–88. It added the step of "acting on your decision" to the reflective decision making model Engle and Ochoa (1988) advocate. Consequently, some Alberta teachers have had their students inquiring into a wide range of social issues, culminating their inquiry with varied forms of direct and indirect action. Some examples will provide a contrast to the passive knower method and to its implicit vision of good citizen and good society.

Programs that stop short at reflectively inquiring into issues and making decisions on them offer a version of citizenship that models knowing and deciding, but not acting: passivity.

Spraying mosquitoes

Taylor and Moore (1983) described a four-and-a-half-month study of the use of chemical sprays for mosquitoes by their grade five and six students that culminated in some students preferring increased use of chemicals, some wanting to replace chemical use with spraying insect predators of mosquito larvae on ponds and ditches, and a third group advocating no control programs at all. The two classes requested time to present their findings and recommendations during a city council meeting, and, using effective forms of persuasion, put predators into an aquarium full of mosquito larvae to show how voraciously predation followed. They read passionate poetry concluding "please spray not, we'd rather swat," and showed a slide-tape presentation on the effects of chemicals on the food chain and ecosystem. These teachers were influenced by the Hungerford and Peyton (1976) conception of citizen who is both competent to take action on issues and willing to take that action. After the project, many of these students had a stronger sense of political efficacy than they'd had four and a half months before. When asked how likely it was that they would really do something about changing an unfair school rule, they made statements such as the following:

> I think it would be likely because after the mosquito project I learned that even grade five kids can change council's minds.

> Very likely, because I have had experience with my school.

We learned that you have to stick up for your rights, so I would go out and do it.

> Well, now that I know how to go about trying to get something done right that I think is wrong, I would probably try and change it. (Chamberlin, Connors & Massey, 1983, pp. 34–35)

Further, parents who were interviewed at the city council meeting were very positive about the depth of knowledge students had acquired and their confidence in making their cases before the august authorities on city council. The hidden curriculum in this program had involved learning roles and self-concepts, but not that of the passive knower.

Ban the bars

Bev Priftis had gotten to the section of Bruner's *Man—A Course of Study* where they learn about the behavior of baboons when she decided to take her Calgary grade seven class to the zoo to observe the nature and behavior of a baboon troop. When her students found the primates kept in individual cages, they were upset by how this contradicted what had been learned about the social organization and territoriality of these animals. They wrote letters of protest to the Zoological Society, the Mayor, the Queen and the editors of the *Calgary Herald* and the *Albertan*. At first, the head of the Zoological Society charged that the students were uninformed, childish, and irresponsible. The "Ban the Bars" movement grew in the city, however, and eventually the baboons were removed from the zoo because a suitable environment could not be provided. Students' sense of political efficacy was reinforced by seeing that their actions could be effective in making their community a better place for all to live in (Dueck, Horvath & Zelinski, 1977).

Clean up the dump

Three grade six and seven classes in rural Rimbey spent two months learning about provincial law on solid waste disposal, surveying other towns to learn about their dumps, observing the dripping pesticide cans and lamb carcasses in their dump, reading newspapers and magazines, surveying residents for their opinions, interviewing the district agriculturist, home economist and mayor, and reading government studies on disposal. Finally, they were ready to propose a set of solutions. They wrote letters to the *Rimbey Record*, entered a float in the rodeo parade, wrote several letters to the town and country councils, put out more garbage cans on the rodeo grounds, made posters to advertise the issue and presented their proposals at a town council meeting (Johncox, 1983).

Save our park

When city planners proposed putting a freeway through a ravine in an Edmonton community, the whole school set out to prepare a submission to the Transportation Task Force hearings. Teachers from grade one to grade six worked with their students to write letters, draw posters and speak to the hearings. Eight student representatives carried the school messages to the hearings, gave brief speeches on why they didn't want the ravine destroyed and submitted picture books bearing their submissions. Later, the Task Force recommended the ravine be developed as a community park and that no freeway be routed there. City council later incorporated these recommendations into their transportation and parks plan, and today the ravine is preserved as a park (Chamberlin, 1979).

Many more examples could be added to this list to illustrate how Alberta students have learned that the desired role of a citizen is to know what's going on, be part of it and do something about it. The passive knowing model of citizenship seems to ignore the importance of a sense of political efficacy and its class-based distribution. In failing to include it, many teachers also fail

---

If students learn that it is enough to make an informed decision on an issue without acting on it, how can we expect them to say, "Well, now that I know how to go about getting something done right that I think is wrong, I would probably try to change it?"

---

to adequately strive for the moral principle of equality Newmann argued is essential to human dignity. The passive knower model of citizenship leaves the school and social studies open to the charge that they do too little to end the role of the school in reproducing a society in which a rich, well educated elite dominate a passive working class. They seem to have ignored the work of such critics of the school as Apple, Bernstein, Bowles and Gintis, Giroux and Freire who point out how the school transmits passivity and acceptance of the status quo to working-class students. The omission of an action component also seems to ignore the work on developing a sense of political efficacy and an internal locus of control done by Ehman, Verba and Nie, Massialas, Peyton and Miller and others.

If students learn that it is enough to make an informed decision on an issue without acting on it, how can we expect them to say, "Well, now that I know how to go about getting something done right that I think is wrong, I would probably try to change it?"

TEN REASONS FOR QUESTIONING THE ACTIVIST CITIZEN MODEL OF ELEMENTARY SOCIAL STUDIES

LARRY GLASSFORD

In the inaugural edition of *Canadian Social Studies*, Chuck Chamberlin (1991) argues for a vigorous emphasis on political action as an indispensable part of the elementary social studies curriculum. Pre-teen students, he asserts, should be encouraged to move far beyond the acquisition of passive knowledge of their world. In Chamberlin's view, they ought to be trained as active doers, not just in the classroom, but also in the political arena. As examples to be emulated, he reviews several instances in Alberta where "teachers have had their students inquiring into a wide range of social issues, culminating their inquiry with varied forms of direct and indirect action." In one case, a grade four class wrote letters to the provincial premier concerning a proposed pulp mill, and then was interviewed before TV news cameras. In another case, grade five and six students presented findings about the chemical spraying of mosquitoes to a city council meeting. Chamberlin is delighted that the teachers of these elementary classes utilized a decision-making model that culminated in taking public action. "Alberta students," he concludes, "have learned that the desired role of a citizen is to know what's going on, be part of it, and do something about it."

What could be wrong with that? Actually, there are a number of reasons to question this activist citizen model. First, though, let us be clear on one matter. As writer of this rejoinder, I do not hold up the traditional passive learner model as the ideal instructional situation. Active learning is, generally, more effective learning. And what about elementary students taking direct or indirect political action? Certainly, as Chamberlin describes the Alberta social studies curriculum, "if feasible and desirable." It's a big "IF"!

I now move to some objections to the activist model, listed here in descending numerical order.

10. Our kids are not always on the side of the angels.

Any conscientious parent knows this. Children are much the same blend of selflessness and selfishness as the adults they eventually become. But oh, how the news media love children, especially in the assumed role of *informed innocence*, questioning some established authority. Not even the advertising might and savvy of McDonald's could withstand the battering of Toronto-area elementary schoolchildren in one recent instance. Brought by their teacher to stand in the shadow of the golden arches, they politely protested the use of styrofoam containers before the eager news cameras. Never mind that the hastily-summoned replacement packaging is deemed by some experts to pose just as daunting an environmental challenge. The kids are back at their favorite restaurant, munching fries and burgers much as before. A triumph of the active citizenship model? I don't think so!

9. Do real teachers picket City Hall?

Are there really an infinite number of absolutely clear-cut, white-hat-vs.-black-hat causes around, so that every elementary social studies teacher in every community can in clear conscience guide succeeding classes, year after year, to take meaningful action in the political arena? And what of the teacher who believes simulating the real world of politics in the classroom is a valid active learning approach? According to Chamberlin, the absence of direct or indirect political action at the end of the research and decision making process is an alarming omission. Teachers who failed to lead their students all the way to community action would not be doing their job. They would be guilty of encouraging their pre-teen students "to know about the world, but not to act on it."

8. To everything there is a season.

The activist model as presented by Chamberlin is built on two questionable assumptions. First, in order to have a participatory citizenry, people must be trained for activism by the schools. Second, this activist training must be fully implemented by grade six. Otherwise, he writes, "teaching students to be passive knowers rather than active doers defeats the key principle of democratic government, consent of the governed." To choose an historical example, would Chamberlin mean to imply that Thomas Jefferson and company waged resistance to British rule largely because their schools two or three decades earlier had specifically trained them in confrontational tactics? In fact, one assumes the American patriots took direct action because they decided it was both "feasible and desirable." With regard to the second assumption, why the insistence that the political action model be fully implemented by grade six? Does all effective learning end then? Or is it simply the case that preadolescent children are less apt to think critically for themselves, and therefore more likely to reach the conclusions indicated for them by their well-meaning activist teachers?

7. What happens when political action fails?

Chamberlin writes "unless students believe their efforts will be effective, all the knowledge in the world is unlikely to lead them to be responsible citizens who participate constructively." It is vital, he maintains, that elementary students acquire a strong sense of political efficacy. And yet, many of these classroom initiated campaigns are bound to fail. Even if every protest, every petition, every letter writing project were totally valid (a most unlikely possibility), some of them would encounter opposing political forces of greater strength, and consequently would fail to achieve the children's objectives. Moreover, most public issues cannot be reduced to such stark good-vs.-evil terms. Political choices generally involve a complex assessment of possible outcomes, with no ironclad guarantees of right or wrong. Students who celebrated an apparent victory in grade four might come to see, with the passage of time, that the outcome they advocated and helped produce was turning out to be the wrong one. In either case—on the side of right but unsuccessful; or, successful but ultimately on the side of wrong—the students' sense of political efficacy would be diminished, not augmented.

6. Do real citizens picket City Hall?

Imagine a society where everyone is extremely active politically. This may be a vision of the perfect polity for Professor Chamberlin and the authorities he cites (chiefly F. Newmann and G.E. Wood), but others might see it as a recipe for chaos. In fact, one might argue that high rates of political activity by the citizenry is a sign not of a thriving political system, but of precisely the opposite: a political system that is not functioning well at all in the interests of its citizens. Most people in functional societies find other legitimate pursuits to occupy the bulk of their time: family, recreation, culture, religion and community service. What happened to the "Big Chill" generation of 1960s-style activists? They grew up, got jobs, started families, took on mortgages and assumed responsibility for running the institutions they once confronted. Direct democracy, with every citizen participating actively and continuously in the political process, does not seem to offer a viable long-term alternative. It must be remembered that ancient Athens, often seen as a role model for democratic citizen participation, disenfranchised both women and slaves, who together formed the great majority of the adult population (Kitto, 1957).

5. Balance efficacy with trust and support.

Professor Chamberlin stresses the great importance of nurturing in students a sense of political efficacy, which he rightly associates with "active citizenship," but nowhere does he mention trust or support, also vital elements in a successful political system (Almond & Verba, 1965). In fact, he is all but contemptuous of "these 9 to 10-year-olds [who] agreed with the importance of obedience, good manners, loyalty, hard work, and respect for Canada's institutions." Such apparently unworthy values are dismissed as mere evidence of "passive citizenship." Furthermore, he takes the schools to task for their success, along with the children's own parents, in developing these attributes. And yet, can we imagine a livable society without such qualities as loyalty, respect, and trust?

4. Power culture or counterculture?

"Picketing, protesting, democratic takeovers" were the core of 1960s-style radical campus politics. Are these really the most effective ways to achieve meaningful political change? In point of fact, these are marginal strategies, often the last resort of interest groups who have failed in more conventional attempts to influence the political process (Van Loon & Whittington, 1987). Certainly students need to know that picketing and

Use this as a learning process- what can we do next?

protesting are options one may select. It is not clear that every elementary student needs a direct experience in placard-carrying by the age of 12. Furthermore, teachers owe it to their students to acquaint them with the deeper realities of political power. Most of it is wielded out of sight, not in the streets or on TV. No amount of instructional manipulation at the elementary level is likely to change that fact. Equating political efficacy with letter writing and public demonstrations may actually do students a disservice if it misleads them about who really gets what, when, how in this country.

> Equating political efficacy with letter writing and public demonstrations may actually do students a disservice if it misleads them about who really gets what, when, how in this country.

3. Don't forget organized interest groups.

Professor Chamberlin argues that Canadian politics are typified by "working-class passivity," a state of affairs he finds intolerable. Evidence to sustain this conclusion is apparently based, at least in part, on an American study conducted some two decades ago. One wonders if this view takes proper account of the growth in profile and influence of such broad-based interest groups as the Canadian Auto Workers, the National Action Committee for the Status of Women and the Assembly of First Nations. Surely factory workers, women and Native people qualify as valid representatives of the working class in its broader sense. "Passive" does not come to mind as an accurate description of these groups in recent years (Sheppard & Valpy, 1982).

2. English-speaking Canada is a distinct society.

The political culture of English-speaking Canada differs from that of the United States. Basic assumptions developed about American society do not necessarily apply in this country. The activist citizenship model is an apt illustration. The political sociologist S.M. Lipset, for instance, has written convincingly of the significantly higher levels of deference to constituted authority evident north of the Canadian-American border, as compared with south of it (1970). One may applaud or deplore this essential difference, but not ignore it. When Chamberlin states that this is "a country that prides itself on being a democratic society where political participation is essential," he may be describing the United States more than Canada. This land of the maple leaf is, after all, the country that placed "peace, order and good government" prominently in its founding constitution, rather than "life, liberty and the pursuit of happiness." The difference is significant and persistent.

1. Let us not confuse ideology with pedagogy.

"Responsible citizenship" is the announced goal of the activist education model, but achieving fundamental changes to a perceived "class-based" society appears to be the real agenda. "The passive knower model of citizenship," Chamberlin writes, "leaves the school and social studies open to the charge that they do too little to end the role of the school in reproducing a society in which a rich, well educated elite dominates a passive working class." The egalitarian ideal is appealing in theory, but one searches in vain for working models in countries the size of Canada. In recent years, several self-described parties of the working class have been driven from power in eastern Europe and the former Soviet Union, after spectacularly failing to deliver the goods, either politically or economically. Marxian analysis of the failings of bourgeois capitalism and bourgeois democracy was, and is, perceptive (Marx & Engels, 1959). Marxist prescriptions for a better society have been thoroughly discredited. As an alternative to the creation of a classless society of extremely active political participators, perhaps one might substitute the development of effective cooperation and leadership qualities in our students as a more realistic goal of citizenship education.

To know and then to act is insufficient. To know, and then to act wisely: there's the problem.

WHAT VISION OF DEMOCRACY SHOULD GUIDE CITIZENSHIP EDUCATION? A RESPONSE TO LARRY GLASSFORD

CHUCK CHAMBERLIN

In spite of Professor Glassford's list of 10 objections to the activist conception of citizenship education, it is clear that the root of our disagreement lies in our conceptions of the good society and the role of the school in preparing Canada's youth for citizenship in that society. Professor Glassford correctly recognizes that my vision of a good society is a democracy in which all citizens feel competent, confident, and responsible to participate in shaping the direction of change. To be competent, they must be knowledgeable about why the world is as it is and how it could be changed to make it better. To be confident they must have had life experiences in being accepted as legitimate participants in governance of classroom, school, community or broader areas. To be responsible they need to see some of the positive and negative consequences of their decisions and feel the effects.

Contrasted to this conception of participatory democracy is one implied in Professor Glassford's article. He refers to participation as chaotic, points to the importance of loyalty, obedience and respect for institutions and suggests that simulating action is as good as real participation in social issues.

Two of the principles of democracy that mandate a social action model of citizenship education are consent of the governed and equal opportunity for all to actively participate in governance. Consent is not the same as passive acceptance of others' proposals, but rather informal and positive espousal. Newmann (1975) has developed this rationale, as have Oliver and Shaver (1967), Barber (1984), Wood (1984) and others. Freire (1972) uses the Spanish term *autogestion* in a similar way, meaning that a community takes responsibility collectively for the planning and action needed to shape their future together. At the school level, *autogestion* and consent of the governed means that students take an active role in openly debating what goals, rules and projects will constitute their future, as Kohlberg (1981) described in his concept of a "Just School," and as currently required by law in Denmark. At the community level, it means that current issues such as using chemical sprays for mosquitoes in Red Deer, or solid waste disposal in Rimbey be seen as public issues that all citizens feel responsible for helping resolve.

It must be noted that contrary to Professor Glassford's conclusion that black-white or good-evil issues would be used, these are complex issues involving competing values, long-term consequences, and are part of global as well as local dilemmas. Having spent last week with Danish primary school children who had just returned from two weeks in Minsk, Belorussia, and who spoke knowledgeably about how Denmark could help, I am convinced Canadian children are equally capable of learning to accept responsibility for understanding the social issues facing their communities and taking informal action. This is reinforced by having listened to Red Deer students show city council that they were much better informed about the economic, environmental, health, recreational and social consequences of using chemical sprays than their elders were.

Central to the argument for a social action model of citizenship education is the importance of a sense of political efficacy. This feeling that our efforts to affect decisions about the future of our communities will be fruitful is not inborn, but is socially learned, and as Newmann (1975) shows, is primarily learned by children from wealthier families whose parents are used to effectively exerting influence. Children from poorer families are more likely to learn from their parents that "you can't fight City Hall," so why waste your time trying? Schools that provide no opportunity for all children, rich and poor, to develop a sense of political efficacy are contributing to the maintenance of a society where the wealthy confidently pick up the phone and invite the mayor to lunch at their country club to discuss changing the zoning of residential land to commercial use, while the poor despair of being heard. By providing children with an opportunity to see themselves as responsible for and capable of participating in social decisions, the school is taking a role in contrib-

uting to the kind of democracy in which active consent of the governed is more equally distributed among children of the rich and poor. Otherwise, schools by default contribute to inegalitarian participation in making social decisions where the children with a strong sense of political efficacy who are from wealthier families will be the movers and shakers.

I was pleased that Professor Glassford spoke up for the status quo and for passive citizenship education goals as it may provoke further critical reflection among Canada's citizenship educators about the kind of society they value and the role of the school in preparing students for their future in that society. To the extent that teachers more clearly think through the alternatives, they can accept conscious responsibility for their decisions and teaching acts, thus being good citizens as well as good teachers.

REFERENCES

Alberta Education. (1989). *Social studies teachers' resource manual*. Edmonton: Alberta Education.

Almond, G. A. & Verba, S. (1965). *The civic culture: Political attitudes and democracy in five nations*. Boston: Little, Brown.

Barber, B. (1984). *Strong democracy: Participatory politics for a new age*. Berkeley, CA: University of California Press.

Chamberlin, C. (1979). A whole elementary school takes social action. *One World*, *17*(4), 13–14.

Chamberlin, C. (1991). Citizenship as the goal of social studies: Passive knower or active doer. *Canadian Social Studies*, *26*(1), 23–26.

Chamberlin, C., Connors, B. & Massey, D. (1983). Project Athens: Can schools teach active citizenship? *One World*, *22*(2), 33–39.

Dueck, K., Horvath, F. & Zelinski, V. (1977). Bev Priftis' class takes on the Calgary Zoo. *One World*, *17*(4), 7–9.

Engle, S. & Ochoa, A. (1988). *Education for democratic citizenship*. New York: Teachers College Press.

Freire, P. (1972). *Pedagogy of the oppressed*. New York: Herder & Herder.

Hungerford, H. & Peyton, R. (1976). *Teaching environmental education*. Portland, ME: J. Weston Walsh.

Johncox, B. (1983). Rimbey environmental action project. *One World*, *22*(2), 25–29.

Kitto, H.D.F. (1957). *The Greeks*. Harmondsworth, UK: Penguin.

Kohlberg, L., *et al*. (1981). Evaluating Scarsdale's "Just Community School" and its curriculum: Implications for the future. *Moral Education Forum*, *6*, 31–42.

Lipset, S.M. (1970). *Revolution and counter-revolution: Change and persistence in social structures*. New York: Anchor.

Marx, K. & Engels, F. (1959). *Basic writings on politics and philosophy*. Lewis S. Feuer (Ed.). New York: Anchor.

Newmann, F. (1975). *Education for citizen action*. Berkeley, CA: McCutcheon.

Oliver, D. & Shaver, J. (1966). *Teaching public issues in*

the high school. Boston: Houghton Mifflin.

Sheppard, R. & Valpy, M. (1982). *The national deal.* Toronto: Fleet.

Taylor, D. & Moore, R. (1983). Red Deer environmental action project. *One World, 22*(2), 8–13.

Van Loon, R. J. & Whittington, M.S. (1987). *The Canadian political system: Environment, structure and process* (4th ed.). Toronto: McGraw-Hill Ryerson.

Wood, G.E. (1984). Schooling in democracy: Transformation or reproduction? *Educational Theory, 34*(3), 219–239.

These articles, reprinted with the permission of University of Toronto Press Incorporated, appeared originally in 1991 in *Canadian Social Studies, 26*(1), 23-26 and in 1992 in *Canadian Social Studies, 27*(1), 28-29 and 30. Minor alterations to the original articles have been made for stylistic and format purposes.

29

All Talk and No Action? The Place of Social Action in Social Studies

Penney Clark

It is generally agreed that the preparation of citizens is the *raison d'être* of social studies. However, establishing that citizenship education is the ultimate purpose of social studies doesn't tell us very much. The crucial question to address is—what exactly are the qualities of a good citizen? It can be argued that it is insufficient to develop the capacity for informed debate on social issues; effective citizenship also requires developing the will and the ability to *act* to address local, national and global problems.

In fact, nurturing students' ability to engage in social action has a long tradition both in the scholarly literature and in social studies curricula. William Kilpatrick (1918) in the United States and Hubert Newland (1943) in Canada, both influenced by John Dewey, were pioneers in the area of progressive education. Kilpatrick advocated an integrated curricular approach which he called the "project method." This activity-oriented approach included community concerns, with learning taking place both in the school and community settings. Newland, Supervisor of Schools for Alberta, spearheaded curriculum innovations in the 1930s and '40s in that province. In these curricula, Kilpatrick's "project" method appeared as the "enterprise" approach, in which social studies formed the core of an integrated approach to subject matter. The classroom was to be a mini-democracy in which decision-making was shared between students and teacher. Students were to develop a sense of social responsibility which would carry over from the classroom into the broader community. Action projects included school gardens, school and community beautification projects and community newspapers. Versions of the "enterprise" approach appeared in curricula across Canada.

Following the wave of progressive curricula in the 1930s and '40s, Canadian provincial departments of education retreated to a more content-focussed "academic" curriculum in the 1950s and '60s. In the 1970s a conception of citizenship as reflective inquiry gained prominence in social studies, particularly at the secondary level. Various programs, such as the *Canadian Critical Issues Series* (Eisenberg & Levin, 1972-1981), developed at the Ontario Institute for Studies in Education, provided students with case studies of current Canadian social issues for analysis and discussion. Students were expected to explore various perspectives and reach decisions as to their own positions, but the focus was on issue analysis and not on the further step of social action.

Fred Newmann (1975) and John Goodlad (1984), two prominent American educators, have been vocal in calling for students to proceed beyond discussing social issues to acting on them. In Canada, monographs such as Kenneth Osborne's *The Teaching of Politics: Some Sug-*

gestions for Teachers (1982) offer suggestions for carrying out social action projects. Increased emphasis on social action also became apparent in provincial curricula. The 1981 Alberta curriculum incorporated this notion with the seventh (optional) step of its inquiry model, "applying the decision," which encouraged students to "create a plan of action to apply the decision (e.g., work for an improved school or classroom environment, provide services to a community group on a close interpersonal basis, express ideas in social settings, or participate actively in a political process)" (Alberta Education, 1981, p. 9). A more recent curriculum in Alberta endorses instead what it calls "responsible citizenship" (Alberta Education, 1988). The Manitoba social studies curriculum recommends social action activities such as volunteer work with the elderly and participation in a political campaign (Manitoba Education, 1985). *The Common Curriculum* of Ontario refers to service activities in the home or school community, as well as at the global level (Ontario Ministry of Education, 1993). British Columbia's *Integrated Resource Packages* for social studies ask students at almost every grade to plan and implement a course of action to address an issue of personal or social concern (British Columbia Ministry of Education, Skills and Training, 1996a, 1996b, 1996c).

The call to action can take many forms and hold many rewards; there are, however, pitfalls to be avoided. Students need to be taught both how to make sound decisions about social problems and how to responsibly plan and carry out action projects based on those decisions. This article focusses on the second part of this challenge—developing students' ability to plan and carry out social action projects. It discusses direct and indirect approaches to social action and explores criteria for selecting and conducting social action projects.

DIRECT AND INDIRECT SOCIAL ACTION

Social action projects can be seen to belong on a continuum from the two poles of *direct action*—directly addressing a problem oneself, at the one end, and *indirect action*—influencing, or using as intermediaries, those who hold power and who are in a position to affect change, at the other. Both direct and indirect action can occur at either the local or global level. Examples of direct local action include cleaning up the school grounds or a local park, raising money for playground equipment, setting up a "buddy" system for new students, visiting the elderly at a senior citizen's home or caring for animals at a local wildlife habitat. An example of indirect local action is lobbying school or community authorities to change an undesirable rule or policy.

Several efforts of elementary students in North Vancouver to improve their community are described in the box "Cleaning Up Their Act." These are examples of indirect action because students lobbied officials in political and government positions who had the authority and influence to take action if they could be convinced to do so.

The difference between direct and indirect action at the global level is less clearcut. An example of a direct action project at the global level involved a grade 9/10 mechanics class in Prince George, British Columbia, which constructed twelve hand-operated water pumps for a rural development project in northern Kenya. Students were provided with both general information about East Africa, and specific information such as the fact that women in rural Kenya spend an average of four hours per day gathering water, which is most often contaminated. After the pumps were sent to Kenya (through a development agency) the class received an

---

CLEANING UP THEIR ACT

Elementary students in two North Vancouver schools engaged in social action as a result of problems they examined in their social studies program. A grade four and five French Immersion class at Ross Road Elementary made a presentation to North Vancouver District officials advocating the suspension of a proposed residential development in an inter-river wilderness area. Prior to the presentation students toured the district hall and met with the Mayor, and also a forest industry representative to discuss forest management. They also performed a play involving a developer who wanted to cut down trees in a small town.

Kindergarten and grade four students from Maplewood Community School in the same school district engaged in indirect social action against the planned development of Vancouver Port Corporation-owned land in the Maplewood mudflats. These students sent letters to the port corporation, the North Vancouver District Mayor, the federal Transport Minister, the Prime Minister, the provincial premier, and environment critics from the provincial NDP and Liberal parties. One grade four student wrote in his letter, "Without the mudflats no one will see the animals again. The only time you will see birds is when they pass by. How would you like it if animals took away your buildings? I do not think you would like that."

The Maplewood kindergarten teacher commented that, "Our environment is endangered and the children need to realize that their voices count. This process is a good one for them to learn how to think persuasively and act on something that they feel strongly about."

These examples of social action were described in "Students wake up to environmental concerns," by Michael Becker in the North Shore News.

audio film which showed their pumps being assembled, and later a photograph of a Kenyan villager drawing clear water from the first installed pump. "Adopting" a child from a developing country can also be an example of direct action to the extent that students have direct involvement and a degree of control from the initial planning and fund-raising through to the end results. They have personal information about the "adoptee" and are aware of the family's living circumstances. In addition, students normally have personal contact in the form of letters and photographs. They know how the money is to be used, can see its effects and can send additional money or goods if they wish. Collecting and sending books to a school or library in a developing country is another example of direct global action. PROJECT LOVE, sponsored by CODE (Canadian Organization for Development through Education), involves Canadian students in sending kits containing basic school supplies to classrooms in developing countries. A final example of direct global action involved a group of students from three school districts near Victoria, British Columbia ("BC Students Team Up," 1996, p. 5). These students raised $6,000 to build a school in a Kenyan village as a way of commemorating the 1994 Commonwealth Games, which took place in Victoria. They gathered information by communicating with a Canadian development worker in Kenya and interviewing Kenyan athletes who were attending the Games. Fund-raising efforts included a benefit concert.

An example of indirect global action is fund-raising in order to send money to a relief organization. Students know they are helping in a general sense, but there is no direct contact with the people being helped, and they have no control over how the funds are administered. There is also no opportunity to observe specific results of their actions.

SELECTING SOCIAL ACTION PROJECTS

Social action projects must be selected carefully. Several criteria are worthy of consideration:

- Will the project promote a sense of empowerment on the part of students?
- Will the project develop a range of civic competencies?
- Will the project promote academic learning?
- Is there a high degree of student interest and personal commitment?
- Is the cost in teacher time worth the potential benefits?
- Is there a high probability of success in the eyes of students?

Student empowerment

"You know, I didn't think something I did could really matter. Now I know that I can make a difference" (reported in Reindl, 1993, p. 44). This was the message given by many students in a grade four and five class to their teacher following an extensive direct social action project. These students conducted food drives to help the needy in their local community, persevering in spite of heckling from older students, because the project was important to them. They also "adopted" a battered women's shelter and raised funds to purchase a swingset for children staying at the shelter. In the teacher's words:

> I found myself trusting them more and more as the year went on and seeing that they could handle it, that it wasn't going to be devastating for them because they were having the opportunity to do something about it. With children you just can't let them feel hopeless. I think they can deal with almost anything as long as they know it doesn't have to be that way. (p. 44)

If students do not feel they have the abilities and resources to affect change, they are unlikely to wish to participate.

These students saw situations which disturbed them and, with the encouragement of their teacher, did something about them. As a result of their actions, they developed a feeling of empowerment, a sense that they could indeed change the world around them for the better. A second interesting point in this regard, as illustrated by the following comment, is that the teacher too, felt a sense of empowerment: "If I never do anything else with kids for the rest of my life, I will feel that, in letting these kids do this, I made a contribution" (p. 46).

If students do not feel they have the abilities and resources to affect change, they are unlikely to wish to participate. For this reason, particularly for young children, it may be worthwhile to focus their social action on the classroom or school environments. These are places where they should feel comfortable and where they can actually see the changes which their actions have wrought. Such projects include forming a "Green Team" to promote recycling, sponsoring a bicycle safety program, forming a team of crosswalk guards or tutoring other students who are experiencing difficulty.

Involvement in social action projects seems to develop both assertiveness and self-esteem (Kohn, 1990). Students who work in projects where they see that they have made a difference feel valued and involved (Yaeger & Patterson, 1996). Although there is much discussion of empowerment in educational literature (Apple, 1982; Giroux, 1988) few have studied it in the context of empowering students in classrooms. Rahima Wade (1995) is an exception. She spent most of a school year in a grade four classroom and assisted students in a number of social action projects. She concluded that student ownership of a project is central to the development of a sense of empowerment. Students must see a connection between the activity and their own interests. Other critical factors were the teacher's willingness to relinquish some control of classroom decision-making, and the teacher's actions in fostering empowerment, such as providing choices and including time in the school day for student-initiated projects. Wade cautions that these findings do not necessarily indicate that students will become socially proactive adults. As she points out, this is dependent on a number of factors such as family influences and other experiences, students' own personalities and interests, as well as additional school opportunities to hone their social action skills.

Development of civic competencies

Social action projects schould provide opportunities to develop and refine various civic competencies. These include competencies in the areas of organization of information, writing of proposals and reports, delivering public presentations, cooperating with others to achieve a shared goal, listening thoughtfully to the ideas and opinions of others, constructing a compelling argument and interacting effectively with adults.

Grade two teacher Syma Solovitch-Haynes (1996) has detailed the successful efforts of her students in Central Harlem, New York, to rename a street as Mary McLeod Bethune Place, after they noticed that there were no streets in their area named after African American women. In the course of working to achieve the goal of their indirect social action project students learned how to conduct research in order to find the information they needed, how to access the legislative process, how to organize and get signatures on a petition and how to prepare and present testimony in public forums.

McCall (1996, p. 206) has suggested a list of competencies for discussing social issues and planning social action projects:

- One person talks at a time; all listen to the speaker.

- Each person voices his or her views, even if disagreeing with others.

- The views of others must be clear to all participants, even if there is disagreement.

- Speakers must strive to build confidence in others and not use put-downs.

- The contributions made to the class discussions are confidential.

- All participants should challenge themselves to take risks during the discussion and present their opinions.

- All may pass at any time during the discussion if they prefer not to contribute.

The value of all of these civic competencies cannot be underestimated. Not only will they be of use to students throughout their lives, but they contribute to the sense of empowerment discussed earlier.

Development of academic learnings

Academic learnings are also promoted through social action projects. For instance, academic peer-tutoring projects in reading and math have been shown to have a positive effect on the achievement scores in these subject areas for both tutors and those being tutored (Hedin, 1987). This is probably because these social action projects are directly related to academic learning. Although research findings about academic achievement are less conclusive for other types of social action, it is clear that social action projects can provide opportunities for academic skill development. Examples include honing mathematics skills when keeping track of money received through a fund-raising project, developing language arts skills when organizing and synthesizing information and writing reports, and improving social studies skills when analyzing and evaluating data for bias and stereotyping. Social action projects also develop knowledge. Lewis (1991) describes the academic skills and knowledge promoted as her elementary students sought to eliminate hazardous waste sites in Utah. Students honed their speaking and writing skills as they learned to communicate effectively by means of telephone calls, letters and proposals. When they decided to try to change a state law, she taught them the process of passing a bill. They used math skills when they compiled survey data and when they calculated the possible profits from their fundraising efforts.

Student interest and commitment

There is little point in attempting to pursue a project for which students are unenthusiastic. Wade (1995) found, when working with a grade four class in a suburban American school over the course of a school year, that unless students saw a meaningful or enjoyable connection between a social action project and their own lives, they had little interest in further involvement. In a direct social action project at the global level, Wade tried to interest students in fund-raising to purchase a goat for a poor family in Haiti. Most students voted to engage in the project, but only three students came to an out-of-school meeting to plan a course of action. She abandoned the project, concluding that it was too far removed from their own interests and life experiences, and therefore not meaningful to them.

Lewis (1991) describes how her upper elementary students from a low-income area became excited about school when they had a real social action project to pursue. As she says, "it was not an imaginary situation or a case study in a textbook—it existed in their neighborhood" (p. 47). She tells how engagement in social action made the curriculum relevant for these students and promoted their interest:

Children anxiously await answers to letters, and track legislation. No one knows for sure what will happen next. When the Jackson children sat in the Utah Legislature watching the votes for their hazardous waste fund flash on the wall, they exhibited as much enthusiasm as if they had been counting points on the scoreboard at a basketball game. (p. 49)

A grade eight class that wanted to help starving children in Africa, invited a speaker from the Eritrean Relief Society to speak to them (reported in Ashford, 1995). Because getting aid to the starving in wartorn countries can be difficult, the speaker suggested that the class send food through established agencies such as the Red Cross or UNICEF, but students wanted a more personal sense of contact. The speaker mentioned pen-pal exchanges, a possibility students had not considered. They were intrigued by the opportunity to establish contacts across the globe, and to assure children in Eritrea that they had not been forgotten by the world. As for providing food, students took on a project to help local homeless people. These students explored possibilities until they found projects that were personally satisfying to them.

It is not necessary that all students in a class participate in a particular project. Nor is it necessary that those who do not wish to become involved prevent others from having the opportunity to do so. Some students may not feel committed to an idea which has gripped other students. If this is the case, they can be provided with alternative activities. Also, some students, although committed to acting on the issue, may not be comfortable with the course of action chosen by the majority of the class. These students can be encouraged to choose other courses of action.

We should not presume that students will always be enthusiastic about the same projects that would interest adults (Wade, 1995). For example, in the context of creating a class Bill of Rights, students in a grade four class decided to write letters to their principal requesting permission to chew gum and wear hats in class. Most adults would not consider these issues of great importance, but the grade four students felt differently and decided to act on their concerns. Students' sense of empowerment can result only when they take ownership of, and feel enthusiasm about, a project.

Teacher time

Social action projects are time consuming. They often require considerable in-class and/or out-of-school time on the part of both students and teacher. Even student-initiated projects can involve a great deal of teacher time in providing guidance and assistance, particularly with elementary students. Wade (1995) concluded that, over the course of a school year, and with the involvement of both the classroom teacher and herself as researcher, it would be possible to support only a few grade four students in completing individual community service projects, in addition to class projects.

Wade found that students responded enthusiastically to projects where they were closely supervised and assisted by their teacher or other adult. Students did not carry carry through on projects where they were left to their own devices. For instance, students planned to write letters to American soldiers in Saudi Arabia, after one student suggested the plan; but, no-one followed through. However, most students were enthusiastic and participated in, a project initiated, organized and supervised by Wade, which involved making puppets to be sent to India to teach villagers to make a simple solution for curing diarrhea, a common killer of children.

Probability of success

There is a risk that students will feel that, in spite of all their efforts, they were ultimately unsuccessful in achieving their goals. There is risk of discouragement

We should not presume that students will always be enthusiastic about the same projects that would interest adults . . .

at every stage of a project. Lewis (1991) gives a description of one boy's discouragement very early on in his project:

> Successful phone calling is a simple place to begin. Students often fail at this initial step. For example, Joe may get access to use the school phones (which might require a notarized letter from his parent). He dials the main number for the Department of Transportation seeking information on the placement of a street light near the school. It takes four transfers before he reaches the correct party who can help him. Ms. So-and-So says she will mail some information to Joe and asks for the school address.

> Joe panics. Although he can instantly recall all the states in the NFL, he doesn't know the school address. He asks Ms. So-and-So to wait, then runs into the secretary's office to find out the address. Seven people are lined up at the secretary's desk. By the time Joe gets the address and returns to the phone, Ms. So-and-So has hung up. Joe can't remember how to get through to her again and gives up. His first attempt to become involved in citizenship, and he stubs his toe and loses interest. (p. 48)

Two ways to reduce the likelihood of perceived failure are to teach students the skills required to carry through the steps necessary to complete the project, and to encourage students to define "success" very broadly. The topic of developing the skills and competencies necessary to complete a social action project has been discussed previously. In terms of students' definition of success, it need not mean that the intended change is achieved. It can simply mean that students develop a sense of efficacy by actively participating in the process to affect change, even if, ultimately, that change does not occur. If students feel proud that they acted on their convictions, they are likely to want to engage in more such projects. Students should also be reminded that even though no immediate consequences stemmed from their social action, change may yet occur over the longterm.

Conducting Social Action Projects

There are many things to think of when guiding students through a social action project. Five particularly significant considerations for conducting social action projects are:

- Garner administrative and parental support prior to embarking on a project.
- Be well informed before proceeding.
- Anticipate major consequences of the social action.
- Use a structured procedure for conducting social action.
- Engage in systematic reflection on the experience.

Prior administrative and parental support

Social action projects can attract criticism. There are several reasons for this. First, they are more 'public' than many other school activities. Second, some people consider it inappropriate for students to be involved in social action projects in school time, when they should be engaged in activities which are more obviously curriculum-related. Third, some issues in which students become involved may be controversial.

Teachers need to judge the maturity of the students beforehand, as well as the community and curricular support for their actions. It is important to keep parents and the school administration informed as much as possible as to intents of the project and the methods which will be used to carry it out. It may be wise to clear the project beforehand with the school administration by pointing out the congruence of project objec-

---

Monkey Business

Bev Priftis took her grade seven students to the Calgary Zoo in order to extend inquiry into the nature and behaviour of baboons and other animals as part of a study of the unique characteristics of humans. The purpose of the unit, which was called *Man: A Course of Study*, was to promote student inquiry into the question, "What is human about human beings?"

As a result of their field trip experience, many students became concerned with the contradiction between what they had learned in class about social organization and territoriality, and the practice of caging baboons and other animals. The students decided to write letters of protest to the Zoological Society, the mayor of Calgary, the Queen and the editors of two daily papers.

The newspapers printed stories on the students' actions. One paper, in particular, emphasized the conflict between the attitudes of the Zoological Society and those of the students. The teacher was portrayed as incompetent, the students uncontrolled, and the zoo keeper inflexible. The head of the Zoological Society wrote a three-page letter charging that the students' criticisms were childish and irresponsible and that they had not been properly prepared for their field trip.

The response to her students' actions could have had negative repercussions on the career of the teacher. It was only her second year of teaching and permanent certificates were not granted until the end of two years teaching experience. Fortunately, she had laid the groundwork. She had become acquainted with the program, *Man: A Course of Study* by means of a professional workshop conducted by a member of the executive of the Social Science Education Consortium and western regional consultant for MACOS. The program was clearly consistent with the provincial curriculum and the supervisor of social studies had promised to purchase the material in order to pilot the program in the Calgary school system. Parents had been given an opportunity to become familiar with the program through informational meetings. Many were pleased at the enthusiasm it generated in their children, particularly those children who had not previously been interested in social studies. She also received a great deal of support from colleagues, including her principal and the professor who had originally introduced her to the program.

The teacher made use of the controversy which surrounded her students' social action to advance student learning. For instance, students compared the story as it appeared in the newspaper with the notes the teacher kept when the newspaper reporter interviewed her for the article. They examined the story for contradictions and evaluated it for bias and personal motives.

Largely because of the prior ground-work, this story has a happy ending. The Zoological Society and the community as a whole eventually endorsed the "Ban the Bars" movement. The baboons were removed from the zoo because it was not a suitable environment for them. MACOS continued to be taught in Calgary schools. Bev Priftis was recognized for her expertise in social studies methodology and became a social studies consultant with the Calgary Board of Education.

This example of social action is based on an article by Dueck, Horvath & Zelinski (1977).

---

tives with the curriculum. By doing this, if there is any negative parental or public response, the school administration is already aware of the project and its justification, and will not be taken by surprise (Kreisberg, 1993). Informing parents by letter of the proposed activities in which students will be engaging allows them to air concerns and helps to garner their support. This is preferable to explaining after the fact if there is some controversy. It can also be helpful to involve parents and others in discussions or as panel members when presenting different perspectives on the issue at hand.

It is inappropriate for a teacher to encourage students to engage in a project which violates the values of the community. For instance, a teacher should not lead students in an action which constitutes civil disobedience. The uproar caused by such an action could negate students' feeling of efficacy and make them unwilling to engage in future projects.

In the example opposite, a grade seven teacher and her class were criticized in the press for questioning the ethics of keeping animals in cages. Support for the actions of the class came by pointing to the congruence between objectives of the social action project and curriculum objectives, and by securing approval ahead of time from the school administration, curriculum specialists and parents.

Be well informed

I recently read a logger's description of his feelings as he walked into the local elementary school for a coach's meeting and encountered walls lined with posters depicting "barren landscapes dotted with stumps" (Warren, 1997). His reaction was shock and hurt. He wondered whether the teacher had taken the time to acquaint students with the benefits of logging or simply made them aware of the negative consequences before embarking on the poster project.

This account reminds me of an incident involving a grade one girl on the Sunshine Coast of British Columbia who came home from school and accused her logger father of being a murderer because his tree-cutting was eventually going to kill everyone. The little girl had been read a story at school about British Columbia's Carmanah Valley and environmentalists' efforts to save the old-growth trees there. Officials in the local of IWA-Canada were concerned about what they saw as an unbalanced treatment of logging and took the issue up with the local school board (Rees & Fraser, 1992).

This child should have been reminded that she used wood, in various ways, every day of her life. She needed to be helped to understand that loggers do no simply 'murder' trees, but chop them down in order to meet very real human needs. Even at six years old, a child can begin to appreciate the complexity of environmental issues, and that their solutions are more often a matter of balance than of taking an either-or position. Teachers have a responsibility to see that their students are well informed about opposing views and why people hold them. They require such information before

they can make responsible decisions to engage in social action.

Not only do students need to be well informed about different perspectives related to the issue with which they are dealing, they also need to be as informed as possible regarding the potential impact of various action options. Students in Toronto were highly successful in their efforts to have fast-food giant McDonald's change from its styrofoam "clamshell" packaging to paper (Roth, 1991). However, scientific experts, as well as environmentalists, have since argued that McDonald's has caused more harm than good by this move. For example, James Guillet (1990), Professor of Chemistry at the University of Toronto, stated that his own 25 years of research, as well as other scientific studies, simply did not support students' understanding that when plastic disintegrates, there is a chemical produced that has been associated with a breakdown of the Earth's ozone layer. As well, the volume of trees which would have to be cut down to provide the new paper packaging, and the magnitude of pollution produced through paper production, may be worse than the effects of plastics used in packaging. Guillet concluded with the following caution,

> Environmental problems are extraordinarily complex. There is no magic solution to pollution. What we must do to minimize environmental damage is to make informed and intelligent choices. Media-supported campaigns such as this make great television, but they also exploit the natural altruism of young children and do little to inform the public. Children's crusades should have no place in the formulation of public policy. (p. D7)

Not only may there be undesirable social consequences, but if students are misinformed when they begin a social action project or hold stereotypical viewpoints, the experience may fail to provide greater understanding or develop social action skills. In fact negative stereotypes can be reinforced. One researcher, after observing volunteer students at community food provision programs for three years, concluded that social action skills were not promoted through these experiences (Willison, 1994). When asked why they thought people went to the programs to obtain meals, students responded that clients were "hungry, homeless, excessive users of drugs and alcohol, unemployed, sick, uneducated, and do not want to work. On some occasions, students responded that the clients 'did not have any self-respect'" (p. 89). These negative stereotypes were reinforced by a teacher who made comments such as, "See how much sugar these people take, they need sugar because of drug addictions" (p. 88). Willison points out that these stereotypical notions were true for only a portion of the clients. Many were actually employed, but their income was insufficient to meet their needs. He suggests that preparation for a social action experience involving feeding the hungry should include an examination of poverty, and issues related to it, both historically and in a contemporary context.

He also suggests that students examine the history of local food provision programs and their sponsoring organizations. This kind of examination would enlighten students as to the social conditions of the community as a whole.

Anticipate major consequences

While it is impossible for students to anticipate all consequences of their proposed action, they should carefully consider possibilities and likely courses of action under various circumstances. An example of careful consideration of an action project is a grade eight class that decided to "adopt" a child in Africa (reported in Ashford, 1995). After carefully considering this plan class members realized that the project was not as desirable as it had initially seemed. It was a longterm project which could not be continued when students left grade eight, and there was no guarantee that the incoming grade eights would be willing to carry on with the commitment.

Recently grade five students in Surrey, British Columbia sent letters to *The Vancouver Sun*, expressing concern about the exploitation of Indonesian factory workers who make Nike products. These students were justifiably angry at Nike for paying their workers wages of $2.20 per day, while at the same time paying the basketball superstar Michael Jordan 20 million dollars a year for representing the company. Many of the students called for a boycott of Nike products. These students thought it worthwhile to take the time to write the letters in order to air their concerns in a public forum. They may well have chosen the best action under the circumstances. However, I hope that they investigated the situation before reaching the conclusion that a boycott was the best alternative. For instance, I hope they considered the possibility that driving up wages in Indonesia might result in Nike moving its factories to another country where labour costs are lower. The economic effects on the Indonesian workers could be devastating if this happened. (In fact, another article in the same newspaper mentioned that Nike is planning to move to Vietnam, where wages are lower.) Other large corporations considering options for locating their factories would also avoid Indonesia. Alternatives to a boycott of Nike may include encouraging the natural competition of the marketplace or getting all companies or countries in the region to establish minimum wage laws. Perhaps, as more large corporations build factories in Indonesia they will compete for the labour that is available and wages will rise. Canadian businessman, Subhash Khanna, who imports clothing from South Asia, has been quoted as saying, "If you don't do business with Third World countries you will increase their poverty and have more kids dying of hunger" (cited in Vincent, 1996, p. 50). It is important that students consider potential consequences before reaching a decision.

In similar vein, advocates for the banishment of child labour in Third World countries, such as thirteen-year-old Canadian, Craig Kielburger, have been cautioned by UNICEF about the complexity of the issues involved. UNICEF officials point out that child factory workers in developing countries are often the sole support of their families. If all child labour was banned, the families may starve and these children may be forced to turn to even less desirable sources of income such as prostitution. Many aid workers advocate, instead, that efforts be directed at the improvement of the children's working conditions, and provision of health care and educational programmes, rather than the outright ban of child labour (Vincent, 1996). A recent UNICEF report has recommended that governments focus their efforts on increasing educational opportunities, the enforcement of their own labour laws, and addressing social problems such as caste and ethnic divisions which are exacerbating the problem (Stackhouse, 1996). Clearly social action is complex and consequences must be considered carefully.

Use a structured procedure

It is recommended that, in learning to plan for social action, students follow a systematic approach to the issues they consider. Here is an example of such a procedure:

Identify the problem or issue
- Should we help disadvantaged people in our community?

Explore the nature of the problem and potential solutions. Pose research questions
- Are there people who need help in our community? Who are they?
- What services are provided now?
- What are ways we can help?

Conduct research
- Identify information sources such as community service agencies, nursing home personnel, and Christmas Bureau staff.
- Divide students into investigative groups and divide tasks accordingly.
- Use information sources to answer questions.

Synthesize, present and evaluate findings
- Groups prepare and present their findings to the class.

Make a decision about a particular course of action
- Students decide whether they wish to engage in a particular social action project to help the needy at this time.

Formulate an action plan (if decision is positive)
- Decide how the action will be carried out.

Determine feasibility of action plan
- Predict possible consequences of the action plan.
- Discuss the plan with information sources listed above.
- Finalize the plan.
- Check to see that most students are comfortable with the plan.

- Plan an alternative activity for those who are not comfortable with the action plan.
- Inform parents of the plan and obtain their permission if necessary.

Carry out the action plan

There are possibilities for both direct and indirect action.

- *Direct Action*: Collect and distribute goods and provide services to target groups and individuals.
- *Indirect Action*: Make a presentation to city council on the necessity to provide better services to the needy in the community and suggest ways this can be done.

Evaluate the action plan

Assess outcomes and procedures. Ask questions such as:

- Did we meet our objectives?
- Did we gain access to sufficient sources of information?
- Were there unforeseen consequences?
- What problems occurred?
- How could these problems have been avoided?
- Did we choose the best form of action to fit the needs of the people we were trying to help?[1]

Engage in systematic reflection

In order to make the social action experience as valuable as possible, students need to assess their decisions and actions in light of their own opinions, the opinions of other students, the responses of those who were affected by the action project, and both short- and long-term consequences. They also need to review the steps taken in order to determine whether they missed any which would have helped them to achieve their purposes more quickly or effectively. They need to review the alternative courses of action they might have chosen in light of their experiences. Ultimately, they need to ask themselves whether the course of action chosen was the best one under the circumstances. If willing to repeat it, under what circumstances would they do so?

FINAL THOUGHTS

There is no doubt that engaging in social action involves some risk. It can place both teachers and students in situations where they are unfamiliar with the circumstances and unsure how to proceed. Social action can be much more visible, and also more controversial, than other social studies activities and therefore invite criticism from outside sources. Nevertheless, there are many benefits. Prominent among these is a sense of empowerment, possession of which increases the likelihood that students will continue to be activists in their adult lives. In the final analysis, it is difficult to conceive of social studies as citizenship education without the possibility of social action. The "cost" of a social studies program that is all talk and no action, is the preparation of citizens who are unqualified and unwilling to work to improve their community, their nation or their world.

ENDNOTE

[1] For a structured process to plan and carry out a social action project, see Dueck's (1980) description of a project to reduce paper use in an elementary school.

REFERENCES

Air Jordan comes in for a crash landing with Surrey students. (1996, June 25). [Letters to the editor], *The Vancouver Sun*, p. A11.

Alberta Education. (1981). *1981 Alberta social studies curriculum*. Edmonton, AB: Author.

Alberta Education. (1988). *Junior high social studies teacher resource manual*. Edmonton, AB: Author.

Apple, M. (1982). *Education and power*. Boston: Routledge & Kegan Paul.

Ashford, M-W. (1995). Youth actions for the planet. In R. Fowler & I. Wright, (Eds.), *Thinking globally about social studies education* (pp. 75-90). Vancouver: Research and Development in Global Studies, University of British Columbia.

BC Students team up to build school in Kenyan village. (1996, April). *BC Education News*, p. 5.

British Columbia Ministry of Education, Skills and Training. (1996a). *Social studies K to 7 integrated resource package, Review document*. Victoria, BC: Author.

British Columbia Ministry of Education, Skills and Training. (1996b). *Social studies 8 to 10 integrated resource package, Review document*. Victoria, BC: Author.

British Columbia Ministry of Education, Skills and Training. (1996c). *Social studies 11 integrated resource package, Review document*. Victoria, BC: Author.

Conrad, D. & Hedin, D. (1991). School-based community service: What we know from research and theory. *Phi Delta Kappan, 72*(10), 743-749.

Dueck, K. (1980). Social action in elementary social studies. *History and Social Science Teacher, 15*(4), 245-251.

Dueck, K., Horvath, F. & Zelinski, V. (1977). Bev Priftis' class takes on the Calgary zoo. *One World, 17*(4), 7-8.

Eisenberg, J. & Levin, M. (Eds.) (1972-1981). *Canadian critical issues series*. Toronto: OISE.

Giroux, H.A. (1988). *Schooling and the struggle for public life*. Minneapolis: University of Minnesota Press.

Goodlad, John. (1984). *A place called school*. New York: McGraw-Hill.

Guillet, J. (1990, December 1). Kids' crusades bad idea. (Letter to the editor) *Globe & Mail*, p. D 7.

Hedin, D. (1987). Students as teachers: A tool for improving school climate and productivity. *Social Policy, 17*, 42-47.

Kilpatrick, W. (1918). The project method. *Teachers College Record, 19*, 319-335.

Kohn, A. (1990). *The brighter side of human nature: Altruism and empathy in everyday life*. New York: Basic Books.

Kreisberg, S. (1993). Educating for democracy and community: Toward the transformation of power in our schools. In S. Berman & P. La Farge (Eds.), *Promising practices in teaching social responsibility* (pp. 218-235). Albany, NY: State University of New York Press.

Lewis, B.A. (1991). Today's kids care about social action. *Educational Leadership, 49*(1), 47-49.

McCall, A.L. (1996). Making a difference: Integrating social problems and social action in the social studies curriculum. *Social Studies, 87*(5), 203-209.

Manitoba Education. (1985). *Social studies: K-12 overview*. Winnipeg: Author.

Newland, H.C. (1943a). Education and social reconstruction, part I. *B.C. Teacher, 23*, 18-20.

Newland, H.C. (1943b). Education and social reconstruction, part II. *B.C. Teacher, 23*, 57-61.

Newland, H.C. (1943c). Education and social reconstruction, part III. *B.C. Teacher, 23*, 98-101.

Newmann, F. (1975). *Education for citizen action*. Berkeley, CA: McCutcheon, 1975.

Ontario Ministry of Education. (1993). *The common curriculum: Grades 1-9*. Toronto: Queen's Printer.

Osborne, K. (1982). *The teaching of politics: Some suggestions for teachers*. Toronto: Canada Studies Foundation.

Reindle, S. (1993). Bringing global awareness into elementary school classrooms. In S. Berman, & P. La Farge (Eds.), *Promising practices in teaching social responsibility* (pp. 27-49). Albany, NY: State University of New York Press.

Rees, A. & Fraser, K. (1992, February 20). Book turns 6-year-old against her father. *The Province*, p. A3.

Roth, A. (1991, April). Battle of the clamshell. *Report on Business Magazine*, pp. 40-43, 45-47.

Scoten, J.A. (1988). *Integrating development education into industrial arts: A pilot project*. (Explorations in Development/Global Education, Occasional Paper #8). Vancouver: Centre for the Study of Curriculum and Instruction, Faculty of Education, University of British Columbia.

Solovitch-Haynes, S. (1996). Street-smart second-graders navigate the political process. *Social Studies & the Young Learner, 8*(4), 4-5.

Stackhouse, J. (1996, December 12). Hazardous child labour increasing. *Globe & Mail*, pp. A1, A12.

Vincent, I. (1996, November). The most powerful 13-year-old in the world. *Saturday Night*, pp. 40, 42-44, 46, 48, 50, 138.

Wade, R.C. (1995). Encouraging student initiative in a fourth-grade classroom. *Elementary School Journal, 95*(1), 339-354.

Warren, K. (1997). *Social action: At what cost?* Unpublished paper, Simon Fraser University, Burnaby, BC.

Willison, S. (1994). When students volunteer to feed the hungry: Some considerations for educators. *Social Education, 85*(2), 88-90.

Yaeger, E.A. & Patterson, M.J. (1996). Teacher-directed social action in a middle school classroom. *Social Studies & the Young Learner, 8*(4), 29-31.

SUPPLEMENTARY READINGS

Alter, G. (1995). Transforming elementary social studies: The emergence of curriculum focused on diverse, caring communities. *Theory and Research in Social Education, 23*(4), 355-374.

Association for Supervision and Curriculum Development. (1990). *Educational Leadership, 48*. This issue is devoted to the theme, "social responsibility."

Baydock, E., Francis, P., Osborne, K. & Semotok, B. (1984). *Politics is simply a public affair*. Toronto: The Canada Studies Foundation.

Berman, S. (1990). Educating for social responsibility. *Educational Leadership, 48*(2), 75-80.

Berman, S. & La Farge, P. (Eds.). (1993). *Promising practices in teaching social responsibility*. Albany, NY: State University of New York Press.

Botting, D., Botting, K., Osborne, K., Seymour, J. & Swyston, R. (1986). *Politics and you*. Scarborough, ON: Nelson.

Chamberlin, C. (1979). A whole elementary school takes social action. *One World, 17*(4), 13-14.

Chamberlin, C. (1985). Knowlege + commitment = action. In J. Parsons, G. Milburn & M. Van Manen (Eds.), *A Canadian social studies*, rev. ed. (pp. 231-248). Edmonton, AB: Faculty of Education, University of Alberta.

Chamberlin, C., Connors, B. & Massey, B. (1983). Project Athens: Can schools teach active citizenship? *One World, 22*(2), 33-39.

Conrad, D. (1991). School-community participation for social studies. In J.P. Shaver (Ed.), *Handbook of research on social studies teaching and learning* (pp. 540-548). New York: MacMillan.

Engle, S. & Ochoa, A. (1988). *Education for democratic citizenship*. New York: Teachers College Press.

Lyman, K. (1995). "AIDS—you can die from it." Teaching young children about a difficult subject. *Rethinking Schools, 10*(2), 14-15.

Nickell, P. (1997). Big lessons for little learners. *The Social Studies Professional: Newsletter of the National Council for the Social Studies, 127*, 3-4.

Nykolaychuck, J. (1979). Grade 5's clean up Grande Prairie. *One World, 17*(4), 12.

Shaheen, J.C. (1989). Participatory citizenship in the elementary grades. *Social Education, 53*(6), 361-363.

Van Scotter, R. (1994). What young people think about school and society. *Educational Leadership, 52*(3), 72-78.

Wade, R.C. (1994). Community service-learning: Commitment through active citizenship. *Social Studies and the Young Learner, 6*(3), 1-4.

Wade, R.C. (1996). Prosocial studies. *Social Studies and the Young Learner, 8*(4), 18-20.

Wade, R.C. & Saxe, D.W. (1996). Community service-learning in the social studies: Historical roots, empirical evidence, critical issues. *Theory and Research in Social Education, 24*(4), 331-359.

— ✦ —

30

Cooperative Learning in Social Studies

Tom Morton

Two decades ago, cooperative learning was on the radical margins of teaching. Since then it has marched—sometimes with considerable fanfare—to the centre stage of accepted educational practice. Researchers and practitioners alike applaud cooperative learning for its power to improve academic achievement, especially among children who have traditionally not done well in school, and for its potential to enhance interpersonal relations, especially among ethnic groups and between handicapped and able students.

Unfortunately, the centre stage role for cooperative learning has more often been in journal articles, teachers' guides and policy documents than in ordinary classrooms. In speaking of the United States, Seymour Sarasan (1995) suggests, rather bluntly, that what passes frequently for cooperative learning is a charade, often a misnomer for traditional group work. Although research on the current status in Canada is sparse, cooperative learning especially in our secondary schools may still be a fringe festival play—creative, exciting but marginal.

Although cooperative learning is a relatively recent term, coined by Morton Deutch (1949), the idea of group learning has been around much longer. At the beginning of the twentieth century, John Dewey recommended that students work together on problems that had relevance to their lives. However, the barriers to effective group work are longstanding and deeply rooted, often extending to the very core of teaching beliefs. Dewey (1916) once wrote of his attempt to buy work tables for his elementary school. He could not find anything other than individual desks. Finally, a salesperson identified the problem: "I am afraid we have not what you want. You want something at which the children may work. These are all for listening!" Similar practical and philosophical barriers impede effective implementation of cooperative learning.

This article seeks to clarify key elements of effective cooperative learning and to suggest ways of implementing cooperative approaches in social studies. Especially important is the need to appreciate that cooperation is not merely a teaching technique, but a fundamental commitment to a set of core values. I begin by offering three reasons why cooperative learning should play an important role in our subject and then explore three challenges to its implementation. The bulk of the article focusses on two of the best known among the many approaches to cooperative learning—the Johnsons' Learning Together model and Spencer Kagan's Structural Approach. I explore the principles of each, offer sample lessons and distinguish these models from each other and from traditional group work and direct instruction.

WHY COOPERATIVE LEARNING IN SOCIAL STUDIES?

Cooperative learning is an approach to teaching in which students work together in small groups that are carefully designed to be cohesive or positively interdependent. At the same time, group members are individually accountable for their own learning and for contributing to the group's learning. This approach to learning can contribute to the goals of social studies in at least three ways:

- **academic achievement**. Considerable research suggests that cooperative learning, properly implemented, promotes academic achievement—in the case of social studies, the acquisition of a body of knowledge in the social science disciplines and the ability to investigate and communicate these ideas. Two notable reviews, a meta-analysis of 475 research studies (Johnson & Johnson, 1989) and a similar review with stricter selection criteria of 60 studies (Slavin, 1989), concluded that cooperative learning produced moderately large gains in achievement when compared to control conditions.

- **constructivist learning**. There is considerable cognitive research suggesting that learners must "construct" knowledge if it is to be internalized and integrated with other background beliefs. Cooperative learning facilitates the transaction or construction of ideas. One of the more effective ways of making personal sense of ideas is to explain them to others. Perhaps this contemporary approach was expressed earliest by the Roman philosopher Seneca when he said, *Qui docet, discit*—whoever teaches, learns (also translated, when you teach, you learn twice).

- **citizenship values and attitudes**. Cooperative learning promotes the values and dispositions of a responsible citizen. Well planned cooperative lessons offer students opportunities to express and reflect on what the National Council for the Social Studies (1994, p. 5) calls civic competence—the abilities and values of citizenship. Since its early years, cooperative learning has been closely linked with promoting mutual respect and liking regardless of differences of intellectual ability, ethnicity, race, gender, handicapping conditions, social class or gender. It does this by encouraging students to appreciate their own background and those of others, and by fostering commitment to a set of foundational values including respect for civic responsibilities, freedom of expression, fairness and equality.

CHALLENGES TO COOPERATIVE LEARNING

The prominent researcher, Robert Slavin had warned during the rise to popularity of cooperative learning in the 1980s that it was being "oversold and undertrained." At the time, many teachers were encouraged to implement an approach to teaching that they may have inadequately understood and possibly was at odds with some of their existing beliefs and practices. If cooperative learning is to be more than the charade that

Sarasan describes we must recognize and commit to several basic principles.

Need for teacher commitment and study

One of the preconditions for cooperative learning is recognition of the level of commitment and study required of us to implement it competently. Cooperative learning is not a mere technique to vary the usual instructional bill of fare. An occasional group task or a lesson or two on cooperation in the midst of business as usual, will not create a learning community and improve interpersonal relations. As David and Roger Johnson (1992, p. 45) note: "Simply placing students in groups and telling them to work together does not in and of itself result in cooperative efforts—or positive effects on students."

We must anticipate that implementing cooperative learning will raise problems and questions: What do I do about students who resist being in the same group? What about the quiet students? What about the group that doesn't get down to work, finishes early or talks too loudly? Most of us will need help in resolving these problems and, over time, forging a learning *community* from what may be very diverse and reluctant learners. Help may be self-help from a cooperative support group formed by teachers themselves—much like the ones in which we expect students to participate—through independent self-study or outside help from a school board consultant or support teacher. (Addresses of two cooperative learning groups are listed in the Additional Resources section at the end of this article, as is an annotated bibliography of resources on cooperative learning in social studies.)

Align classroom practices and values

The basic values of cooperative learning, such as collaboration, equality and inclusion, may conflict with teaching philosophies, curriculum content and classroom organization. Because of these conflicts, some teachers may be reluctant to extend cooperative learning beyond a few token lessons. One source of value conflict is the importance in cooperative learning given to social or interpersonal goals. Most cooperative models teach interpersonal skills and encourage group self-reflection, both to help students for academic purposes and for their own sake. In contrast, the norms in some classrooms, especially in secondary schools, affirm that learning means *academic* learning only. Although lip service may be paid to values and interpersonal skills, evaluation usually reflects textbook learning not the ability and willingness to work with others. In fact, social goals may not merely be downplayed, they may be actively suppressed by factors such as the way seating is arranged into rows so as to minimize student interaction and maximize teacher control.

As well, cooperative learning may conflict with deeply-held beliefs about the value of individualism and competition. In a cooperative classroom, common watchwords are "Two heads are better than one" and "You have a right to ask any group member for help and a duty to help anyone who asks." Students sit facing each other, they know the names of their classmates, and they may ask for a chance to study together before a test or have a partner for a project. Teachers who believe strongly in individual learning and competition may be uncomfortable with this kind of a classroom.

Even if students are not separated from each other in classrooms, they are often pitted against each other. We send enduring messages that fellow students are potential barriers to success whenever we grade by the curve, display only the best papers on the wall, sort children into winners and losers in spelling bees and encourage students during a teacher-led discussion to compete to get the answer quickest. In his book *No Contest: The Case Against Competition*, Alfie Kohn (1992) summarizes the empirical literature on the effects of these sorts of classroom practices: competition is associated with less generosity, less inclination to trust, less willingness to see other viewpoints and poorer communication. Cooperative learning will never be more than a fringe methodology or a charade unless the practices and embedded values operating within our classrooms support cooperation. We must recognize that almost everything we do or say in our classes may influence cooperation (Sapon-Shevin & Schniedewind, 1992).

One way cooperative values can be fostered is by making themes such as competition, participation, collaboration and conflict focusses of study within various social science disciplines. In other words, as suggested in the box below, Studying about Cooperation in Social Studies, cooperation becomes part of the curriculum as a topic of academic study in its own right.

Build student skills and habits of cooperation

If cooperative learning is to be effective, we need to include considerable instruction and student reflection

---

STUDYING ABOUT COOPERATION IN SOCIAL STUDIES

Cooperation can be more than a teaching approach, it is an important concept and value to use when examining the world. Students should study about cooperation and competition though the various disciplines which make up social studies. Particularly valuable cooperative themes include competition, compassion, belonging, interdependence, conflict resolution, equality, democracy, group and individual identity, diversity and participation.

- **History.** History has traditionally been preoccupied with competition and conflict through the study of war and oppression. Yet most conflicts in history have been resolved far short of war. A balanced curriculum would match attention to wars with topics such as the establishment of the United Nations peace keeping force for which former Prime Minister Lester Pearson won the Nobel Prize. Making peace can be as exciting as waging war. Students' experiences in their own school can be starting points for examining the roles of competition in causing wars and of cooperation in keeping peace. Moreover, even violent conflicts often reflect themes of caring and struggles for equality and democracy. For example, blacks and whites, slaves and citizens, Americans and Canadians worked together to build the Underground Railroad. In the years before the American Civil War they risked their lives in an intricate cooperative network in order to bring slaves to freedom. The role of collaboration in human history must be explored more thoroughly and self-consciously. A half century ago Bertolt Brecht asked: "Who built the seven towers of Thebes? The books are filled with the names of kings. Was it kings who hauled the craggy blocks of stone?" Our teaching of history should reflect the extent to which many of our greatest achievements are the result of collaboration and not just the work of a few rugged individualists.

- **Geography.** Cooperative classrooms are built on interdependence. Likewise, interdependence is a major theme in geography, especially in human-environmental interaction. Our current environmental challenges may be the result of a collective refusal to recognize our interdependence—an overemphasis on competing against and dominating nature rather than on cooperating with it. Here too, students can extend their personal understanding of group interdependence to environmental issues. Moreover, local environmental issues are a common focus for student action and service projects.

- **Civics/Political Science.** Students can also apply their personal experiences to civic society and government. Key themes common to both politics and the cooperative classroom are trust, decision-making and participation. Many of the same issues for Canada as a nation—especially, cultural diversity vs. unity and rights vs. responsibilities—are enacted everyday in Canadian classrooms and schools.

- **Economics.** On one level, economic systems are highly competitive: they are centrally concerned with issues of distribution and scarcity. Yet such systems also contain elements of interdependence and conflict resolution as governments, labour and business cooperate to make the system work and to protect fair competition. The hand of cooperation may often seem invisible in classical economic explanations of the market, but there are countless examples of caring and interdependence from child rearing to helping a neighbour, all of which contribute to our economy. Moreover, most modern workplaces stress teamwork even when they embrace the competition of free enterprise. Many cooperative learning teachers cite preparation for employment as one of the reasons for using cooperative learning.

on interpersonal skills and attitudes. When problems occur, such as a conflict or a reluctant participant, students and the teacher should discuss them. One motto of the Johnsons' has been "Turn problems back to the group to solve," and they insist that cooperative groups put their academic tasks to one side and address personal problems first. By teaching social skills and establishing the habit of reflection on group dynamics, students can recognize that they have the power to make cooperation work. Moreover, academic achievement and increased social skills go hand in hand: research evidence suggests that reflection on group process improves academic performance, especially when students are engaged in complex learning tasks.

FORMS OF COOPERATIVE LEARNING

Describing the essence of cooperative learning can be like "The six blind men of Hindustan," the old poem about the blind men who touch various parts of the elephant—the leg, the trunk, the tusk, etc.—and declare the animal to be just like a tree, a snake, a spear and so on. There are by one account more than 20 cooperative learning models (Myers, 1991). In the remaining sections of this article I explore two of the more popular ones: Johnsons' Learning Together model and Kagan's Structural Approach. Our purpose is to understand the key ingredients involved in cooperative learning, recognize how it differs from traditional group work and appreciate that there are different ways to implement cooperative learning.

Elements of the Learning Together model

The Johnsons' model is one of the best known explanations of the principles of cooperative pedagogy (Johnson, Johnson & Holubec-Johnson, 1990). According to their model, five elements are essential for effective cooperation:

- **Establish positive interdependence**. Group work will be cooperative only if there is positive interdependence: group members must believe that their success depends on the success of others or, as the Johnsons say, "We sink or swim together." Positive interdependence can be seen as both an element of lesson design and as a spirit of mutual helpfulness. In a lesson design the teacher might create positive interdependence by asking small groups to come up with a single product or to share a limited number of resources such as one instruction sheet, paper, felt pen, glue stick or pair of scissors. Planning for positive independence is especially important in the early months of the year when students may not have developed the skills or motivation to cooperate.

- **Require individual accountability**. Individual accountability can be seen as both an element of lesson planning and, over time, a spirit that everyone contributes to the group effort and is valued for that contribution. When students know that they are accountable for their own learning and for helping the group learn, both group productivity and individual achievement are enhanced. On the other hand, resentment is likely if all members are not pulling their own weight. If some hitchhike on the efforts of others, hard-working group members may lessen their effort to avoid being "suckers." To encourage individual accountability we might require each student to be ready to explain the contents of a common product or assign each student a specific section of a shared product.

- **Encourage face-to-face promotive interaction**. Cooperative learning requires face-to-face interaction where the conversation helps students advance their own thinking on the matter before them. Cooperative learning educators in Ontario often refer to this element as purposeful talk and emphasize the role of talk in thinking. To achieve a high level of academic achievement, students must meet in groups to discuss and refine their thinking. To achieve a feeling of caring and commitment, students must encourage and help each other. Sitting together but working independently and occasionally copying each other's notes is not promotive interaction.

- **Teach interpersonal or social skills**. Social skills refer to behaviours like sharing, listening and encouraging that enable a group to work together. Students do not necessarily know how to behave cooperatively. In the first few weeks of cooperative work, we may have to teach what might simply be called "good classroom manners": moving quickly and quietly to groups, using a person's name, talking in quiet voices, staying with the group, not wandering around and sitting so that students face each other. In classes with many impetuous students it may be several months before we can introduce more advanced social skills such as encouraging participation, active listening, checking for understanding or criticizing ideas constructively. The timing and particulars may differ, but the need to teach rather than assume social skills is crucial.

- **Allow for processing**. Students require the time and procedures to analyze their functioning as a group and their mastery of the requisite social skills. Research suggests that academic achievement is greater when cooperative groups reflect on their process. It is advisable to regularly devote between five and fifteen minutes of group time for students to write about or discuss group interactions. The Participation Pie activity described in the box on the next page is one strategy for facilitating reflection about group interactions.

Planning an effective Learning Together lesson may take considerable time to master. The suggested sequence of steps outlined in the following box is one way of helping us attend to key considerations in implementing cooperative learning.

PLANNING A LEARNING TOGETHER LESSON

Specify lesson objectives
- academic content
- social skills

Decide about operational details
- group size
- assignment to groups
- room arrangement
- materials
- student roles

Introduce the lesson
- explain the academic task
- structure positive interdependence
- create individual accountability
- explain expected use of social skills
- set criteria for success

Monitor students
- observe for evidence of the expected social skills (by student or teacher observation)
- provide opportunity for processing

Evaluate
- academic achievement
- group functioning

In addition to planning a lesson around the five elements of the model, consideration needs to be given to group composition and, in some cases, seating arrangement and materials.

A feature of most cooperative learning models is the use of heterogeneous groups, where student groups are mixed according to academic level, ethnicity, gender and socio-economic status. Compatibility is another ingredient in the mix. Considerable research and teacher experience suggest that heterogeneous groups enhance class cohesiveness, intergroup relations and academic achievement for all students. When unaccustomed to cooperative learning, students often want to choose their own groups which frequently means including only their friends. Consequently, there may be tension when teachers choose groups. We may want, therefore, to explain the need for mixed groups along the lines of the following reasons:

- social studies class is where we learn how to be good citizens and part of that is learning to work with others who may be different from us but with whom we share this classroom and share this planet;

- when hired for a job, we do not choose our fellow employees and certainly not the customers; learning to work with others whom we do not know well is learning for life;

- often we work better with those who are not our friends, there's less social talk about sports or movies and the like;

- when we explain something to someone, we help that person learn, but we also learn ourselves because we think through and organize our ideas;

- each student will probably work with everyone in the class at some point during the year.

During the early part of the year when we are unfamiliar with our students or for a break at any time of the year, random choice is often best. There are several enjoyable, creative ways to do this such as counting off the names of famous figures, counting off in a foreign language, distributing playing cards with the common cards sitting together, or lining up according to birth date without talking—a challenge—and then grouping students next to each other. As a class develops into a learning community, one that is inclusive by habit, we may want students to choose their own groups.

PARTICIPATION PIE

Divide the pie to illustrate how much each member of your group participated in the task. Write down your names in the appropriate section. Below give reasons why you divided up the pie as you did and suggest things you might do to improve the cooperative sharing in the group.

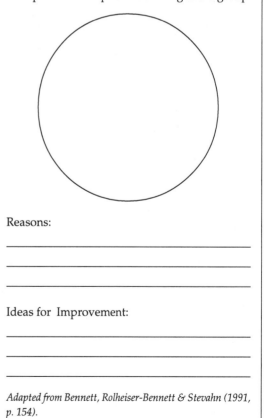

Reasons:

_____

_____

_____

Ideas for Improvement:

_____

_____

_____

Adapted from Bennett, Rolheiser-Bennett & Stevahn (1991, p. 154).

Contrasting Learning Together
with traditional group work

The significance of the Johnsons' Learning Together model can be seen by contrasting its five elements and key decisions with traditional group work. In the following example, students are asked to use a study sheet using the PAID strategy to analyze a primary document which, in this case, is a pair of political cartoons with contrasting views of women's attempts to gain the right to vote early in this century. Let us explore how the analysis of the cartoons through traditional group work might differ from a cooperative group approach.

CONTRASTING VIEWS OF WOMEN'S SUFFRAGE

Cartoon courtesy of Charles Hou.
Illustrated by Lou Skuce, *Toronto World*,
March 3, 1912.

Cartoon courtesy of Charles Hou.
Illustrator unknown,
Montreal Herald, circa 1912.

Selection of group

If this were traditional group work, students might be asked to choose their own groups and the size might vary from two to twenty. Choosing a group of 20 is not a joke. I have observed a class that divided itself into three groups: about 20 students of Chinese origin, four white students and one First Nations boy who had no one to work with. Self-selection based on ability, ethnicity, gender, friendship and the like is the common result when students choose their own groups. With such homogeneous groups, few of the social goals of cooperation will be realized and probably neither will the academic goals in some groups. In contrast, the Learning Together teacher will carefully select groups to include a high achiever with a low achiever and one or two middle-level achievers. In addition, she would consider gender, ethnicity and general compatibility.

Positive independence and individual accountability

The Learning Together teacher would next set the interdependence. Each group might have *goal interdependence*, the common goal of completing the PAID form for analyzing political cartoons. There could also be *resource interdependence* if each group has a single set of handouts to share and *role interdependence* if there are different, complementary roles such as those described in the box on this page. Individual accountability exists if the teacher randomly asks students to explain their answer. The roles also give special responsibilities to each student.

If this were traditional group work there would be little positive interdependence or individual accountability. All students would have their own set of handouts and the groups would be instructed to complete the PAID questions and share their answers. Even if the teacher instructs them to share, without structured interdependence there would be little impetus for students to cooperate; and if they did share answers, little motivation to refine and develop them. In addition, without individual accountability, some students would say and do little and may merely copy the work of others.

Social skills

In traditional group work social skills are either omitted entirely or superficially addressed in the form of general admonitions: "I want you folks to share." In the Learning Together model the teacher discusses why sharing is a good idea and teaches specific strategies by, for example, asking "What might you say to someone who is a bit shy in your group to encourage him or her to give some ideas?" The teacher might write down responses and make a poster of them or ask three or four students to role play positive and negative examples. Understanding the importance of social skills and to be able to use them well are major learning objectives for the Johnsons.

Processing

At some point, the cooperative groups would be given an opportunity to reflect on how well they worked together so they might improve their social skills, resolve any group problems or simply celebrate their success. This reflection might be done in various ways: students keep a journal, the teacher makes observations and reports on them to the class, the group discusses what they did well and areas for improvement or individuals complete a self-reflection form such as the Pair Reflections described on the next page. Typically, in traditional group work, student reflection at the end would be solely about the content of the lesson.

COOPERATIVE CARTOON ANALYSIS

PAID Strategy

Instructions: Discuss and write out an answer to the following questions for each cartoon. All group members should agree with the answers and be ready to explain them.

P = Point of View. What is the point of view of the cartoon? What message is being communicated?

A = Assumption. What assumptions does the cartoonist make about his or her subject? What values and value judgments are apparent?

I = Information. What relevant information about this topic do you already know? Does that information support the cartoonist's point of view? Does the cartoon's message seem to make sense based on your own experience?

D = Device. What cartoon devices does the cartoonist use (for example, light and dark, line, size, caricature, symbols, exaggeration, and stereotyping)?

Cooperative Roles

Instructions: Divide the following roles among group members. Each person must fulfill a role as the group completes the questions.

- **Reader/Checker.** Begin by reading these instructions and the PAID questions to your group, then as the group answers each one, check that everyone agrees with what is written and can explain it.

- **Recorder.** Write down the group's answers then read what you have recorded to your group to check for accuracy.

- **Encourager.** Ask students who are silent or say little if they have any ideas to share. Try to motivate the team if it gets bogged down.

- **Gatekeeper.** If one student is talking too much, politely ask the person to give someone else a turn.

The Structural Approach

Another popular cooperative learning model, Spencer Kagan's Structural Approach, has a different starting point but includes similar elements to the Johnsons' approach. Kagan offers a rich repertoire of cooperative structures or lesson formats suitable to different teaching situations. At first look, it may appear to be a "cookbook" but each structure has a solid cooperative foundation. What follows is a description of common structures and an explanation of how a lesson using direct whole class instruction can be converted to a cooperative learning lesson using a structures approach.

Types of cooperative learning structures

The number of structures in Kagan's model appears daunting. His encyclopedic teacher's guide (1992) explains 92 of them plus 20 "lesson designs" or series of structures. In addition, recent Kagan publications and training programs describe new structures and variations developed by innovative teachers and Kagan's team of trainers. However, there is no need for us to use all or even most of these. In fact, Kagan advocates teaching students one structure a month. The large repertoire simply provides flexibility in our choosing of a practical cooperative procedure for a specific topic or learning objective.

Kagan defines structures as content-free ways of organizing social interaction for the classroom. They are the "how" of instruction while the lesson content is the "what." Structures can be as simple and brief as Think-Pair-Share, which can take mere minutes to complete its three steps. The teacher poses a problem or a significant question. Students think, write or draw an answer then share their ideas with a partner and then with the whole class. A structure can be as involved as Co-op Co-op, the structure for group research projects that has ten steps and involves considerable student autonomy. Co-op Co-op may take a full semester to complete. With this structure students form groups with others who share an interest in a topic, research an aspect of that topic, then pool their knowledge to prepare a class pres-

entation. Other Kagan structures include:

- **Pairs View.** The teacher stops a videotape at five to ten minute intervals and students in pairs take turns summarizing the main ideas of the video.
- **Team Discussion.** Students work as a team to decide on a common answer or create a single product.
- **Numbered Heads Together.** Students number off in their teams. The teacher asks a question which has multiple answers and the teams discuss possible answers. The teacher calls a number and students with that number explain their group's answer.
- **Values Line.** Students are given a values issue and then order themselves in a line according to their opinions on that question. Next, they fold the line to talk to a partner about their reasons for their choice. Before they give their opinion they must paraphrase what their partner has said.
- **Blackboard Sharing.** Each team selects a representative or the teacher chooses one. The representatives go to the blackboard and write or post their teams' best answers simultaneously. The teams can continue working while this is going on.
- **Carousel Sharing.** One person from each team stays at the team's work place to be a spokesperson. The others rotate from team to team learning as much as they can to incorporate later into revisions of their own work. The spokesperson stays behind to explain the team's work to the other teams as they rotate through.

Each Kagan structure incorporates the same positive interaction and individual accountability as the Johnsons, but Kagan offers the additional principles of *equal participation*—the use of strategies such as taking turns that promote broad involvement of all students—and *simultaneous interaction*—that is, as many students as possible contributing at the same time. The acronym for Kagan's principles is PIES: Positive interdependence, Individual accountability, Equal participation and Simultaneous interaction.

PAIR REFLECTIONS

Name: _____   Name of Partner: _____

	Never				**Always**
I made certain my partner and I both understood the material we were studying	1	2	3	4	5
I listened to the contributions of my partner	1	2	3	4	5
I felt that my partner listened to me	1	2	3	4	5
We stayed on task	1	2	3	4	5

Give two adjectives to describe how you feel about your work together

1 _____   2 _____

Contrasting the Structural Approach
with direct instruction

To better understand a structure and its four principles let us contrast direct instruction of a class studying a video with cooperative instruction using Kagan's model. A typical form of direct instruction using a video might appropriately be labeled the "Whole Class View-Question-Answer" approach. It has three parts:

- the teacher shows the video;
- students complete worksheets or answer questions individually during or after the showing;
- when the assignments are completed, the teacher calls on students one-by-one for their answers to the questions.

In this approach, during the showing of the video, there is little interaction among students nor with the teacher, at least if the class is orderly. If a section of the video is confusing or complex, students get little or no help until the end. The question and answer session is intended to help all students learn, but in many classes it may be competitive if students are vying for the teacher's attention with cries of "Me! Me!" and hands jabbing the air. Student-to-student interaction is competitive when strong students triumph, while those who are not quick with the answer or not aggressive enough to win the teacher's attention lose.

This approach is quite different from a cooperatively structured activity that uses the steps of Pairs View (Morton, 1996) described below:

PAIRS VIEW
- The teacher pairs students A and B and explains to the pairs that they have a common goal: to generate a clear set of notes for each partner that contains the main ideas of the video (or answers to assigned questions).
- The teacher shows the video and stops it every ten minutes or so (five minutes for younger students).
- When the video is stopped for the first time, A performs three roles:
  — summarizes for B the information and ideas presented so far,
  — tells B what s/he finds most interesting about what was presented (or answers the assigned questions),
  — identifies anything that was confusing and tries to clarify, with B's help.
- Both A and B take notes.
- After the explanation and notes for that section are completed, the video is turned on again.
- After a suitable period, the pause is repeated but with B completing the three tasks.
- The cycle repeats and the roles reverse with every pause until the film is finished.
- With the whole class, the teacher randomly calls on different As and Bs to explain the main ideas or answers.

The Pairs View strategy illustrates the four key principles of Kagan's approach:

- **positive interdependence**. Pairs View has both role interdependence because students have complementary and alternating roles and goal independence because students have the common goal of each completing a set of notes.
- **individual accountability**. In Pairs View students are accountable in three ways: their roles require them to explain to each other what they have learned, each is to have a set of notes and they are accountable because anyone can be called upon to respond to questions on the video.
- **equal participation**. Learning teams can deteriorate quickly if one person dominates or someone else withdraws. In Pairs View the requirement that each person take turns talking ensures involvement of both partners.
- **simultaneous interaction**. In the final stage of the traditional approach, Whole Class View-Question-Answer, only the teacher or one student at a time talks about the video. The rest sit idle. At each pause of Pairs View, however, half of the class is talking simultaneously.

Comparing Learning Together and the Structural Approach

There need not be any differences in a lesson taught following the Johnsons' model or Kagan's. The key difference between them is in the planning steps before the lesson is taught. Nonetheless, because of the different emphases of these two models, dissimilar lessons may result.

Let us imagine that we are planning a lesson on interpreting graphs. Following the planning steps of the Learning Together model outlined earlier, we would begin by deciding on the lesson objectives, group size and selection procedure, then consider how to create interdependence. We might choose goal interdependence (e.g., a single list of answers) or resource interdependence (e.g., each group member has a different graph). We would then consider individual accountability such as each student taking turns writing an answer or being ready to respond to the teacher's question. The next decision would be on a social skill: checking for understanding or taking turns seem appropriate here. Throughout the lesson we would monitor the use of those skills. A student might even be assigned to act as an observer. Finally, we would consider how best to facilitate student reflection on the group process. The Participation Pie would work well with our graphing assignment.

In contrast, the Kagan model would have us ask, "What kind of structure fits with this content and my learning goals?" The Think-Pair-Share structure would be best if we wanted tight control of the activity whereas Team Discussion would give greater autonomy to students to organize themselves, but it may not result in equal participation of all students. Numbered-Heads-

Together with its strong individual accountability might be a good compromise. If this is early in the year, we would teach the purpose and procedure of the structure. Otherwise, we need only tell students that they are going to follow a Think-Pair-Share or Numbered-Heads-Together structure. Specifying the social skills and processing are very important for the Structural Approach, but they are not as explicit a part of every lesson as they are with Learning Together. However, because simultaneity and equal participation are important for Kagan, the final answers might well be shared by group representatives writing their answers on the blackboard at the same time (Blackboard Sharing structure) or with the team representatives making a tour of other groups (Carousel Sharing structure).

The Johnsons and Kagan have also grafted additional strategies and approaches to the core of cooperative learning. For example, both spend considerable time in their training programs on team and class building to create a sense of community of learners. Both have developed teaching materials for social studies. Together, these two models give social studies teachers a rich source of practical techniques and principles to which they can refer when implementing cooperative learning.

References

Bennett, B., Rolheiser-Bennett, C. & Stevahn, L. (1991). *Cooperative learning: Where heart meets mind*. Toronto: Interactive.

Deutch, M. (1949). A theory of cooperation and competition. *Human Relations, 2*, 129-152.

Dewey, J. (1916). *Democracy in education*. New York: Macmillan.

Johnson, D. & Johnson, R. (1989). *Cooperation and competition: Theory and research*. Edina, MN: Interaction Books.

Johnson, D. & Johnson, R. (1992). Approaches to implementing cooperative learning in the social studies classroom. In R. Stahl & R. VanSickle (Eds.), *Cooperative learning in the social studies classroom* (pp. 45-51). Washington, DC: National Council for the Social Studies.

Johnson, D. & Johnson, R. (1994). In R. Stahl (Ed.), *Cooperative learning in social studies: A handbook for teachers*. Menlo Park, CA: Addison-Wesley.

Johnson, D., Johnson, R. & Johnson-Holubec, E. (1990). *Cooperation in the classroom* (4th Ed.). Edina, MN: Interaction Books.

Kagan, S. (1992). *Cooperative learning*. San Juan Capistrano, CA: Resources for Teachers.

Kohn, A. (1992). *No context: The case against competition*. Boston: Houghton Mifflin.

Myers, J. (1991). Cooperative learning in history and social sciences: An idea whose time has come. *Canadian Social Studies, 26*(2), 60-64.

Morton, T. (1996). *Cooperative learning and social studies: Towards excellence and equity*. San Juan Capistrano, CA: Kagan.

National Council for the Social Studies. (1994). *Expectations for excellence: curriculum standards for social studies*. Washington, DC: National Council for the Social Studies.

Sapon-Shevin, M. & Schniedewind, N. (1992). If cooperative learning's the answer, What are the questions? *Journal of Education, 174*(2), 11-37.

Sarason, S. (1995). Some reactions to what we have learned. *Phi Delta Kappan, 7*(1), 84.

Slavin, R.E. (1989). *Cooperative learning: Theory, research, and practice*. Englewood Cliffs, NJ: Prentice-Hall.

Additional Resources

Groups

BC Cooperative Learning Association
BC Teachers' Federation
100-550 West 6th Avenue
Vancouver, BC V5Z 4P2

GLACIE (Great Lakes Association for the Study of Co-operation in Education)
Winchester Public School
15 Prospect Street
Toronto, ON M4X 1C7

Journals

Several journals and magazines in Canada and the United States have featured cooperative learning. Those relating to social studies include the following:

The International Association for Cooperation in Education (IASCE), a group of teachers and researchers from around the world, produces a magazine *Cooperative Learning*. A theme issue on social studies (Volume 12, Number 3, 1992), edited by John Myers at the University of Toronto, includes lesson plans and classroom examples such as "Teaching for the Bleachers" (T. Morton) that includes a creative controversy on the Pig War, the almost-war when James Douglas ordered the British navy to blast American soldiers off of San Juan Island, and "Who Killed JFK?" (H. Foyle), using group investigation.

A special issue of *Social Studies and the Young Learner* (Volume 2, Number 3, 1990) published for kindergarten to grade 8 teachers by the National Council for the Social Studies (NCSS) features cooperative learning and illustrates the use of Co-op Co-op and jigsaw in several articles.

The History and Social Science Teacher, now called *Canadian Social Studies*, produced a theme issue on cooperative learning in 1991 (Winter issue) edited by Tom Morton and John Myers. Among the articles is a piece called "Getting Started Strategies" (J. Myers, L. Cox & R. Evans) using Kagan's structural approach and an article on the use of group investigation (R. Evans). Other individual articles in *The History and Social Science Teacher* on classroom practice of cooperative learning include a creative controversy in "Decision at Dieppe" (Volume 21, Number 4, 1986), a mystery game structure on buffalo hunting (Volume 25, Number 4, 1990) and a look at native North Americans using jigsaw (J. Myers & C. Lemon; Volume 24, Number 1, 1989).

Social Education, the major publication of NCSS, contains numerous articles on cooperative learning applied to social studies classrooms. Most of these have focussed on the use of jigsaw such as a lesson on modernization in Meiji, Japan (P. Ferguson; Number 5, Volume 52, 1988).

The Social Studies features jigsaw in "Where in Western Europe Would You Like to Live? A Cooperative Lesson for World Geography' (R.W. Richburg & B.J. Nelson; Volume 82, Number 3, 1991).

Books

Robert Stahl and Ron VanSickle (1992) have edited a collection of essays for the National Council for the Social Studies (NCSS), *Cooperative Learning in the Social Studies Classroom: An Introduction to Social Study*. This is not a "how-to book," but rather a look at research and issues in the use of cooperative learning in social studies. (NCSS Publications, c/o Maxway Data Corp, 225 W. 34th St, Suite 1105, New York, NY 1001. Phone: 1-800-683-0812.)

Cooperative Learning in Social Studies: A Handbook for Teachers, edited by Robert Stahl (1994) is the practical companion to the NCSS book above. Most of the major schools of cooperative learning are discussed. Jeanne Stone and Spencer Kagan explain structures in "Social Studies and the Structural Approach" and the Johnsons discuss their model in a chapter on Learning Together. Other chapters look at forms of jigsaw, Robert Slavin's Teams-Games-Tournament and Student Teams-Achievement Divisions, and the Johnsons' Creative Controversy. The book gives thorough descriptions of the various models but does not include lesson plans. (Addison-Wesley, Jacob Way, Reading, MA 01867. Phone: 1-800-447-2226.)

Tom Morton's *Cooperative Learning and Social Studies: Towards Excellence and Equity* (1996) is based on Spencer Kagan's cooperative structures. It includes explanations of 24 structures with lesson narratives, blackline masters and numerous ideas for further applications. The guide also includes chapters on implementation and evaluation. (Kagan Cooperative Learning, 27128 Paseo Espada, #602, San Juan Capistrano, CA 92675. Phone: 1-800-WEE-COOP.)

Bert Bower, Jim Lobdell and Lee Swenson in *History Alive* (1994; Addison-Wesley) have applied the work of Elizabeth Cohen's Program for Complex Instruction (PCI) to history teaching. PCI combines cooperative learning with activities that use multiple intelligences. Although not a cooperative learning guide, *History Alive* has a strong cooperative focus. The authors also run an institute that provides curriculum materials and training. (Teachers Curriculum Institute, 201 San Antonio Circle, Suite 105, Mountain View, CA 94040. Phone: 1-800-497-6138.)

The Stanford Program on International and Cross-Cultural Education (SPICE) produces some of the richest and most rigorous curriculum material available,

much of which builds on cooperative learning. Especially worthwhile are the materials based on the Program for Complex Instruction such as *Nationalism and Identity in a European Context* (R. Steinbeck, 1993), *Why Do People Move? Migration from Latin America* (L. Nunez, 1993) and *Along the Silk Road* (R. Chu, 1993). (SPICE, Institute for International Studies, Room 14 C, Stanford University, Stanford, CA 94305-5013, Phone: 415-723-1114.)

A popular teacher's guide with an international focus is Graham Selby and David Pike's *Global Teacher, Global Learner* (1988). Along with explanations of global education concepts such as human rights and interdependence, the authors draw together a collection of extremely creative activities for team building, role playing, discussion and the like. (Hodder and Stoughton, Mill Road, Dunton Green, Sevenoaks, Kent, England, TN13 2YA.)

Cooperative Learning, Cooperative Lives (N. Schniedewind & E. Davidson, 1987; W. C. Brown Co.) includes a number of lessons and worksheets suitable for upper elementary and middle school students that teach content related to themes of cooperation, competition and respect for diversity while using a cooperative approach. The lessons start with classroom and school issues, such as the use of put-downs and peer pressure, and expand to national and international topics, such as food and workers' cooperatives, trade, and war and peace. It is American oriented. (Order from Circle Books, 30 Walnut Street, Somerville, MA 02143. Phone: 617-623-7863.)

Elizabeth Coelho is the author or co-author of several powerful books for developing a community of learners in a multicultural classroom at the middle and high school level: *Learning Together in the Multicultural Classroom* (1994; Pippin), a teachers guide; *Jigsaw* (1991; Pippin), student materials and lesson plans that focus on reading skills and constructive controversy with a reading level of grades 3-7; *All Sides of the Issue* (with J. Winn-Bell Olsen & L. Winer, 1989; Alemany Press), the American version of *Jigsaw*; and *Jigsaw Plus* (1991; Pippin), similar to *Jigsaw*, but at a higher reading level, grades 6-10. (Pippin Publishing, 150 Telson Road, Markham, ON, L3R 1E5. Phone: 416-513-6966. *All Sides of the Issue* can be ordered from Prentice-Hall, PO Box 11071, Des Moines, IA 50336-1071. Phone: 1-800-223-1360.)

Another source of strategies and teaching materials is *Creative Controversy* (D. Johnson & R. Johnson, 1992). The book includes a number of short, involving exercises designed to encourage perspective-taking, processing forms, a self-evaluation questionnaire and student materials on diverse controversies such as the debate over the hunting of the timber wolf and whether James Wolfe was a hero or not. (Interaction Book Co, 7208 Cornelia Drive, Edina, MN 44535. Phone: 612-831-9500.)

Lesson Plans for Cooperative Learning (M. Alberts, J. Caldwell & C. Schmidt, 1989) provides secondary social studies teachers with five detailed lessons based on the Johnsons' Learning Together model for topics such as three world religions and propaganda. (Learning Incentives, Rt. 1, Box 104, Monticelloe, MN 55362. Phone: 612-878-2336.)

Other useful resources for teachers who use team learning to develop quality thinking about public issues are the booklets on religious freedom, immigration and the New Deal from the Public Issues Series of the Social Science Education Consortium (SSEC). There is some treatment of discussion skills but the focus is on critical thinking such as using analogies or identifying and weighing values. Cooperative structures would enhance this focus. SSEC also produces the CREST series—role playing exercises on science-related social issues such as nuclear fuel storage and AIDS and drug research. (SSEC Publications, 3300 Mitchell Lane, Suite 240, Boulder, CO 80301-2272.)

— ✧ —

SECTION THREE :

IMPLEMENTATION

▶ INSTRUCTIONAL PLANNING

▶ LEARNING RESOURCES

▶ STUDENT ASSESSMENT

31

COURSE, UNIT AND LESSON PLANNING

ROLAND CASE

In this article I offer a framework which tracks teacher planning in social studies from the most abstract and general aims for an entire course to the most specific decisions as to which method and resource to employ in a particular lesson. The framework consists of four levels: the vision for the year, a course plan, unit plans and individual lesson plans. Before examining each level in detail I offer four overall principles to guide our deliberations. I introduce these principles by drawing parallels between successful planning and the practices of experienced hikers on a long-distance wilderness trek. The image of a journey through boundless, often unfamiliar territory is a particularly apt metaphor for the challenges of course, unit and lesson planning.

GUIDING PRINCIPLES OF PLANNING

Those with orienteering experience will know that hikers must be clear both about where they are starting from and where they want to get to ultimately. Otherwise they are likely to lose their bearings in what may well be dense and confusing terrain. Without a clear sense of direction, even if they do not become completely lost, hikers may waste considerable time and energy and, possibly, not reach their intended destination. Although the ultimate destination may not be inview until near the end of their trip, which may be many days or weeks in length, hikers will always know the general direction to head towards in order to reach this long-term objective. Typically, they plot their route in outline form. They anticipate that these plans will change, but they recognize the value of having a clear plan, even if it is provisional. To keep themselves on track hikers identify prominent features or landmarks within intermediate reach that will keep them working towards their final destination. These landmarks may be off in the distance, several or even many kilometers ahead, but they nevertheless serve as a beacon—as the clear visible focus of their travel. If a landmark is vaguely defined, for example, if they select a feature as vast and undefined as a mountain range or an ocean, it will not keep them on a consistent path. From time to time, especially if conditions change or the going becomes very rough, hikers may reconsider whether or not heading towards the designated beacon is the best course to follow. Of course, the bulk of hikers' time is spent attending to their most immediate objectives—getting up the ravine, finding a suitable place to stop, checking their resources, making sure morale among the hikers is positive and so on. They look for easy routes or pre-established paths that can expedite their travel and they take detours if a route seems easier or if there is a site that offers an enticing diversion. They supplement the supplies they carry with resources found on the way, and they improvise should the need arise. Although, much of the trip consists of these moment-to-moment choices about which way to turn or where to step next, there is no point in staying on a path or turning towards a hill if it does not lead in the desired direction. Consequently hikers continually double check—often in an intuitive or reflexive manner—that the specific choices they make are aligned with the more distant beacon they have set. Accordingly, they will follow a pre-established path only so long as it leads in the desired direction, and they may rejoin the path sometime later if it turns back towards their destination. Consistently, the direction hikers take is informed by the beacon they have set because, if clear and properly determined, heading for it means they are on the track of their ultimate destination.

There are many insights about effective planning to draw from this analogy with trekking though wilderness terrain. These insights can be consolidated into four general principles of planning: be destination driven, build thoughtfully, draw widely and wisely, and plan loosely.

Be destination driven

The principle that planning should be destination driven is perhaps the most significant recommendation I offer. It emphasizes the need to decide where we want to take our students and to use that destination to orient everything we do. Without a clear and conscious direction, our teaching is aimless—likely amounting to little more than a string of activities leading nowhere in particular and serving no important purposes. Just as with trekkers, so too as teachers we need to set and be guided by long-, intermediate- and immediate-term destinations:

- our ultimate destinations are our *rationale*—our ideals or ultimate vision—for society and for our students;
- our intermediate destinations are our *goals* for an individual unit and course;
- our immediate destinations are our *objectives* for specific lessons.

The principle of being destination driven does not presuppose a "teacher-driven" approach to planning and teaching in social studies. The need to set a clear destination is not incompatible with extensive student involvement in setting destinations by consensus or, to the extent feasible, in encouraging individuals to strike out in different directions. Given students' different preferences and abilities it often makes sense, even for those heading for the same general ultimate destination, for individuals to pursue common goals by different paths.

Effective implementation of the principle of destination-driven planning implies four conditions:

- **clear, focused destinations**. Both in the long-term

and in the short-term, we should know what we hope to achieve with our students. Vaguely understood goals and objectives do not provide the sense of purpose that effective teaching requires.

- **manageable destinations**. We should not expect to do it all and if we try to do too much—for an entire course or for an individual lesson—we may end up doing a superficial job that makes no lasting difference.

- **justifiable destinations**. We cannot simply decide to pursue our own preferred direction without seriously considering students' best interests, parents' rights and other curricular and professional responsibilities.

- **aligned destinations**. Our long- and short-term destinations must be in alignment, so that we are continually working towards our ultimate destination. This requires that:

Our rationale inform our goals.

Our goals orient our objectives.

Our objectives determine our day-to-day decisions about the methods to employ, the resources to select and what to look for in our assessments.

Build thoughtfully

The principle of building thoughtfully emphasizes the importance of anticipating the intermediate steps to be taken and developing the resources and tools needed to achieve our ultimate educational goals. The expression by the Chinese philosopher Lao Tzu that a journey of a thousand miles starts with a single step is especially relevant. It is not enough that we have a grand plan, we must attend to how we will get there. Just as the trekker must decide what equipment is needed to ford a river or what supplies to sustain the team, so too as teachers we must consider what our students will need to reach the desired goals and what we must do to support this growth.

Effective implementation of the principle of building thoughtfully includes at least three considerations:

- **nurture a conducive environment.** We must work to develop the type of classroom and school environment that supports the desired learning. If we want to develop student autonomy, we must nurture it by establishing a climate that encourages students to take risks and to make up their own minds. The mere planning of thoughtful lessons will not lead very far if the conditions in the classroom undermine these efforts. For example, inviting students to debate a very controversial issue before classroom trust and civility have been adequately established may lead to bitter and counter-productive results.

- **provide meaningful contexts for learning.** A concern expressed by many social studies teachers is students' lack of perceived relevance of the subject. We can help student better appreciate social studies by carefully planning activities that are motivating and by framing our units and lessons in contexts that will resonate with students.

- **teach the prerequisites**. Just as it is unfair to expect someone to construct an elaborate house without having the basic tools to do the job, so too it is unfair to expect significant educational achievement without providing students with the intellectual tools they need for success. We must think through what students require for success at each step—for example, what knowledge, abilities and attitudes are needed for students to become good researchers. Then we must plan how to assist students in acquiring each of these prerequisites.

Draw widely and wisely

The principle of drawing widely and wisely from many sources draws attention to the value of an eclectic approach to planning for content, teaching methods and learning resources. Preoccupation with a narrow theme and over reliance on a single method, such as lectures, or on a single resource, such as a text-book, are analogous to staying on pre-established paths long after they cease to lead in the direction that we want to head towards. We must draw imaginatively from varied sources in our quest for better ways to help our students get where we want them to go.

Effective implementation of the principle of drawing widely and wisely involves the following considerations:

- **integrate the content of different disciplines and subjects**. We should help students make meaningful links among the disciplines within social studies, draw insights from other subjects to inform social studies and connect what they study in school with their own experiences and concerns.
- **use diverse learning resources**. We should plan to make effective use of diverse resources from computers to cartoons, from textbooks to picture books and from feature films to guest speakers.
- **use varied teaching methods**. We should plan for a rich array of activities from teacher-directed to student-directed, from written work to small-group conversation and from seatwork to fieldwork.

Plan loosely

The principle of planning loosely arises because there is no guaranteed path for all students for all times. Planning is too messy and uncertain an affair to be reduced to a fixed plan. Not only will one path not work for all students, but conditions change, our students change and we change. We should be prepared to reformulate our plans to accommodate these eventualities and the countless unanticipated turns that arise half way though the year or in the middle of a lesson. However, this lack of predictability does not imply that planning is fanciful or useless. Planning is a deeply practical matter—the point of planning is to identify what is most worthwhile to teach and then to design a course, a unit or a lesson that increases the likelihood that our teaching will be successful.

Effective implementation of the principle of planning loosely involves the following considerations:

- **expect diversity.** Always expect and, to the extent possible, accommodate diversity in student interests and abilities.
- **allow for student choice.** Entrench opportunities for student choice and self-direction as a feature of our teaching.
- **stay flexible.** As teachers we will be more effective if we remain open to change. Instead of viewing a lesson or unit plan as the fixed menu for the day or the month, we should look upon planning as the *ongoing* vehicle for scrutinizing where are we going with our teaching and what is a good way to get there.

I believe these four principles should permeate all of our planning, from decisions about the ultimate destinations to our most immediate objectives. To assist in planning that embodies these principles I offer a four-level framework: the vision for the year, a course plan, unit plans and individual lesson plans. These levels are akin to progressive snap shots of the earth beginning with the broadest global view and zeroing in on a particular site. Each provides increasing detail of a progressively smaller area of instruction. I begin by describing the most general level and proceed to the most specific level. Despite sequencing my discussion of the model in this order, planning should *not* necessarily proceed in a "general to specific" manner. Those who like to begin with the concrete will find it more productive to start with particular lessons and resources, and work from there to the more general vision. Regardless of where we start, all of us will likely move back and forth between levels as our ideas become clearer and more specific. Thus the four levels imply no particular planning sequence; but regardless of how we proceed, by the end of our planning deliberations, the issues raised at each level of the model should have been thought through in a coherent way.

Realistically, a *fully completed* set of plans as outlined in this framework would involve years of thinking about and trying out ideas. Nevertheless, I believe that all of us, and especially new teachers, can benefit from a deeper understanding of the considerations involved in the kind of comprehensive planning suggested by this framework. In this respect the framework is an ultimate destination. It is an invitation to strive for an ideal—even if never fully reached, only by attempting it will we come closer to where we want be.

CREATING A VISION FOR THE YEAR

The most general level of planning involves creating a vision for the entire year. In effect, it involves asking ourselves the following question: "In a hundred words of less, what am I really attempting to achieve in social studies this year?" The point of planning at this level is to give focus and direction to a course. The box on the next page illustrates a form that might be used to articulate the most general level of planning. A vision for the year may consist of three main components:

- **rationale**. Our rationale should be a clear and defensible account of our educational ideals—the underlying reasons or ultimate purposes for our efforts as educators.

- **priority goals**. Our priorities goals are the handful of educational goals which will be the *major focus* of attention for the year. These goals represent our priorities for the year—mindful that we cannot do everything well. If our goals were met we would have gone some way towards moving students closer to the ideals set out in our rationale.

- **classroom climate**. The classroom climate refers the defining qualities and procedures of the learning environment within which we hope to promote the priority goals and, ultimately, our rationale.

Formulating a rationale

Educational rationales are descriptions of the ideal individual or society we hope to promote through education. Two earlier articles in this collection—"Elements of a Coherent Social Studies Program" and "Four Purposes of Citizenship Education" identified four broad categories of rationales for social studies, positioned along two continuums:

Social acceptance /social change spectrum

- **social initiation**. Transmitting the understandings, abilities and values that students will require if they are to fit into and be contributing members of society.

- **social reformation**. Promoting the understandings, abilities and values necessary to critique and improve society.

Student-centred/subject-centred spectrum

- **personal development**. Fostering the personal talents and character of each student so that they develop fully as individuals and as social beings.

- **academic understanding**. Developing understanding of and appreciation for the bodies of knowledge and forms of inquiry represented in the social science disciplines.

These rationales, in effect, are ways of categorizing the types of ideals that are typically offered for social studies. In the sample vision for the year in the box on the following page are elements from each of these four categories.

In thinking about our own rationale we should be guided by two considerations: Am I clear about the ideals I am striving for? Are these justifiable ideals?

Clarity of focus

Many of the ideals found in rationales for social studies—such as personal autonomy, critical thinking, productive citizen or tolerant society—are potentially vague. Unless we are clear in our own minds what we mean by notions such as these, they will not serve as useful guides to our planning. Does a tolerant society mean that we will begrudgingly accept differences? And what sort of differences will we tolerate? Religious views? Alternative lifestyles? Political and economic ideologies? Or, perhaps, we want to focus largely on racial, ethnic and cultural differences. We may also want to pursue a more embracing vision, not merely putting up with differences but actually welcoming and accepting people because of the cultural contributions that they bring to mainstream society. These are different emphases and we must be clear about the particulars of our rationale if it is to be of use in planning.

VISION FOR THE YEAR			
Theme for the Year			Grade
Rationale			
PRIORITY GOALS			**CLASSROOM CLIMATE**
Content Knowledge	Personal & Social Values		
Critical Thinking	Individual & Collective Action		
Information Gathering & Reporting	Other		

Theme for the Year

Canada before and after Confederation

Grade
middle/high school

Rationale

My ideal citizen:

- is able to cope with a complex, uncertain world
- is willing and trained to think things through rigorously
- is knowledgeable about a wide range of issues
- is committed and willing to work to make the world better for all
- is emotionally mature and socially adept

PRIORITY GOALS

Content Knowledge

- understands the complexities and interrelations of many of the historical and contemporary problems in Canada
- has knowledge of both the ennobling and the regrettable events in Canada's past

Critical Thinking

- can competently analyze controversial issues
- sees issues from varying perspectives
- possesses the tools of a good critical thinker

Information Gathering & Reporting

- can plan and conduct independent research
- can effectively use media and other local sources of information

Personal & Social Values

- has empathy and respect for others
- is committed to social justice
- is respectful of different viewpoints
- has tolerance for ambiguity
- is independent-minded

Individual & Collective Action

- is able and willing to work cooperatively with others, even in difficult situations
- can plan thoughtfully to solve demanding problems

Other

CLASSROOM CLIMATE

- respectful, safe environment
- challenge students in non-threatening ways
- emphasis on self-directed learning—independent projects, peer- and self-assessment
- abundant opportunities for student choice
- students expected to form personal opinions and support with reasons

Justified ideals

In deciding whether or not our rationale is justifiable we should be guided by the following considerations:

- the broad needs of our students;
- the broad needs of the local community;
- the broad needs of society generally;
- our own values as an educator.

The value of a clear justifiable rationale is that it helps us to recognize and keep to what really matters. I certainly remember as a teacher of an especially troubled group of grade six-seven students that whenever I got bogged down in the minutia of the curriculum or frustrated by the day's events, I would remind myself of why I was there. Long before I knew to call it my "rationale," I knew that my *raison d'etre*—my reason for persisting—was to help these students learn to take personal responsibility for their lives. I had seen too many of their peers fall by the wayside, driven by a lack of trust of others and a lack of respect for themselves into a world of glue sniffing and other forms of self-destructive escapism. I hoped I could teach them about literature and science along the way, but not if pursuing these goals interrupted my more pressing mission of helping them take control of their lives. My justification for this "personal development" rationale was obvious—when I thought about what these students most needed in their lives and what their parents most hoped for them, of paramount importance were notions such as functional literacy, personal responsibility and self-respect.

Establishing priority goals

The priority goals identify our key educational emphases for the year. If we could make a real difference in several areas what would we hope to achieve over the year? With the students described above, my priorities included teaching them to read at a level required to understand the newspaper, learning to commit to a task and complete it, learning to treat each other with respect and developing pride in themselves.

In deciding what to emphasize in a given year it is useful to consider how our rationale could be advanced through the general goals for social studies. Throughout this collection of articles, the following have been identified as representative of the range of goals social studies typically seeks to promote:

- **content knowledge.** The breadth and depth of factual and conceptual knowledge students should possess about their world.
- **critical thinking.** The ability and inclination to competently assess what to believe and how to act.
- **information gathering and reporting.** The ability to identify information needs, extract information from varied sources and represent this information in appropriate forms.
- **personal and social values.** The desired values that individuals are to hold about themselves and towards others.

- **individual and collective action.** The ability to analyze problems in students' lives and in society, plan appropriate courses of action individually and in collaboration with others, put into action their plans and evaluate the efficacy of their efforts.

We need not be bound by these categories of goals, and may prefer to use the terminology provided in our provincial curriculum or some other document. If we are teaching an integrated course we would want to include goals not exclusively from social studies but from all of the subjects to be integrated into the course. The important consideration is not the terminology, but to identify a *manageable* number of priority goals that will be our emphasis for the year. We will of course pursue many other goals, these merely represent the handful of goals that we have set as the most productive and pressing avenues to promote our ideals. Often our rationale overlaps with our priority goals because some of the ideals in our rationale are aims that are directly promoted in social studies. Typically, however, ideals are broader aspirations, and we will emphasize only some aspect of these. For example, a "social reformation" rationale might include the ideals of promoting a world without poverty, hunger and war. In a given year, we might emphasize only a few goals that promote these ideals, for example, teaching students to treat one another respectfully and to use peer-mediation and other non-violent forms of interpersonal conflict resolution.

The criteria for justifying a rationale are relevant to justifying our priority goals, although the focus in justifying priority goals is more on examining how social studies and we, as teachers of social studies, can best further ideals embedded in our rationale. In deciding upon this we should consider the following factors:

- the needs and expressed wishes of our students;
- the expectations embedded in the provincial curriculum;
- the nature of social studies as a subject and the range of purposes that social studies is expected to serve;
- the expressed wishes of parents and the local community;
- the needs of society generally;
- our own priorities and strengths as an educator.

Shaping the classroom climate

Although classroom climate has not traditionally been seen as part of the defining vision of a course, it is becoming increasingly obvious that this factor plays a significant role in supporting or impeding the achievement of social studies goals. Many of us will have been frustrated by our inability to get students, say, to think critically about issues or to take responsibility for their learning because the prevailing mood in the class undermined our efforts. The point of including classroom climate is to identify the basic principles that ought to guide the conduct of our class if we are serious about our rationale. For example, in the sample vision for the year, one of the elements of the rationale is to promote students' willingness and ability to think things through with rigour. Students are likely to take the risks involved in thinking for themselves only if the classroom is a safe and respectful place and only if the inevitable "challenging," required to help students probe their thinking more deeply, is done is a non-threatening manner. These features must, therefore, be important operating principles for this classroom. Identifying operating principles is a matter of thinking through the sorts of routines and norms that must be part of the daily business of our classrooms if we are to have any likelihood of advancing our rationale.

DEVELOPING A COURSE PLAN

Although the vision for the year is our ultimate destination and should always be in the back of our minds, like trekkers we will often not have that vision constantly in our sights. Our conscious focus will likely be more immediate: deciding what we would have to teach in September, or in November, in order to get where we want to be in June. The purpose of the second level of the planning model—the course plan—is to set out the general sequence and structure of the pursuit of our goals by plotting the more specific objectives or outcomes that will be promoted in each unit. Just as a long trip may be broken into phases, so too the journey through the curriculum is typically divided up into units of study—usually between three and five units over the course of a year. The box below contains a form that might be used to lay out a course plan. The tasks in developing a course plan include:

- deciding upon an appropriate focus for each unit;
- identifying specific objectives for all unit goals;
- sequencing objectives across units.

Focusing the unit

Typically, the planning of course begins by identifying the unit topics or unifying ideas for each phase of the course. The topic provides the context or vehicle for promoting the goals and specific objectives that will eventually be set for each unit. Selecting a topic is a common beginning step in deciding upon an appropriate focus for a unit. Surprisingly, however, identifying a topic need not determine in any definitive way

COURSE PLAN

UNIT DESCRIPTION	UNIT OBJECTIVES				
	Content Knowledge	Critical Thinking	Information Gathering & Reporting	Personal & Social Values	Individual & Collective Action
UNIT #1: SYNOPSIS: MAIN GOALS:					
UNIT #2: SYNOPSIS: MAIN GOALS:					
UNIT #3: SYNOPSIS: MAIN GOALS:					
UNIT #4: SYNOPSIS: MAIN GOALS:					
UNIT #5: SYNOPSIS: MAIN GOALS:					

what will be taught in a unit. For example, a unit on the topic "Ancient Egypt" might focus on any number of studies:

- learning about human-environmental interactions (e.g., impact of the Nile);
- exploring the religious and cultural practices of other groups (e.g., embalming, reincarnation);
- appreciating the mathematical and engineering features of this African people (e.g., building of pyramids);
- thinking critically about ethical issues (e.g., Is it fair to judge the actions of people in ancient times by our own standards?);
- learning about archaeology (e.g., carrying out a simulated dig).

In an important respect, a unit topic is the shell within which the contents of a unit will develop. Although the most common type of topic is what is typically referred to as a theme, there are other types of unifying or central ideas of a unit. The chart on the next page identifies six types of unit organizers.

The choice of type of topic influences the shape or direction of a unit. For example, a unit organized around a theme—say, on Simon Fraser—provides a different orientation than a project-based unit—say, to research, write and mount a play about Simon Fraser's travels—or an issue-based unit—say, on deciding whether Simon Fraser was a hero or a rogue. Although there will be overlap in what is learned from these three units there will likely be important differences in the outcomes. Accordingly, we should select unit topics that will best advance the goals we want to foster in each unit.

An important step in getting clear about a unit is to decide upon three or four goals that will be the main emphasis of the unit (other goals will be promoted but not stressed in the way the main goals will be) and, using these goals as a guide, to think through how the topic might best be handled. (As a theme or an issue? And what theme or issue in particular?) The sample of a partial course plan in the box on page 298 contains a synopsis, main goals and the objectives for the first unit in a course on nineteenth century Canada. The main foci of this unit are to help students learn to work effectively together in groups, to teach them about conducting independent research and to develop a broad understanding of key events leading up to Confederation. The unit organizer—a project to create a giant timeline of events during this period—was chosen because it is a good vehicle to serve these three goals.

Identifying specific objectives

As we think about our unit topic and main goals, we will inevitably begin to identify specific content. At some point it becomes necessary to outline more systematically and specifically the objectives or learning outcomes for the unit. At this stage we are not concerned about teaching methods—what we will have students do during the unit—but rather on what we hope students will learn. (Research suggests that many teach-

ers prefer to begin with the activities then decide what the objectives might be. This simply means that once deciding on a unit focus some teachers may want to jump to the next, more specific level and think about the activities that students will be involved in before identifying the specific objectives that the unit will address.)

The key challenge in identifying the specific objectives is to unpack what is involved in promoting the goals we have set for the year, and especially the main goals that we have identified for the unit. Objectives are simply more specific elements of a goal—objectives often take a lesson or two to cover whereas goals typically refer to general aims that may take an entire unit or longer to achieve. In developing the sample unit plan we would want to think through what is involved in promoting independent library research? What are the crucial sub-skills or tools that students will need to develop this ability and which of these are best taught in this unit? Should my students learn to use library reference aids (e.g., card catalogue, reference index), or should I introduce them to the Internet and the various tools available for electronic research? Perhaps, my students already know how to locate information sources. In which case, I might be better advised to help them improve at extracting information from these sources?

Although it is difficult to do, the best place to begin this articulation process is by developing lists of the more specific objectives that are implied by the goals for each unit (but especially the main goals for the unit). Often the curriculum guide or other professional materials are helpful in providing details about the objectives for specific goals. Of course, we will not be able to do it all in any one unit—we must set priorities about the most important objectives to pursue. As a general rule, we are well advised to do a smaller number of things very well, rather than attempt too many things in one unit. This is why a few goals (perhaps, three or four) should be designated as the main goals for the unit. If we run out of time we will make sure that the key objectives associated with our main goals are not sacrificed.

The following factors are particularly relevant considerations when deciding the specific objectives for a unit:

- the overall rationale for the course and the main goals for the unit;
- our students' interests and prior learning;
- the requirements of the provincial curriculum;
- our own interests and competencies as teachers;
- the resources available in the school and district;
- the possibilities of integration with other areas of study.

Sequencing objectives across units

The final task in developing a year overview is to develop a *scope* and *sequence* of objectives from unit to unit. The scope of objectives should be comprehensive so that over the course of a year the entire set of cur-

TYPES OF TOPICS OR UNIT ORGANIZERS

theme: A theme is an idea or feature that is shared by, or recurs in, a number of separate elements. The connection among elements in the unit is that they are in some way associated with a common theme. Some types of themes are:

places—(e.g., Egypt, our neighbourhood, deserts, the moon)

events—(e.g., making the pyramids, building the A-bomb)

eras—(e.g., the Depression, pre-Copernican Europe)

concepts—(e.g., friendship, harmony, time, creativity)

generalizations—(e.g., man is a social animal, history repeats itself)

phenomena—(e.g., biological change, war, growing up)

entities—(e.g., bears, atoms, multi-national companies)

narrative: A narrative (Kieran Egan calls it a storyform) is a series of episodes that uses a familiar structure for building upon and connecting elements in a unit. The elements are united in that each must fit the story being told. Some sample narratives are:

- developing story of a country, province or city
- tale of a people, family or person
- evolutionary steps in a discovery or invention
- account of a quest or adventure

issue: An issue identifies a specific question whose answer is a value judgment about what ought be the case. The elements are united in that each is necessary to competently address the issue. Entire units might focus on issues such as:

- Should students have a right to select their textbooks?
- Are large families better than small families?
- Should further technological innovation be encouraged?
- Which innovation arising from ancient Greece has had the most significant influence on our lives?

inquiry: An inquiry identifies a specific question whose answer is a description of how things actually were, are or are likely to become. The elements are united in that each is necessary to competently undertake the inquiry. Entire units might focus on inquiries such as:

- What motivated/drove famous people to greatness?
- How does the natural environment deal with its "waste"?
- What will my life be like thirty years from now?
- Is the United States more like ancient Sparta or Athens?

problem: A problem identifies a specific question whose answer is a course of action. The elements are united in that each is necessary to competently solve the problem. Instead of merely talking about what should or might occur, entire units could lead students to act on problems such as:

- Can we reduce the amount of paper wasted in school?
- How can our school be made more personal/safe?
- What can we do to protect our parks and wildlife?
- What can we do to improve working conditions in developing countries?

project: A project involves creation of a "product" of some kind. The elements are united in that each is necessary to competently complete the project. Entire units might focus on producing objects or events such as:

- models or replicas
- a play or performance
- diorama or mural
- written or audiovisual piece

Sample (Partial) Course Plan

UNIT DESCRIPTION	UNIT OBJECTIVES				
	CONTENT KNOWLEDGE	CRITICAL THINKING	INFORMATION GATHERING & REPORTING	PERSONAL & SOCIAL VALUES	INDIVIDUAL & COLLECTIVE ACTION
UNIT #1: *Timeline - The lead-up to Confederation* **SYNOPSIS:** The class is divided into five teams to re-search and prepare a giant illustrated time-line that would be posted around the entire classroom depicting the major social, political, cultural and economic events and people in Canada from 1815 to Confed-eration. Each team has responsibility for researching, documenting and illustrating major landmarks and key figures for a 10-year period. Groups must decide by consensus on the basis of agreed-upon criteria the most significant events/persons of their time period. Students are expected to share their findings orally and prepare a background sheet that all students receive. The unit concludes with a student-created exam on events and people depicted in the timeline. **MAIN GOALS:** 1. Learn to work effectively and cooperatively in groups. 2. Learn to conduct independent library research. 3. Develop a broad overview of events leading to Confederation.	• Overview of the political, economic, social and geo-graphical factors leading to Confederation. • Knowledge of key events and persons in the development of Canada.	• Ability to assess appropriateness of information source for purpose. • Ability to use criteria to reach a reasoned decision.	• Uses library refer-ence aids to locate sources (e.g., biblio-graphy, catalogue, electronic search engines). • Uses textual aids to locate information (e.g., table of contents, index, glossary, keywords, headings, legend). • Summarizes ideas in one's own words. • Uses graphics (e.g., timelines, charts, graphs) to present information. • Oral and visual communication is clear and accurate.	• Takes pride in preparing quality work. • Respects opinions and is supportive of others. • Engages res-pectfully in group discussion.	• Understands collaboration, cooperation, compromise, consensus. • Respects the rights of everyone in the group. • Plans how to organize the group, divide up the tasks, and schedule and monitor the work plan. • Fulfills roles and responsibilities effectively and fairly.

ricular objectives are adequately addressed. The sequence should be reasonable, for example, we should not teach objectives in an early unit that presuppose mastery of outcomes that we had planned for teaching later in the year. In many cases, there may be no obvious prerequisites—for example in teaching students to interpret visual documents it may make no difference whether we start with photographs or maps—the sequence may depend entirely on the availability of resources for the unit topics we have selected. In other cases, the sequence may be crucial. For example, we should teach simple procedures for using the Internet, such as finding sites where the address is provided, prior to introducing more sophisticated variants involving student-designed searches. Although there are no hard and fast rules, the following are different ways of thinking about the scope and sequence of objectives over the course of a year:

- proceed from simple to more difficult
- proceed from concrete to abstract
- proceed from general to specific
- proceed in chronological order (especially relevant with content objectives)
- process in reverse chronological order (i.e., from present working back)
- proceed from near to far
- proceed from far to near.

OUTLINING UNIT PLANS

A more specific level of planning occurs when we take each of the units described in the course plan and begin to develop the details of them. As illustrated on the form on the box below, unit plans typically consist of summary notes outlining the objectives, the proposed methods or activities, the anticipated resources that will be needed and the suggested assessment strategy for each lesson. A unit might contain anywhere from 10 to 20 lessons. A sample of a partial unit plan is found on the next page. The following sequence is one way to proceed when developing a unit plan.

- Brainstorm possible teaching strategies and resources that would promote the identified goals and objectives. Supplement your own ideas by looking for teaching resources in a local school library, in a teacher's resource centre or in catalogues of print and multimedia resources. Talk to others who have taught this topic and may be in a position to suggest ideas or resources. Assemble as many ideas and resources as you can find.

- Identify an introductory activity or activities. We all know that first impressions are important. This same principle applies to the way new units of study are introduced. The introductory lesson(s) to a unit can serve several important purposes:

  - arouse student interest in the topic and provoke student questions;
  - provide students with background information and set the context for what is to follow;
  - provide the teacher with diagnostic information as to the extent of student's present knowledge about the topic and attitudes toward it, as well as related skill levels;

UNIT PLAN

UNIT TOPIC			Grade	Unit #
UNIT GOALS	1.			
	2.			
	3.			
	4.			

Lesson Title	Specific Objectives	Methods/ Activites	Resources	Assessment Strategies & Criteria

SAMPLE (PARTIAL) UNIT PLAN

UNIT TOPIC	Our school community		GRADE	One	UNIT	#1

UNIT GOALS
1. Develop students' ability to read simple maps
2. Increase students' familiarity and comfort with the school setting and staff
3. Develop students' appreciation of the contributions that others make to the school
4. Develop students' ability to use criteria in thinking critically

Lesson Title	Specific Objectives	Methods/Activities	Resources	Assessment Strategies & Criteria
Making school our home	• learn the layout of the school; • learn the meaning of the concept "criteria"; • learn to use criteria in making a decision;	Read *Welcome Back to Pokeweed Public School*. Introduce map of school and, just as in the story, students will tour their school. Make a list of people and places encountered. Brainstorm what might be done to make school more "homey" (e.g., what something "looks like" or "sounds like" when it is done right. Introduce concept of "criteria"— what something "looks like" or "sounds like" when it is done right. Assist students in generating criteria for sound actions (i.e., realistic, safe, serves desired purpose). Discuss which options for making school more "homey" meet the criteria for sound action. Plan how the class might carry out some of these options.	• *Welcome Back to Pokeweed Public School* by John Bianchi;	• assess if students recognize when a possible option clearly meets or clearly does not meet the criteria;
Learning to read maps	• learn to read symbols and locate sites on simple maps;	Read *Mandy's Flying Map* to introduce the idea of maps. Discuss the concept of a "bird's-eye" view. Walk students through a classroom map pointing out things on the map and in the classroom. Play a game where students think of things in the classroom and give clues on the map to help others guess the object.	• *Mandy's Flying Map*; • overhead or poster-sized map of the classroom;	• using a game format, assess if students correctly move to places identified on the classroom map; • assess if students correctly point on the map to classroom objects;
Touring our school	• learn to follow simple maps and locate objects on the map;	Working in small groups and accompanied by a parent or helper, student go on another tour of the school. They are trace the route followed and add features to their map as they come to key spots in the school.	• copies of simple school map;	• assess if students correctly locate their location on the map and draw on their map objects in the school;
Who are the people in our school?	• learn who works in the school;	Read *Who's Behind the Door at Our School?* Students list the people in their school and the position they have (i.e., Mr. Chan, custodian; Ms. Smith is the principal; Mrs. Jones, the learning assistance teacher). Paste photographs of each person on a poster next to their name and position.	• *Who's Behind the Door at Our School?* by Michael Salmon; • staff photographs;	• assess if students correctly match the name, picture and position of each staff member;
What do the people in our school do?	• learn the duties performed by each staff member;	Brainstorm questions students might ask to learn more about each person and what they do. Discuss the criteria of a good question (i.e., is clear, gives lots on information—not "yes" or "no," may be unexpected). As a class, decide upon a common set of questions to use to interview each staff member. Students interview their designated person. Students trace route to the interview on their map.	• interview question and recording sheets for each pair of students;	• assess if students recognize when a possible option clearly meets or clearly does not meet the criteria; • assess if students correctly trace their route on the school map;
Who's contributing the most?	• appreciate staff contributions to school; • learn to support their position with a reason;	Record information gathered from interviews on poster next to each person's picture. Discuss criteria for deciding who contributes most (i.e., protects safety, affects largest number of students). Students vote for the three people who are doing the most to make the school a positive place, asking for a reason for each choice.	• "ballot" to vote for three most significant contributions;	• using the "ballot," assess if students offer a relevant reason for each choice; • observe informally during class discussions if students show appreciation for staff contributions;

This partial plan is adapted from a unit by primary teachers Janis Chappell, Robin Johnson, Kerrin McLeod and Danielle Doucette.

- help the teacher and students formulate a plan of action for studying about the topic of the unit.

The box on this page and the next offers various suggestions for beginning new units of instruction in an engaging and effective manner.

WAYS OF INTRODUCING A UNIT

- **Audio-Visuals.** Viewing an audio-visual material is motivating and provides students with information on which to build. Do not expect that students will necessarily attain a strong grasp of its contents on the first viewing. It can be viewed again at a later point in the unit. When choosing audio-visual material to introduce a unit the priority should be to stimulate interest rather than to provide a great deal of information immediately.

- **Brainstorming.** Brainstorming is a useful way to informally diagnose the depth of students' knowledge about a topic before beginning instruction and to help them organize the information they already have into a framework. The teacher's role is to accept and record all responses without criticism, help students expand on others' ideas, and set a time limit and stick to it. Following the brainstorming sessions the teacher helps students sort the ideas into categories using approaches such as webbing or data retrieval charts. The final organization should be retained so that students can examine it at the end of the unit to see how much they have learned.

- **Discrepant Event.** A discrepant event is a description that points out unusual aspects of a situation in order to provoke student thought. For example, tell students that as the people in a sleepy town of 500 inhabitants left church one Sunday, they heard much shouting and general hilarity issuing from the direction of the harbour. As they raced down for a look, they saw a steamship containing 400 men entering their harbour. Many of the men wore bright red shirts and carried backpacks with supplies. Some had picks and shovels. Ask students why they think these men descended on this town. After students have advanced a number of possible explanations, tell them that the sleepy town was called Fort Victoria and it was the future capital of the province of British Columbia. The men who arrived on the ship had just come from San Francisco because they had heard that gold had been found on the Fraser River. They intended to purchase supplies in Fort Victoria and then continue on to seek their fortunes. It was the influx of new people due to the gold rush which was the first step toward British Columbia becoming a colony and then a province.

  Here is another example. Tell students that a civilization began on the banks of a river which flooded regularly; it was surrounded by a desert; and was in a climate that was dry and hot. Ask them for their predictions as to the likelihood of survival of this civilization and for their guesses as to what civilization this might have been. If students are not able to guess correctly, tell them that the civilization was that of ancient Egypt and that it flourished on the banks of the Nile River in Africa for thousands of years. Ask students to hypothesize reasons why the civilization of ancient Egypt established itself in this particular location. They can then begin data gathering activities to verify or refute their hypotheses.

- **Displays.** A teacher created display can be useful for arousing interest and for providing initial information about a topic. The display should be set up a week or more prior to beginning the unit so that students will have plenty of time to browse among the items in the display and to talk about them informally with other class members. Alternatively, students can create their own displays by bringing pertinent items, newspaper articles and magazine illustrations to school, or the teacher and students can contribute jointly to the display.

- **Field Experience.** A field experience is often considered to be most effective at the end of a unit because students have a greater understanding to bring to it at that point. However, such an experience can also be useful at the beginning of a unit because of its value in piquing interest and in the information it can provide, which can serve as a springboard to the acquisition of further information.

- **Guest Speaker.** Invite a guest speaker who has special knowledge about the unit to speak to students. Often, students' parents are willing to speak to the class about their occupations, countries of origin or other areas of expertise. A way of finding out whether there are parents willing to make themselves available for this purpose is to send a questionnaire home at the beginning of the school year. Other sources of guest speakers include retired people's organizations, consulates, government departments and agencies, and public relations departments of large companies.

- **Music.** Play a tape which is representative of the time, place or topic. For instance, if studying a particular country, music commonly enjoyed by people there could be played. Songs from Canadian children's singers such as Raffi; Sharon, Lois and Bram; Fred Penner or Charlotte Diamond could be chosen to illustrate topics such as friendship, family relationships, and roles and responsibilities of family members. "The Wreck of the *Edmund Fitzgerald*" by Gordon Lightfoot is an example of a song which could be used in connection with Canada's transportation links.

- **Mystery Box.** Show students a gift wrapped box containing several objects related to the unit. Let each student handle the box. Have students use a "twenty questions" approach to ascertaining what objects you have selected to include in the box; that is, they will be limited to twenty questions, and therefore must begin with very general questions in order to eliminate as many possibilities as they can as quickly as possible. Record the guesses on the blackboard. When twenty questions have been asked, open the box and tell students a little about each object.

- **Simulation.** A simulation can provide an ex-

tremely motivating introduction to a unit. Examples are beginning a unit on the growth of industrialization by having students simulate an assembly line or a unit on local government with a simulation in which they become members of a city council making a decision related to commercial versus recreational uses of land. The simulation should be followed by a discussion in which the simulation experience is related to understandings which will arise from the unit.

- **Story.** Stories can engage student interest in a unit of study and bring unit understandings to life. Examples are the use of *Maxine's Tree* by Diane Leger-Haskell to begin a unit on the environment or perhaps a Greek myth to begin a unit on ancient Greece.

This list of unit openers was developed by Penney Clark.

- Identify a culminating activity or activities which summarize or draw attention to the main goals and provide an occasion to demonstrate and celebrate students' learning. Often the culminating activity may refer back to the introduction or be previewed at the outset of the unit so that the unit is "framed" in an coherent manner.

- Begin to flesh out the rest of the unit plan by indicating the specific lessons and order in which the unit will unfold. Specify objectives for each lesson. Check to see that all relevant objectives listed on the course plan for that unit are addressed. From the list generated above, select the teaching strategies, student activities and learning resources that will best serve the objective(s) for each lesson. Also, specify the assessment techniques (e.g., a one-page report, an oral presentation, a poster) that will reveal how well students have met the objectives for that lesson. It is also very useful to specify what qualities will be looked for when assessing students' work—in other words, indicate the criteria that will be used to assess students' work (e.g., the report is well organized, shows evidence of empathy for the people described, is historically accurate).

- Finally, review the draft unit plan with another person to ensure the following:
  - **adequate emphasis on each goal.** Verify the match of the activities and objectives described in the unit plan with the main goals identified in the course plan. Has the unit shifted in a direction that does not do justice to the originally proposed emphasis? If so, either bring the unit back in line so that it promotes the main goals adequately, or change the proposed focus for the unit.
  - **appropriate sequence.** Check to see that the lessons are ordered in such a way that the prerequisite objectives are taught in a reasonable sequence

and that the unit builds towards a culminating activity, with a sense of completion for students.

- **reasonable flow.** Look to see if the transitions between lessons and over the unit as whole are connected or disjointed. Although every lesson will not follow directly from the prior one nor lead smoothly to the next, the greater the flow of lessons, the less likely that students will be confused by the progress of the unit.

- **rich variety.** Review the proposed activities, resources and assessments strategies to ascertain if they contain sufficient variety and range. Without realizing it the unit may rely excessively on one or two activities (e.g., answering questions from a textbook) or assessment strategy (e.g., journal reflections).

CREATING LESSON PLANS

The most specific level of planning occurs at the individual lesson level. This is where we think through in considerable detail exactly what, when and how things will be done for each lesson. The more experienced we become, the less detailed our lesson plans need be. Although lesson planning may take different forms, I recommend dividing the planning of a lesson into seven tasks described below.

- **formulate lesson objectives.** Objectives specify the outcomes we hope to produce (i.e., what we expect students to learn from the activities that we plan for them). These objectives will already be identified if a unit plan has been developed. Although there is no hard and fast rule, it may be unwise to have more than three objectives for any given lesson, especially if they are not closely connected to one another. Generally speaking, promoting one or two outcomes well is to be preferred over doing many things superficially. It is important not to confuse objectives with methods: an objective specifies the hoped for outcome of having students complete the learning activity. Statements such as "Students will debate an issue" and "Students will experience what it is liked to be discriminated against" are both statements of method. A statement of the objectives is generated by asking what will students learn by engaging in the debate (e.g., learn to express their ideas clearly or to develop persuasive arguments to support their position) or by experiencing the discrimination (e.g., acquire greater sensitivity to the feelings of minorities).

- **introduce the lesson.** The introduction should provide an engaging and illuminating launch into the lesson. Its purpose is to create a "mindset" which will motivate students and focus their attention in ways that will increase the likelihood of their benefiting from the lesson. Suggestions for creating mindset include:
  - Establish a connection with a previous lesson.
  - Explain the purpose and value of what is to be learned.
  - Provide an overview of what will take place.
  - Invite students to share what they know of the topic for the day's lesson.
  - Involve students in an enjoyable activity or pose

a question or dilemma that will arouse curiosity and set a context for what students are about to learn.

- **develop and sequence the body of the lesson.** The body of the lesson refers to the teacher instructions and student activities that will occur during the lesson. Suggestions for planning the body of the lesson include:
  - Break down the component parts of each objective into teachable elements and think of how each can be taught.
  - Vary the types of activities so there is a change of pace.
  - Think about dividing the tasks/sessions into tightly orchestrated segments (of between 10 and 20 minutes duration) to reduce the likelihood of students tiring of activities that go on for a long time.
  - Although this sequence is not always appropriate, as a rough rule it is useful to think of six stages in the body of a lesson:
    — *instructional input:* students are given new information or are introduced to a new notion (by the teacher or students, through reading or viewing);

LESSON PLAN

Lesson title

_____

Objectives

By the end of the lesson students will:

1.
2.
3.
4.

_____

Introduction

_____

Body of lesson

_____

Closure

_____

Assessment

_____

Extension

— *modelling*: a demonstration (by the teacher or by students) of what is to be done with this new knowledge;

— *trial run*: on their own or in small groups, students try one or two examples (or the first steps) to see if they have grasped the task;

— *group feedback*: issues and difficulties encountered during the trial are discussed as a class;

— *application of knowledge*: students then proceed with the main assignment for the lesson;

— *coaching*: as students work on their assignment, the teacher or students (in pairs or in cooperative groups) provide individual advice as problems and questions arise.

- **prepare resources.** Resources refer to the instructional materials, activity sheets, readings, questions, etc. that will be used to support the lesson.

- **draw closure.** Closure refers to the proposed means for debriefing the lesson and helping students consolidate what they have learned. Closure often involves the following sorts of task:
  - students summarize what they have learned;
  - students apply learning to a new situation;
  - the teacher synthesizes key ideas and draws connections.

- **assess student learning.** Assessment tells us how well the objective(s) have been met. Students should be provided, *prior* to completing an assignment, with a clear indication of the assessment including:
  - the criteria that will be used as the basis for assessment of student learning;
  - the standards or levels of performance for each criteria (i.e., What does "very good" on the assignment look like, and how does it differ from "good," etc.?).

- **extend or follow-up on the lesson.** The extension part of a lesson is a way of providing for those students who invariably finish early. Unless we plan educationally enriching activities for this eventuality some students will often waste considerable class time. Extension activities are useful when the proposed lesson goes more quickly than anticipated. Extension is also useful to encourage students who may want to further pursue ideas raised by the lesson.

The following sample lesson plan, Simon Fraser: Hero or Rogue?, illustrates many of the suggestions just described. The focus of the lesson is the concept of inference—that is, interpreting or drawing conclusions from accepted facts. In this lesson, students consider whether or not Simon Fraser is a bona fide hero by reading an historical account of his explorations and dealings with the First Nations people he encountered.

SAMPLE LESSON PLAN

Lesson title

Simon Fraser: Hero or Rogue?

Objectives

By the end of the lesson students will:

1. understand the concepts of "directly observed fact" and "inference" and be able to identify inferences draw by an author;

2. understand that different inferences may be drawn from the same event (and the most defensible inference is the one that is most plausible given the facts);

3. be able to generate and defend an interpretation of a historical event;

4. know of Simon Fraser's experiences with First Nations people.

Introduction

Mention to students that Simon Fraser is a famous Canadian explorer—among other forms of recognition, a major river and a university have been named after him. Suggest that there is some reason to suspect that history been too kind to Simon Fraser—that possibly he really doesn't deserve his fame. The point of the lesson will be to find out exactly what sort of person he was. Before doing that, students must learn how to interpret facts.

Body of lesson

1. *Teaching about inferences* (i.e., difference between directly observable fact and an inference). With little or no prior explanation perform the following gestures and ask students to explain what you are doing:
   - Point finger at a student and motion to come.
   - Put up your finger to your mouth to indicate silence.
   - Pretend to be thinking.

After students have answered, suggest that they have interpreted or drawn an inference from what you were doing. Ask them to tell you exactly what they saw you doing. Use a chart such as the following to record student answers.

Directly observable facts	Inferences
directing index finger at student and curling it inward	*teacher wants student to come to her*
putting index finger to your lips	*teacher trying to quiet class*
stretching out arm and pointing index finger	*teacher sending student out of room*

2. *Reinforcing understanding.* Ask class to come up with a definition of: (a) a directly observable fact and (b) an inference. Ask students for examples of a directly observable fact and possible inferences to be drawn. Provide several examples and discuss the inferences implied in the statements (include some that are contentious inferences).

3. *Modelling the assignment.* Direct students' attention to the first paragraph of the reading for this lesson "The Descent of the Fraser River." Invite students to identify either directly observed facts or inferences in this paragraph. Ask students to speculate about other inferences that might be drawn from these events. For example, it is stated that "The route was so rough that a pair of moccasins was worn to shreds in one day of portaging." The wearing out of a pair of moccasins in one day is the directly observable fact. The author's inference seems to be that Fraser and his men were determined, preserving and willing to endure great sacrifice.

4. *Application of learning.* Direct student attention to the *Student Instructions* sheet (for younger students present them orally) and the *Data Recording Chart.* Explain the tasks (which may be done individually or in small groups). Ask one-half of the class to focus on Simon Fraser and the other half of the class to focus on the First Nations people. Confirm that students understand what is expected before setting them to work.

5. *Sharing of insights.* After students have had sufficient time to complete the

---

STUDENT INSTRUCTIONS

Simon Fraser: Hero or Rogue?

Simon Fraser is a famous Canadian explorer—a major river and a university have been named after him. Has history been too kind to Simon Fraser? Does he really deserve this fame? What sort of person was he? What sort of people were the First Nations people that Simon Fraser encountered on his travels? Read the attached historical report, *The descent of the Fraser River,* and complete the following tasks.

Step 1

Circle all the statements in the attached report that provide any obvious insights about the character (personality traits, and personal strengths and weaknesses) of Simon Fraser and/or the First Nations people he encountered.

Step 2

Use the data recording sheet to summarize what the report tells us about Simon Fraser and the First Nations people. The entries in the left-hand column should be *descriptions* of what occurred, the entries in the middle and right-hand column are *character traits* that the author and you attribute to the character of the person(s). In many cases, the author does not present directly observed facts, but simply provides his inferences. In these situations, indicate what you imagine are the facts that would have been observed. Examples have been provided on the data recording sheet.

1) *Simon Fraser's character*: In the left-hand column, list any *directly observable facts abo*ut the events and actions involving Simon Fraser. For each directly observable fact, indicate in the middle column what the *author* infers from the facts about his character, and in the right-hand column indicate what *you* infer from these facts about his character.

2) *Characteristics of First Nations people*: In the left-hand column, list any *directly observable facts* about the events and actions involving First Nations people. For each directly observable fact, indicate in the middle column what the *author* infers from the facts about their character, and in the right-hand column indicate what *you* infer from these facts about their character traits.

Step 3

1) List approximately five words or phrases which portray your assessment of Simon Fraser's character. Be prepared to defend your assessment.

2) List approximately five words or phrases which portray your assessment of First Nations peoples' character Be prepared to defend your assessment.

DATA RECORDING CHART

SIMON FRASER'S CHARACTERISTICS		
Directly observable facts	*Author's inferences*	*Your inferences*
Example: *The places where they had to carry their canoes were so rough that a pair of moccasins was worn out.*	*Simon Fraser is a very determined individual— nothing will stop him.*	*Fraser may be determined but, perhaps, he just doesn't know how to walk in this kind of countryside.*

FIRST NATION'S CHARACTERISTICS		
Directly observable facts	*Author's inferences*	*Your inferences*
Example: *The First Nations people said the river could not be canoed and Fraser believed them.*	*The First Nations people were truthful.*	*Perhaps, the First Nations were trying to scare Fraser.*

assignment, invite students to share their findings. Begin by asking about the more interesting facts and inferences that students encountered in the text. Then ask individuals to share their assessments of the character of Simon Fraser and the First Nations people. Encourage debate and ask students to defend and qualify their answers on the basis of consistency with the evidence found in the text. Be careful to note that all First Nations people may not have the same character—some may be friendlier than others, and so on.

6. *Summative assignment.* Based on their own deliberations and on the class discussion, ask students to list five or six words or phrases that they believe fairly describe Simon Fraser's character and five or six words or phrases describing the First Nations character(s). Students must support their character description by referring to their interpretations of the events. Remind students that events may have several plausible interpretations, and their task is to decide which is the most defensible interpretation. For older students expect them to defend their interpretations of specific events in light of other evidence in the text.

Closure

*   Discuss how differences of opinion about what sort of person Simon Fraser was could be resolved by finding out more about Simon Fraser from others sources (e.g., Simon Fraser's diary, the diaries of some of his men, what is know about Simon Fraser from his friends, employers and competitors).

*   What do these differing stories about tell us about the study of the past? Consider the following question: *What is the true nature of history: Fact or inference?* In your own words, explain what the question is asking and support your position by referring to examples drawn from the report about Simon Fraser's trip and an account of the trip from a First Nations perspective.

Assessment

*   Evaluate student's character profile in light of the following criteria: adequacy of support for overall conclusion, sensitivity to alternative inferences, ability to support particular inferences in light of other textual evidence.

*   Present students with the drawing of Simon Fraser and his men. Pose the following questions:
    *   Which one of the men in the drawing is Simon Fraser? Explain the reasons for your choice.
    *   What impressions does this drawing suggested about these explorers and about the region that they are travelling through?
    *   Draw your own picture of Simon Fraser and his men as seen from a First Nations perspective. On the back of your picture explain the key differences in perspective on the explorers and the region between your picture and the drawing provided.

    Criteria for assessment of picture study
    *   Correctly identify middle person (in front canoe) and suggest that clothing, physical appearance and lack of paddle are key reasons why this person is different from the rest.
    *   The number of plausible inferences that student suggests (e.g., region is dangerous, uncivilized and largely uninhabited, and the explorers are daring, afraid and determined).
    *   Assess students' pictures (and explanation) in terms of the number and plausibility of inferences drawn as seen from the First Nations perspective. An additional criterion might be imaginativeness of inferences drawn.

Extension or follow-up activities

*   Have students write a two-page detailed account of Simon Fraser's trip from the perspective of one of the First Nations people that Simon Fraser would likely have encountered. Their account should be consistent with the directly observable facts in the attached historical report. (It is expected that they will draw different inferences from these facts.) *Criteria for assessment*: The major criteria are the plausibility of inferences drawn and sensitivity to alternative inferences when facts are seen from different perspective. Other criteria might include accuracy of chronological sequence, imaginativeness of inferences drawn and completeness of account of all the major events.

*   Discuss factors that affect the credibility of reports (e.g., were the witnesses physically present, do they have an obvious self-interest, are they trustworthy sources). Why might Simon Fraser's diary not be completely credible? Why might he be motivated to distort the truth, consciously or unconsciously? Perhaps, introduce concepts of primary and secondary sources.

THE DESCENT OF THE FRASER RIVER

On May 28, 1808 Simon Fraser led 23 men to find a route from the interior of British Columbia to the Pacific Ocean along the river which Fraser imagined to be the Columbia River. Day after day they encountered obstacles as they paddled down the river. The river was a continuous series of rapids and the carrying places were extremely dangerous or very long. The places where they had to carry their canoes to get around the rapids were so rough that a pair of moccasins was worn to shreds in one day. Fraser decided the Indians he had met were correct in saying that the river was not passable for canoes. So Fraser and his men set out on foot, carrying packs weighing eighty pounds each. In his diary, Fraser wrote that they experienced "a good deal of fatigue and disagreeable walking" but he and his men continued on their journey.

Soon they met Indians who told them ten more days would bring them to the sea. One villager said that he had been to the sea and had seen "great canoes" and white men. When Fraser and his party proceeded, many of the locales walked with them. Two days later, at a large village (near present day Lillooet), Indians told them that the river was navigable from their village to the sea, whereupon Fraser bargained for two canoes. At another village (now Lytton) the people were so friendly that Fraser was called upon to shake hands with twelve hundred of them. In return he and his men were well fed and were able to get two wooden canoes.

Despite what the Indians had about the river being navigable, the explorers soon found their way blocked by numerous rapids. Two canoes were lost. More canoes were obtained from the natives. During this time, the explorers toiled over the roughest country they had ever seen:

We had to pass over huge rocks assisted by the Indians . . . As for the road by land, we could scarcely make our way with even only our guns. I have been for a long period among the Rocky Mountains, but have never seen any thing like this country. It is so wild that I cannot find words to describe our situation at times. We had to pass where no human being should venture; yet in those places there is a regular footpath impressed, or rather indented upon the very rocks by frequent travelling. Besides this, steps which are formed like a ladder . . . furnish a safe and convenient passage to the Natives; but we, who had not the advantage of their education and experience, were often in imminent danger when obliged to follow their example.[extract from Fraser's *Journal*]

At Spuzzum, Fraser was much impressed by a number of totem poles, each fifteen feet high and "carved in a curious but rude manner, yet pretty well proportioned." Friendly Indians living in large frame houses presented them with roast salmon. Near where the town of Hope now stands, they were entertained at a large village where there was a huge community house built of cedar planks. Some Indians warned that the natives of the coast were "wicked" and would attack them, but Fraser would not alter his plan. When these Indians refused to lend him a canoe Fraser took one by force. For a short while canoes from the village followed them, their occupants waving weapons and shouting war songs, but Fraser and his men ignored them. Soon after, another group came at them "howling like wolves" and swinging war clubs, but they did not attack Fraser's group. Fraser ordered his men to paddle farther along to a second village, but the behaviour of the Indians forced them to turn back. On July 2, near what is now New Westminster, Fraser decided to return up the river in order to secure provisions before attempting to resume his descent to the ocean. This was the farthest distance reached by the explorers. Fraser's reception by the natives on his return up the river was far from friendly—one group seized a canoe and began to pillage the baggage. Fraser forced a canoe from them and left a blanket in return. For several days hostile Indians followed them. They finally reached friendly villages and were guided over rough bridges and swaying ladders by natives who "went up and down these wild places with the same agility as sailors do on board a ship."

Fraser finally arrived back at Fort George on August 6. Although Fraser had not accomplished his purpose of exploring the Columbia River, he really was the discover of the river that bears his name. Because of his voyage the confusion between the Fraser River and Columbia River was cleared up.

This is a shortened version of "The descent of the Fraser River" by Malcolm G. Parks in Discoverers and Explorers in Canada—1763-1911 (Portfolio II #4), *illustrated by Charles W. Jefferys and published by Imperial Oil Ltd. Reprinted with permission of the National Archives of Canada.*

CLOSING REMARKS

As suggested by the analogy offered at the outset of this article, the challenges to thoughtful planning are a lot like trying to negotiate through a wilderness. Just as it easy to lose one's way in the forest, so too it is easy to become disoriented when planning for instruction at any level. We are especially likely to stumble if we fail to articulate or we lose sight of our important educational destinations. The danger, if you will pardon the forced metaphor, is that we may lose sight of the forest through the trees. The immense volume of choices about what and how to do it and our desire to do it all may result in plans that are scattered and rather superficial. Setting a modest number of challenging goals and doing them well may be the best course to follow.

Having just emphasized the importance of a strong guiding direction to one's teaching, let me also caution that we should not feel bound to follow a preordained set of steps and activities when circumstances change. We need to monitor student reactions as we go, changing plans in mid-stream when appropriate. In addition, as we learn more about teaching, we should revisit our plans from year-to-year.

32

Story Forms and Romantic Perspectives: Alternative Frameworks for Planning in Social Studies

Kieran Egan

In the curriculum of teacher-preparation programs a prominent place is usually given to teaching students how to organize lessons and units. This usually involves some model derived from the procedure recommended by Tyler (1949) and elaborated in a variety of ways during the last quarter century or more. Often there are segments on stating aims and objectives, organizing the content and methods of teaching so that the aims and objectives will be achieved, and evaluating to see whether or not, or to what degree, they were in fact achieved. There have been some criticisms of Tyler's particular formulation (Kliebard, 1970; Stenhouse, 1975), but it is commonly accepted that equipping student teachers with an objectives/content/methods/evaluation scheme for planning is to provide them with an important and useful skill.

The desire to improve this scheme and make it more readily accessible to students has led to what one might call an increasing technologizing of the original procedure. Each section has been the focus of large-scale research efforts and more elaborate and explicit techniques have been recommended as a result. There is, for example, a huge body of literature on the need for, or the need to resist, stating objectives in behavioral terms; on the structuring of content, either to lead precisely to the behaviors aimed for, or to ensure understandings, knowledge, skills and so on; on teaching-methods, which are characterized in detail and labelled as discrete "models;" and on quite remarkably elaborate instruments of evaluation. All this research and implementation literature has tended to reinforce the sense of the utility and appropriateness of Tyler's basic scheme.

What this overall scheme brings to the fore is a particular way of thinking about teaching. It is a way which comes along quite subtly with the scheme, and the apparent common-sense of the objectives/content/methods/evaluation scheme makes us think that this way of thinking is generally appropriate. My contention is that the elaboration and technologizing of Tyler's basic rationale as a planning procedure taught to student teachers, while an excellent preparation for some aspects of teaching, is rather poor at, and suppresses, others. Unfortunately, it is some of the more important aspects of teaching that are suppressed and rather less important ones that are promoted to centre-stage in their place.

When planning a unit or lesson according to the currently dominant procedure we are encouraged to select our topic—say, North American Indians at Grade Four—and then state our objectives for that topic. These may include a general aim, such as that children will become familiar with an earlier culture and form of life that prevailed before Europeans came. Such objectives are typically arranged under headings of clothing, shelter, food, social structure and so on. Materials and procedures to be used may then be listed. The teaching may go forward in a variety of ways. Some teachers may use didactic procedures based on standard texts, others will include building a model First Nations village, fishing with the old First Nations methods, having a First Nations person address the class about past and present details of the life of his or her society and so on. The evaluation will involve methods of testing how well the objectives were achieved. These evaluative procedures can vary from the behavioral to ethnomethodological surveys; they will seek to test whether and to what degree children have mastered the appropriate knowledge and skills, can use the requisite concepts and have enhanced their intercultural understanding.

What is missing? Nothing is missing as a matter of necessity. This planning procedure does not require that we ignore something important. Rather it *tends* to encourage certain things to be focussed on and others to be neglected or suppressed. What, then, does this procedure tend to neglect? Meaning. It tends to focus the planner's mind on clarity of organizing content to ensure the learning of certain specified material. It tends to neglect what it is about that material that can be made most meaningful and engaging to the particular children to whom it will be taught. Now clearly these are not incompatibles. My concern, however, is with the "fit" of the procedure used and the job at hand. The dominant procedure does not fit equally well all aspects of the educational job, and seems to fit only with strain crucial aspects of that job which have tended to receive less than their due while use of this procedure has predominated. Children's access to meaning in the curriculum has, it seems to me, become a matter of too slight concern.

Rather than try to elaborate this point in the abstract it might be better to propose an alternative and by example show in what ways important features of the educational task which are suppressed in the traditional procedure can be brought into focus. So I will contrast the traditional procedure for planning units and lessons—objectives/content and methods/evaluation with that for telling a story and, for somewhat older students, with taking a romantic perspective on the content to be learned. The procedure I am recommending encourages the teacher to think of the lesson or unit as a good story to be told and as emotionally important, rather than as a set of objectives to be achieved and evaluated. Perhaps it might be thought that what I am doing is simply recommending a more or less novel way of organizing content and methods that can fit within the traditional procedure. I think that rather more is involved, and acceptance of the value of the story form and a romantic perspective has implications which go beyond a small recommendation for improving an element of the traditional procedure. Let me introduce the new planning tools by way of a discussion of why it makes sense to draw on the use of stories and of romance in teaching.

THE MYTHICAL FOUNDATIONS OF UNDERSTANDING

In oral cultures people know only what they can remember. Once something is forgotten by living memories, it is lost for ever. In oral cultures, then, techniques that can assist the memory and so help preserve the tribe's lore securely are of great social importance. It has been discovered in nearly all oral cultures that by using rhyme, rhythm and meter it is possible to make messages and social lore more easily memorable. Similarly all oral cultures have discovered that if the lore can be encoded into stories it can be made more memorable than by any other technique. It is not too much to say, then, that the story is one of the most important social inventions. It ensured memorization of social lore and stimulated an emotional commitment to that lore, and to the social group, and so helped to establish individuals' sense of identity. Education or socialization in oral cultures centered on learning the lore of the tribe as it was encoded in the sacred myth stories. All oral cultures that we know of used or use myth stories for this purpose (Blumenberg, 1985; Lévi-Strauss, 1966; Malinowski, 1954).

> The procedure I am recommending encourages the teacher to think of the lesson or unit as a good story to be told and as emotionally important, rather than as a set of objectives to be achieved and evaluated.

We tend to forget that until children have internalized literacy in Western culture, they live in an oral culture and they have available for use the techniques of orality. This does not mean that their thinking is generally like that of people in oral cultures, but only that they use certain techniques of thinking in common. But these techniques affect how people make sense of the world and of experience. It is not coincidental, then, that we find young children using in their activities such techniques as rhyme, rhythm, meter and, very prominently, stories. We can see these at work whenever we examine the intellectual engagements of children (Egan, 1987). Let us consider just three features of the kinds of stories children seem most readily engaged by, and see later what we may infer from them about the kind of understanding of social studies that is accessible using these features.

- The basic structure of the classic fairy stories or folk tales which children find readily engaging most commonly is binary. Children's stories use powerful and abstract binary opposites, such as good/bad, brave/cowardly, security/fear. That is, young children deploy some of the most powerful abstract concepts in making sense of the world. We are commonly told that young children's thinking is concrete; that they cannot use abstractions. Indeed, they commonly do not *articulate* abstractions, but clearly they *use* them prominently in making sense. If they did not have such abstract concepts available for use they would be unable to make sense of the kinds of stories they find most engaging. This observation suggests that when planning teaching we need to be sensitive to what powerful abstract concepts we can structure the concrete content on. It seems not too much to say that it is only through connecting concrete con-

---

Children's stories use powerful and abstract binary opposites, such as good/bad, brave/cowardly, security/fear. That is, young children deploy some of the most powerful abstract concepts in making sense of the world.

---

tent with powerful abstract binary opposites that we can hope to make it meaningful to young children (Hayek, 1970).

- The content of the fairy stories or folk tales that young children find engaging is rather odd. Such stories are commonly made up of creatures like middle-class talking bears or rabbits, witches and giants. Why should children find such impossible creatures so engaging if, as we are told, their thinking is bound to what they perceive? Consider how children gain conceptual control over a wide range of phenomena in their environment. Usually they first learn binary opposite concepts—in learning conceptual control over the temperature continuum, for example, they learn first the concepts "hot" and "cold." Then they learn a mediating concept, like "warm." Then they mediate between "warm" and "cold" and learn the concept "cool," and so on. This procedure works very well for all kinds of phenomena in their environment. If you look at the world through the eyes of a child you note some clear binary discriminations. Some things are alive and some dead, for example. If you use the same procedure that serves so well making sense of the physical world, you seek a mediating category; that is you look for things that are both dead and alive, as warm is both hot and cold. So the category of ghosts and spirits is generated; they are both alive and dead. Similarly, between nature and culture, you generate a menagerie of creatures who are both natural and cultural, such as middle-class talking bears and rabbits. That is, this procedure helps to account for the contents of children's fantasy stories.

- The story-form itself is worth reflecting on. What, after all is a story? Stories are narratives that fix for their hearers how to *feel* about the events that make them up. Life and history cannot do this very successfully, because we keep reassessing how we feel

about things as future events affect us. But once a story is ended there are no further events to affect the meaning of the story's events. It is a complete world which provides us with a security and satisfaction rarely available outside of fiction (Frye, 1957; Kermode, 1966).

These are three techniques children up to about age seven or eight use readily in thinking, which are easily verified by any observer. The phenomena are uncontentious; the task then is to infer from them what kind of social studies material would be accessible and engaging to children on the one hand, and what method of teaching would stimulate the development of understanding on the other. I will return to this task after similarly discussing some of the characteristics of older students' learning. What does it mean to take a Romantic perspective, for students from about ages seven or eight to about fourteen or fifteen?

TAKING A ROMANTIC PERSPECTIVE

With the internalizing of literacy, which commonly takes place around the age of seven or eight in the schooled cultures of the West, some further sense-making techniques or, to borrow a term from Lévi-Strauss, *bons-à-penser*, come into play. By "internalizing" literacy I mean becoming sufficiently fluent that students begin to take it and its capacities for granted in their intellectual lives. Again, I will consider just three characteristics of students' sense-making, and will infer them from some of the commonest intellectual engagements that are readily observable.

- A significant change occurs in the kinds of stories that students find most engaging after about age seven or eight. Perhaps the most general way to characterize this change is to say that students' thinking becomes engaged with and constrained by reality. This is rather a general way to put it! To take pervasive American examples, with a male orientation, students commonly become interested in stories with characters like Superman. Superman differs significantly from Cinderella, in that while both are impossible characters, Superman requires a context of plausibility to make him acceptable. That is, we have to know that Superman was born on the planet Krypton and was sent through space to land in America, and that his superpowers are due to the difference between his home planet and its sun and those of earth and our sun. Children are quite unconcerned about the means of locomotion used by Cinderella's Fairy Godmother or the physical processes whereby she changes mice into horses and the pumpkin into a coach. More commonly, we find students become interested in more realistic stories, such as *Anne of Green Gables* or *The Adventures of Huckleberry Finn*.

Student's initial engagement with this reality that seems to become intellectually engrossing after the internalizing of literacy is with its extremes. There is not a gradual expansion of interests; in some sense there seems to be almost the reverse. In the earlier layer of understanding, children's intellectual engagement with their fantasy worlds seems only incidentally concerned with reality. With the internalizing of literacy and the engagement with reality we see first their engagement with extremes—with what is most strange, exotic and bizarre in the world and in human experience. In the English-speaking world one of the most engaging books for students during this layer is *The Guinness Book of Records*—lists of the extremes of the real world and of human experience. It is the biggest, the smallest, the fattest, the thinnest, the fastest, the slowest and so on, that are most readily engaging.

- Another evident characteristic of student's intellectual lives at this time is the development of associations with heroes and heroines. Perhaps it would be truer to say that the association is not so much with heroes or heroines so much as with the transcendent human qualities that they express. That is, it is with such qualities as courage, ingenuity, patience, power and so on that students associate. These are the human qualities required to overcome the threats of the everyday world that bear down on students. As they grow to consciousness of reality, and of its autonomy and independence from their wishes, hopes and fears, they need to build defences against

---

Students from about ages eight to fifteen in Western cultures are relatively powerless in society, while becoming increasingly conscious of society and while developing a sense of their independent selves. By associating with transcendent human qualities—in heroes or heroines, in film stars or football teams—they associate with, and grow towards, those things best able to help them feel less powerless in society.

---

this threatening reality. Students from about ages eight to fifteen in Western cultures are relatively powerless in society, while becoming increasingly conscious of society and while developing a sense of their independent selves. By associating with transcendent human qualities—in heroes or heroines, in film stars or football teams—they associate with, and grow towards, those things best able to help them feel less powerless in society.

- A further item might be noted. Students during these middle-school years tend to develop obsessive interests—hobbies, or collections, or diary keeping. Students commonly engage something in great detail, and they seek to complete sets of things, whether collections of dolls, football cards, postage stamps and so on. Commercial interests are very good at exploiting this drive. I think we may see it as a part of students' discovery of reality. While on the one hand they search for the extreme limits of reality and its most strange and exotic features, they seem also

to explore it by trying to get some sense of its *scale*. By finding out exhaustively about something in detail, one gets a sense of security that the world is not limitless, and one gets some sense of the scale of things. The search for the extremes and for details can be compared to the kind of interest we have in looking through telescopes and microscopes. Both give us a perspective on reality that adds to our understanding of its scope and scale. Students during their middle-school years seem inclined to do this intellectually too, seeking macro- and micro-scopic views of the world they find themselves in.

SOME PRINCIPLES FOR TEACHING SOCIAL STUDIES

I would like here just to list a few principles that we might infer from the above observations for teaching, and then I will try to design a couple of models or frameworks that teachers might use in planning their history or social studies lessons. Most of the educational research that deals with children's and students' thinking tends to focus on their logical or logico-mathematical capacities. At least this is the case in North America, and also is the case with Piaget's interesting work. Important as this is, it tends to neglect those imaginative capacities, in which indeed we tend to see children's and students' intellectual activity at its most engaged and energetic. What I have tried to do above is focus rather on imaginative intellectual life, and so the principles I will note below are concerned with how we might engage children's and students' imaginations in social studies material.

If we wish to engage children's and students' imaginations, then, we might be wise to use the following characteristics in our teaching of young children:

- affective orientation
- abstract binary opposites
- the heroic
- detail and distance
- the exotic, wonder and awe
- humanizing knowledge

Affective orientation

Children's imaginations tend to be more readily engaged by materials that are organized and presented so that they not only convey information but also involve children affectively or emotionally. The most common and powerful technique that enables us to do this is to organize the material into the form of a story. This does *not* mean having to fit the content into a fictional story, but rather it invites the teacher to shape the factual content into a story shape. (I will indicate one method of doing this in the next section.) The teacher's task, if this principle is to be used, is to first reflect on what is affectively engaging about the content to be taught.

Abstract binary opposites

We saw earlier that affectively orienting children's understanding is achieved more readily if we organize our content using abstract binary oppositions. This tool is particularly useful in providing clear access to the meaning of the content. To use this principle teachers must reflect on what fundamental binary opposites can be located in the content to be taught — survival/destruction? fear/security? love/hate? cooperation/competition? and so on endlessly. I should perhaps emphasize that use of this principle does *not* require that we present the world to children in constant black and white or in simplistic terms. Consider that we all use such binary affective orienting techniques constantly, and that the purpose of beginning with such opposites is that they provide access to the content and we can then mediate between them and make understanding more sophisticated. But initial access is crucial.

The following items are particularly relevant to students during the middle-school years, but may suggest ideas for teaching younger children too.

The heroic

This does not mean teaching about male heroes performing superhuman deeds. But the quality of heroism is an effective catcher of our imaginations, and particularly so during early adolescence. We create a sense of the heroic when we emphasize those qualities that overcome the everyday constraints that hem us in. Heroic qualities can be found in anything. They need not only be located in people acting or suffering. An institution can embody heroic qualities. Even a plant can be seen as heroic, as when we focus on, for example, a weed's tenacity in maintaining itself in hostile conditions. A rock formation can be "heroized" by focusing on its stability, its stubbornness or its towering strength and sheer persistence. This "heroizing" of whatever we wish to engage students' imaginations in does not necessarily require falsification; rather it is a matter of emphasizing those qualities of the chosen content that transcend the everyday and conventional sense of them that we might unthinkingly hold.

Detail and distance

Another potential stimulant to students' imaginations is to shift perspectives now and then. Teachers might take an opportunity in a lesson or unit of study to pursue some topic in great detail, and occasionally to stand back and see the whole area within a wider context. Remember how common it is for people to enjoy looking through microscopes and telescopes when they have a chance.

The exotic, wonder and awe

Adolescents' imaginations are readily engaged by the extremes of reality, with what is most strange and exotic about the world and human experience. Teachers are often told to begin with what is familiar to students. This principle suggests that we might try quite the opposite. If we want to engage students' imaginations, beginning with the most exotic and least familiar seems a better principle. As with the heroic, there is potentially something strange and exotic about everything—if we can only see it in the right light. Even the most commonplace features of our environment can be seen as the products of amazing ingenuity, struggles, immense natural forces and persisting energy.

Teachers are often told to begin with what is familiar to students. This principle suggests that we might try quite the opposite. If we want to engage students' imaginations, beginning with the most exotic and least familiar seems a better principle.

Wonder is a kind of surprize mingled with admiration or curiosity or bewilderment. A significant feature of wonder is the combination of exclusive attention to the object of one's wonder and the desire to know more about it. Pointing up some features of a topic that can stimulate students' sense of wonder is occasionally useful in keeping their imaginations engaged.

Awe is a little different from wonder. Awe is the emotion resulting from the perception of something mysterious underlying the everydayness of things. It can be evoked by pointing to some mystery within what might normally be taken for granted. Most basically we might feel awe in response to the occasional clear and profound sense of there being something rather than nothing, existence rather than non-existence. The stimulation of a sense of awe also seems to me educationally important because it can help to provide a proper humility about the limited intellectual grasp we gain on reality.

Humanizing knowledge

The imagination helps students' understanding of knowledge if the knowledge is embedded in contexts of human emotions, human struggles, hopes and fears. Whatever content we wish to teach has a place in human lives and human purposes. By locating it, by seeing it, as meaningful in others' lives, students can gain a better imaginative sense of its meaning. In addition we might note that knowledge will engage students' imaginations more readily if it is clear that the teachers are imaginatively engaged by it. So "humanizing knowledge" can be read in two senses; one, concerning the context of human lives in which the content is embedded, and, two, concerning its place in the imaginative life of the teacher. This latter suggests that, in planning, teachers should reflect on the imaginative meaning in their own lives of the material to be taught.

IMPLICATIONS FOR TEACHING

We might infer a number of implications for teaching from these principles. I will first try to outline frameworks that might help the planning of teaching. I will present two frameworks; the first, called the Story Form framework, will be most appropriate for use in planning teaching up to about age eight, and the second, called the Romantic framework, from about age eight to fifteen. In each case the frameworks will draw on the principles outlined above and be articulated in terms of a set of questions, answering which will produce a lesson or unit plan. These conflict somewhat with the planning frameworks that are currently most common in English speaking countries. Those usually begin by requiring the teacher to state objectives, then to select content, then methods and then decide on means for evaluating whether the objectives have been achieved. Such a model is derived from industrial procedures, and particularly the assembly line method of production (Callaghan, 1962). The alternative frameworks I suggest are at least derived from educational considerations. (Unfortunately I do not have space here to show more than a single example that uses the first of these frameworks, but a number of examples of both are available in Egan, 1987, 1988, 1990, 1992 & 1997.)

These are not intended to be rigidly followed in planning all teaching. Rather they are offered as heuristic frameworks that attempt to capture some significant principles of how students' imaginations can be engaged in learning. No doubt other frameworks could be designed drawing on the principles articulated earlier in the paper. Teachers might find that parts of each of these frameworks might be drawn on in planning particular lessons or units. (This blending of elements that seem to work well for particular teachers has been quite common among those teachers who have worked with these frameworks so far.)

THE STORY FORM FRAMEWORK

1. **Identifying importance**
   - What is most important about this topic?
   - Why should it matter to children?
   - What is affectively engaging about it?

2. **Finding binary opposites**
   - What powerful binary opposites best catch the importance of the topic?

3. **Organizing content into story form**
   - What content most dramatically embodies the binary opposites, in order to provide access to the topic?
   - What content best articulates the topic into a developing story form?

4. **Conclusion**
   - What is the best way of resolving the dramatic conflict inherent in the binary opposites?
   - What degree of mediation of those opposites is it appropriate to seek?

5. **Evaluation**
   - How can one know whether the topic has been understood, its importance grasped and the content learned?

THE ROMANTIC FRAMEWORK

1. **Taking a romantic perspective**

   What images are brought into sharpest focus by viewing the topic romantically? What transcendent human qualities with which students can form Romantic associations are prominent and accessible?

2. **Organizing the content into a story form**
   - *Providing Access* - What content with which students can Romantically associate most vividly exemplifies the Romantic qualities of the topic?
   - *Organizing the unit/lesson* - What content best articulates the topic into a developing story-form, drawing on the principles of Romance?
   - *Pursuing details and contexts* - What content can best allow students to pursue some aspect of the topic in exhaustive detail? What perspectives allow students to see the topic in wider contexts?

3. **Concluding**

   What is the best way of resolving the dramatic tension inherent in the unit/lesson? How does one bring a satisfactory closure, that opens to further topics, the Romantically important content of the topic?

4. **Evaluating**

   How can one know whether the topic has been understood and the appropriate Romantic capacities have been stimulated and developed?

An example of the story form framework

I am recommending that teachers should approach a unit on North American Indians as a story that is to be told, rather than as a set of objectives to be attained. We need to remember that stories can be true as well as fictional, and that shaping events into a story form may involve simplifying events but need not involve falsifying them. Also we need remember that in a well-wrought story there is room for detailed knowledge, and inference and discovery processes together.

The first task then is to decide on the most important and profound meaning that is to be conveyed. First we *identify importance*. We will not be concerned with a story in the sense of following a fictional "Little Talker" or "White Cloud" through a cycle of the annual activities of their tribe—though if written using the principles sketched here these could form a part of our unit. Rather we are looking for the story in the sense that a newspaper editor asks, "What's the story on this?" What is it that is important about it, and — for our next step of *finding binary opposites*—how is that importance brought out in the clearest and most dramatic way. Any complex content will involve many stories, so we must make choices about which to tell.

These first two procedural steps will usually be taken

close together. They direct us to think first about what is truly important about this content. This is primarily a question about justifying the place of that content in our curriculum. If we cannot identify its importance in terms of profound concepts that are meaningful to young children then we need go no further. That content has no place in the curriculum. The related second step of finding binary opposites directs us to try to see the content through the prominent conceptual and affective forms whereby the child can have most meaningful access to it.

In the case of our unit on North American First Nations societies, then, we must ask first, what is important about this topic for young children? What are we teaching them? Why should it matter to them? How do we deal with the aboriginal peoples of North America in a manner which engages children affectively? What is important is learning something about what a culture is and why there are different cultures. We cannot deal with all aspects of this, nor provide the complexity of answers social anthropologists seek to express. We must focus on a part, but it must be a central and important part of the answer. Our choice will need to be expressed in the binary opposites we find in order to articulate our story. Let us, then, take as binary opposites "survival/destruction," and tell our story on those. What we are choosing thereby to teach children about cultures, and about a North American First Nations culture in particular, is that they are, as it were, machines designed to maximize chances for survival against the various threats of destruction that face them. This is not, of course, all that is to be said about cultures, but it is important and it will allow us to say much else as well. Also our choice of binary opposites provides us with a principle for the selection of relevant content. (In cases where the range of content is undetermined, any standard technique, such as concept mapping or webbing, can be used.)

Now we need to set about organizing the content in a story form. There are two parts to this. First is the choice of a particularly vivid example of our binary opposites in order to provide direct access to the heart of what we intend to teach. We must look at the range of content that falls within our topic and consider what can be used to show the culture of a particular North American aboriginal society most dramatically as a struggle for survival against destruction; what aspect of the life of the society we are teaching about would vividly exemplify the theme of survival against destruction? We could begin with a dramatic account of Plains Indians hunting; they took a food supply that could last for three days and it is the third day; the hunters grow weak, the village waits for fresh meat—what will happen? Or we might dramatize the problems of the Cree facing a brutal and late winter, waiting to move south. Our beginning, that is, will be designed to engage children's affective response in a struggle between survival and destruction which they understand profoundly. (While children may not be able to articulate such concepts, it is clear that they are grasped profoundly at the level of our basic animal existence. We can know they are clearly grasped because children clearly understand stories articulated on them. That is, such concepts are prerequisite to the stories making sense. *Robin Hood*, for example, cannot be meaningfully followed unless children understand concepts like survival/destruction, honor/betrayal, fear/security and so on.)

The second stage of building the story is the longer activity of building the content onto the binary opposites that provide our story line. Even though the general choice of content might be no different from that made using the traditional model, its organization and focus will be rather different. Also the abstract storyline, stretching between our binary opposites, allows us a much more precise principle for determining exactly what aspects and details should be included and what excluded. The key to telling a good story, as Aristotle tells us in *The Poetics*, is that the incidents should be carefully chosen to body forth the plot in a causal sequence. The worst kind of plot is what he calls "episodic;" by this he means stories in which the incidents follow each other as in a more or less random list. They may all be relevant to the plot, but they are not tied to each other in any clear way which enables the reader or hearer to be engaged by them. It is as if in, say, *The Empire Strikes Back* we were to follow the activities of Yoda for ten minutes before Luke Skywalker arrives on the planet. Interest would wane because the hold of the story line would be loosened. Exactly the same principle is important in designing a unit of study or a lesson. Once it becomes episodic, interest will be loosened, engagement will flag. The traditional model of unit planning strongly tends towards "episodic" units; in teaching about North American aboriginal societies the sections on clothing, food, and shelter are treated, indeed, as *sections*, as more or less discrete bits.

Having chosen the basic structure of our story as the binary opposites survival/destruction, we must tie the rest of the content to the structural line that they offer. Thus, when we examine "shelter," we will be concerned to see the particular shelters of our chosen society as parts of the struggle to survive against the particular threats of destruction which they faced. This will constantly focus our attention on the limits of the protection offered. In the case of shelter, we will focus

> The worst kind of plot is . . . "episodic." . . . It is as if in, say, *The Empire Strikes Back* we were to follow the activities of Yoda for ten minutes before Luke Skywalker arrives on the planet. Interest would wane because the hold of the story line would be loosened. Exactly the same principle is important in designing a unit of study or a lesson.

on each feature which protects against particular threats, and so we will see the form of their shelters as a part of a system determined by natural threats. We will thus consider, for example, against how many weeks of what winter temperatures such shelters would protect their inhabitants. The teacher might look up weather reports for the area and see if or how often during the period for which we have records lower temperatures prevailed for longer periods. Similarly when discussing food, our focus will not simply be on what was available at what time of year. The typical account of North American First Nations life in textbooks at present suggests a harmonious and rhythmic swing through a mostly leisurely year. Our focus will be on what food supplies were available in the context of what is needed for health and survival. The relatively brief normal lifespan of North American aboriginal peoples in the past needs to be tied in to what was usually an insufficiently varied and inadequate diet. We will again focus on the limits of the food supply to provide for survival. What happened when a particular crop was late or diseased or killed by late or early frosts? How often did such weather conditions prevail?

That is, we choose the content which can be fitted to our binary opposites and which the binary opposites in turn weld into a coherent order. Each element is tied to this basic structural feature and there are no "episodic" elements which do not further that particular story-line. We do not, that is, decide to include a section on, say, the particular designs they weave into mats or baskets just because that is a part of their culture. If we want to include such a topic we have to tie it into our story-line. Perhaps the designs have religious significance, and represent charms to enhance the contributions the baskets or mats make to the survival of the tribe. Perhaps we will focus on the survival-function of the baskets, and show the designs incidentally to that. If we cannot find a plausible and clear relationship between a topic and our organizing binary opposites, then we should leave it out. It will slacken interest and dissipate the lesson we are teaching. If we cannot attach it to our story-line structure but nevertheless think it is important that children should learn it, then we should use different binary opposites to organize our unit: binary opposites that would enable us to include such other topics.

We cannot teach everything about any aboriginal society in North America. Our choice of binary opposites involves a choice of what to include and what to exclude. But it is a choice that provides a clear principle for making decisions about inclusion and exclusion. The trouble with using the traditional model is that it provides no such principle. Any things that seem relevant may be included, and there are no strong and clear structural relationships built into the array of content to ensure that it is being made meaningful to chil-

dren. When each element is tied to the same powerful structure, and that structure is made from binary opposites that are affectively engaging, we have an organizing tool that can add clarity and ease of access to the content.

By using the survival/destruction binary opposites, children will learn both that First Nations cultures were systematic interrelated activities all of which were closely tied into survival techniques in particular environments, and also that, for most societies most of the time, that survival was won often tenuously and at the cost of brutal and unremitting hardship. This particular important lesson is what is brought to the fore by the choice of the survival/destruction organizers. I am not arguing here that this is the most important or the only way of organizing a unit on North American aboriginal peoples. It is one useful way, however, because it allows us to deal with a great amount of the content of their lives and focusses attention on something important to learn about a culture. Cultures are not sets of arbitrary differences in human behavior; they are in large part responses, and elaborations of those responses, to particular threats from nature and other peoples. If other lessons about First Nations life are considered by any teacher as more important, then they may be focussed on by the choice of different binary opposites. Indeed one could use the survival/destruction organizers for one unit and choose, say, cooperation/competition or adventurous/conservative or some other binary opposites to exemplify other aspects of a society's life or compare different social groups.

> Our choice of binary opposites . . . is a choice that provides a clear principle for making decisions about inclusion and exclusion. The trouble with using the traditional model is that it provides no such principle. Any things that seem relevant may be included, and there are no strong and clear structural relationships built into the array of content to ensure that it is being made meaningful to children.

My point, here, is about how one needs to tie all the content of a unit onto a powerful binary organizing structure in order to make it most accessible and engaging and meaningful. To ignore this principle is the educational equivalent of including "episodic" elements, like Yoda wandering around his swamp before Luke Skywalker arrived, in a story. This is not a principle concerned with making things entertaining, but with making them meaningful. To ignore it is to dissipate meaning. It is ignored in much teaching practice at present and I think this helps to account for a great deal of children's failures to learn.

Good stories do not just stop; rather they reach some kind of resolution of the conflict that started them off. Similarly our unit should not simply peter out, but must find some way either of resolving or moving toward mediation of the binary opposites which have provided our story-line so far. In true Hegelian fashion we might use our mediated conclusion as one pole of a binary pair on which we can begin our next unit. There are a number of alternative ways of concluding the kind of unit I have sketched here.

One way might be to consider what happened to the First Nations society(ies), whose way of life we have been studying, with the coming of Europeans. In so many cases this is unrelievedly tragic. Such historical facts, however, fit precisely and meaningfully into the unit as structured so far. The conclusion, then, is an examination of ways in which the survival techniques of particular aboriginal cultures were unprepared for, and inadequate to, the threats presented by a rapacious, land-hungry, expansive culture with a developing technology. The cultural defences broke down in the face of displacement for cultures tied closely to particular environments, of diseases against which there was no immunity, of hostile armies. In some cases, the conclusion is not so unrelievedly tragic. We may reach mediation in some societies' persistent attempts to survive and maintain their culture in alien environments. The particular conclusion in the above cases would depend on the history of the particular social group. An alternative is to reach a mediation by developing the concept of equilibrium—whether one uses that term or not—between culture and environment. It would be an image of the culture accommodating with more or less success to a somewhat unstable environment. The greater the flexibility of the culture, the more able it is to deal with greater environmental threats and instability.

How does one evaluate a unit such as this? Does our principle provide us also with new forms of evaluation? No, I do not think it does. One might, however, pause to consider how one might evaluate whether *The Return of the Jedi* had been properly learned, understood or appreciated. One could ask factual questions, record how well narrative themes were understood, seek clues about how much it was enjoyed. Much of that would be idle because we know that a typical child will successfully *follow* a well-crafted story. What is entailed in *following a story* is the use of a variety of intellectual skills, having a sense of causality, understanding relationships and what underlying concepts were embodied in particular characters and so on. If the meaning is clear and the content is articulated on binary opposites to expose and elaborate that meaning constantly, we feel fairly confident that children are "getting the message." We really do not worry if a detail of *The Return of the Jedi* is missed because the whole story carries the message forward consistently. This is to suggest that in a well-crafted unit structured on clear binary opposites we might well be less concerned with elaborate evaluation procedures. We may seek in the process of the unit evidence that children are following the unit; that

they see aspects of the aboriginal culture as parts of a machine against destruction. Apart from that, evaluation may go forward however teachers or administrators wish it to go forward. The only caveat is that the procedures for evaluation should not assume such importance that they affect the organization of the unit or its teaching. If the evaluation procedures, for example, are inadequate to provide precise measures of whether children have followed the story, we do not simplify or dilute or degrade our teaching to the primitive level of available evaluation procedures. If we do this, there is no incentive to make evaluation procedures more so-

> We must recognize that at the moment procedures of evaluation of learning are vastly cruder than learning itself. We should be ever aware, then, that we will be unable to get any but the vaguest evaluation of the most important things children can learn, and ever wary of the temptation to make learning cruder so that we can more securely measure it.

phisticated. (If I seem to labor an obscure point here, I should explicitly note that one of the constant dangers in education seems to be the replacement of ends by means. The means of using certain evaluation procedures to measure the results of teaching, has led in the case of the behavioral objectives movement among others, to the evaluation procedures requiring particular forms of objectives which in turn affect the method of teaching.) The clearer our teaching, the less complex is the task of evaluation. We must recognize that at the moment procedures of evaluation of learning are vastly cruder than learning itself. We should be ever aware, then, that we will be unable to get any but the vaguest evaluation of the most important things children can learn, and ever wary of the temptation to make learning cruder so that we can more securely measure it.

CONCLUSION

Teaching is a tough business, and education is a serious enterprise. What is tough about teaching is only in part the stress and strain of interacting with groups of children in often difficult environments. If this were all there was to it our technologies could come to our aid in a major way. What makes it tough at the best of times and in the best of circumstances is the constant imaginative effort required to convert our knowledge into their understanding. It is the problem of communicating meanings from mind to minds that is at the tough heart of teaching, and it is the importance of the range of meanings for making individual lives better that makes education a serious enterprise.

The fit of procedures that can help teachers plan units and lessons with the central tough part of their job is to be measured by how prominently they focus on the meanings to be communicated and on how access can be best provided to them. It seems to me that the technological elaboration of Tyler's rationale has led to techniques displacing somewhat the meanings. This alternative procedure is one which has grown from an attempt to keep the meanings central and the techniques subservient.

REFERENCES

Bettelheim, B. (1976). *The uses of enchantment*. New York: Knopf.

Blumenberg, H. (1985). *Work on myth*. Cambridge, MA: MIT Press.

Callaghan, R. (1962). *Education and the cult of efficiency*. Chicago: University of Chicago Press.

Egan, K. (1979). *Educational development*. New York: Oxford University Press.

Egan, K. (1986). *Teaching as story telling*. London, ON: Althouse Press; Chicago: University of Chicago Press.

Egan, K. (1987). Literacy and the oral foundations of education. *Harvard Educational Review, 57*(4), 445-472.

Egan, K. (1988). *Primary understanding: Education in early childhood*. New York: Routledge.

Egan, K. (1990). *Romantic understanding: The development of rationality and imagination, ages 8- 15*. New York: Routledge.

Egan, K. (1992). *Imagination in teaching and learning: The middle school years*. London, ON: Althouse Press; Chicago: University of Chicago Press.

Egan, K. (1997). *The educated mind: How cognitive tools shape our understanding*. Chicago: University of Chicago Press.

Frye, N. (1957). *Anatomy of criticism*. Princeton, NJ: Princeton University Press.

Hayek, F. A. (1970). The primacy of the abstract. In A. Koestler & J. R. Smythies (Eds.), *Beyond reductionism*. New York: Macmillan.

Kermode, F. (1966). *The sense of an ending*. Oxford: Oxford University Press.

Kliebard, H.M. (1970). The Tyler rationale. *School Review, 78,* 259.

Levi-Strauss, C. (1966). *The savage mind*. Chicago: University of Chicago Press.

Levi-Strauss, C. (1969). *The raw and the cooked*. New York: Harper & Row.

Malinowski, B. (1954). *Magic, science and religion*. New York: Anchor.

Stenhouse, L. (1975). *An introduction to curriculum research and development*. London: Heinemann.

Tyler, R.W. (1949). *Basic principles of curriculum and instruction*. Chicago: University of Chicago Press.

33

TEACHING THE GENERAL LEVEL STUDENT

HISTORY AND WORK— REWRITING THE CURRICULUM

BOB DAVIS

PART 2

In Part 1 I dealt with what it is like to teach "general level" (non-university bound) students in Ontario high schools. I focussed particularly on the responses of my fellow teachers to the working class background of their charges and how these teachers coped with their students' resistance to being "taught." For a great many of these teachers it was only too clear that what these kids actually learned in school was not of much importance.

I concluded by saying I start with the premise that despite the obstacles many working class kids face that come from lack of money, they can learn just as well as middle and upper class kids and deserve to have a curriculum and learning standards as serious and as challenging. When we examine the General Level curriculum, however, and we keep in mind what economic class its students largely come from, we soon notice some big problems with the curriculum. (Problems which are even bigger at the Basic Level—the stream below General.)

I am mostly a history teacher and the missing ingredients are more obvious to me in the history curriculum, where I want to start this section, and in the changing nature of work, with which I want to conclude through a proposed classroom unit on work for Grade 9 History.

Does it not seem likely that children of foot soldiers, stonemasons, cooks, factory workers and clerks identify poorly with a history which fails to mention foot soldiers, stonemasons, cooks, factory workers and clerks?

All our children should be learning about the trials, struggles, frustrations and accomplishments of these missing heroes, but the children of the working class especially suffer from their absence from our history books.

This is not the place to explain why these "peoples'" stories are absent these books, but it is the place to point out that the teacher, who understands what socioeconomic class his lower stream kids come from and who wants to affirm the dignity of their background, will understand that all courses must be revamped to correct this monumental silence.

Once again, let me emphasize two things: (1) Everybody, including upper and middle income kids, need to hear the history of all classes. (2) Working-class kids by the same token do not just need a package of "working-class" curriculum, especially an ersatz version—a bunch of S.E. Hinton novels, like *The Outsiders*, for instance, combined with some hip social history focussed on flappers and model T's. To add challenging curriculum to lower stream history courses is not a matter of adding "social colour" (like costuming in early Ontario), but rather of incorporating the roles "ordinary people" have played in the central activities of the society—in politics, family, work, etc.

The following is a poem on my classroom wall that is a motto for what I think is missing in traditional school history.

So Many Questions
by Bertolt Brecht

Who built the seven gates of Thebes?
The books are filled with the names of kings.
Was it kings who hauled the craggy blocks of
    stone?
And Babylon so many times destroyed,
Who built the city up each time? In which of
    Lima's houses,
That city glittering with gold, lived those who
    built it?
In the evening when the Chinese Wall was fin-
    ished
Where did the masons go? Imperial Rome
Is full of arcs of triumph. Who reared them up?
    Over whom
Did the Caesars triumph? Byzantium lives in
    song.
Were all her dwellings palaces? And even in
    Atlantis of the legend,
The night sea rushed in,
The drowning men still bellowed for their slaves.
Young Alexander conquered India.
He alone?
Caesar beat the Gauls.
Was there not even a cook in his army?
Philip of Spain wept as his fleet
Was sunk and destroyed. Were there no other
    tears?
Frederick the Great triumphed in the Seven Years'
    War.
Who triumphed with him?
Each page a victory —
At whose expense the victory bell?
Every ten years a great man.
Who paid the piper?
So many particulars.
So many questions.

The Scope of the Task

If what I have in mind were to be done right, it would be a very extensive job. It means, at its most extreme, the rewriting of all courses to include the dimension of ordinary people's history. It does not mean tacking on a "social history" chapter at the end of each unit, which happened in one of Ricker and Saywell's famous old texts, *The Modern Era*. That approach gives students the impression that ordinary peoples' history is a kind of relief from the mainstream history of politics and economics—a pause that refreshes; more flappers and model T's. Neither is it satisfactory to do "easier" G-level versions of the prescribed courses. They may ease some teacher/student anxiety by simplifying the reading material, but they do not solve the problem of what's missing in the course content itself.

But if the full task of this curriculum reform is daunting, it is not so difficult to make a start with a specific new unit, which I want to talk about in a short while. First though, I'd like to lay out what seem to me some basic principles for the rewriting of classroom history.

As a preface, let me say that when such a central element of our history is so absent from most of our courses, proper change cannot happen merely by the introduction of a nibble here and a dabble there. Some changes must happen slowly, but many very small changes are so unnoticeable that we are not necessarily better off with them than we were without them. In *The Modern Era*, for example, you are left with the impression that the only time "workers" get on to history's stage is when they're living it up or causing trouble (Model T's, flappers and strikes). Current texts are no better. Other books push this line even further: workers are pictured as boozing pleasure-seekers, who periodically turn into a violent mob. It is essential to introduce experimental units and courses which correct this neglect and distortion.

I should add here that if extensive changes were to take place in the regular courses, these experimental units might cease to be needed. They should not be thought of as models for a whole program; they are meant to highlight elements missing in the regular program. They are not concerned, for example, with the central process of political development and change, which must, of course, be part of a total history program.

First Principles for a History Rewrite

The dignity of ordinary lives and work

If you spend most of your historical study learning about famous missionaries, explorers, kings and queens, politicians, financiers, writers and inventors, you pick up the message that the life of the average peon is unimportant. If, in addition, you are from a humble background yourself, you pick up the additional message that you and your own folks are not that memorable either. So my first principle is that a corrected version of history would stress the lives and histories of ordinary people; this is primarily to offer them proper recognition and dignity. Fortunately, there has been a burgeoning of social history in the last ten years in Canada, England and the United States, so that the number of available sources for improving our high school history texts have increased significantly.

The history of conflict is central

Battles over hunger, wages, work conditions, housing, children, schooling, politics, transportation, possession of property, etc., have always been a central part of the history of ordinary people. Conflict has always had a primary place in history teaching, but some kinds of conflict have generally been more acceptable to record than others: conflicts between religious sects, barons and kings, colonies and mother countries, dictatorship and democracies. These are the central conflicts we find in our history books.

The conflicts that are underplayed or are virtually absent include conflicts between slaves and owners, peasants and lords, soldiers and officers, workers and management, tenants and landlords, rich and poor. These are conflicts which suggest serious division within our own societies and, worse still, some of these conflicts continue today. When these conflicts are present in our history books, they are there so infrequently and in so chaotic a form that the message students get is that there is little historical rhyme or reason to them; they appear as mindless mob violence. A point appreciated by those who have power in our own society.

Exploitation is an ongoing fact of history

History books that set out basically to defend the status quo do not present exploitation as an ongoing fact of history. Yet once you begin to present the history of ordinary people in any systematic way, you find it difficult to avoid putting exploitation centre stage.

You do not have to be a socialist to come to this conclusion. With enough distance between present and past, exploitation is usually accepted as a root interpretation by historians of all political affiliations.

Most historians agree, for example, that peasants were exploited in the Middle Ages or that North American Indians were exploited in the 17th, 18th and 19th centuries.

Ordinary people fight back

If you take ordinary peoples' battles out of the mob violence category and put them into the category of a natural response to being exploited, you inevitably get into a coherent history of the riots, strikes and organizations ordinary people have formed to gain new rights or hold on to old ones.

The union movement is a central part of the story

The best known working class organization is the union. The union movement is central to the struggle by working people for a decent life. Certainly, this movement has many problems and weaknesses, which ought to be dealt with plainly in school, but to have its history popping in and out of our curriculum the way it does, suggests it is largely insignificant. This is a serious distortion.

Political parties are also key to the history of ordinary people

When ordinary workers and farmers have been very angry about conditions—and have not obtained suffi-cient satisfaction through their unions—they have sometimes formed new political parties to look after their interests. Our history text writers acknowledge this to some extent. The strength of farmer-worker parties after World War I is often mentioned as is the rise of radical farmer parties in the West during the 1930s. What's usually missing—a depoliticizing absence—are two major elements of our political party system: (1) the extent to which ordinary people's demands, mostly moving in a left-wing direction, are reflected in all political parties, and (2) the extent to which popular support has arisen, at the same time, for parties at both ends of the political spectrum (communist and fascist parties in the 1930s, for example).

An Experimental Unit on "Work" for Grade Nine General History

I now present a ninth grade General Level history unit on "Work," which I designed and still teach in my Scarborough, Ontario high school. I have given it for many years now to students who are streamed by local elementary schools into what amounts to a "self-contained" General Level program. The class invariably reflects the predominantly working-class makeup of this program, which was identified in our school's Every Student Survey. Let me once again remind you (too often?) that I believe students of all social classes and academic levels would benefit from this unit, but working class students benefit especially from it.

Sparking interest

I get students started by asking them to write down what they consider the five most dangerous jobs, the five most boring jobs, the five most unhealthy jobs, the

> History books that set out basically to defend the status quo do not present exploitation as an ongoing fact of history. Yet once you begin to present the history of ordinary people in any systematic way, you find it difficult to avoid putting exploitation centre stage.

five most physically exhausting jobs and the five jobs which most produce nervous stress.

I learn a lot about them from this, and we have a good discussion. I bring in some information I have from surveys of dangerous jobs by organizations like the Ontario Federation of Labour or the National Farmers' Union. What do I learn? Such things as this: none of my city kids has ever listed farmer as a dangerous job, yet it rates in the top three jobs in Canada for deaths and bad accidents. I have also realized that students are heavily influenced by TV so that a common dangerous job they listed was "stunt man," a job not known to employ many full-time people but big in TV hype.

Jobs which students list as producing stress are also commonly affected by TV, so that doctor and nurse crop up a lot, but keypuncher does not appear and neither do factory jobs.

At the same time many students have stories from home about jobs that are unhealthy and unsafe. We discuss whether the government ads suggesting that unsafe or unhealthy conditions are the fault of workers for not taking care or for not wearing safety boots, a mask or a helmet.

Work terms

I then ask my students to explain each of the following terms from the world of work.

1. Blue collar job
2. White collar job
3. A strike
4. Equal pay for equal work
5. Equal pay for work of equal value
6. Fringe benefits
7. Collective bargaining
8. Overtime pay
9. Getting fired
10. Layoff
11. Pregnancy leave
12. Assembly line job
13. Piece work
14. Management
15. Shop steward
16. Minimum wage law
17. Seniority
18. Workmen's compensation
19. U.I.C. (unemployment insurance)

Students are expected to learn the meaning of these work terms, if they don't know them already. We discuss them in class. Then they do a test on them. There is a common assumption by conservative critics of liberal school reform that "new curriculum" is just gazing at your navel and telling each other how it feels. In fact, the topic of "work" has lots of precise knowledge con-

nected with it, as much as any "science."

Your rights under Ontario's labour code

I then turn to look at the rights of Ontario workers under the law, going through the work sheet (below). In working out this sheet students are to ask for information from their parents. Later they learn where this information can be obtained from government information services, usually a single phone number. Precise information here is combined with a knowledge of personal rights. This opens up a very solid discussion, and the writing tasks focus on how these rights came about and whether they are adequate.

Organizing a union: The film Maria

The next unit starts with a film called *Maria* written for TV by Rick Salutin and directed by Alan King. An Italian textile worker in her mid 20s, after 10 years in a Toronto plant where her sister and mother also work, decides to try to start a union. The story shows the tough organizing battle, which unfolds at the plant, as well as the opposition Maria encounters first from her father and then, especially, from her boyfriend, when she takes on this "man's job." *Maria* is just one hour long. It is a totally absorbing personal story and very informative about union organizing, the law which frames it, and the attitudes and responses of companies, unions and male workers to new organizing among low paid immigrant women. It is also a film that gives a very clear view of the difference between labour code rights and the protection that only a union can obtain.

Apart from the new topic here, I also judge that students are ready to deal with a more artistic project after two sheets of factual terms and labour law. Op-

---

THE RIGHTS OF ALL WORKERS IN ONTARIO BY LAW (ON PAPER ANYWAY) —WHAT ARE THEY?

Minimum wage required to be paid: adult _____ student _____ waiter _____

Minimum number of hours of work per week before overtime pay must be paid _____

Amount of overtime pay must be at least _____

Pregnancy leave rule for management _____ Is it paid leave? _____

Vacation—number of weeks after how long _____ Vacation pay _____

What is "pay equity?" _____

Is it guaranteed by law in Ontario? _____

Are any seniority rights guaranteed for all workers? _____

How about paid sick leave? _____

When is a person entitled to UIC (unemployment insurance)? _____

How much do you get for how long? _____

The regulation about when and how long a compulsory break must be given _____

Is this more favourable to management or the workers? _____ Give reason. _____

What are the statutory paid holidays that all workers must be given? _____

What kind of benefits and rights can a good union get for workers that they don't have from the Ontario labour code?

QUOTATIONS FROM THE MOVIE, MARIA

From each of these quotations from *Maria*, write the following:

    a. Who said it?

    b. To whom?

    c. The place and situation in the movie at the time the statement was made.

    d. The significance of the statement. (Sometimes this part will need two to three sentences.)

NOTE: DON'T WORRY IF YOU DON'T RECOGNIZE LOTS OF THESE THE FIRST TIME YOU GO OVER THEM. WE'LL GO OVER THEM TOGETHER AND HELP EACH OTHER!

1. Wouldn't you want a wife who leads a strike? No, you wouldn't.

2. Now, give me a dollar to make it legal.

3. Hey, come back, you forgot the cards.

4. We're peanuts in a dying industry. The government doesn't listen to us. They listen to the big corporations, not us.

5. If the union comes in, we'll probably have to let a few people go especially the newer ones.

6. Look, there are 800,000,000 human ants all over there willing to work for a few pennies a day. Can we compete against that?

7. You're a bunch of Judases. You've sold us all out. Whore!

8. March? That's two months! What's Gloria supposed to do for two months?

9. You're two hours past eight o'clock. It's not the union. I don't want you to be like a streetwalker in Napoli.

10. I want her to join. It'll cost $1000 in sleeping pills for me and for her another $1000 in sleeping pills. But I want her to join.

11. I don't want to buy any today, thank you. Maybe later on.

12. We're going to join, Maria. But naturally we expect appropriate compensation for joining.

13. Where's Gina?

    She's on piece work. She doesn't want to miss any more time. She's going to the hospital.

    She's going to get more money.

14. Don't give me tears! I know how you people use your emotions.

15. In this factory, Mr. Slinger, you do not talk to employees in that tone of voice.

16. You think I'm a Greek?

17. Has your work permit come through yet? My father and I know your problems. We were immigrants too.

18. We make the money. If we join, the others will.

19. They don't own the banks, they don't own the railroads, the airlines. They don't own Eatons and Simpsons.

20. You should see the bathroom. It's painted. There's a new mirror.

21. I may be a woman, but you're the one who should be wearing a dress!

22. If you had to chose, would it be me or the union? That's no choice.

23. Don't vote tomorrow or I'll cut your heart out.

24. Don't put a wedge between members of this family.

25. We're giving the company one more chance.

26. The Board has questioned some of the cards, so we don't get automatic certification. They've ordered a vote.

27. You can't make a union of immigrants and women. If we sign, the rest will.

28. You're going to win? Why? Because you're tough. Because you're Carlo's daughter. And because you're right.

29. We scared the hell out of them. We'll go at them again in six months.

posite is my concluding assignment on this movie.

Work songs

I now introduce the following work songs:

Bud the Spud, Stompin' Tom Connor

Pickin' for a Dollar, David Campbell

Dark as a Dungeon, Dolly Parton

9 to 5, Dolly Parton

The Maintenance Engineer, Sandra Kerr

The Farmer's Song, Murray MacLachlan

Black Fly Song, Wade Hemsworth

These songs are taken from various records and converted to a single cassette tape. I give students copies of the lyrics. I always add current songs and the work songs they bring to class. I focus on difficult words, and students are tested on their knowledge of the lyrics. Labour curriculum must be integrated with art as any other successful piece of curriculum must be. Songs also open up the chance to discuss why songs about work am so rare in the mainstream radio, record and video businesses. It also opens up the possibility for students to write a work song of their own.

Interviews of two people who work full-time

It has struck me for some time that schools usually fail to make good use of the human resources available to students. Libraries and vertical files are not students' only source of information. Indeed, they are often out of date and extraordinarily boring.

In my experience reliance on libraries and vertical files has produced two miserable travesties of education: the "Research Essay" and the "Term Project." The Research Essay, much beloved by many teachers as a training for university, usually turns out to be a mostly undigested, pretentiously-worded pastiche of slightly reworked quotes from fat textbooks. Of course, that's what many university essays are as well, and that's what many professors actually like. So I guess I shouldn't be so hard on teachers who hold up the same ideal to their

high school students. The Term Project is often worse than the Research Essay. The essay at least insists on words and sentences. The Term Project, however, is often nothing more than a glossy duotang collection with cover photograph, coloured headlines and lots of vertical file quotes, which are entirely undigested by the student. These essays and projects pass as our high school contribution to the "information society."

I'm not opposed to formal research, provided it's serious, but in the context of a normal school schedule good human resources will often get students much better information much faster. Students are an obvious source of information for each other, though they are rarely tapped as such. The surrounding community is equally, if not more, fertile ground, though with limited class time it's hard to get out collectively to this community. Classroom guests from the community are essential, and they should be paid. And, obviously, students should be encouraged to do it on their own, particularly with their parents. This is what I do in my next unit. In this unit I assign students the task of interviewing two people—parents or guardians, relatives or friends—about their work. I've prepared a sheet of 29 questions for students to use (which readers can have by writing to me c/o OS/OS[1]). At the head of this questionnaire is a note to those being interviewed (see below).

Working by Studs Terkel

After the interviews I move on to a book called *Working* by Studs Terkel. Terkel interviewed hundreds of "ordinary Americans" about their jobs and their off-hours, and the book is a compendium of these lively and honest statements. Terkel knows how to get people talking, and his characters include everyone from prostitutes to steelworkers. I don't use much of this fat book for my Grade 9 class. I require them to pick out any five selections, however short. Almost all of them pick the prostitute, and some of them pick the next four shortest selections, which is fine with me. With 30 students doing the choosing, they end up covering a lot of the material, which helps extend their general know-

---

NOTE TO INTERVIEWEES

This class is now taking a unit on WORK. They are discussing what different kinds of work there are—also the pay and the working conditions. They have been discussing the different interests of workers and management. They have been learning about some of the problems of health and safety in jobs. They are also considering whether men and women are treated differently in jobs in ways that are unjust.

They will write about these things to develop their writing ability.

They are also reading books about the topic to improve their reading ability.

These interviews are part of this work. They have two purposes:

(1) To help the students to realize that they can learn a lot from people around them like relatives and friends.

(2) To develop their abilities in interviewing and in getting on paper the main things that you say. (A few kids will be using a tape recorder.)

Note: No names are needed in these interviews and the information is confidential. Each student is to interview any two adults.

---

ledge when we come to discuss the reading with the whole class. Individually, I require each student to write a paragraph on each person they have chosen, mentioning "the main things that stand out about them." I also require them to write another paragraph telling who their favourite character was (or "least hated"— picking favourites is often a lie for many students, who might not like anything about what they've experienced or read).

Your own story

I now give an assignment that requires delicate preparation and encouragement. I tell them that they should imagine that they are older and already have full-time jobs and that Studs Terkel is going to interview them for his book. Their task is to write out a selection about themselves as it might have appeared in Terkel's book. They must decide whether they are married or living with someone, whether they have children, whether they are single. How do they spend their spare time? What are their bosses like? How about their fellow workers? What, in detail, do they do in their job? Is there a union at work. Are they workers or management? What happens in breaks? Do they like their jobs? What were some funny or miserable incidents at work? There are a lot of questions that can be asked.

For those students who say "I can never do those imagination assignments," I suggest they get a detailed rundown of the job of a parent, guardian, brother or sister or friend, pretend they have that job themselves and add their own feelings.

What usually comes out of the assignment is a revealing spread of TV dream world jobs (beauty salon operators, professional hockey players, stunt men, night-club dancers) through pretty bizarre stuff (one South American kid was a big time gun runner on the Amazon River with a harem of women) to the most painful and dull jobs. The writing is sometimes remarkably strong and almost always leads to deeper thinking on the subject of work and the students' future.

Below and on the next page are recent and representative examples of student work on this topic.

Field trip

Next we visit some instructive place like the General Motors Van Plant, which was near our school in Scarborough. Here we are shown around by company personnel, but we also get together with a union representative after the visit to the plant. One inevitable feature of a visit to an auto factory is the shouting, cat calls and hyena screams the workers make to the group from a distance and through the protection of various production lines. A union person explained this phenom-

---

LAWYER

by Gino Damiano

I am an ordinary man who works minding my own business. I am twenty-nine years of age and married to a beautiful woman. I have two children who are as beautiful as my wife.

Now, continuing on with my job, I like my job some of the time when the other workers aren't bothering me.

I get a good salary because I receive a lot of clients. People like me because they think I work so well. I work five days a week and nine hours a day. I take the weekend off and enjoy it with my family.

I work in a full-sized office with a few secretaries and bosses. Our building is pretty big, filled with criminal lawyers such as myself and business lawyers (corporation) and family lawyers. Even though there are a lot of people working in this building, we are not a union. We work with our own clients and make money off them. I like this job very much because I get to associate with different people.

On special occasions at work I like to take some of my friends out to lunch. We celebrate during lunch somewhere fancy. I sometimes take my wife along with me so she can associate with my secretaries and bosses too.

One time, if I can remember long enough, there was an incident that took place at the Supreme Court of Law. I was hired to help this innocent person accused of murder and theft. I gave it all I had. But even though he was innocent, he was sentenced to jail for two years or five thousand dollars bail.

This job took me five years through university and four years through law school. I never really had time for other jobs, because I was too busy studying every night. But I did have jobs when I was younger and, believe me, those jobs don't come anywhere near the job I have now.

I feel like a new man now that I've passed through school and, though it was years of hard work and studying, I pulled through.

When I have my holidays I take about two weeks off. My family and I run away somewhere far like the Bahamas or Italy, Greece or Africa and have fun in the sun.

Though I'm not really a lawyer I sure wouldn't mind being one.

---

enon to my students: (1) the job is boring, (2) from a distance workers are safe from management reprimands, (3) our visits make them feel like zoo animals so they act the part for a lark. Without this analysis, students often mistook these actions as simply whistling at girls.

On field trips to factories and other workplaces a teacher must always try to go beyond the glossy management view of the operation or the natural attraction to students of a free coke or a free chocolate bar.

Historical novels, bean bakes, models and murals

I end this unit with two historical novels for young people by Bill Freeman, *Shantymen of Cache Lake* and *Last Voyage of the Scotian,* and with the projects which follow their reading. These two books about 19th century lumbering and fishing are remarkably popular. I won't exaggerate to you. There are no stampedes or pleas for extra homework to get at them. But when five or six students out of twenty-five mention on their own that they like these books, or that "this book is starting to get good" or that "this book is better than the usual stuff we have to read," you know you have a find.

For four years one project that emerged from this reading was a massive iron-pot wood-fire bean bake. It was a real shantyman bean bake, produced over 24 hours by 40 Grade Nine General Level students and their teachers to feed 1500 high school and elementary students. And after the meal we even managed an old time hoedown to the music of a top fiddle band. The biggest scare every year was that the beans would either be too hard or burned. The taste we could adjust during the last few hours by adding ingredients. But if the fire was not hot enough, the beans would burn. Our guests would let us know if they didn't like the meal, and 1500 complaining students equals a failed project. This added an air of deadly seriousness to an event full of raucous fun and wild fatigue.

My students and I were also led to model building (of ships and shanties, rafts and log chutes, houses of rich owners and poor workers) and mural painting as we tried to create a physical setting in our classroom for both of these books. On our first try, with help from two senior art students, we produced 3 panels of 8' x 4' plywood, the left hand one being Cache Lake, the scene of the lumbercamp, the centre one being 19th century Ottawa, and the third, Quebec City in the same period. These three scenes we chose because the logs flowed through the Madawaska from Cache Lake, into the Ottawa River, and in turn into the St. Lawrence and down to Quebec City. The mural sat on three tables the same length as the plywood which then became the surface on which to put a paper mâché continuation of the murals. All models eventually sat in place on the painted paper mâché in front of their appropriate picture—the model shanty, sleighs and log chute in front of Cache Lake; the houses big and small in Ottawa; and three model ships anchored in front of Quebec. Each model was made by a group of 2–4 students but since the class contained 30 people, some students collected pictures and made slides of lumberjacking and sailing, some made the paper mâché and one group even wired up the whole set-up so that all shanties, houses and ships lit up in the dark.

I had permission of my department head to give over our daily class for the entire month of May to this project. After about ten days' work, I realized the students were liking this, and there was a fine sense of calm starting to develop. I then got the idea that this would be an excellent project to invite their parents to see.

Meeting the parents

We sent home an invitation to an inside sit-down party with bean supper (cooked inside this time!), a bit of music by students and myself (with the principal on hand to sing "My Daddy Was A Logger"), the presentation of the project (which we carried with great hazard and great commotion to the staff lounge the night before the party), and finally the showing of the Alan Ladd movie—*Two Years Before The Mast*. (This film was part of my actual curriculum since it gives an excellent picture of 19th century conditions for seamen and also a good depiction of the sailors fighting back to improve their conditions. And the students know this is Cheryll Ladd's father being the hero.)

Would the parents show up? Very few parents of General level students come on the regular parents' night. "Would you come if you had bad memories of school and were going to be told your kid 'had to apply himself ', etc." was the way one friend put it to me.

With each invitation we sent out new copies of *Working* by Studs Terkel, and our two historical novels and a letter. The letter read: "Have a look at these. Your kids are taking them in history class, and we'd love to get your reactions." With two weeks to go, we had only received back five confirmation forms from parents.

I then made the decision that tipped the balance. I decided to visit each of the thirty homes personally. I did it over two evenings, usually stayed only a couple of minutes at each home. One parent and I had a great debate about the language in the Terkel book. Another was sitting at the back door when I was let in by her daughter. "I just wanted to invite you to a free party and movie when you can see Karen's work," I said. "I didn't read the books!" the mother shot back from her perch. She was obviously thinking: "Not only are they giving students homework; now they're giving it to parents." "That doesn't matter," I said. She showed up with Karen's younger brother as well.

On June 7th at 6:30 pm 78 people arrived, counting the class of 30, parents and brothers and sisters. The event went very well indeed and was sealed as a success for me by the way the students presented the project to their parents and colleagues. Three days before the Big Night I decided to ask each group to appoint one person to explain to the assembled people what they had done and why. We got a microphone hooked up on a long cord so people could move around to the different models, maps, cartoons and drawings.

I swear to you that the people who described the life of shantymen and sailors as shown in the slides they had made were so good, so natural, that most teachers could have learned from them. I had taken the risk of asking the students to talk, knowing that they might get stage fright or might say things that were dull and maybe embarrassing. I took the risk because I didn't want that kind of parents' night where all you see are pretty projects and slides clicking away by themselves. That kind of show is a lot like the way most books teach about work processes. They talk about coal mining, steelmaking or clothes making as if no people are involved. "First coal is taken," etc. By whom? To whom?

With what human energy? At what cost to human health and emotion and life?

As Brecht says: "So many questions. So many particulars." And so many students, too, who have something important to say and who can say it loud and clear to their parents and peers.

ENDNOTE

[1] Bob Davis, c/o *Our Schools/Our Selves*, 5502 Atlantic St., Halifax, NS, B3H 9Z9.

This article, which is reprinted with permission, appeared originally in 1989 in *Our Schools/Our Selves*, 1(3), 55–76. Minor alterations to the original article have been made for stylistic and format purposes.

34

Integrating the Curriculum: Getting Beyond the Slogan

Roland Case

Over the past decade curricular integration has again garnered considerable support across North America. Countless official documents, educational writers, workshop presenters and others urge teachers to integrate the curriculum. Unfortunately much of this enthusiasm is not a thoughtful, focussed call to address a clearly delineated problem, but an outburst of educational sloganeering. The danger with slogans—and positive-sounding "buzzwords" are ubiquitous in education—is that they are seductive and urge action without providing much direction. As a result, the potentially important aims behind the call for curricular integration are often lost behind the cloud of what Fullinwider (1991) refers to as "numbing education-speak." Concerns about curricular integration as an empty slogan are not new. Repeatedly during this century, critics have warned of the potential vacuousness and disguised confusion lurking behind the call to integrate the curriculum (cf., Knudsen, 1937; Aiken, 1942; Dressel, 1958; Taba, 1962; Pring, 1973, Jacobs, 1989; Werner, 1991). Despite the warnings, many advocates continue to promote an amorphous conception of curricular integration, promising to solve a myriad of educational problems.

In this article I examine the pitfalls of these vague proposals to integrate the curriculum. To combat this confusion and to provide more useful guidance to teachers, I distinguish three forms of curricular integration, and the different aims that each seeks to promote. I then consider appropriate strategies to meet these differing demands for greater integration. In the process, I expose the limitations of the two most popular integrative strategies—thematic units and interdisciplinary courses.

Curricular Integration as a Slogan

Consistently vague accounts of curricular integration undermine the educational value of many efforts to integrate curriculum. Often the sole defining feature offered by advocates is that integration involves making "connections" (cf., Brandt, 1991; Fogarty 1991; Drake, 1991, 1992; British Columbia Ministry of Education, 1992; Ontario Ministry of Education and Training, 1993). Yet, the mere joining together of topics under the rubric of a common theme does not integrate the study in any educationally meaningful manner—many connections may be contrived and trivial. For example, I have heard of proposals to integrate the curriculum around the theme of "sidewalks" because they lead everywhere: a sidewalk may lead to a store, which might prompt students to study about commerce, and to a vacant lot so students can learn some biology. But we do not further students' understanding of either commerce or biology by lumping them under this common theme.[1]

The dubious value of many integrative proposals is worsened by advocates who encourage teachers to plan integrated units by freely brainstorming a sprawling web of ideas (cf., Drake, 1992; Schwartz & Pollishuke, 1990). The result is often an overwhelming number of disparate topics thinly related to a common theme. What is worse, many professional publications imply that integration can and should mean whatever individual educators wish it to mean (cf., British Columbia Ministry of Education, 1993, p. 11; Fogarty, 1991, p. 65). The open-ended and ambiguous nature of many so-called definitions of integration may mislead teachers into concluding that they are already integrating their curricula (Hargreaves, 1993, p. 124). The lack of a rigourous definition fuels "false clarity" (Fullan, 1991)—a situation where educators believe that they have successfully changed their practices but, because of their lack of understanding of the fundamental principles and rationale, merely adopt the "superficial trappings" of an innovation.

A further example of pseudo-integration arises at the secondary school level where subjects such as English and social studies are purportedly integrated into a new "interdisciplinary" subject, called humanities. On many occasions, virtually no integration of curricular content occurs. Instead "humanities" may amount to little more than having the same teacher deal with English for half of a double-blocked class and with social studies for the other half. Yet many advocates seem to believe that the mere "repackaging" of the courses serves to integrate them.

The limitations of interdisciplinary courses were also noted during the Eight-Year Study—an impressive curricular experiment involving thirty high schools across the United States during the 1930s. Reservations about fusing social studies and English included concerns that English often became "the handmaiden" of history, that the literature from certain historical periods was too scarce to justify devoting much time to it, and that collapsing subjects created considerable "artificial integration"—a predicament worse than the situation which integration sought to eliminate (Aiken, 1942, p. 53). These experiences caused most teachers in the study to question the wisdom of their attempts to "put subjects together." Instead teachers found alternative strategies for promoting integration that did not require complete fusion of subjects. Unfortunately, these strategies have been largely overlooked in contemporary recommendations for curricular integration.

In response to criticism about vagueness, some advocates of integration encourage teachers to promote only "*natural* connections" or only those connections that have a "*natural* fit." Yet it is not clear that the notion of "natural" provides any useful guidance. Con-

sider a recent British Columbia Ministry of Education document (1992, p. 10), encouraging the making of "natural" connections. It invites teachers to integrate language arts with social studies by introducing a unit on ancient Egypt with the picture book, *The Egyptian Cinderella*. This book is a straightforward relocation of the classic Cinderella story into an Egyptian setting. But what contribution does the use of this book provide? Most students will already know the basic story, very little is added to the characters and plot by changing the geographical details, and drawings of Egyptian scenes which would have greater educational payoff could easily be found elsewhere. It is difficult to comprehend, if this example qualifies as a "natural fit," what would *not* count as a "natural fit" between two subjects. And yet this Ministry-recommended example is typical of superficial understandings of the nature and conditions for educationally sound integration of the curriculum. Regrettably, the compulsion to draw connections often legitimates the use of inferior resources simply because they happen to fit the chosen theme. Lack of clarity about the meaning of integration—a legacy of its usage as a slogan—undermines the very purposes for which it is proposed.

Another common failing among advocates of integration are naive and exaggerated claims about the potential benefits and the prospects for success (cf., Schwartz & Pollishuke, 1990, pp. 49-50). Alleman and Brophy (1993), two of a handful of researchers to write in the professional literature about their reservations about curriculum integration, reject the seemingly prevalent maxim that the more integration the better (p. 287). In addition, some proponents of integration exhibit a stereotypical and unproductive tendency to characterize disciplines as the antithesis of integration—as "territorial spaces carved out by academic scholars for their own purposes" (Beane, 1991, p. 9; see also, Drake, 1991). According to one professor, teachers who do not base all instruction on students' questions and concerns are dismissed as imposing on students "the interest of the teacher" or the "manipulation of subject areas" (Beane, 1991, p. 12). Ironically, organizing curriculum around loosely defined themes may increase the amount of curricular fragmentation. The disciplines, for all of their narrowness, provide integrative principles—disciplines are fields of inquiry that share standards for evidence, fundamental explanatory concepts and methodological procedures. The same intellectual integrity can not be claimed for many interdisciplinary units which indiscriminately lump together disparate kinds of questions and fields of inquiry. This concern is captured rather humourously in the following quip in

> "Humanities" may amount to little more than having the same teacher deal with English for half of a double-blocked class and with social studies for the other half. Yet many advocates seem to believe that the mere "repackaging" of the courses serves to integrate them.

a teacher magazine (*The Teacher* 2(4), 1990): "I used to teach *Who Has Seen the Wind?* and *Breaking Smith's Quarterhorse*. Now, with integration, I'll teach *Who Has Seen Smith's Quarterhorse Breaking Wind!?*"

Despite all these concerns, there are important benefits to be gained by greater integration of the curriculum, but discourse that does not rise above sloganeering severely inhibits the possibilities for achieving these payoffs. If integration is to be more than a fad, we need to more thoughtfully attend to what it means to integrate the curriculum—its different forms and aims—and to be more guarded and realistic about the expected results. If we do this, our efforts to integrate the curriculum may actually enrich the educational experiences of elementary and secondary students.

FORMS OF CURRICULAR INTEGRATION

A useful place to begin to appreciate the complexity and requirements for thoughtful integration is by distinguishing (admittedly, rather crudely) between three forms of curriculum:

- the *formal* curriculum—the explicit objectives for each subject typically outlined in formal policy documents;
- the *personal* curriculum—the personal sense or relevance that individuals make of what they study;
- the *hidden* curriculum—the often unarticulated norms that underlie the practices and structures that operate in schools and classrooms.

In each case, the call for integration is an invitation to reduce the particular fragmentation—or dis-integration—within that form of the curriculum. As I see them, each form presents a different set of concerns and, consequently, may require different strategies for implementation. My reading of the main goals for each form of curricular integration is as follows:

- the aim of integrating the *formal* curriculum is to help students make connections between topics within and among subjects which will improve the coherence of what is learned and increase transfer of learning across the curriculum;
- the aim of integrating the *personal* curriculum is to help students relate what goes on in school with their personal world so as to increase the perceived relevance of the curriculum;
- the aim of integrating the *hidden* curriculum is to harmonize school and classroom practices and routines so as to reduce the inconsistencies and contradictions in students' school experiences.

Integration of the formal curriculum

The most frequently advocated form of curricular integration, what I have called integration of the formal curriculum, is a plea for enhanced coherence and

transfer across the curriculum. Coherence refers to the unity of the curriculum—seeing parts of the curriculum as contributing to an interlocking, mutually supporting whole. The world is complex and students cannot understand many phenomena from a single disciplinary perspective. In many cases, valuable insights can be gained by drawing upon varying subjects. For example, students can come to a rich understanding of the environment only by studying it from aesthetic, cultural, geographic, biological and health science points of view. Notice, however, this does not mean that it is necessary to draw upon all subject areas for every topic. Rather, it implies that when warranted on educational grounds students should be assisted in seeing the supporting links across multidisciplinary inquiries. Transfer across the curriculum seeks to help students make meaningful inter-subject use of what they have learned. For example, inviting students to apply outlining strategies learned in language arts when developing a speech in social studies is an attempt to enhance transfer across the curriculum.

Indication of the need for integration of the formal curriculum in found in the following remark: "Isolating one subject from another, creating separate subjects within subjects, and specifying discrete learning within each subject has given rise to disintegration of personal knowledge and fragmentation of school experiences" (British Columbia Ministry of Education, 1990a, p. 89). We have done such an effective job of divorcing subjects from each another that students often comment: "This is a language arts activity. Aren't we supposed to be doing social studies?" The effect of excessive differentiation of subjects is to dissuade students from seeing the interlocking connections among subjects and from using ideas and skills gathered in one subject to inform another. Consider the following remark from a student in a New York integration project: "I learned the strategy in this class and I use it in another class, I wonder if the teachers have figured it out" (personal communication, Jamie McCloud & Giselle Martin-Kniep). This comment—that it might be against the rules to transfer learning across subjects—is a shameful indictment of the curricular fragmentation that we have created in the minds of many students.

Integration of the personal curriculum

A second form of integration, what I have called integration of the personal curriculum, refers to attempts to integrate what students study in school with students' *own* concerns, desires, needs, queries, aspirations, dilemmas, questions and so on. The focus of this form of integration is to improve the match between the school curriculum and what students care about so that students can appreciate the relevance of what they study. For example, showing students how geometry

> If integration is to be more than a fad, we need to more thoughtfully attend to what it means to integrate the curriculum—its different forms and aims—and to be more guarded and realistic about the expected results.

might be useful to them in pursuing an outside interest of theirs would be an attempt at personal integration. Attention to this form of integration is suggested by the following British Columbia Ministry of Education statement: "Through involvement in learning experiences that are centered around a powerful issue, idea, or dimension of experience, students have the opportunity to see their learning activities as related and significant to their personal lives" (1990a, p. 91). Too often, students fail to see how anything they study in school has "real-world" connections. As indicated above, the primary aim of personal integration is increased perceived relevance of schooling.

Integration of the hidden curriculum

The third form, integration of the hidden curriculum, refers to attempts to integrate all school-related experiences—practices, routines, methods, rules and so on—that influence what students learn. Much has been written about the pervasiveness of the hidden curriculum in determining what students actually learn from schooling. For instance, despite verbal support for the importance of critical thinking, many teacher-made tests focus extensively on recall of factual information. In fact, Benjamin Bloom estimates that ninety percent of test questions that U.S. students confront deal largely with information recall (Raizen & Kaser, 1989, p. 720). This tacit message about what "really" counts influences what students regard as important: despite our verbal assurances that critical thinking matters, our assessment practices tell students that it is not necessary for success in school and, consequently, students are dissuaded from taking it seriously. So too, differences in the cultures of elementary and secondary schools, including the way classes are scheduled and taught, are disruptive for many students. Although, the creation of a single humanities course may do very little to integrate the formal curriculum (if the mingling of ideas from socials studies and English is minimal), it may integrate the hidden curriculum by reducing the number of different teachers and courses that students must cope with each week. This reduction in the shuffle and anonymity of schools may enhance students' sense of belonging, which in turn may positively affect their ability to learn. Integration of the hidden curriculum is a call to harmonize school and classroom practices so that we do not unwittingly undermine the educational goals that we hope to promote. It aims to reduce the inconsistencies and contradictions in students' educational experiences.

STRATEGIES FOR INTEGRATING CURRICULUM

If we recognize the different forms of curriculum integration each with different aims, we can readily appreciate that different strategies may be required. Two approaches to integrating the curriculum typically offered as *the* ways of integrating the curriculum are, at the elementary level, use of thematic units and, at the secondary level, fusion of separate subjects into an interdisciplinary course—for instance, teaching English and social studies through a double-blocked humanities course. I want to explore the utility of these strategies in promoting each of the forms of curricular integration discussed above, and offer alternatives that may more appropriately and sensitively serve the defining aims of each form.

Integrating the personal curriculum

Personal integration (the integration of the school curriculum and student interests) may not always be advanced by thematic units and interdisciplinary courses. Themes that do not raise issues or questions that excite students, or that do not come eventually to be seen as significant by students, will not increase students' perceptions of the relevance of the curriculum. (I am not implying that all topics must be clearly perceived by students as relevant before they are defensible, merely that units which are not perceived to be relevant cannot be said to promote personal integration.) Ironically, some uses of thematic units and interdisciplinary courses have decreased perceived relevance because students tire of the same theme and of the unrelenting connections made among subjects. For example, a pre-service teacher reported the following experience as an elementary student during an earlier period when integration was popular:

Ironically, some uses of thematic units and interdisciplinary courses have decreased perceived relevance because students tire of the same theme and of the unrelenting connections made among subjects.

My memories of grade six are strictly recollections of pyramids. It seems everything I did revolved around pyramids. I thought about them in Social Studies; I read and wrote about them in Language Arts; I drew and modelled them in Art; and I considered their preservation in Science. I have studied pyramids *ad nauseam*. Would I consider (as a student teacher) writing lesson plans on the grade six Social Studies topic, Ancient Civilizations, using the Egyptians as the sample study? The answer is no. My grade six experience offered me enough pyramids to last a lifetime! (reported in Craig, 1987, p. 31)

As this example suggests, teaching through thematic units may undermine the perceived relevance of the curriculum. The notion of *perceived* relevance is crucial: relevance, like beauty, is in the eye of the beholder. It is not sufficient that the topics students study are somehow relevant to their lives, the key is in helping students see this relevance. This, of course, does not mean that students must accept that everything they do has obvious relevance; on the other hand, we must not be satisfied with the perception of many students that virtually nothing they do in school has significance in their lives. Several strategies for increasing perceived relevance are suggested in the box on the facing page.

INTEGRATING THE PERSONAL CURRICULUM

- Wherever fruitful, draw connections so that students can see the value or point of what they are learning (merely telling them that it is important is not sufficient):

  — *connect with contemporary events*, for example, when studying about the conditions during the Industrial Revolution in eighteenth century England have students draw parallels with the conditions in modern-day developing countries such as Thailand or Korea;

  — *set the study in the context of a larger theme*, for example, treat the study of a particular community or historical event as an illustration of a larger phenomenon—a study of the diverse effects of the Black Death or of the Crusades may be used to exemplify the ripple effect of unanticipated results;

  — *connect with students' personal situation or experiences*, for example, invite students to imagine their own reactions if they were to live under a given set of circumstances, say, during the Depression or as a new immigrant.

- To increase interest, frame studies around an appealing issue, problem, dilemma or case study. For example, instead of studying, for its own sake, about different Canadian communities, present students with a challenge which requires learning about these communities. The study might be framed by proposing the following scenario:

  Your mother has just been offered a job transfer to either Prince George, British Columbia or Weyburn, Saskatchewan (or other appropriate communities). She asks you to help decide which option to accept by researching these two communities and making a recommendation as to the more desirable destination for your family. You will have to decide on the criteria for choosing a desirable place to live (e.g., pleasant climate, essential services, ample recreational opportunities, healthy living conditions, interesting sites) and gather information to determine how well the communities fare on each criterion.

  Alternatively, a factual survey of the geography of a region can be made problematic, and likely more engaging, by asking students to gather data about the region to confirm or refute a particular geographic theory (e.g., To what extent are the locations and features of settlements in Ancient Greece consistent with the theory of environmental determinism?).

- To the extent feasible, provide meaningful opportunities for informed student choice as to what they study or how they study it.

- Make sure it is important to learn. Often we teach topics because we have always taught them, or because they were taught to us. We should continually ask ourselves, especially when students question why they have to learn it, whether or not it is absolutely necessary that we spend time on the topic. Often the topics students complain about *need* not be covered, or could be covered in much less detail.

Integrating the hidden curriculum

It should be obvious that integration of the hidden curriculum may be only partially promoted through theme-based teaching and interdisciplinary courses. Many of the practices and routines that are not consistent with overall educational goals may not be harmonized merely by reorganizing instruction. In fact, it is possible that inappropriate practices, say a preoccupation with factual recall, may actually be intensified if all instruction revolves around a single theme. Volumes have been written on attempts to restructure schools and classrooms so that they encourage and support desired learning. Serious discussion of the strategies for harmonizing the hidden curriculum is beyond the scope of this paper, however a few general suggestions are offered in the box on the right.[2]

INTEGRATING THE HIDDEN CURRICULUM
- **modelling good practice**—ensure that our actions model the sort of behaviour we expect from our students.
- **harmonize practices among teachers**—work with other teachers in a school to develop a consistent approach to shared activities, such as researching and writing essays, and set shared priorities which all teachers will actively promote.
- **scrutinize classroom practices**—ensure that the way we run our classes supports our important educational values, for example, if we care about critical thinking then we must provide for wait time, encourage students to challenge the perspective in the textbook and so on.

Integrating the formal curriculum

Integration of the formal curriculum can be viewed along two temporal dimensions, reflected in the following spatial metaphor:

- **vertical integration**—integrating areas of study that students encounter over time—from one grade to the next;
- **horizontal integration**—integrating areas of study that students encounter at any given time—among subjects within a given grade.

We promote vertical integration by referring to what students studied in previous months (or years) to assist them in making sense of current topics of study (e.g., noting the similarities and differences among cultures, or political systems, studied in consecutive units). We promote horizontal integration by helping students see how what they are currently studying in one subject, say English (e.g., the personal tragedy resulting from the feuding families in *Romeo and Juliet*) can enrich their understanding of a current topic in another subject, say social studies (e.g., developing historical empathy for the human costs of inter-group conflict). It is worth noting that the concern for greater horizontal integration is accentuated when students are no longer taught predominantly by one teacher—for this reason, the fragmentation of the formal curriculum is often most acute at the secondary school level. Although the major focus of formal curriculum integration is integrating the various subject areas, we should also be concerned that the elements within a subject or discipline are integrated. This is especially important in social studies where history and geography are often taught in isolation from each other and from other social science disciplines.

Clearly, integration of the formal curriculum along the vertical dimension (i.e., integration over time) is not likely to be advanced by theme-based units and inter-disciplinary courses. In fact, it has long been recognized that a preoccupation with integrating (horizontally) around themes may undermine the vertical integration of the curriculum (Knudsen, 1937, p. 22). If everything students study in one unit is closely tied to the theme for that unit, say of "early settlers," and the next unit has "bears" as its theme, students may become increasingly confused about the connections between their studies from unit to unit. In other words, increased horizontal integration of content may be purchased at the cost of decreased vertical integration.

As I suggested at the outset of the article, even when integrating the formal curriculum horizontally (i.e., at a given point in time) there is no guarantee that it will occur in any *meaningful* way through thematic units or interdisciplinary courses—the topics falling within a particular theme may not provide greater educational coherence. We can better recognize when themes and interdisciplinary courses succeed or fail to promote integration by distinguishing between an *organizing* and an *integrating* principle (Coombs, 1991):

- an *organizing principle* is a thread or feature which various elements happen to have in common (e.g., all topics deal with change, or have something to do with Egypt);
- an *integrating principle* is a characteristic which contributes to an interlocking, mutually supporting whole (e.g., the study of the art, music and literature of a era informs, and is informed by, our understanding of the social history of the period).

A study is organized, but not integrated, if the topics do not build on each other to produce an interlocking, mutually supporting picture. For example, suppose we *organize* the curriculum alphabetically according to the first letter of the topics to be taught. Our first unit, dealing with letter "A" objectives, would include study of "abbreviations," "algebra," "apostrophes," "archaeology," "atlases" and so on. This unit is not *integrated* because the principle for inclusion—that all topics in each unit start with the same letter—provides no educational coherence. In this case, the connections within and among the units are superficial and trivial. While this example is obviously a silly suggestion, it helps us to see that the mere joining together of various topics under the rubric of a common theme does not necessarily integrate the studies educationally. The content of unit "A" is integrated only to the extent to which study of, say, atlases assists students in understanding archaeology.

In the box below is an actual example of a thematic unit on forests, found in a British Columbia Ministry of Education document (1990b, pp. 317-333). Although all of these activities are associated in some way or another with forests, they are not *integrated* because increased understanding of any of the topics contributes little to an understanding of the other, supposedly related topics. For example, the only thing that Emily Carr, edible plants and making paper have in common is a tangential connection to forests. Merely because we use the

---

A "RECOMMENDED" UNIT ON FORESTS

Subject	Activities
art	make paper;
social studies	write letters to the editor about environmental issues;
language	listen to stories by and about Emily Carr;
music	dance to music from the "Four Seasons" by Vivaldi;
nutrition	write a guide for the library about edible plants in the forest;
science	make a class terrarium;
mathematics	use natural objects from the forest environment to develop concepts such as estimation and seriation.

same general theme ("forests") to connect diverse phenomena is not sufficient to presume that the topics falling under this broad concept are integrated. In other words, while all themes imply some sort of connection between the topics addressed, there is no guarantee that the topics are *meaningfully* connected; i.e., that they contribute to the coherence of the curriculum. A study is integrated when the bringing together of the parts contributes to a better understanding of the individual topics and to a clearer picture of the unity—as a jigsaw puzzle comes together to reveal the whole picture.

To more sharply contrast the difference between organizing and integrating a unit, consider the hypothetical example of two units both with an environment theme. Unit "O" (for Organized) and Unit "I" (for Integrated) both deal exclusively with topics that are, in some way or another, connected with the environment. It should be clear that most topics in Unit "O" are not connected in any educationally significant way with each other. Learning about composting and looking at the geometric shapes found in nature—although on their own valuable topics of study—do not contribute to any larger, common understanding. On the other hand, all of the topics in Unit "I" are directly concerned with human's relationship to the environment—each part of the study contributes to a larger and richer understanding of how we should stand in relation to our environment. To this extent, Unit "I" is integrated—the separate topics are connected in an educationally coherent way.

A second area of concern about integration of the formal curriculum was raised in the earlier discussion about artificial integration, where subjects are integrated for the sake of integration and not for the sake of a greater educational purpose. The result is frequently a watering down or distortion of curricular content or a sacrificing of one subject to serve the educational goals of another—for example, the use of mediocre literature or trivial learning activities solely because they fit the required theme. A related concern is the neglect of the goals of one subject—for example, even if exemplary literature is involved, it may be studied exclusively for its historical and political lessons, at the neglect of the literary or aesthetic values. The treatment of one subject as the handmaiden to another is not good integration. Rather, as the metaphor of the interlocking pieces of the puzzle implies, the insights from one subject should inform and be informed by the insights from other subjects. For example, in the "Integrated" unit on the environment mentioned above, the teaching through the art curriculum about images and metaphors furthers students' understanding of these notions in the English curriculum, and may help students' appreciate in social studies how different cultures see their relationship to the environment. Conversely, the study of other cultures' environmental philosophies may expand students' repertoire of ideas when developing their own artistic representation. One of the richest *symbiotic* relations in an integrated study I encountered was an art-social studies unit on the horror and glory of war using historical photographs and paintings of Canadian war scenes. Students learned to "read" the composition and imagery of these works both to advance their visual literacy and to help them unpack the powerful scenes which furthered the social studies objective of encouraging a more thoughtful attitude towards the then recently concluded Gulf War. Each subject enhanced and was enhanced by the integration. This was curricular integration as it should be.

There are many strategies for integrating the formal curriculum. Over the long history of this idea, three general approaches or *modes of integration* have been most widely discussed. Fusion is a viable mode of inte-

---

TWO UNITS ON THE ENVIRONMENT

UNIT "O"

Subject	Activities
mathematics	looking at tables with statistics on number of trees cut and number planted in the last year;
English	reading stories about survival in the wilderness (e.g., Farley Mowat's *Lost in the Barrens*);
social studies	analyzing the green revolution of the 1960's;
art	drawing landscapes;
music	explore reactions to New Age "wilderness" music;
science	building a compost.

UNIT "I"

Subject	Activities
mathematics	graphing trends in human consumption, population growth and resource depletion;
English	writing about human's place in nature;
social studies	exploring the attitudes of different cultures towards the environment;
art	drawing images/metaphors about human's relation to nature (e.g., in harmony with nature, nature's master);
music	listening to Sting songs about the fragile environment;
science	studying key biospheric cycles (e.g., water, air, food) and the stresses on those cycles.

Integrating the Formal Curriculum

- **fusion:** Fusion occurs by melding subjects into a new single curricular entity. Thematic units and interdisciplinary courses are examples of a fusion approach to integration because discrete disciplines or subjects are fused into a new course or unit of study (e.g., the social studies and language arts curricula are joined to create a new humanities course; several subjects are woven within a single thematic unit). A unit focussed on "publishing" an historical biography provides a powerful vehicle for learning to write with depth and detail in language arts and to explore in social studies the lives of great historical figures (described in Parker & Jarolimek, 1997, pp. 358-371). Fusion need not require the amalgamation of courses for an entire unit or semester. Fusion may occur over a relatively short time period, for example during a special interdisciplinary "global awareness" day or an integrated mini-project—e.g., preparation for a joint science-social studies fair on technological innovation.

- **insertion:** Insertion refers to a mode of integrating that involves infusing selected aspects of one subject to another subject area (e.g., introducing a chapter from the novel *Tale of Two Cities* into a history unit on the French Revolution; occasionally examining historical paintings or music during a unit on the Renaissance). Insertion is achieved by fitting a topic from one subject into the framework of another subject. Generally, the integrity and structure of the subject into which the insertion occurs remains largely unchanged, thus facilitating the teaching of both the unique features of the discipline and the relevant points of intersection with other disciplines.

- **correlation:** Correlation implies drawing connections and noting parallels among topics taught in separate courses (e.g., having teachers in various subjects deal with a common theme at the same time; teachers in one subject referring to material that students have learned in another subject). Correlation is achieved by synchronizing and drawing connections between discrete subjects which typically are taught by different teachers, for example, by organizing the timing of topics so that the history and literature or art of a particular period are taught concurrently in different courses. Alternatively, teaching about metaphor in English could be orchestrated to correspond with a social studies assignment where students devise an original metaphor to explain the underlying dynamics of a particular historical period or event.

gration—there are numerous exemplary thematic units and interdisciplinary courses.[3] However, the two other modes—insertion and correlation—have received insufficient attention in contemporary discussions about integration. Although there are limits to these alternative approaches, they are more measured responses to the challenge of integrating curricular content and they mitigate some of the problems with fusion. As I suggested earlier, entire subjects need not be integrated in order to serve the aims that integration is intended to promote. The danger is that in an effort to fuse subjects, one subject becomes the handmaiden of another. Besides, not all teachers are interested in and competent to teach all the required subjects.

Concluding Comments

I am not against theme-based units or interdisciplinary courses as approaches to curricular integration.

Aphorisms on Curricular Integration

- **Don't lose sight of the forest through the trees.** Curricular integration is not an end in itself, but a means to an end—which is to assist students in their understanding and in their appreciation of the nature and relevance of what they are studying. Keep these goals in mind. Don't reduce subjects to handmaidens. The use of inferior activities or resources, or the inclusion of marginal or trivial topics, merely because they fit with a theme is counterproductive.

- **It is not all or nothing.** There is a "golden mean" between complete separation and complete integration of subjects. Integrate when and to the extent that it makes an educationally significant contribution. Determine which curricular outcomes can be more effectively promoted through integrated study, and teach them in concert. Those that can competently be done in an independent context can be taught on their own.

- **Things are not always as they appear.** Organizing a unit is not the same as integrating a unit. We must be wary of false clarity—that the connections between subjects do not actually contribute to a more coherent picture.

- **There are many ways to skin a cat.** Interdisciplinary courses or the collapsing of all subjects into a thematic unit are not the only way to integrate the curriculum—more selective insertion and correlation of topics may be advisable in many cases.

- **There are other fish to fry.** Do not let a preoccupation with integrating the formal curriculum overshadow the need to integrate the hidden and personal curriculum.

These two strategies are *potentially* powerful means of integrating the formal curriculum. My purpose has been to indicate that (1) thematic units and interdisciplinary courses are unlikely to serve our students' needs for greater curricular integration in all its forms—personal, hidden and formal—and dimensions—vertical and horizontal; and (2) these strategies sometimes fail to integrate the formal curriculum in any educationally coherent way.

As I have tried to illustrate, vague understandings of the nature and rationales for curricular integration have meant that many integrative efforts miss the mark. I close with five general principles—offered in the form of aphorisms (on page 336)—to guide teachers' decisions about when and how to integrate the curriculum. If we were to adopt them, we would go a long way to getting beyond mere sloganeering about curricular integration.

ENDNOTES

[1] Other equally scattered recommendations for thematic units include "flight" (Jacobs, 1989), "patterns" (Fogarty, 1991), "consumerism" (Palmer, 1991) and "My travels with Gulliver" (Kleiman, 1991).

[2] Other articles in this collection deal with the hidden curriculum, notably the discussion of creating a community of learners in the Case and Wright article, "Taking Seriously the Teaching of Critical Thinking," and the discussion of the role of the social environment in Case's article, "Nurturing Social and Personal Values."

[3] An exciting example of an integrated primary unit on bears (integrating formal and personal curriculum) is described in MacIntosh (1989).

REFERENCES

Aiken, W.M. (1942). *The story of the Eight-Year Study.* New York: Harper.

Alleman, J. & Brophy, J. (1993). Is curriculum integration a boon or a threat to social studies? *Social Education, 57,* 287-291.

Beane, J. (1991). The middle school: The natural home of integrated curriculum. *Educational Leadership, 49*(2), 9-13.

Brandt, R. (1991). On interdisciplinary curriculum: A conversation with Heidi Hayes Jacobs. *Educational Leadership, 49*(2), 24-26.

British Columbia Ministry of Education. (1990a). *The Intermediate Program: Learning in British Columbia.* Victoria, BC: Author.

British Columbia Ministry of Education. (1990b). *Primary Program resource document.* Victoria, BC: Author.

British Columbia Ministry of Education. (1992). *Curricular integration: An outline for discussion.* Victoria, BC: Author.

British Columbia Ministry of Education. (1993). *The Intermediate Program policy: Grades 4 to 10.* Victoria, BC: Author.

Coombs, J. (1991). *Thinking seriously about curriculum integration.* (Forum on Curricular Integration Occasional Paper #4). Burnaby, BC: Tri-University Integration Project, Simon Fraser University.

Craig, C. (1987). Addressing subject integration. *History and Social Science Teacher, 23*(1), 31–34.

Drake, S.M. (1991). How our team dissolved the boundaries. *Educational Leadership, 49*(2), 20-22.

Drake, S.M. (1992). Integrating curricula through transdisciplinary webbing. *Canadian School Executive, 12*(5), 3-6.

Dressel, P.L. (1958). The meaning and significance of integration. In N.B. Henry (Ed.), *The integration of educational experiences: The fifty-seventh yearbook of the National Society for the Study of Education* (pp. 3-25). Chicago: University of Chicago Press.

Fogarty, R. (1991). Ten ways to integrate curriculum. *Educational Leadership, 49*(2), 61-65.

Fullan, M.G. (1991). *The new meaning of educational change.* Toronto: OISE Press.

Fullinwider, R. (1991). Multicultural education. *Report from the Institute for Philosophy and Public Policy, 11*(3), 12-14.

Hargreaves, A. (1993). Curriculum integration. In K. Leithwood, A. Hargreaves & D. Gérin-Lajoie (Eds.), *Exemplary practices in the transition years: A review of research and theory* (pp. 123-138). Toronto: Queen's Printer.

Jacobs, H.H. (Ed.). (1989). *Interdisciplinary curriculum: Design and implementation.* Alexandria, VA: Association for Supervision and Curriculum Development.

Kleiman, G.M. (1991). Mathematics across the curriculum. *Educational Leadership, 49*(2), 48-5l.

Knudsen, C.W. (1937). What do educators mean by "Integration?" *Harvard Educational Review, 7,* 15-26.

MacIntosh, E. with Martell, G. (1989). Bears and collective learning. *Our Schools/Our Selves, 1*(3), 41-54.

Ontario, Ministry of Education and Training. (1993). *The common curriculum: Grades 1-9* (Working document). Toronto: Queen's Printer.

Palmer, J.N. (1991). Planning wheels turn curriculum around. *Educational Leadership, 49*(2), 57-60.

Parker, W.C. & Jarolimek, J. (1997). *Social studies in elementary education* (10th ed.). Upper Saddle River, NJ: Prentice-Hall.

Pring, R. (1973). Curriculum integration: The need for clarification. *New Era, 54*(3), 59-64.

Raizen, S. A., & Kaser, J. S. (1989) Assessing science learning in elementary school: Why, what, and how? *Phi Delta Kappan, 70*(9), 718-722.

Schwartz, S. & Pollishuke, M. (1990). *Creating the child-centred classroom.* Toronto: Irwin.

Taba, H. (1962). *Curriculum development: Theory and practice.* San Francisco: Harcourt, Brace.

Werner, W. (1991). Defining curriculum policy

through slogans. *Journal of Educational Policy, 6*(2), 225-238.

This article is based on two earlier works: a 1991 article "Integrating Around Themes: An Overemphasized Tool?" in *The Bookmark, 32*(2), 19-27, and a 1994 article "Our Crude Handling of Educational Reform: The Case of Curricular Integration" in *Canadian Journal of Education, 19*(1), 80-93.

35

Between the Covers: Exposing Images in Social Studies Textbooks

Penney Clark

The textbook plays an important role in Canadian social studies classrooms. In fact, it has a habit of becoming the *de facto* curriculum with 'covering' the textbook an important goal (Hodgetts, 1968; Cassidy & Bognar, 1991; Case, 1993). Consequently we must carefully attend to what textbooks communicate to their readers. We need to get beneath their surface discourse and expose their implicit as well as explicit messages. They portray particular world views and perspectives. Both by what they include and what they omit, textbooks represent choices made from among many possibilities. Generally speaking, however, students do not question their textbooks. As one high school social studies student commented, "You can't disagree with it [the text] . . . it's what you are supposed to learn" (Seixas, 1994, p. 93). The presumed sanctity of the text disinclines students to question its contents.

In view of these concerns, teachers are often dissuaded from using textbooks. Some teacher education programs encourage student teachers to avoid them completely, and develop original instructional activities and materials (Loewenberg Ball & Feiman-Nemser, 1988). Given the wide range of other materials available, it may be thought feasible simply to abolish textbooks from the classroom; however, a more practical and worthwhile approach is to learn to use them sensitively and critically. A textbook provides material presented by an author who has a degree of content mastery which most teachers would not have, and could not acquire without a great deal of work. Given the pressures on teacher time, it is unlikely that most teachers have sufficient opportunity, even if they wished, to assemble materials that were as competent as the text. Teachers can accept, reject, modify or supplement textbooks, but they do provide a basis from which to begin instruction. Since they are likely to continue to have a significant instructional role, it is important for teachers to learn to deal with them in ways that help students recognize their limits and overcome the biases inherent within them.

Textbook discourse can be examined for a variety of purposes. In this article I consider the depiction of gender, race and ethnicity, the elderly and the disabled.[1] I focus on social studies texts officially approved for use in British Columbia elementary and secondary schools from 1983 to 1995, but I refer to studies of other Canadian texts as well. After exposing what I see to be significant images—especially distortions and omissions—in these texts, I discuss three ways to deal with their unavoidable and often biased representations of the world.

CANADIAN TEXTBOOK STUDIES

Since Marcel Trudel and Genevieve Jain's (1970) landmark study for the Royal Commission of Bilingualism and Biculturalism compared versions of Canadian history presented to Francophone and Anglophone students, there has been an avalanche of textbook studies in Canada. The vast majority of the studies carried out during the 1970s and early 1980s focussed on portrayal of race. The first of these studies to receive national attention, an analysis of 143 social studies textbooks authorized in Ontario, reported many examples of bias and stereotyping (McDiarmid & Pratt, 1971). One of the conclusions was that "we are most likely to encounter in textbooks devoted Christians, great Jews, hardworking immigrants, infidel Moslems, primitive Negroes, and savage Indians" (p. 45). A major area of concern was textbook portrayal of Native peoples (Nova Scotia Human Rights Commission, 1974; Manitoba Indian Brotherhood, 1977; Paton & Deverell, 1974). These studies found errors of fact, glaring omissions and negative stereotyping about Native peoples.

Depiction of gender did not receive much attention in studies of social studies textbooks prior to the mid 1980s. Early gender studies of basal readers and children's literature found that females were presented as inferior to males. Little girls were fearful and incompetent, in contrast to confident and resourceful boys. Adult women had servile roles in the family and were largely confined to their kitchens (Wright, 1976/1977; Lorimer & Long, 1979/1980; Pyke, 1975). In a 1989 examination of 66 Canadian history texts, historians Beth Light, Pat Staton and Paula Bourne found a range of women's content from less than one percent to just over forty-three percent. There was a less serious tone when describing women's activities, accompanied by a tendency to blame female family members for men's faults and failures. Patricia Baldwin and textbook author Douglas Baldwin (1992) analyzed four grade seven Canadian history textbooks, concluding that women are relegated to minor roles of supporting men's endeavours. They suggested that traditional categories and periodizations of history be abandoned in favour of new formats which allow for a fairer portrayal of women. In addition, they recommended that both teachers and students be taught to recognize bias and how to counteract it.

There has been little interest in disabled people in social studies textbook studies other than in provincial assessments to determine which books were suitable to remain on approved lists (Curriculum, Alberta Education, 1985). Seniors have received slightly more attention. Patrick Babin (1975) found little bias in depiction of seniors in his examination of 1,719 textbooks approved for use in Ontario schools.

As a result of studies such as these, each province developed social awareness criteria to be used to assess potential resources before they are officially approved for use in public schools. The intention is to authorize only those materials which accurately depict the racial and ethnic pluralism of Canada and show people of various races and ethnic groups, both genders, the elderly and the disabled, making positive contributions to Canadian society, past and present.

David Pratt boldly declared in 1984 that the publication of Ontario's social awareness criteria "virtually ensures the elimination of racial, ethnic, cultural, and religious bias in future Ontario textbooks" (p. 153). Had his prediction proved true, there would be no need to

---

David Pratt boldly declared in 1984 that the publication of Ontario's social awareness criteria "virtually ensures the elimination of racial, ethnic, cultural, and religious bias in future Ontario textbooks" (p. 153). Had his prediction proved true, there would be no need to write this article. Unfortunately, this is not the case.

---

write this article. Unfortunately, this is not the case. Despite the rigorous criteria now applied to textbooks, there are lingering distortions, as well as omissions of particular groups. In addition, we now recognize that any author will unavoidably write from a particular perspective formed from experiences and personal values, whether we choose to call that perspective 'bias' or not. Hence, we will always need to recognize and assess the adequacy of the representations found in any textbook, including those that are not overtly "biased."

DEPICTION OF GENDER

Distorted representations of gender appear in elementary texts in the form of a reverse stereotyping, where little girls are depicted engaging in activities such as tree-climbing, which also often interest boys, but not in those activities which have come to be viewed as stereotypical, such as playing with dolls. In terms of gender omissions, women have come out of the shadows and into the full light of social studies textbooks to some extent only. While elementary textbooks abound with examples of females pursuing both traditional and nontraditional careers, engaging in challenging recreational activities and offering opinions on social issues, such is not the case in secondary texts. Many of these texts are largely devoid of women and discussion of gender-related issues. When women do appear in secondary texts, it is typically in the role of queen.

Prior to the 1980s, depiction of gender was stereotypical. For example, in *How Families Live*, a 1970s era prescribed grade one picture set, contemporary Canadian women's activities are centered around child care and household tasks. In the six booklets in the *Explorations* series, prescribed for grade one in the 1980s, contemporary women are depicted in a much wider range of activities, including child care, food preparation and other household tasks, but also changing a tire, talking on the telephone in an office setting, using blueprints at a construction site and hammering nails into a floor.

It is not only women's roles which have expanded. Men, too, are shown in a greater variety of activities in the newer texts. In the *Explorations* series men are shown caring for children, as well as engaging in household tasks such as vacuuming, preparing meals, loading a dishwasher, doing carpentry work and outside home maintenance and grocery shopping, as well as various kinds of paid employment.

Previously invisible in elementary Canadian history texts, females became evident even in these, in the 1980s. For instance, the presence of white women at the Cariboo gold rush is acknowledged. A grade five text, *Canada: Building Our Nation,* tells about a woman who started up a pie business, selling her pies from a tent; a washerwoman; a woman who accompanied her husband to work a mining claim; and a woman who planned to build her own hotel. Texts also acknowledge the presence of women on the journeys of the European explorers. In fact, in *The Explorers: Charting the Canadian Wilderness,* a grade four text, a journey by Anthony Henday is described from the perspective of Grey Goose Woman, an imaginary name given by the author to a Native woman whose presence on the trip has been documented.

Issues concerning gender roles are discussed in elementary texts. For instance, *Exploring Our World,* a grade six text, asks students to consider two points of view on the importance of education for girls in Peru. A twelve year old girl presents the case for an education and her father presents points against it. Two twelve year old French girls take different positions on the question of staying home to care for children versus remaining in the work force.

Secondary texts, on the other hand, ignore women to a rather surprising extent. For instance, in the grade ten text, *Our Land: Building the West,* the index has only three references to women (Susanna Moodie, Queen Victoria and women in the labour force) and 90 to men.

It is interesting to note how one generation's taboos are replaced by those of the next generation. While it is now accceptable to portray children in a single-parent family, it seems as though it is no longer acceptable to portray little girls dressing up in their mother's discarded clothing or playing with their dolls.

This is slight representation for a text 432 pages in length. The grade nine text, *Thinking About Our Heritage,* has only three references to women and 81 to men. The grade nine text, *Patterns of Civilization,* Volume Two, has 14 references to women and 204 to men.

In spite of sincere attempts on the part of elementary textbook authors and publishers to include women, I do have a concern with instances of reverse stereotyping. This concern was expressed best by June Callwood, who quoted a former textbook editor as saying, "Every jet pilot has to be female. . . . and I don't think you can find a book any more in which a little girl cries. They've

all got to be tough as nails" (1987, p. A2). The suggestion here is that newer texts may have overreacted to the stereotyping of the past, where little girls were depicted as subordinate to their male brothers and friends; where it was the males who engaged in the most challenging activities and who made the important decisions. Callwood's point is epitomized by Morgan, the androgynous figure who takes the reader from community to community in the grade three text, *Exploring Our Country.* Morgan's very name is ambiguous. Morgan wears various t-shirts and a pair of ubiquitous blue overalls. The activities she enjoys are limited to those generally deemed acceptable for either a boy or a girl: "She liked making angels in the snow and eating birthday cakes. She liked collecting bugs and climbing trees. She hated being tickled" (Wood, 1983, p. 6). No playing with dolls for Morgan. In fact there is not a picture of a little girl playing 'house' or dolls to be found in any of the texts. Girls are shown playing street hockey, riding a horse, riding a tractor, going fishing and riding a bike. We do not see girls in activities in which boys do not also usually engage. It is apparently no longer acceptable to depict such activities. It is interesting to note how one generation's taboos are replaced by those of the next generation. While it is now accceptable to portray children in a single-parent family, it seems as though it is no longer acceptable to portray little girls dressing up in their mother's discarded clothing or playing with their dolls. We can only hope that, in future texts girls will be allowed to drag out their tea sets or put their dolls to bed. Perhaps, in those future texts, girls will be portrayed in a greater variety of roles and activities, including those in which they have traditionally, and still do, engage.

Instead of including 'ordinary' women, as the elementary texts make an effort to do, secondary texts focus almost exclusively on royalty, with an occasional saint thrown in for good measure. For instance, the three women in the index of *Thinking About Our Heritage* are two queens and a saint (Joan of Arc). Of 14 references to specific women in the grade eight text, *Patterns of Civilization,* Volume One, 13 are members of royalty and the other is Joan of Arc once again.

Should social studies texts attempt to present a realistic or an idealistic view of gender roles? The Federation of Women Teachers of Ontario believes that texts should indeed portray an ideal, non-sexist vision. This group believes that children need to encounter females and males in equal numbers who are intelligent, independent and competent. They need to see males who are receiving help, friendship and advice from females as often as females receiving these from males. As well, human failures should be cast as learning or growth experiences and not as events which stigmatize individuals for life (Gaskell, McLaren & Novogrodsky, 1989, p. 37).

The rationale for this position is understandable: proponents want positive role models and goals for students to work towards. On the other hand, critics point to two problems with this view. First, any portrayal of a traditional woman, or of a woman participating in traditional activities, reinforces a stereotype and is therefore problematic. The reality is, according to every survey, that women still do the majority of the child care and housework, whether or not they work outside the home. A second problem relates to the insistence on "positive growth experiences." It would seem to preclude discussion of negative topics such as the holocaust, slavery and racism. Critics of the idealized view do not want texts to portray a world of "androgynous superpeople" nor to exclude all material showing women in traditional roles (Gaskell, McLaren & Novogrodsky, 1989, p. 38).

In spite of the improved depiction of gender—and textbooks have improved in this regard—concerns remain. Authors of elementary texts make every effort to include women, but in doing so, there are instances of reverse stereotyping. Secondary textbooks have serious gaps in terms of inclusion of women. I believe that text readers should see females in a range of roles, and that range should include 'ordinary' women engaging in routine day-to-day tasks such as childcare and running a household. Avoiding such depictions because earlier texts placed far too much emphasis on them, results in a different kind of distortion.

DEPICTION OF RACE AND ETHNICITY

The major change in the nature of Canada over the last three decades has undoubtedly been the move from a predominantly bicultural to a multicultural population. The concept of multiple facets of national identity, as J. Donald Wilson (1994) reminds us, forms the basis of Canadian multicultural policy. Wilson makes the point that "national identity is something invented, constructed, contested, and constantly changing" (p. 6) and that Canada's multicultural policy is its latest manifestation. This policy recognizes that Canadians can have many identities simultaneously, yet contemporary texts reflect Canada's changing cultural reality and the possibility of multiple identities in a very limited way. Again, the elementary texts do a better job than the secondary. Elementary texts typically depict faces of different colours and people wearing ethnic clothing and participating in activities which celebrate their ethnicity. Ethnic and racial diversity is reflected in photographs. Developers have gone so far as to consult census data to determine that illustrations convey a representative mix of people. In many cases, immigrants are no longer the cardboard cut-outs they were in earlier texts. They are presented as diverse people with many characteristics. The contributions of immigrants to the his-

torical development of Canada are also acknowledged. However, although diversity is acknowledged, it is only at a superficial level. It is not explored in a rich way.

While contemporary texts acknowledge Canada's multicultural nature, indepth discussion of what it means to be a Canadian within this unique multicultural reality is negligible. The grade ten text, *Our Land: Building the West*, devotes one and one-half, of 432 pages, to the topic of recent immigration to British Columbia, exclusively in the context of links between Canada and the Pacific Rim region. This treatment consists largely of statistics regarding numbers of immigrants from vari-

---

Again, the elementary texts do a better job than the secondary. Elementary texts typically depict faces of different colours and people wearing ethnic clothing and participating in activities which celebrate their ethnicity. Ethnic and racial diversity is reflected in photographs. . . . However, although diversity is acknowledged, it is only at a superficial level. It is not explored in a rich way.

---

ous groups. A highlighted section discusses the effects of immigration on Vancouver's school system, although the focus is on how the system is *accommodating* the influx of students whose first language is not English, The perspective is reminiscent of the 'problems' approach taken in earlier texts, where Oriental immigrants were discussed only in the context of the problems they were causing the dominant Canadian society (Clark, 1995). Only one paragraph is devoted to a discussion of effects of immigration more generally.

Desmond Morton, in the grade eleven text, *Towards Tomorrow: Canada in a Changing World, History*, provides a thoughtful, if brief, discussion of multiculturalism, building on the notion of multi-faceted identity. According to Morton, each of us must decide, from a range of choices, what it means to be a Canadian in a multicultural society. He invokes Maurice Careless's concept of "limited identities," describing Canadians as "people who could identify with an ethnic heritage, a region, a province, and a community, with economic interests, and with ideas and a religious faith, and still be good Canadians" (p. 220). He also discusses Pierre Elliot Trudeau's views on the value of individualism and multiculturalism, and the interplay between the two. Unfortunately, Morton's discussion suffers from the usual limitations of the textbook format; there is space to present ideas but not to explore them in any depth.

Examination of earlier texts reveals that they tended to ignore or downplay contributions of Oriental immigrants and ways in which Orientals were unfairly treated in Canada (Clark, 1995). Authors of contemporary texts, both elementary and secondary, acknowledge the historical presence and contributions of Orientals in Canada. The grade five text, *Canada: Building Our Nation*, uses simulated journal entries to convey a sense of the experience of Chinese railway workers. The grade ten text, *Our Land: Building the West*, discusses Chinese workers in the construction of the Canadian Pacific Railway, as well as in British Columbia mines and canneries. The presence of Japanese in the commercial fishery until World War Two is also noted in this text.

Texts published after 1980 often highlight previously unmentionable occurrences such as the wartime internment of Japanese Canadians, although discussion is typically superficial. They rarely give students any inkling of the circumstances and broader issues surrounding these events. For instance, readers are told that "the Canadian government made Japanese Canadians move away from the west coast" (Bowers & Swanson, 1985, p. 306) without being informed of the persistence of British Columbians through letters, petitions and public rallies, in driving the federal government to take that position. Nor are readers told about the bombing of Pearl Harbour and fears for personal safety during the horrors of wartime. If mentioned, an event such as this should be explored in greater depth, or at least the reader should be given some indication of its complexity and referred to other resources which can provide more detail.

There has been a marked change over the years in terms of the way Canada's Native peoples are presented in the texts. The often extremely negative and patronizing depiction found in earlier texts has evolved into a respectful tone in contemporary texts (Conner & Bethune-Johnson, 1984; Siska, 1984). The assistance of Native people to European explorers is acknowledged. Intermarriage between white fur traders and Native women is also acknowledged—another new development.

While contemporary texts are more positive than earlier texts, the elementary texts in particular are not as realistic. In terms of their treatment of Canadian history, newer texts focus primarily on the positive aspects of European/Native interaction and what each learned from the other. Earlier texts, on the other hand, acknowledged the disruptions to Native life caused by the introduction of European technology, as well as the epidemics and other negative effects of the arrival of Europeans on their shores. One popular grade four text referred graphically to "the frenzy and the horrors of the nineteenth century" (Symington, 1970, p. 23).

In terms of their treatment of contemporary life, earlier texts focussed too much on problems experienced by contemporary Native communities, to the point where the communities were defined by their problems. For instance, Frobisher Bay was referred to as "a rather sorry mess" (Martin, 1969, p. 47). Contemporary elementary texts tend to focus on the positive with no hint of the poverty and self-destructive behaviour sometimes found on reserves and in Inuit communities (Conner & Bethune-Johnson, 1984). Secondary texts are more realistic. The grade eleven text, *Towards Tomorrow: Canada in a Changing World, History*, devotes six pages to discussion of issues of concern to contemporary Canadian Native people.

Shortly after the publication of the grade two text, *Exploring Mount Currie*, Lisa Fitterman, writing in the *Vancouver Sun*, criticized the text for its positive portrayal of the community of Mount Currie, which is a reserve. Fitterman made the point that the text presented only one reality of life on the reserve. It ignored the other reality which is "a town where icicles hang from the ceiling of the clapboard houses in winter and fewer than 150 homes shelter up to 1,000 people; where the unemployment rate hovers around 74 per cent and the suicide rate is three or four times the national average" (1984, p. C20). Carol Langford, editor of the *Explorations* series, responded at the time that the text was intended to depict the reality of Tanina, one grade two child, not the total reality of the community (p. C20). The community series, of which this text was a part, was intended to portray actual students' milieus in four communities, so student readers could get a sense of similarities and differences across the communities. The texts accomplish this, and perhaps this is quite enough for texts intended for seven and eight year olds. A per-

> *There has been a marked change over the years in terms of the way Canada's Native peoples are presented in the texts. The often extremely negative and patronizing depiction found in earlier texts has evolved into a respectful tone in contemporary texts . . . The assistance of Native people to European explorers is acknowledged. Intermarriage between white fur traders and Native women is also acknowledged— another new development.*

ennial dilemma for social studies textbook developers and teachers is the extent to which primary students should be exposed to negative aspects of the world. Another point made by Langford more recently, was that it was the wish of the people of the community to have its positive aspects conveyed. She believes publishers must consider the wishes of the people they are portraying (Interview by author, 19 April, 1995, Kamloops). This adds another dimension for teachers to consider in deciding on which "faces" of a community or culture to portray.

Textbooks published following the textbook assessments of the 1970s and early 1980s do acknowledge Canada's contemporary multicultural reality. The faces in illustrations are no longer all white. Cultural differences are celebrated and derogatory statements have been removed. However, there is little attempt to explore this diversity and what it means to be a Canadian within this reality. This is due, in part, to the space restrictions of the textbook format, where topics are touched on and then the text moves on.

With regard to depiction of Native peoples, the elementary texts present a very positive, but not entirely realistic picture. Historically, the ways in which Native people assisted European explorers are acknowledged without discussion of the disruption to Native cultures caused by that contact. Life on contemporary reserves is presented as a celebration of Native culture, with little reference to problems to be overcome. This is in contrast to earlier texts, which tended to define contemporary Native communities by their problems.

DEPICTION OF DISABLED PEOPLE

Inclusion of mentally and physically disabled people in textbooks is a phenomenon unique to contemporary texts and found only in the elementary textbooks. Disabled people are included in these texts in both implicit and explicit ways.

The implicit message in these texts is that individuals who happen to have physical disabilities can be fully functioning members of society who do not need to be defined by their disabilities. Photographs frequently depict people with disabilities engaging in day-to-day tasks: a teacher has a walking cane; two of the individuals who work in an imaginary space community are in wheelchairs (Gordon, 1983a, pp. 100, 37, 77); a young woman is standing at a sink washing dishes with her metal crutches leaning against the counter beside her (Sauder, 1983f, p. 2); and a child in a wheelchair is surrounded by friends (Wood, 1983, p. 58).

> The implicit message in these texts is that individuals who happen to have physical disabilities can be fully functioning members of society who do not need to be defined by their disabilities.

The most innovative depiction of a disabled person is found in the grade two text *Exploring Prince George*. Each of four grade two texts is about a different British Columbia community. Each community is viewed through the experiences of a particular child who lives in the community, as in the example of Tanina in *Exploring Mount Currie*, discussed earlier. *Exploring Prince George* is about Lara, a grade two child who appears to have Down's Syndrome. The text itself does not mention this, although the teacher's guide refers to the fact that she has disabilities. Lara is shown engaging in a variety of activities, including participating in a group art project in her classroom, working in a backyard vegetable garden, doing gymnastics, playing dress-up with friends, riding a bike and playing miniature golf. The implicit message to the student reader is: This child has a disability. Yet, this disability is only part of the person that she is. She has a family as you do. She attends school and enjoys many of the same recreational activities as you, and likes to enjoy them with other people. In all of these ways she is similar both to the student reader and to the children featured in the three other community texts.

In terms of explicit inclusion, the primary text, *Exploring Your School and Neighbourhood*, devotes two pages to photographs of disabled people experiencing problems of access because they are confined to wheelchairs. The caption asks, "How could a neighbourhood help these people?" (Gordon, 1983, pp. 26-27).

The omission of disabled people in textbooks prior to those prescribed in the 1980s was a reflection of the social circumstances in which the texts were written. Prior to the 1980s mentally and physically disabled people tended to be 'invisible'. Disabled children lived at home and either did not attend school, or attended 'special' schools or 'special' classes in public schools, or were institutionalized as permanent or semipermanent residents. They had little contact with other children. Disabled adults tended to be either institutionalized or living at home with elderly parents or other caregivers. Their involvement in the community was minimal. The first Canadian census to ask for specific information about disabled Canadians was not until 1986. The lack of interest in them on the part of Canadian government information gathering agencies is evidence in itself for the 'invisible' state of disabled Canadians in earlier years.

Mainstreaming of disabled children in the public school system is a phenomenon of the eighties in Canadian schools. Disabled adults, too, have become a more visible part of Canadian society. In 1984, 42 percent of disabled Canadians were employed. This is a reasonably high percentage when one considers that only 67 percent of the non-disabled population were employed in the same year (Statistics Canada, 1988, p. 30). Disabled adults in the 1980s and 1990s usually live in private homes with their families or in small group homes in the community, rather than in large institutions (Statistics Canada, 1990, p. 16).

The elementary texts reflect these changing realities. It is unfortunate that secondary texts, particularly those depicting contemporary society, do not include disabled people. This is a serious omission.

DEPICTION OF CANADA'S SENIORS

The depiction of senior citizens in elementary textbooks changed somewhat with the advent of new texts in the 1980s. This is not true of secondary texts. Seniors were absent in earlier texts and remained so in the new texts prescribed for use in secondary schools in the 1980s.

When found on the pages of earlier elementary texts seniors have been depicted in one of two ways—as dependent on younger adults or as a loving companion to young grandchildren. They exist without friends, or obligations and interests outside the family circle. In *How Families Live*, one of the primary picture sets in the One World series, an elderly Inuit woman is shown being assisted to walk by her adult grandson. The teacher's guide asks the question, "Why does the lady need help? Why is her grandson holding her arm? Why does she have a stick? Who might help her if her grandson wasn't close by?" (Owen, 1972, p. 89). This is elderly as weak, disabled and helpless. Other pictures in this set show a grandmother rolling pastry with a little granddaughter and another grandmother watching television with her two young grandchildren (pp. 60, 81).

Although contemporary texts continue to focus on the activities of middle-aged and younger members of society, seniors appear more frequently and are engaged in a slightly broader range of activities. There are many examples of seniors with other family members, particularly of seniors teaching children. For instance, Tanina, the little girl in *Exploring Mount Currie*, enjoys the companionship of her two grandmothers. One teaches her Lil'wat dances, while the other takes her out to dig cedar roots. In *Exploring Our Country* we see an elderly woman in a wheelchair being assisted by a volunteer, a stereotypical representation of the elderly as weak and dependent on others. However, in the same text we meet Mrs. Parker and W.O. Mitchell, both of whom convey the sense that the elderly contribute to society. Mrs. Parker is celebrating her one hundred and twelfth birthday in Burgeo, Newfoundland, where she has lived all her life. She is being interviewed by a television reporter about how life in Burgeo has changed over the years. The text asks the reader, "What did Morgan learn from Mrs. Parker? What could you learn from older people in your community?" (Woods, 1983, p. 96). The text makes the point that W.O. Mitchell is a well respected Canadian author from whom people can learn about life on the Canadian prairies in the past.

Despite the increased frequency of appearance of seniors, their range of activities is still very limited. They tend to exist only in the role of family member—W.O. Mitchell being an exception. It would be a great step forward to see seniors doing something besides teaching grandchildren, posing for family portraits and taking part in family birthday celebrations. It would be refreshing to see someone over sixty-five driving a car, in paid employment, engaging in volunteer work instead of the recipient of such, socializing with friends or engaging in recreational activities other than family picnics.

DEALING WITH TEXTUAL REPRESENTATION

Three types of concerns related to textbooks have been identified in this article: distorted images, gaps in terms of accurate representation of various groups and the unavoidability of a perspective inherent in any textbook. Since there is no promised land where textbooks come without bias, or, at least, perspective, students need to be taught to view a text as representing particular perspectives rather than as *the* objective authority on a topic. This section discusses three ways to use textbooks to expose and overcome these concerns:

- teach students to directly confront the biases found in their texts by means of examining both their written content and illustrations from a critical stance in order to locate and analyze the distortions and omissions, as well as author perspective;
- use source materials to "demystify and dethrone the textbook" (Osborne, 1995, p. 155);
- use sets of alternative texts, instead of one class set of the same textbook, so that students can see and compare their varying perspectives.

Textual analysis

Students can engage in activities which directly confront the biases found in their texts by analyzing text contents. They could examine their texts to determine how women are depicted, or use up-to-date census information on racial groups in Canada as a basis for assessing the proportional depiction of various groups in textbook illustrations. (Note that the text as a whole would be assessed for this representation. It would be unreasonable to expect balance in each individual illustration.) An example of author perspective, which is found in the history textbook *Patterns of Civilization*, Volume Two, depicts a detail from a famous painting called *The Battle of Bunker's Hill* by American artist John Trumbull. The portion of the painting found in the textbook shows an American soldier who seems to be bravely facing the British soldiers. An examination of the entire painting gives quite a different message. In fact, the painting centres on an heroic act by a British officer, who is preventing one of his soldiers from killing an injured American general. The American soldier is merely staring in astonishment. Students can be asked to consider what the choice of this detail from the painting tells us about the pro-American perspective of the text on this historical event (Case, Daniels & Schwartz, 1996, pp. 124).

Source materials

Ken Osborne (1995) outlines four ways to use primary and secondary source materials:

- present an account which contradicts that in the text;
- use two or more sources which differ among themselves;
- provide background information to support and

> *Despite the increased frequency of appearance of seniors, their range of activities is still very limited. They tend to exist only in the role of family member . . . It would be a great step forward to see seniors doing something besides teaching grandchildren, posing for family portraits and taking part in family birthday celebrations.*

expand the generalizations in the text;

- have students construct their own historical accounts and, in so doing, deconstruct the textbook.

When students are presented with sources which differ, either from the text or among themselves, they can begin to see that texts, like other accounts, are written from particular perspectives. For example, Osborne provides three differing perspectives on the Winnipeg General Strike—from a strike leader, the *Toronto Globe* and the *Manitoba Free Press*—accompanied by questions intended to help students consider the interpretation of sources in the construction of historical accounts.

Because texts must cover, in a restricted number of pages, the required content specified in provincial curriculum documents, they are limited in terms of the depth of the coverage they can offer. Supplementing the textbook with additional sources can provide that depth. For instance, Osborne provides a description by George Simpson, governor of the Hudson's Bay Company, of an encounter with men from the rival Northwest Company. Canadian history textbooks mention the rivalry, but a description from an individual who was directly involved can help students appreciate the intricacies of the interaction between the two companies.

Additional source materials can also be useful in infusing into the historical and contemporary record the contributions of marginalized groups such as women and racial minorities. For example, as an approach to including women's contributions, Nel Noddings (1992) suggests that students investigate topics such as family membership and even homemaking. In addition to practical aspects of homemaking, students might address philosophical questions such as: "What does it mean to 'make a home'? Must a home's occupants be members of a nuclear family? Why is a 'home for the aged' not considered a home by many of its occupants?" (p. 235). The use of supplementary sources can help fill gaps such as the one noted by Noddings that students frequently study about war but rarely investigate peace movements. Our social studies texts have tended to ignore the activities of organizations such as the Women's International League for Peace and Freedom in favour of the activities of admirals and generals.

It may be particularly effective to invite students to write their own historical accounts either by using a teacher-chosen selection of sources around a common theme or by having students conduct original research to develop family, school or local histories.

The use of additional or conflicting sources does not pertain exclusively to history texts, they apply to any social studies materials. For instance, we can use maps, graphs, charts and surveys to extend and make problematic textbooks' representations of geographic information.

Other forms of representation such as film, paintings, poetry and music also help students challenge and compare information. Marcy Gabella (1994) found that while students would not question the historical information found in their textbooks, they would question historical sources such as paintings, music and poetry. She concluded that they were more willing to question artforms because they were aware of the human face of their creators. They viewed the voice of their textbooks as disembodied, and therefore could not envision a human voice with whom they could engage in dialogue. One critical thinking resource for social studies includes exemplars of the use of painting and poetry in order to have students compare the portrayal of events from different perspectives (Case, Daniels & Schwartz, 1996). For example, students compare a reporter's despatch describing the Battle of Balaclava during the Crimean War with the poem, "The Charge of the Light Brigade" by Tennyson, for their perspectives on valour. As Gabella (1994) points out, having students critically assess artforms, which they recognize as subjective, is a step toward helping them recognize subjective features in seemingly objective representational forms such as textbooks.

Multiple textbooks

Using several sets of textbooks can be more effective in removing the text from its pinnacle than providing alternate source materials because students are already willing to accept that the alternate source materials may present different perspectives (Gabella, 1994). Since students are inclined to view a textbook as the final word on a topic, it can be more unnerving to see a different perspective presented in each of several texts. Alternate textbook sets allow students to examine and compare the treatment of particular topics in

---

Using several sets of textbooks can be more effective in removing the text from its pinnacle than providing alternate source materials . . . Since students are inclined to view a textbook as the final word on a topic, it can be more unnerving to see a different perspective presented in . . . several texts.

---

the different texts. They can look for distortions, omissions, degrees of emphasis, tone of presentation and the perspectives from which information is presented. As an example, on a topic such as the fur trade, students might look for the presence or omission of women; whether the emphasis of the discussion tends to be social, economic or political, or some combination; and what tone pervades the inclusion of Native people and whether the discussion is entirely from a European perspective.

Another advantage of using several different sets of texts is that omissions with regard to a particular group in one text may be filled by another. Texts can atone for one another's flaws.

From a practical standpoint, using several sets of texts does not mean, in an era of tight budgets, that several class sets of new texts must be purchased. It might mean holding on to old, supposedly outdated, texts as alternate information sources or purchasing partial class sets of alternate texts instead of relying exclusively on one class set of a single text. It may also mean sharing several different text sets among two or three classes.

In the final analysis, we must direct our attention to the textbooks' intended audience, rather than striving for perfection in the texts themselves. The task of teachers is to tear down the sanctity of the text and help students learn to probe surface discourse for the latent messages texts deliver. As Cleo Cherryholmes suggests, "encouraging students themselves to engage in criticism may be simultaneously a step away from social studies instruction and a step toward social studies education" (1991, p. 55).

ENDNOTE
[1] For a more detailed discussion of the points raised in this article, and to see how depiction of gender, race/ethnicity, disability and age have changed over time, see Clark (1995). That historical study examined 169 social studies textbooks approved for use in British Columbia schools since 1925. Texts were examined for views of Canadian identity inherent within them and how these views were redefined over time. A profile was created for each textbook based on eleven selected aspects of Canadian identity, including the four examined here. Research was funded by a doctoral fellowship from the Social Sciences and Humanities Research Council of Canada.

REFERENCES
Elementary textbooks
Bowers, V. & Swanson, D. (1985). *Exploring Canada: Learning from the past, looking to the future*. Vancouver: Douglas & McIntyre (Educational).

Carriere, M., James, M. & Koleszar, S. (1983). *Explorations teacher book, grade one*. Vancouver: Douglas & McIntyre (Educational).

Collins, J. (1983a). *Exploring Elkford*. Vancouver: Douglas & McIntyre (Educational).

Collins, J. (1983b). *Exploring Naramata*. Vancouver: Douglas & McIntyre (Educational).

Collins, J. (1983c). *Exploring Prince George*. Vancouver: Douglas & McIntyre (Educational).

Conner, D.C.G., with Bethune-Johnson, D. (1985). *Canada: Building our nation*. Scarborough, ON: Prentice-Hall Canada.

Conner, D.C.G. & Bethune-Johnson, D. (1984). *Native people and explorers of Canada*. Scarborough, ON: Prentice-Hall Canada.

Gordon, H. (1983a). *Exploring a space community*. Vancouver: Douglas & McIntyre (Educational).

Gordon, H. (1983b). *Exploring your school and neighbourhood*. Vancouver: Douglas & McIntyre (Educational).

Langford, E. (1984). *The explorers: Charting the Canadian wilderness*. Vancouver: Douglas & McIntyre (Educational).

Martin, T.H.W. (1969). *Then and now in Frobisher Bay*. A Gage World Community Study. Toronto: Gage.

Neering, R., Usukawa, S. & Wood, W. (1986). *Exploring our world: Other people, other lands*. Vancouver: Douglas & McIntyre (Educational).

Owen, E.E. (1972). *Year 1, How families live*. One World Series. Toronto: Fitzhenry & Whiteside.

Sauder, K. (1983a). *Families are people*. Vancouver: Douglas & McIntyre (Educational).

Sauder, K. (1983b). *Families are special*. Vancouver: Douglas & McIntyre (Educational).

Sauder, K. (1983c). *Families change*. Vancouver: Douglas & McIntyre (Educational).

Sauder, K. (1983d). *Families have feelings*. Vancouver: Douglas & McIntyre (Educational).

Sauder, K. (1983e). *Families have needs*. Vancouver: Douglas & McIntyre (Educational).

Sauder, K. (1983f). *Families share*. Vancouver: Douglas & McIntyre (Educational).

Siska, H. (1984). *The Haida and the Inuit: People of the seasons*. Vancouver: Douglas & McIntyre (Educational).

Symington, D.F. (1970). *Seafaring warriors of the west: Nootka Indians*. Ginn Studies in Canadian History. Toronto: Ginn.

Williams, L. (1983). *Exploring Mount Currie*. Vancouver: Douglas & McIntyre (Educational).

Wood, D. (1983). *Exploring our country*. Vancouver: Douglas & McIntyre (Educational).

Secondary textbooks
Beers, B.F. (1984). *Patterns of civilization, Vol. 1*. Scarborough, ON: Prentice-Hall Canada.

Beers, B.F. (1985). *Patterns of civilization, Vol. 2*. Scarborough, ON: Prentice-Hall Canada.

Bowers, V. & Garrod, S. (1987). *Our land: Building the west*. Toronto: Gage.

de Leeuw, G.J.A., Money, J. & Murphy, S.G. (1985). *Thinking about our heritage: A Hosford study atlas*. Edmonton, AB: Hosford.

Morton, D. (1988). *Towards tomorrow: Canada in a changing world, history*. Toronto: Harcourt Brace Jovanovich Canada.

Other references
Babin, P. (1975). *Bias in textbooks regarding the aged, labour unionists, & political minorities: Final report to the Ontario Ministry of Education*. Ottawa: University of Ottawa.

Baldwin, P. & Baldwin, D. (1992). The portrayal of women in classroom textbooks. *Canadian Social Studies, 26,* 110-114.

Callwood, J. (1987, March 18). Sanitized texts reflect a pious parade that never was, *Globe & Mail*, p. A2.

Case, R. (1993). *Summary of the 1992 social studies needs assessment*. Victoria, BC: Queen's Printer.

Case, R., Daniels, L. & Schwartz, P. (Eds.). (1996). *Critical challenges in social studies for junior high students*. Burnaby, BC: Faculty of Education, Simon Fraser University.

Cassidy, W. & Bognar, C.J. (1991). *More than a good idea: Moving from words to action in social studies*

1989 British Columbia assessment of social studies provincial report. Victoria, BC: Assessment, Examinations and Reporting Branch, Ministry of Education.

Cherryholmes, C.H. (1991). Critical research and social studies education. In J.P. Shaver (Ed.), *Handbook of research on social studies teaching and learning* (pp. 41-55). New York: Macmillan.

Clark, P. (1995). *'Take it away youth!' Visions of Canadian identity in British Columbia social studies textbooks, 1925-1989.* Unpublished doctoral dissertation, University of British Columbia.

Curriculum, Alberta Education. (1985). *Teacher reference manual for learning resources identified as 'unacceptable' or 'problematic' during the curriculum audit for tolerance and understanding.* Edmonton, AB: Alberta Education.

Fitterman, L. (1984, October 16). Mount Currie: A textbook case of reality. *The Vancouver Sun,* p. C 20.

Gabella, M.S. (1994). Beyond the looking glass: Bringing students into the conversation of historical inquiry. *Theory and Research in Social Education, 23,* 340-363.

Gaskell, J., McLaren, A. & Novogrodsky, M. (1989). *Claiming an education: Feminism and Canadian schools.* Toronto: Our Schools/Our Selves Education Foundation & Garamond Press.

Hodgetts, A.B. (1968). *What culture? What heritage? A study of civic education in Canada.* Toronto: Ontario Institute for Studies in Education.

Light, B., Staton, P. & Bourne, P. (1989). Sex equity content in history textbooks. *History and Social Science Teacher, 25,* 18-20.

Loewenberg Ball, D. & Feiman-Nemser, S. (1988). Using textbooks and teachers' guides: A dilemma for beginning teachers and teacher educators. *Curriculum Inquiry, 18,* 401-423.

Lorimer, R. & Long, M. (1979/1980). Sex role stereotyping in elementary readers, *Interchange, 10,* 25-45.

Manitoba Indian Brotherhood. (1977). *The shocking truth about Indians in textbooks.* Winnipeg, MN: Textbook Evaluation and Revision Committee of the Manitoba Indian Brotherhood.

McDiarmid, G. & Pratt, D. (1971). *Teaching prejudice: A content analysis of social studies textbooks authorized for use in Ontario.* Toronto: Ontario Institute for Studies in Education.

Noddings, N. (1992). Social studies and feminism. *Theory and Research in Social Education, 20,* 230-241.

Nova Scotia Human Rights Commission. (1974). *Textbook analysis - Nova Scotia.* Halifax, NS: Queen's Printer.

Osborne, K. (1995). *In defence of history: Teaching the past and the meaning of democratic citizenship.* Our Schools/Our Selves Monograph Series no. 17. Toronto: Our Schools/Our Selves Education Foundation.

Paton, L. & Deverell, J. (Eds.). (1974). *Prejudice in social studies textbooks.* Saskatoon, SK: Saskatchewan Human Rights Commission and Modern Press.

Pratt, D. (1984). Bias in textbooks: Progress and problems. In R.J. Samuda, J.W. Berry & M.

Laferriere (Eds.), *Multiculturalism in Canada: Social and educational perspectives* (pp. 145-166). Toronto: Allyn and Bacon.

Pyke, S.W. (1975). Children's literature: Conceptions of sex roles. In R.M. Pike & E. Zureik (Eds.), *Socialization, stratification and ethnicity: Vol II. Socialization and values in Canadian society* (pp. 51-73). Toronto: McClelland and Stewart.

Seixas, P. (1994). Preservice teachers assess students' prior historical understanding. *Social Studies, 85,* 91-94.

Statistics Canada. (1988). *Canadian social trends.* Ottawa: Canadian Government Publishing Centre.

Statistics Canada. (1990). *Focus on Canada: A profile of the disabled in Canada, 1990.* Ottawa: Ministry of Supply & Services.

Trudel, M. & Jain, G. (1970). *Canadian history textbooks: A comparative study. Royal Commission on Bilingualism and Biculturalism, Staff Study No. 5.* Ottawa: Queen's Printer.

Wilson, J.D. (1994). Multiculturalism and immigration policy in Canada: The last twenty-five years. *Siirtolaisuus - Migration, 21,* 5-12.

Wright, V. (1976/1977). Hidden messages: Expressions of prejudice. *Interchange, 7,* 54-62.

— ◇ —

36

Promoting the Aesthetic Experience: Responding to Literature in Social Studies

Roberta McKay

The idea of incorporating literature into the social studies program is not a new one. Many teachers know that young people enjoy stories and poems that relate to social studies topics and some teachers integrate literature to a greater extent by using it to directly teach content. In this article I address the role of literature from a different point of view, arguing that literature has an essential place in social studies because of its *aesthetic* qualities—qualities that educate the heart and complement a subject area that cannot be mere facts, but includes human feelings and emotions. I hope to communicate the importance of, and share some of the understandings required, in order for teachers to incorporate literature as aesthetic experience into social studies.

The first section of the article briefly considers what literature is and why it engages us so powerfully. This is followed by an overview of the role of literature in the social studies program from an aesthetic stance. I then discuss specifically how literature as aesthetic experience contributes to major knowledge, skill and attitude dimensions of social studies. There is an enormous number of pieces of literature that may enhance the social studies; far more than could be listed by any one source and certainly more than could be listed in an article of this length and nature. The danger in listing only a few titles is that these stories risk being overused to the point of abuse. For this reason, I discuss general considerations in choosing literature for aesthetic purposes in social studies and sources of annual lists of quality literature related to the social studies. As well, I identify characteristics and criteria for selection of particularly relevent categories of literature, including contemporary realistic fiction, historical fiction and biography, and folktales. In the final section, I suggest an approach to encouraging an aesthetic response to literature. The article concludes with lists of references to help teachers incorporate literature aesthetically into social studies.

The Power of Literature

Charlotte Huck and her co-authors, noted experts in children's literature, define literature as "the imaginative shaping of life and thought into the forms and structures of language" (Huck, Hepler & Hickman, 1993, p. 6). Pictures are often part of literature and work with language to evoke in the reader what Huck et al. describe as an inner experience of art, an aesthetic experience. Huck et al. suggest that this aesthetic experience may be a reconstruction, extension or the creation of an experience that enables the reader to perceive patterns, relationships and feelings. The subject matter of literature is the human condition and the experience of literature is the coming together of text and reader.

Literature for children and young people exhibits similar qualities to adult literature. In this respect, Huck et al's broad definition of children's literature is most appealing: "a child's book is a book a child is reading." Huck et al. suggest that the only limitations that seem binding on literature for children are that it appropriately reflect children's emotions and experiences.

The power of literature rests in its ability to engage simultaneously with the feelings and thoughts of the reader or listener. Young people need to be introduced to literature as a source of wonder, delight, joy and sorrow, as a window on the human condition.

The power of literature rests in its ability to engage simultaneously with the feelings and thoughts of the reader or listener. Young people need to be introduced to literature as a source of wonder, delight, joy and sorrow, as a window on the human condition. Literature engages us at an affective and aesthetic level, connecting us with our own experiences and the experiences of others. Literature helps us to shape and understand our human experience on affective and cognitive dimensions simultaneously. Literature connects us to the human community through time and space as we gain insights into human behaviour and develop a sense of the universality of experience.

Harold Rosen (1986) suggests that the human mind is essentially a narrative or storying device and that much of the knowledge of the world we remember is in the form of story. As Huck et al. comment, "storytelling is as old as human history and as new as today's gossip" (1993, p. 9). Narrative seems to be a way of making sense of our human experience, or put another way, narrative is a way of thinking. Rosen believes that narrative is universal in its use as a "primary and irreducible form of human comprehension" (1986, p. 230) and that narrative form is characteristic of children's thinking. Rosen points out that children take on narrative very soon after language development and that they get better at it depending on how much it is fostered in their specific cultural setting.

Literature also engages us because it provides a doorway to other worlds. Imagination and curiosity are fueled by literature. As young people enter other possible worlds, they encounter new perspectives on people, events, places, times and ideas. The realms of possibility are widened and deepened on every dimension as children engage with literature. "Whether reading takes them to another place, another time, or an imaginary world, young readers will return home enriched. Reading gets us out of our own time and place, out of ourselves; but in the end it will return us to ourselves, a little different, a little changed by the experience" (Huck et al., 1993, p. 12).

In addition to engaging children at a profoundly aesthetic level, literature simultaneously develops language on several crucial dimensions. Oral language is enhanced by listening to stories and poetry and engaging in conversation about them. Literature provides experience with abstract language patterns and structures that are similar to those encountered in school. A sense of story is developed and there is exposure to a vast vocabulary. Reading fluency is increased by reading many and varied books and the content, structure, vocabulary and conventions in young people's writing reflects the amount and type of reading to which they are exposed. Because there is a definite link between growth in language and growth in thought, literature also plays a role in the development of higher level thinking abilities. Ralph Waldo Emerson is quoted as saying, "If we encounter a man of rare intellect, we should ask him what books he reads."

THE ROLE OF LITERATURE IN SOCIAL STUDIES

Although literature can enhance social studies knowledge and attitudes, its primary purpose is to engage us aesthetically. This is a very different purpose than that of a textbook which has been primarily written to transmit information and we must not violate this purpose by utilizing literature as a textbook to "teach" social studies (McKay, 1995). Literature should be used in social studies for literature's sake—to provoke an aesthetic response, to stir an affinity with the human condition, to capture our hearts and imaginations as well as our minds, and to connect us to ourselves and others. This is a primary purpose of literature and these qualities of literature can make a lasting contribution to the social studies program. Literature is not a substitute for the textbook; each serves different purposes and requires different teaching and learning responses. While literature often includes considerable information about the world both past and present, it should not be used as a textbook. Or as Huck et al. assert, "literature should never be distorted to fulfill the purposes of an informational lesson" (1993, p. 693).

Louise Rosenblatt (1991) distinguishes along a continuum from the efferent stance, reading for information, to the aesthetic stance, reading for the aesthetic experience. Rosenblatt asserts that all readings are a mix of efferent and aesthetic stances. For example we may read a story, such as *Sadako and the Thousand Paper Cranes*, that deals with the aftermath of war, and experience the poignancy in the death of Sadako while also acquiring some information about World War Two. Because readings have this mix of efferent and aesthetic stances, it is essential that teachers be clear on the purpose for which they are having students read. She suggests that we should view text as being written for a predominant reader stance, either efferent or aesthetic. Unlike nonfiction, literature is written predominantly from an aesthetic stance. This suggests that young people should first experience the piece, then recapture and reflect upon it, followed perhaps by further aesthetic responses such as talking, drawing, singing, writing or engaging in dramatic forms such as tableaux, mime, reader's theatre or role. Rosenblatt suggests that secondarily to the aesthetic responses, the text may be discussed efferently for informational purposes. But she states, "first, if it is indeed to be 'literature' for these students, it must be experienced" (1991, p. 447).

Even though the primary role of literature in social studies should be to evoke the aesthetic response in children, literature can offer considerable factual background and provide unique human perspectives on historical, scientific and technological phenomena. Such books should not be used to gather facts or do research on topics but rather should be used as a way for children to acquire the human context of these events or issues. Huck et al. suggest that "it is especially impor-

---

Literature is not a substitute for the textbook; each serves different purposes and requires different teaching and learning responses. . . . as Huck asserts, "literature should never be distorted to fulfill the purposes of an informational lesson"

---

tant for children to confirm what they are learning from informational sources by meeting similar ideas in the more human frame of literature" (1991, p. 695). The primary purpose is to read the literature to experience pleasure and insight and the secondary purpose, sometimes but not always, may be to garner information. For example, when studying Canadian history, a novel about prairie settlement may be valuable, but primarily as an aesthetic experience, as a way of experiencing what it would have been like to live at that time. Factual information contained in the literature may be recalled at a later time as a starting place for further research or to enrich prior information by adding the human dimensions.

Poetry is a category of literature that can enrich the social studies program because the use of language is particularly vivid, intense and aesthetically evocative. Contemporary poetry for young people often reflects experiences of hurt, fear and sadness, as well as experiences of happiness, satisfaction and expectation. In social studies, poetry can be introduced in conjunction with prose. Huck et al. provide one listing of thematically arranged poetry/prose connections that includes such themes as being yourself, family, death/loss, change, decisions, courage and holocaust/war (1993, pp. 500-505). Poetry in social studies must be presented as aesthetic experience. Required memorization, detailed analysis and selection of poetry that is too difficult, sentimental and abstract are to be avoided (Huck et al., 1993). By selecting modern contemporary poems that reflect student interest in familiar experiences and

humour and by selecting poetic forms such as narrative verse, limericks and rhymes, social studies teachers can deepen learning and foster delight in poetry.

There is one exception to my stance that the role of literature in social studies is first to evoke aesthetic response. Informational books are a category of literature for children that is slightly different in that while informational books are not textbooks they are also not fiction. These books characteristically have aesthetic value as a result of being finely written and illustrated and thereby evoke satisfaction and delight in the reader. But such informational books also fulfill a specific teaching function in that their primary purpose is to provide information, usually on a single topic. These nonfiction books often provide depth, richness of detail and recency of facts about a topic that is unlikely in a textbook. These books are written with a predominantly efferent stance and while they may also have some aesthetic value as noted above, they certainly may be utilized for primarily efferent (information gathering) purposes. The pairing of informational and fiction books in relation to a social studies topic or theme is a powerful way to introduce children to the use of a wide variety of sources to understand topics and issues.

LITERATURE AND SOCIAL STUDIES OBJECTIVES

Incorporating literature into the social studies as aesthetic experience enriches the curriculum both directly and indirectly. Knowledge, skill and attitude dimensions of the social studies all benefit from immersing young people in related literature. Knowledge outcomes are enhanced as people, events and situations are personalized and contextualized. Factual information and concepts are developed through the familiar format of story. Literature enables young people to relate facts, concepts and generalizations to their own lives, thereby facilitating individual construction of meaning. Literature offers entry into many possible worlds and provides vicarious experience that enables young people to gain insight into people, places, events, situations and times far removed from their immediate experience. Their world view is expanded. Literature often acts as a springboard for research as inquiries generated from a story motivate a quest for further information.

Many skills outcomes of the social studies can be realized through literature. Creative thinking and problem solving are stimulated in a variety of contexts. Reading is an individual meaning-making activity, providing opportunity to draw conclusions, speculate and imagine and make self-initiated discoveries. Comparing, contrasting, analyzing, synthesizing and evaluating are all required when listening to and reading stories and poetry. Communication and participation skills are meaningfully utilized as young people respond to literature individually and collectively through talking, writing, drawing and dramatizing. Reading as an enjoyable and thoughtful experience is promoted in the context of the content area. The use of literature in social studies capitalizes upon opportunity in the school day to read to young people and/or to have them read silently. Young people get further exposure to language structures and vocabulary present in literature and become acquainted with additional authors and memorable characters, plots and moods.

It is perhaps in the area of the value and attitude outcomes that literature makes its most profound impact and powerful contribution to the social studies. Literature evokes feeling, stimulates emotion and is a way of shaping our human experience. Values and attitudes are personalized in literature and are treated as living forces that motivate human behaviour and are intrinsically embedded in complex situations.

It is perhaps in the area of the value and attitude outcomes that literature makes its most profound impact and powerful contribution to the social studies. Literature evokes feeling, stimulates emotion and is a way of shaping our human experience. Values and attitudes are personalized in literature and are treated as living forces that motivate human behaviour and are intrinsically embedded in complex situations. Conflict, change and ethical dilemmas are presented as part of what it means to be human. Through aesthetic engagement with literature, young people can come to understand their own lives more fully by seeing that they share areas of conflict in their lives with other human beings who for better or for worse have responded to these conflicts in their lives. Empathy and the ability to view life from different perspectives are promoted. Through literature, young people experience that our actions typically reflect what we value. They identify and analyze the values and attitudes of characters in literature and often relate these to their own experiences, past, present or future. This can develop positive attitudes towards themselves, and towards others both in their immediate as well as global environment.

Literature can be a vehicle for considering many sensitive social issues. Contemporary authors writing for young people deal with a wide range of contemporary topics including sibling and peer relationships, divorce, death, adoption, sex roles and discrimination. Reading or listening to stories and poetry about the feelings and responses of other young people in similar situations can be very beneficial to young people in the classroom who are facing these situations as real-life experiences. Literature can provide models of alternative behaviours that are removed from an individual and personal context. Folk tales and fairy tales also provide a rich array of value-laden dilemmas and conflicts to stimulate reflection and discussion.

Literature can also contribute to a sense of classroom community. The focus for developing citizenship goals through classroom community is on human relationships and literature is one powerful way to focus on the qualities required for living with others (Orr, 1995). Literature often celebrates uniqueness, considers friendship and acceptance, and deals with concepts of sharing and caring for others. These aspects of human relationships can be catalysts for young people to reflect individually and collectively upon the meaning of these for community in their own classroom. For instance, literature that reflects themes of caring for and about others may encourage young people to examine their own behaviour towards one another in the classroom. Providing opportunites for listening to, reflecting upon and responding to literature may help young people develop a sense of what a classroom community should be.

Literature can be at the heart of multicultural education in social studies by celebrating and building upon the diversity in young people's backgrounds and experiences. Rosenblatt has argued that aesthetic responses evoked by literature, such as heightened sensitivity to the needs and problems of others and greater imaginative capacity, are "part of the indispensable equipment of the citizen in a democracy" (Pradl, 1991, p. 274). It is currently popular to promote multicultural education through literature and many professional resources are available (Radinski & Padak, 1990; Ramirez & Ramirez, 1994; Zarrillo, 1994; Bieger, 1996). The four-level model proposed by James Banks (1989) is helpful when integrating ethnic and cultural content into the curriculum because it reduces the likelihood of superficial treatment of multicultural concepts.

The Banks' model for integrating ethnic and cultural content into the curriculum is hierarchical, based on the degree to which multicultural issues are central to the curriculum, the extent to which changes occur in the traditional curriculum, and the extent of teacher and student commitment to diversity and social justice. The Banks' model provides a theoretical framework for incorporating literature into multicultural education. Making use of literature at the transformative and decision-making/social action levels can assist young people in understanding and valuing cultures and experiences different from their own.

CHOOSING LITERATURE FOR SOCIAL STUDIES

There are several considerations when choosing literature for the social studies. Many of these are particular to the genre of literature, and, as such, these criteria will be discussed within the category of literature. However, because of my emphasis on literature as aesthetic experience, the first criterion for choosing literature in social studies is literary or aesthetic qualities. These qualities in fiction are traditionally judged by the elements of plot, setting, theme, characteriza-

INCORPORATING LITERATURE INTO MULTICULTURAL EDUCATION

Banks' level of integration of ethnic/cultural content in the curriculum	Use of literature	Relationship to social studies curriculum	Nature of commitment to diversity and social justice
Contributions	• In February reading literature about Chinese New Year.	• Cultural concepts and content are *separate* from curriculum and are introduced as a result of special ethnic/cultural holidays, heros, customs or contributions.	• Eurocentric perspective is used as a basis for selection of elements to be studied. • May reinforce stereotypes and mistaken beliefs. • A focus on visible aspects of a culture may lead to superficial understanding.
Additive	• During Canadian history unit, reading about European immigration.	• Cultural concepts and content from a Eurocentric perspective are *added* to social studies curriculum.	• Diverse views of events and issues are presented.
Transformative	• During Canadian history unit, reading literature, including historical fiction and biography, about immigration, that incorporates perspectives of diverse cultural groups (e.g., Native, Ukranian, Chinese, German).	• Cultural concepts/content *alter* structure of curriculum as perspectives of various ethnic/cultural groups included.	• Diverse cultures are recognized and presented in curriculum.
Decision making and social action	• During Canadian history unit, reading literature about immigration that identifies and deals with social issues (e.g., discrimination). • Social issues are discussed in relation to students' own school or community leading to social actions.	• Cultural concepts and content *alter* structure of curriculum by including diverse perspectives *and* related social issues.	• Diverse views and social issues are recognized and explored through problem solving, decision making and social action.

tion, style, point of view and format. According to Huck et al., quality fiction for children includes "a well-constructed plot that moves, a significant theme, authentic setting, a credible point of view, convincing characterization, appropriate style and attractive format" (1993, p. 32). They provide an excellent expanded explanation of each of the above elements and an extremely useful chart (pp. 34-35) that includes guidelines for the evaluation of literature for children. They also provide specific guidelines for evaluating the literary merit of poetry (p. 464). Young people evaluate literature by their responses to it and as teachers we need to value their interpretations and judgments while also acquainting them with the qualities in story and poetry that make it acclaimed for literary, aesthetic merit.

Professional organizations such as the International Reading Association (IRA) and the National Council for the Social Studies (NCSS), publish annual annotated bibliographies of children's books that have been selected for their literary and aesthetic qualities. The NCSS annual listing, "Notable Children's Trade Books in the Field of Social Studies," appears in their journal, *Social Education*. The books are grouped in subject categories such as biography, memoir and diary, contemporary issues, folktales, legends, and myths, geography, people, place, social interactions and relationships, and world history and culture. While many of the titles could be placed under more than one category, the review panel which consists of teachers and other professionals from both NCSS and the Children's Book Council, have categorized the books in ways they see as most useful in social studies education. The criteria utilized to select the literature included in this yearly list reflect attention to both literary and aesthetic quality and to social studies concerns. Criteria for selection include: are written primarily for children in grades K-8; emphasize human relations; represent a diversity of groups and are sensitive to a broad range of cultural experiences; present an original theme or a fresh slant on a traditional topic; are easily readable and of high literary quality; and have a pleasing format and, where appropriate, illustrations that enrich the text (*Social Education*, April/May 1996). IRA annual listings appear in their publication, *The Reading Teacher*, and the books are selected for literary, aesthetic qualities as well as potential for use across the curriculum. In addition to these annual listings of quality material, the journals *Social Education*, *Social Studies and the Young Learner* and *The Reading Teacher* often publish excellent practical articles for teachers on ways to incorporate literature into the social studies. (See the resource list at the end of this article.)

Although the listings and articles I have mentioned here originate in the United States, many of the titles and ideas are applicable to Canadian social studies.

Teacher librarians, public librarians and school district and professional associations can provide local and provincial listings of available literature for use in social studies. The April, 1992 issue of *The Reading Teacher*, featured a column exclusively on Canadian literature for children and young people and cited organizations such as the Canadian Children's Book Centre which publishes an annual listing of the best Canadian books published for children.

A second criterion to consider when choosing literature for social studies is "curriculum fit," that is suitability to the specific content and issues in the social studies curriculum. Selecting books for social studies is a serious responsibility because the best books can enhance social studies understandings while poor selections reinforce misconceptions and stereotypes. Sullivan (1996) offers four criteria to guide literature selection to enhance global understanding: shows our common humanity; provides sound geographic, social, historical, political, economic and/or religious informa-

The best books can enhance social studies understandings while poor selections reinforce misconceptions and stereotypes. . . . four criteria to guide literature selection to enhance global understanding: shows our common humanity; provides sound geographic, social, historical, political, economic and/or religious information; shows that other people have different but valid approaches to our common human concerns and needs; and increases understanding, empathy and the ability to learn from other people and cultures.

tion; shows that other people have different but valid approaches to our common human concerns and needs; and increases understanding, empathy and the ability to learn from other people and cultures.

As previously discussed, stories and poetry may present only one perspective on an event, issue or topic and several selections may be chosen to represent varying points of view. While suitability to the age and reading level of the students is a third consideration, student interest is often the more important criterion. Many stories and poems that young people express interest in, enjoy and understand may be too difficult for individual reading, but can be read out loud by the teacher. Quality picture books that may appear to be suitable for a younger audience can stimulate discussion and writing, art and drama projects with older students.

Choosing literature for social studies is both challenging and rewarding. More quality material is available for young people than ever before. The professional listings and considerations I have outlined serve as a starting point as you consider such criteria as literary and aesthetic qualities, social studies curriculum fit and the interests and needs of your students.

CATEGORIES OF LITERATURE

There are several categories of literature for children that are particularly powerful in promoting the aesthetic dimension in social studies. These are contemporary realistic fiction, historical fiction and biography, and folk literature. The nature and criteria for each are explored separately.

Contemporary realistic fiction

Contemporary realistic fiction can make a powerful contribution to the social studies program because of the nature of the story content and the topics explored. Contemporary realistic fiction is imaginative writing that accurately reflects life as it could be lived today, including its problems and challenges, its values and attitudes (Huck et al., 1993). Through contemporary realistic fiction young people may experience the social issues of our times in relation to growing up, coping with problems of the human condition and living in a diverse world. Through such literature, young people experience models, both good and bad, that may assist them in making sense of their own life experiences and ultimately of the human condition. Contemporary realistic fiction has changed dramatically in the last thirty years in its depiction of contemporary life and studies of young people's preferences consistently show it to be the most popular category of story (Huck et al., 1993). Because its realistic content addresses issues such as family and peer relationships and changes, developing sexuality, physical and mental disabilities, aging and death, and ethnic and racial diversity, this category of books is often controversial and is closely scrutinized for bias and stereotyping.

Multicultural literature is a type of contemporary realistic fiction and deserves particular attention in social studies. There are several definitions of the term multicultural literature and I have chosen one from Junko Yokota because of its inclusiveness: "literature that represents *any* distinct cultural group through accurate portrayal and rich detail" (1993, p. 157). Contemporary multicultural literature provides young people with opportunities to enhance their self concepts and to understand and develop pride in their own cultural heritage. It also provides opportunities for experiencing cultures other than their own in ways that foster respect, appreciation and sensitivity. Multicultural literature should meet the general criteria for literary and aesthetic value I have previously outlined, as well as some specific criteria for both text and illustrations. Cultural accuracy is a major criterion in selection. Since no single book can portray the full range of experience in a culture it is important to provide a collection that portrays members of a culture in a wide spectrum of occupations, educational backgrounds, living conditions and lifestyles. Young people need to understand that within any culture there is diversity. Illustrations should reveal differences in individual appearances while portraying distinctive characteristics of a group or race. Stereotyping of appearance, artifacts and occupations in the text and illustrations of multicultural literature should be avoided. Authors of contemporary realistic fiction are increasingly sensitive to such stereotyping and the number of books that positively and fairly depict our diverse population is increasing. Historical realistic fiction and traditional literature such as folktales, present cultures and ethnic groups from views and values of times past and are considered biased and stereotypical when evaluated by criteria for selection of contemporary multicultural fiction. However, Huck et al. maintain that these forms should not be eliminated from classrooms when they may actually be historically authentic or true to traditional genre. Issues related to historical fiction and folktales are discussed later in this article.

Historical fiction and biography

Historical fiction and biography are categories of literature for children that are in particular demand in social studies. Although neither of these are as popular as contemporary realistic fiction, there are many outstanding books available that not only enhance social studies but also expand young people's experiences with a category of literature that they may not choose on their own. Historical fiction and biography draw upon both fact and imagination. Historical fiction encompasses "all realistic stories that are set in the past" (Huck et al., 1993, p. 601) and depends on the author's ability to present the facts of the past accurately while also being able to speculate imaginatively on what it was like to live during that time. Biography is a life story that reads like fiction but centers on facts and events

---

Contemporary multicultural literature provides young people with opportunities to enhance their self concepts and to understand and develop pride in their own cultural heritage. It also provides opportunities for experiencing cultures other than their own in ways that foster respect, appreciation and sensitivity.

---

that can be documented. Huck et al. suggest that the best biographies "combine accurate information and fine writing in a context that children enjoy—the story that really happened" (p. 650). Both historical fiction and biography embed the facts that young people encounter in social studies textbooks in human affect. As discussed previously, this elicits an aesthetic response that enables the content to be experienced on a more personal dimension.

Historical fiction helps young people develop a sense of what history is and a feeling of continuity as they realize through story that their lives and times are linked individually and collectively to past lives and times. This linking of past to present helps young people see themselves as part of a continuum of human experience; the current way of life is a result of the past, and will have an impact on our way of life in the future. Historical fiction offers vicarious experience of past conflicts, accomplishments, tragedies and high points along the journey of what it means to be human. Higher level thinking skills are stimulated as comparisons with the present are inevitably created and conflicting points of view on issues are presented. Through the aesthetic experience of historical fiction, young people experience that while change is inevitable there are certain aspects of being human that remain constant through time. Our interconnectedness as a human community is reinforced.

In selecting historical fiction, the first consideration, as discussed previously, is aesthetic quality, that it engages us in story. There are several other considerations and issues in the selection and use of historical fiction. While the factual details should be accurate and authentic, it should be background to the story, blended with the fiction. At the same time, contradictions and distortions of the actual record of history must be avoided. In addition to accurate and authentic portrayal of the facts, the story must also reflect the values and spirit of the times as accurately as possible. Huck et al. state, "historical fiction can't be made to conform to today's more enlightened point of view concerning women or minorities or knowledge of medicine" (1993, p. 603). Teachers have a rich opportunity to help students examine the values and attitudes of today in light of those reflected in historical fiction. The language of the times also reflects values and attitudes. While authenticity of language is important in historical fiction, some vocabulary used in previous times is considered offensive by today's standards. Derogatory and demeaning labels for particular people and cultural groups are examples of language that may have reflected previous times but is unacceptable today. The use of these labels in historical fiction is helpful in understanding characters and events of the past provided they accurately and authentically reflects the values and attitudes of the times. Young people should be taught to respond to these labels in the context of the past and make links to the present. Young people can reflect upon the hurt and damage that derogatory and demeaning labels inflict and realize that while some people in the past may have used these terms, others were hurt by their use. In this way another essential feature of good historical fiction is realized—insight into the problems of today as well as those of the past is stimulated.

A final consideration when including historical fiction in social studies relates to recognizing that there are many and varied points of view on the issues and events of the past as well as the present. The use of different pieces of historical fiction on a particular topic or event can assist young people in recognizing that there is never only one point of view on any historical event. Events such as the Riel Rebellions need to be understood from the perspectives of the Metis and other native Canadians, as well as from the perspectives of the Canadian government and European settlers. The perspectives of women have often been ignored in Canadian history, as well as the perspectives of native Canadians, Asian Canadians and other cultural groups. As discussed previously in this article in relation to the Banks' hierarchical model, in order for literature to make a meaningful contribution to social studies learnings, it must be incorporated at the transformative and social action levels. In terms of historical fiction, this may require using multiple pieces of literature on any historical event in order to present the event from the points of view of the various peoples and cultures involved.

Folk literature

Folk literature is another category of literature that can profoundly impact social studies because it is "literature derived from the human imagination to explain the human condition" (Huck et al., 1993, p. 309). Huck et al. include folktales, fables, myths, epics and legends in this category and suggests that this literature is the foundation of the understandings about the human condition that are reflected in modern literature. Folk literature derives from oral tradition as human beings sought to explain themselves and their world—in short, it is oral history. It is, say Huck et al., "the literature of the fireside, the poetry of the people, and the memory of humankind" (p. 307). Bruno Bettelheim (1976), noted child psychologist, suggests in his book, *The Uses of Enchantment: The Meaning and Importance of Folktales*, that there is more to be learned from this literature about our inner problems and possible solutions to our predicaments than from any other type of story that a child can comprehend. Folk literature can provide insights into inherent cultural values and beliefs, as well as into human motivations and inner feelings. It can have a profound impact in social studies because it engages young people with universal patterns of experience.

Folk literature is popular with young people because the engaging stories demand full use of the imagination. They tend to be short, fast-moving, concrete and deal with the imponderables of life such as truth, beauty, good, evil and justice. They often include inspirational concepts like courage, nobility of character, accomplishment, tenderness and optimism. Folk literature is a compelling resource because it deals with universal issues and problems of daily life that have embedded within them ethical and moral dimensions.

Every culture has folk literature that can provide insights into the beliefs, values, jokes, lifestyles and his-

> Teachers have a rich opportunity to help students examine the values and attitudes of today in light of those reflected in historical fiction. The language of the times also reflects values and attitudes.

tories of that culture. In this way, folk literature can help young people understand other cultures. Because similar types of stories can be traced from country to country and continent to continent, a cross-cultural study of folk literature can help young people see universal patterns that show the similarities in our experiences of being human. Cinderella-type stories are a good example of folk literature that appears in many versions across many cultures. Huck et al. (1993) list a number of cross-cultural folktale versions as well as cross-cultural motifs, for example the motif of magical powers that appears in folk literature from many cultures.

Folk literature has been criticized for being violent, sexist and even agist (sorcerers and witches are often portrayed as old men and women). But, as previously suggested, experts in the area of literature for young people maintain that folk literature should not be eliminated for being true to the genre of such traditional literature. As with historical fiction that is authentic for the historical period, folk literature must be introduced as stories that present cultures, views and values from times long past.

RESPONDING TO LITERATURE FROM AN AESTHETIC STANCE

Throughout this article I have stressed that literature be incorporated into the social studies program to evoke an aesthetic response—to stir an affinity with the human condition, to capture our hearts and imaginations, as well as our minds, and to connect us to ourselves and others. In this section, I outline an approach to responding aesthetically to literature. In the language arts, engaging young people with literature in this way is called a reader response perspective. In the reader response perspective, the major focus is on reading the literature for its own sake. This stance encourages engagement, personal involvement and connection with the literature, and the use of personal response to build further interpretive response (Tompkins, 1993). Although not widely held by social studies educators, this stance toward literature is receiving increased recognition and attention within social studies (Lamme, 1994; Kornfeld, 1994; Koeller, 1996).

Responding to literature in social studies from an aesthetic stance involves three essential components; the opportunity to experience the literature aesthetically, the opportunity to respond personally, and the opportunity to revisit the piece in ways that enable personal response to be connected to broader concepts, issues, values and attitudes about self, others, and ultimately about the human condition, past, present and future.

Whether young people personally read the stories, poems and novels, or have them read to them, literature related to social studies topics and issues should first be encountered whole, not in parts or in fragments

as textbooks. That is, literature should be engaged in aesthetically—its flow and complexity should not be interrupted by predetermined questions, probes and activities. In this way, young people can experience and respond to literature for the sheer joy and pleasure it evokes.

Responding to literature aesthetically means acknowledging and valuing the personal connections, meanings and questions young people construct as they read and listen to stories and poems. Students will respond differently to the same piece of literature depending on age, life experience and literary and reading experience. Answering other people's questions, taking someone else's perspective and aiming for someone else's purposes do not facilitate aesthetic response. Our role as teachers is to enable young people to express their responses and then to revisit the literature with a range of activities that deepen and enrich personal meanings by connecting them to understandings about other people and the world.

Tompkins (1993, p. 137) suggests that the aesthetic reading is stimulated by questions that focus on personal meaning: What did the story or poem remind you of? What images came to mind as you read? What were your feelings as you read? What do you think? Questions such as these provide opportunities to express personal responses in conversations and in expressive writing such as journal writing. Although the sharing of personal responses should never be forced, indi-

Responding to literature in social studies from an aesthetic stance involves three essential components: the opportunity to experience the literature aesthetically, the opportunity to respond personally, and the opportunity to revisit the piece in ways that enable personal response to be connected to broader concepts, issues, values and attitudes about self, others, and ultimately about the human condition, past, present and future.

vidual meaning is enriched by hearing the range and diversity of response evoked by a piece of literature. Where young people feel that their personal responses are valued by the teacher and classmates, most of them, over time, will want to share personal meanings and connections.

After young people express their personal responses to literature, it is important to "revisit" the piece. Revisiting experiences are defined by their relevance to students' interests and questions. This means allowing for student choices in how to engage with the piece. Revisiting experiences are characterized by active learning and open-endedness and by their ability to reflect that "inner experience of art" evoked by the piece. While the possibilities for this type of experience are almost endless, Huck et al. (1993), Hoyt (1992) and Tompkins (1993) provide outstanding descriptions of a wide range of specific revisiting experiences to engage young people. These include art and media, writing and reading, collecting and constructing, drama and talk, singing and movement. In the articles mentioned previously, Lamme, Kornfeld and Koeller provide examples of the application of personal response and revisiting experiences directly to social studies topics.

SAMPLE AESTHETIC RESPONSE

The new land: A first year on the prairie

This beautiful Canadian piece of historical fiction, written by Alberta author Marilynn Reynolds and illustrated by Stephen McCallum of British Columbia, details a family's journey by boat, train and wagon to their new home on the prairies and their first year there. The story begins in the springtime as the family leaves the old country and takes us along with them through the long voyage, coming to their homestead's iron stake, finding water, building a house and surviving their first winter. As spring comes to the prairies the family plants apple trees, "that would bloom every spring, just like the trees they had left behind."

Purpose
- To experience what it was like for one family who moved to the western prairies from the old country.

Experiencing the story
- Prior to reading the book, read the title to students and show them the cover of the book (an illustration of the family on their ox-drawn wagon). Ask them what they think this story might be about and what in the title and picture makes them think this.

- Ask if any of them has ever moved to another country or province and how they felt. Alternatively, they could be asked to speculate on how they might feel if they did move. Ask students to listen to the story and imagine what it would have been like for students in the story.

- Read the book through once without interrupting the flow of the text, even to show the pictures. Read the book a second time and show students the stunning pictures that complement the text on each page, giving them ample time to enjoy and comment on the details.

Responding personally
- Personal response to the book will have begun in the form of questions and comments students have as they listen to the story and look at the illustrations.

- Questions that facilitate personal response may include:
  - Did the story remind you of anything that has happened to you or that has happened in another story that you know?
  - What was the most significant or important part of the story for you and why?
  - What feelings did you have as you listened to the story? Why?

- Alternatively, students could be asked to write in their journals in response to one of these questions or more generally on what they liked about or learned from the story.

Revisiting the story
- Have students recreate the sequence of the story in a series of tableaux scenes:
  - the voyage by sea
  - the ox-cart journey over the prairie
  - finding the iron stake on their homestead
  - finding water
  - building a house
  - surviving the winter
  - spring arrives

Divide students into seven groups and assign each group the task of creating a "frozen picture" or tableaux of one of the scenes. Students use facial expression, placement of body, gesture and stance to convey the scene. Give students enough time to discuss the aspect of the story their tableaux will involve and how they will do it, and to prepare their expression, placement and stance. When they are ready each group "freezes" in their picture (no talking, no movement) and the rest of the groups observe. The teacher may ask the observing students to comment on what the scene shows and how this is conveyed.

- Have students choose from the following revisiting possibilities:

  - Write an I" poem from the viewpoint of the father, mother, the boy John, or the little girl Annie. For example:

    I am Annie, a little girl.
    I am scared to leave my friends.
    I am only six years old.
    I was sick for 14 days on the boat.
    I loved the train ride to the prairie.

  - Draw a picture which interprets the story or some aspect of it.

  - Create a collage of words and/or pictures that represent the experiences of the pioneer family in the story.

  - Construct a "soddie" like the first home of the family.

  - Read another book, informational story or poem about pioneer family life.

CONCLUSION

Social studies is about the human condition in all its complexity, and literature is one way to enable young people to access that complexity. Literature should not be used as the textbook in social studies, nor should it replace the textbook. "In social studies classes, literature is a work of art enabling the study of character issues and relationships between persons sharing contexts or ideas" (Koeller, 1996, p. 102). The role of literature in social studies is to evoke the aesthetic response—to illuminate, inspire, inform perspective and educate the heart as well as the mind. Promoting the aesthetic experience through the use of literature in social studies is necessary for the full development of humane and responsible citizens.

REFERENCES

Banks, J.A. (1989). Integrating the curriculum with ethnic content: Approaches and guidelines. In J.A. Banks & C.A.M. Banks (Eds.), *Multicultural education: Issues and perspectives* (pp. 189-207). Boston: Allyn and Bacon.

Bettelheim, B. (1976). *The uses of enchantment.* New York: Knopf.

Bieger, E. M. (1996). Promoting multicultural education through a literature-based approach. *Reading Teacher,*49(4), 308-311.

Hoyt, L. (1992). Many ways of knowing: Using drama, oral interactions, and the visual arts to enhance reading comprehension. *Reading Teacher, 45*(8), 580-584.

Huck, C., Hepler, S., & Hickman, J. (1993). *Children's literature in the elementary school.* (5th ed.). Orlando, FL: Harcourt Brace Jovanovich.

Koeller, S. (1996). Multicultural understanding through literature. *Social Education, 60*(2), 99-103.

Kornfeld, J. (1994). Using fiction to teach history: Multicultural and global perspectives of World War ll. *Social Education, 58*(5), 281-286.

Lamme, L.L. (1994). Stories from our past: Making history come alive for children. *Social Education, 58*(3), 159-164.

McKay, R. (1995). Using literature in social studies: A caution. *Canadian Social Studies, 29*(3), 95-96.

Orr, J. (1995). *Classroom as community.* Unpublished doctoral dissertation, University of Alberta, Edmonton.

Pradl, G.M. (1991). Reading literature in a democracy: The challenge of Louise Rosenblatt. In J. Clifford (Ed.), *The experience of reading: Louise Rosenblatt and reader-response theory* (pp. 23-46). Portsmouth, NH: Boynton/Cook.

Ramirez, G. & Ramirez, J.L. (1994). *Multiethnic children's literature.* Albany, NY: Delmar.

Rasiniski, T.V. & Padak, N.V. (1990). Multicultural learning through children's literature. *Language Arts, 67*(6), 576-580.

Reynolds, M. & McCallum, S. (1997). *The new land: A first year on the prairie.* Victoria, BC: Orca.

Rosen, H. (1986). The importance of story. *Language Arts, 63*(3), 226-237.

Rosenblatt, L. (1991). Literature-S.O.S.! *Language Arts, 68*(6), 444-448.

Sullivan, J. (1996). Real people, common themes: Using trade books to counter stereotypes. *Social Education, 60*(7), 399-401.

Tompkins, G. & McGee, L. (1993). *Teaching reading with literature.* New York: Macmillan.

Yokota, J. (1993). Issues in selecting multicultural children's literature. *Language Arts, 70*(3), 156-167.

Zarillo, J. (1994). *Multicultural literature, multicultural teaching.* Orlando, FL: Harcourt Brace, Jovanovich.

RESOURCE LISTING

Literature in social studies (general)

Alter, G. (Ed.). (1995). Varieties of literature and elementary social studies. [Special issue]. *Social Studies and the Young Learner,* 8(2).

Billig, E. (1977). Children's literature as a springboard to content areas. *Reading Teacher, 30*(8), 855-859.

Combs, M. & Beach, J.D. (1994). Stories and storytelling: Personalizing the social studies. *Reading Teacher, 47*(6), 464-471.

Cullinan, B.E., Scala M.C. & Schroder, V.A. (1995). *Three voices: An invitation to poetry across the curriculum.* York, ME: Stenhouse.

Eeds, M. & Wells, D. (1991). Talking, thinking and cooperative learning: Lessons learned from listening to children talk about books. *Social Education, 55*(2), 134-137.

Farris, P. J. & Fuhler, D.J. (1994). Developing social studies concepts through picture books. *Reading Teacher, 47*(5), 380-386.

Fredericks, A.D. (1991). *Social studies through children's literature: An integrated approach.* Englewood, CO: Teacher Ideas Press.

Hennings, D.G. (1982). Reading picture storybooks in the social studies. *Reading Teacher, 36*(3), 284-289.

McGowan, M.J. & Powell, J.H. (1996). An annotated bibliography of resources for literature-based instruction. *Social Education, 60*(4), 231-232.

McGowan, T., Guest Editor. (1996). Telling the story of citizenship. [Theme Issue]. *Social Education, 60*(4).

Needham, R.L. & Sage, C. (1991). Intermediate children and notable social studies picture books. *Social Studies and the Young Learner, 4*(2), 11-12.

Woll, C.B. (1991). Support resources for whole language lovers. *Social Studies and the Young Learner, 4*(2), 26-27.

Zarnowski, M. & Gallagher, A.F., (Eds.). (1993). *Children's literature and social studies: Selecting and using notable books in the classroom.* Washington, DC: National Council for the Social Studies.

Contemporary realistic fiction (general)

Barnes, B.R. (1991). Using children's literature in the early anthropology curriculum. *Social Education, 55*(1), 17-18.

Gallagher, A.F. (1991). Peace (and war) in children's literature. *Social Studies and the Young Learner, 4*(2), 22-23.

Hoffbauer, D. & Prenn, M. (1996). A place to call one's

own: Choosing books about homelessness. *Social Education, 60*(3), 167-169.

McGowan, T., McGowan, M., & Lombard, R. (1994). Children's literature: Empowering young citizens for social action. *Social Studies and the Young Learner, 7*(1), 30-33.

McGowan, T., McGowan, M. & Lombard, R. (1994). Children's literature: Social education as the curriculum integrator: The case of the environment. *Social Studies and the Young Learner, 6*(3), 20-22.

Rule, A. & Atkinson, J. (1994). Choosing picture books about ecology. *Reading Teacher, 47*(7), 586-591.

Reed, C.A. (1992). Children's literature and antiracist education: A language-planning project. *Alberta Teachers' Association Multicultural Education Journal, 10*(2) 12-19.

Contemporary realistic fiction (multicultural)

Au, K.H. (1993). *Literacy instruction in multicultural settings.* Orlando, FL: Harcourt Brace Jovanovich.

Bieger, E.M. (1996). Promoting multicultural education through a literature-based approach. *Reading Teacher, 49*(4), 308-311

Finazzo, D. (1997). *All for the children: Multicultural essentials of literature.* Albany, NY: Delmar.

Galda, L. (1992). Exploring cultural diversity. *Reading Teacher, 45*(6), 452-460.

Gillespie, C., Powell, J., Clements, N., & Swearingen, R. (1994). A look at the Newberry Medal books from a multicultural perspective. *Reading Teacher, 48*(1), 40-50.

Hillard, L.L. (1995). Defining the "multi-" in "multicultural" through children's literature. *Reading Teacher, 48*(8), 728-729.

Koeller, S. (1996). Multicultural understanding through literature. *Social Education, 60*(2), 99-103.

Madigan, D. (1993). The politics of multicultural literature for children and adolescents: Combining perspectives and conversations. *Language Arts, 70*(3), 168-176.

Mikkelsen, N. (1984). A place to go to: International fiction for children. *Canadian Children's Literature, 35/36,* 64-68.

Pang, V.O., Colvin, C., Tran, M., & Barba, R.H. (1992). Beyond chopsticks and dragons: Selecting Asian-American literature for children. *Reading Teacher, 46*(3), 216-224.

Ramirez, G. & Ramirez, J.L. (1994). *Multiethnic children's literature.* Albany, NY: Delmar.

Rasiniski, T.V. & Padak, N.V. (1990). Multicultural learning through children's literature. *Language Arts, 67*(6), 576-580.

Stewig, J.W. (1992). Using children's books as a bridge to other cultures. *Social Studies, 83*(1), 36-40.

Yokota, J. (1993). Issues in selecting multicultural children's literature. *Language Arts, 70*(3), 156-167.

Zarillo, J. (1994). *Multicultural literature, Multicultural teaching.* Orlando, FL: Harcourt Bracejovanovich.

Historical fiction

Caldwell, J.J. (1988). Historical fiction as a modern tool. *Canadian Journal of English Language Arts, 11*(1), 24-32.

Danielson, K.E. (1989). Helping history come alive with literature. *Social Studies, 80*(2), 65-68.

Drew, M.A. (1991). Merging history and literature in teaching about genocide. *Social Education, 55*(2), 128-129.

Drew, M.A. (1995). Incorporating literature into a study of the holocaust: Some advice, some cautions. *Social Education, 59*(6), 354-356.

Freeman, E.B. & Levstik, L. (1988). Recreating the past: Historical fiction in the social studies curriculum. *Elementary School Journal, 88*(4), 330-337.

Galda, L. (1993). Stories of our past: Books for the social studies. *Reading Teacher, 46*(4), 330-338.

Handley, L.M. (1991). *Sarah, plain and, tall:* A model for thematic inquiry. *Social Studies and the Young Learner, 4*(2), 24 - 25.

Harms, J.M. & Lettow, L.J. (1993). Bridging time and space: Picture books with historical settings. *Social Education, 57*(7), 363-367.

Harms, J.M. & Lettow, L.L. (1994). Criteria for selecting picture books with historical settings. *Social Education, 58*(3), 152-154.

Johnson, N.M. & Ebert, M.J. (1992). Time travel is possible: Historical fiction and biography— Passport to the past. *Reading Teacher, 45*(7), 488-495.

Kazemek, F.E. (1994). Two handfuls of bone and ash: Teaching our children about Hiroshima. *Phi Delta Kappan, 75*(7), 531-534.

Kornfeld, J. (1994). Using fiction to teach history: Multicultural and global perspectives of World War 11. *Social Education, 58*(5), 281-286.

Lamme, L.L. (1994). Stories from our past: Making history come alive for children. *Social Education, 58*(3), 159-164.

Tunnell, M.O. & Ammon, R. (1996). The story of ourselves: Fostering multiple historical perspectives. *Social Education, 60*(4), 212-215.

Folk literature

Hickey, M.G. (1995). Focus on folk tales. *Social Studies and the Young Learner, 8*(2), 13-14.

Spagnoli, C. (1995). These tricks belong in your classroom: Telling Asian trickster tales. *Social Studies and the Young Learner, 8*(2), 15-17.

Taub, D.K. (1984). The endearing, enduring folktale. *Instructor, 94*(4), 61-70.

Wason-Ellam, L. (1988). Making literacy connections: Trickster tales in Canadian literature. *Canadian Journal of English Language Arts, 11*(1), 47-54.

— ✧ —

37

Training the Eye of the Beholder: Using Visual Resources Thoughtfully

Penney Clark

The statement, "a picture is worth a thousand words," is a truism. Photographs, paintings, films and other visual resources *can* convey immense detail at a glance—detail that would take pages of print to describe. They can depict nuances of colour, texture and facial expression which are difficult to convey in words. They may also be artifacts which provide rich historical insights. Certain photographs are so powerful that they come to represent an era, such as the poignant image of John Kennedy Jr. saluting his father's coffin, Pierre Elliott Trudeau pirouetting behind the queen or the sole Chinese student in front of sixteen tanks in Tiananmen Square. Much of Canada's early history (and other countries, too, for that matter) has been recorded for posterity by painters before photography came into common use. For example, Paul Kane produced over 100 oil paintings of Native peoples based on sketches done in his travels from the Great Lakes to Vancouver Island between 1845 and 1848. We are indebted to Frances Hopkins, whose husband was the secretary to George Simpson, Governor of the Hudson's Bay Company, for her detailed paintings of the voyageurs on several canoe journeys which she took with them between 1858 and 1870.

Given all of this, visual resources should be a key part of a social studies program. If students are to make effective use of visual resources, they first need to appreciate their worth as data sources. They need to see them as an important part of the variety of resources that are available to them. Yet, often visuals are overlooked. For instance, pictures in textbooks are ignored while students scour the print segments for information. Second, students need to learn to examine pictures from a critical perspective. They are not only a rich source of information and insights, but deliberate constructions, rather than mere reflections, of reality; and as constructions, they represent the purposes and perspectives of their creators. Coupled with this is the need to actively examine visuals for the meanings which underlie their surface images. In order to make them yield all that they have to offer, students must spend time studying them and learn to ask compelling questions of them.

This article discusses the thoughtful classroom use of photographs and paintings, as well as visual resources with an audio component, such as videos, films and CD-ROMS.

Paintings and Photographs

The most abundant and accessible visual resources are photographs and paintings. Most textbooks are full of them. Other sources include:

- travel brochures
- newspapers
- government departments
- consulates and embassies
- store advertising displays
- archives
- art books
- public relations departments of commercial firms

- calendars
- magazines
- discarded textbooks
- personal collections
- CD-ROM encyclopedias
- internet
- family albums
- National Film Board and its distributors

In this section I look at concerns about taking paintings and photographs at face value and offer a few strategies for "interrogating" these visual resources.

Paintings

Paintings (and other art forms) can give students a powerful sense of what was important in the age and place in which they were produced.

However, students need to be aware that paintings do not necessarily represent events as they actually happened. For instance, a famous painting showing the death of the French commander, the Marquis de Montcalm at the Siege of Quebec, shows him dying on the battlefield. In fact, he died the next morning in Quebec. An equally famous painting of the death of General Wolfe, the British Commander, depicts people who weren't actually present, and some who were there are not shown. Students should discuss why artists do not choose to always represent events as they actually happened. One of the reasons for altering the details is to represent the social and political purposes of their creators. The influence of national perspective on an artist's depiction of events can be shown by having students compare two famous paintings of the death of the American commander Richard Montgomery during the 1775-76 American invasion of Quebec. The painting by American artist John Trumbull shows Montgomery as the centre of attention. The painting by a British artist shows a chaotic battle scene with many things happening at once. It is interesting to note that neither painting is authentic in that Montgomery died on the battlefield on December 31st, but his frozen body was not found until the next day.

Students can use historical paintings to construct a written account of life in a particular place at a particular time in the past. For instance, Peter Rindisbacher, a Swiss settler at Red River from 1821 to 1826, created numerous drawings and paintings depicting the activities of Native peoples in the area. (*Life at Red River: 1830-1860*, a text in the Ginn Studies in Canadian History series, has several Rindisbacher paintings.) Students could examine some of these and then write a few paragraphs describing what they see. They might also compare the information extracted from the drawings and paintings to information extracted from written sources and attempt to account for any differences.

It is important for students to be aware that paintings, like other visual sources, need to be interrogated for the messages which lie beneath the surface. In one activity students are asked to examine two Early Renaissance Flemish paintings depicting weddings—Jan Van Eyck's *Giovanni Arnolfini and His Bride* and *The Peasant Wedding* by Pieter Bruegel—for their symbolism, and then create their own art form using symbols from the period. Students are provided with background information about the symbolism in the paintings. For instance, Van Eyck's painting uses religious symbolism such as a burning candle in the chandelier, which stands for the ever-present, all-seeing Christ; the couple's shoes have been removed, which suggests that they are standing on "holy ground;" and a little dog symbolizes faithfulness. Bruegel has painted his peasant wedding scene in a solemn, respectful way that suggests that he saw peasant life as desirable to city life of the time. Students are asked to identify the actions, gestures and expressions of people; choice of colours and objects used as symbols in the paintings; speculate about the symbolic meaning behind each and provide a plausible explanation for each symbol. Students then create an art form using symbols from the Renaissance period to portray an aspect of that age. Finally, they write a commentary on the symbolism in the work of another student (Case, Daniels & Schwartz, 1996, pp. 49-54). Other strategies for deconstructing these messages will be presented in a later section of this article.

Photographs

"While photographs may not lie, liars may photograph" (Hine, quoted in Everett-Green, 1996, p. E1). Students (and many others) tend to take photographs at face value, while they are ready to accept that drawings and paintings represent the perspectives of their creators (Gabella, 1994). It is difficult to repudiate the visual evidence of a photograph because it is a record of a particular moment in time. Students may not stop to consider that even photographs are not always what they seem and that the person behind the camera will likely have constructed the picture to suit particular purposes.

Photographs can be misleading and, as a result, the viewer may draw erroneous conclusions. Photographic evidence may be unreliable in four ways:

- photographers or subjects may stage photographs in order to deliver a particular message;
- photographs may depict an atypical situation or event, one which is not representative of the people or circumstances shown;
- photographs may be deliberately altered;
- photographs may exclude important aspects of a situation.

Staged photographs

Photographers may arrange subjects or objects in a photo in order to deliver a particular message. An example of this is the famous photo by Alfred Eisenstaedt of the sailor and the nurse kissing in the middle of a crowd on VJ Day (official end of the fighting between the Allies and Japan in World War II). The photographer had two people pose for the shot. He did not serendipitously happen upon a spontaneous eruption of joy, as most people who see the photograph imagine. Such photos are clever and capture the imagination, but they are not 'real', in that they would not have happened without the photographer's intervention. They are created by photographers just as paintings are created by painters.

instance, the photograph below shows children dressed in ragged and dirty clothing, yet with freshly scrubbed faces. Someone has done what they could to prepare the children for this photograph. Students have to be aware of such anomalies so that they do not take such photographs at face value (no pun intended). It is interesting to speculate about the photographer's motives and the effect on the audience of seeing poorly dressed children with fresh faces.

A photograph may also, in some sense, be staged by its subjects. Joy Kogawa, in *Obasan*, a novel about a Japanese family which was transported first to an internment camp and then to an Alberta beet field, says of a photograph of another Japanese family taken at the time: "'Grinning and happy' and all smiles standing

GRAFLEX CAMERA PHOTOGRAPH

The Shame of the City. Can We Give Our Children No Better Playing Space? — Winnipeg, 1912

National Library of Canada (C-030947)

Photographs can be 'created' in much less dramatic ways than the VJ Day example. It was common practice for 19th Century photographers, intent on preserving traditional images of Native peoples for posterity, to stage their photographs. For instance, Edward S. Curtis, who photographed tribes from Alaska to the American Southwest, used wigs and costumes, as well as other props, so his subjects would appear as he imagined Native people would have looked before being affected by white culture.

In other cases, it is not so much that the photos have been deliberately staged, but rather that the reality they are intended to convey has been slightly altered to suit the momentous occasion of the photograph itself. For

around a pile of beets? That is one telling. It's not how it was" (1981, p. 197). The photo did not reflect the reality of the lives of the subjects of the photo. The camera can create its own reality.

Students need to learn to look beyond distortions created by photographers or subjects to examine other evidence which photographs may offer. J. Robert Davison (1981-82) describes a photograph labelled *Indians, Fraser River*, taken about 1868 by photographer Frederick Dally. The photograph which appears on the following page shows a group of Native people "praying." However, the photographer contradicts the evidence of the photograph by writing underneath, "Indians shamming to be at prayer for the sake of pho-

Indians, Fraser River, c. 1868
Provincial Archives of British Columbia
(HPO83074)

tography." Above the photo is written, "At the priests [*sic*] request all the Indians kneel down and assume an attitude of devotion. Amen." Even without the help of the caption, close examination of the photograph reveals that it is a sham:

> the two priests have set a fine, holy example, but their spiritual and physical distance from the group is palpable; they are easily picked out standing (here kneeling) apart—curiously not aloof, for in this case it is the native group that is aloof. They have gone along with the play, but there is little conviction. Some emulate the priests, but only tentatively, as if they were unsure of what exactly constitutes an "attitude of devotion." A few others seem to have thought it barely worth the effort. They have pulled their dignity and their pride around them like their blankets, refusing the pious assault on their spirit. (Davison, 1981-82, p. 2)

Much can be ascertained from such a photograph and its captions. It can be used to demonstrate to students that critical examination of a visual resource can reveal messages which are not evident at first glance. Students could discuss why it might be in the best interests of the priests to have such a photograph taken and how it might be used. Also, it would be interesting to consider why the photographer, in writing his captions, refused to go along with the sham. Students could examine other photographs and their captions to determine how a caption can alter the message conveyed by a photograph.

Unrepresentative images

A second way photographs lead viewers to draw unwarranted conclusions occurs when they are highly unrepresentative of the reality of the person or the situation. The famous photograph showing candidate for Prime Minister, Robert Stanfield, fumbling a football kick-off during a national election campaign is an example of this. The photograph, which was widely reprinted, left the impression that Stanfield was an incompetent bungler. Other evidence does not support this impression. Students could be shown such a photograph and asked to locate additional evidence which supports or refutes the impression conveyed by the picture. They could then be asked to draw a conclusion about the person or event based on the wider array of evidence which they now have at hand. They should also consider the power of such impressions, where connections can be made which are not warranted. In this case, competence in football is not related to competence in politics or, for that matter, governing, but these connections were made.

Daniel Francis (1996) points out that early photography technology was instrumental in developing an image of nineteenth century Native peoples that was less than accurate. Francis says:

> A masklike quality was particularly pronounced in early photographs, because exposure times were prolonged and subjects had to keep themselves and their expressions immobile for up to half a minute. Since photographs were often the only glimpse most non-Natives got of Native people, this simple technological imperative may have contributed to the stereotype of the grim, stoical, cigar-store Indian. (p. 2)

Here, the camera has created rather than captured, unrepresentative images. The result is the same—a misleading impression is created.

To help students appreciate that photographs may lead viewers to draw unwarranted conclusions, students could role-play particular historical events while another student takes photographs at particularly dramatic moments. Have students examine the photographs and discuss what they convey about the event and what is misleading. Students might also speculate about conclusions historians using family photo albums as evidence might draw about contemporary family life. Using their own family albums as an example, students may conclude that an historian would judge the family to be avid travellers and party-goers, without realizing that these were the types of events which family members recorded by means of photographs. Such albums often do not record the more typical routines of the family. Students should consider what cautions need to be exercised when examining historical photographs of family life based on this contemporary example.

Altered photographs

With the advent of digital technology, photographs are "as malleable as clay" (Grady, 1997, p. A23). People can be moved from one location to another, objects can be placed in the photograph, unwanted people can be removed and so on. However, these sorts of alterations did not suddenly appear with the advent of the computer. They have occurred since photography was invented. Stephen Jay Gould (1981) describes his unearthing of "conscious skulduggery" (p. 171) in the work of psychologist, H.H. Goddard. Goddard maintained that the 'feeble-minded' could be recognized by their facial characteristics and 'proved' this point by means of photographs of poor families. Seventy years after publication of the photographs, examination by experts revealed that facial features had been altered to make the people appear mentally disabled. Communist regimes have rather routinely altered historical evidence, including photographs, to suit current political thinking. For instance, in *The Book of Laughter and Forgetting*, Milan Kundera (1980) describes a scene on the balcony of a palace in Prague in 1948, where Communist leader Klement Gottwald was addressing hundreds of thousands of Czechoslovakian people. Photographs of the group on the balcony were reproduced widely in posters and textbooks. However, after Vladimir Clementis, who was on the balcony and in the photographs, was executed for treason in 1952, his presence was removed from the photographs, which once doctored, showed a bare palace wall where he had stood.

DECONSTRUCTING THE LAST SPIKE

C.P.R.—Driving the Golden Spike, The Hon. D.A. Smith (Lord Strathcona). Ed Laughan, photographer.

National Archives of Canada (C-003693)

C.P.R.—The Last Spike. Ed Laughlan, photographer.

National Archives of Canada (C-014115)

Questions to ask about these pictures:

* What is happening in these two photographs?
* What features signal that an important event is occurring?
* What faces do you recognize in the first photo (William Van Horne, who was in charge of the project to build the railway, Donald Smith, a financial backer and Sanford Fleming, an engineer)?
* Do you recognize anyone in the second photo?
* Why would there be recognizable faces in the first photo but not the second?
* Why do you think the labourers were not featured in the more famous photo?
* Why do you think the labourers chose to stage their own ceremony?
* Why do you think the first photo has been included in many Canadian history books and the second has not?
* Who is missing from the labourer's photo?
* Who 'built' the railway?
* What does this tell us about our perspectives on history?

More commonly, a photograph intended for publication will be cropped before printing in order to suit layout requirements; sometimes radically altering its meaning in the process. Students can apply two L-shaped frames to photographs from magazines and newspapers in various ways in order to see for themselves how the meaning can be altered by the practice of cropping.

Selective focus

Photographs can also exclude; that is they may only represent *part* of a story. An example of this is the famous photo, which has appeared in many textbooks, of Donald Smith and other dignitaries at the last spike ceremony to mark the completion of the Canadian Pacific Railway at Craigellachie, British Columbia. It is important in such a case to ask who is included and who excluded. Another, less famous photo, shows the labourers who had built the railway holding their own last spike ceremony while they waited for the train that would take them back east. A comparison of these two photographs, which appear on the page 366, can be used to show that our historical record is selective. However, it is not only the first photo that excludes. Encourage students to note who is missing from the photograph of the labourers as well. Even though there was a large contingent of Chinese workers on the railway, they are not represented in the second picture. This, too, tells students something about historical perspectives. Many textbooks dwell on the activities and achievements of prominent Caucasian men, while ignoring those of working class people, people of other races and women.

In the box on the previous page is a question sequence which could be used with the two Last Spike photographs. Similar questions aimed at helping students consider who is excluded, as well as who is included in the photos, could be posed about many historical pictures. For instance, there is a photo showing the Fathers of Confederation at the Charlottetown Conference. Since historians (Cuthbert Brandt, 1992) have acknowledged that the social aspects of the Conference were key to its success, it seems fair to ask why the political wives who organized these social events, do not appear in official photographs.

Students can also take their own photographs, as a way of helping them understand that photographs are a selective view of the world. Primary students can be assigned a word which describes a quality of their community (e.g., cooperation, safety, peace). Then they can take a photograph within the school grounds or in the neighbouring community that captures the particular quality. Photographs and captions can then be separately taped to the board and class members guess which caption belongs with each picture and explain why they think it fits. The students who take each photograph are expected to provide an adequate explanation as to why it is an appropriate photograph for their caption. Finally, students may create a neighbourhood montage with magazine photographs representing the original captions. (This activity is described in greater detail in McDiarmid, Manzo & Musselle, 1996, pp. 5-6.)

Strategies for interrogating photographs and paintings

There are at least seven types of questions that we might use with students to help them critically examine photographs and paintings (as well as other visual resources). These questions ask students to:

- attend carefully to detail
- consider geographic data (e.g., climate, landscape)
- consider historical data (e.g., type of clothing, hairstyles, furniture)
- consider sociological data (e.g., social class, relationships)
- consider emotional context (e.g., feelings of people depicted)
- consider aesthetic qualities (e.g., general appeal, use of colour, light, texture)
- consider photographer's or artist's perspective and purpose (e.g., intended audience, messages conveyed).

Questions which fit within one category may not necessarily be asked all at once. The teacher needs to follow a sequence that stems logically from students' responses.

Two examples of the use of these types of questions to interrogate visuals are shown on pages 368 and 369. The first one, which is intended for secondary students, uses the painting *Canoe Manned by Voyageurs Passing a Waterfall* by Frances Ann Hopkins. The second is intended for elementary students and uses a contemporary photograph.

The following strategy (adapted from Ontario Ministry of Education, 1989, pp. 137-138) can be used to examine photographs and paintings from an aesthetic perspective. The questions are concerned with such techniques for highlighting some aspects of a picture and subduing others as use of light, focus and frame. Students could apply these questions to any of the visuals provided in this article.

- **Subject**. What is the photograph or painting about? Does the photographer or painter wish us to think about an object, a place, a person, an event or an idea? Is the subject unusual or revealing? Does the subject have an impact on the viewer? Is the subject representational or universal?
- **Frame**. In what way has the subject been isolated from its surroundings? Are there particular objects that become more interesting to us as a result of the frame established by the photographer or painter? What new meaning between objects or people is created within the frame? What comparisons, contrasts, or tensions are created by the framing? What effects has the point of view had on the meaning of the subject?

INTERROGATING A PAINTING

Canoe Manned by Voyageurs Passing a Waterfall, Ontario, 1869—Frances Anne Hopkins

National Archives of Canada (C-002771)

Attend carefully to detail
- Describe the people you see in this painting. Note the clothing and various types of headgear.
- What are the people doing?
- What objects do you see? Describe them.

Geographic data
- What is in the foregound of the painting? The background?
- Where do you think these people are?

Historical data
- What can you learn about the voyageurs from this painting?
- What questions would you like to ask the artist about the lives of the voyageurs?

Sociological data
- Who do you think the woman and man in the centre of the canoe are? What clues suggest this?
- Why do you think they are not paddling? Is this explanation supported by anything in the painting?

Emotional context
- How do you think the voyageurs felt about having the well-dressed man and woman in the canoe with them? How might their presence affect the behaviour of the voyageurs?
- What aspects of this painting convey a sense of tranquillity?

Aesthetic qualties
- How is light used in this painting? What is the purpose of this use?
- What are some of the ways the artist has made the painting artistically pleasing?

Photographer's or artist's perspective and purpose
- Why do you think the artist chose to paint a journey by voyageurs?
- Why might the artist have chosen to convey the voyageurs amid such a tranquil scene?
- Do you think the artist has a positive feeling for voyageurs?

INTERROGATING A PHOTOGRAPH

Grandparent and Child

—Photo by Penney Clark

Attend carefully to detail
- What do you see here?
- What do you see in the foreground? the background?
- What do you think the people are doing?

Geographic data
- What natural objects do you see? What is the land like?
- What do you think the weather was like on the day the photo was taken? What clues help you to answer this question?
- Where do you think they are?

Sociological data
- What can you tell about the people by the way they are dressed?
- Do you think the man and the little girl are related? If so, what might be their relationship? Why do you think this?

Emotional context
- What words could be used to describe how these people are feeling? Hurried? Relaxed? Comfortable? Anxious?

Aesthetic qualities
- What are some ways that the photographer has used to make this photo artistically pleasing?

Photographer's or artist's perspective and purpose
- Who do you think might have taken the photograph? Why do you think it was taken?
- Do you think the people in the photo knew it was being taken? Why or why not? If not, why would the photographer choose to take the photo when the people weren't aware it was being taken?

- **Light**. Students should examine the use of light in terms of its quality (sunlight or artificial light), quantity (under- or overexposure), and angle (e.g., how the subject is lit, whether a flare was used). Guide their discussion with questions such as the following: How has light been used creatively to create the overall effect? Is the subject lit from a specific angle? Do lines of light and shadow create or enhance the meaning? What reasons do you think the artist had for using light the way he or she did?

- **Focus**. How much detail is in focus in the picture? Did the artist isolate certain elements and leave the rest fuzzy? Has the artist used "sharp" or "soft" focusing to create a specific mood? Did the artist make the best choice in the details emphasized in the photographs? Is the picture too "busy" with sharply focussed details?

AUDIO-VISUALS

Audio-visual resource—CD-ROMS, videos, slides—have many positive features which make them useful in teaching social studies. Students with different learning styles can make effective use of them because they deliver information through both auditory and visual means. They provide an alternative way to gather information for less capable readers. In some cases they can be more useful for data gathering even than field trips because they focus on the most important aspects of the experience and eliminate extraneous details. They can convey a great deal of information in a relatively brief span of class time. Through such methods as animation, slow motion, time-lapse photography and microphotography, they allow students to view scenes they would otherwise not have an opportunity to observe. Those that use motion have their own advantages. For instance, processes that can be difficult to visualize when described in print can be seen in action. Motion can also add to student interest. Finally, they can be more motivating than many other resources; they are usually less intimidating than textbooks, as well as being colourful and appealing.

Historian Graeme Decarie has warned us to "beware of technologies standing under streetlights, calling, 'Hi, sailor'" (1988, p. 98). He was referring to the production and indiscriminate classroom use of poor quality (both technically and in terms of meeting curriculum objectives) audio-visual aids of various kinds. He urged teachers to choose such resources carefully and use them selectively. With the advent of computer technology, there are many more audio-visual materials available now than there were a decade ago. Therefore, it is more important than ever that they be chosen carefully and used selectively.

The type of audio-visual technology chosen will depend on its accessibility and the purpose for which it is being used. The chart on the next page summarizes advantages and disadvantages of various types of audio-visual technology.

Specific audio-visual resources should be selected for classroom use based on criteria such as: interest, accuracy and currency of content, conceptual level, whether content fits intended purposes, quality of photography and sound and the way in which information is organized for presentation.

Helping students become critical viewers

As with other visual resources, it is important to help students see that these resources have been created by human developers with particular perspectives and for particular purposes. Like the other resources, these must be actively investigated in an effort to reveal the messages which lie underneath the surface. Below are sample questions (adapted from Cates, 1994) for deconstructing an audio-visual resource:

- **Dialogue.** Notice consistent use of words which have positive or negative connotations. What is the effect of using the word, "cheap" instead of "inexpensive," or "conceited" in place of "high self-esteem," or "forthright" instead of "domineering"?

- **Actors.** Is there any relationship between the type of character played and the physical appearance of the actor? For instance do homely actors play "bad guys," while attractive people play the upstanding characters" Are people of a particular race over-represented among the evil characters?

- **Character development**. Are characters stereotypical (e.g., Native people presented as uniformly good or uniformly bad; attractive blonde women presented as unintelligent)

- **Colour and lighting.** Is the depiction light and airy, dark and brooding or some variation of this? Are some scenes lighter and brighter than others? What is the content of these scenes? What about the darker scenes? Are any scenes in black-and-white? Why do you think this is the case?

- **Music**. Can you find examples where the choice of music or its volume influences the way you view particular characters or events?

- **Camera angle and choice of shot.** Is the action ever shown from the viewpoint of a character? If so, in what cases and for what purposes?

- **Selection and arrangement of scenes.** Does the film alternate among different viewpoints, places, people? Are different viewpoints given equal time and emphasis?

- **Overall impression.** What is the developer of this resource attempting to convey through use of some of the devices presented here?

Audio-visual resources do not necessarily have to be limited to those developed specifically for classroom use. The use of popular film in the classroom has been advocated as a way of helping students learn to deconstruct a medium to which they receive constant exposure in their daily lives. This is important to do for

CONSIDERING AUDIO-VISUAL RESOURCES

Resource	Advantages	Disadvantages
Filmstrip/ Tape Set	• easily used by students independently • since they are inexpensive, schools often have their own collections • machine can be easily stopped for discussion or close examination of one frame • filmstrip is easily reversed to re-examine an earlier frame • useful in presenting sequential information; e.g., steps in getting a food product from farm to grocery store shelf, or architectural changes over time in a particular region of the country	• no motion • when not accompanied by sound, students can lose interest quickly • content is often dated because these are not as popular as they once were
Slide/Tape Set	• since they are inexpensive, schools often have their own collections • machine can be easily stopped for discussion or close examination of one frame	• no motion • when not accompanied by sound, students can lose interest quickly • not easily used independently by students • cannot move forward or backward quickly
Videotape	• widely available • motion adds interest and realism • machine can be easily stopped • machine can be easily reversed or fast forwarded • easily used by students independently	• can be expensive • does not move forward or backward to a desired segment as quickly as a laserdisc
Film	• widely available • motion adds interest and realism	• not flexible in terms of moving quickly backwards or forwards to a desired segment • not easily used independently by students • expensive
CD-ROM	• motion adds interest and realism • holds a great deal of information • can access information readily by means of menus • can be used independently by students	• schools have computers but usually in insufficient numbers for ready individual access • expensive
Laserdisc	• motion adds interest and realism • holds a great deal of information • bar codes allow instant access to desired segment • can be used independently by students	• equipment is expensive and not yet widely available in schools • few appropriate laserdiscs available for school use

the following reasons: many people are predominantly visual learners; films present details graphically that may not necessarily be communicated through writing; their dramatic telling can amplify and illuminate themes and ideas from history; they are an important art form in their own right because of their pervasiveness in our culture; and they are a guage of the tastes and ideologies prevalent in North American culture (Johnson & Vargus, 1994).

Peter Seixas (1994) has used the 1989 Kevin Costner film, *Dances With Wolves*, in conjunction with the 1956 John Ford film, *The Searchers*, to determine how students' ideas about a currently popular historic film would be challenged by viewing an older film with differing moral perspectives on Native-white interactions. Students endorsed segments in *Dances With Wolves* as "true" windows on the past because they were congruent with their own views. The moral stance of the movie, with its critical view of the U.S. Army and westward expansion and the Sioux as their victims, was in keeping with revisionist popular culture. *The Searchers*, on the other hand, with its depiction of Native peoples as violent and vengeful, represents an earlier view of Native-White interaction during the period of settlement of North America. The contrasting historical interpretations posed a moral dilemma for most of the students. While Seixas used the two films for research purposes, contrasting film clips can be used to develop students' sense of the problematic relationships between historical evidence and historical interpretation. The use of popular film is an engaging way to help students develop such understandings.

Ideas for using audio-visual resources

This section discusses pre-viewing, viewing and follow-up activities for use with audio-visual resources. It is, generally speaking, not enough merely to turn on the video machine and let students sit back and watch the show. These activities are very important to the effective use of audio-visuals because they turn what may simply be an entertaining interlude into an educational experience.

Pre-viewing activities

Pre-viewing activities should arouse interest in the topic of the audio-visual, build background knowledge, clarify purposes for viewing and reveal what students already know about the topic. In order to arouse interest and build background knowledge, teachers might briefly describe the topics to be explored in the audio-visual and ask students to bring pertinent newspaper and magazine pictures and articles to class. These materials could form part of a bulletin board display which will continue to evolve throughout the unit of study. In order to clarify purposes for viewing, students can be given key questions which identify main ideas, establish relationships among different aspects of a topic or help students examine the material for accuracy, authenticity or bias. These questions need not be numerous; one general question may be quite sufficient. The important point is that students are given the questions prior to, rather than following, the viewing. Pre-posed questions give students a purpose for viewing. Note that every student need not have the same purpose. Students can have different purposes and their information can be pooled following the viewing. A pre-viewing

PRIOR KNOWLEDGE DATA CHART REGION OF CANADA : _____		
	Prior Knowledge	Additional Knowledge
Topography		
Climate		
Vegetation		
Natural Resources		
Industries		
Major Cities		
Transportation & Communication		
Wilderness Preserves		

VIEWING GUIDE

- **SURVEY.** Listen to your teacher read you a brief summary of the video. List five topics you think will be addressed in this video.

  1. _____
  2. _____
  3. _____
  4. _____
  5. _____

- **QUESTION.** Create a question about an important aspect for each of the above topics. Write your questions on the lines below.

  1. _____
  2. _____
  3. _____
  4. _____
  5. _____

- **VIEW AND RECORD.** View the video to find the answers to your questions. Record your answers below. All of your questions may not be answered in the video. You may want to check other sources for those answers.

  1. _____
  _____
  2. _____
  _____
  3. _____
  _____
  4. _____
  _____
  5. _____
  _____

- **REVIEW.** Review your answers above. Use this information to write a summary of the video.

  _____
  _____
  _____
  _____
  _____

activity might also consist of a discussion of what students already know about topics dealt with in the audio-visual. They could record what is already known in a retrieval chart such as the one on page 372, intended to be used with an audio-visual about a Canadian region.

After viewing, students can refer back to their charts to add to and confirm the accuracy of the information they recorded prior to viewing.

Pre-viewing activities signal to students that the viewing is to be an educational rather than a recreational experience. Because videotapes in particular, and also CD-ROMS, are accessible in many homes, students develop a mindset that such materials are for pleasure use only. Unless reminded by means of such pre-viewing activities, students may not view them with the same intensity that they might read a textbook or other "serious" information source.

Viewing activities

The purpose of viewing activities is to give students a focus while encountering the resource. It is preferable that students not take detailed notes during the viewing because there is a danger that the recording task will occupy their attention to such an extent that they will miss important points. Audio-visuals can be stopped frequently in order to check on student comprehension and to discuss and clarify points made. The entire audio-visual need not be viewed if only a portion is appropriate to curricular intents. If the entire audio-visual is pertinent, one viewing can be insufficient to allow students to cope well with the information. It may be best to view it in its entirety once and then show selected portions a second time, or as many times as necessary.

Follow-up activities

Following the viewing students might record and then compare their responses to questions asked during the pre-viewing phase. If there are discrepancies, pertinent sections of the audio-visual can be viewed again to determine why. If students have recorded hypotheses prior to viewing, they might confirm their accuracy. Other follow-up activities might relate the material in the audio-visual to the ongoing unit of instruction in which they are engaged. For example, students might use an audio-visual resource as one of a set of information sources to prepare for a talk or a report that they will prepare.

The example on the previous page (adapted from Clark, 1991) of an approach to pre-viewing, viewing and follow-up activities is an adaptation of the well-known SQ3R (Survey, Question, Read, Record, Review) strategy for dealing with print material. Its purpose is to provide students with a structured format which gives them purposes for viewing, ways to record information and ways to summarize the information once recorded. Students can then proceed to more sophisticated strategies involving probing underneath the sur-

face discourse for author's purpose, and so on. They may also wish to view the resource a second time.

CONCLUDING REMARKS

Visual resources should be a key part of a social studies program. They add interest and variety. Their use teaches students that the print medium is not the only means by which information is attainable. However, visual resources, like other learning resources, represent the perspectives of their creators. Visual resources are particularly seductive sources of misleading information because of the powerful effect they can have on the viewer. Therefore, students need systematic strategies for interrogating this source of information and they should view these resources with the same healthy scepticism with which we would want them to view any other resource.

REFERENCES

Case, R., Daniels, L. & Schwartz, P. (1996). *Critical challenges in social studies for junior high students.* Burnaby, BC: Faculty of Education, Simon Fraser University.

Cates, W.M. (1990). Helping students learn to think critically: Detecting and analyzing bias in films. *Social Studies, 81,* 15-18.

Clark, P. (1991). *Government in Canada: Citizenship in action.* Montreal: National Film Board of Canada.

Cuthbert Brandt, G. (1992). National unity and the politics of political history. *Journal of the Canadian Historical Association, 3,* 2-11.

Davison, J.R. (1981-82). Turning a blind eye: The historian's use of photographs. *BC Studies, 52,* 16-35.

Decarie, G. (1988). Audio-visual aids: Historians in Blunderland. *Canadian Social Studies, 23*(2), 95-98.

Everett-Green, R. (1996, November 9). Photography's white lies. *Globe & Mail,* pp. E1, E5.

Francis, D. (1996).*Copying people, 1860-1940.* Saskatoon, SK: Fifth House.

Gabella, M.S. (1994). Beyond the looking glass: Bringing students into the conversation of historical inquiry. *Theory and Research in Social Education, 22*(3), 340-363.

Grady. M. (1997, May 17). Photography as 'monster'. *Vancouver Sun,* p. A23.

Gould, S.J. (1981). *The mismeasure of man.* New York: Norton.

Johnson, J. & Vargus, C. (1994). The smell of celluloid in the classroom: Five great movies that teach. *Social Education, 58*(2), 109-113.

Kogawa, J. (1981). *Obasan.* Boston: David R. Godine.

Kundera, M. (1980). *The book of laughter and forgetting.* New York: Knoff.

McDiarmid, T., Manzo, R. & Musselle, T. (1996). *Critical challenges for primary students.* Burnaby, BC: Faculty of Education, Simon Fraser University.

Seixas, P. (1994). Confronting the moral frames of popular film: Young people respond to historical revisionism. *American Journal of Education, 102*(3), 261-285.

Wilson, K. (1970). *Life at Red River: 1830-1860*. Toronto: Ginn.

SUPPLEMENTARY READINGS

Adams, D.M. (1986). Developing critical viewing skills with student video production. *Educational Media International, 23*, 81-84.

Allen, R. (1994). Posters as historical documents: A resource for the teaching of twentieth-century history. *Social Studies, 85*(2), 52-61.

Allen, R.F. & Molina, L.E.S. (1993). Snapshot geography: Using travel photographs to learn geography in upper elementary schools. *Canadian Social Studies, 27*, 62-66.

Braun, J.A. & Corbin, D. (1991). Helping students use videos to make cross-cultural comparisons. *Social Studies & the Young Learner, 4*(2), 28-29.

Considine, D.M. (1989). The video boom's impact on social studies: Implications, applications, and resources. *Social Studies, 80*(6), 229-234.

Downey, M.T. (1980). Pictures as teaching aids: Using the pictures in history textbooks. *Social Education, 44*(2), 92-99.

Felton, R.G. & Allen, R.F. (1990). Using visual materials as historical sources: A model for studying state and local history. *Social Studies, 81*(2), 84-87.

Hennigar-Shuh, J. (1988). Learn to look. *History and Social Science Teacher, 23*(3), 141-146.

Jackson, D. (1995). A note on photo CDs: A valuable resource for the classroom. *Canadian Social Studies, 30*(1), 28-29.

Ministry of Education, Ontario. (1989). *Media literacy resource guide*. Toronto: Queen's Printer.

Morris, S. (1989). *A teacher's guide to using portraits*. London: English Heritage Education Service.

Nelson, M. (1997). An alternative medium of social education—The "horrors of war" picture cards. *Social Studies, 88*(3), 100-107.

Osborne, K. (1990). Using Canada's visual history in the classroom. In *Canada's visual history* (pp. 4-19). Ottawa and Montreal: National Museum of Civilization and National Film Board of Canada.

Sunal, C.S. & Hatcher, B.A. (1986). How to do it: Studying history through art. *Social Education, 50*(4), 1-8.

OTHER RESOURCES

An Internet Resource

Le WebLouvre

To get there go to: http://mistral.enst.fr/-pioch/louvre/

Then go to: The Famous Painting exhibition. User can view paintings from a variety of periods and categories including:

- Baroque (1600-1790)
- Revolution and Restoration (1740-1860)
- Impressionism (1860-1900)
- Cubism to Abstract Art (1900-1960)

Then select: Les tres riches heures du Duc de Berry. This will let you view and read about a rare exam-ple of a medieval Book of the Hours.

Options within this website will vary over time.

Films Using Paintings

National Film Board of Canada. (1972). *Paul Kane goes west*. Montreal: Author.
A source of Paul Kane paintings depicting Canada's early history.

National Film Board of Canada. (1980). *A visit from Captain Cook*. Montreal: Author.
Illustrates how European artists projected their own ethnocentric perspectives on what they observed and recorded.

National Film Board of Canada. (1977). *Pictures from the 1930s*. Montreal: Author.
Juxtaposes paintings produced during the Depression with newsreel footage about both domestic and international events. Features female artists such as Emily Carr and Paraskeva Clark.

Slides on Canadian History

National Film Board of Canada. *Canada's visual history* (Vols. 1-80). Montreal: National Museum of Civilization and National Film Board of Canada. This rich source of visual information deals with Canada's social and economic history. Each of the 80 volumes contains 30 slides and a teachers' manual. Each manual includes a brief essay providing background information, a discussion of the historical significance of each slide, a recommended reading list and suggested extension activities.

For catalogues of National Film Board resources contact:

National Film Board of Canada
P.O. Box 6100
Montreal. Quebec H3C 3H5

38

Bringing the Outside In: Using Community Resources to Teach Social Studies

Penney Clark

The community can be a valuable and readily available learning resource in social studies. Students can explore nearby places or those further afield. They can have personal contact with people in the community, both by going to see them on-site and by inviting them to the classroom. They can also take advantage of the availability of a wide variety of materials developed by noneducational organizations.

Community resources are not only valuable, they are readily available. We sometimes forget to look around us and appreciate the intellectual value of what is accessible close at hand. Garnet McDiarmid (1970) tells the story of a teacher in a university course he taught who wrote that he did not have science in his elementary school because the school did not have any textbooks or laboratory equipment. McDiarmid points out that the school where this teacher taught was located in an area of uranium mines, moraines and other postglacial deposits, running water, ponds and abundant flora and fauna—all of which could have been exploited as fascinating sources for student investigation. Students in an urban area can step outside the school and investigate traffic patterns or recreational facilities. All schools have access to people in the community who are willing to come to the school to share their interests and expertise. Many organizations are very willing to send their materials free-of-charge.

There is no guarantee, however, that making use of the community will necessarily have educational benefit. Bremer suggests field trips may involve

> isolated experiences of wandering in a long line (rather like a snake that has just shed its skin and is doubtful about its boundaries) through museum corridors with half-minute halts to gape at an exhibit or collect stragglers. (quoted in Oliver, 1970, p. 22)

This bleak description of field experiences is reminiscent of an episode of the television show *The Wonder Years* in which the junior high school protagonist Kevin Arnold and his classmates visit a museum. In the show, teacher and students have very different agendas. The teacher, of course, views the trip as an opportunity for students to steep themselves in the richness of the past. For Kevin and his friends, however, the exhibits become merely a backdrop to the more important concerns of life—who likes whom, who is going to which party on the weekend and so on.[1]

The use of community resources has questionable value when they are "isolated experiences" which are unrelated to curriculum learning outcomes. If students do not have clear purposes in mind when embarking on a community experience, and a curricular context in which to place it, it can become a mere diversion from classroom routine—a welcome relief perhaps, but ultimately not one which furthers the goals of social studies.

This article discusses the value of, and strategies for, "bringing the outside in[to]" the curriculum—and making resources found in the community an important educational experience. Three types of community resources are examined. Field experiences are discussed in terms of types of trips appropriate to social studies topics; planning; strategies at the site, including interviewing and surveying; and follow-up and assessment activities. The use of guest speakers is also considered, including sources of speakers, organization of the session and follow-up activities. Finally, the article discusses sources of materials developed by non-educational agencies (e.g., consulates, environmental groups, business organizations) and how they should be critically examined.

FIELD EXPERIENCES

Field experiences, with the direct involvement which they entail, can foster rich understandings not available from, for example, a textbook study. During a unit on pioneer life a grade three-four class in Alberta visited a typical pioneer home, a wealthier pioneer home, an historical costume collection and the first schoolhouse built in their school district over one hundred years earlier (McKay, 1990). In the typical pioneer home, they chopped wood, carded wool and made butter, ice cream, scones and candles. In the home of the wealthier family, they did needlework, baked cookies and acted as guests in the drawing room. When viewing the historical costume collection, students imagined what it would be like to wear corsets and stiff collars. During the morning spent in the schoolhouse, they enacted a typical 1881 school day with a teacher "in role." Through these simulated experiences, students gained a great deal of insight about life during pioneer times in their community. This is evident from three students' journal reflections following the field experience in the schoolhouse (McKay, 1990, pp. 153-154).

- **Penney**
  Today at the 1881 School I learned how things were back in the 18S mostly. Such as reading, games, aned a spelleing B. the teacher called us lassies and ladies. I also learned that there wre severeal additions to the school because the amount of children was growing alot the games were called Anti-I-over, marbles jacks, count the rabbits and fox and geese. I also learned that the old school was once a House and the people that lived in it loved walpaper and I learned that the school house was down by saskatchewan river and it flooded so they tied it down by a hool on the back of it so it wouldn't float away. I also learned that the first legestlatetive building was in the gym of Macy avenue school.

- **Adam**
  I lrnd that 1881 school is srikt with the kids. The kids

play anty anty I over and the boys playd kech and rabits

- **Timothy**
  it was scarry when adam was talking to Jason and the teacher turned around and smacked the stick on the desk and said put your hands on the desk and I thought she was going to smack adams nuckles but she didn't. then she turned to me and said stand up and put your hands on your desk and then I thought she was going to smack me on the bum but she didn't.

  I also was intereted and thought that was neet was the little kinds of porjectors, one you would put a candel in it and that would be the light and you would put a little sort of film and it would show up on the wall.

Timothy's relief that both he and Adam were spared the wrath of the teacher is palpable. Because they actually *were* pioneer children for a time, all three students gained a more powerful understanding of what it was like to be children in a pioneer school than they might have attained through reading about, or viewing, such a scene. The students also acquired historical information on a variety of topics including the games played by children of the time, the first legislative building in the province, audio-visual techniques used by 19th Century teachers and disciplinary methods used. This information enabled students to build their impressions of what life was like during the period—impressions which would expand as they engaged in follow-up activities upon their return from the trip.

When conducted in the context of an ongoing unit or theme, a field trip becomes much more than a pleasant break from daily routines. It can provide accurate information and direct experience that can enrich many social studies topics, such as:

- roles of community members
- community services
- community rules and laws
- cultural makeup of the community
- local government
- transportation networks
- industry and commerce
- architecture
- zoning
- recreation.

Field experiences in such locations as art galleries and museums can enrich more wide-ranging topics such as ancient civilizations or pioneer times. Field experiences, particularly those involving overnight stays, are ideal for outdoor studies and the investigation of environmental topics as well.

Field experiences must be carefully planned. Activities which take place prior to and following the field experience may be of equal importance to those which take place during it. Prior activities set the context for the experience and help students participate with an enquiring attitude. Follow-up activities allow students to clarify impressions, share ideas and apply what they have learned. On this and the following pages I discuss considerations for choosing a field experience over other approaches to reaching curricular objectives, deciding on a site and developing preparatory, on-site and follow-up activities.

Choosing to go on a field trip

Two key factors should govern the decision to include a field experience in a social studies program: feasibility and educational cost-effectiveness. Feasibility refers to the ability to engage effectively in the learning activity within prevailing constraints. With a field experience, constraints can include transportation problems, insufficient availability of adult supervisors, expensive admission fees, safety considerations and parents who discourage their children's participation due to lack of understanding of the connection between the experience and curriculum objectives. Careful planning is necessary if curricular goals are to be attained and constraints effectively overcome. If constraints cannot be overcome, it may be best to abandon the plan. Clear communication is necessary in order to assure parents, students and school (and school board) administration that a field experience is the best way to meet those goals.

A second consideration is whether the benefits outweigh the risks and drawbacks. Will the gain in educational learning match the time and effort involved? Cost-effectiveness is a very important consideration for field experiences because they are invariably expensive in terms of class time. Ask the question—could the same learning outcomes be attained as richly and efficiently by staying in the classroom? A field experience should be chosen only if there are important benefits to be gained which could not be achieved in the classroom.

Choosing the site

The key criterion in choosing a field trip site is that it advance curricular objectives by extending and enriching areas of investigation which are being (or will be) pursued in the classroom. Field experiences are one more data source to be used in a unit, albeit a more intriguing source than some.

We need not limit our choices of field site to settings such as museums, local historical sites or other typical tourist destinations. A field experience might be as simple as a walk around the neighbourhood to observe and record the range of home types, or a trip to the shopping mall to observe product marketing, if these will help attain curriculum objectives. One of the most successful field experiences I am aware of took place at a construction site around the corner from the school and involved the building of new government offices in a small town. Several grade two students observed the beginning of construction on the way to school one morning and reported this event to the class. The teacher, eager to capitalize on this serendipitous lesson on community change, took students to the site almost every day during construction. Students observed construction plans, materials and methods and interviewed construction workers. After the building opened, and government workers had moved in, students interviewed them to find out how well their new offices met their needs. What made this experience so successful was the uniting of keen student interest with the achievement of social studies objectives.

In considering alternatives, a possible site should not be rejected out-of-hand merely because most students may have been there many times. I remember my surprise when I learned that a little boy in my grade four class in a suburb of Vancouver had never visited Stanley Park. In the nine years of his life his family had never climbed into a car or onto a bus and travelled there to spend the day in the zoo or aquarium, or simply exploring the seaside. We cannot assume that all students will have had these seemingly common experiences. As well, a family excursion can and should be quite a different experience than a structured field experience. Students on a field experience observe with particular purposes in mind, which guide their information gathering. Also, field trips offer more opportunities for indepth activities. For instance, it is always enjoyable to visit an aquarium, but it is a much richer experience when students are invited behind-the-scenes to observe feeding routines or attendants caring for a sick animal.

The box on the following page outlines the kinds of field sites available in many communities, and suggests questions or tasks which could provide a focus for the experience. There has been no attempt to differentiate possible sites according to intended grade level. Many sites visited in the primary years for one purpose may well be revisited in the secondary grades for other purposes.

Preparatory activities with students

Prior activities set the context for the experience and help students participate with an enquiring attitude. First and foremost, students need to be aware of field trip objectives. For instance, one objective for a trip to a local branch of the public library might be to discover what special services are offered to particular groups in the community such as children and seniors and how these services are delivered. A second objective might be to explore how these services or their delivery could be improved to better meet people's needs. Such a trip might be part of a larger unit on services offered in the community. Prior to the trip, it must be clear to students how the trip fits within the larger unit so they can make the connections between their experiences on the trip and other learning activities. It is not enough to assume that this awareness is present simply because the field experience is in the context of a particular unit and, therefore, is one way of helping to attain unit objectives. This needs to be made explicit through discussion.

To help students develop a clear sense of purpose provide specific information about what to expect at

RANGE OF FIELD SITES

Field sites	Focus Questions or Tasks
School • Physical layout • Roles of various staff members	• What types of rooms are in our school (e.g., classrooms, offices, gym)? How is each one used? • What types of occupations are there in our school? What tasks do people do? How are these tasks important? • How could the physical layout be altered to better meet the needs of the people who use the school?
Local neighbourhood • Modes of transportation • Safety measures (e.g., crosswalks, sidewalks, signs, fire hydrants)	• How do people get to work and to school in our neighbourhood? What do people in the neighbourhood think of the transportation services? How could they be improved to better meet people's needs? • What safety features are in our neighbourhood? What is the function of each? Are there other safety features which we should have? How could we go about getting them?
Public services • Fire station • Police station • Public library • Public health unit	• What places in our community provide services? Which services are provided by the government? Which services are special to our community and which are provided in most communities? Are there other services which are needed in our community? How could we go about getting them?
Retail businesses • Grocery store • Bakery • Shopping mall	• Which places sell goods? Are there enough goods and services available in our community? Do all communities need goods and services from other communities?
Manufacturing or commercial sites • Assembly line • Newspaper plant • Warehouse • Advertising agency	• What is the product(s) here? Where does the facility fit in terms of the product's production, distribution, marketing or sale? What happens at this site? What happened to the product before it arrived at this site? What happens next? Would I like working here? Why or why not?
Community celebrations • Multicultural festivals • Remembrance Day ceremonies • Heritage days	• What things do people in our community choose to celebrate? Why are these celebrations important to people in this community?
Historical sites • Restored homes, forts and villages • Graveyards and monuments • Museums (local and provincial)	• What can we learn about the past at this site? How authentic is what you see here? Is it important to maintain sites like this one? Why or why not? What might life have been like when people lived and worked here?
Resource development sites • Mines • Lumber mills • Farms • Refineries	• What resource is being developed here? Give a step-by-step description of the process used to develop this resource. What are the environmental effects of development of this resource? What environmental protection measures are used here? Are these measures sufficient? Where does the product(s) go? How are transportation systems used to transport the product from this site?
Environmental preservation sites • Fish hatchery • Water treatment plant • Landfill facility	• What happens at this facility? How does it contribute to environmental preservation?

Government operations	• All-candidates meeting: Choose two election issues. What is each candidate's stance on these issues? Which issues seem to be of most concern to the audience? Who are the strongest candidates, in your opinion? Why?
• All-candidates meeting prior to an election • Provincial legislature in session • City council in session • Ratepayer meeting on a local issue • Mock trial in a courtroom	• Simulated City Council meeting: What strategies did you use to try to win others over to your point of view? How successful were you? Did you change your position in any way based on what others said? Describe the decision-making process used by the city council. Were points in favour of each argument taken into consideration? Did some opinions seem to carry more weight than others? What recommendations would you offer to city councils about the process of making decisions?
Transportation and communication venues • Railway station • Bus depot • Port facilities • Television station • Post offices • Airport	• How is this venue organized so that employees work together to keep things running smoothly? Draw a flow chart. Describe what it would be like to work at a job in one of these venues. What are some examples of technology that is used at this facility?

the site. Many sites provide pamphlets, posters, kits of sample items or video programs which can be used to preview what will be available during the field experience. Students can use these materials to create questions which will guide their observations at the site. They can also be given key questions by the teacher.

Prior to the trip, a permission form providing basic facts about the trip should be sent home. (See box below for an example.)

If interviews or surveys are to be conducted at the site, there are many aspects which need to be consid-

FIELD PERMISSION TRIP FORM (SAMPLE)

In conjunction with their local history study, grade five students will be spending the day at McAdam Heritage Home. Volunteers at the home will be involving students in a series of activities in which people living in the home would have engaged in the late 1800s.

Date of trip _____Oct. 3, 1998_____

Destination _____McAdam Heritage Home_____

Duration _____All day_____

Transportation _____Bus_____

Time leaving school ___9:00___ Time of return ___3:00___ Cost to student ___$10.00___

Items to bring _____Bag lunch, rain jacket_____

Teacher's Name _____Ms. Clark & Mr. Case_____ Phone _____683-1211_____

— —

Please return this section.

I give my permission for_____to participate in the trip to the McAdam Heritage Home on October 3, 1998.

Signature _____ (parent/guardian)

Address _____

Phone number _____

ADVICE ON CONDUCTING INTERVIEWS

Preparation

- Research background information before the interview. The more information you have, the more pertinent your questions are likely to be.
- Clearly state who you are, what your purpose is and how long the interview is expected to take.
- Prepare questions beforehand. Avoid questions which could be answered with a simple "yes" or "no" because these may not be particularly enlightening.

Interview

- Allow the interviewee time to think about your questions before responding.
- Clarify ambiguous responses. Restate your question using other words. Or say, "Is this what you meant?" and state what you consider to be the intended meaning of the response.
- Ask new questions which grow out of the interviewee's comments. If you stick to the questions which you planned beforehand, you may miss valuable opportunities to delve deeper and explore ideas which you had not considered.
- Use a tape recorder (with the interviewee's permission) or notes to record the interview. Use the interviewee's exact words in your notes. Choice of words may be an important indicator of feelings.
- Summarize the main points for the interviewee at the end of the interview. Don't offer comments that could be interpreted by the interviewee as placing a value judgement on the responses.
- Explain to the interviewee how the information will be used.
- Visit with the interviewee for a few minutes before and after the interview. This will help you to see the interviewee as a person and to make the interviewee feel comfortable.
- Thank the interviewee at the end of the interview.

Follow-up

- Summarize impressions in writing as soon as possible after the interview.
- Send a thank you note to all interviewees. Send a copy of your report to all those who wish to have it.

ADVICE ON CONDUCTING SURVEYS

- Decide what information is needed to answer the question(s).
- Consider whether a survey is the best way to obtain the required information. A survey will be best when a minimal amount of information is needed from a fairly large number of people.
- Decide if you want to ask the type of questions where people can write YES\NO or AGREE\DISAGREE, or the type where people explain their answers. Obviously the latter approach will involve more work, because responses will be more difficult to interpret and categorize.
- Decide if questions will be asked of each respondent or if they will fill out the form on their own. The response rate will be lower if respondents are asked to fill out their own forms because some will not do so.
- Decide whether responses will be anonymous. This will depend on type of questions and respondents' wishes.
- Generate a list of possible questions. Choose the best questions from the list. These will be the questions that most clearly and directly address the key desired information. Explain how the reader can find out the results of the survey.
- Provide information on the survey, in an accompanying letter, on why the survey is being conducted and who is conducting it.
- Decide on the "sample" (the group who will answer the questions).
- Tabulate the results by adding up the totals of similar answers and clustering common themes contained in open-ended answers.
- Draw conclusions from the survey results.
- Prepare an oral and/or written report of the survey results.

ered ahead of time. The boxes on page 382 contain considerations for planning and carrying out both interviews and surveys.

Activities at the site

An ideal field experience is structured and purposeful. Students observe and record their observations in an organized manner. Here are some approaches to recording information at the site:

- **Tally sheets**. If students are looking for specific information which can be counted, then tally sheets are useful. For instance, students might be interested in finding out how much traffic goes over the school crosswalk during a specific period of time, or in soliciting opinions for a survey.

TRAFFIC OVER OUR CROSSWALK

Time Periods	Number of persons
8:00-8:15	I I I
8:15-8:30	JHT
8:30-8:45	JHT THH THH JHT THH HH
8:45-9:00	THH
etc.	

- **Maps.** Students could be given a simple street map of the community on which to record the location of different housing types (e.g., apartments, single-family dwellings, duplexes).

- **Notetaking sheets**. These are sheets with teacher or student-made questions, on which students record responses during the field experience. The questions should help students make observations which are key to the understandings which are intended to develop as a result of the experience. They should also direct students' attention to aspects of the experience which they may not notice otherwise.

- **Photographs.** One or more students could be asked to record important aspects of the trip by means of photographs. These could be used for activities involving detailed observations following the trip. They could also be used to assist in the presentation of data following the trip in the form of a bulletin board or a class booklet.

- **Sketches.** These can also be a useful way to record information because students can focus on particular details rather than record everything as a camera would.

- **Journals.** Students could record their impressions in a journal. They could also use their imaginations and write in the role of someone living in an historic house, for instance,

- **Interviews**. Often, it may be appropriate for students to conduct interviews at the site. See articles by Alan Sears "Using Interviews in Social Studies" and Tony Arruda " 'In Their Own Voices and In Their Own Times': Exploring Social History Through Oral Narrative," both in this volume, for discussions on interviewing. A form like the one below could be used to record interview information while on a field trip.

STRUCTURED INTERVIEW FORM

Interviewer _____   Interviewee _____

Date _____   Place _____

1. Question _____

   Response _____

   _____

   _____

2. Question _____

   Response _____

   _____

   _____

Other points made during interview

   _____

   _____

   _____

Follow-up activities

Field experience follow-up activities are of at least three kinds: students organize and interpret the data they have gathered, students share their findings with others and students review and assess the experience itself, including its preparatory and follow-up activities.

The first set of activities can involve a variety of different strategies, depending on the purposes of the experience and the onsite activities. Students should review their notes, diagrams, photographs, drawings or whatever other form their data is in and then select and organize their data coherently and logically. It may be that the questions with which students were armed prior to the trip, or the data charts which they used, in themselves provide an organized format for the data and there is little work to do at this stage. Once the data is organized in a way that makes sense, students interpret it and make some judgements about it. This might include asking questions such as the following, where appropriate:

- Is there a particular point of view from which this information was presented?

- Is there another side to this story?

- What conclusions can I draw from this information?

- Was I able to answer all my questions or do I need to go to other sources now?

- Do I have other questions now that my original questions have been answered?

Next students need to decide how to present their findings and conclusions in a way that will be both understandable and interesting to others. This could be an individual or a group activity. Presentation formats include bulletin board displays, models, photo albums, stories, reports, letters, poems, tape recordings, journals, articles in the school newspaper, a play to be put on for other classes and so on. Choices are as varied as for any other kind of research. (See Penney Clark, "Escaping the Typical Report Trap," in this volume.)

The final set of activities involves review and assessment of the experience itself. This may simply be a class discussion which reviews the intents of the experience followed by an assessment of how well those intents were met from both the students' and the teacher's perspectives. Students could ask questions such as:

- What were our purposes in engaging in this community experience?

- Did we achieve our purposes? Was the trip interesting?

- Are there things we could have done differently in order to achieve our purposes?

- Was the trip the best way to obtain the needed information?

- What were some of the pleasant and unpleasant surprises we encountered? How could we reduce the possibility of encountering the unpleasant surprises in another field experience?

Students could write a letter reviewing the experience and send it as a thank-you note to coordinators at the site.

On the following page is found a checklist of logistical and educational considerations for planning, carrying out and following up on a field experience.

GUEST SPEAKERS

Many people within the community have special knowledge and expertise which they would enjoy sharing with students, if given the opportunity. This interaction serves to provide students with a unique opportunity for data gathering, as well as to initiate friendly relationships with adults they would not normally have an opportunity to meet. Students enjoy opportunities to ask their own questions, to receive firsthand responses to those questions and to make their own judgements.

Having a guest speaker can also dispel stereotypes. In the grades three-four unit on pioneer life discussed earlier, the class had a local senior who had lived in the community as a child come to speak to them. For one child a predominant impression from the experience was how healthy the speaker was. This child could not explain why he had drawn this conclusion. However, the teacher decided that the child must have been surprised when the speaker announced to the class that the reason she had come a day early was because she was going skiing the next day. He had not expected a 76 year old woman to be so physically healthy and active (McKay, 1990). Clearly, this child's concept of 'elderly' was broadened considerably through the experience of having a guest speaker in the classroom.

Sources of speakers

Many people are willing to come to the classroom and share their expertise with students. Sources of speakers can include:

- **Parents.** It is easy to forget this rich source of speakers that is so close at hand. Every classroom will have parents who have travelled to places of interest. In many cases there will be parents who have come to Canada as immigrants. Parents will also have a variety of occupations and interests. It can be useful to send a form home at the beginning of the year outlining topics which the class will be exploring, and asking for parents who have some related expertise to share.

- **Industry and commerce.** Chambers of Commerce, public relations departments of large firms, business lobby groups, owners of small businesses and professional people such as doctors and lawyers are often prepared to send speakers to schools or to arrange for interviews.

- **Interest and service groups.** Community organizations such as local historical societies, environmental lobby groups, veterans' organizations and ethnic group associations are also often prepared to speak to students.

CHECKLIST FOR TRIPPING

Early Preparation

- ❏ Review school and district policies regarding field trips.
- ❏ Obtain information about trip, including talking to other teachers who have done it.
- ❏ Clarify objectives. Make them as concrete as possible.
- ❏ Obtain permissions from principal and on-site authorities.
- ❏ Book trip. Arrange transportation.
- ❏ Make students aware of objectives. Solicit student input.
- ❏ Visit site. Could take along a student committee.
- ❏ Arrange for helpers.
- ❏ Inform parents of the purpose of the trip, departure and arrival times, eating arrangements, costs, supervision arrangements and any special clothing or equipment requirements.
- ❏ Obtain permission from parents.

Just Prior to Trip

- ❏ Provide checklist for students:
  - money
  - equipment
  - clothing
  - food
- ❏ Collect money.
- ❏ Prepare students logistically:
  - discuss safety issues
  - could role-play expected behaviour
  - review rules of conduct
  - establish work groups and buddy system
- ❏ Brief helpers:
  - discuss purposes of trip
  - discuss duties
  - discuss safety issues
- ❏ Prepare students educationally:
  - review objectives
  - review what students already know about the place
  - determine individual and group tasks

On the Trip

- ❏ Make the trip to the site part of the experience (e.g., have students take note of types of buildings, industries and means of transportation observed enroute).
- ❏ Once on site, point out boundaries and key spots (e.g., washrooms, meeting area, lost and found space).
- ❏ Elicit questions and discussion from students.
- ❏ Remind students about gathering and recording data:
  - go over charts to be filled in or questions to be answered
  - have one or more students take photographs as a record of the trip
  - create field sketches
  - interview people on-site
- ❏ Plan for return trip (e.g., plan to take a different route back to the school to capitalize on the commuting and what can be observed from the windows of the bus).

Follow-Up

- ❏ Organize, synthesize and present collected data.
- ❏ Formally thank hosts and helpers.
- ❏ Evaluate trip.

- **Government.** Politicians are often willing to visit schools to present their perspectives on pertinent issues and to answer student questions. Museums sometimes provide speakers, as well as kits of materials for classroom use. Embassies and consulates are other possibilities.

- **Special people.** Some people may have unique life experiences to share. Such people might include survivors of the Holocaust, refugees from war-torn countries, people who have worked for humanitarian organizations in developing countries and so on. Of course, the possibilities are limitless.

Preparation

Having a guest speaker is a profitable experience only if both students and speaker are adequately prepared for the experience. In the box below are points to keep in mind to increase the likelihood that the encounter with a guest speaker will be a worthwhile experience.

Follow-up activities

Follow-up activities should provide students with an opportunity to make comparisons between information provided by the speaker and previously acquired information, to interpret the information, to synthesize it, to draw conclusions and to develop further questions. The visit should be acknowledged with a written thank you letter or letters. Students could also make copies of pictures, stories or other projects completed after the session and send them to the visitor.

COMMUNITY-DEVELOPED MATERIALS

In addition to the community resources already discussed—field experiences and resource people—organizations in the community have an amazing variety of materials available to those teachers who want them. Sources of materials include the following:

- Consulates. Quantity varies from country to country. However, a vast array of materials is available from some countries (e.g., Japan, Switzerland).

CHECKLIST FOR GUEST SPEAKERS

Students

- ❏ Discuss objectives of the visit with students.

- ❏ Emphasize that the speaker is volunteering valuable time. Therefore students should be on their best behaviour.

- ❏ Help students formulate questions ahead of time. The questions should be in keeping with previously established objectives. They could be listed on the blackboard and then students could choose the most appropriate. These could be recorded on chart paper.

- ❏ Appoint recorders to record the speaker's responses.

- ❏ Have class choose students to introduce and thank the speaker.

- ❏ Allow unstructured time at the end of the session for more casual interaction between students and speaker.

Speaker

- ❏ Consider whether the speaker is the best source of information for students about this particular topic. Consider alternatives such as audio-visual materials, library resources and so on.

- ❏ Consider timing. In most cases, it is better to schedule the speaker for the end of a unit of study rather than the beginning so students will have adequate background information. This will make the session more rewarding for both students and speaker.

- ❏ Discuss with the speaker the purpose of the talk, how it fits into the theme of the unit of study and what the speaker can offer to students. Point out aspects which are of particular interest to students.

- ❏ Discuss the length of the talk. The speaker may not be used to talking to students at this grade level. Also alert the speaker to questions which students may ask.

- ❏ Help the speaker prepare content and visuals. Point out the value of visual aids to provide additional information and to increase student interest.

- ❏ Determine whether the speaker requires specific directions to the school or if transportation arrangements need to be made.

- ❏ Determine audio-visual equipment needs and arrange for necessary equipment to be available.

- ❏ Arrange to meet the speaker in advance of the scheduled time.

- ❏ Thank the speaker in writing.

- Canadian federal government (e.g., National Archives, National Film Board, National Library, Canadian Citizenship and Immigration, Canada Customs, government departments).

- Provincial and local government (e.g. museums often have kits of materials which schools can borrow; government departments such as the Department of Fisheries).

- Political parties.

- Resource industries often have provincial associations which have worked with teachers to develop teaching materials (e.g., provincial mining or forestry associations).

- Environment organizations (e.g., Greenpeace, Western Canada Wilderness Committee).

- Local fire and police departments.

These resources can be particularly useful in two ways. They often provide information that is more current than that found in textbooks because they are usually updated more frequently and they may present an alternative perspective to that found in other classroom materials that students are using.

Because these materials may have been originally intended for use in classrooms it is important that teachers and students carefully scrutinize the information and ideas contained in them.

The following questions may be useful in helping teachers examine these materials from a critical perspective:

- What are the aims of the organization? Are these acceptable in a public education system?

- How are these aims reflected in the materials available to teachers and students?

- Does the organization have any formal ties to education or the production of educational materials?

- How suitable are the materials for classroom use and what levels might they be appropriate for? Can they be adapted for use?

- Which curricular objectives can these materials be used to help attain?

- If the organization provides human resources for classroom or professional purposes, how can these resources be used to enhance social studies?

Concluding Remarks

A rich social studies program requires access to a wide array of resources, including those in the community. Community resources are an important source of data which can deepen student understanding of social studies. Careful preparation is the key to making the most of such resources. Preparation includes choosing a field trip site or resource person carefully, making students aware of purposes for using the resource and helping students develop questions to guide their dis-

covery. Most importantly, let us not be like that teacher in Bancroft and ignore the exciting possibilities all around us.

Endnote

[1] I would like to thank Marjorie Redbourn, a student in a Simon Fraser University social studies methods class, for reminding me of this episode of *The Wonder Years* and its applicability to field experiences.

References

McDiarmid, G.L. (1970). The value of on-site learning. *Orbit*, *1*(3), 4-7.

McDiarmid, T., Manzo, R. & Muselle, T. (1996). *Critical challenges for primary students.* Burnaby, BC: Faculty of Education, Simon Fraser University.

McKay, R. (1990). *Children's construction of meaning in a thematic unit.* Unpublished doctoral dissertation, University of Alberta, Edmonton.

Oliver, H. (1970). Philadelphia's Parkway Program. *Orbit*, *1*(3), 22-23.

Supplementary Readings

Alleman, J. & Brophy, J. (1994). Taking advantage of out-of-school opportunities for meaningful social studies learning. *Social Studies*, *85*(6), 262-267.

Bischoff, H. (1987). A walking tour of an ethnic neighborhood: Communities as outdoor classrooms for teaching immigration history. *Social Studies*, *76*(5), 202-205.

Carter, J.C. (1985). Community museums and schools: An annotated bibliography of resource and reference materials. *History and Social Science Teacher*, *21*(2), 89-93.

Cook, S.A. (1988). Linking the social science classroom with the community: A sample curriculum project. *History and Social Science Teacher*, *24*(1), 30-31, 34.

Cox, C.C. (1993). The field trip as a positive experience for the learning disabled. *Social Education*, *57*(2), 92-94.

Cuthbertson, S. (1985). Museum education: A British Columbia perspective. *History and Social Science Teacher*, *21*(2), 80-85.

Da Silva, B., Proctor, J. & Calvori, L. (1985). Field trips in social studies education. *Horizon*, *24*(1), 44-55.

Downs, J.R. (1993). Getting parents and students involved: Using survey and interview techniques. *Social Studies*, *84*(3), 104-106.

Guyton, E.M. (1985). The school as a data source for young learners. *Social Education*, *49*(2), 141-144.

Jorgensen-Esmaili, K. & Rosalind, S. (1986). Intergenerational interviews. *Social Education*, *50*(4), 288-290.

Kazemek, F.E. (1985). Stories of our lives: Interviews and oral histories for language development. *Journal of Reading*, *29*(3), 211-218.

McGugan, D. & Terry, E. (1977). Out-of-classroom experiences. *Curriculum ideas for teachers.* Toronto: Ontario Ministry of Education.

Moffat, H. (1988). The educational use of museums: An English case study. *History and Social Science Teacher, 23*(3), 127-131.

Sears, A. & Bidlake, G. (1991). The senior citizens' tea: A connecting point for oral history in the elementary school. *Social Studies, 82*(4), 133-135.

Sutter, D.S. (1993). Historical visit to the site of the Canard River skirmishes. *Canadian Social Studies, 27*(3), 102-106.

Terigni, J.F. (1990). The Donnellys revisited: The importance of field studies in the teaching of history. *History and Social Science Teacher, 25*(3), 130-133.

— ✧ —

39

Principles of Authentic Assessment

Roland Case

There is a common saying in educational circles that "What is counted counts." In other words, the only learning objectives that are, in fact, important are the ones we assess. Student sensitivity to this maxim is implied by their common refrains: "Is this on the exam?" and "Will it be for marks?" Consequently, if we value, for example, promoting students' abilities to think critically and to apply their knowledge in novel situations, then we should be concerned that our assessment practices reflect this goal. Yet, as John Goodlad (1984) reports, the vast majority of questions on teacher-made tests are limited to recall of information. The effect of this is to signal to students that what really matters is memorizing information.

This shortcoming will not be redressed simply by devoting more attention to assessment of other goals. In fact, many commonly employed ways of assessing thinking abilities are self-defeating. The "timed" nature of many tests and the "once-over and one-time nature" of many assignments do not invite in-depth thoughtful reflection. Even much of the rhetoric about raising standards may be counter productive. Advocates of "higher" standards typically call for raised expectations of student performance and for expanded testing of students. It is not obvious that these steps result in enhanced student learning. Students who are motivated by grades may already be trying their best, and many others may not be moved by raising further an educational "high jump" that is already out of their horizon. It is arguable that many of the most important educational goals—such as getting students to take responsibility for their actions, competently solve real-life problems, develop as reflective, considerate individuals—are rarely if ever measured by standardized tests. What is worse, in the rush to teach to the test less time may be devoted to these goals. The amount of effort and considerable financial cost of developing and administering standardized tests may detract from more promising efforts to improve student performance—such as putting better resources into teachers' hands and providing for sustained professional development. In truth many of our system-wide and classroom-based assessment practices may actually inhibit genuine learning.

This concern to overcome what many regard as the pervasive effects of common assessment practices is the driving motive for what is referred to "authentic assessment."[1] The notion of *authentic* assessment refers to measuring the real, actual or genuine thing as opposed to measuring a poor substitute. Traditional classroom assessment practices are being supplemented with "alternative" approaches that seek richer, more productive ways of assessing students. Although there are many interpretations of authentic assessment, three inter-related purposes underlie this movement (Case, 1992):

- **greater "authenticity."** Advocates of authentic assessment seek a closer fit between the attributes and abilities actually measured by an assessment device and the educational goals that we most value. Too often we have assessed what is easiest to measure (e.g., whether or not students can remember information) and have neglected to assess what is more difficult yet more important (e.g., students' ability to think critically and to use their knowledge to solve realistic problems).

- **supporting learning.** Advocates of authentic assessment are committed to using assessment data to support student learning. Often assessment interrupts or discourages learning. We can enhance learning by making assessment tasks more meaningful, by de-mystifying the process, and by involving students in assessing their efforts and those of fellow students.

- **fairness to all students.** Advocates of alternative assessment are concerned that some students are penalized by current assessment practices, not because these students know less, but because of the assessment devices and the conditions under which assessment occurs. For example, some students may not be able to communicate what they know on a subject under the pressure of a single, timed written examination.

In this article I explore four principles for guiding our assessment practices in more authentic ways. In a follow-up article—"Assessment Methods"—I discuss how to develop assessment tools that embody these principles. But before proceeding further with these principles I invite you to assess an assessment device that I used when teaching a grade six social studies unit.

ASSESSING MY ASSESSMENTS

Years ago, after having just graduated with my teaching certificate, I proudly developed a marking sheet (below) to accompany a research project my students

---

RESEARCH REPORT ASSESSMENT

1. Bibliography: (1 mark for each book)   **/ 4**

2. Notes: very good   _____ (3)
           good   _____ (2)
           satisfactory   _____ (1)
           poor   _____ (0)   **/ 3**

3. Charts, maps, drawings, etc.:   #1   #2   #3
   a) neat: _____   _____   _____
   b) accurate: _____   _____   _____
   c) relevant: _____   _____   _____   **/ 9**

4. Text:
   a) neatness: / 2
   b) spelling, grammar, punctuation: (1/2 mark off per error)   / 5
   c) coverage of major points:
          all   _____ (5)
          almost all   _____ (4)
          most   _____ (3)
          some   _____ (2)
          few   _____ (1)   / 5
   d) well written:
          good   _____ (2)
          satisfactory   _____ (1)
          poor   _____ (0)   / 2   **/ 14**

5. Comments:

                                                                 _____
                                                                  / 30

---

had just completed. Towards the end of a unit on India, I asked my students to select an aspect of India (e.g., climate, religion, geography, customs) that they wished to pursue though independent research. I instructed them to consult several library resources on the basis of which they were to prepare a written report. The report was to include several visuals (e.g., charts, graphs, maps) and, unlike previous efforts, these visuals were to bear obvious relation to the ideas in the text. To discourage the mere copying of reports from published sources I required that research notes be submitted with the final report. When the project was completed, I assessed and returned their work with the Research Reports Assessment sheet attached to the front of each of their assignments.

Take a moment to study my marking sheet. Make a written list of its positive features and its areas of weaknesses. Imagine that I am a student teacher and that you are supervising my teaching practicum. Decide the grade you would assign to my assessment practices based on the following scale:

outstanding (A/A+ range)
very good (B+/A- range)
good (B-/B range)
satisfactory (C/C+ range)
poor (C-/D range)
very poor (F)

Over the past few years in a variety of contexts I have asked over 250 pre-service and practicing teachers to complete this assessment of my assessment. The grades assigned to my marking sheet have ranged the entire spectrum from "outstanding" to "very poor" with the vast majority (approximately 90% of responses) dividing fairly evenly between "good," satisfactory" and "poor." Although I offer this anecdote as a provocative and not as a representative example, it is cause for some concern. As professionals, how can we have confidence in our assessment practices if there is such latitude in judging the quality of my marking scheme? This lack of agreement is especially disturbing since our assessments have potentially profound effects on our students. For example, if I was a secondary student and *if* this assessment was typical of my evaluations it would have the following consequences:

- an "outstanding" would enable me to be eligible for university scholarships;
- a "very good" would enable me to attend the university of my choice, but not on scholarship;
- a "good" would allow me to get into a university, but perhaps not my first choice;
- a "satisfactory" would mean I would be lucky to get into a community college;
- a "poor" would prevent me from directly continuing post-secondary studies;
- a "very poor" would require that I repeat the grade.

Although I do not wish to infer too much from my somewhat contrived example, it is suggestive of a con-siderable inconsistency in our understanding of what counts as good assessment. As indicated above I believe there are a four principles which, if better understood and implemented, would improve this predicament. My present purpose is to explain the implications and importance of the following principles:

- Focus assessment on what really matters.
- Assessments must provide valid indications of student competence.
- Use assessment to encourage student learning.
- Assessment practices must use teacher time efficiently.

Although there are other principles and other ways of expressing the ones I suggest, the above principles seem to be a defensible and reasonably comprehensive set of considerations for improving the authenticity, support for learning and fairness of our assessment practices.

At the close of the article, I will ask you to revisit your assessment of my assessment in light of what I hope will be a clearer, more thorough grasp of these key principles. Just as we should use criteria to assess our students' work, so too should we use the principles of authentic assessment as the basis for judging our assessments. The implicit message in my article is that we should neither be satisfied with nor confident of our assessments of student work until we have seriously scrutinized our own assessment practices. Let us now look in turn at four principles that I recommend as a basis for this assessment.

FOCUS ON WHAT REALLY MATTERS

The most significant question to ask ourselves when judging our assessment practices is whether or not we are assessing what really matters. Are the criteria we are using—consciously or not—to judge students' work reflective of the most important educational objectives? As suggested above, what teachers assess has important implications for what students consider important and ultimately what students learn. Do our assessment practices do justice to the breadth and complexity of the goals of social studies? Assessments that are skewed towards a limited range of desired outcomes, say outcomes related exclusively to factual knowledge, fail to assess and possibly inadvertently discourage student growth along other desired dimensions.

The most shocking realization for me when I first had occasion to look back at my marking sheet was how skewed my assessment was. One-third of the total mark for the project (10 marks out of 30) dealt with mechanics (i.e., neatness, spelling and punctuation). Although these are appropriate criteria to use, it now strikes me as mistaken that I would weigh these twice as much as I did the content of the report (the extent to which the report addressed the main ideas accounted for only 5 out of 30 marks). Notice the consequences of this kind of weighting: students who knew a lot about their topic, but who did not write proper English, might fail the assignment. On the positive side, the fact that I placed some value on information gathering (i.e., the use of multiple references and the taking of competent notes) and on content knowledge (i.e., the need for students to cover the main points of the topic) showed some sensitivity to the importance of these goals. Regrettably I did not appear to attach any special importance to students' ability to think critically about the material they were researching.

Over the course of a unit or the entire year (not necessarily on any given assignment) we should assess for all relevant goals, and the emphasis assigned to each of these goals should reflect their importance. Completing what is called a *table of specifications* is one strategy for checking that each goal for the unit receives an appropriate weighting. After completing a unit (or at the end of a term) list all the graded assignments and tests. Record in a table similar to the one illustrated on the bottom of this page, the amount of marks devoted to each unit goal. In this sample table, the unit had five main goals indicated in the left-hand column, and employed five different assessment strategies indicated across the top of the chart. The column on the far right indicates the percentage of marks assigned to each goal, for example, understanding of key concepts was worth 40% of unit marks (160/400). Be prepared for a surprise when you discover the importance you actually attached to the various goals. The actual weighting of marks should be matched against the importance these goals deserve according to the curriculum and your own professional sense of what really matters, given the students you teach. Although not always possible, setting up a table of specifications beforehand, or part way through a unit, is more useful than waiting until the end. These tables can provide an emerging sense of how ongoing assignments are contributing to goal achievement, and allow for adjustments to be made along the way.

Provide Valid Indications

A second key consideration in authentic assessment is validity. Although validity has a long history as a complex technical term, in the context of authentic assessment it can be defined as a close fit between the kinds of attributes actually measured by an assessment device and those educational goals that we value. In simplest terms, an assessment strategy is valid if it actually assesses the outcomes that it claims to assess.

My intention with my marking sheet was to assess students' ability to identify and use multiple sources of information in conducting independent research. I now doubt that my assigning marks for the number of references in the bibliography measures this ability. Students could score very well on this part of the assignment even if they did not actually use more than one of the books listed in their bibliography. For that matter, I could not know if students knew how to find books on their topic—perhaps someone had obtained the books for them. My reliance on the number of references in the bibliography was not a valid indicator of students' research abilities. I could have better measured their ability to use multiple sources of information by having them indicate in their final report the source of their information, and by assigning a mark for the use of several sources of relevant information. The outcome measured in the "coverage of the main points" section of my marking scheme is equally problematic. Students may have written on all the main points without really understanding what they had put down. If I was serious about finding out if they had gained any understanding of the topic I would have been better advised to ask students to tell me orally in their own words what they had found out.

The importance of validity was first brought home to me when I was preparing my grade six students for a day-long field trip. Several weeks before beginning to plan for a picnic lunch on our field trip, we practiced answering word problems like the following:

If there are thirty students in the class and students want on average two sandwiches each, how many slices of bread will be required? How many loaves of bread will we need if there are 20 slices of bread

Table of Specifications

UNIT GOALS	ASSESSMENT STRATEGIES					Total marks	% of unit
	quiz	textbook assignment	group project	in-class observation	essay		
critical thinking about issues	15	–	–	20	25	**60**	15
information gathering	15	–	20	–	25	**60**	15
recall of factual information	50	30	–	–	–	**80**	20
understanding of key concepts	20	20	70	–	50	**160**	40
cooperation with others	–	–	30	10	–	**40**	10
TOTAL	**100**	**50**	**120**	**30**	**100**	**400**	**100**

in each loaf? What will be the total cost if bread sells for $1.25 per loaf? How much must each student contribute to cover the cost of the bread?

Despite their ability to successfully solve these kinds of word problems (as determined by a unit quiz), my students were incapable of determining how much money each would have to bring for lunch on our field trip. They made no connection between the arithmetic we had been doing and the challenge before them. Even after the connection was explained, they were unable to solve the problem. In the word problems I had provided, all of the mathematical "ingredients" had been supplied to them. Not only did they not know the answers to the real-life questions (i.e., the number of sandwiches we would want, the number of slices in an actual loaf and the current cost of bread), beyond getting an adult to tell them, they had no ideas as to how they could come up with the answers.

Although I had taught my students to solve word problems on costing lunches, I had not taught them how to cost the lunch. As Grant Wiggins (1989) suggests, "school tests make the complex simple by dividing it into isolated and simplistic chores—as if the students need not practice the true test of performance, the test of putting all elements together" (p. 706). My students' mastery of all the requisite competencies involved in this task and their ability to integrate them successfully were tested only when they were charged with planning the actual lunch. Significantly, I would never have realized the gaps in their abilities, and subsequently addressed them, unless I had assigned this "real-life" assessment task. If we do not assess beyond isolated competencies in artificial situations, we are unlikely to know of, and less likely to promote, our students' abilities to use their knowledge in significant ways.

Another factor affecting assessment validity is the conditions under which the assessment occurs. The use of "surprise" tests and a failure to make clear to students the basis upon which they will be judged may impair students' abilities to show what they actually know—instead, students may be rewarded for anticipating what the teacher wants. As well, traditional timed tests reward students who perform well in on-the-spot situations and may discriminate against students who are equally knowledgeable but are unable to perform under contrived conditions. A very common concern for validity, especially acute with students whose first language is not English, is that students' answers may be a function of their written fluency and not their understanding of the content. Although this obstacle cannot be completely overcome, there may be ways to mitigate its effects:

- assignments and questions should be explained orally to students, perhaps have someone translate the instructions and make frequent use of visual aids and other low vocabulary prompts;
- whenever feasible allow students to represent their answers in graphic form, orally, in written point form

or, perhaps, even in their native tongue;

- whenever appropriate offer alternative assignments, reduced expectations in terms of volume or additional assistance to offset the language impediment.

Besides being careful when developing measures to devise questions or tasks that capture what we intended, validity may also be enhanced by using several devices of different sorts to gather information about student achievement. The point of considering a variety of approaches is to increase the likelihood of finding a rich way to assess the desired outcomes. If, for example, the ability to solve real-life problems is an important goal then, at some point, we should assess student's ability to act on a real problem and not be satisfied, in an hypothetical context, merely to ask students to list the factors that they should consider. An observation checklist or rating scale may be particularly effective in assessing student performance in group projects and class presentations. Having students keep a journal while participating in a field project or a simulation activity may provide rich information about student attitudes towards themselves and others. For example, while preparing for a debate, students might comment on their reflections about expressing and defending their positions, or about working with others.

USE ASSESSMENT TO SUPPORT LEARNING

Advocates of authentic assessment are emphatic about using assessment to enhance learning—especially to enhance the full range of goals that we value highly. Greater validity of assessment measures is in itself an aid to increased use of assessment to support learning. As suggested by the example about planning for the field trip lunch, if an assessment does not capture what it is we really value, then we are less likely to know when we have succeeded (or have failed to succeed) in reaching our objective. Only after the real-life task did I realize that my students could not calculate the cost of our lunch. As teachers, our assessment practices can support learning in at least three other important ways:

- communicate effectively about expectations and results;
- involve students in the assessment process;
- use assessment to create opportunities and incentives for students to improve.

Effectively communicate expectations and results

If students know clearly what is expected of them they are more likely to succeed at the task. One of the most obvious ways in which I could have used my assessment practices to support learning was by presenting students with the marking sheet *before* they embarked on the research assignment. As it was, they saw the criteria only after they had completed their report. If my measure had validity and had focussed on the important goals, I would be signalling to students what was important and what they were required to do to demonstrate their learning. Because of its flaws, had I distributed beforehand my original marking sheet, unwittingly I would be encouraging students to attend to the technical dimensions and downplay the content. I did draw students' attention beforehand to the need for their graphs, charts and maps to relate to their text and the fact that I assessed for this encouraged students to attend to these features in their reports. Also on the positive side, by providing students, albeit after the fact, with a detailed breakdown of how well they did on each aspect, with place for general comments, I may have helped them understand what they did well and where more attention was needed.

Students may be even clearer about expectations if they are informed specifically about the *criteria* upon which they will be marked and the *standards* for achievement of these criteria. Because the concepts of criteria and standards are often used interchangeably, let me explain the distinction drawn between these two terms. (For additional discussion, see the next article in this volume—Assessment Criteria and Standards.)

- **criteria**: the features or attributes that provide the grounds for judging quality. Sample criteria include:
  - historical accuracy
  - originality of ideas
  - use of multiple sources
  - clarity of presentation
  - depth of analysis
  - active participation in project
  - openness to new ideas
  - flow/structure of the paper
  - neatness
  - spelling accuracy

- **standards**: the benchmarks, performance levels or degrees of achievement of a given criterion (i.e., "high" and "low" standards). Standards can be binary (correct/incorrect; pass/fail; above average/below average) or have multiple levels (A+ to F; outstanding to atrocious; vastly superior to vastly inferior; top 1% to bottom 1%). Sample standards for three criteria are listed in the box below.

My grade six students might have been better able to succeed had I clearly indicated all the criteria and standards for assessment. When assessing their notes I merely indicated whether they were "very good," "good," etc. without indicating the basis for this assessment. What criteria was I using? Was it the neatness of the notes? Conciseness? Amount of notes taken? Or, perhaps all of these? Furthermore, even if they knew the criteria for this assessment, I should not have assumed that students would know what distinguished a "good" from a "satisfactory" standard of notes. And yet, if I wanted them to improve, this is precisely the understanding they require. I did a slightly better job of communicating the criterion and standards for the "main points": my criterion was the amount of coverage and my standards were distinguished by the number of main points covered (e.g., all, most, a few). Besides supporting learning, another powerful reason for providing clearly articulated standards is that it reduces inconsistency and arbitrariness in assessments. I now wonder when I look at the standards I offered for "coverage of main points" if there is any *real* difference between "almost all" and "most" points and between

---

SAMPLE STANDARDS

Criterion	Standards	Descriptions of Performance Levels
historical accuracy	excellent	no factual inaccuracies
	good	at most, a few minor factual inaccuracies that do not substantially impair the writer's position
	satisfactory	several minor factual inaccuracies, and one or two major inaccuracies that damage the writer's position
	unsatisfactory	several or more major factual inaccuracies that completely undermine the writer's position
depth of analysis	in-depth	all main topics are analyzed in a probing and careful manner
	modest depth	although there is evidence of careful analysis, some aspects are not addressed in much depth
	superficial	for the most part, topics are addressed superficially
spelling accuracy	excellent	zero errors
	very good	at most 2 errors
	good	between 3 and 5 errors
	satisfactory	between 6 and 9 errors
	poor	10 or more errors

"some" and a "few" points. If there is no clear distinction between these performance levels how can I have reliably distinguished among them?

In the spirit of living the principles I preach, I offer on the following page detailed descriptions of the four criteria which I believe form an important basis for judging our assessments. As well I articulate performance levels or standards for each criteria. After you have finished reading about all four of these principles, and have a clear understanding of what each involves, I will ask you to use this assessment rubric to re-assess your original judgment of my marking sheet. For the time being, I offer this as an example of a way in which we can support learning by providing clear accounts of our assessment criteria and the standards for each. Read my descriptions of each standard and decide if you would recognize what each involves.

One of the most inspiring examples of the use of criteria to enhance student learning is a lesson, described in the box to the right, about teaching primary students to develop "powerful" questions. More generally, we can help students understand the criteria and standards for assessment in a variety of ways:

- Provide students with actual samples of previous students' work at each performance level.
- Provide students with concrete indicators of what may be involved in satisfying the criterion: "I know I am being *friendly* when I . . .
  — compliment others on their work;
  — offer to help others before they ask me to;
  — use friendly words and smiles;
  — am willing to share my supplies and my ideas.
- Provide students with criteria and ask them to articulate these criteria in concrete or operational terms: What does it look like? sound like? feel like?
- Provide students with a set of standards and have them assess their own work and identify what would be required to bring it up to the next level.
- Have students prepare a range of sample answers that satisfy each performance level on the scale. For example, students might write a weak, good and excellent answer to a question.
- Invite students to generate and explain in their own words the criteria for the assignment.

Learning is enhanced if students are clear about how they can improve. Feedback on how well students have met each criterion can be provided through a variety of methods including written teacher comments, teacher interviews, use of fellow students to explain areas of weakness, additional instruction and practice, large and small group discussion of answers and providing exemplars of student work. We are unlikely to help students learn from the assessment if we provide only a letter grade or a terse comment at the top of their assignment.

Involve students in assessment

Another way to use assessment to support learning is by involving students more directly in the assessment process. Students can be involved in at least three ways: in setting criteria and standards, by creating assessment tasks and by assessing themselves and their peers.

Setting criteria and standards

Greater understanding of criteria and standards, and ultimately of students' performance in light of them, may be encouraged by joint teacher and student negotiation of the criteria upon which students are to be judged. Criteria can be justified on two grounds:

- by being shown to be relevant or likely to contribute to the desired purpose or function (e.g., essays should be well organized and clearly written because

---

DEVELOPING POWERFUL QUESTIONS

In preparation for a visit by a classroom guest, students in a K-3 class at Charles Dickens Annex in Vancouver, British Columbia brainstormed criteria for a really good question—a really *powerful* question. Below are the criteria they developed as a class.

Criteria for powerful questions
- give you lots of information
- are specific to the person or situation
- are open-ended—can't be answered by yes or no
- may be unexpected
- are usually not easy to answer

These criteria were then posted on the wall. In pairs, students brainstormed and then assessed questions they might ask of a World War II veteran who was soon to be a guest visitor. Using the criteria as their guide, students discussed how they could make their questions more powerful. Finally students selected powerful questions to ask of their guest, some of which are listed below:

Sample powerful questions
- Why did you fight in the war?
- Do you remember some of your friends from the war?
- Which countries did you fight over?
- Where did you live during the war?
- Were there any women in World War II? If so, what were their jobs?
- What started the fighting?
- Why was Canada involved?
- What was your safe place?

Needless to say the guest was greatly impressed with the quality of these young students' questions, aided in large measure by their consideration of the criteria of a powerful question.

This lesson was developed by Tami McDiarmid and is described in McDiarmid, Manzo & Musselle (1996).

CRITERIA	STANDARDS			
	excellent	competent	flawed	very poor
Focuses on the important goals	**6** The objectives of the assignment and the weighting of marks closely reflect a warranted sense of educational importance	**4** The objectives of the assignment and the weighting of marks are reasonable, but reveals some significant imbalance in importance	**2** The objectives of the assignment and the weighting of marks reveal significant imbalances in importance	**0** Virtually all important objectives are absent or seriously under-represented
Provides valid indications of student ability	**6** The assignment and the marking scheme address in a direct and highly revealing way student ability on all intended objectives	**4** The assignment and the marking scheme address in a fairly direct and revealing way student ability on important intended objectives	**2** The assignment and the marking scheme are unlikely to be revealing of student ability on key intended objectives	**0** Virtually all intended objectives are measured in a superficial, contrived or distorted manner
Supports student learning	**6** The instructions and feedback are extremely clear about the criteria and standards of student achievement/areas for improvement; holds significant potential to reinforce and encourage important student learning	**4** The instructions and feedback are generally clear about the criteria and standards of student achievement/areas for improvement; holds potential to reinforce and encourage student learning in some major areas	**2** The instructions and feedback contain significant gaps or ambiguities in communicating the criteria and standards of student achievement/areas for improvement; key aspects of the assessment fail to reinforce and encourage student learning	**0** The instructions and feedback offer no useful feedback about the criteria and standards, and may mislead; offers nothing to support, and may discourage, significant learning
Uses teacher time efficiently	**3** The assessment and feedback method is very efficient in use of teacher time and effort relative to significant learning it encourages	**2** The assessment and feedback method is somewhat efficient in its demands on teacher time and effort relative to the rewards	**1** The assessment and feedback method is quite inefficient in its demands on teacher time and effort	**0** The assessment and feedback method requires very extensive teacher time and effort for what it communicates

Outstanding (A+/A)	19 - 21	Satisfactory (C+/C)	8 - 11
Very Good (A-/B+)	16 - 18	Poor (C-/D)	5 - 7
Good (B/B-)	12 - 15	Very Poor (F)	0 - 4

Total	/21
Grade	_____

the purpose of an essay is to communicate and these features assist in that purpose);

- by being required by other more general educational or cultural expectations (e.g., essays should not contain foul language or should use established conventions for references and footnotes).

Students can also be involved in deciding upon standards—by articulating what might be required in order for the work to be regarded as excellent, good and so on.

Creating assessment tasks

Another way to involve students in assessment is by having them assist in developing the tasks by which they will be assessed. One of the most exciting examples of student-created assessment tasks was reported to me by Karen Barnett, a junior high humanities teacher in Sooke school district on Vancouver Island. Borrowing an idea from Bob Friend (a fellow Vancouver Island teacher) Karen has her students *create*, not simply answer, the end-of-unit exam questions. (See "Creating the Exam.")

Self- and peer-assessment

Involving students in self- and peer-assessment can greatly enhance their learning. The very exercise of assessing their peers on the specific criteria related to the lesson would likely reinforce students' own understandings of what is expected of them. Furthermore, involving students in assessment encourages students to take greater ownership of their learning.

However there is no point in involving students in self- and peer-assessment without ensuring that they will be well prepared and appropriately disposed to take on this significant responsibility. The following are suggestions for grooming students as self- and peer-assessors:

- Emphasize peer- and self-assessment as critique—seeing the positives, not just the negatives.

- Begin by critiquing the work of those not in the class, and before asking students to put their work on the line have the class critique something that you have done (e.g., an essay you wrote as a student, a class presentation that you made). When it is time for peer-critique, consider starting with group assignments so the responsibility is shared among several students.

- In the early days of peer critique do not allow negative comments—only allow remarks on positive features. A good indication of the time to make the transition to include concerns/weaknesses is when students start asking each other for what is "wrong" with their work.

- Model and set a few simple guidelines for giving peer-critique: perhaps insist that each student start with two (or more) positive comments before offering a (single) concern, and that negative comments be phrased in the form of a query (e.g., I'm not sure I understand why you did it this way. Could you help me see what you had in mind?).

CREATING THE EXAM

Students are assigned a chapter in the social studies textbook to read and asked to prepare six questions (and sample answers) for inclusion on the end-of-unit test. When framing their questions students are to consider criteria such as the following:

- must be clear so that fellow students will understand what is required;
- should address a non-trivial aspect of the content of the chapter;
- can be answered within a half page (or twenty minutes);
- must require more than mere recall of information.

The draft questions and sample answers are graded—the questions are assessed on how well the above-mentioned criteria for a good exam question are met, and the sample answers are assessed on the adequacy of the response. A short-list of student-generated questions are duplicated and handed out to the class well before the test. Students are informed that the exam would be drawn from these questions. Since the questions go beyond mere recall, studying for the test requires thinking about the questions posed. Karen insists that had she posed the very questions her students came up with, she would have been bombarded with complaints: "How do you expect us to know this? You never told us the answers to this." Instead, not only do students take seriously the assignment to create the questions—in some cases reading the textbook for the first time—they are more motivated to study for the test since the questions come from them. The following is Theo's uneditted set of questions on the English Revolution:

1. *Compare the ideas of Thomas Hobbes and John Locke on government?*
2. *Do you think Cromwell was correct in chopping off the king's head, and what advantage did government gain over royalty because of that?*
3. *What was the affect of the civil war on the monarchy and the peasants of the country.*
4. *If you were the king how would you handle the pressures of government and the people?*
5. *Compare the power of the government in the early 1600's to the power it has today.*
6. *What do you think would have happened if the people never rebeled against the king.*

- Ensure that the early instances of critique are low risk, relatively easy to perform and have an obvious benefit (e.g., bonus marks).
- Make sure students understand the criteria and the standards they are to use in assessing their work and the work of others. Rubrics are a very effective way in helping students recognize the assessment standards. Provide feedback to students about the quality of their assessment judgments.
- Until students have demonstrated the ability and commitment to assess conscientiously and fairly, do not use their assessments for awarding marks.
- Because teachers have the ethical and legal responsibility for assigning grades, reserve the right to veto any student-assigned mark that is clearly unwarranted.

Provide opportunities and incentives to improve

Where feasible teachers should use assessment to encourage students to learn on their own and to revise and rethink their work. Possible strategies include establishing a routine of re-assessing key course objectives in subsequent units, and making it clear to students that certain abilities will be assessed routinely. Offering supplemental tests or assignments for those students who make some effort to improve their understanding may also motivate students. Perhaps one of my most counter-productive assessment habits as an elementary teacher was my penchant for "one-shot" efforts. Rarely did I ask students to seriously revise their work—if work was revisited it was only to tidy up typos or add a missing sentence or two. Now, in my university teaching, I no longer have one-time assignments. In my graduate class, for example, students are expected to write three papers—in effect they write the same paper three times. The first and second draft are distributed to everyone in the class for critique. My impression is that the significant learning—the deeper, more insightful learning—occurs only after the first draft. In the first draft students show largely what they could do before the course, the subsequent revisions reveal what they have learned from the course.

Before inviting students to undertake serious revision we should ensure that they have meaningful input as to how they did initially and what they might do to improve. Since elementary and secondary students may be less motivated to engage in subsequent revisions than are students in graduate school, we must be imaginative in encouraging them in this regard:

- students might redo only a part of the original assignment, say the two worst (or preferred) answers, or the opening and closing paragraphs of an essay;
- a new, additional incentive could be added after the initial draft, for example the revised assignments might be exhibited in a fair, submitted to the newspaper, published in a book or otherwise shared with adults or other students;
- the initial mandatory draft might be commented upon but not marked, only the revised draft would "count" for marks;

- weeks or months after, students might be asked to revisit an earlier work to see how much they have progressed in the intervening time.

Using Teacher Time Efficiently

The final, perhaps one might say the bottom-line criterion of good assessment is efficient use of teacher time. Although efficiency has no direct relationship to authentic assessment, we know that the incredible press on teachers' time means that changes, however desirable, are unlikely to occur if they are more time consuming. Generally speaking, marking sheets, including the one I developed for the independent research project, are efficient assessment tools. Once familiar with the layout, it is easy to quickly complete the sheet because it keeps the assessor focussed and saves having to repeatedly write out the same comments. Rubrics are great savers of marking time, but they require considerable up-front development time. For this reason I am inclined to develop rubrics only for major projects during the year—starting with the one that causes the biggest marking headache.

Clearly articulated criteria and standards, communicated beforehand to students, increase the likelihood of students providing what the teacher is looking for, and help focus the teacher's attention when marking assignments. Clear expectations reduce the likelihood of protracted discussions with students who complain that they did not know what was required of them.

Peer- and self-assessment can save teacher time provided students are adequately trained in the practice. It saves time because it means that students are giving each other feedback that otherwise the teacher would have to give. Developing students' abilities to assess their own work and their peers' work may be one of the more efficient *instructional* strategies. In my university teaching, I marvel at how much graduate students learn about (and improve upon) their own writing from frequent opportunities to critique the work of fellow students. Not only are they better able to appraise their own writing after noting the same strengths and weaknesses in others' writing, but they also benefit considerably from critiques of their work because they have a richer context for making sense of others' comments. But perhaps the biggest efficiency arising from self-assessment comes from a shift in the perceived ownership of learning. When students truly realize that they, and not the teacher, have primary responsibility for the grade they get, the relationship between student and teacher changes. Students acquire more independence, self-reliance and, often, more commitment—and, not surprisingly, more is learned.

A Final Reflection

In closing, let us return to your initial assessment of my marking sheet. While reviewing any notes you took, consider the merits and oversights in your earlier thoughts about my device. Use the assessment rubric presented earlier to re-assess my marking sheet. What grade do you now judge that it is worth? Even if your assessment is largely unchanged, do you now have greater confidence in the grade you assigned? Is it a fairer, more valid assessment? Are you clearer about how you might help me improve my assessment practices? I hope the answer is yes to all these questions, and to one further question: Do you have a better understanding of principles to follow in making your assessment practices more authentic?

ENDNOTE
[1] The term *authentic assessment* is the emerging general label for a cluster of overlapping innovations, including notions such as "alternative assessment" (Maeroff, 1991), "whole assessment" (Nickell, 1992), "performance assessment" (Boykoff Baron, 1990, p. 127), "performance testing" (Boykoff Baron, 1989, p. 8), "performance-based assessment" (Boykoff Baron, Forgione & Rindone, 1991), "portfolio assessment" (Wolf, 1989) and "naturalistic assessment" (Reithaug, 1992).

REFERENCES

Boykoff Baron, J. (1989). *Whole assessment: Moving toward assessing thinking in situ.* Paper presented at the Second National Conference on Assessing Thinking, Baltimore.

Boykoff Baron, J. (1990). Performance assessment: Blurring the edges among assessment curriculum, and instruction. In A.B. Champagne, B.E. Lovitts, & B.J. Calinger (Eds.), *Assessment in the service of instruction* (pp. 127-148). Washington, DC: American Association for the Advancement of Science.

Boykoff Baron, J., Forgione, P.D. & Rindone, D. (1991, March). *Performance-based assessment at the state level: Developing and implementing high school mathematics and science assessments.* Paper presented at the American Educational Research Association Annual Meeting, Chicago.

Case, R. (1992). On the need to assess authentically. *Holistic Education Review, 5*(4), 14–23.

Goodlad, J.I. (1984). *A place called school.* New York: McGraw-Hill.

McDiarmid, T., Manzo, R. & Musselle, T. (1996). *Critical challenges for primary students.* Burnaby, BC: Field Relations, Faculty of Education, Simon Fraser University.

Maeroff, G.I. (1991). Assessing authentic assessment. *Phi Delta Kappan, 72,* 273–281.

Nickell, P. (1992). Doing the stuff of social studies: A conversation with Grant Wiggins. *Social Education, 56*(2), 91–94.

Reithaug, D. (1992). Naturalistic assessment: Capturing success in reading. *Research Forum, 9,* 46–50.

Wiggins, G. (1989). A true test: Toward more authentic and equitable assessment. *Phi Delta Kappan, 70,* 703–713.

Wolf, D.P. (1989). Portfolio assessment: Sampling student work. *Educational Leadership, 46*(7), 35–39.

— ✧ —

40

ASSESSMENT CRITERIA AND STANDARDS

ROLAND CASE

I n this article I explore a few key considerations in identifying and justifying the criteria and standards we use when assessing our students. Criteria refer to the qualities that we look for in student assignments and performances; standards specify the degree to which the criteria are present. Because they apply to all assessment, regardless of method, it is important to understand the nature and issues surrounding the effective use of criteria and standards.

IDENTIFYING AND JUSTIFYING CRITERIA

Inevitably when we assess we rely on criteria: if I announce that a particular movie was great, I will have some reason or reasons for this assessment. I might feel that the plot was exciting, or the cinematography was breathtaking or the actors were engaging. These reasons reveal the implicit criteria that I use as the bases for my assessment—whether or not features of the movie were exciting, breathtaking and engaging. When assessing student work it is important to be especially conscious of the criteria we use. Otherwise we may rely on a narrow and questionable set of considerations. The easiest criterion to assess is, of course, factual accuracy— Is the answer correct? Not surprisingly, this is the most common criterion for teacher assessment (Goodlad, 1984). The challenge in developing more authentic assessment practices is to base our assessments on a *relevant* and *comprehensive* set of *appropriately articulated* assessment criteria. These three considerations—relevant, comprehensive and appropriately articulated— are, in effect, the criteria for identifying and justifying assessment criteria. If we want our students to develop competence in setting their own assessment criteria, then we must help them learn to recognize when these three considerations are present. Without this understanding of what good assessment criteria looks like, student-generated criteria may often be irrelevant, incomplete and crudely stated.

Relevant criteria

The *relevance* of criteria depends largely on the purpose of the assignment. For the most part, the goals of the subject should direct what we look for when assessing students' work. In social studies it would not be relevant to evaluate a report or other piece of extended writing largely on the basis of grammar and punctuation. An emphasis on this set of assessment criteria is more appropriate in language arts or English composition because one of the *main* goals of these subjects, unlike in social studies, is mastery of the technical aspects of written expression. Rather, a piece of extended writing in social studies should focus (for the most part) on criteria that are centrally connected to the main goals of the subject, such as clarity of position, ability to use information to support a position, accuracy of information and depth of analysis. In the box on the next page are a sampling of criteria related to each of the main goals in social studies. On any individual assignment, the criteria should relate directly to the particular purpose or objectives for that assignment, which in turn should be connected to the more general goals of social studies.

Comprehensive set of criteria

The importance of a *comprehensive* set of criteria stems directly from the effects of a preoccupation with assessment on content knowledge—and even then on a narrow aspect of that, namely recall of facts. As the sample criteria for each goal suggests there are additional considerations within content knowledge (e.g., depth and clarity of understanding) and there are other goals that ought to be assessed (e.g., critical thinking, information gathering). A failure to address the full range of goals, in effect, discourages students from taking them seriously. Although any one assignment would not address the full range of criteria, over the span of a unit or a semester, criteria should be drawn from most goal areas.

Appropriate articulation

A final consideration in identifying and justifying assessment criteria is the need for appropriate articulation. Obviously students will be assisted in understanding both what is wanted of them and how well they have succeeded after completing their assignment if the bases for assessments are clearly specified. One factor in effective articulation is the number of criteria to specify for any given assignment. Obviously, younger students will be able to deal with fewer criteria than older students. But even with older students it may be counter-productive to have many criteria to consider at any one time. One way to avoid overburdening students with too many criteria is to frame them in broader, more general terms that subsume several specific criteria. For example, "effective presentation manner" may be used in lieu of specifying several more detailed criteria such as clarity of presentation, audibility of voice, correctness of posture and effective eye contact. However, if presentation were a major objective of the assignment, then it may be unwise to lump these more specific criteria under the broader heading.

Another issue surrounding articulation concerns the use of *descriptive* versus *qualitative* terms to specify criteria.

- **Descriptive criteria** specify the desired features in directly observable terms—in terms of immediately identifiable or quantifiable ingredients of the piece or performance. For example, descriptive criteria for assessing a paragraph may include: (a) have at least ten sentences, (b) open with a statement of position, (c) include at least three reasons in the body, (d) close with a summary statement and (e) provide a bibliography.

- **Qualitative criteria** specify the desired features in evaluative terms—in terms of attributes or qualities that are embodied in the constituents of the piece or performance. For example, qualitative criteria for assessing a paragraph may include: (a) the opening sentence *clearly* and *engagingly* states a position, (b) the body of the paragraph contains *well-supported*, *relevant* reasons for the position and (c) the closing sentence offers a *clear* and *powerful synthesis* of the position.

The advantage of articulating criteria in descriptive terms is that it is easier to recognize when these criteria

SAMPLE CRITERIA FOR EACH SOCIAL STUDIES GOAL	
Content knowledge	• Is the information *factually accurate*? • Do the answers reveal *depth of understanding*? • Did students *explain clearly in their own words* what the concept means?
Critical thinking	• Were students able to *offer a plausible reason* for their answer? • Were the reasons *well supported with evidence*? • Have students *anticipated counter-arguments* to their position?
Information gathering and reporting	• Are their research questions *focussed* and *clear*? • Have they identified the *main ideas* in a passage? • Is the oral presentation *thoughtfully structured* and presented in a *clear* and *engaging manner*?
Personal and social values	• Did students *apply themselves* to the task? • Were students *willing to take turns*? • Did students show *sensitivity to the feelings of others*?
Individual and collective action	• Were students *active listeners*? • Did students *attempt to reach consensus*? • Were the anticipated consequences of the proposed action *realistic*?

have been met—for example, we simply count the number of sentences and reasons, and look to see if the closing sentence offers a summary. Descriptive criteria are more appropriate when there is a single acceptable or preferred way to do something (e.g., in order to be able to confirm the sources used by an author, a report must contain a bibliography of some sort). The disadvantage of descriptive accounts is that they may not allow us to distinguish when the desired feature has been satisfied in a competent manner. For example, the three "reasons" provided may be largely irrelevant to the position taken, or the opening sentence may offer a very confusing position statement. Qualitative criteria, as the term suggests, would indicate the qualities that we want to see present in the reasons offered and in the opening sentence. The disadvantage with qualitative terms is we must make a judgment when deciding how well each criterion has been met. For example, what would count as a *clear* synthesis or a *well-supported* reason? With younger students and generally in the early stages of students' work with criteria, it may be appro-

priate to specify criteria largely in descriptive terms—simply expecting students to come up with three reasons (for that matter, even one reason) for their position. But over time, the infusion of qualitative criteria allow us to identify those qualities that we are most interested in promoting. After all, it is not just any three reasons that we seek, but three *well-supported* and *relevant* reasons.

A common strategy to help students generate assessment criteria is to ask what success on a particular task or assignment "looks like" and "sounds like." As suggested in the box on this page, students can be aided in making the transition from use of descriptive to qualitative criteria by adding a third question: "What are the underlying qualities that make these actions and words effective?"

The next challenge, that of deciding what counts as meeting the criteria, is essentially a matter of articulating the standards for each criterion. As we said earlier, standards specify the levels of achievement for criteria.

GENERATING CRITERIA

As a first step in generating criteria, students might brainstorm as a class what success on a task looks like and sounds like. In this example, the focus is on harmonious group work. These suggestions about looks and sounds (which typically identify descriptive criteria for a task) can be recorded in two columns as indicated below. Students might then be asked to look for the qualities underlying these sights and sounds. For example, what is really happening when students nod at each other or say "That's a good idea?" The underlying qualities identify the qualitative criteria for the task (e.g., students are supportive of each other). Finally, students might be asked to double-check their lists of criteria: Are all the suggestions relevant (e.g., it might have been suggested that the "look" of a harmonious group is everyone sitting down)? Are their lists comprehensive (i.e., have all the important features of harmonious group work been mentioned)? Is each criterion clearly stated (i.e., does everyone know what each means)?

HARMONIOUS GROUP WORK

Underlying qualities

are supportive/encouraging of each other
are interested in the ideas of others
are sensitive to each others' feelings

Looks like

students smile at each other
students look at each other
students nod to each other

Sounds like

"What do you think about this?"
"That's an interesting idea."
"Are you O.K.?"
"That's a good idea!"

This example was suggested by Tom Morton, a secondary school teacher in Vancouver.

ARTICULATING AND JUSTIFYING STANDARDS

The task of articulating standards is a matter of deciding the degree to which a criterion has been met. What would a "somewhat clear" position statement look like? How would this differ from a "very clear" position statement? Articulating standards is important for at least two reasons: their educational value and for grading purposes. Students may know that their report will be assessed on certain criteria, say that of clarity and organization, but it is another matter for them to appreciate what a very clear or moderately well-organized paragraph looks like. Standards tell students what is required to succeed (partially or completely) in meeting these criteria. The educational benefit of knowing this is obvious.

Articulating standards is also necessary if we are to translate performance on an assignment into a grade or other summative judgment. How good is 30 out of 35? Is it "outstanding," warranting an A or an A+? Or is it "very good," warranting a B or B+? Or, perhaps, some other grade? Teachers and students should have some idea of the basis for these performance levels. Which means we need to be clear about the standards we are using.

Articulating standards is especially important if we want to engage student in peer- and self-assessment. Making more explicit the bases for our assessments assists in changing students' mindsets from one of "What grade did you *give* me?" to one of "Where along this scale does my work fall?" If the standards are very well articulated and students are trained in making careful, fair-minded assessments of their work and that of their peers, the teacher's role in assessment becomes less prominent, relegated largely to checking the soundness of students' assessments.

Justifying standards

Judgment is inevitable in justifying standards. Standards, whether in the form of letter grades or in terms such as "excellent" and "poor," can be justified on either *norm-referenced* or *criterion-referenced* bases.

- **Norm-referenced standards** are determined by how well a particular product or performance matches against a "normal" or typical population (e.g., Would this be within the top 10% of the province? Is this an "average" performance for a grade six student? Would only about 30% of the class meet this level?). Norm-referenced judgments are based on the percentage of students likely to achieve each level. Notice, with norm-referenced standards if the class as a whole did very poorly a student's work could be "mediocre" and still be in the top 10%. Since norm-referenced standards are determined relative to other members of the comparison group, it is theoretically impossible for all students to get a top score.
- **Criterion-referenced standards** are determined by benchmarks that are not directly dependent of how well others in the population perform but on some

external reference (e.g., what would be needed in order to read the newspaper or to be understood by a stranger). Criterion-referenced judgments are based on what is necessary or appropriate to expect. With criterion-referenced standards it is theoretically possible that everyone achieves a high score.

Neither norm-referenced nor criterion-referenced standards should be arbitrary—there should be a reasonable basis for setting each level. Criterion-referenced standards may be justified in terms of what would likely be required in order to be employable, or to read and understand the newspaper or complete a task (e.g., by grade 10, students should be able to write a clear, well organized paragraph; after completing the unit, students should have mastered 80% or better of the content on this exam; by the end of secondary school, if they are to be functional citizens, students should be able to draw warranted inferences from newspaper articles). Norm-referenced standards may be justified in terms of a "normal" distribution of the population (e.g., the Bell curve—the top 10 percent get "A," the next 20 percent get "B," etc.) or a comparison with what an "excellent" or an "average" student had done in previous years.

There is no simple solution to arriving at justifiable standards. We should be sensitive to both norm-referenced and criterion-referenced considerations. There seems to be little merit in adopting a criterion-based standard that either no student could meet because it is too demanding or would challenge no one because it it too easy. We have to temper this standard with norm-referenced expectations. Conversely it seems counterproductive to decide beforehand on norm-referenced grounds that on a given assignment only 20 percent of students will be allowed to do "very well" and at least 20 percent must do "poorly." Rather, we should rely on our professional intuitions about what are fair and educationally productive expectations of achievement that grow out of norm- and criterion-referenced considerations. In justifying the standards articulated in the "thoughtful report" example appearing below, I adjusted my image of a truly masterful essay to accommodate the reasonably expected abilities of secondary students—I do not expect them to be able to challenge competing claims to the extent that I would graduate students. As well, in justifying the setting of this standard it would be appropriate to ask students about the fairness and reasonableness of my expectations.

Articulating standards

There is immense educational value in helping students recognize when their work meets or fails to meet certain standards. Learning simply that they did well, is not as helpful to students as is learning what "doing well" means, and what doing even better would involve. This requires that we describe what performance looks like at each level, or standard. The most common way of articulating standards is through use of an assessment *rubric* which is a marking scale describing the criteria and standards for an assignment or test. Two types of scales are used in rubrics:

- **Holistic scales** cluster criteria so that the description of standards for all criteria are aggregated—the assessor makes a global judgment about an assignment taking into consideration all of the criteria. The rubric at the bottom of this page offers a holistic scale for judging which one of five descriptions best characterizes the overall thoughtfulness of a report on a social issue students have analyzed.

- **Analytic scales** specify the standards for criteria separately, and the assessor makes judgments about the assignment on several criteria. The rubric on the following page is an analytic scale used to assess students' contributions to a group project on two criteria—contribution to the final product and contribution to the group dynamic.

An advantage of holistic scales is that we need make one judgment only. This often reduces the amount of teacher time involved in assessing student work. On the other hand, there may be a tendency for students to miss the forest through the trees—to strive directly for the individual criteria but fail to see the broader picture of successful performance. Analytic scales allow teachers to focus students' attention on particular aspects. Students may find it easier to begin with self assessment using analytic rubrics because they need only attend to one criteria at a time. Having said this, the difference between analytic and holistic scales may be more a matter of degree since specific criteria may be clustered into a more general category, thereby modifying an analytic scale so that it more closely resembles an holistic scale. The rubric on the following page is an example of a modified analytic scale. I have lumped more detailed criteria under two general categories—contribution to the final product and contribution to the group dynamic.

Rubrics may be more or less detailed in the descriptions of performance levels:

- **Fully articulated rubrics.** The most elaborate rubrics richly describe each level of performance. Both samples—Thoughtful Report and the Individual Contribution to the Group Project—are examples of "fully articulated" rubrics. These kinds of rubrics are deceptively difficult to develop, requiring numerous revisions before balanced and precise descriptions are produced. Unless the descriptions of standards are clear and mutually exclusive (i.e., no overlap between descriptors), the rubric is unreliable. Fully articulated rubrics may be well worth the effort, especially for major projects involving student self- and peer-assessment. The elaborate descriptions provide considerable guidance, clarity and consistency, which are especially needed if students are to responsibly adopt an assessors' role.

However, because they are difficult to produce, it may be wise to reserve use of fully articulated rubrics for regularly recurring assignments or major projects where the time required to develop the rubric will pay off in terms of enhanced student understanding and achievement.

HOLISTIC RUBRIC: THOUGHTFUL REPORT

Mark	Description of Report
4	**Accomplished and insightful.** The report clearly addresses the essential arguments in the pute. Discussion deals with the important matters with considerable insight and sensitivity. Personal opinions are well explained and supported with compelling examples and/or reasons.
3	**Competent and thoughtful.** The report addresses much of the essence of the dispute. Discussion deals with most of the important matters in a fairly thoughtful manner. Personal observations are generally supported with relevant examples and/or plausible reasons.
2	**Some thoughtfulness, but flawed.** The report is vague or confusing on key aspects of the pute. Discussion is frequently superficial, seeming to state the obvious or overlook basic points. Support or elaboration for personal opinions is very modest.
1	**Little or no thoughtfulness.** The report is very vague or misrepresents the main aspects of dispute. Discussion is confused and very superficial. Personal opinions show little or nor evidence of being thought through with care.
0	**Not done.** No report submitted.

ANALYTIC RUBRIC: INDIVIDUAL CONTRIBUTION TO GROUP PROJECT

Assess *each member* of your group and *yourself* on the basis of the following rubric. For each person, assess the contribution to the final product and to the group dynamic by indicating the box that best describes his/her actions within the group.

STANDARDS

CRITERIA	very poor	weak	competent	accomplished	outstanding
Contribution to the final product	Individual contributed no useful ideas and did little or no work;	Individual contributed very few productive ideas and did much less than his/her equal share of the work;	Individual contributed productive ideas and did his/her equal share of the work;	Individual regularly contributed productive and thoughtful ideas and was generous in the amount of work done for the project;	Individual regularly provided extremely productive and thoughtful ideas that profoundly shaped the project OR did far in excess of his/her share of the work;
	0	3	6	9	12
Contribution to group dynamic	Individual was a major and constant impediment to the friendly and efficient operation of the group;	Individual often seriously impeded the friendly and efficient operation of the group;	Individual may only occasionally have impeded the friendly and efficient operation of the group, and participated most of the time but was not a key factor in shaping the group dynamic;	Individual almost never impeded the friendly and efficient operation of the group and most of the time was a positive force in shaping the group dynamic;	Individual regularly made significantly empowering or nurturing contributions to the friendly and efficient operation of the group;
	0	2	4	6	8

GRADING SCALE			
Outstanding	17 - 20	Weak	5 - 8
Accomplished	14 - 16	Very Poor	0 - 4
Competent	9 - 13		

Total	/20
Grade	_____

- **Skeletal rubrics.** On a more regular basis it may be advisable to use less elaborate rubrics where the descriptions for each level are not articulated in detail. In most of these cases, standards will be delineated by using a single word or phrase for each level—"always," "often," "occasionally" and "rarely"—or a set of words or phrases at polar ends of a spectrum. Where possible, use words that clearly communicate the nature of the basis for distinguishing each level (e.g., quantity of correct answers, degree of clarity, extent criterion is present). In the skeletal rubric on the next page students might use standards describing the extent to which each criterion is present to self-assess their efforts during an independent project. Standards described in terms such as "excellent," "satisfactory" or "poor" which are very general evaluative terms may be less expressive of the differences between levels.

GUIDELINES FOR DEVELOPING FULLY ARTICULATED RUBRICS

- **Generating criteria.** Begin by brainstorming criteria for assessing the assignment for which the rubric is being developed.

- **Prioritizing criteria.** Select the most important and relevant criteria, justified in light of the main purposes for the assignment.

- **Consolidating criteria.** Cluster criteria around common themes. Consider rephrasing some criteria more generally to reduce the number of specific criteria. Make a provisional selection of a manageable number of criteria, organized into helpful categories (e.g., presentation, content, research).

- **Setting levels.** Decide on the number of performance levels or standards to specify. With younger students three levels may be most appropriate. More than five levels may be too difficulty to distinguish for any students. Besides it is always possible to assign a mark mid-way between two levels.

- **Draft polar descriptors.** Begin by describing the standards at the very top and the very bottom of the scale—What would the best performance look like? What would the worst level of performance look like? Decide whether the performance is better articulated in a single paragraph (making it a holistic scale) or whether, for ease of preparation and clarity, discrete descriptions are more useful (making it an analytic scale).

- **Draft intermediate descriptors.** Next try to describe the in-between standards. It may be helpful to look at existing rubrics for ideas on the kinds of words to use in distinguishing different gradations of performance. An advantage of using an odd number of performance levels (three or five levels) is that the intermediate levels can be distinguished by splitting the difference between the poles. For example, on a five-point scale, the third level would be mid-way between the descriptions of a "one" and a "five," and the second level would then be mid-way between the descriptions of a "one" and a "three." With an even number of levels it is necessary to divide the distance between the poles into equal intervals. For example, on a four-point scale, the second level is one-third of the distance between the descriptions of a "one" and a "four," and the third level is two-thirds the distance between a "one" and a "four."

- **Refine draft.** After developing an initial version of the rubric, check that the descriptors are *mutually exclusive* and *precise* and that the intervals between the levels are *approximately equivalent* (i.e., the amount of improvement between any two levels should be roughly the same). This step is the most demanding and frustrating since is often difficult finding precise words to distinguish each performance level for each criterion. Very subtle changes in wording may make all the difference between a reliable rubric and one that provides little guidance.

- **Finalize the performance levels.** Assign labels to each level and decide, in light of the relative importance of the criteria, the weight to be attached to each criterion. If appropriate, decide on the grade to be awarded for each range of marks by asking the following sorts of questions: "If a student received 15 out of 20 marks on this assignment what grade does this mark deserve?" "What about a 10 out of 20?" and so on. Translating a mark to a grade requires deciding whether to use criterion- or norm-referenced standards. Will it be based on what percentage of the class will be allowed to receive an A, B, C, etc. (hence norm-referenced), or is there an independent benchmark to which we can refer (hence criterion-referenced) or should it involve a balancing of both considerations?

- **Pilot the rubric.** Before using the rubric in an actual assessment situation try to score a sample of assignments to determine any unanticipated problems or flaws. If this is not feasible, at least share it with individuals who have not participated in developing the rubric and ask for their critical feedback (e.g., Based on the descriptions would you know what "good" or "fair" required? Does the weighting of marks seem reasonable? Are the levels clearly distinguished?).

Skeletal Rubric: Assessing Independent Learning

	definitely not true	partly true	mostly true	most definitely true
I stayed "on-task" until all my work was finished				
I thought carefully about what I was expected to do				
I asked for help whenever I needed it				
I tried to help other students when they needed help				
I tried my best				
I have done a very good job				

Concluding Comment

There are, of course, many other factors to consider and issues to explore in learning to use assessment criteria and standards to support student learning. As well, there are many practical hurdles to overcome as we open up the "black box" of assessment. In my own teaching I continue to experiment—often with mixed success—with the use of student-developed rubrics and with peer- and self-assessment. Despite the difficulties, I am convinced of the importance, for educational and ethical reasons, of students clearly understanding the basis for assessments of their work. I am no longer satisfied when my reliance on vague criteria and unarticulated standards when assessing my students. Discussions about assessment criteria and standards have been a focal point for probing examination by me and my students about what it is they need to learn. Being crystal clear as to what is involved in truly successful achievement of a task has improved both teaching and learning in my classes.

References

Goodlad, J.I. (1984). *A place called school.* New York: McGraw-Hill.

41

ASSESSMENT METHODS

ROLAND CASE

In this article I explore five general methods for assessing social studies outcomes. These methods are the traditional short-answer and extended-answer questions, and three forms of "alternative" assessment—performance assessment, portfolios and naturalistic assessment. My focus is on learning to develop methods that support the four principles that I discussed in a previous article, "Principles of Authentic Assessment." These principles which I believe ought to guide our assessment practices are:

- Focus assessment on what really matters.
- Assessments must provide valid indications of student competence.
- Use assessment to encourage student learning.
- Assessment practices must use teachers' time efficiently.

SHORT-ANSWER QUESTIONS

Short-answer questions refer to closed-ended questions such as multiple choice, true or false, labeling and matching columns as well as open-ended questions that can be answered in a few words or sentences. These are very common assessment formats because of their ease both in student completion and in teacher marking. Although there is much that could be said about developing these kinds of question formats, I want to make two points only:

- short-answer questions can assess beyond mere recall of information;
- when using short answer questions we must be careful about validity.

Assessing beyond recall

A common criticism of multiple choice and other short-answer questions is that they are used almost exclusively to assess recall of information. This need not be so, they can be used to assess depth of understanding, critical thinking, social and personal attitudes and other social studies goals. Certainly, there are limits to what short-answer questions can assess. For example, because of their format, multiple choice questions can only measure students' abilities to select correctly from a set of supplied answers. Also, multiple choice questions reduce complex learning outcomes to atomistic units, whereas we may be concerned with students' abilities to integrate what they know in realistic situations. While these limitations provide powerful reasons for using "alternative" measures, there is a role for multiple choice assessment beyond the measure of information recall. For instance, open-ended short-answer questions can be used to assess student reflection by inviting students to revisit initial ideas or opinions af-

SUBSEQUENT REFLECTION QUESTIONS

Cuthbert: Hero or Scoundrel?

After reading the story, *It's So Nice to Have a Wolf Around the House* by Henry Allard (1977), students are asked to decide whether the main character in the story, Cuthbert Q. Devine, is a hero or a scoundrel. In groups, students then explore more carefully the evidence in the story for each option. Based on these further deliberations students reconsider their initial assessment of Cuthbert.

Second thoughts about Cuthbert

My first opinion was that Cuthbert was a   ❑ hero   because . . .
                                             ❑ scoundrel

_____

_____

I have   ❑ changed   my opinion of Cuthbert because . . .
          ❑ NOT changed

_____

_____

This assessment activity is described in McDiarmid, Manzo and Musselle (1996, pp. 27-29).

Democracy in Canada

Pre-unit questions

Before we begin our unit on democracy in Canada consider the following questions:

1. If you were about to vote for a federal politician, what issues should you consider?

2. Make a list of the various ways that people can participate in the political decision-making process. Which one or two ways do you think are more effective and why do you think they are more effective than other ways?

3. Do you think that *you* have a responsibility to participate actively in the political decision making process? Explain the reasons for your answer.

End-of-unit reflections

At the start of the unit you were asked about your opinions on three topics. Your answers to those questions are being returned to you. Please reread each question and your response. Consider two things:

• additional comments to further support or clarify your initial remarks;

• changes in your initial opinions and the reasons for those changes.

Write any additions or changes to each of your initial responses in the spaces provided below—do NOT write anything on the pre-unit sheet.

1. _____

_____

_____

2. _____

_____

_____

3. _____

_____

_____

ter they have had a chance to study and think more about the matter. Responses can be marked by assessing post responses in terms of the accuracy of their answers, the insightfulness of their reflections and their open-mindedness. In the box on the previous page are two "subsequent reflection" questions: pre- and post-lesson reflections for primary students on a character in a story, and a pre- and post-unit reflections for upper elementary and secondary students on democracy in Canada.

As the examples in the box below illustrate, short-answer questions can also be used to gather information about personal and social attitudes. Although we may not want to assign marks for attitudes it may be important to provide students and parents with feedback about student attitudes on matters related to the curriculum. The questions in the first example focus on open-mindedness. The second example was developed by Margaret Chapman, a British Columbia primary teacher, to assess her children's empathy for people in other countries. Before and after studying the needs of people in Chile, Margaret read the questions to her grade one students and they circled the appropriate face depending on whether they agreed (the "happy face"), were not sure (the "so-so face") or disagreed (the "sad face") with each statement.

Watching for validity

In using short-answer questions we may be mislead into thinking that we are measuring something that we are not. It is important to be vigilant in checking that the things we think we are measuring are the things we actually measure.

A common oversight with short answer questions is that of presuming to assess students' *understanding* of a concept by asking students to offer a definition of the word. Understanding a concept is a much broader notion than knowing the definition. For example, understanding 'equality' requires understanding that treating people equally does not always mean treating every one exactly the same (e.g., providing equal opportunity to a blind person requires treating them differently in some respects from a sighted person). This notion that 'equal' does not necessarily mean 'same' explains why affirmative action (i.e., giving preferential treatment to people who have historically been discriminated against) is often justified in terms of equality: certain groups need special treatment to compensate for the social barriers put in their place. Assessing conceptual understanding requires more than asking for a definition that students may have memorized. Students need to provide fresh examples of the concept or explain why certain situations are not ex-

---

ASSESSING ATTITUDES

Open-Mindedness

EACH OF US SHOULD	strongly agree				strongly disagree
1. Be open to changing our minds when new reasons are presented	1	2	3	4	5
2. Have very clear, very firm opinions on most issues	1	2	3	4	5
3. Believe that there is always one answer that is better than all of the other possible answers	1	2	3	4	5
4. Believe that there may be more than one acceptable position on most issues	1	2	3	4	5
5. Consider what those who disagree with us would say	1	2	3	4	5
6. Often question matters that many people accept	1	2	3	4	5
7. Often question our own reasons and motives	1	2	3	4	5

Empathy

1. I want all my friends to be like me

2. We should help other, poorer countries even if it means we have to give up some things

3. I like learning about people who live in other countries

4. It is only important to me what happens to people I know

amples of the concept. In the case of 'equality,' a more valid strategy would be to set the following task: "Give a definition of 'equality' and explain why affirmative action, but not 'the old boys' network, is an example of concern for equality." Analogously when assessing younger children's understanding of the concept of 'community,' we might ask them to explain whether or not a beehive is an example of a 'community.'

EXTENDED-ANSWER QUESTIONS

The use of extended-answer questions such as essays, reports and position papers is another common assessment method. They are generally a more holistic measure of learning than short-answer questions. There are, however, several limitations. They are heavily dependent on students' writing fluency, students may be overwhelmed by the demands of a large writing project and they are time-consuming to mark. For these reasons it is worth reconsidering whether or not the traditional research report merits the prominence it has in some social studies classes. Personally, as a secondary student I remember disliking most reports I had to write and, generally speaking, I transcribed ideas with little alteration and limited understanding straight from reference books. I would have welcomed and benefited from many of the suggestions contained in Penney Clark's article, "Escaping the Typical Report Trap." But even then, I might have learned from smaller, less daunting, assignments that placed greater emphasis on multiple revisions of my writing. Certainly I would have put more effort into my reports if I had been engaged by the topics and had been expected to think for myself about ideas more than merely assemble what others had said.

The merits of any given extended-answer assessment depend on the quality of the question or task. At the very least this requires providing students with explicit, unambiguous directions on assignments and tests. For example, the question "Research and defend your personal position on mandatory supervision" could be made to focus more clearly on thinking critically about the ideas (rather than rehashing undigested arguments found in books) if the question stated:

Defend your personal position on mandatory supervision by:

1) explaining in your own words what mandatory supervision refers to;

2) identifying and explaining the major reasons that proponents of mandatory supervision offer in support of their position;

3) identifying and explaining the major reasons that opponents of mandatory supervision offer in support of their position; and

4) justifying your position by arguing why the reasons for are more compelling than the reasons against your position.

When framing essay questions we should not assume that there are generic formats that invite critical thinking. For example, asking students to *evaluate* the justification for Canada's immigration policy may not necessarily assess critical thinking. The validity of this question as a measure of critical thinking depends on what students were taught during the unit. If students studied the pros and cons of immigration, then the question may be largely one of regurgitation of previously presented material. Alternatively, if students had not had any instruction and practice in identifying appropriate criteria for evaluating legal policies and had no way of knowing the reasons that might be offered for or against immigration, it is questionable whether they are engaging seriously in critical thinking. Without some grounding in the appropriate considerations, student answers are more likely to be instances of guesswork or naive reactions. A more valid examination question that assesses students' ability to think critically about an issue is suggested below.

DEFEND YOUR POSITION

The following are four arguments commonly offered in support of increased immigration policy and four arguments commonly offered in opposition to this policy.

Pro	*Con*
• many immigrants may be in desperate economic need;	• increased immigration puts too great a burden on our medicare, welfare and education systems;
• many immigrants may need protection from war and political prosecution;	• increased immigration discourages integration of ethnic groups into mainstream society;
• many immigrants bring talents and human resources that benefit Canada;	• increased immigration fuels racial/ethnic tensions in Canada;
• immigrants provide a pool of workers to fill low paid jobs that may otherwise go unfilled;	• immigrants take jobs which people who are already here need and want.

All things considered where do you stand on the issue of increased immigration to Canada? Defend your answer with specific reference and critical analysis of the arguments above. Justify why your position is more defensible than opposing positions.

PERFORMANCE ASSESSMENT

A newly-emphasized alternative approach to assessment, referred to as performance assessment, focusses on students' completing realistic tasks that a person would typically face as a citizen, writer, businessperson, scientist, community leader, historian and so on. These tasks may involve performing a feat or developing a product:

performing a feat

- perform a dramatic scene of an historical event,
- hold a formal parliamentary debate on a controversial piece of legislation,
- teach fellow students about family traditions,
- organize and run a school fund-raising event,
- conduct a trial around an historical incident,
- adjudicate between nominees for an award,
- make a presentation to city council on a proposed change to local laws,

developing a product

- build a model logging site or ancient village,
- make a film about promoting racial harmony,
- create a set of exam questions and sample answers for an end-of-unit test,
- prepare a "consultant's report" on a local pollution problem,
- develop a foreign-language script for a radio play,
- create "museum" displays depicting local history,
- create a web page on the history of the school,
- publish a (contemporary or historical) class newspaper or journal.

Because they typically involve realistic tasks, performance assessments are more likely than traditional methods to measure students' ability to apply a complex set of "real-life" abilities and understandings. The emphasis in performance tasks is on knowledge-in-use, as opposed to regurgitation of "school" knowledge. Also important is their potential as a learning opportunity and not exclusively as an assessment tool: the working through of the tasks should enhance—not simply measure—student understanding. A performance task to plan a summer vacation (described in Heckley Kon & Martin-Kniep, 1992) illustrates these features. In this assessment, pairs of students are given a map of California and a list of state parks with camping facilities, and asked to plan the details of a family camping trip from the San Francisco area to any state camping facility in northern California. Students must measure distances, calculate traveling time, describe particulars of the travel route, and develop a contingency plan in the event of a strike by workers on the Golden Gate and Bay bridges. As well, they have to negotiate with their partner the destination and route that best accommodate the interests of family members.

As this example suggests performance assessments can be engaging. Some students do poorly on evaluations because they are unmotivated. The perceived irrelevance and drudgery of, for example, an extended written report may discourage some students from trying to do well. If we want to assess what students are *capable* of doing, it is only fair that we provide opportunities where students are likely to want to do well.

Because performance tasks are complex, they provide opportunities to assess a variety of outcomes using many assessments strategies, including:

- interview students about their experiences during the project and about their conclusions;
- analyze students' preparatory materials for quality of research;
- analyze group discussions for thoughtfulness in preparing products and in justifying decisions;
- assess students' written or oral reports for quality of language use and presentation, and for content knowledge;
- score classroom discussions or debates for evidence of students' ability engage in respectful dialogue.

Key features in developing performance assessments are choosing the task, setting the context and providing appropriate direction. A performance task should allow students to integrate what they have been studying into a culminating performance or product. It is unfair to assess students on matters that they have not been working with during the term—the novel dimension of the performance assessment is the need to draw together various elements they have studied in order to solve a realistic problem. Setting a realistic context for the task provides a rich opportunity for students to think through their options. Students also require appropriate direction about the nature and requirements of the task. The sample performance assessment described on the two pages which follow involves adjudicating political cartoons about Canada-American relations. It provides students with extensive direction about factors to consider and suggestions for proceeding. The main outcomes addressed by this task, as well as some of the more specific criteria, include:

knowledge of American-Canadian relations

- accuracy of knowledge of key events and issues;
- breadth of knowledge of key events and issues;

ability to think critically

- thoroughness of analysis of the cartoons;
- ability to judge merit in light of criteria;
- adequacy of support for conclusions;
- fair-minded assessment of each cartoon's strengths and weaknesses;

understanding of visual representation

- knowledge of cartooning techniques;

ability to communicate ideas orally

- sensitivity to audience (including the candidates for the award);
- clarity of presentation;
- ability to organize an oral presentation.

JUDGING CARTOONS

The task

You have been asked by a local media organization to determine which of two cartoons deserves an award for the better political cartoon on American-Canadian relations. You are expected to announce and justify your decision in a five-minute oral adjudication to a public audience which may include the creators of the cartoons.

What to consider

You must judge the *form* of the cartoon (i.e., as an example of a *genre* of communication) and the *content* or message presented. In making your decision, consider the following techniques of cartooning:

- captions;
- relative size;
- use of light and dark (shading);
- lines;
- composition or arrangement;
- symbolism;
- caricature (distortion/exaggeration/stereotyping).

The cartoons should be judged on various criteria, including the following (Add other criteria, if desired):

- immediate impact (i.e., "gut response" to the cartoon);
- originality or freshness of the techniques;
- clarity of the message;
- importance of message;
- ironic, satiric or humorous effect.

Suggestions for proceeding

To assist in reaching your decision, the following approach is suggested:

1. Familiarize yourself with each cartoon—decide what each is saying and how the specifics of each cartoon fit into the whole.

2. Use the following chart to list elements of each cartoon that pertain to the criteria provided. Circle the number which best represents your judgment for each criterion.

	Cartoon #1					Cartoon #2				
	very strong				very weak	very strong				very weak
immediate impact	2	1	0	-1	-2	2	1	0	-1	-2
originality or freshness	2	1	0	-1	-2	2	1	0	-1	-2
clarity	2	1	0	-1	-2	2	1	0	-1	-2
reveals important aspect	2	1	0	-1	-2	2	1	0	-1	-2
ironic, satiric or humorous effect	2	1	0	-1	-2	2	1	0	-1	-2
other criteria (if applicable)	2	1	0	-1	-2	2	1	0	-1	-2
SCORE										

3. Calculate the score for each cartoon and consider which are the most significant positive and negative features of each cartoon. On the basis of this assessment, decide which is the better cartoon.

4. In preparing your presentation, do not ridicule anyone's efforts, but do concentrate on explaining why your selection meets the criteria of cartooning better than does the other one.

JUDGING CARTOONS

(CONT'D)

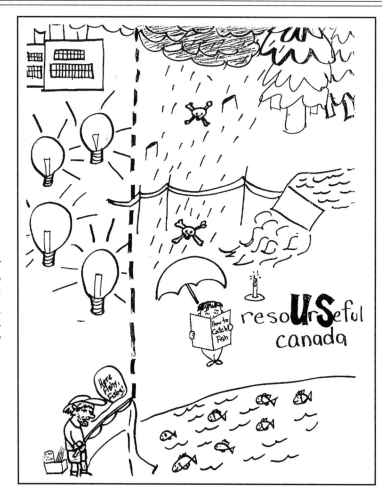

► Cartoon created by
Cindy Frasier and
Kathi Dickie-Bell,
pre-service teachers at
Simon Fraser University

▼ Cartoon created by
Erika Walsh and
Cindy Rogers,
pre-service teachers at
Simon Fraser University

SUGGESTIONS FOR DEVELOPING PERFORMANCE ASSESSMENTS

- Identify the important outcomes for a unit or course.

- Think of "real-life" feats or products that, if completed successfully, would represent exemplary achievement of several of these outcomes.

- Determine more precisely the details of the performance assessment, including:
  - the realistic nature and the context of each task;
  - the amount of direction to provide students regarding what they need to consider to complete the task and how they might proceed.

- Orally or in writing provide students with a clear articulation of the requirements and parameters of the task.

- Consider what students must know in order to successfully complete the task. Ensure that there has been sufficient prior instruction to allow students a reasonable chance of competently undertaking the task. Assessment tasks can be made easier by providing detailed direction or additional instruction.

- For each of the desired outcomes that the performance assessment addresses, determine the criteria to be used in assessing students' feats or products. Share the criteria with students prior to their completing the task.

- Determine how information about the criteria will be collected (e.g., through observation, conferencing, analysis of written products). Where appropriate devise rubrics, checklists or other making sheets.

- After using the performance assessment consider how it may be improved for next time. Asking students for their comments may be helpful in this regard.

PORTFOLIO ASSESSMENT

A second form of alternative assessment involves students in compiling a collection or portfolio of work they have completed over a period of time. Portfolio assessment draws heavily on the practices of artists and designers, who carefully assemble samples that represent key characteristics of their work for use in demonstrating to others particular competencies. Assessment portfolios are characterized in a similar vein, as "a purposeful collection of student work that exhibits the student's efforts, progress, and achievements in one or more areas" (Paulson, Paulson & Meyer, 1991, p. 60).

Because portfolios are based on cross-sections of student work completed over time, they offer a richer portrait of a wider range of student achievements than, say, a single end-of-unit test. Also, unlike traditional forms of assessment, where assignments are marked and then forgotten, portfolios encourage both teacher and students to monitor growth over time. Typically, students are involved to varying degrees in selecting, analyzing, assessing and reporting on the products that make up their portfolio. This involvement often results in significantly greater personal ownership of their learning. These benefits are particularly likely when portfolios are used as the focus for conferences where students explain to their parents or teacher what the portfolios show about their progress and levels of achievement. In fact, it has been suggested that portfolios be seen primarily as "a reason for talking" (Murphy & Smith, 1990, p. 1)—that is, the collection of products is essentially a means to engage students, teachers and parents in informed dialogue about learning.

There are five phases in a portfolio assessment.

- **Accumulation of products**. At the beginning of the term when portfolios are to be used, procedures should be in place for collecting and storing all student work. The date when work is completed should be indicated on every assignment. If it is decided beforehand that a specific set of outcomes is to be the theme for the portfolio, then there should be varied opportunities during the term for students to produce work in these areas. The range of materials produced by a student over a unit, term or year may include the following:

- annotated bibliographies of books/documents
- artwork (preliminary sketches and final products)
- audio tapes
- book reports
- charts and graphs
- drawings
- essays (drafts and final copies)
- evaluations of self and peers
- group reports
- interview results
- journals or diaries
- maps
- notes (classroom, laboratory or field)
- peer evaluations
- photographs of projects, models, displays or murals
- reading inventories

- tests and quizzes
- videotapes of presentations, debates, interviews or simulations
- worksheets.

- **Selection of portfolio pieces.** From the total array of products, a sampling is to be selected for inclusion in a portfolio. Near the end of a unit, discuss with students how they are to select those work samples. A range of student discretion is possible in selecting portfolio contents: students may be given very precise instructions about what to include and why, or they may be allowed to select on any basis that they desire. The selected products may represent the student's best efforts, or be indicative of typical performance. They may focus on a particular theme such as growth as a critical thinker, development of a global perspective or appreciation of culture. It may be important to limit the *number* of pieces to include in a portfolio, as thoughtful analysis becomes unwieldy if there are too many pieces to examine. A summary or checklist (possibly a table of contents) may be helpful.

- **Reflection.** Alone or in collaboration with peers, each student reviews the portfolio contents as a vehicle for assessing achievement or progress over the term. These reflections might involve identifying criteria and standards, analyzing patterns or key features, diagnosing strengths and problem areas, and setting personal plans and targets. Providing samples of other students' work at various performance levels may assist students in assessing their own work.

- **Reporting.** Students should be expected to report (orally or in writing) on what they observe about their learning and to recommend a plan of action.

Student-led conferences with the teacher, and often with parents, are common ways of student reporting. Alternatively, students might prepare audiotaped analyses of their portfolios. It may be helpful for students to prepare and practice their oral reports with fellow students. For young students the reporting might be a simple as the example at the bottom of the page.

- **Feedback.** Feedback from the teacher (and parents) may occur on two fronts: (1) on student achievement or progress over the term as evidenced in the portfolio and (2) on the quality of student analysis and reporting, since the portfolio is itself a product representing students' capacity for critical self-assessment and personal accountability. For young students the feedback might be a simple as "two stars and a wish"—noting two positive aspects and an area for improvement.

Portfolio creator _____

Two stars:

★ _____

_____

★ _____

One wish:

☞ _____

PORTFOLIO REPORT

The topic for my portfolio is:

_____

The two pieces I selected that show my learning are:

1. _____
2. _____

Things I did well	Things I might improve upon
1. _____	_____
_____	_____
2. _____	_____
_____	_____

My plan for next time is _____

_____

NATURALISTIC ASSESSMENT

A third form of alternative assessment refers to assessment occurring during the normal course of classroom activities—as opposed to during completion of specially set performances or as a result of specially compiled student portfolios. Naturalistic assessment, which draws heavily from anthropological methodologies, involves the teacher as a participant-observer—collecting information about student learning while engaged in the normal duties of teaching. In some respects, teachers are involved in naturalistic assessment every time they confirm that students have understood a lesson, or check to see which students have done their work, or ask students to explain any trouble they are having. The differences between these *ad hoc* assessment strategies and naturalistic assessment are the extent to which they rely on systematic data and whether or not records are kept for use in student grading.

Naturalistic assessment is seen to be particularly appropriate for assessing student abilities and attitudes not measured by traditional pen-and-paper assignments or by isolated assessment tasks. In addition, as with student portfolios, the extended basis of naturalistic assessment is more likely than one-shot tests to provide rich accounts of student learning and insightful indications of factors that may influence learning. Naturalistic assessment makes use of various information-gathering strategies:

• making regular anecdotal "field notes" about significant comments or incidents—for example, by noting the strategies that a particular student uses to solve a problem, or by watching over several months for indications of students' growth in self-esteem or attitudes towards school work;

• using student-teacher conferences as a means of gathering information about students while helping them learn;

• systematically observing through use of checklists or other devices the incidence of particular behaviour—such as completion of work, the number of books read, the frequency of students' cooperative participation in group assignments. The checklist below records students' ability to use various aids to locate information.

Often, like the anthropologist, the teacher will seek to "triangulate" evidence, using several sources of information to corroborate judgments about students. For example, in drawing conclusions about students' critical thinking abilities, a teacher may use information obtained from peer- and self-assessment of students' willingness to entertain alternative opinions, analyses of selected products for the quality of reasoning and suggestive anecdotal comments about attitudes toward "thinking things through."

A promising and important trend is to involve students more actively in naturalistic assessment—monitoring and reflecting upon their learning as they work. The assessment device on the following page is an example of naturalistic assessment for use by students (although, the device could be used by teachers). The focus is on peer-assessment of thoughtful habits of mind during cooperative group work.

LOCATING INFORMATION CHECKLIST

Uses information locating aids:	Students									
	Saul	Pam	Chan	Naim						
locate section in table of contents	/	0	✓	✓						
locate page in index	✓	0	✓	✓						
find word in glossary	✓	/	✓	✓						
find word in dictionary	✓	/	✓	✓						
skim paragraph to locate information										
use headings to locate information	0	/	✓	✓						

Uses information locating aids:
0 = not at all
/ = somewhat
✓ = adeptly

COOPERATIVE DECISION-MAKING

Your name: _____   Group member's name: _____

1. For each criterion listed below, circle the number which most accurately reflects each person's behaviour while carrying out the project.

2. Wherever possible, describe an actual situation or identify a typical behaviour that is supporting evidence for your assessment.

3. Use a separate sheet for each person. Do not show or discuss your assessment with anyone else.

	rarely or never in evidence		in evidence about half the time		consistently in evidence	not enough information to decide
1. *Willingness to reconsider position*	1	2	3	4	5	NEI

Supporting evidence _____

_____

_____

2. *Willingness to defend personal opinion*	1	2	3	4	5	NEI

Supporting evidence _____

_____

_____

3. *Respectful of persons who disagree*	1	2	3	4	5	NEI

Supporting evidence _____

_____

_____

4. *Challenges in responsible ways*	1	2	3	4	5	NEI

Supporting evidence _____

_____

_____

5. *Works towards establishing consensus*	1	2	3	4	5	NEI

Supporting evidence _____

_____

_____

6. *Accepts disappointment graciously*	1	2	3	4	5	NEI

Supporting evidence _____

_____

_____

CONCLUDING COMMENT

By no means has this discussion of assessment methods been exhaustive. There are many other matters to consider and other approaches to be explored. I have tried to suggest some of the issues and strategies that deserve careful and imaginative consideration when developing assessment tools consistent with the principles of authentic assessment. By embodying these principles in our assessment practices through methods such as those suggested in this article, we will be meeting our professional responsibility to assess students in a valid and fair manner that richly supports their learning.

REFERENCES

Allard, H. (1977). *It's so nice to have a wolf around the house.* (Illustrated by J. Marshall). Garden City, NY:

Heckley Kon, J. & Martin-Kniep, G. (1992). Students' geographic knowledge and skills in different kinds of tests: Multiple choice versus performance assessment. *Social Education, 56*(2), 95–98.

McDiarmid, T., Manzo, R. & Musselle, T. (1996). *Critical challenges for primary students.* Burnaby, BC: Field Relations, Faculty of Education, Simon Fraser University.

Murphy, S. & Smith, M.A. (1990). Talking about portfolios. *The Quarterly, 12*(2), 1–3, 24–27.

Paulson, F.L., Paulson P.R. & Meyer, C.A. (1991). What makes a portfolio a portfolio? *Educational Leadership, 48*(5), 60–63.

ABOUT THE AUTHORS

Tony Arruda is a secondary school social studies teacher who is currently completing his doctorate in the Department of Educational Studies, University of British Columbia. He used oral history in both his magistral and doctoral work. His 1992 Master's thesis is entitled *Growing Up in Portuguese Canadian Families*.

Roland Case is an Associate Professor in the Faculty of Education, Simon Fraser University. His books include *Thinking About Law: An Issues Approach* (IPI Publishing) and *Understanding Judicial Reasoning: Concepts, Controversies and Cases* (Thompson). He is co-editor of the *Critical Challenges Across the Curriculum* series (TC²/SFU).

Charles Chamberlin is a Professor Emeritus, Department of Elementary Education, University of Alberta. Although no longer teaching, he continues his interest in social activism.

Penney Clark is a recent recipient of a doctorate from the University of British Columbia. She has taught social studies curriculum and instruction courses at the University of Alberta, the University of British Columbia and Simon Fraser University. She is co-author of *Canada Revisited: A Social and Political History of Canada to 1911* (Arnold).

Bob Davis is a secondary school social studies teacher in Toronto, Ontario. He recently published *Whatever Happened to High School History? Burying the Political Memory of Youth Ontario: 1945-1995* (James Lorimer).

Heather Devine, at the time of writing, was a Public Education Officer with the Archaeological Survey of Alberta, Government of Alberta

Harry Dhand is a Professor in Curriculum Studies at the College of Education, University of Saskatchewan. He is a frequent contributor to *Canadian Social Studies*.

Kieran Egan is a Professor in the Faculty of Education, Simon Fraser University. His publications include *Educational Development* (Oxford), *Primary Understanding: Education in Early Childhood* (Routledge) and *The Educated Mind: How Cognitive Tools Shape Our Understanding* (University of Chicago Press).

Margaret Ferguson is currently a teacher-on-call in Quesnel, British Columbia. She has a law degree from the University of Alberta. She held the position of School Reorganizing Coordinator for the Legal Resource Centre, Faculty of Extension, University of Alberta for thirteen years, and has published numerous articles on law-related education.

John Friesen was a Professor in the Department of Educational Policy and Administrative Studies, University of Calgary, at the time of writing.

Susan Elaine Gibson is an Assistant Professor in the Department of Elementary Education, the University of Alberta. Her area of specialization is social studies curriculum and instruction. Recently she was guest editor of a theme issue of *Canadian Social Studies* on women's issues in social studies. She has published in *Journal of Technology and Teacher Education* and *School Libraries Worldwide*.

Larry Glassford is an Assistant Professor at the University of Windsor. He is author of *Reaction & Reform: The Politics of the Conservative Party Under R.B. Bennett, 1927-1938* (University of Toronto Press).

Susan Hargraves is a secondary school social studies teacher in Victoria, British Columbia. She has been involved in the design and development of several curriculum projects dealing with social justice issues.

Todd Horton is a former secondary school social studies teacher who taught in elementary and secondary schools in Frederiction, New Brunswick. He is currently completing his doctorate in the Department of Curriculum Studies, University of British Columbia.

Michael Ling is from Ottawa and is currently completing his doctorate in the Faculty of Education, Simon Fraser University. His particular area of interest is the influence of popular culture on young people.

Milton McClaren is a Professor in the Faculty of Education, Simon Fraser University. He is co-author of *A Thematic Guide to Learning About Global Change* (Royal Society of Canada) and *Connections* (Ginn).

Roberta McKay is an Associate Professor in the Department of Elementary Education, University of Alberta. She is a recent recipient of the Rutherford Award for Excellence in Undergraduate Teaching. She is co-author of the secondary social studies textbook, *Canada Revisited: A Social and Political History of Canada to 1911* (Arnold).

Dennis Milburn was a Professor in the Faculty of Education, University of British Columbia. His particular interests were geography and early childhood education. His article is published here posthumously.

Tom Morton is a secondary school social studies teacher in Vancouver, British Columbia, who makes extensive use of cooperative learning in his classroom. He is author of *Cooperative Learning & Social Studies: Towards Excellence & Equity* (Kagan).

Ken Osborne is a Professor Emeritus, University of Manitoba. He recently received the Prix Manitoba Award for Heritage Education from the provincial Ministry of Culture, Heritage and Citizenship. He is author of *In Defence of History: Teaching the Past and the Meaning of Democratic Citizenship* (Our Schools/Our Selves).

Jim Parsons is an Associate Professor in the Department of Secondary Education, University of Alberta. He is author of *What Works: Ideas to Teach By* (Les Editions Duval) and co-author of *Playing with Language* (Les Editions Duval).

Alan Sears is an Associate Professor in the Department of Curriculum and Instruction, University of New Brunswick. His primary interest is citizenship education and he is the author of numerous articles on this topic in scholarly journals. He is co-editor of *Trends and Issues in Canadian Social Studies* (Pacific Educational Press).

Peter Seixas is an Associate Professor in the Department of Curriculum Studies, University of British Columbia. His particular area of interest is in how students construct their understanding of history. He has published articles on this topic in journals such as *Curriculum Inquiry*, *Theory and Research in Social Education* and *The History Teacher*.

Neil Smith is an instructor of social studies curriculum and instruction courses at Malaspina University College in Nanaimo, British Columbia. His particular area of interest is global education.

Jane Turner is a secondary school social studies teacher in Burnaby, British Columbia. She is currently completing her Master's degree at Simon Fraser University. Her research work is concerned with conceptualization of the role of women in social studies.

Walt Werner is an Associate Professor in the Department of Curriculum Studies, University of British Columbia. His particular areas of interest are curriculum implementation and global education and he has published articles on these topics in numerous scholarly journals.

Ian Wright is an Associate Professor in the Department of Curriculum Studies, University of British Columbia. He is author of *Elementary Social Studies: A Practical Approach* (Nelson) and co-editor of *Trends and Issues in Canadian Social Studies* (Pacific Educational Press). He is a frequent contributor to the journal, *Canadian Social Studies*.

Journals and Professional Resources

Journals for Teachers

Canadian Council for Geographic Education Newsletter
CCGE Office
c/o Faculty of Education
Queens University
Kingston, ON
K7L 3N6
(613) 545-6221

Canadian Social Studies
Althouse Press
Faculty of Education
University of Western Ontario
1137 Western Road
London, ON
N6G 1G7
(519) 661-2096

Focus
Social Studies Council of the
    New Brunswick Teachers' Association
650 Montgomery Street
P.O. Box 752
Fredericton, NB
E3B 5R6
(506) 452-8921

The Green Teacher
95 Robert Street
Toronto, ON
M5S 2K5

Horizon
British Columbia Social Studies Teachers' Association
British Columbia Teachers' Federation
#100-550 West 6th Avenue
Vancouver, BC
V5Z 4P2
(604) 871-2283

Magazine of History
Organization of American Historians
112 North Bryan Street
Bloomington, IN 47408-4199
U.S.A.

The Manitoba Social Science Teacher
Social Science Teachers' Association
Manitoba Teachers' Society
191 Harcourt Street
Regina, MN
R3J 3H2
(204) 888-7961

The Monograph
Ontario Association for Geographic
    and Environmental Education
Treasurer, OAGEE,
Box 507, Station "Q"
Toronto, ON
M4T 2M5

The New Zealand Journal of Social Studies
Waikato Social Studies Association
P.O. Box 4127
Hamilton East
New Zealand

One World
Alberta Social Studies Council
Alberta Teachers' Association
11010 142 Street
Edmonton, AB
T5N 2R1
(403) 453-2411

Our Schools/Our Selves
5502 Atlantic Street
Halifax, NS
B3H 9Z9
1-800-565-1975

Perspectives
Saskatchewan Council of Social Sciences
Saskatchewan Teachers' Federation
2317 Arlington Avenue
Saskatoon, SK
S4J 2H8
1-800-667-7762

Rapport
Ontario History and
    Social Science Teachers' Association
Ontario Teachers' Federation
#700-1260 Bay Street
Toronto, ON
M5R 2B5
(416) 966-3424

Social Education
3501 Newark Street, NW
Washington, DC 20016
U.S.A.
(202) 966-7840

The Social Studies
Heldref Publications
1319 Eighteenth Street, NW
Washington, DC 20036-1802
U.S.A.
(202) 296-6267

Social Studies & the Young Learner
3501 Newark Street, NW
Washington, DC 20016
U.S.A.
(202) 966-7840

Teaching Geography
343 Fulwood Road
Sheffield, England
S1O 3BP
44-114-267-0666

Teaching History
Historical Association
59A Kennington Park Road
London, England
5E11 4JH
01-71-735-3901

Theory and Research in Social Education
3501 Newark Street, NW
Washington, DC 20016
(202) 966-7840

JOURNALS FOR STUDENTS AND TEACHERS

The Beaver: Exploring Canada's History
#478-167 Lombard Avenue
Winnipeg, MN
R3B 0T6
(204) 988-9300

Canadian Geographic
Royal Canadian Geographic Society
39 McArthur Avenue
Vanier, ON
K1L 9Z9

Just in Time
IPI Publishing
708-50 Prince Arthur Avenue
Toronto, ON
M5R 1B5
(416) 944-1141

National Geographic
National Geographic Society
P.O. Box 2395 STN A
Toronto, ON
M5W 9Z9
1-800-647-5463

National Geographic World
National Geographic Society
P.O. Box 63002
Tampa, FL 33663-3001
U.S.A.
1-800-647-5463

Time Machine: The American History Magazine for Kids
29 West 38 Street
New York, NY 10018
U.S.A.
(212) 398-1550

METHODOLOGY TEXTBOOKS
Canadian
Kirman, J.M. (1996). *Elementary social studies* (2nd ed.).
  Scarborough: Prentice-Hall.
Wright, I. (1995). *Elementary social studies: A practical
  approach* (4th ed.). Scarborough: Nelson.
Wright, I. & Sears, A. (Eds.). (1997). *Trends & issues in
  Canadian social studies.* Vancouver: Pacific Educa-
  tional Press.

American
Banks, J. (1990). *Teaching strategies for the social studies:
  Inquiry, valuing, and decision-making* (4th ed.). New
  York: Longman.
Chapin, J.R. & Messick, R. (1989). *Elementary social
  studies: A practical guide.* New York: Longman.
Ellis, A.K. (1991). *Teaching and learning elementary
  social studies* (4th ed.). Boston: Allyn and Bacon.
Farris, P.J. & Cooper, S.J. (1994). *Elementary social
  studies: A whole language approach.* Madison, WI:
  Brown & Benchmark.
Hennings, D., Hennings, G. & Banich, S. (1989).
  Today's elementary social studies (2nd ed.). New
  York: Harper and Row.
Kaltsounis, T. (1987). *Teaching social studies in the
  elementary school: The basics for good citizenship.*
  Englewood Cliffs, NJ: Prentice-Hall.
Martorella, P. (1985). *Elementary social studies: Develop-
  ing reflective, competent and concerned citizens.*
  Boston: Little, Brown.
Maxim, G.W. (1991). *Social studies and the elementary
  school child* (4th ed.). New York: Macmillan.
Michaelis, J.U. (1992). *Social studies for children: A guide
  to basic instruction* (10th ed.). Englewood Cliffs, NJ:
  Prentice-Hall.
Naylor, D. & Dien, R. (1987). *Elementary and middle
  school social studies.* New York: Random House.
Parker, W.C. & Jarolimek, J. (1997). *Social studies in
  elementary education* (10th ed.). Upper Saddle River,
  NJ: Prentice-Hall.
Seefeldt, C. (1997). *Social studies for the preschool-
  primary child* (5th ed.). Columbus, OH: Prentice-
  Hall.
Social Science Education Consortium, Inc. (1996).
  *Teaching the social sciences and history in secondary
  schools: A methods book.* Toronto: Wadsworth.
Welton, D.A. & Mallan, J.T. (1992). *Children and their
  world: Strategies for teaching social studies* (4th ed.).
  Toronto: Houghton Mifflin.
Zarnowski, M. & Gallagher, A.F. (1993). *Children's
  literature & social studies: Selecting and using notable
  books in the classroom.* Washington, DC: National
  Council for the Social Studies.